Transition to the Knowledge Society

The Institute for European Studies Research Series

The Institute for European Studies is part of UBC's ongoing mission to advance international knowledge and research. Located in the Faculty of Graduate Studies and emphasizing an interdisciplinary approach, the Institute promotes an exchange of ideas, students, and scholars between Canada and Europe and provides a public forum for debate on European issues through research seminars, workshops, lecture series, and international conferences.

With the publication of *Transition to the Knowledge Society: Policies and Strategies for Individual Participation and Learning* we are launching the Institute for European Studies Research Series. Future contributions to the series will focus on issues of social change, cultural interaction, and economic transformation facing Canada and Europe in the new millennium.

Edited by Kjell Rubenson and
Hans G. Schuetze

Transition to the Knowledge Society: Policies and Strategies for Individual Participation and Learning

UBC
INSTITUTE
FOR EUROPEAN
STUDIES

UNIVERSITY OF
BRITISH COLUMBIA

Printed in Canada on acid-free paper ∞

ISBN 0-88865-532-0

Canadian Cataloguing in Publication Data

Main entry under title:

Transition to the knowledge society

   Includes bibliographical references and index.
   ISBN 0-88865-532-0

   1. Information technology – Social aspects. 2. Information society. I. Rubenson, Kjell, 1944- II. Schuetze, Hans, 1939- III. University of British Columbia, Institute for European Studies.

T58.5.T72 2000   303.48′33   C99-911154-X

The publication of this book was funded by Human Resources Development Canada/Développement des ressources humaines Canada.

Publication coordinator: Garnet Grosjean
Project editor: Janet Atkinson-Grosjean
Copy editor: Francis Chow
Typesetting and cover design: Artegraphica Design Co.
Institute for European Studies logo: Iris Communications Inc.

Institute for European Studies
University of British Columbia
1855 West Mall
Vancouver, BC V6T 1Z2

Contents

Preface

This volume owes its existence to an international conference that took place in November 1998 in Vancouver, British Columbia. A joint venture involving several partners, the conference was sponsored by Human Resources Development Canada (HRDC). Together with four other federal departments, HRDC is engaged in a broad exercise of defining the elements of the knowledge-based society and of identifying the various agendas for research and policy. The problem of access to and active participation in the knowledge-based society is of particular interest. Directorate-General V (DG V) of the European Commission was the international partner. The Directorate is responsible for employment and social affairs and, like HRDC, is concerned about both the impacts of the new information and communication technologies (ICTs) on employment, working conditions, and skill requirements and the larger issue of civic participation and social cohesion.

Two units of the University of British Columbia were involved in the definition of the themes and the organization of the conference. The Institute for European Studies, founded in 1998 with the help of a major grant from the German Academic Exchange Service (DAAD), is charged with facilitating the understanding of European issues through research, teaching, and dialogue with European scholars and artists. The Centre for Policy Studies in Higher Education and Training (CHET) – an interdisciplinary research unit, as the name suggests – focuses its work on postsecondary and training issues, linking these to broader developments in society and the world of work.

The Vancouver conference brought together some 120 researchers, policy analysts, and high-level administrators from 12 countries. Over the course of three days, they discussed the challenge of the emerging knowledge-based economy and society (KBES). One focus was the impact of the KBES on wages and skill requirements. The other was access to ICTs, work opportunities, and education and training activities. The broad themes and varied backgrounds of the conference participants generated a stimulating international exchange of ideas, information, and perspectives as well as a multidisciplinary dialogue.

This book offers a selection of the papers presented at the conference. All of the chapters have been thoroughly edited or rewritten by the authors. The introduction and first chapter present an overview of the book as a whole. The editors' introduction lays out the design of the volume and provides a brief summary of the individual chapters. The first chapter, by Charles Edquist and W. Craig Riddell, the two rapporteurs of the conference, reviews the role of knowledge and innovation for economic growth and employment, and refers to more specific discussions of this theme in the chapters that follow.

Without diminishing the importance of any of the individual contributions, it is fair to say that the keynote chapter by Richard Lipsey is of central relevance to the entire book. This is due not only to the eminence of the author, one of the originators of a new theoretical approach to the process of technological change and innovation, but also to the broadness of his topic, which establishes the theoretical foundation of knowledge-based economics and links it to public policy.

The editors wish to thank all the contributors to this volume for their willingness to edit and rewrite parts of their original conference papers, under a very short timeline. We also appreciate the work of the rapporteurs, who faithfully recorded and summarized the discussions from the various working groups. The friendly and efficient cooperation, support, and many helpful comments from Jean-Pierre Voyer, François Weldon, and Philippe Massé from the Applied Research Branch of HRDC must also be noted. Finally, great thanks are due to CHET researchers Garnet Grosjean and Janet Atkinson-Grosjean, who provided project coordination and editorial expertise. Without them the task of bringing together the various contributions into one coherent volume would have been impossible to accomplish.

Introduction:
Towards the Knowledge Society
Kjell Rubenson and Hans G. Schuetze

It is generally accepted that industrial nations are undergoing a period of economic and social transformation in which knowledge and information are becoming the foundation for the organization and development of economic and social activity. At the core of this transformation is the rapid introduction of information and communication technologies (ICTs) and the growth of global competition.

The significance of ICTs in driving the emergence of the knowledge society lies in their ability to codify information and knowledge. They enable knowledge to be manipulated to meet a multitude of needs and to be transmitted instantly the world over. The capacity of ICTs to contribute to diffusion of knowledge is enhanced by two facts: they are more pervasive than previous technologies; and their prices are falling and their capabilities increasing more rapidly than for any other technology in history.

As a result, ICTs are an important force behind the intensification of globalization. Their impact has been most noticeable in the financial sector, where, in combination with a process of liberalization and deregulation, they have enabled financial capital to become an internationally mobile factor of production. They have also increased the tradeability and geographic mobility of many services – such as programming, retailing, and travel services – by providing opportunities for their establishment in locations with low-wage labour. At the same time, the development and diffusion of ICTs and other modern technologies are themselves being driven by the intensification of global competition as firms and nations seek to become leaders in the process of technological change.

While these changes hold the promise of increased productivity and an improved standard of living, they also introduce a new set of transitions and adjustment challenges for society and individuals. They affect organizational structures, the nature and level of skills required in the workplace, and the nature of work itself. As a result, these developments have raised concerns over job security and the quality of jobs. There are also concerns over the capacity of individuals to acquire, maintain, and develop the competencies necessary to adapt to new technologies and to take advantage of the opportunities arising from globalization. In these conditions, innovation is increasingly key to growth and comparative advantage is considered to be related to the quality of human capital. The context is one where lifelong learning, to many, becomes fundamental to meeting the adjustment challenges arising from a changing industrial base and culture.

These adjustment challenges also raise crucial distributional and equity considerations – particularly with respect to disparities involving class, gender, ethnicity, age groups, skill levels, and regions. Further expansion of world trade and widespread adoption and use of ICTs can potentially lead to a society in which all citizens can experience the benefits of inclusion. At the same time, there is the risk that these developments could lead to a society of "haves" and "have-nots," where important segments of the population face the prospect of permanent exclusion or marginalization.

As the advent of the knowledge society is changing the current social and economic landscape, the foundations of the social contract that supported the welfare state are also being challenged. Economic restructuring, increasing globalization, and rapid technological change combine with high and persistent unemployment in many countries to undermine the consensus on how roles, responsibilities, and rewards should be distributed in our societies. The question then is how to rebuild a consensus based on current realities that will underpin enhanced economic prosperity and social cohesion.

These themes are addressed in the five parts of this book. The first part, *Economic and Social Policy for the Knowledge Society,* provides an overview of the broader economic and societal foundations and dimensions of the knowledge society and economy, laying the foundations for the chapters that follow. *The Global Market, Regions, and Communities* focuses on the spatial dimensions of innovation and economic development and discusses how ICTs not only are at the core of the globalization of markets but also change the role of regions and communities in economic development. Part 3, *Work in the Knowledge Economy,* looks at the effects of ICTs on employment and work, including the impact of far-reaching changes in both on individual jobs, working conditions, and income. Part 4, *Participation and Inclusion in the Knowledge Society,* addresses different facets of these two key aspects of the knowledge society. Finally, Part 5, *Measuring the Knowledge Society,* is concerned with methodological questions of measuring the impact of ICT use on employment, income, working conditions, and human resources development.

Economic and Social Policy for the Knowledge Society

The emergence of the knowledge society challenges established theoretical explanations of the economic process and growth. In particular, the emergence of knowledge as the key factor of industrial innovation and economic growth puts into question both neoclassical models and their understanding of the role of policy in the economic process.

Furthermore, the knowledge-based economy and society (KBES) challenges the foundations of the social contract that provided the glue for industrial societies after the Second World War. The foundations of the new social contract are not yet clear, but many see the likelihood of a new consensus, based on current realities, that enhances economic prosperity and social cohesion.

In the first chapter, the rapporteurs of the conference, **Charles Edquist** and **W. Craig Riddell**, primarily provide a broad overview of the economic themes addressed in this volume. The analysis focuses on the nature of ICTs, the way they change traditional ways of producing goods and services, and their effect on the organization and nature of work. Linking the emergence of ICTs as a central factor of production to industrial innovation, Edquist and Riddell stress the skill bias of new technologies and the role of knowledge in economic innovation, development, and growth. The central theme concerns the impact of ICTs and innovation on employment, with regard to both the quantity of jobs and the quality of work. The authors stress the importance of distinguishing between productivity and economic growth. Drawing on the papers presented at the conference, they address the role of public policies and private strategies in the process of transformation and change.

In his keynote paper on new growth theories and economic policy for the KBES, **Richard Lipsey** reviews the implications of these theories for economic policy, and in particular for technology or innovation policies. He shows how new theoretical insights into the nature and role of knowledge in the economy change both the understanding of innovation and technological change, as well as the parameters of classical policy interventions. Because of the non-rivalrous nature of knowledge and the uncertainty associated with innovation and technological change, Lipsey argues that there is no unique optimum of resource allocation for research and development (R&D) or the development of a particular technology. In contrast to neoclassical theory, he concludes that policy cannot be "neutral" and that there is no single "best" technology policy. Rather, every policy is context-dependent and requires decisions based on a mixture of theory, measurement, and subjective judgement. Providing examples from economic history and different countries, he illustrates the technology-specific and context-dependent nature of decisions made in support of private sector innovations and technology development.

In their chapters, **John Richards** and **Tom Wall** address the role of a new social contract in the evolving learning society from Canadian and European points of view, respectively. Richards presents what he sees as an appropriate way to think about the social contract and the welfare state in a knowledge society. While there is much to celebrate in the advance of the knowledge society and the growth of the welfare state over the last half-century, there have been costs as well as benefits. The author discusses important adverse consequences arising from the interaction of the knowledge society and the current social contract in the context of some broad economic and social developments. The chapter provides suggestions of what needs to be done to address the adverse effects. He focuses, in particular, on the poverty traps that exclude many from the learning opportunities, and hence the knowledge and skills, that are prerequisites for full participation in the knowledge society.

Tom Wall examines the impact of changes on employment, income disparities, social cohesion, and democracy. He highlights the role social dialogue plays in the process of change and readjustment within the European Union (EU). Wall argues that social-contract accords, or partnership agreements, have contributed greatly to the transformation of some European economies. Despite some evidence to the contrary, the author suggests that through dialogue involving the social partners, ICTs have the potential to facilitate greater levels of economic, social, and political participation.

The Global Market, Regions, and Communities

It is apparent that ICTs have a pivotal role in the globalization of markets for goods and services. The realization of their potential depends on a number of factors, however. One of these is the speed and the extent of their dissemination and use, which is dependent on both the level of investment and adoption by firms. As the potential of ICTs can be realized only if concomitant changes take place in the organization of work and management practices, the adoption of such changes at the firm level is an indispensable prerequisite for their efficient use.

While innovation must ultimately take place in firms, it is now generally accepted that this process depends to a considerable extent on a "system of innovation": an understanding that puts the emphasis not only on the individual firms but on different agents and their interplay. Often consisting of networks of regional or local agents, partners, or members, innovation systems have a strong spatial dimension – a seeming paradox in increasingly globalized markets.

Someshwar Rao and **Ron Hirshhorn** examine the links between ICTs and globalization. They conclude that, overall, Canada's experience with ICT-related globalization has been positive. They note a number of concerns, however. One is the slow implementation by firms, particularly small firms, of advanced technologies. Another is their slow adoption of innovative organizational and human resource practices, both of which are strongly correlated with enterprise performance. As well, despite high penetration rates of ICTs in Canadian households, there remain barriers to access for certain segments of the population, in particular low-income or low-skilled individuals.

In his chapter on European regional development and innovation, **Nicola De Michelis** argues that there are sizeable disparities among regions of the EU in terms of scientific infrastructure, the technical capacity of the local enterprise base, and the nature and level of skills available in the local labour market. These differences lead to what he calls "technology gaps" between regions, and contribute to disparities in overall regional competitiveness and the potential for economic development. Policies to address this problem were rendered largely ineffective by their piecemeal introduction and their predominant focus on large public infrastructure projects and subsidies for individual firms. Recently, however, the emphasis of policy initiatives has shifted at both the local and regional level, as well as at the level of the European Union. There is now a concentration on measures to strengthen endogenous potential and ability to innovate.

Covering the theme of regional innovation and development from a Canadian perspective, **David Wolfe** emphasizes the critical role of knowledge and learning in the process of activating endogenous regional potential. In line with this emphasis, he suggests that the emerging paradigm is more appropriately described as a "learning economy" than as a "knowledge-based economy," as the building of new competencies, the acquisition of new skills, and the capability to learn are central to success in the global economy. Cultural and institutional features, leadership, civic-mindedness, and the interaction between a region's industry and its science and technology infrastructure are stressed by the author as requisites for the "learning region" and its capacity, through institutions and firms, to absorb, apply, and create knowledge.

Luigi Orsenigo focuses on the relationship between innovation and competitiveness in a global economy. The author identifies three sources or levels of innovation as key determinants of competitiveness: individual firms, groups or networks of firms, and systems of innovation. He argues that the key to innovative performance is the development of "organizational capabilities" at all levels. Organizational capabilities define how firms, sectors, regions, and countries put together individual pieces of knowledge – whether codified or tacit – through organizational innovations. Orsenigo suggests that the slow rate of adoption of organizational innovations among European firms may present a possible explanation for what has been called the "European paradox" – the fact that European countries arc less competitive than the United States and Japan, not in their ability to generate knowledge through basic research and R&D but in their ability to transform that knowledge into innovation and ultimately into marketable products.

Work in the Knowledge Economy

There is a growing body of evidence that investments in workplace organization and human resource management practices are necessary if firms are to ensure optimal use of ICTs and other production technologies and to respond to growing competitive pressures from domestic and international sources. At the same time, it appears that the introduction of new forms of work organization is associated with changes in the pattern of employment, as evidenced by increased reliance on part-time and temporary employment. These changes are associated with improved job quality and human resource development opportunities for some workers; for others, however, they have contributed to increased labour market insecurity and reduced opportunity. As such, changing workplace practices may have the effect of polarizing individual economic prospects.

Pascal Petit compares the growing importance accorded to skilled labour in the present situation with the previous phase of mechanical automation, which led to a massive deskilling of work. With respect to this skill bias of the ICTs, he emphasizes aspects such as the rationalization of unskilled jobs, the drop in relative wage rates, and the unstable and precarious nature of jobs, especially of unskilled and older workers. He points out, however, that it is very difficult, and often impossible, to distinguish the effects of the introduction of ICTs from those of corporate restructuring. The latter may have more to do with the firm's competitive situation and business strategy than with new technologies. Petit reasons that in order to use ICTs to their full potential, firms must radically rethink their work patterns in order to link them to the individual learning processes required by the new work setting.

Caroline Weber's and **Henri Rouilleault's** chapters address two themes: the relationship between technological change, human resource practices, and innovation, and the organization of work and the new ICTs. Starting with the latter, Rouilleault notes that ICTs represent a major global change because the merger of the computer, telecommunications, and media industries will give rise to a single industry involving a networking of communications. In comparing the 1980s with the 1990s, he notes three areas of change: technological, organizational, and social. He concludes that there is no absolute link between technology and an explicit model of organizational change. The model of change can be adapted to the needs of the organization. In fact, the new ICTs offer enhanced flexibility because a variety of configurations can be adopted.

Weber's chapter addresses the question of the relationships between the implementation of new technology, human resource practices, and innovation by focusing on technological and organizational change, and on human resource practices. Using the data from the Workplace and Employee Survey (WES; see the chapter by Krebs et al.), she finds that new technology implementation is associated with increased employee training, more employee participation programs, greater organizational decentralization, and less employee turnover. Contrary to popular perception, it thus appears that organizations that implement new technologies tend to have more stable and traditional work environments.

The chapter by **Yves Gingras**, **Philippe Massé**, and **Richard Roy** deals with the changing skill structure of employment in Canada. Their findings support a bias in labour demand towards knowledge and management occupations – those in which the primary task is the production of ideas. This phenomenon is due mainly to the substitution of knowledge occupations for other groups of occupations, and was more pronounced in the 1980s than in the 1970s. Their work provides insight into what skills are required in knowledge occupations. Cognitive, authority, management, and communication skills appear to be key features. Cognitive skills are the most valued assets on the market today, as evidenced by the fact that occupations requiring these skills pay substantially more than average. Cognitive skills emphasize the importance of work experience and specific training. As a result, building bridges between schools and workplaces (e.g., through co-op programs) is an investment that appears to pay off.

These authors show that there is a sufficient supply of highly educated people in Canada to meet the requirements of the labour market, but **John Van Reenen** suggests that the supply of educated people may not be keeping up with increased demand in the US and in several European countries. Examining the microeconometric evidence on skill-biased technological change, Van Reenen finds a strong relationship between technology (computers, R&D) and increases in the employment or wage bill shares of educated or nonproduction workers. Whether skill-biased technological change is the main cause of the deterioration in the position of less-skilled workers is less clear. In the United Kingdom and the United States, the wages of the low-skilled have fallen significantly relative to the high-skilled, while they have been stable in European countries such as Germany, France, and Italy, where wages tend to be less flexible.

Participation and Inclusion in the Knowledge Society
It is widely accepted that the ability of workers to adapt and benefit from the new technologies depends on the extent to which they can acquire, develop, and maintain the requisite skills throughout their life. Given the close links between learning and the ability to work efficiently in the new environment, the workplace is a key link in the learning chain for most working people. This puts the focus on who will benefit from firms' decisions on training. It also brings up the more general question of who is engaged in lifelong learning. Further, the impact of ICTs on workers and the labour market adds a new dimension of social inequality, defined by the

extent to which one possesses the necessary skills and resources to access and use new ICTs in order to participate in society.

Investment by firms in human resources is the common theme of the first two chapters. Despite the general acceptance of the principle that human resources are critical to economic outcomes, **Gordon Betcherman**, **Norm Leckie**, and **Kathryn McMullen** show that in Canadian firms, access to training and learning is very uneven and training is still largely concentrated in individuals with high levels of education, income, and full-time work. In other words, it is increasingly less likely for employers to invest in training if there is no clear business rationale to do so. Therefore, the authors suggest that some form of public policy intervention is needed to address the concerns of access, equity, and inclusion. There is an increased role for labour market intermediaries (sector councils, labour force boards, unions, employment agencies) in helping to make this new market function better.

Gerhard Bosch argues that there are a number of factors influencing firms' decisions to provide training for their workers. As other authors in this volume stress (see Betcherman et al., and Rubenson and Schuetze), work organization plays an important role, as does the supply of a well-educated workforce, which leads to more flexible structures. Other factors are labour market regulation, the existence of an external training infrastructure, support, and well-developed standards and certificates to assist small and medium-sized firms in training. Important as well is a climate of "high-trust" industrial relations, which leads to a negotiated adoption of new work arrangements and contributes to the reduction of learning costs by exchanging information on experiences and practices.

A central issue around the KBES is its effect on women's opportunities in the labour market. **Brenda Lipsett**'s chapter examines the major issues related to employment and working patterns and conditions of women from a Canadian perspective. Starting from the premise that occupational segregation has been declining over the last decades, the author concludes that research to date does not establish a clear picture of the effects of the transition to the KBES on women. She identifies three issues that determine women's role in the new labour market: the availability of flexible work arrangements, access to training opportunities in the workplace, and education and further learning. Lipsett concludes that policy has an important role to play in facilitating the adjustment of women in these areas.

Ursula Huws argues that the ICTs have no intrinsic features that would affect men and women differently, and that their impact will therefore be affected by a person's "place" in society. Women as a group are affected unequally only insofar as their existing social position is unequal. In apparent contrast to Lipsett, Huws cites evidence from Europe that women's positions are indeed unequal with regard to income, education, leisure time, and occupation. Looking at emerging forms of "telemediated" work, such as home-based work, she sees strongly gendered patterns that not only reproduce existing patterns of segregation but in some cases add new dimensions to them. This situation is exacerbated by profound differences between regions, as Huws sees a new polarized industrial geography emerging in the information society. Huws concludes, however, that in spite of this evidence the new model offers possibilities for making work more autonomous and creative, allowing greater individual scope for designing a more flexible work pattern that fits personal and family needs; it also has the potential to enhance equality of opportunity between men and women.

Despite the fact that lifelong learning has risen to prominence in the policy literature, **Kjell Rubenson** and **Hans Schuetze** stress that the concept is vague and broad. Policy documents have often simply substituted lifelong learning for adult education and training; they do not look systematically at lifelong learning as a whole. The authors distinguish a number of fundamental factors that need to be addressed by policies for lifelong learning. They argue that selective/targeted policy interventions will help ensure lifelong learning for all, whereas a general policy to encourage training will help only those able and willing to take up learning opportunities. Furthermore, their analysis suggests that policies need to be developed between different ministries.

Vincent Mosco focuses on the links between education, citizenship, and the knowledge society. He notes that while the ICT phenomenon is taking place in the developed world, cyberspace is empty space for most of the world's people. He argues that the primary emphasis has been on technical education, that is, on teaching people how to use technology. When attention *is* paid to content, most is directed towards teaching people how to be consumers of products and services. Mosco's chapter presents an argument for treating cyberspace as a public space or "new commons" to which all people have rights of access and participation, and identifies examples of programs that promote this new form of citizenship.

Measuring the Knowledge Society

As is evident from the analyses presented in the first four parts of this volume, there are growing concerns regarding the adequacy of existing measurements and their ability to inform our understanding of the consequences of the present economic and social transformation. For example, human capital has historically been measured using useful, low-cost proxy measures: years of education or educational attainment. These measures are inadequate for several reasons. First, skills and competencies are not congruent with education; proxies using initial education ignore the accumulation of skills throughout life and the attrition of skills due to disuse, and assume that the acquired qualifications are equivalent across jurisdictions and countries. Further, while much of the focus is on the changing nature of work, few good datasets exist to capture recent workplace developments.

In his chapter, **Albert Tuijnman** presents two new sets of data developed with the intention to provide direct measures of skills. The first of these, the International Adult Literacy Survey (IALS), has been a breakthrough in the methodological capacity to measure skill profiles in countries. The aim of the survey was to develop an assessment framework, measurement instruments, and reporting scales that would permit valid and useful comparisons of literacy – one important element of human capital. The IALS measures prose, document, and quantitative literacy. The International Life Skills Survey, patterned on the IALS, aims to measure the distribution of a broader range of skills: prose and document literacy, numeracy, problem solving, practical cognition, teamwork, and computer literacy. While some progress has been made in the area of skill measurement, Tuijnman suggests that the next evolutionary step in understanding the link between human capital and economic growth would be a better measurement of productivity.

Two chapters examine some recent survey instruments that have been used in Canada and Europe to monitor workplace developments in work organization practices. **Kevin O'Kelly** describes three surveys commissioned by the European Union. Their intent is to monitor developments and trends in the organization of work and job design, and to identify problems arising in the employment relationship.

H. Krebs, **Z. Patak**, **G. Picot**, and **T. Wannell** describe the methodology of the Workplace and Employee Survey (WES). This innovative survey links information on workplaces – such as the adoption of technology, organizational change, training, and other human resource practices – to information on employees in those workplaces, such as wages, hours of work, job type, and skills. Because of its longitudinal nature, the WES has the potential to provide a better understanding of the relationship between business strategies, technology, organizational change, and changes in the world of work. The authors point out the dilemmas in undertaking surveys of this kind, especially the communication gap between employers and employees.

In summary, because of the genesis of this book, the five themes are addressed from the perspectives of both Canadian and European researchers and policy analysts. This often provides an interesting insight into the varying cultural and societal contexts in which the transformation to a knowledge-based society and economy is taking place. The chapters reflect the different approaches and traditions with respect to the role that policy plays or is expected to play in alleviating the negative impacts of this transformation.

Part 1
Economic and Social Policy for the Knowledge Society

1

The Role of Knowledge and Innovation for Economic Growth and Employment in the Information and Communication Technology (ICT) Era[1]

Charles Edquist and W. Craig Riddell

Introduction

This chapter provides an overview and synthesis of several of the main issues that are addressed in the contributions in this volume. Rather than attempt to cover all of the topics examined in the individual chapters that follow, we focus on the interaction between technological change, economic growth, and labour market outcomes such as quantity and quality of employment, the distribution of income, and the nature of work. We devote particular attention to the mechanisms by which major changes in the technology of production, distribution, and consumption – such as those taking place due to the current revolution in information and communication technologies (ICTs) – affect the economy and society. We also discuss the role of public policies and individual strategies in this rapidly changing environment.

Technological Change, Economic Growth, and the Productivity Paradox

Long-term economic growth (increased production and higher living standards over time) is driven by technological change and innovation (changes in the goods and services we produce and the way we produce them). Technological change takes place in several forms: (1) continuous small, incremental changes, (2) discontinuous radical inventions, and (3) massive shifts in some pervasive or "general purpose technology" (GPT).[2]

Examples of GPTs include: ICTs such as writing, printing, and current electronic technologies; materials such as bronze, iron, and steel, as well as made-to-order materials; and power-delivery systems such as domestication of animals, the waterwheel, the steam engine, electricity, and the internal combustion engine (Lipsey 1996). The discovery and adoption of a new GPT transforms the entire economic system and society. As noted by Lipsey (1996, 21), the study of history "tells us that, along with the masses of incremental changes in technology that are important sources of economic growth from year to year, every once in a while comes a new GPT that causes deep structural adjustments and massive changes in our way of life as well as rejuvenating the growth process by presenting a whole new research program for finding improvements in and new applications for the new basic technology."

Long-term economic growth is not the same as productivity growth. The most general measure of productivity growth is growth of "total factor productivity" (TFP), which reflects, on the output side, the quantity and quality of all of the goods and services produced in the economy and, on the input side, the quantity and quality of all factors of production utilized. An important component of TFP is labour productivity: the ratio between the value of all goods and services produced and the amount of labour used in production. Thus labour productivity growth can come about because of either increased production or decreased employment (or both). TFP growth is necessary for long-term economic growth, and growth in labour productivity has generally been an important source of TFP growth.

An important issue arising in this context is the so-called "productivity paradox" – the fact that the apparently high rates of technical advance associated with the ICT revolution have not resulted in significant gains in measured productivity advance. As stated by Robert Solow, "computers are everywhere except in the productivity statistics."

At the outset it is important to note – as discussed in Richard Lipsey's chapter in this volume – that there is not necessarily a contradiction between technological changes that result in massive structural changes and low productivity growth. New technologies are introduced because they promise to be better than the ones they replace. There is no guarantee how much better they will be, however. Some technologies, such as the first water-powered factories, bring about massive structural change but only modest productivity gains, while others, such as the second-generation steam-driven factories, bring substantial gains (Lipsey, this volume).

One potential resolution of the productivity paradox is associated with the concept of a general purpose technology described above. The recent literature on GPTs suggests that their introduction may cause shifts in the temporal pattern of productivity growth, with initial productivity slowdowns followed by productivity booms (Helpman and Trajtenberg 1998). The slowdown and subsequent boom are due to the development of, and experimentation with, technologies complementary to the GPT, and learning-by-doing with the new technology.

As documented in Paul David's well-known study of electrification in the latter part of the 19th century, realizing the productivity and economic growth benefits of a new GPT may take a very long time – as with the replacement of mechanical power with the dynamo or electric motor. The delay was due to slow diffusion of the innovation, adjustment of workplaces and production facilities to the new technology, design and adoption of complementary inputs into production, changes required in the education and training systems, and other factors (David 1991). In the case of the dynamo, it took almost 40 years for the benefits of electrification to show up in the form of measured productivity gains and associated increases in living standards. As summarized by David (1991, 315), at the time one would have noted that "the electric dynamos were to be seen everywhere but in the economic statistics."

This explanation is important, not only because it provides a resolution of the "productivity paradox" consistent with at least one historical episode of massive technological change, as well as with some recent theoretical models of GPTs, but also because it suggests that we may experience a future "technology/productivity boom" associated with the ICT revolution. According to this hypothesis, the massive structural adjustments now being experienced in many industrialized countries are indeed worthwhile, although the benefits of these adjustments will accrue in the future rather than the present.

As suggested by the experience with electricity, an important part of the GPT explanation is that the productivity benefits come with a lag because of the need to develop complementary organizational structures in addition to complementary production techniques. That is, for the current investments in ICTs, we need to develop new organizational structures and new ways of managing and structuring the workplace – a central theme of the conference on which this volume is based.

Another potential explanation of the "productivity paradox" is poor measurement of productivity growth, principally due to inadequate (and perhaps increasingly inadequate) measurement of the economy's real output of goods and services. A number of factors could account for the substantial and increasing understatement of real output and productivity growth.[3] The first is associated simply with the substantial sectoral shift of output and employment from sectors such as agriculture and manufacturing, where the measurement of outputs and inputs is both conceptually straightforward and carried out with considerable accuracy. Associated with the decline in the relative importance of agriculture and manufacturing is the sectoral shift towards services. In this sector, many outputs are not measured but are treated simply as a function of measured inputs, and some outputs are not conceptually straightforward to define. As discussed by Griliches (1994), the aggregate economy is increasingly dominated by the "unmeasurable sector," which according to his estimates now accounts for approximately 70 percent of total output in the United States. Comparable estimates for Canada are almost identical to those for the US, while those for the European Union (EU) are approximately 10 percentage points less

(OECD 1994, 6). Differences in measured productivity trends in the "measurable" and "unmeasurable" sectors are substantial enough that even the existence of a productivity growth slowdown, beginning in the 1970s, is called into question.

A second measurement issue is the problem of accounting for "new products" – an aspect that, while always present, is likely to be quantitatively more important in periods of rapid technological advance. The third principal reason real output and productivity measurement may be seriously understated is associated with accounting for quality improvements in goods and services.[4] As economies shift towards more emphasis on knowledge-based production, many of the associated improvements show up not as increases in the quantities of goods and services but as improvements in their quality. Yet there is considerable doubt that these quality improvements are being adequately captured in national economic statistics (Nordhaus 1997).

These issues related to the measurement of the productivity gains (if any) associated with the transition to the knowledge-based economy and society (KBES) arise in several other parts of this summary.

The Shift to the Knowledge-Based Economy

The industrialized countries are currently undergoing a fundamental transformation associated with the movement from the previously established technology of production and consumption to a new GPT based on ICTs, the silicon chip, and the digitization of information. The principal focus of this volume is not how best to define the concept of a KBES, or how to measure its extent and rate of evolution. Rather, it is the strategies and policies that individuals and organizations might best adopt in adjusting to the KBES. Nonetheless, evidence on the extent of the shift towards the KBES is presented in several chapters, and is briefly summarized here.

The emergence of the KBES is marked by several product-market dimensions. These include the following:

- Both large and small firms are increasingly able to carry out business internationally.
- The role of intermediaries is shrinking in many industries.
- Firms are placing greater emphasis on their "knowledge capital."
- Discrete segments of the "value-added chain" can increasingly be carried out by teams operating in diverse locations, such as the design of the Boeing 777 aircraft, which was completed by numerous development teams in many countries.
- Electronic commerce (e-commerce) is growing at a rapid rate.

Because of these and related developments, globalization and ICTs are en-hancing competition in product markets. Firms are responding to this more competitive environment by focusing on their core business, in order to facilitate a rapid response to innovations and product-market developments.

These product-market developments have potentially important implica-tions for the organization of work and employee skills. Smaller, more flex-ible firms that are closer to the client's needs are often appropriate in this environment. Indeed, such organizations may frequently combine together for a specific project and then dissolve at the project's conclusion. Smaller firms are more likely to rely on outsourcing for many inputs, leaving the organization to focus on its core competencies. These organizations are typi-cally less hierarchical, more horizontal, and more organic. Skilled workers are in a position to assume greater responsibility in these smaller, more flexible organizations. Related developments include greater emphasis on employee responsibility and teamwork in order to improve organizational performance. In successful firms, the introduction of new technology is often accompanied by innovations in management systems and in com-pensation and incentive arrangements. These issues relating to the organi-zation of the workplace and associated skill requirements arise throughout this volume, and are discussed in more detail in subsequent sections.

The principal evidence emanating from the labour market relates to sectoral shifts in output and employment towards more knowledge-intensive pro-duction. As is well known, the Canadian and European Community econo-mies have been characterized by a sectoral shift in production and employment from manufacturing and primary industries to services. Even within these sectors, however, there is evidence of significant shifts in out-put and employment towards more technologically advanced and more knowledge-intensive production. In his chapter, Pascal Petit summarizes such evidence at the level of industries and occupations in the European setting, while the Canadian evidence is summarized in two chapters, one by Gordon Betcherman, Norm Leckie, and Kathryn McMullen and the other by Yves Gingras, Philippe Massé, and Richard Roy.

For example, Gingras, Massé, and Roy classify occupations into five cat-egories: data, knowledge, goods, services, and management occupations. Data and knowledge are "information" occupations while goods and serv-ices are "non-information" occupations. Management is treated as a sepa-rate "information" category because it requires different skills from those used in knowledge and data occupations. Employment trends over the 1971-96 period differ substantially across the five occupational groups, with rapid growth occurring in management (7.6 percent per year) and knowledge (4.1 percent per year), much slower growth in data (2.2 percent) and serv-ices (2.6 percent), and very slow growth in goods-producing occupations (0.6 percent).[5] Although knowledge occupations displayed a rapid growth rate, they remain a relatively small proportion of total employment, increasing from 5.1 percent of employment in 1971 to 8.5 percent in 1996.

The International Adult Literacy Survey (IALS), carried out in Canada and several European countries, also shows a strong positive correlation between employment growth in an occupation and the average literacy level in that occupation. Similarly, the industries that have experienced more rapid employment growth are those whose employees have relatively high levels of literacy skills, while those industries that are declining are characterized by employees with lower literacy levels (Statistics Canada et al. 1996).

Although there is clear evidence that output and employment are shifting towards more knowledge-intensive activities, there remains uncertainty about whether this trend is accelerating. Most research points to a steady growth in the share of output and employment devoted to knowledge-intensive production, consistent with an underlying steady rate of technological progress, at least during the decades of the 1960s, 1970s, and 1980s (see, for example, Gera and Mang [1998] for evidence for Canada). Some evidence, however, suggests an acceleration of the rate of structural change in employment in Canada and the United States during the 1980s and 1990s relative to previous decades (Baldwin 1993; Riddell 1997). It is unclear to what extent this increase in "downsizing" and restructuring is associated with a more rapid transformation towards the knowledge-based economy, or with other economic shocks occurring during the 1980s and 1990s.

Different Kinds of Innovations

The central theme of this volume is the way employment and workplace organization are changing in the transition to the KBES, and how they are being influenced by the diffusion of ICTs. Knowledge as such is of no great economic and social importance, however. Only when transformed into innovations does it become significant for economic growth and employment. Thus, a central issue is how such innovations influence employment and workplace organization. To address this issue, we begin by discussing what is meant by innovation.

As has been stressed by many of those who have studied the process of technological change, innovation is certainly not a homogeneous category (Rosenberg 1982; Lipsey et al. 1998b). Certain kinds of innovations can even have oppositional effects on the number of jobs available and on the skills required in the labour force. It is futile, therefore, to talk in a general way about the effects of innovations on employment and skills. Similarly, it is misleading to talk about "jobless growth as a result of rapid technological change." The reason is that the impacts of innovations generally work in both directions. They both create and destroy jobs and increase and decrease skill requirements; the net effect of any particular set of innovations can be either (Edquist et al., forthcoming). We will therefore supplement the macro-level discussion above with one pursued at the meso level of aggregation.

A Taxonomy

We divide the broad category of innovation into subcategories. For the purpose of discussing the relations between innovations and employment, we use the following taxonomy:

INNOVATIONS

PROCESS   PRODUCT

Technological   Organizational   Goods   Services

Process innovations are a matter of how things are produced; product innovations are a matter of what is produced. Technological process innovations and goods are material; organizational process innovations and services are intangibles. Except for that qualification, the subcategories are fairly self-explanatory.[6]

The distinction between process and product innovations arises either explicitly or implicitly in several of the chapters, such as those by John Van Reenen and Tom Wall. It is useful to make these kinds of specifications systematic and explicit; otherwise, it is difficult to understand the complex relationships between knowledge, innovations, employment, skill requirements, education, and other forms of learning. And if these relations are not well understood, we will not be able to design policies that can solve or mitigate problems in the area of innovations, growth, and employment.

With regard to employment, we will use the standard dichotomy between quantity of employment (number of jobs) and quality of employment (character of jobs). Process innovations and process technologies are emphasized most in this volume. There is also more emphasis on organizational process innovations than is often the case. The chapters also talk more about quality of employment than quantity. We will balance this bias somewhat by addressing product innovations and the quantity of employment. One reason is that we cannot deal with the issue of quality of employment if we do not also talk about quantity. And we cannot analyse the relations between innovations and employment if we do not address product as well as process innovations.

The importance of addressing quantity of employment is also obvious from many of the chapters, particularly those from Europe, which probably reflect the slow employment growth and mass unemployment that has been plaguing Europe for quite some time. From a European point of view, the magnitudes of employment and unemployment are crucial.

This issue is addressed in the chapter by Luigi Orsenigo, who points to the so-called "European paradox." By this, he means that Europe is *not* lagging behind the US and Japan in R&D and the generation of scientific knowledge, but *is* behind in terms of product innovation.

This suggests that the European systems of innovation are less efficient in transforming scientific knowledge into product innovations. Orsenigo blames a weaker "organizational capability" – that is, the capability to put different pieces of knowledge together – for this situation. This inability to generate enough product innovations may also partly explain the fact that the rate of unemployment is much higher in Europe than in the US and Japan.

Relations Between Categories of Innovation

The relationships between the different kinds of innovations are complex. First, there is a relationship between product and process innovations. Sometimes the production of a new product requires new process technologies. This is, for example, the case with a new integrated circuit with a smaller line breadth, which requires new lithographic process technologies. In other cases, a new product can be produced with the old process technology. For example, a new mechanical pump can be produced in the same factory as an old one.

Second, a product innovation can later be transformed into a process innovation. An industrial robot, for example, is a product innovation when it is produced by ABB (Asea Brown Boveri) and becomes a process innovation when used by Volvo. It has two "incarnations."

Third, there is a close relation between technological and organizational process innovations. When a new technological process innovation is introduced, it is often also necessary to change the organization of work as well. Organizational innovations are frequently required to reap the productivity benefits of technological innovations.

This relation between technological change and organizational change is the focus of the chapters by Caroline Weber and Henri Rouilleault. Weber concludes that more training and employee participation occurs in firms that implement new process technologies. Rouilleault addresses the links between technological and organizational change and argues that they are not absolute; a certain technology is compatible with several organizational forms. In addition, it has been argued that employee participation is very important when new process technologies are being implemented.

Finally, there is obviously also a close relation between new goods and new services. One example is the relation between a mobile telephone system and the service of mobile phone calls.

Employment Consequences of Innovations

Let us now examine the employment consequences of innovations, dealing first with the number of jobs created and destroyed (i.e., quantity of employment) and later with the quality of employment.

Quantity of Employment

Process Innovations

The initial or direct consequence of process innovations is that they destroy jobs. This consequence occurs because such innovations increase labour productivity (the ratio between production volume and quantity of employment).

The literature on technological change stresses that there are also compensating or offsetting mechanisms. Increased productivity leads to a decrease in production costs, which in turn lead to lower prices for the product or service under consideration. Lower prices then lead to increased demand and thereby increased employment, possibly compensating for the initial job loss. The increased demand has two components: an "own-price effect" on the good or service under consideration, and a "general equilibrium effect" on other goods and services. The "own-price effect" refers to increased demand for the particular product or service due to the price reduction because of the lower production costs associated with the process innovation.

The size of the increased demand associated with the own-price effect is dependent upon the price sensitivity of the product. This is what economists call the product's "price elasticity of demand." If this elasticity is large (for example, above 1), the compensation effect is likely to exceed the initial job reduction. If it is small (for example, significantly below 1), the compensation mechanism will typically be too weak to balance the initial job destruction.

So how large are these price elasticities? Looking at various empirical estimates, Edquist et al. (forthcoming) conclude that they are often below 1.[7] This suggests that the net employment effect of process innovations in the industry in question may often be negative.

A general finding in economics is that price elasticities of demand are smaller in the short run than in the long run. The difference in responsiveness occurs because consumer expenditure patterns display considerable inertia in the short run due to habits, imperfect information, and related factors. In the longer term, however, price elasticities are higher because consumers adjust more fully over time to changes in relative prices. As a consequence, the magnitude of any particular employment reduction related to process innovation will depend on the time period over which adjustment to the resulting changes in prices takes place.

The general equilibrium effects arise because the consequences of technological change are not confined to the industry or sector in which it occurs. As summarized by Robert Allen (1986, 77-78):

Raising efficiency in the production of one commodity lowers its price. Two consequences follow. First, the real incomes of all consumers increase. This is the process by which the benefits of technical change (i.e. rising real incomes) are distributed over the community. Second, because the real incomes of consumers rise, the demand for most goods in the economy rises. As a result, the demand for labour in most industries increases. These increases in the demand for labour provide job opportunities for the workers initially displaced by the technological change.

The conclusion is that process innovations often lead to decreased employment in the industry or sector in which the innovation is introduced. This reduced labour demand is offset by increased labour demand in other sectors of the economy, associated with the higher real incomes of consumers. A central issue, both for the individuals affected by such changes and for public policy, is how smoothly this adjustment of labour – from sectors that are declining in employment to sectors that are expanding – takes place. A related and equally important issue is the extent to which the costs of such adjustments to technological and other economic change are borne by the individuals affected by such adjustments or by society as a whole through income support and social insurance programs.

Examples of such adjustments to technological change are familiar. During much of this century, rapid technical progress in agricultural production (much of it process improvements) implied both declining employment in agriculture and rising real incomes, which fuelled growing demand for manufactured products and services. As a consequence, manufacturing and services were expanding sectors in terms of employment over much of the past century. More recently, in the postwar period, technological progress in manufacturing resulted in this sector being one whose relative share of employment declined in many OECD countries. The higher real incomes associated with productivity growth in manufacturing resulted in growing demand for services, a sector in which relative employment has grown.

This complex set of forces associated with technological change helps explain why simplistic predictions about rising technological unemployment – predictions that are frequently heard during periods of substantial economic and technological change – typically fail to be realized, as Tom Wall notes in his chapter.

We conclude this discussion of the relationship between process innovations and employment with two observations. First, the overall or net effect of a process innovation on employment is clearly an empirical matter, because there are offsetting positive and negative effects. Furthermore, obtaining good estimates of the net impact on employment in any particular case is difficult, because of differences in both the timing and location of the innovation's employment consequences. The negative impacts on employment occur mainly in the short to medium term and in the industry or sector in which the process innovation is introduced. For these reasons, they are typically the easiest to identify and measure. The positive impacts occur principally in the medium to long term and are widely diffused throughout the economy. For these reasons, they are much more difficult to identify and measure.

A second general observation is that there is nothing automatic about the mechanisms we have described. In particular, in order for the community as a whole to realize the benefits of a process innovation – especially the general equilibrium consequences, which tend to expand employment in other sectors of the economy – adjustments in prices, wages, output, and employment are needed. If these adjustments do not take place, or take place only slowly, the negative own-sector employment-reducing effects will dominate, and the process innovation's contribution to improved standards of living will be reduced or delayed. The fact that the benefits of process innovations do not accrue automatically highlights the importance of the mechanisms by which individuals and organizations adjust to technological change, the central theme of this volume.

Product Innovations
The initial or direct consequence of product innovations is that they create jobs. The reason is that production of new products means the establishment of new production capacity, the creation of new markets, and the satisfaction of new demand – all of which leads to new employment. Counteracting and general equilibrium forces operate here also, however. Again, there are both own-industry and general equilibrium effects. The own-industry effects occur because a new product might replace an old product in the same industry or sector, and may be produced in a less labour-intensive way than the old product. The general equilibrium effects occur because increased expenditure on the new good will result in reduced expenditure by consumers on other goods and services throughout the economy.

The counteracting own-industry forces are generally weaker here than in the case of process innovation. The result is that product innovation can be a major creator of new jobs in the industry under consideration (Edquist et al., forthcoming). On the other hand, these generally positive net effects on employment in the industry where the product innovation occurs are offset by reduced demand and employment in other sectors.

In summary, there are important differences between process and product innovations in terms of their effects on employment. Process innovations generally have negative net employment effects in the industry in which the technological change occurs, whereas the reverse is true for product innovations. These own-industry effects are offset by general equilibrium effects that occur throughout the rest of the economic system. In the case of process innovations, these general equilibrium effects increase employment in other sectors, thus offsetting the negative net effects within the industry in which the innovation is introduced. In contrast, in the case of product innovations, general equilibrium effects typically reduce employment elsewhere in the economy, thus offsetting the positive own-industry effects.

Some of these forces are illustrated in the chapter by Pascal Petit. He notes that, overall, while the number of jobs has dropped or remained constant in industry, there has been a rise in employment in services. More importantly, he also shows the heterogeneity of the picture at a more disaggregated level. In some industrial sectors, the number of jobs has actually increased, albeit modestly, notably in high-technology sectors like ICT production, biotechnology, pharmaceuticals, and new materials. In these sectors product innovation is very important. The chapter by Gingras, Massé, and Roy shows that knowledge and management occupations have grown much faster than other occupations during the 1971-96 period.

Petit also points out that development has been very uneven in the various subsectors of the service industry. Employment growth has been modest in the spheres of transport and commerce. At the same time, it has increased sharply in the financial, hotel and catering, social services, and business services sectors.

In other words, employment has increased in some industrial and service sectors and decreased in others. Thus, although it is true that on the whole employment is decreasing in manufacturing (industry) and increasing in services, subsector disaggregation is necessary for a more complete understanding of the effects of technological change.

Structural Change

As discussed above, both process and product innovations result in changes in employment within the industry in which they are introduced as well as general equilibrium effects throughout the economy. New products are added to the production bundle and some old products are phased out. New methods of producing existing products are introduced and old methods decline in usage. As a consequence of these innovations, structural change in the composition of production is a continuing feature of economic life.

What kinds of products are most interesting, then, from the point of view of employment creation? We mentioned earlier that some product innovations become process innovations in a second incarnation. As new products they (initially) create jobs, but as new processes they (initially) destroy jobs.[8] From the point of view of employment creation, those product innovations that never become process innovations are perhaps most interesting. These are the consumer products. Investment products become process innovations when they are used. Since consumer products – both goods and services – never become process innovations, they do not destroy jobs in a second incarnation.

In this respect there is an important difference between goods and services. Service products rarely become investment products. It is therefore possible that, among the product innovations, intangible services – on average and in a net sense – generate more employment than material goods. As well, service sectors now account for the bulk of employment in the OECD countries – on average two out of three jobs – and have been responsible for the bulk of job creation in these countries, particularly since the 1970s.

In reference to the discussion about economic growth and productivity growth in the section "Technological Change, Economic Growth, and the Productivity Paradox" earlier in this chapter, let us say a few words about different kinds of growth and their relation to innovation and employment. The relationship between technology, productivity growth, economic growth, and employment is addressed in several of the chapters in this volume (Petit; Wall; Gingras, Massé, and Roy).

We have seen that process innovations normally lead to productivity growth in the industry in which the innovations occur and that sectoral job destruction is the other side of that coin. These types of innovations, however, release economic forces that create net employment growth elsewhere in the economy. Product innovation is a net creator of jobs in the sector in which the innovation occurs – in spite of substitution. The employment-creating effects of these innovations are offset, however, by employment-reducing effects elsewhere in the economy. Thus both types of innovations lead to economic growth (growth in the standard of living) and both have complex effects on employment. Direct effects in the sector in which the innovation occurs and indirect effects elsewhere in the economy produce the overall net effect.

For the above reasons, it is important to distinguish between *productivity* growth and *economic* growth. Politicians, policymakers – even researchers – often fail to do so. At the macro level, in order to achieve net employment growth we need economic growth large enough to compensate for the productivity growth occurring through technological change. Another way of expressing this is to say that the employment intensity of growth must be high for net employment generation to occur. As noted by Tom Wall, the employment intensity of growth has actually been higher in both Europe and North America during the decades of the 1980s and 1990s than during the 1960s and 1970s, when productivity growth was higher.

It is also worth noting that although the distinction between product and process innovations is useful for many conceptual and analytical purposes, technological change is varied and complex and in some circumstances the distinction becomes blurred. For example, many new products require new processes (although others do not); as these products are changed and improved over the decades through successive innovations, so are the processes by which they are produced, changed, and improved.

Quality of Employment

Let us now deal with quality of employment, against the background of what we have said about quantity of employment. Jobs can be destroyed for several reasons. First, they disappear because of labour-saving process innovations, as discussed above. The jobs that disappear are normally those that are easiest to mechanize and automate. These are often, but not always, the ones that require less skill and qualifications.[9] Earlier in the postwar period, these were often manual tasks in manufacturing. Because of ICTs, this replacement of labour by capital equipment is now also increasing in some of the service sectors, such as banking and financial services with the introduction of automatic teller machines. A second reason jobs disappear is that production of old products is terminated. Either the needs satisfied by them disappear, or new products satisfying similar needs replace them.

Skill Requirements

We have stressed that technological change involves a process of "creative destruction" – reducing the number of (or even eliminating) some jobs and increasing the demand for others, even creating jobs that previously did not exist. In addition to these effects on quantities of jobs in the economy, technological change alters the skill requirements of employers and, in some cases, the nature and organization of work itself. In some circumstances skill requirements are enhanced, while in others new jobs require fewer skills than old jobs. The overall effect of technological change on skill requirements thus depends on the net effect of these potentially offsetting forces. In some situations, the net effect will raise overall skill requirements, while in others the net effect will lower labour force skill requirements as a whole.

Two historical episodes illustrate this general point. The industrial revolution created some new skills, particularly in the engineering industry, but it is generally accepted that mechanization during this period lowered skill requirements overall (Allen 1986). Evidence from the automation debate of the late 1950s and early 1960s indicates that technological change caused deskilling in some cases and the opposite in others, with no evident tendency for the average level of skill in the labour force to rise or fall (Globerman 1986).

The current period associated with innovations and diffusion of ICTs appears to be one of generally rising skill requirements. Evidence supporting this claim appears in several chapters in this volume. For example, Rao and Hirshhorn show that the ICT sectors in Canada grew at five times the rate of gross domestic product (GDP) growth between 1990 and 1996 and that this meant considerable job creation. Recent experience indicates that the skill requirements are often much higher for these new jobs. They may even require skills that were sometimes previously unheard of.

Gingras, Massé, and Roy examine the skill requirements of the most rapidly growing occupations – knowledge and management occupations – as well as those of their slowly growing counterparts. Workers with the highest levels of literacy skills are concentrated among knowledge and management occupations, whereas workers with the lowest literacy skills are dominant in the most slowly growing occupations – data manipulation, services, and goods occupations. This suggests that literacy requirements are rising as firms shift employment towards knowledge and management occupations and away from other occupations. Furthermore, Gingras et al. report evidence that knowledge and management occupations require significantly more cognitive, authority-management, and communication skills than other occupations. Employment is thus shifting in a way that raises the demand for these skills and lowers the demand for others, such as gross motor skills.

At the same time, the structural changes that have been occurring in OECD economies cannot be characterized simply as high-growth in sectors employing relatively skilled workers and low-growth in sectors employing the relatively unskilled. As Petit notes in his chapter, the experience of the last two to three decades has been rather more complex. Within industrial sectors, the characterization generally holds: employment has increased somewhat in high-tech sectors such as electronics, biotechnology, pharmaceuticals, and new materials while declining in more traditional industries such as shipbuilding, textiles, and iron and steel. In the service sector, however, employment has grown rapidly in finance, hotels and tourism, social services, and business services, but has been comparatively modest in transportation, communications, and commercial and government services. Unlike the industrial sector, one cannot characterize the service sector as expanding those activities most involved in the production and use of the new technologies.

The magnitude of job turnover in a modern industrial economy is substantial. For example, analysis of longitudinal data on individual establishments in the manufacturing sectors of Canada and the United States indicates job creation rates of approximately 10 percent per year (i.e., 10 percent of all jobs existing in a given year did not exist in the previous year) and job destruction rates of a similar magnitude (Baldwin 1993, Chapter 6). Thus, gross job turnover within the manufacturing sector is approximately 20 percent per year, in contrast to net job creation or destruction, which typically lies in the 1-3 percent per year range. With such high rates of job destruction and creation, the potential for significant changes in skill requirements is clear if the skills needed in the newly created jobs differ from those of jobs that are destroyed. Structural change of this magnitude clearly puts emphasis on a flexible and adaptable labour force, as well as education and training systems that can adjust to the evolving needs of the workplace. (See the introduction to this volume by Rubenson and Schuetze.)

Skill-Biased Technological Change and Income Inequality
One of the most striking labour market developments of the past several decades has been the reduction in employment and/or earnings of relatively unskilled workers – those with the least education and/or labour market experience. In several countries – including Canada, the United States, and the United Kingdom – earnings inequality between the less skilled and the more skilled has widened substantially.[10] Unemployment and non-employment among the less skilled has also risen relative to that experienced by the more skilled. In much of Europe, unemployment has increased (and employment decreased) more among the unskilled than the skilled, although earnings inequality has not increased as in North America. Nonetheless, although there are important differences in the way various individuals and groups are affected, in both Europe and North America a substantial decline in the relative demand for the less skilled has occurred (Katz and Murphy 1992; Nickell and Bell 1995).

A great deal of research has been devoted to understanding these developments. Perhaps the leading explanation has been "skill-biased technological change" – that is, technological change that raises the relative demand for more-skilled workers and lowers the relative demand for the less skilled. Competing explanations include: increased trade and globalization of production; organizational and institutional changes such as the extent of unionization and the level of minimum wages; and macroeconomic conditions that adversely affect particular groups, such as the young and the least educated. Assessing the quantitative importance of the contribution of these various factors is crucial to understanding the implications of the transition to the KBES for many economic and social outcomes, and is a major theme of this volume (see in particular the chapters by Petit; Gingras, Massé, and Roy; and Van Reenen).

As discussed earlier, it is important to note that not all technological change need be skill-biased. Just as technological change destroys some jobs and creates others, it raises some skill requirements and lowers others. In some time periods, the net effect of such change may be to lower skill requirements while in other periods the net effect may be to raise skill requirements. According to the skill-biased technological change (SBTC) theory, the current period of technological change associated with the ICTs is one in which the overall net effect is to raise skill requirements.

One appeal of the SBTC theory is that it is capable of accounting for widening income inequality along all three general dimensions of "skill" – educational attainment, experience, and "within-group" skill differences within age, education, and gender groups. The widening earnings differences can thus be explained as a general increase in the economic returns to skill along all these dimensions.

Perhaps the leading alternative explanation for the higher premium being placed on skill in the labour markets of developed economies is increased trade with low-wage countries and globalization of production. As noted by Petit, this explanation is very difficult to disentangle from the pure technological change view because changes in technology and globalization of production are interrelated.

Although the complex interrelationships between technological change and globalization of production make it difficult to distinguish among competing explanations, the simple view that rising imports from the Third World are the principal cause of the decline in demand for less-skilled workers does not fit well with the evidence. The reason is that this "trade explanation" would be associated with an inter-industry shift in the composition of output in the industrialized countries, as production in these economies shifts out of unskilled labour intensive sectors (reflecting growing imports of goods produced in countries with abundant unskilled labour) and into skill-intensive sectors (reflecting growing exports of goods produced with skilled labour). Such shifts in the industry composition of output have not been observed. Rather, employment of more-skilled workers has increased within most industries in the economy. This intra-industry shift in relative demand towards more-skilled workers is consistent with the SBTC theory but inconsistent with the simple trade explanation.

The chapter by Gingras, Massé, and Roy provides evidence for Canada along these lines. They find that over the 1971-91 period much of the growth in employment of knowledge and management workers (the two occupations growing most rapidly during this period) can be attributed to substitution towards these types of employees within firms and industries. That is, for given levels of firm or industry output and employment, firms have been using more of these types of workers and less of other types. Cross-industry factors – differences in productivity growth and output growth across industries – were less important. Such findings are consistent with the view that technological changes associated with ICTs are raising the demand for certain types of workers across a wide range of firms and industries, rather than being confined to a few sectors of the economy.

Labour market institutions – and changes in the importance of such institutions – have also evidently played a role in changes in inequality. Recent research (e.g., Fortin and Lemieux 1997) concludes that the sharp decline in unionization and the decline in the real value of the minimum wage can together account for about one-third of the rise in earnings inequality in the United States during the 1980s. Countries such as the United States and the United Kingdom, which have experienced significant declines in union representation, have experienced larger increases in earnings inequality than, for example, Canada and many European countries.

Furthermore, as noted by both Petit and Van Reenen in this volume, even if it is the case that technological change is currently skill-biased in nature, this only affects labour demand, raising the demand for the more skilled and lowering that for the less skilled. Changes in relative supplies matter also, and these can be expected to respond to changes in the returns to skill acquisition. The changes in relative demand will alter the relative income and employment of different skill groups only if they outpace changes in relative supplies.

In their analysis of changes in inequality in the US labour market from the early 1960s to the late 1980s, Katz and Murphy (1992) conclude that observed behaviour can be accounted for by a steady increase in relative demand for the more skilled (which they attribute to skill-biased technological change), together with observed supply shifts of more- and less-skilled workers. For example, the premium to a college education (the ratio of earnings of a college-educated worker to those of a high-school educated worker) rose in the 1960s, declined in the 1970s, and then rose steadily during the 1980s and 1990s. The authors attribute these different trends to moderately slow growth of college-educated labour in the 1960s, followed by rapid growth during the 1970s and slow growth during the 1980s and 1990s, together with steady growth in relative demand due to skill-biased technological change. Using a similar methodology, Murphy et al. (1998) found that the relative demand for more educated workers grew at a similar rate in Canada as in the United States. They attribute the absence of a rise in the premium to higher education in Canada to the more rapid growth of the supply of university-educated workers there than in the US.

These findings relating to the role of the supply of more-skilled workers are important because many policies for responding to the opportunities and challenges associated with the KBES operate on the supply side of the labour market. Policies that encourage human capital formation – whether in the form of education, training, or lifelong learning – are important not only because they help to meet the increased demand for more-skilled workers, thus reducing upward pressure on the wages of this group, but also because they reduce the supply of less-skilled workers, thus reducing downward pressure on their wages.

This section has dealt mainly with labour market evidence on the possible relationship between technological change and wage inequality, evidence that is often at a fairly high level of aggregation (for example, separating the total labour force into two groups, "the skilled" and "the unskilled"). In most of this literature, technological change is not observed directly, but is taken to represent the "residual" of forces that cannot be accounted for by observed factors. There is also a growing microeconometric literature that investigates these issues at the industry, firm, plant, and individual levels.

Van Reenen's chapter in this volume provides a useful survey of this literature, focusing on studies that use direct measures of technology instead of associating technological change with unobserved factors such as a residual time trend. He concludes that there is a strong positive effect of technology on skills in cross-sectional data (on firms, plants, or individuals); this positive effect appears to be quite robust to different statistical approaches to analysing the data. He also finds a strong positive effect of technological diffusion on wages, although this effect is not robust to different statistical specifications. Finally, he concludes that at the firm level, product innovations appear to raise employment growth, but there is no clear effect (either positive or negative) of process innovations or R&D on job creation. This latter finding supports the distinction made earlier between the own-industry effects of process and product innovations.

Polarization and Social Cohesion
Closely related to concerns about rising income inequality are fears that the KBES may have a tendency to be characterized by greater polarization in a variety of economic and social outcomes. Indeed, a common theme of the conference on which this volume is based was the importance of avoiding a scenario in which society becomes increasingly polarized into the "haves" and "have-nots," or into "those who know" and "those who don't know."

Evidence to support such fears about increasing polarization comes from several sources, including changes in the nature of work and in the employment relationship. The growing importance of unstable or insecure forms of employment – such as contract work, temporary and casual employment, part-time work, and self-employment – is noted in several chapters, including those of Ursula Huws, Brenda Lipsett, and Pascal Petit. A perhaps related development is the substantial rise during the 1980s and 1990s in feelings of employment insecurity among members of the labour force in many OECD countries (Petit, this volume).

At the same time, it is important to note that such developments do not simply represent a trend towards an economy with "good jobs" – those with stable, secure employment; high wages and benefits; and opportunities for learning and advancement – and "bad jobs" – those with the opposite characteristics. Reality appears to be considerably more complex than this simple characterization. Much part-time work reflects the desire of the employee for a better balance of family life and career, and much self-employment reflects a desire for independence and control over the flow of tasks and the work environment (Huws; Lipsett, this volume). Changes in the nature of work and in the employment relationship reflect not only competitive pressures on firms and their desire for greater flexibility and reduced costs but also the preferences of workers. What are now referred to as "atypical work arrangements" hold out the promise of better matching between the needs of employers and the desires of employees, at the same time as they point to the danger of a society increasingly polarized into "good jobs" and "bad jobs."

A related point is that work arrangements are becoming more heterogeneous. As a consequence, "average behaviour" is increasingly less meaningful as a summary statistic. In those countries that have experienced an increase in income inequality, this development is evident with respect to earnings: fewer workers receive average earnings, and larger numbers earn both more than and less than the mean level of earnings. Similarly, in Canada the average duration of jobs has been remarkably stable over the past two decades, yet there has been both an increase in the amount of short-term employment (jobs that last less than one year) and an increase in the amount of long-term employment (jobs lasting more than 10 years) (Green and Riddell 1997). In a labour market in which work arrangements are becoming more heterogeneous, it is important to examine the distribution of outcomes because summary statistics such as the average outcome are less meaningful than in the past.

Meaning and Measurement of Skills

As discussed previously, there is considerable evidence that the current wave of technological change is increasing the demand for more-skilled workers and reducing the demand for the less skilled. This increased premium on human capital is generally attributed to the complementarity between high-skilled workers and ICTs (Van Reenen; Petit, this volume). But what are the skills that are most valued in the emerging knowledge-based society? An important theme of the conference was that relatively little is known about the answer to this important question.

Most of the social science research on the economic returns to human capital investments uses only crude measures of skill: educational attainment (often measured by years of education or highest level of educational attainment) and labour market experience (often measured by years since completing schooling). However, individuals with the same number of years of education and labour market experience may have widely different skills, depending on their innate abilities, the quality of their schooling, their home environment and parental involvement in schooling, their field of study, the nature of their work experience, and many other factors.

For addressing issues such as whether there are skill deficiencies in the labour force and which particular skills have the highest returns, it is clearly necessary to go beyond crude measures such as educational attainment and labour market experience. Similarly, in order to assess the success or failure of alternative educational policies that may affect the quality of schooling, it is necessary to have direct measures of educational outcomes in terms of the skills and knowledge of students. Putting this point in a way that will be familiar to students of technological change, it is important to get inside the "black box" of human capital in order to see what its various components are. We also need to better understand the relationships between these components and the various economic and social outcomes in which we are interested.

The International Adult Literacy Survey (IALS), described in the chapter by Albert Tuijnman, is a breakthrough in the measurement of the literacy and numeracy skills of the labour force in a manner that permits international comparisons. Three measures are obtained: document literacy, prose literacy, and quantitative literacy (or numeracy). Building on earlier work on international comparisons of student achievement and on previous surveys of literacy skills in the United States and Canada, the IALS methodology has now been applied in more than 20 countries. In those countries in which the survey has been carried out, the results have received substantial attention from researchers, policy analysts, and policymakers.

Design work is currently progressing on the International Life Skills Survey, a successor to the IALS that attempts to measure several "employability skills" and "life skills" in addition to prose, document, and quantitative literacy, including problem solving, interpersonal skills and teamwork, and computer familiarity (Tuijnman, this volume). The social benefits of such innovative investments in data collection appear very large in the current environment.

Massive Change versus Steady but Substantial Change
Several of the contributions in this volume talk about significant changes in the nature and organization of work being associated with the transition to the knowledge-based economy and society. Trends and developments argued to be associated with this transition include: less-hierarchical forms of work organization, more employee involvement in decision making, shared responsibility and teamwork, innovative compensation practices such

as profit sharing and team-based and other incentive pay, and innovations in human resource practices in order to create "learning organizations" (Betcherman et al., this volume).

Although evidence does support the validity of such claims of substantial changes in the organization of work and in the employment relationship between firms and their workers, these developments appear to be taking place gradually rather than rapidly. Thus there is an apparent "disconnect" between accounts, often anecdotal, of massive organizational and structural adjustment and most empirical evidence, which points to steady, albeit significant, change. For example, Brenda Lipsett notes in her chapter that one of the distinct labour market trends in Canada over the past two decades has been a gradual shift towards nonstandard work forms (part-time, temporary, and own-account self-employment) and other work arrangements (home-based, shift work, flextime) that expand working time options and flexibility as well as contribute to firm performance. Over the 1976-97 period, "nonstandard employment" (defined as part-time, short-tenure, and own-account self-employment) rose gradually from about 25 percent to approximately 32 percent of total employment (Betcherman et al. 1998).

Similarly, in their analysis of training practices in Canada, Betcherman et al. (1998) report that despite much talk about "high-performance workplaces" and greater emphasis being placed on the skills and knowledge of employees, only 20 percent of Canadian enterprises could be accurately described as "learning organizations." Others train in response to events, while in most Canadian organizations little or no formal training takes place (Betcherman et al., this volume).

In summary, it is easy to get caught up in the "hype" about the transition to the KBES. Fundamental changes are occurring, but many of these are taking place gradually rather than dramatically. Nonetheless, it is important to keep in mind that there is not necessarily a conflict between the empirical evidence of gradual change and the view that the changes associated with ICTs are transforming the economy and society in profound ways. The industrial revolution brought about massive changes in turning a predominantly rural society into an urban one, but it took nearly 100 years. Similarly, electricity fundamentally transformed almost all aspects of working and living, but this process also took almost a century and those living through the transformation would describe it as gradual rather than abrupt change.

Policy Implications

This section examines policy issues in the context of the KBES. We begin by discussing the general stance of economic policy, including the role of government in the knowledge-based economy. The discussion then proceeds to policies that are more directly related to both the quantity and quality of employment, including policies that may affect earnings inequality, human capital formation, lifelong learning, and workplace organization.

Economic Policy for the Knowledge-Based Society

The implications of the "new growth theory" for economic policy are examined in Richard Lipsey's chapter in this volume. The new growth theory emphasizes the point that technological change responds to economic incentives; that is, technological change is endogenously determined within the economic system, rather than exogenously determined, as had been assumed in previous generations of aggregate models of economic growth. As Lipsey emphasizes, although incorporating endogenous technical change in aggregate macroeconomic models is a new development, scholars who study the microeconomics of research and development and technology have long emphasized that both the discovery of new inventions and the adoption and diffusion of innovations respond to economic incentives.

Perhaps the most important, and certainly the broadest, policy implication of the new growth theory has to do with the role of government in the economy. In particular, in the case of knowledge the standard neoclassical conditions for achieving an optimal allocation of resources – where the role of government is to correct any market failures – do not hold. The reason is that knowledge is not a standard private good like bananas or motorcycles. Rather, knowledge is non-rivalrous – one of the characteristics of a public good – in that one person can benefit from new knowledge without reducing the benefit received by others. Yet knowledge is not a pure public good in that it is at least partially appropriable. It is important to have sufficient incentives for the creation of new ideas and inventions (for example, through patents), and the creation of such property rights on new discoveries will contribute to the appropriability of the knowledge so created. Government has a role, therefore, in determining the institutional and legal forms these property rights may take.

Scholars studying the microeconomics of technological change have reached similar conclusions about the role of government, but for different reasons. These scholars stress the enormous uncertainty associated with the search for inventions and innovations and the "path-dependent" nature of the choices made. As a consequence, there is true uncertainty in the Knightian sense and the conditions for optimal decision making under risk do not hold.[11] In the presence of true uncertainty and path dependency, policy choices tend to be context-specific, so that different countries or regions may make different choices due to differences in their historical development and institutional arrangements. For these reasons, Lipsey concludes that both aggregate models of endogenous growth and detailed microeconomic analysis of technological change lead to the same general conclusion: that no unique set of scientifically determined, optimum public policies exist with respect to technological change in general and R&D or human capital in particular.

This general observation and the detailed study of growth and technological change summarized and discussed by Lipsey lead to several conclusions for policy. Perhaps the most general conclusion is the need for judgement when dealing with technological (and, for that matter, institutional) change. Theory and evidence are important and valuable, but these cannot be relied upon alone.

An implication is the importance of encouraging experimentation. The absence of optimal policies and the fact that policy choices are context-specific imply that governments should try to maximize the amount of experimentation, learn from experience, and alter behaviour in the light of experience. This approach is best accomplished by relying on the private sector for wealth creation, with government providing the background for a dynamic, competitive society.

An important question that arises in science and technology policy is whether particular technologies should be singled out for government support or encouragement. Lipsey's view is that this cannot be avoided. He cites several examples – from agricultural land-grant universities in the United States to breakthroughs in computer hardware and software – in which selectivity has played a key role and in which reliance on the private sector alone would not likely have produced the desired outcomes. In innovation policies it is common to single out particular technologies for public support. And such policies have actually produced many of the crucial technological breakthroughs in the US.

Lipsey cites the airframe for the Boeing 707 and the engines for the 747 as examples where publicly funded military versions were developed first, then transferred to the civilian sector, as were electronic computers, atomic energy, and semiconductors. According to Lipsey, "knowing when and how to ... encourage really important new technologies in their early stages" is "an important condition for remaining technologically dynamic."

He concludes that there is no such thing as a neutral (nondistorting) technology or innovation policy. While he presents theoretical arguments for this conclusion, there are also common sense arguments.

If you pursue a regional policy, you do so because there is unequal economic development of different regions. In other words, you want to support certain regions more than others at the policy level. And such a policy can never be neutral or general. If you pursue an R&D policy, you will have to target resources towards certain areas of science. Should the resources be used in the areas of nuclear research or biotechnology? Such policies must be selective. In Lipsey's scheme, the so-called "facilitating structure" is crucial. This structure is similar to "the system" in what is called the Systems of

Innovation approach.[12] Both approaches deny the existence of optimality, and are also similar in many other respects.

In these perspectives, innovation policy is a matter of influencing the "facilitating structure" or "system," and in this mediated way influencing innovation processes. In this scheme, while the situation can be improved compared with the present, we can never be certain that we are pursuing an optimal policy. This is not to imply that policymakers can do as they please, however. In order to avoid costly mistakes, policy objectives must be clearly specified. The policy must also be based on a detailed diagnostic analysis identifying the "problem" to be mitigated, which factors in the "system" or "facilitating structure" can help achieve these improvements, and how these factors can be influenced from the policy level.

For Europe, for example, this means that policymakers need to confront the issues and problems related to making transitions to new product technologies and markets, because of what Luigi Orsenigo, in his chapter in this volume, calls "the European paradox." We discussed previously the positive direct effects of product innovations on employment. Product innovations could thus be stimulated in Europe if the objectives are to increase employment as well as enhance economic growth.[13] Such a policy would involve identifying and strengthening those manufacturing and service sectors where there appears to be the greatest potential for product innovations. These sectors are often new or young, and they are often characterized by a high R&D intensity, which tends to lead to considerable product development and renewal. In other words, a policy for increased economic growth and employment should stress structural economic change in the direction of new sectors.

At the same time, we noted that the positive employment impacts of process innovations arise from the indirect or general equilibrium effects. Thus an employment-oriented economic growth policy for Europe would stress the importance of achieving these general equilibrium effects as rapidly as possible. This outcome is most likely to occur when there is wage and price flexibility, and rapid transfer of labour and other resources from sectors with declining employment to sectors with expanding employment.

Can these policy directions best be achieved at the country or national level, however? Structural change in the composition of production always occurs at a lower level of aggregation, e.g., in a regional context. Interaction between firms – they might be customers, suppliers, and even competitors – is a crucial source of product innovations. Also important are interactions between firms and other organizations such as universities. These interactions take place in systems, and proximity still matters for such interactions.[14] Therefore innovation policies are often best pursued at the regional level. These issues are discussed in the chapters by David Wolfe and Nicola De Michelis.

Wolfe points to several examples where product innovation in ICTs has been instrumental in transforming regions from old-fashioned and inward-looking into dynamic and advanced areas. Besides physical and educational infrastructure, he stresses community leadership as being important in these processes. Nicola De Michelis addresses the structural funds of the European Union as a redistributing policy instrument. To a certain extent, these funds are used to support product innovation in less favoured regions.

If the proportion of the structural funds used for the purposes of product innovation policy increases, they may be an important instrument in transcending the "European paradox," thereby transforming the EU economy for the benefit of growth and employment.

Perhaps the most important contrast between North America and Europe in this area is the lack of policy coherence between levels of government. Both continents have national, state/province, and local forms of government, but in North America (and especially in Canada), there is little policy coherence and coordination of regional economic development activities among the three levels. Wolfe's chapter identifies some of the factors that appear to underlie successful regional development, such as physical and educational infrastructure and strong community leadership. Successful local development also probably requires greater vertical coordination among governments as well as greater horizontal coordination of stakeholders across many areas.

Employment, Human Capital Formation, and Workplace Policies

The performances of the economies of Europe and North America have differed substantially on a number of key dimensions during the past four decades. During the 1950s and 1960s, Canada and the United States were high-unemployment regions, whereas unemployment rates in Europe were generally quite low. During the 1970s, 1980s, and 1990s, however, unemployment rose sharply in most of Europe but changed relatively little in the United States (apart from ups and downs related to the business cycle).[15] Canada has been an intermediate case, with unemployment rates drifting upward but to a lesser extent than in Europe. Relative to North America, Europe has changed from being a low-unemployment region to a region characterized by high and persistent unemployment.

There have also been significant differences between the two regions in employment creation. Both Canada and the United States had high rates of employment growth during the four decades from the 1960s to the 1990s. In contrast, much of Europe experienced little or no employment growth during this period. As a consequence, the fraction of the population employed (the employment rate) rose during the past four decades in both Canada and the United States but declined significantly in Europe.

A third key dimension on which the Canadian, American, and European economic experience has differed has been in terms of income inequality. Earnings inequality rose sharply in the United States but changed little if at all in most of Europe. Canada is again an intermediate case, with some increase in inequality in certain dimensions but less than that observed in the US.

These significant differences in economic performance result in very different policy concerns in Europe and North America. In the United States, much of the policy attention focuses on income inequality, whereas in Europe the focus has been on employment creation and reducing unemployment. Canadian policymakers have been concerned with both issues.

One policy response to widening income inequality in North America has been heightened interest in earnings supplementation (ES) programs. Although the details of such programs vary, their general purpose is to supplement the employment earnings of low-income families – the so-called "working poor." Because the supplement is based on employment earnings, these programs also have the effect of "making work pay" relative to other forms of income support such as welfare. The latter programs support poor individuals and families independent of their employment earnings; indeed, most welfare programs implicitly "tax back" any employment earnings at rates close to 100 percent, because they reduce welfare payments by the amount of work-related earnings. Earnings supplementation programs thus have stronger work incentives than traditional income support programs such as welfare, because the supplement is conditional on work activity.

The role of ES programs in the context of labour market trends associated with the transition to the knowledge-based economy is discussed in the chapter by John Richards, with particular reference to the Canadian situation. As he notes, earnings supplementation has become a significant policy instrument in the United States due to the substantial expansion of the Earned Income Tax Credit, a program that provides (through the tax system) a large subsidy to the employment income earned by poor families with children. The current Labour government in the UK has also introduced such a program.

In Canada, two provinces (Quebec and Saskatchewan) introduced ES programs during the 1990s. There is also a major social experiment under way in British Columbia and New Brunswick (funded by the federal government), testing whether an earnings supplement can be successful in encouraging single parents on welfare to enter the labour market. As Richards notes, however, ES programs remain a minor part of the Canadian income security system at present. The principal federal income supplementation program for poor families – the Canada Child Tax Benefit –

provides income transfers based on total family income rather than on employment income. Although this program helps to alleviate poverty among Canadian families with children, it does not "make work pay" relative to nonwork forms of income support. Richards argues that Canada should substantially redirect its social security system towards ES programs – in particular, that the country should "experiment aggressively with programs that subsidize earnings among low-income families with children." He also proposes major changes to the Canada Child Tax Benefit. We concur that earnings supplementation programs deserve serious consideration in the current environment. In addition, there are strong reasons for most European Union countries to do likewise.

Although there is support in many of the chapters in this volume for policies to encourage human capital formation, there is less agreement on priorities for bringing this about. One view is that lack of resources for education is not the principal problem. Rather, the challenge is how to obtain better educational outcomes with existing levels of funding. According to this view, there is a need to orient the educational system in many countries towards a more "performance-based system," in which greater effort is devoted to measuring and assessing educational outcomes and greater attention is devoted to determining how educational practices can best achieve desired outcomes.

Similar concerns are raised in several chapters in the areas of training within the firm and lifelong learning more generally. The lack of concrete evidence on rates of return to investments in these activities is an important obstacle. Without such evidence, how can one adequately assess claims that there is underinvestment in lifelong learning and employer-based training? As discussed in the chapter by Betcherman, Leckie, and McMullen, governments can play a valuable role in providing and brokering information in these areas. This type of suggestion is an important shift in emphasis away from more traditional policy levers such as taxes and subsidies.

Finally, several chapters (such as those by Brenda Lipsett and John Richards) draw attention to pressures on the family in the KBES. Although the shift to the knowledge-based economy and society presents many opportunities, it also presents challenges. Maintaining an appropriate work/life balance and strong families are among the more important such challenges.

Notes

1 We are grateful to Richard Lipsey and Philippe Massé for helpful comments on an earlier draft of this chapter.

2 See the essays in Helpman (1998) for further discussion of the concept of a GPT and some analysis of the role of these pervasive technologies in economic growth. Lipsey, Bekar and Carlaw (1998a) discuss related concepts in which pervasive technologies play a central role, such as "enabling technologies" and the "techno-economic paradigm."

3 See Nordhaus (1997) and Harris (1998) for reviews and assessment of these issues in the international and Canadian contexts.
4 This reason is obviously related to the problem of accounting for "new products," since an improved version of an existing product can be considered a new product.
5 Average annual employment growth in Canada over this 25-year period was 2.1 percent.
6 The taxonomy is elaborated on in Edquist et al. (forthcoming).
7 Exceptions are luxury products and products that are new, i.e., at an early stage in the product cycle.
8 The industrial robot is an example.
9 For example, many observers have argued that many of the jobs created during the industrial revolution required less skill than the jobs of the workers displaced by the new technologies (Allen 1986).
10 In Canada this has mainly taken the form of widening income inequality between younger and older workers (i.e., by labour market experience), whereas in the United States widening income inequality between more- and less-educated workers has been a more important factor.
11 Knightian uncertainty refers to the situation in which it is not possible to assign probabilities to the various outcomes that may occur as a result of a set of choices or decisions. In these circumstances, optimal decision making under uncertainty (such as maximization of expected utility) is not well defined.
12 The emergence and characteristics of the Systems of Innovation Approach are addressed in Edquist (1997).
13 Such stimulation does not have to take the form of subsidies. It may, for example, take the form of creation of institutions (in the sense of "rules of the game"). One such institution was the Nordic Mobile Telephony (NMT) standard in mobile telecommunications. It gave a competitive advantage to Finland and Sweden and crucially assisted Nokia and Ericsson in their entry into mobile telephony. It was of crucial importance to these two firms in attaining the global leadership that they have today (Edquist et al. 1998, 48-49).
14 These are sometimes called "regional systems of innovation."
15 For example, in the late 1990s the US unemployment rate (approximately 4 to 5 percent) is essentially the same as that at the beginning of the 1970s.

References
Allen, Robert C. 1986. "The Impact of Technical Change on Employment, Wages, and the Distribution of Skills: A Historical Perspective." In W. Craig Riddell, ed., *Adapting to Change: Labour Market Adjustment in Canada*, 71-110. Toronto: University of Toronto Press.
Baldwin, John R. 1993. *The Dynamics of Industrial Competition: A North American Perspective.* Cambridge, UK: Cambridge University Press.
Betcherman, Gordon, Kathryn McMullen, and Katie Davidman. 1998. *Training for the New Economy.* Ottawa: Canadian Policy Research Networks.
David, Paul. 1991. "Computer and Dynamo: The Modern Productivity Paradox in a Not Too Distant Mirror." In *Technology and Productivity: The Challenge for Economic Policy.* Paris: OECD.
Edquist, Charles. 1997. "Systems of Innovation Approaches – Their Emergence and Characteristics." In Charles Edquist, ed., *Systems of Innovation: Technologies, Institutions and Organizations.* London: Pinter/Cassell.
Edquist, Charles, Leif Hommen, and Maureen McKelvey. Forthcoming. "Innovations and Employment in a Systems of Innovation Perspective: The Role of Process and Product Innovations."
Edquist, Charles, et al. 1998. "The ISE Policy Statement: The Innovation Policy Implications of the 'Innovation Systems and European Integration' (ISE) Research Project." Linköping: Department of Technology and Social Change, Linköping University, Sweden.
Fortin, Nicole, and Thomas Lemieux. 1997. "Institutional Changes and Rising Wage Inequality: Is There a Linkage?" *Journal of Economic Perspectives* 11(Spring): 75-96.

Gera, Surendra, and Kurt Mang. 1998. "The Knowledge-Based Economy: Shifts in Industrial Output." *Canadian Public Policy* 24(June): 149-84.

Globerman, Steven. 1986. "Formal Education and the Adaptability of Workers and Managers to Technological Change." In W. Craig Riddell, ed., *Adapting to Change: Labour Market Adjustment in Canada,* 41-70. Toronto: University of Toronto Press.

Green, David A., and W. Craig Riddell. 1997. "Job Durations in Canada: Is Long Term Employment Declining?" In Michael G. Abbott, Charles M. Beach, and Richard P. Chaykowski, eds., *Transition and Structural Change in the North American Labour Market,* 8-40. Kingston, ON: IRC Press.

Griliches, Zvi. 1994. "Productivity, R&D, and the Data Constraint." *American Economic Review* 84: 1-23.

Harris, Richard. 1998. "Long Term Productivity Issues." In Thomas J. Courchene and Thomas A. Wilson, eds., *Fiscal Targets and Economic Growth,* 67-90. Kingston, ON: John Deutsch Institute for the Study of Economic Policy, Queen's University.

Helpman, Elhanan, ed. 1998. *General Purpose Technologies and Economic Growth.* Cambridge, MA: MIT Press.

Helpman, Elhanan, and Manuel Trajtenberg. 1998. "A Time to Sow and a Time to Reap: Growth Based on General Purpose Technologies." In E. Helpman, ed., *General Purpose Technologies and Economic Growth,* 55-84. Cambridge, MA: MIT Press.

Katz, Lawrence F., and Kevin M. Murphy. 1992. "Changes in Relative Wages 1963-1987: Supply and Demand Factors." *Quarterly Journal of Economics* 107(February): 35-78.

Lipsey, R. 1996. "Economic Growth, Technological Change and Canadian Economic Policy." C.D. Howe Institute, Benefactors Lecture. Toronto: C.D. Howe Institute.

Lipsey, Richard G., Cliff Bekar, and Kenneth Carlaw. 1998a. "What Requires Explanation?" In E. Helpman, ed., *General Purpose Technologies and Economic Growth,* 15-54. Cambridge, MA: MIT Press.

–. 1998b. "The Consequences of Changes in GPTs." In E. Helpman, ed., *General Purpose Technologies and Economic Growth,* 193-218. Cambridge, MA: MIT Press.

Murphy, Kevin M., W. Craig Riddell, and Paul M. Romer. 1998. "Wages, Skills and Technology in the United States and Canada." In E. Helpman, ed., *General Purpose Technologies and Economic Growth,* 283-309. Cambridge, MA: MIT Press.

Nickell, Stephen, and Brian Bell. 1995. "The Collapse in Demand for the Unskilled and Unemployment Across the OECD." *Oxford Review of Economic Policy* 11,1: 40-62.

Nordhaus, William D. 1997. "Traditional Productivity Estimates Are Asleep at the (Technological) Switch." *Economic Journal* 107(September): 1548-59.

OECD (Organization for Economic Cooperation and Development). 1994. *The OECD Jobs Study: Evidence and Explanations.* Paris: OECD.

Riddell, W. Craig. 1997. "Structural Change and Adjustment in the Canadian Labor Market." In Horst Siebert, ed., *Structural Change and Labor Market Flexibility: Experience in Selected OECD Countries,* 223-56. Tubingen: Mohr Siebeck.

Rosenberg, Nathan. 1982. *Inside the Black Box: Technology and Economics.* Cambridge, UK: Cambridge University Press.

Statistics Canada, Human Resources Development Canada, and National Literacy Secretariat. 1996. *Reading the Future: A Portrait of Literacy in Canada.* Ottawa: Minister of Industry.

2

New Growth Theories and Economic Policy for the Knowledge Economy[1]

Richard G. Lipsey

In this chapter, I review the implications of the "new growth theory" for economic policy. Since the aspects of the theories that I will consider here deal primarily with technological change, most of the policies I discuss are technology-enhancing policies – policies usually covered under such rubrics as "S&T policies," "technology policies," and "innovation policies." A further investigation, and it seems to me a potentially fruitful one, would be to study what lessons are implied for human capital, the main topic of the "Transition to the Knowledge Society" conference that generated this volume. But that topic is the subject for a major research paper rather than a chapter based on a keynote address. What I can do here is lay out the key aspects of the new theories of endogenous growth at both the macro and micro levels, show their general implications for economic policy, illustrate how these apply to technology-enhancing policies, and speculate somewhat on their possible implications for labour markets and human capital.

The key objective of the new macro-growth theory is to make sustained economic growth the result of the operation of endogenous forces rather than of *exogenous* technological change, as it is in neoclassical growth theory. The key objective of the new micro-growth theory is to understand in some detail the processes by which endogenous technological change drives long-term economic growth.

In general terms I argue that the new macro-growth theory – which elaborates on the aggregate production function of Solow's original neoclassical growth model (Solow 1956) – has arrived at the same place as the policy analysts and policymakers who have been dealing with the new globalized and knowledge-driven societies. Micro-growth theory got there earlier, but not being in the mainstream, particularly in North America, its influence on policymakers would not have been large. However, because of its microeconomic structure, this theory is able to go further than macro-growth theory, giving more detailed policy insights.

Thus one of the main results of the new growth theories has been to legitimize conclusions that policy analysts and practitioners (many of them economists) had come to some time ago. This is not a useless contribution. Understanding something in theory gives it a legitimacy in the academic community that can never be conferred by accumulated practical experience, and often generates new insights that were only implicit in accepted practices.

The above assertions will surprise some of my academic colleagues, so I point for corroboration to a book edited by John Dunning (1997), *Government, Globalization, and International Business*. Although the new growth theory is mentioned in only one chapter – mine – virtually all the policy conclusions I will mention here are outlined, in some detail, in the various parts of that volume.

The Neoclassical Background

In most of the applied jobs on which I work, I use my neoclassical toolbox and it serves me well. Indeed, neoclassical theory would not have been around for so long were it not so useful. However, to understand the contribution of the new growth theory, we need to discuss various characteristics of neoclassical theory and offer some criticism of neoclassical policy analysis.

The Theory of Market Behaviour

As is evidenced in any standard general equilibrium (GE) model of the Arrow-Debreu type, the neoclassical theory of market behaviour is devoid of institutions, stages of development, or any other of the many characteristics that, to the ordinary observer, distinguish one economy from another. Of course, its strength lies in its generality. But, as I shall argue, this generality is a weakness when it comes to dealing with endogenous technological change.

Neoclassical theory implies a unique set of policy prescriptions that apply with equal force to all economies and all activities, whatever their differences; this is to remove market imperfections. The job can be done by creating effective property rights, establishing perfect competition, discouraging activities that create negative externalities, and encouraging those that create positive externalities. The exact amount of encouragement or discouragement is determined by what is required to equate the marginal social benefit of each activity with its marginal social cost.

Aggregate Growth Models

The neoclassical growth model, which began with Solow's famous 1956 article, uses an aggregate production function. Inputs are transformed by that function into outputs, specifically gross domestic product (GDP). Neither technology nor any aspect of the economy's structure are modelled.

Technology and structure affect the form of the production function, but the ways in which they do so are hidden inside the black box of the aggregate production function.

In the absence of technological change, the form of the aggregate production function is static and the accumulation of capital is subject to diminishing returns, so that per capita growth cannot be sustained. Sustained per capita growth requires sustained technological change, which is assumed to be given exogenously.

The Treatment of R&D

Since technological change is exogenous in the formal neoclassical growth model, research and development (R&D) designed to change technology has no formal role. Nonetheless, following Arrow's seminal 1962 article, R&D has been studied within the framework of neoclassical market theory.

In neoclassical theory, all agents are assumed to be maximizing expected values under conditions of risk; the expected payoff from all lines of R&D will therefore be equated. Importantly, this allows the micro flows of R&D to be aggregated into a single flow with a well-defined marginal product.

The model then implies that, in the absence of externalities, any total amount of R&D expenditure will be optimally allocated among the various lines of research and development. Following Arrow, however, R&D is recognized as having positive externalities: because of the non-rivalrous nature of knowledge, people other than those who produce it benefit from it.[2] It follows that to obtain an optimal allocation of resources, R&D should be encouraged beyond the level at which private agents would voluntarily engage.

This neoclassical case for R&D support calls for general assistance to all R&D, not for specific encouragement of any particular line of activity. The latter will "distort" market signals and cause a departure from the optimal allocation of resources among the various lines of R&D. The required general support can be accomplished by either an equal subsidy to all R&D or a general strengthening of intellectual property rights. The first lowers the cost of R&D and the second raises its payoff. Both can produce the same results, so policy does not discriminate between them.

Macro Modelling of Endogenous Growth

The macro approach to endogenous growth began with Paul Romer's famous 1986 paper, which was followed shortly thereafter by an equally famous paper by Robert Lucas (1988).

Sustained Growth

Romer's concern was, first, to develop an aggregate model in which long-term growth was self-sustaining and did not require exogenous technological shocks, as it did in the neoclassical models. Second, he wanted to explain the acceleration of growth over the last two centuries. His first model used externalities in investment to create increasing returns to knowledge. The model made growth self-sustaining and explained its acceleration in terms of knowledge externalities – the more you know already, the easier it is to acquire a new increment of knowledge. However, the accumulation of these externalities made the growth rate accelerate continuously, producing the erroneous prediction that the growth paths of various nations would diverge continually. Furthermore, empirical research has so far failed to find compelling evidence of the existence of the required externalities at the macro level of observation.

Romer's later models took a somewhat different tack. In his own words (Romer 1990, S71):

> Growth in this model is driven by technological change that arises from intentional investment decisions made by profit-maximizing agents. The distinguishing feature of the technology as an input is that it is neither a conventional good nor a public good; it is a non-rival, partially excludable good. Because of the nonconvexity [increasing returns to scale] introduced by a non-rival good, price-taking competition cannot be supported. Instead, the equilibrium is one with monopolistic competition.

The macro study then split into two lines, which I can mention only briefly here. The first was represented by linear growth models that make sustained growth purely a matter of accumulating the right kinds of factors, including human capital. According to this view, endogenous growth theory does not need to have recourse to technological knowledge as a special type of input that creates difficult-to-measure externalities. Self-sustaining growth occurs because the aggregate production function, however that is understood, just happens to be homogeneous of degree one in the accumulating factors of labour, physical capital, and human capital. Here is a new knife-edge! If the degree of homogeneity is less than unity, growth peters out; if it exceeds unity, national growth paths diverge continuously. Models in this tradition include those of King and Rebelo (1993), Jones and Manuelli (1990), Becker et al. (1990), and Mankiw et al. (1992).

The second line, championed by Paul Romer, argued that what made new growth theory interesting was that it pointed to something that really was different, the nature of knowledge. (See, for example, Romer 1986, 1990, 1994a, b.) Although this approach has some interesting policy implications, the issue of sustained growth generated from within macro models was given a no more satisfactory resolution in Romer's models than in the other traditions; basically, it was assumed. Romer's growth mechanism is that aggregate output depends on the normal (rivalrous) inputs and a stock of non-rival knowledge whose marginal product increases exactly in proportion to its stock. If it increased by less, growth would peter out; if by more, growth would accelerate indefinitely. Although Romer tells us (1990, S84) that this assumption is made "largely for analytical convenience," he goes on to observe that it "is what makes unbounded growth possible, and in this sense, unbounded growth is more like an assumption than a result of the model." Although this model may not solve the problem of the forces behind sustained growth, it does show that growth models can be constructed that break free from the assumption of perfect competition and incorporate some of the nonconvexities that are associated with the creation of intellectual property. Romer's models can explain accelerating growth in terms of both knowledge externalities and increasing amounts of human capital directed towards invention and innovation.

Policy Implications
Some of the policy implications of macro growth models are model-specific and so have no established general applicability. For example, the main conclusions of Romer's 1990 model are that "[1] the stock of human capital determines the rate of growth, [2] that too little human capital is devoted to research in equilibrium, [3] that integration into world markets will increase growth rates, and [4] that having a large population is not sufficient to generate growth" (Romer 1990, S71; reference numbers added). In contrast to conclusion 4, there are models with scale effects that go back at least as far as Allyn Young (1929) in which increasing the size of the population does generate growth – although few people today would say that a large population was *sufficient*. Regarding Romer's conclusion 3, there are models in which increased integration into world markets can lower growth (see especially Grossman and Helpman 1991). As for conclusion 2, virtually all economists have been agreed since Arrow (1962) that imperfect property rights over intellectual property will lead to too little R&D, without the need to derive that proposition from a formal growth model. Yet this proposition does not necessarily hold in a world in which oligopolistic firms compete with each other by developing new product and process technologies – i.e., in the world in which we actually live (see, for example, Lipsey and Carlaw 1998a). Regarding conclusion 1, different macro models show the growth rate to be determined by different elements of the set of key macro variables, of which human capital is only one. Similar contrasts can be made with just about all the specific policy implications of each of the macro growth models now in the literature.

In Romer's theorizing, however, what really matters is that the knowledge that lies behind technology, and hence much of economic growth, is unlike an ordinary private commodity in that it is appropriable but non-rivalrous. We can see what matters here by inspecting a 2×2 matrix that

Figure 1

Rivalrous/non-rivalrous and appropriable/non-appropriable goods

	Appropriable	Non-Appropriable
Rivalrous	NORMAL GOODS *Apples* *Dresses* *TV sets* *Computers* *A seat on an airplane*	COMMON PROPERTY *Fisheries* *Common land* *Wildlife* *Air* *Streams*
Non-Rivalrous	KNOWLEDGE *All codifiable knowledge,* * pure and applied* *All tacit knowledge that* * adheres to individuals*	PUBLIC GOODS *Defence* *Police* *Public information* *Broadcast signals* *Some navigational aids*

Note: Classes of goods that fall into each cell are shown in upper case; illustrative examples are shown in italics.

combines two distinctions: rivalrous/non-rivalrous and appropriable/non-appropriable (Figure 1). Pure private goods of standard economic analysis are rivalrous (if you eat this orange, I cannot also eat it) and appropriable (if I buy it, it is clearly mine, not yours). Pure public goods, such as neighbourhood police protection, are non-rivalrous and non-appropriable – everyone benefits when the police protect some public neighbourhood, and no one can own that protection in order to prevent others who enter that neighbourhood from gaining the benefit. Knowledge is different from both of these. It is non-rivalrous, since one person's use of it does not diminish another person's ability to use it, and it is (at least partially) appropriable, since much technological knowledge can be converted to intellectual property and some can be kept secret, at least for a time.

The upshot of this is that the famous conditions for an optimum allocation of the nation's resources do not apply to knowledge. With normal goods and services, we need only(!) establish perfect property rights and competitive markets and then sit back and let Adam Smith's hidden hand allocate the nation's resources optimally.[3] But intellectual property is not a normal good (or service). A new idea can be used by the person who develops it and by everyone else at the same time.

Although this characteristic of ideas may seem obvious, it is not a feature of most macro-growth models, which treat knowledge and human capital just like any other rivalrous good. Non-rivalrousness, however, has important implications for modelling and policy. The non-rivalrous nature of knowledge introduces a nonconvexity that rules out perfect competition. The theoretical properties of perfect competition are so attractive, however, that many economists seek to preserve it in their models; to do so they need to exclude the non-rivalrous characteristic of knowledge (see theories in the Mankiw et al. 1992 tradition). In contrast, Romer accepts the need to depart from price taking in order to incorporate what seems to him, and to most micro-theorists in the evolutionary tradition discussed below, a critical characteristic of knowledge: one that needs to be accepted if growth in the real world is to be understood.

Another important implication – one that this line shares with the micro-based structuralist-evolutionary (S-E) theories considered below – concerns property rights. Arrow's seminal 1962 piece might lead one to conclude that perfect property rights would remove any market failure connected with the generation of knowledge. Also, the empirical patents literature can be read as no more than an interesting footnote exception to market efficiency. In contrast, the macro theories in the Romer line, and the micro S-E theories considered below, unite in arguing that the non-rivalrous nature of knowledge challenges the belief in market optimality in all markets and at all times. Far from creating a footnote exception, it transforms our understanding of how markets work, both statically and dynamically.

Romer uses this characteristic of knowledge to make many interesting observations and recommendations about policy that are not tied to any single specific macro-growth model. In "Two Strategies for Economic Development," he contrasts the development policy of Mauritius and Taiwan (Romer 1993a). Mauritius sought to attract foreign firms that would bring with them their ideas (technologies) and use the cheap local labour, largely in garment manufacture. In contrast, Taiwan sought to establish local firms that would initially use the ideas (technologies) of others but quickly move to the position where they could generate their own. Romer points out that "gains from using someone else's ideas come from a source that is different from the classical gains from trade." Although he clearly prefers the policy of Taiwan to that of Mauritius, he recognizes what is not in his or any other macro-growth model: that good policies may be context-dependent. For example, Taiwan's success in highly interventionist policies at the initial stages of its growth depended on, among other things, its political structure and its large pool of Chinese entrepreneurial talent.

Recognizing the importance of institutions in the development of ideas, Romer goes on to recommend a new institution to encourage idea development, designed to work within the US context. His article *Implementing a National Technology Strategy* (Romer 1993b) uses the premise that long-run growth is based on our ability to discover innovative ways to "arrange" our limited stock of objects (physical things); such growth could be enhanced if we were equally innovative in finding new ways to "arrange" our institutions. He recommends a national policy that would allow the majority of firms in an industry to agree to set up a research unit to undertake industry-specific (and largely pre-competitive) R&D. To solve the free-rider problem, a mandatory industry-wide tax would be levied once the majority agreed to set up the institution. Competition is preserved by the ability to set up further institutions should the existing ones not function as desired, and to disband any unit when the majority of firms wishes to do so. This solves many of the bureaucratic problems associated with government-sponsored bodies that often develop a life of their own, independent of their ability to provide sufficient value to clients to justify their costs.[4]

Romer (1994b) argues that the welfare costs of protection are much higher in a model that allows for new goods than in the traditional model where goods are given. This is an important addition to analyses of trade policy. However, as John Rae (1834/1905) long ago argued, once technological change is made endogenous, tariffs have a potential for raising welfare. This conclusion has been elaborated by many in the micro tradition considered below. This result leaves the case for free trade a matter of judgement, rather than something that follows from all "reasonable" models.

In "Idea Gaps and Object Gaps in Economic Development," Romer (1993c) further develops his distinction between normal goods and knowledge. According to conventional theory, economies with low living standards and poor growth rates suffer from an "object gap" – they have insufficient physical and human capital. The policy advice is to accumulate more capital of all sorts, either through private accumulation or foreign borrowing. A group that he characterizes as "dissidents" emphasizes the "notion of an idea gap [that] directs attention to the patterns of interaction and communication between a developing country and the rest of the world. In particular, it suggests that multinational corporations can play a special role as the conduits that let productive ideas flow across national borders" (1993, 544). This dissident group of economists deals with technology and institutions at a micro level and with a degree of complexity that cannot be aggregated into formal mathematical macro models of the whole economy. As a result, much of the research is in the form of case studies and other "partial" analyses. The theory used is often what Richard Nelson calls "appreciative." This is tightly reasoned, often verbal, analysis not in the form of formal mathematical models – a form of analysis often used by historians and philosophers but not regarded as serious by many mainline economists. As Romer observes: "In their efforts at being serious scientists, mainstream economists have advocated both formal mathematical modelling and formal statistical hypothesis testing. Both of these styles of research have something important to offer, but if they crowd out other kinds of theorizing and other approaches to the evidence, they can do serious harm."

Because, by and large, this crowding out has occurred, the "dissidents" have not had the impact on the corpus of mainline economists, particularly in the US, that in Romer's (and my) opinion they should have had.

Micro Studies of Endogenous Growth

The group of researchers that Romer characterizes as dissidents, I call structuralist-evolutionary (S-E). Their work emphasizes the importance of a detailed knowledge of technologies and of the process of technological change – something that is *not* required in order to master all of the complexities of aggregate growth theory, whether it treats technological change as exogenous or endogenous.

Inside the Black Box

These micro treatments go inside that neoclassical black box, seeking to understand how technological change actually occurs. Much has been discovered by such analyses, but for present purposes the most important observations are *endogeneity* and *uncertainty*.

Endogeneity

Because R&D is an expensive activity, often undertaken by firms in search of profit, innovation is partly endogenous to the economic system, altering in response to changes in perceived profit opportunities. Indeed, much interfirm competition in nonperfect markets takes the form of competitive innovations. A firm can survive making a mistake over prices or capacity (the two main variables in most conventional theories of the firm), but falling behind in innovation is often disastrous.

The study of endogenous technological change has a long history in microeconomics. In a volume first published in 1834, John Rae studied endogenous technological change and pointed out that it undermined the case for complete laissez faire in general and free trade in particular. In 1912, Joseph Schumpeter made the innovating entrepreneur the centrepiece of his theory of growth (English version, 1934). However, Schumpeter did not study the process of technological change in detail. As a result, he developed a theory that made too sharp a distinction between innovation (whose perpetrators were his heroes) and diffusion (the work of "mere copiers"). In the early 1960s, Nicholas Kaldor – one of the greatest economists to be passed over for the Nobel Prize – developed models of endogenous growth (see especially Kaldor and Mirrlees 1962). His work influenced a generation of European scholars. Also in the 1960s, the historian Schmookler (1966) provided detailed empirical evidence that innovation was endogenous. Nearly two decades later, Nathan Rosenberg (1982) established endogeneity in his classic work, *Inside the Black Box*. After that date, there could be no doubt that technological change was endogenous at the microeconomic level, in the sense that it responded to economic signals. Rosenberg also made a persuasive case that pure scientific research programs respond endogenously to economic signals (1982, Chapter 7, "How Exogenous Is Science?").

Uncertainty

Long ago, Frank Knight distinguished between risk and uncertainty. Risky events cannot be foretold with certainty but they have well-defined probability distributions and hence well-defined expected values. Economic analysis has no trouble handling risk. Agents merely maximize expected values, rather than the actual values that they would maximize in a world of perfect certainty.

Uncertain events have neither well-defined probability distributions nor well-defined expected values. Because innovation means doing something not done before, it always involves an element of Knightian uncertainty. When major technological advances are attempted, it is typically impossible to enumerate in advance the possible outcomes of a particular line of research. Time and money are often spent investigating specific avenues of research to discover whether they are blind alleys or full of immensely rich pots of gold. As a result, massive sums are sometimes spent with no positive results, while trivial expenditures can produce results of great value. Furthermore, the search for one objective often produces results of value for quite different objectives. All this implies that agents will not be able to assign probabilities to different occurrences in order to conduct risk analysis as conventionally defined.

Uncertainty is involved in more than just making initial technological breakthroughs. There is enormous uncertainty with respect to the range of applications that a new technology may have. As new technologies diffuse, their specifications are improved and sometimes altered beyond recognition. Their range of application is also expanded in ways that are impossible to predict.

Not only are researchers and innovators uncertain about what will be discovered and how useful it will eventually prove to be but they do not know how long their new technologies will go on being useful. No one knows, for example, when some superior alternative will end the useful life of the gasoline or electric engine, just as no one knew, in 1850, how long it would take for the steam engine to be dislodged from its position as the industrialized world's most important power source.

The basic uncertainty surrounding invention, innovation, and diffusion arises not from a lack of information that might feasibly be corrected given enough time and money but from the nature of knowledge. Until new knowledge is obtained about some researched phenomenon, no one can know what the nature of that knowledge will be. (To know this is to have the knowledge already.)

A key characteristic of risky situations is that two agents possessed of the same information, and presented with the same set of alternative actions, will make the same choice – the one that maximizes the expected value of the outcome. A key characteristic of uncertain situations, however, is that two equally well-informed agents presented with the same set of alternative actions may make different choices. If the choice concerns R&D, one agent may back one line of attack while the other backs a second, even though both know the same things and both are searching for the same technological breakthrough. After the results are known, one agent may prove to have made a better decision than the other, but no one can say which agent is making the better choice at the time the decisions are made.

Compelling illustrations of choice under uncertainty are seen when competing Japanese and American firms make different R&D decisions while searching for the next advance in some competing product. Sometimes, as with the fifth-generation computer chip, those making the more adventurous attempt find, after the event, that the technical difficulties are too great, and massive investments are written off. There is no simple behavioural lesson here because at another time the firm that takes a conservative tack loses out dramatically when a technological breakthrough is made with surprising ease by its competitor. Decision making under uncertainty is thus the everyday experience of firms whenever the relevant technology is changing endogenously. Incorporating such decision making into economic theory has enormous consequences, however, as we will see below.

In contrast to the real world's uncertainty, models in the neoclassical and new growth traditions usually assume that firms undertaking R&D know the probability that a specific invention will occur, what its range of applications will be, and when it will be replaced by some new challenger. This allows the expected value of any given line of research to be calculated and the optimal allocation of research expenditures to be made. That this kind of knowledge must be assumed to make the models work shows just how far theorists still have to go to grapple with what is known empirically about the microeconomics of technological change. The assumption that R&D decisions involve only risk is, no doubt, a necessary simplification at the early stages of formal theoretical inquiry into phenomena that are very difficult to model. Care must be taken, however, not to base policies on the results of an analysis that may be profoundly misleading about real-world events.[5]

Non-Maximization and Non-Optimality

Because firms make R&D choices under uncertainty, there is no unique line of behaviour that maximizes their expected profits. If there were, all equally well-informed firms would be seeking the same breakthrough in the same way. In the absence of a unique best line of behaviour, firms are better seen as groping into an uncertain future in a purposeful and profit-seeking manner, rather than as maximizing the expected value of future profits. This approach to the behaviour of firms has a long lineage, going back at least to the work of Herbert Simon. Later, it was pioneered in relation to growth and technical change in a seminal book by Richard Nelson and Sidney Winter (1982).

Profit seeking in the presence of uncertainty, rather than profit maximizing in the presence of risk, implies that technological trajectories are path-dependent and non-unique. If we could return to the same initial conditions and play the innovation game again, there is no guarantee that we would retrace our steps exactly. It also follows that there is no unique optimum allocation of resources. For example, we cannot say in advance that more resources should have been devoted to firm A's line of R&D and less to firm B's line. After the event, we may wish that this had been done, but we may equally well wish that more had been devoted to B's line, or we may conclude that the two got the balance between themselves just about right.[6] More generally, when technology is changing endogenously, there is no unique, welfare-maximizing equilibrium of the sort derived in neoclassical static economics. This in turn has another important implication: *there does not exist a unique set of scientifically determined, optimum public policies with respect to technological change in general and R&D or human capital in particular.*

A Structuralist-Evolutionary (S-E) Model of Technological Change

To discuss technological change and economic dynamism, we need some framework – a theoretical model. The standard neoclassical model, found in Part A of Figure 2, shows inputs passing through a macro-production function to produce the nation's output, as measured by its gross domestic product (GDP). Institutions and other structural components are hidden in the "black box" of the aggregate production function, where, presumably, they help determine its form.

The S-E model, found in Part B of Figure 2, is designed to highlight some of the elements of the neoclassical black box that research in technological change shows to be important for economic dynamism. It shows the economy's *structure* and is in line with much microeconomic research on the *evolution* of technology (hence the term *structuralist-evolutionary,* or *S-E*). Since it breaks open the black box, it is called an "S-E decomposition."

The model separates technological knowledge from the capital goods that embody it, making the latter a part of the economy's "facilitating structure." At any point in time, the facilitating structure, in combination with primary inputs, produces economic performance.[7]

Figure 2

Neoclassical (Part A) and structuralist-evolutionary (Part B) models of technological change

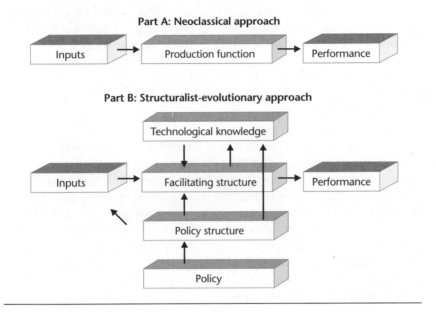

Part A: Neoclassical approach

Inputs → Production function → Performance

Part B: Structuralist-evolutionary approach

Technological knowledge

Inputs → Facilitating structure → Performance

Policy structure

Policy

The six main categories in this model are shown in Part B of Figure 2.

Main Categories

Technological knowledge is the *idea set* of all knowledge on how to create economic value. It includes the specification of products (product technologies), processes (process technologies), and organizational plans for production on the "shop floor" and for the management of firms (organizational technologies). Production includes all economic value – whether design, manufacture, or distribution – of all goods and services, including financial services. Thus the model's concept of technological knowledge is wider than the definition often used.

The **facilitating structure** is the *realization set* of technological knowledge; it embodies that knowledge. To be useful, the great majority of technologies must be embodied in one form or another. The facilitating structure comprises: (1) all physical capital, (2) all human capital (embodied in people), (3) the organization of production facilities, including labour practices, (4) the managerial and financial organization of firms, (5) the geographical location of industries, (6) industrial concentration, (7) all infrastructure, and (8) all private sector financial institutions and instruments.[8]

Public policy is the *idea set* of public policy, covering the specification of policy objectives expressed in such things as legislation and precedent.

The **policy structure** is the *realization set* of public policy, embodying the means of achieving policy. It covers all public sector institutions, rules and regulations, and the human capital of those who administer these public institutions. (Note the parallel between policy and the policy structure on the one hand and technology and the facilitating structure on the other hand.) Public policy, operating through the policy structure, influences inputs, the facilitating structure, and technological knowledge.

Inputs of labour and raw materials are fed through the structure to produce the system's economic performance.

Economic performance covers: aggregate GDP – its growth rate and breakdown among sectors and among such broadly defined groupings as goods and service production; GNP and its distribution among size and functional classes; and total employment and unemployment and their distribution among such subgroups as sectors and skill classes. Economic performance is determined by the interaction between inputs and the existing facilitating structure. That structure is, in turn, influenced by technology and public policy. It follows that changes in technology typically have no effect on performance until they are embodied in the facilitating structure. Furthermore, the full effects on performance will not be felt until all the elements of the structure have been adjusted to fit the newly embodied technology.

Directions of Influence

Changes in technological knowledge cause changes in the facilitating structure embodying that knowledge, as when machines are built to embody new process technologies. Changes in the facilitating structure can lead to changes in technological knowledge, as when new research laboratories are set up. Changes in public policy require changes in the policy structure that gives them effect, as when a new granting body is set up to administer some new subsidy policy. These public policies can then affect the nature of inputs, the facilitating structure, and technological knowledge either directly or indirectly (by altering those parts of the facilitating structure that engage in R&D).

The S-E Analysis of Growth

We cannot explore here the evolutionary modelling of economic growth that had its modern beginning in Nelson and Winter's seminal 1982 book. In the next four subsections, we merely note some conclusions that are important for the topic of this volume. The first concerns the importance of technological change as an engine of growth. The other three follow from the use of macro production functions in growth theory.

Although our points are new, the general concerns were originally expressed by such Cambridge economists as Joan Robinson and Nicholas Kaldor, in their debates in the 1950s and 1960s over neoclassical capital and growth theories. They asked such questions as: What does it mean to assume the existence of a single aggregate production function over the centuries when technologies are changing continuously, and sometimes radically? What does it mean to have (or not to have) constant returns to scale in such an artificial construct as this stable aggregate production function applied over centuries? What is meant by the concept of pure capital measured as a single magnitude, when actual capital is an array of different goods that embody different and changing technologies, and that are used to produce a constantly changing array of final goods and services? Whether or not these questions can be answered satisfactorily, mainline theorists have proceeded to use macro production functions in both neoclassical and new growth theory models.[9]

Technology as the Main Engine of Growth

The first and most important conclusion is that the main engine of long-term economic growth is technological change. S-E theorists do not believe that relevant evidence is provided by the mere data-tracking ability of some constant-returns aggregate models, in which growth is driven by the accumulation of physical and human capital rather than by technological change.

To S-E economists, the historical evidence that technological change is the main engine of long-term growth is conclusive. We can, however, argue for the importance of technological change with a simple thought experiment in which technological knowledge is frozen at the levels existing in 1900, while over the next century 1900-vintage machines and factories are accumulated (at value equal to the actual measured investment over the century) and used to produce more 1900-vintage goods and services. Human capital is also amassed by training more people longer and more thoroughly in the technological knowledge that was available in 1900. Today's living standards would then be vastly lower than those we now enjoy (and pollution would be a massive problem). The contrast is even more striking if we make the same thought experiment comparing today with the knowledge, product, process, and organizational technologies that existed at even earlier points in time.

As I have put it elsewhere (Lipsey 1999):

This thought experiment illustrates what economic historians and students of technology are agreed on: technological change is *the* major determinant of long-term, global economic growth. So the problem of explaining growth over time and across countries is mainly one of explaining the generation, adaptation within one country, and international diffusion of, new product and process technologies. In the long term, these new technologies transform our standards of living, our economic, social and political ways of life, and even our value systems.

We should not conclude, however, that savings, investment, and capital accumulation are unimportant for growth. Most new technologies must be embodied in new capital equipment, whose accumulation is measured as gross investment. This makes technological change and investment complementary, the latter being the vehicle by which the former enters the production process. Anything that slows the rate of embodiment through investment, such as unnecessarily high interest rates, will slow the rate of growth, just as any slowdown in the development of new technology will do the same in the long term.

Sustained Growth

My colleagues and I have argued elsewhere that the problem of explaining why long-term growth can be sustained is an artifact of the aggregate production function. Three S-E propositions put a different light on the issue of sustained growth. First, technological change is driving long-term growth. Second, there is no foreseeable limit to new knowledge. Third, there is no reason new knowledge should obey some postulated law of diminishing returns. It follows that there is no reason growth cannot persist indefinitely, and no general expectation that its rate will follow some smooth path of acceleration or deceleration.

In Lipsey and Bekar (1995, 19-21) we argued the point as follows:

[As] any one technology evolves over time ... its productivity [may] approach an upper limit beyond which further improvements are difficult if not impossible. [However] when there is a shift from one technology to another and then to a third, there is no reason to expect any particular relation between the increments of output that arise in moving between technologies. Consider, for example, successive energy technologies. The factories of the First Industrial Revolution were powered by water power (K_1). Then, in the early nineteenth century, the transition was made to steam (K_2). Then in the period from 1890 to 1930 electricity replaced steam (K_3). At some future time, nuclear fission and/or fusion may replace fossil fuels as the main generators of power for electricity (K_4). Still later, electricity itself will give way to some hard-to-imagine, new energy source (K_5).

Now consider the increment in total constant-dollar value of production $[Y(K_{n-1})-Y(K_n)]$ that is due to each shift from one technology to the next technology. No matter how the impact is measured, there is nothing in physics or economics to suggest that the increments in going from one technology to the next have to be ordered in the following way:

$$[Y(K_2)-Y(K_1)] > [Y(K_3)-Y(K_2)] > [Y(K_4)-Y(K_3)] > [Y(K_5)-Y(K_4)]$$

Indeed, there are no currently known general principles to suggest any particular relation, and we can see many different ones in history. Historical experience suggests that, as time passes, one technological change may bring massive gains, to be followed by another that brings smaller gains, to be followed by a shift that brings larger gains – and that this is true of each of the many fields in which technology is used.

So there is nothing in the economics of ideas to suggest diminishing returns to new knowledge as technological knowledge accumulates. The message is that there are no known limits to economic growth based on technological change (as there are to growth based on capital accumulation with given knowledge). As long as investment in capital goods is continuously embodying new technological knowledge there are no limits to growth based on capital accumulation – since this is merely one important way in which new knowledge gets into productive use.

No Productivity Paradox

Because in neoclassical theory technological change can be observed in aggregate models only by its effects on total factor productivity (TFP),[10] it seems paradoxical to be told that observations outside of those incorporated in this theory show massive information and computer-related technological changes while TFP is registering only small gains. The separation of technological change and economic results in S-E theory suggests two separate reasons that the magnitudes of changes in technology and TFP need not be strongly related.

First, as Paul David has emphasized (see especially David 1991), technological change makes its effects felt only after it has been embodied in the facilitating structure. The required changes are not just in the machines that embody the technology directly but in all the cooperating technologies and organizational structures. This typically takes decades and, in the meantime, big technological changes that eventually bring large productivity gains may not be associated with such gains. Second, and more fundamentally, there is no reason to expect a one-to-one relationship between the magnitude of the technological change and the magnitude of the change in economic results. A new technology is introduced when it is expected to give better results than the one it replaces. But sometimes these gains may be large and at other times they may be small.

So S-E theory suggests that the problem of the productivity paradox arises only because of the artifact of compressing growth into an aggregate model built on a single aggregate production function. When that black box is broken open, there is no expectation whatsoever about the relation between the magnitudes of any technological change and the change in economic performance. For example, the early industrial revolution, in which water-powered factories replaced cottage industries, brought about only small, possibly negligible, changes in productivity and real wages.

Confusion Between Changes in Technology and the Facilitating Structure

Because aggregate models treat both technology and the facilitating structure as a black box, major changes in the facilitating structure are often misconstrued as major changes in technology. For example, the movement out of cottage production into water-powered factories was a major structural adjustment. It transformed ways of life in general and ways of organizing economic relations in particular. Yet the technological changes were not all that dramatic, and neither were the productivity changes. Since the 11th century, the waterwheel had increasingly been used to mechanize European production, and machines for producing textiles and related products had been improving more or less continuously since the late Middle Ages. The point is as important as it is obvious, once an S-E decomposition is set out. Changes in technology, the facilitating structure, and economic performance are seen to be separate phenomena. Related changes in these three, even if they are all driven by the same technological advance, do not have to be of similar magnitude.

An S-E Analysis of Policy[11]

Because it deals explicitly with structure, S-E theory has a lot to say about the details of technology-enhancing policies. I give some examples below. They are designed partly to show the power of S-E theory and partly to show the contrast with the general prescriptions that follow from neoclassical analysis.

Policy Judgement

If because of the non-rivalrous nature of knowledge, as emphasized by Romer, and because of pervasive uncertainty surrounding technological change, as emphasized in S-E theory, we accept the conclusion that there is no unique optimum allocation of resources, there are important consequences for how we view economic policy in the area of growth and technological change. If there is no unique optimum rate of R&D, of innovation, and of diffusion, policy with respect to these matters must be based on a mixture of theory, measurement, and subjective judgement.

As we have argued elsewhere (Lipsey and Carlaw 1998a, 47):

> The need for judgement does not arise just because we have imperfect measurements of the variables that our theory shows to be important, but because of the very nature of the uncertain world in which we live. Although a radical idea with respect to microeconomic policy, the point that policy requires an unavoidable component of subjective judgement is commonly accepted with respect to monetary policy. For two decades from the mid 1950s to the mid 1970s, Milton Friedman tried to remove all judgement from the practice of central banking by making it completely rule-based. When his advice was followed by several of the world's central banks, the monetary rule proved ineffective as a mechanical determinant of policy – just as many of his critics had predicted. Today, the practice of central banking is no different from the practice of most economic policy: it is guided by theoretical concepts; it is enlightened by many types of empirical evidence which are studied for the information that each provides; and, in the end, all of these are inputs into the *judgement calls* that central bankers cannot avoid making.

Rejecting optimality does not imply rejecting science and technology policies in general or an R&D subsidy in particular. What is rejected is the idea that we can determine *the* best amount of R&D and innovation activity by comparing the actual amount against some criterion of optimality. Instead, it is a judgement call that there is a case for policies designed to accelerate the current rate of technological advance, either in general or in specific applications. This is a judgement call that virtually all governments are revealed to make – by virtue of their many technology-enhancing policies – and it is a judgement call that we are prepared to support.[12]

Complex Externalities

Aggregate neoclassical models deal with a generalized externality arising because knowledge has value to parties other than those who pay for its creation.[13] A richer, more complex set of externalities can be revealed in two ways.

First, we can disaggregate and observe externalities, industry by industry or sector by sector. When we do this, we see that what looks at the macro level like a single homogeneous externality associated with the accumulation of technological knowledge is actually composed of many different and complex externalities, some of which are negative – as, for example, when a new discovery in bioengineering turns out to have unexpected harmful effects. Thus giving equal assistance to all technological advancement is a blunt weapon, even if this could be done. It encourages all activities equally, whether externalities are high or low, positive or negative. Even when all other neoclassical assumptions are accepted, therefore, the optimal policy is not to encourage all R&D equally. Instead, the ideal subsidy would be proportional to the amount of the externalities in each line of R&D. This argument shows that aggregated models do not merely suppress a few second-order details; instead they make predictions about some policies that conflict with those arising from an S-E decomposition.

Second, we can make an S-E decomposition, which allows us to see *new classes* of externalities. One such class is among technologies. The development of a new technology will raise the values of some existing technologies and lower the values of others. Another class is externalities between technologies and the facilitating structure. A new technology will alter the values of many of the elements of the existing facilitating structure, in some cases upward and in other cases downward. Conversely, a development in the structure will alter the value of existing technologies. A third class is between performance and technologies. In a process that Rosenberg (1982, especially Chapters 6 and 8) calls *learning by using,* those who use a technology – particularly a new technology – are in effect doing research for the product's makers. Their experience feeds valuable information back to producers, helping them improve their products. In the early stages of important new technologies, such as a new generation of passenger aircraft or computers, this feedback can be highly valuable.

All of these externalities create opportunities for public policy. For example, policymakers may encourage the development of specific elements of the facilitating structure in an attempt to alter the value of the research that makes use of that structure. New research labs may be subsidized and linkages may be encouraged between university, government, and private research centres.[14]

No Neutral Policy

In the neoclassical model, a generalized subsidy to R&D is neutral with respect to private incentives. The expected value of the payoff to the last dollar's worth of R&D will be the same in all lines of activity, both before and after the introduction of the nondistorting R&D subsidy. In the neoclassical, risk-only world, this is *the optimal way* to counteract the externality that arises from the underproduction of knowledge (due to its public-good aspects).

In contrast, when uncertainty is present there are no well-defined expected values. One implication is that there is no unique optimal R&D policy. Neither is there such a thing as a neutral or nondistorting policy. The various instruments of R&D policy will have different effects on the amount of R&D performed, depending on both the technological and the structural contexts within which they operate.

To the extent that the object of technology policy is to provide adequate incentives, ideal public assistance will vary inversely among agents according to their ability to capture the returns of invention and innovation; it would give a return to each inventor/innovator just sufficient to provide the appropriate incentives.[15] The resulting technological knowledge would then be made freely and immediately available. However, S-E theories do not per se preclude policy instruments such as patents, R&D subsidies, or investment tax credits. Rather, they provide an explanation for the effects of these instruments, and a method of going beyond them. In the neo-classical world there is a unique best policy, but in the S-E world the best set of policies is context-dependent, that is, the efficacy of a given policy depends on the specific context in which it is applied. Below, I offer a few of the many possible illustrations.

No Simple Invention/Diffusion Trade-off In simple models, invention and diffusion are separate activities. This creates the appearance of a simple trade-off between more secure property rights to encourage invention and less secure property rights to encourage diffusion. If we give perfect property rights to inventors, we allow them to act as monopolists. They will extract rents, slowing the diffusion of the knowledge of their inventions. If we give no property rights, we maximize diffusion of *existing* inventions but provide little incentive for inventors to risk their time and money on discovering new applied knowledge.

Micro studies of technological change show that inventions are inter-related or bundled, as one piece of new knowledge contributes to the discovery of another. Furthermore, complex technologies do not come into the world fully developed. New technologies usually begin operation in crude form. As they diffuse through the economy, their efficiency and range of application improve and expand. Many of these new uses require the invention of additional supporting technologies. (Steam, electricity, lasers, and computers are typical examples of technologies that started in crude form and took decades, sometimes centuries, to develop much of their potential.) It follows that patents slow not only diffusion but also downstream invention and innovation.

In practice, therefore, invention and diffusion are interrelated. Any measure that slows diffusion will certainly slow the rate at which related downstream inventions occur, making the overall effect indeterminate in the absence of detailed case-by-case knowledge. In terms of policy, we cannot assume that by strengthening property rights we will always accelerate invention (while slowing diffusion). By strengthening property rights, we slow *diffusion of any given pre-existing set of inventions*. In general, however, we cannot know the effect on future inventions, many of which depend on the diffusion of existing inventions, or on the total amount of future diffusion.[16]

R&D versus Intellectual Property Protection   R&D support is independent of results. An R&D subsidy lowers costs equally for everyone doing R&D, whether their efforts succeed or fail, and whether or not successes create externalities. In contrast, stronger intellectual property rights do not raise returns equally, since the ability to extract value from patents varies greatly across types of innovation. In some lines of activity, patents are relatively easy to enforce. Firms in industries such as chemicals and pharmaceuticals are able to internalize enough of the value they create to be strongly motivated to innovate. In other cases, such as consumer goods and processes, patents are of little value in protecting markets. (They are still taken out, but for other reasons; see, for example, von Hipple 1980.)

It follows that for any given amount of aggregate R&D, the allocation among firms will differ according to whether it is induced by an effective patent system or by an R&D subsidy.

Pre-Commercial Research   In some lines of work, the inability to keep the results of pre-commercial research secret discourages firms from engaging in such research; in other lines of work, the ability to keep results secret may lead to too much duplication of virtually identical research (Lipsey and Carlaw 1996). A focused policy that discriminates between situations where the free market produces too much pre-competitive research and where it produces too little is potentially superior to a policy that merely encourages more of whatever is already being done. For example, where individual firms find it difficult or impossible to maintain the secrecy of their research, focused policies can create commitments among firms that encourage them to do pre-commercial research from which they all benefit. (In the past, Japan's Ministry of Trade and Industry [MITI] has been very strong in creating the type of commitment that allows a group of firms to conduct pre-commercial research as a joint venture.)

A broad support policy not only covers some activities that do not need support but also misses some that do. For example, because no clear distinction exists between innovation and diffusion, much activity related to the development and use of new technologies may not be classified as basic R&D. John Baldwin has repeatedly pointed out that while small firms do little recognizable R&D, they spend a lot of time monitoring what larger firms are doing and adapting it to their own uses. This activity may be as important as upstream R&D, but typically it is not covered by broad polices such as R&D tax credits or subsidies. More generally, it is only Revenue Canada's definition of R&D that earns tax credits. The problem is illustrated by recent concerns about the harmful effects of tightening the department's criteria for acceptable R&D. Because any policy is interpreted and administered by civil servants, neutrality is much harder to achieve in practice than on the theoretician's drawing board. This is not a quibble. Once one accepts that there is no unique optimal set of policies, the context-specificity must include the institutional capabilities and biases of those who administer policy – what we call the policy structure.

Technologies Can Be Singled Out   Neoclassical theory calls for a generalized subsidy to all R&D as *the* optimal policy. It is opposed to policies that focus on specific sectors or technologies. We dissent. Many important technologies have been encouraged in their early stages by public sector assistance. US policy provides many examples of this important point. (American examples are chosen because many American economists argue that governments have no part to play in assisting the advancement of specific technologies.)

Many countries, including the US, went through the early stages of industrialization with substantial tariff protection for their infant industries.[17] In the United Kingdom, the subsequent home of free trade, the prohibition on importing Indian cotton goods was critical to the development of the First Industrial Revolution. From their inception in the 19th century, publicly funded US land-grant universities conducted research important to the agricultural industry. The "green revolution" in the 20th century was, to a great extent, researched by public funds. In its early stages, the US commercial aircraft industry received substantial assistance from the National Advisory Committee on Aeronautics (NACA), which, among other things, pioneered the development of large wind tunnels and demonstrated the superiority of the retractable landing gear. Both the airframe for the Boeing 707 and the engines for the 747 were developed in publicly funded military versions before being transferred successfully to civilian aircraft. Electronic computers and atomic energy were largely created in response to military needs and military funding. For many years, support for the US semiconductor industry came mainly from the military, whose rigid procurement standards and quality controls helped to standardize practices and diffuse technical knowledge. The US government's heavy involvement in the early stages of the US software industry produced two major spin-offs to the commercial sector. One was an infrastructure of academic experts, built largely with government funding; the other was the establishment of high and uniform industry standards.

The list can be extended almost indefinitely. As the examples illustrate, an important condition for remaining technologically dynamic, at least in some areas of advance, is knowing when and how to use public funds to encourage really important new technologies in their early stages. I hasten to add that this is no easy task.

No One Optimal Set of Policies for All Countries?   Neoclassical theory produces one unique set of optimal policies. Since these are not context-specific, they apply to all countries no matter what their circumstances. S-E theory recognizes many country-specific influences, one of the most important of which is the country's stage of development.

The problems facing catch-up economies are different from the problems facing those trying to stay on the cutting edge of technological advance. Catch-up economies, especially in their earlier stages, have the advantage of dealing with already established technologies. Although uncertainties associated with local adaptations of generic technologies and the acquisition of tacit knowledge remain, many of the main uncertainties surrounding cutting-edge advances have been resolved.

Whether in catch-up or leading-edge situations, the belief that civil servants knew better than private sector agents, and could efficiently dictate R&D decisions to them, rarely achieved good results. Many catch-up Asian countries, however, championed consultative processes whereby the government agency (MITI in Japan's case) and the main private sector agents pooled their knowledge and came to a consensus on where the next technology push should be. (For further discussion, see Lipsey and Carlaw 1996 and Lipsey and Wills 1996.) The parties then jointly financed the required research. This policy worked well in the catch-up phase and still works well when all private sector agents are pushing for *fairly well-defined* small to intermediate advances in pre-competitive technology. Consensus and cooperation can then reduce wasteful duplication of research. In the search for major breakthroughs at the cutting edge, however, the uncertainties argue for a multiplicity of investigations, each pursued with the minimum required resources. In such cases, it has often been demonstrated that concentrating effort – even after a national consensus has been reached – is worse than the apparent "wastefulness" of uncoordinated free market experimentation. Examples include Japan's costly failures in high-definition TV, overtaken by the digital revolution, and the fifth-generation chip, which proved too big a technological jump to succeed against the more conservative US approach.

Confusion arises when the variance between catch-up and leading-edge economies in what constitutes an appropriate policy is not accepted. First, take the neoclassical prescription of one set of common policies for all, and the World Bank's dichotomy between government intervention and market-friendly policies. These confuse the real issue, which is to find the right set of context-specific policies that avoid laissez faire on the one hand and direct government control over the innovation process on the other hand. Second, when a country's institutions that worked well at the catch-up stage begin to run into trouble at the cutting edge, as are many of Japan's, there is a danger of drawing the wrong lesson. The neoclassical conclusion is often that the policies were bad policies in general, rather than that they were inappropriate to the new circumstances. Third, because many countries have some sectors at the cutting edge and some at the catch-up stage, the wrong lesson can be drawn when policies appropriate to one sector fail in another.

Beyond R&D

Neoclassical analysis recognizes R&D alone as a suitable object for encouragement. Tests of policy effectiveness tend to concentrate on the amount of R&D encouraged or the new technologies established. In contrast, S-E studies of innovation reveal other lines for policy assistance. (For more detail, see Lipsey and Carlaw 1998b.)

Diffusion. Acquiring codifiable knowledge about new technologies, as well as tacit knowledge of how to operate existing technologies, often requires heavy fixed costs. Small firms thus typically operate in "rational ignorance" about the full array of relevant existing technologies.[18] Government bodies can assist the dissemination of technological knowledge by operating on a scale that makes the sunk costs bearable, even trivial, where otherwise they would be prohibitively high for small firms. The institutional design of such programs is critical if they are to succeed in this difficult area. In Canada, the successful Industrial Research Assistance Program (IRAP) is a case in point.

Induced changes in structure. Policies may also indirectly target technological change by altering elements of the facilitating structure. Examples include attempts to integrate university, government, and private sector research activities; create technology information networks; and change private sector attitudes towards adopting new or different technologies. Furthermore, a government can give funds to firms to develop technologies they would have developed anyway, but attach structural conditions to the assistance. More than one government has done this to encourage the development of long-range research facilities, including the Canadian government's Defence Industry Productivity Program (DIPP). All of these initiatives would fail narrow neoclassical tests that evaluate programs only by the direct changes they induce in specified technologies. Wider tests, however, consider structural alterations that would not have occurred without government pressure. A prime example, already referred to, is the US military procurement policy that virtually created the US software industry. A case can be made that DIPP achieved something similar – although on a less ambitious scale – for the Canadian aerospace industry.

Conclusion

The Romer branch of macro endogenous growth theory and the structuralist-evolutionary microeconomic branch are shedding new light on many issues of economic policy. New light may also be shed on the nature and importance of human capital, although so far this has not occupied the attention of researchers in these traditions as much as technology-enhancement policies. Several aspects need fuller investigation:

1   The significance of the non-rivalrous nature of knowledge requires consideration (i.e., rather than treating knowledge as a normal rivalrous good, as in much of the Lucas tradition of new growth theory).
2   The importance of tacit knowledge, whose significance for economics was first emphasized by Nelson and Winter (1982) must be assessed.
3   There is the need for human capital to complement new embodied technologies, whereas capital accumulation is given prime emphasis in neoclassical and Lucas-style endogenous models.
4   The importance of idea generation and rapid idea assimilation as engines of long-term growth requires investigation, both in economies that are at the cutting edge of technological development and in those that are seeking rapid catch-ups.

To conclude, we should note the good news. Economics need no longer be the dismal science it was when growth theory – from Adam Smith to Solow – was dominated by considerations of diminishing returns to the accumulation of capital. As I have put it elsewhere (Lipsey 1994, 351):

> The modern title should become "the optimistic science" – not because economics predicts inevitable growth or the arrival of universal bliss, but because its underlying structure, altered to incorporate the economics of knowledge, implies no limit to real-income–creating, sustainable growth, operating in a basically market-organized society. If we cannot achieve sustained and sustainable economic growth, the fault dear Brutus must lie with ourselves not with some iron-clad economic law that dictates failure before we start.

Notes

1   For comments and suggestions I am indebted to Kenneth Carlaw, Charles Edquist, and Paul Romer.
2   See Demsetz (1969), Hirshleifer (1971), and Dasgupta and Stiglitz (1980) for criticisms and further contributions, and Backhouse (1999) for an analysis of why we stay with Arrow.
3   Never mind that markets are not perfect; economists who use this neoclassical model tend to argue that there is sufficient competition to ensure that the actual allocation of resources will approximate, if not precisely achieve, the optimum. However, this must be taken on faith, since it is not something that can be demonstrated.
4   Romer's proposal also has some problems of its own. Here are two examples. First, the proposal does not deal with the free-rider problem that arises because industries do not operate in airtight compartments in which the ideas developed in one industry are of no interest or value to other industries. Second, the ability to make a "majority" decision to set up such a body to be funded by an industry-wide tax depends on how the majority is defined. Consider an industry with a few big firms and a fringe of many smaller firms. If

the decision procedure is "one firm, one vote," the large firms could be forced by the majority of small firms into financing research that they did not want, or did not anticipate benefiting from. If votes are weighted by size, then large firms could extract research money from the small firms to do research from which only the large firms benefited.

5 For examples of this kind of theorizing, see Chapters 3 and 5 in Helpman (1998), and for an elaboration of the points made in the text paragraph, see Chapters 2 and 8 in the same book. Although the authors of these abstract theories are aware of the extreme nature of their simplifying assumptions, I worry that many of their readers will be less well informed. Students who struggle to grasp the difficult mathematics used in the models may come to believe that the models provide an adequate description of the process of technological change.

6 In Lipsey (1994) I have analysed in more detail why endogenous technological change at the micro level destroys the concept of an optimum allocation of resources.

7 This model lies at the core of the analysis found in the forthcoming book by Lipsey, Bekar, and Carlaw, and is used in all their existing publications on growth and technological change.

8 We are sometimes criticized for making this too embracing. We mean it to be embracing. It covers all realizations that go towards creating economic value. The theory requires that we can distinguish the idea set from the realization set, not that we can fully enumerate the elements of the latter set.

9 When economists tried to test the various versions of aggregate growth models, microeconomists were skeptical about the value of the exercise. They pointed out that these models could not be explanations of very long-term growth because backward projection created anomalies. A model of divergent growth rates projected backward puts all countries at identical growth positions a century or two in the past. A model of convergent growth rates shows vast and growing differences when projected backward. The evidence of long-term growth is that economies diverged at some times and converged at other times. A minimum requirement for an adequate theory of long-term growth is that it can explain alternating periods of divergence and convergence. None of the existing aggregate growth models seeks to meet this minimum condition.

10 TFP is the amount of the increase in measured output that cannot be statistically associated with increases in measured inputs (usually physical and human capital and labour).

11 This section uses conclusions reached in Lipsey and Carlaw (1996, 1998a, b).

12 The need to encourage technological advance through public policy can be thought of as a response to a market failure, so there is no need to ban this concept from S-E theory. Whereas in neoclassical theory the market fails when it does not achieve the unique optimal equilibrium, in S-E theory it fails when it does not lead to some desired and attainable state.

13 To summarize what has gone before, in the neoclassical, microeconomic, risk-only world, each and every activity is carried out until its expected marginal benefit equals its marginal cost. It follows that a dollar's worth of R&D expenditure has the same expected value everywhere in the economy. This allows the aggregation into a macro model in which a non-differentiated body of knowledge is a factor of production and the optimal policy is to increase its acquisition until the marginal cost equals the social value of another generalized unit of knowledge. The knowledge externality results in too little R&D everywhere. It follows that the optimal policy is to provide a generalized subsidy to R&D, lowering its costs by the amount of the social externality. Furthermore, it does not matter whether a subsidy is used to reduce the cost of R&D or whether improved intellectual property rights are used to increase the payoff to R&D. Both give that same smooth acceleration in the acquisition of knowledge in all lines of activity. Since they lower costs or raise returns equally everywhere, they are, in the technical jargon, "nondistorting" or "neutral" interventions.

14 Policies of this type are studied in more detail in Lipsey and Carlaw (1998b), Chapters 2 and 4.

15 In the neoclassical model with smoothly variable R&D expenditure, it is optimal to internalize all externalities. In an S-E model that recognizes empirical lumpy expenditures with

uncertain and lumpy results, paying the social value of some major new technology to its originator is usually unnecessary.

16   James Watt's patent on his steam engine provides an example in which a patent slowed invention as well as diffusion. Watt opposed high-pressure engines and, until his patent expired in 1800, the further development of his engine was prevented. Within two years of its expiry, Trevithick had produced a high-pressure engine whose favourable power/weight ratio was essential to expanding the uses of steam. The invention of the railway and the iron steamship, along with many other applications, was held up by Watt's patent, which not only slowed the existing steam engine's diffusion but, more importantly, stalled the invention of many new technologies that required high-pressure engines.

17   It is worth noting, although we do not have space to go into it in detail here, that the standard infant industry argument for tariff protection is altered when technology is recognized as being endogenous. In the standard model with known technology, the only reason for imposing an infant-industry tariff is to assist the industry in moving along a downward sloping long-run cost curve (i.e., to exploit economies of scale) when capital markets are imperfect. With endogenous technology, tariff protection serves many purposes, including providing time to develop activities that confer major externalities and to develop the kinds of structures conducive to technological diffusion and advance.

18   Rational ignorance occurs when the cost of obtaining knowledge exceeds the expected value of that knowledge. There would be no rational ignorance if the cost of obtaining knowledge were zero.

References

Arrow, K. 1962. "Economic Welfare and the Allocation of Resources for Invention." In *The Rate and Direction of Economic Activity: Economic and Social Factors*. Princeton: NBER.

Backhouse, Roger. Forthcoming. *Modelling Invention: The Use of Models in the Neoclassical Literature*. Birmingham, UK: University of Birmingham.

Becker, G., K. Murphy, and R. Tamura. 1990. "Economic Growth, Human Capital, and Population Growth." *Journal of Political Economy* 98,5 (Part 2): S12-S137.

Dasgupta, Partha, and Joseph Stiglitz. 1980. "Industrial Structure and the Nature of Innovative Activity." *Economic Journal* 90: 255-93.

David, Paul. 1991. "Computer and Dynamo: The Modern Productivity Paradox in a Not-Too-Distant-Mirror." In *Technology and Productivity: The Challenge for Economic Policy*, 315-47. Paris: Organization for Economic Cooperation and Development (OECD).

Demsetz, Harold. 1969. "Information and Efficiency: Another Viewpoint." *Journal of Law and Economics* 11: 1-22. Reprinted in Charles K. Rowley, ed., 1972, *Readings in Industrial Economics, Volume 2: Private Enterprise and State Intervention*, 237-62. London: Macmillan.

Dunning, John. 1997. "Globalization and National Government Policies: An Economist's View." In John Dunning, ed., *Governments, Globalization, and International Business*, 73-113. Oxford: Oxford University Press.

Grossman, Gene, and Elhanan Helpman. 1991. *Innovation and Growth in the Global Economy*. Cambridge, MA: MIT Press.

Helpman, Elhanan, ed. 1998. *General Purpose Technologies and Economic Growth*. Cambridge, MA: MIT Press.

Hirshleifer, Jack. 1971. "The Private and Social Value of Information and the Reward to Inventive Activity." *American Economic Review* 61: 561-74.

Jones, Lawrence, and Rodolfo Manuelli. 1990. "A Convex Model of Equilibrium Growth: Theory and Policy Implications." *Journal of Political Economy* 98,5 (Part 1): 1008-38.

Kaldor, Nicholas, and J. Mirrlees. 1962. "A New Model of Economic Growth." *Review of Economic Studies* 29: 174-92.

King, Robert G., and Sergio Rebelo. 1993. "Transitional Dynamics and Economic Growth in the Neoclassical Model." *American Economic Review* 83,4: 908-31.

Lipsey, R.G. 1994. "Markets, Technological Change and Economic Growth." In *The Pakistan Development Review* 33,4: 327-52. Reprinted in Lipsey (1997).

–. 1997. *The Collected Essays of Richard Lipsey, Volume I: Microeconomics, Growth and Political Economy*. Cheltenham, UK: Edward Elgar Publishing.

–. 1999. "Sources of Continued Long-Run Economic Dynamism in the 21st Century." In Wolfgang Michalski, ed., *21st Century Economic Dynamics: Anatomy of a Long Boom.* Paris: OECD.

Lipsey, R.G., and C. Bekar. 1995. "A Structuralist View of Technical Change and Economic Growth." In *Bell Canada Papers on Economic and Public Policy* 3: 9-75. Kingston, ON: John Deutsch Institute.

Lipsey, R.G., C. Bekar, and K. Carlaw. Forthcoming. *Time, Technology and Markets: Explorations in Economic Growth and Restructuring.*

Lipsey, R.G., and K. Carlaw. 1996. "A Structuralist View of Innovation Policy." In Peter Howitt, ed., *The Implications of Knowledge Based Growth,* 255-333. Calgary: University of Calgary Press.

–. 1998a. "Technology Policies in Neoclassical and Structuralist-Evolutionary Models." In *STI Review* 22 (Special Issue).

–. 1998b. *A Structuralist Assessment of Technology Policies: Taking Schumpeter Seriously on Policy.* Industry Canada Working Paper No. 25. Ottawa: Industry Canada.

Lipsey, R.G., and R.M. Wills. 1996. "Science and Technology Policies in Asia Pacific Countries: Challenges and Opportunities for Canada." In Richard Harris, ed., *The Asia-Pacific Region in the Global Economy: A Canadian Perspective,* 577-612. Calgary: University of Calgary Press.

Lucas, Robert E., Jr. 1988. "On the Mechanics of Economic Development." *Journal of Monetary Economics* 22,1: 3-42.

Mankiw, N. Gregory, David Romer, and David N. Weil. 1992. "A Contribution to the Empirics of Economic Growth." *Quarterly Journal of Economics* 107: 407-37.

Nelson, R., and S. Winter. 1982. *An Evolutionary Theory of Economic Change.* Cambridge, MA: Harvard University Press.

Rae, John. 1905. *The Sociological Theory of Capital.* New York: Macmillan. First published in 1834 as *Statement of Some New Principles on the Subject of Political Economy Exposing the Fallacies of the System of Free Trade and of Some Other Doctrines Maintained in the Wealth of Nations.*

Romer, Paul M. 1986. "Increasing Returns and Long-Run Growth." *Journal of Political Economy* 94,3: 1002-37.

–. 1990. "Endogenous Technological Change." *Journal of Political Economy* 98: S71-S102.

–. 1993a. "Two Strategies for Economic Development: Using Ideas and Producing Ideas." In *Proceedings of the World Bank Annual Research Conference 1992.* Supplement to *World Bank Economic Review,* March 1993: 63-91.

–. 1993b. "Implementing a National Technology Strategy with Self Organizing Investment Boards." *Brookings Papers on Economic Activity* 2: 345-89.

–. 1993c. "Idea Gaps and Object Gaps in Economic Development." *Journal of Monetary Economics* 32: 543-73.

–. 1994a. "The Origins of Endogenous Growth." *Journal of Economic Perspectives* 8,1: 3-22.

–. 1994b. "New Goods, Old Theory, and the Welfare Cost of Trade Restrictions." *Journal of Development Economics* 43,1: 5-39.

Rosenberg, N. 1982. *Inside the Black Box: Technology and Economics.* Cambridge, UK: Cambridge University Press.

Schumpeter, Joseph. 1934. *The Theory of Economic Development, English Translation.* Cambridge, MA: Harvard University Press. First published in German in 1912.

Schmookler, J. 1966. *Invention and Economic Growth.* Cambridge, MA: Harvard University Press.

Solow, Robert M. 1956. "A Contribution to the Theory of Economic Growth." *Quarterly Journal of Economics* 70: 537-62.

Von Hipple, E. 1980. *The Sources of Innovation.* New York: Oxford University Press.

Young, Allyn Abbatt. 1929. "Increasing Returns and Economic Progress." *Economic Journal* 38: 527-42.

3

The Social Contract in a Knowledge Society[1]

John Richards

Both *social contract* and *knowledge society* are frustratingly vague terms.

That knowledge is important to economic development is hardly a new idea. Over the last two centuries, now-rich countries have created "knowledge societies" – at least to the extent of providing near-universal elementary and secondary schooling. The spread of literacy and simple mathematical skills was crucial in enabling the majority of the population to move from farming into the higher-productivity occupations generated by the industrial revolution. That there is a link between economic development and the extension of basic knowledge to the majority is one of the few fundamental lessons to be learned by governments of Third World countries currently trying to industrialize. Given the complex market failures involved, efficient provision of universal schooling should rank very high among their policy priorities.

What is meant here by knowledge society is something different. It is the claim that, over the last quarter of this century, technologically induced shifts in the demand for labour have accelerated, thereby increasing the earnings premium associated with acquisition of technical skills and knowledge, and reducing the supply of "good jobs" for those with physical strength or manual dexterity but little formal education. A recent Organization for Economic Cooperation and Development (OECD) report summarized this as follows: "One clear dimension to structural change has been, and continues to be, a systematic shift away from the employment of low- or narrowly skilled labour, both in manufacturing and in services. This reflects both demand and supply-side factors but the most important cause has apparently been technical progress, which is increasingly being reflected in a move towards a more knowledge-intensive economy" (OECD 1994, 2).

The term *social contract* has been applied to certain broad agreements struck between representatives of major interest groups, agreements that may or may not involve the state. It is also a long-established metaphor used by political philosophers to describe what is entailed in governing. Except in totalitarian states, politics entails a set of shifting Hobbesian social contracts whereby society avoids the anarchy of unconstrained conflict between competing individuals and interest groups. Among other provisions, these implicit contracts limit the inequality of economic rewards and form a more or less cooperative solution in an ongoing prisoners' dilemma game over distribution of income and wealth. More narrowly, the term summarizes the political consensus – to the extent one exists – that underlies government expenditures on welfare state programs. It is this last, more narrow meaning that is relevant to this discussion.

This chapter proceeds as follows. Part 1 suggests an appropriate way to think about a social contract and the welfare state. Part 2 discusses important adverse consequences arising from the interaction of the knowledge society, the current social contract, and several independent sets of variables. Part 3 makes two recommendations pertinent to the Canadian context: to experiment with earnings-supplement programs and to universalize targeted child benefits. Part 4 offers a brief conclusion.

Part 1: "Wasted Effort"

The term *welfare state* is also vague. Nicholas Barr (1993, 742) concludes that "much high-grade effort has been wasted in the effort [at definition]." He informally defines *welfare state* as "shorthand for the state's activities in four broad areas: cash benefits; health care; education; and food, housing and other welfare services."

My own contribution to this wasted effort is to define the welfare state as an ongoing work in progress, comprising the set of government programs that register along one or more of the three dimensions outlined below. In turn, the social contract is the central tendency at any point in time – for distributions that may have high variance – in three broad public debates corresponding to each of these dimensions:

- *Income redistribution:* The first and most obvious dimension concerns programs that redistribute income from the nonpoor to the poor. Hence the first source of debate: how much redistribution to undertake?
- *Correction of inefficient market outcomes with a simultaneous redistributional impact:* Many social programs simultaneously improve economic efficiency by overcoming a failure inherent in particular markets and redistributing "merit goods" such as health care and education. This dimension invites debate about the extent to which programs actually achieve efficiency gains.
- *Realization of certain widely shared values:* A third dimension is to realize certain paternalistic values with redistributional consequences. This third dimension generates passionate debate over the extent to which it is legitimate, in a liberal society, for the majority to impose values on dissenting minorities.

An Example: Mandatory Health Insurance

An example may help us understand this view of the welfare state and the social contract underlying it. In Canada, no major political party opposes universal state-run health insurance programs. Here, as in most industrial countries, universal health insurance has become integral to any definition of the contemporary social contract.

Canada has no national health insurance program; it has 10 provincial programs, loosely constrained by federal guidelines contained in the Canada Health Act. Funding for these programs derives primarily from the provinces' respective own-source tax revenues, supplemented by some federal transfers; citizens do not pay actuarially fair premiums. These programs redistribute towards low-income and high-risk citizens (two overlapping but not identical groups).

In these programs, the welfare state is used to correct several market failures, such as the inefficiency associated with buying and selling private health insurance. In a private market, insureds want maximum coverage at minimum cost; they have a strong incentive to hide risk factors that point to a high probability of expensive claims. Insurers have a strong incentive to refuse high-risk applicants, and to deny liability in particular situations. The result is cheating by both parties, costly monitoring to discourage fraud, and far from universal insurance coverage for high-risk patients. As is evident from the much lower per capita health insurance administrative costs in Canada relative to the United States, pooling all provincial residents into a single plan was an efficiency-improving policy (Richards 1997, Chapter 7).

Health policy is accordingly debated over the first two dimensions: the extent to which governments should redistribute and the extent to which they can improve efficiency in an important sector of the economy. The third dimension is also relevant. Universal health insurance may currently be integral to the Canadian social contract. In the early 1960s, when the government of Saskatchewan first introduced it, this was far from being true. In effect, the provincial government imposed a widely shared but far from universally endorsed value regarding the desirability of mandatory universal health insurance.

Part 2: Creating an Excluded Minority

There is much to celebrate in the advance of the knowledge society and the growth of the welfare state over the last half-century. However, there have been costs as well as benefits. Combined with changing public attitudes towards the family and a social contract that favours generous but highly targeted benefits to families with children, the declining reward from what the OECD describes above as "low- or narrowly skilled labour" is creating a serious social problem: a sizeable minority of the population is increasingly excluded from the world of work and stable family life.

The discussion in this section is organized around four sets of variables: (1) factors inducing a decline in market earnings among those with little formal training, (2) changes in attitudes towards the "traditional family," (3) ghetto effects due to the geographical concentration of the poor, and (4) poverty traps arising from highly targeted social programs. In many cases, these variables interact with one another in a way that augments the negative effect.

Consequences Due to the Knowledge Society

The first of these dynamics is widely acknowledged. The knowledge society has reduced the supply of "good jobs" requiring physical strength or manual dexterity and little formal education. In most industrial countries, the number of people looking for such jobs has declined, but less quickly than the supply of such jobs. A typical result is that between 1973 and 1989, real annual earnings among the bottom fifth of male wage-earners in Canada declined by 16 percent (Morissette et al. 1995, 28).

In explaining this decline, the most important factor has probably been the shift in labour demand brought on by the knowledge society. New technologies have simultaneously created a demand for high-skill workers (such as computer technicians and programmers) and low-skill workers (as in telemarketing) while destroying many moderate-skill jobs (manual letter sorters). Also, contemporary low-skill jobs require less physical strength than in previous decades. This may account for why increased wage polarization in Canada has affected men but not women (Beach et al. 1996).[2] (See Figures 1 and 2.)

Most analysts conclude that technological change – i.e., the knowledge society – is the principal explanation for the increased earnings polarization evident in many industrial countries. Although less important, several other factors also matter.

First, trade liberalization permits a greater exploitation of international comparative advantage, one aspect of which is the Third World advantage in low-skill, labour-intensive manufacturing activities. Second, prolonged laxity in fiscal policy combined with bouts of monetary restriction generated recessions in the early 1980s and early 1990s that were more serious, in Canada, than any since the Great Depression of the 1930s. Recessions are particularly bad for wage and employment trends among the low-skilled. Finally, over time, unions and other occupational organizations have probably become more entrenched and able to segregate labour markets. Segregation has resulted in increased wage premiums and employment security for "inside" workers relative to "outsiders." In many cases, these benefits go

Figure 1

Polarization of male wage-earners in Canada, 1971-92

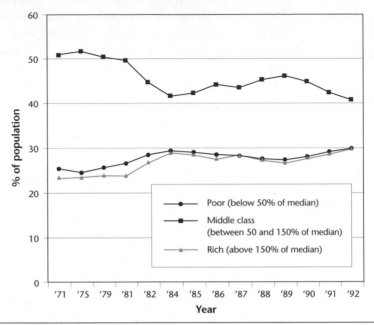

Source: Beach et al. (1996).

well beyond what is warranted by relative productivity. Young workers tend to be outsiders; older workers are far more likely to be insiders. This final factor helps explain the declining relative ratio of earnings between young families and older families since the 1960s (Picot and Myles 1995).

Consequences of Abandoning the "Traditional Family"

The second set of variables can be summed up as a declining commitment among individual citizens and the state to the traditional two-parent family with children. *Le revers de la médaille* has been the rise of single-parent families. The proportion of Canadian children living in such families has roughly doubled over the last quarter-century. (The increase throughout OECD countries has been of a similar magnitude.) By the 1996 Canadian census, 16 percent of children lived in single-parent families, 11 percent lived in common-law families, and 73 percent with married couples (OECD 1997, 14; Canada 1998, 5).

Declining family size combined with rising life expectancy means that child rearing now occupies a smaller share of adult time than in any previous era in history. In Canada, as late as the 1970s, only one in three married women with young children (under age six) was in the paid labour force; by

Figure 2

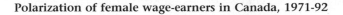

Polarization of female wage-earners in Canada, 1971-92

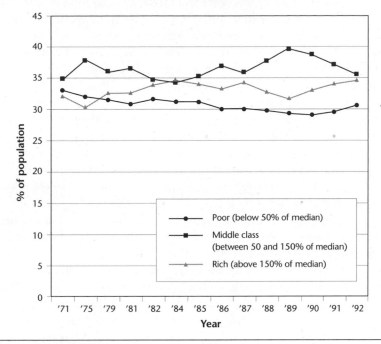

Source: Beach et al. (1996).

the 1990s, this ratio had become two out of three (Canada 1994, 4). One consequence has been the massive growth of care for young children by adults other than parents. Another aspect is manifest in a trebling of the Canadian divorce rate since the 1960s. This increase can be attributed to changing social values and their reflection in no-fault divorce laws.[3]

Much of this change is for the good. Working mothers increase family incomes. Paid work also carries more subtle benefits that women quite reasonably want. It may stimulate learning and allow women to build a network of supportive friends. Also, by providing a source of independent income, it may help women achieve equality with their husbands.

Some hard-to-determine fraction of the increased number of divorces is also to be welcomed. It reflects the rejection of abusive partners. To insist upon this as the sole cause for family break-up, however, is a serious oversimplification. To take a limiting case, nearly half of all aboriginal families in Canada's Prairie cities are now headed by a single parent. While this is three times the national average rate (Canada 1998, 5), it would surely be wrong to conclude that one in two aboriginal fathers is abusive or three times worse than non-aboriginal fathers.

Not all results of changing attitudes are for the good. The most convincing evidence of adverse effects comes from longitudinal studies that attempt to assess intergenerational effects of parental choices on children. Such studies seem to confirm the wisdom of our grandparents. Adjusting as much as possible for other variables, traditional families – comprising a father and mother, with at least one parent working – generate better outcomes for children measured by criteria such as high school completion, avoiding teenage pregnancy, and avoiding dependence on welfare as adults.

In Canada, the incidence of poverty among single-parent families in 1996 was 57 percent, roughly five times that among two-parent families (Canada 1997b, 41). Not surprisingly, roughly half of single-parent families rely to a greater or lesser extent on social assistance.[4] But this raises another factor: source of income matters. The role-model effect of working parents seems to influence children positively and, independent of income levels, reliance on welfare is conducive to poor outcomes for children.[5]

The argument that traditional families, on average, raise children better is subject to vigorous debate. On one side of the debate, the prominent American analyst Walter Mead (1997, 14-15), writing about inner-city family poverty, states: "Most children acquire a sense of possibility not because society is fair to them but because adults near to them are. By identifying with parents and teachers, they internalize values. By meeting their expectations, they also derive a sense of mastery that makes them approach life hopefully, without defeating themselves. The wider world has no comparable influence. If parents are effective, children will be well formed even if the surrounding society is unfair." Mead believes that the main task of social policy today is not to reform society but to restore the authority of parents and other caregivers. He says that while this is not an easy task, government can make a start by restoring order in the inner city and by requiring poor parents to work, "because employment failures are the greatest cause of family failures. If parents do not work, no program to help the children is likely to achieve much."

Many disagree with Mead's conclusion that "the main task of social policy is no longer to reform society but to restore the authority of parents and other mentors who shape citizens."[6] In a book that gained wide attention, Judith Harris (1998) argued that peers, not parents, matter in explaining what happens to children. Parents can affect choice of peers by choosing to live in a particular neighbourhood. To that extent, parents remain the ultimate independent variable. But in Harris's analysis peer influence swamps that of parents.

The family debate poses a dilemma for the conduct of social policy. Broad public debates must take place that will cumulatively define the social contract underlying social programs. Yet neither the politicians, the mandarins, nor the general public can claim specific expertise in this area. The best that can be done is to advance ideas carefully, admit that they may be wrong, and try to avoid doing harm.

Consequences of Ghetto Formation

Policy interest in ghettos arises from interaction effects attending the abnormally high incidence of several adverse factors present in a community, which augment the severity of consequences relative to what would be expected were the effects additive. For example, a community with a low employment-to-population ratio will probably experience a higher incidence of social problems than a comparable community with high employment. However, if a community simultaneously experiences low employment, high poverty, and high dependence on transfer income, the consequences are likely to be more severe than if the incremental effect of each factor were simply added.

The obvious reference is to neighbourhoods in large US cities with multiple social problems that have become an intractable feature of American poverty over the last half-century.[7] As with many issues, what happens first in the US arrives with a lag elsewhere. Ghetto-like neighbourhoods are becoming more significant in most industrial countries – from bidonvilles around Marseilles to north end Winnipeg. While blacks are overrepresented in US ghettos and aboriginals in analogous communities in western Canada, this argument is not about racially based differences. The outcomes are similar in areas of East Montreal and East Vancouver, neighbourhoods with fewer racial distinctions relative to the surrounding metropolitan region.

In an attempt to describe more rigorously the formation of ghetto-like communities in Canada, Michael Hatfield (1997) identified "distressed neighbourhoods" by an abnormal incidence of five social indicators:

- a high individual poverty rate (above 28 percent)
- a high proportion of total household income coming from government transfers (above 17 percent)
- a low proportion of the 15-24 age cohort attending school full time (below 43 percent)
- a low proportion of adult males employed full time (below 36 percent)
- a high incidence of families with children headed by a single parent (above 31 percent).

It is far from clear why the poor are becoming geographically concentrated in ghetto-like neighbourhoods, but the trend is certainly under way. Between 1980 and 1990 (two years in which income was recorded in national censuses), the proportion of poor Canadian families living in distressed neighbourhoods, defined by the above criteria, rose from 12 percent to 17 percent. In Montreal in 1980, 30 percent of the city's poor lived in such neighbourhoods, compared with 40 percent in 1990. Other cities with large increases were Winnipeg (24 percent to 39 percent) and Edmonton (4 percent to 28 percent).

Consequences of Targeted Government Transfer Programs

Essentially, the factors discussed so far concern dynamics within civil society, defined as activities independent of government. This is not to deny the contribution of certain policies to adverse consequences. Relaxed divorce laws have contributed somewhat to the rise of single parenthood. Free trade agreements have contributed somewhat to earnings polarization. Public decisions to concentrate service agencies in poor neighbourhoods have no doubt exacerbated the trend towards ghetto formation. The impact of these public policies, however, has probably been minor relative to the impact of changes arising independently within civil society.

In a manner that needs to be addressed, governments are to blame for adverse consequences. In Canada – and in most other OECD countries – they have erected two serious "poverty traps" that, in combination with the variables already discussed, are key to understanding contemporary poverty.

In any welfare state, governments transfer income to the poor. In Canada, the most important of these transfers are provincial social assistance programs, followed by federal unemployment insurance (whose design makes it redistributive) and a variety of targeted benefit programs offered by both orders of government. Despite the retrenchment of the 1990s, relative to the 1970s Canadian transfer programs to low-income families have either remained constant in real terms or become more generous.[8]

The term *poverty traps* refers to the disincentive to undertake work that arises from the aggressive clawing back of targeted benefits. By design, targeted programs provide less generous benefits to those with positive earnings. By clawing back benefits as earnings rise, governments generate work disincentives similar to those arising from explicit income taxes.

Provincial social assistance creates the first poverty trap. There are acute trade-offs between providing enough income to assure a reasonable standard of living and maintaining incentives for families to gain economic self-sufficiency. For welfare recipients, provinces allow a small earnings exemption, beyond which the clawback rate on incremental earnings is close to 100 percent. If the recipient has one or two children, and if her skills allow her to earn no more than minimum wage, then even full-time work provides little or no additional income relative to social assistance.

Transfers targeted to low-income families have offset the effect of male earnings polarization. Among poor families with children (defined as those with an income of less than half the median), the relative importance of

Figure 3

Polarization of family incomes in Canada, 1972-92

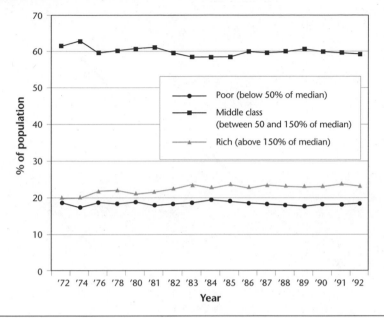

Source: Beach et al. (1996).

earnings to transfers has shifted substantially. In the early 1970s, two thirds of income in such families was derived from earnings and one-third from transfers; two decades later, the ratio was reversed (Figures 3 and 4.) (Beach et al. 1996; Canada 1999b).

Currently, most Canadian families with children start paying personal income tax and payroll-based levies when incomes exceed $15,000. (All monetary amounts shown here are in Canadian dollars.) Provinces attempt to avoid overlap between social assistance and these taxes, but the transition is messy. Some families in this range wind up with marginal tax rates in excess of 100 percent – especially when the phase-out of benefits in kind available to social assistance recipients is taken into account.

At approximately $20,000, Ottawa and the provinces start clawing back targeted benefits other than social assistance,[9] creating the second poverty trap. In most provinces, modest-income families face marginal effective tax rates in excess of 60 percent on incremental earnings over much of the $20,000 to 35,000 earnings range.

In British Columbia a family with two children earning $25,000 currently keeps about $30 from an additional $100 earned. Over most of the

Figure 4

Sources of family income in Canada, 1973-95

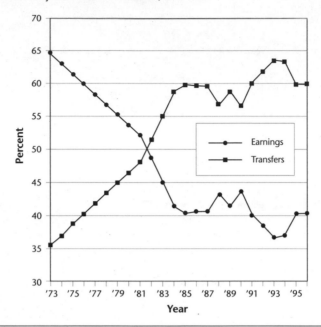

Sources: Canada (1999b, Table 10b); Picot and Myles (1995).

Figure 5

Marginal effective tax rates for families in British Columbia

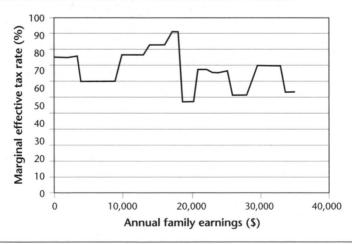

Source: Sayeed (1999, 17).
Note: The family is defined here as a one-wage-earner couple with two preschool children.
Earnings from work and welfare payments are assumed to be the only sources of income.

earnings range illustrated in Figure 5, the combined federal-provincial income tax rate is below 25 percent; the majority of the marginal effective rate is attributable to clawbacks of targeted benefit programs. (Note that Figure 5 refers only to short-term clawback of social assistance transfers. In the long run the clawback becomes more aggressive.) Another way to perceive the severity of this second poverty trap is via the implicit post-tax wage. Based on 1,800 hours of annual work, the pre-tax hourly wage for this family is about $14, whereas the post-tax, post-transfer hourly wage is about $4.30, well below minimum wage.

How important are high marginal effective tax rates in discouraging work effort among low-income families and in encouraging tax evasion? This is an important question, one for which few good answers exist. A few comments can be made. In general, the most severe clawback occurs among recipients of social assistance. Not surprisingly, this group reports low employment earnings.[10] Currently, much attention is being devoted to tax reduction, particularly for the few upper-income tax filers subject to the highest marginal rates. One of the rationales is that high rates create a disincentive for professionals, who either relocate to lower-tax regimes or work less. Often ignored in this discussion is that modest-income families with several children are subject to even higher marginal effective rates.

Authors of the 1998 British budget reached certain "tentative conclusions" from academic studies of work incentives (United Kingdom 1998, paragraphs 4.12 and 4.13):

- in-work credits, such as the [American] EITC and Family Credit [UK program now renamed WFTC], have the potential to raise substantially labour market participation for poorer families, particularly lone parents, both in respect of parttime and fulltime work;
- a fall in [clawback] rates can help more people move up the earnings ladder. But the withdrawal of in-work support as income rises can also reduce modestly the hours worked of those already employed.

In the passage preceding these conclusions, the analytical difficulties in answering questions about work effort were stressed. In attempting to determine the work effects of alternative social policies, Canada enjoys an advantage over countries, such as Britain, with centralized social policy jurisdiction. Because of our decentralization, individual provinces can experiment while the remaining provinces serve as a control group.

Synthesizing the Adverse Effects
The price effect implicit in the changing ratio of welfare benefits available to single parents compared with the potential earnings of male partners offers one means of examining these issues. Reasonably generous but highly

targeted government benefits for low-income families form the numerator; declining wages among low-skilled and/or young men form the denominator. In Canada, this ratio has varied across provinces and over time. Undeniably its overall change has been substantial – a rise in the order of 40 percent since the 1970s.[11]

Do such price effects matter in explaining the growth of single-parent "distressed communities" and reliance on social assistance? Right-wing opinion typically stresses perverse effects from increases in targeted benefits, while those on the left emphasize perverse effects of increased earnings polarization. Realistically, however, both the numerator and denominator matter.

Boessenkool and I attempted to explain trends in welfare use in three provinces from the early 1980s to mid-1990s through three variables: the state of the economy (measured by the provincial unemployment rate), the ratio of welfare benefits to a reference male earnings level available from low-wage employment, and shifts in administrative culture (Boessenkool 1997; Richards 1997).

In Ontario, the normalized welfare caseload (cases per 1,000 population) roughly doubled between 1989 and 1993. During this period, welfare benefits, unemployment, and the reference earnings level all moved in directions that increased welfare use. The recession in the early 1990s mattered: rising unemployment accounted for about 40 percent of the explained increase, increased welfare benefits accounted for another 40 percent, while a decline in the reference wage accounted for the final 20 percent.

In Alberta, welfare use was dramatically different from Ontario: the caseload was halved between 1993 and 1996. Nearly 90 percent of that decline was explained by a series of administrative measures that rendered access to social assistance more difficult. A falling unemployment rate explained about 35 percent of the decline. A decrease in the reference wage offset these effects, and brought the total explained decline to 100 percent.

In British Columbia, the normalized caseload increased by 30 percent between 1991 and 1995. The most important variable was again a change in administrative culture, here operating in the opposite direction from Alberta. Replacement of an ideologically conservative government in 1991 by one markedly to the left led to a relaxation in access to welfare that accounted for about 80 percent of the explained caseload increase. A rising provincial unemployment rate explained about 20 percent of the increase. A minor increase in welfare benefit levels and in the reference earnings level roughly offset one another.

Using a large sample of nationwide data from the years 1981 to 1993, Lefebvre et al. (1998) undertook a far more rigorous analysis of the question: what variables affect the probability that a woman will become a single parent? They found that age matters: for women below age 25, the probability of becoming a single parent is significantly higher than for older women. Both what women earn and the expected earnings of their male partners matter. The higher a woman's earnings, the lower the probability of becoming a single parent; the lower her partner's expected earnings, the higher the probability. Welfare benefits may or may not matter independently of other variables. In those specifications that introduce both provincial welfare benefit levels and a "dummy" variable to capture other province-specific characteristics, welfare benefits do not matter. In those specifications that include provincial welfare benefits but exclude the provincial "dummy," higher provincial welfare benefits do matter: they increase the probability of single-parenthood in that province.

Low-income parents have always faced two options:

- *Option A:* Parents live together and jointly raise their children. While the children are young, the primary source of income will probably be the father's earnings, which, given his limited training, are likely to be low. Unless the extended family provides child care, the cost of paid child care – even in the informal sector – is likely to mean that the mother works part-time at most.
- *Option B:* The parents separate or, if living apart at the time of a child's birth, decide not to live together. In the overwhelming majority of cases, the mother becomes the sole custodial parent. As family head, the mother becomes eligible for a range of transfer programs; the father earns what he can. If there are two or more children, the mother will receive as transfer income more than her partner can earn from full-time work at minimum wage. As the noncustodial parent, the father faces some obligation to support his children. But the probability of the mother realizing consistent long-term financial support from the father is much reduced when the two do not live together, for two obvious reasons: (1) The father may have a reduced psychological link to his children and may start a new family. (2) If the mother receives social assistance, the financial incentive to seek such support is absent. Under most provincial programs, any income from the father reduces dollar-for-dollar the mother's social assistance benefits.

To summarize Part 2, over the past generation more low-income families are choosing option B and fewer are choosing option A. All four sets of variables are probably relevant to an understanding of this choice.

Part 3: What Is to Be Done?
Given the complexity of the reasons underlying poverty, it is foolish to

present one or two policy options as a panacea. With that caveat, I think the time has come for those interested in the social contract underlying the welfare state to address bluntly the perverse effects of poverty traps. With the Canadian context in mind, I make two complementary policy recommendations:

- Experiment aggressively with programs that subsidize earnings among low-income families with children. I label such programs generic earnings supplement (henceforth ES) programs.
- Beyond social assistance, maintain universality (or near-universality) for social programs benefiting families with children. To the extent that a consensus exists to treat families with children more generously than families without, either make benefit programs universally accessible independent of income or apply a low (say, 5 percent) clawback rate starting at a middle-class earnings level.

Earnings Supplement (ES) Programs

A few introductory comments are in order. ES programs are intended to be ongoing subsidies to any and all earnings by family members, and to be accessible by all low-income families with children. As such, they contrast with a host of discretionary programs that subsidize employment income among designated groups of people for a limited period. Since welfare benefits are much more generous for parents with children than for single individuals, the first poverty trap is of more concern among the former. ES programs are intended to shift the welfare/wage ratio faced by low-income parents; they are not intended for single individuals or families without children.

In several countries, ES programs have already become a significant social-policy instrument. The US Earned Income Tax Credit (EITC) is an example. Expenditures on this program were $40 billion for 1994 (OECD 1997, 52). In the UK, the newly elected Labour government gave a high priority in its first budget to enhancing a British equivalent (relabelled the Working Families Tax Credit [WFTC]), with an estimated annual cost of $12 billion when fully phased in by the year 2000 (United Kingdom 1998, paragraph 2.08).[12]

Canadian examples of ES programs also exist. Quebec's APPORT is important as the pioneer. Ottawa included a small ES program in its 1992 reform of child benefit programs, but subsequently terminated it in favour of the expanded Canada Child Tax Benefit. This decade, Ottawa has also undertaken a pilot ES project in regions of two provinces (New Brunswick and British Columbia). Saskatchewan introduced a provincewide ES program in 1998.

Despite these examples, ES programs remain to date a marginal, experimental, and controversial component of Canadian social policy. Opponents include conservatives who fear labour market distortions; anti-poverty advocates who want generous unconditional income transfers; and union leaders who do not want an increase in low-skill workers in the labour market.[13]

In understanding the controversy, the first point to appreciate is that, by construction, ES programs link benefits to earnings from work. They are less redistributive than programs of equal budgetary cost that deliver maximum benefits to those without earnings. The second point is that beneficiaries are poor and usually lack high-level skills; hence, the work subsidized is usually low-wage. ES programs increase the supply of low-skill workers in the labour force, and – subject to minimum wage provisions – lower the cost to employers of hiring them. Low-wage jobs are often menial jobs, involving repetitive tasks and hard physical labour. Although their rationales diverge, conservative supporters of free markets, anti-poverty activists, and left-wing union leaders come together in opposition to ES programs.

Admittedly, many self-described conservatives are prepared to intervene aggressively in the work choices made by the poor.[14] Typically, however, conservatives want less government intervention in the labour market, and view ES programs as exercises in social engineering that distort market signals. It is true enough that all transfers blunt market incentives to work. But no wealthy industrial society has yet been prepared to accept the consequences for children of making parents with low or narrow skills depend solely on the labour market. The working majority have been prepared to tax themselves to bring all families above some, admittedly vague, tolerable standard of living. Even in jurisdictions with low benefit levels (such as conservative-led American states), families with several children are often eligible to receive more via transfers than low-skill workers can earn from full-time employment. The combination of the laissez-faire conservatives' policy bias plus majority preferences leads to large numbers of low-skill parents opting for more or less permanent cycling between social assistance and low-wage employment.

Quite legitimately, union leaders seek to increase members' wages, and an increased supply of low-skill, usually non-union, workers in the labour market does not help: part of any ES benefit goes to employers in the form of a lower net cost of labour.[15] Instead of an employment supplement targeted towards low-skill workers, argue union leaders, increase the income for such families by increasing the minimum wage. To their members, they add that a high minimum wage will reduce employer demand for such labour, in favour of higher-skill union workers. Therein lies the contradiction of this position. As social policy, a major disadvantage of a high minimum wage is that employers avoid those who combine low productivity and low attachment to the labour force. In the past, traditional left-wing governments have accompanied a higher minimum wage with higher welfare benefits. Thus, leaving aside demand and looking at labour supply, the ranking remains the same as under conservative governments: reliance on social assistance transfers is financially more rewarding than reliance on paid work.[16]

The case for ES programs rests on two empirical propositions: first, that financial incentives matter and employment subsidies can (in combination with other programs) significantly increase employment; and second, that the role-model effects from working parents matter a great deal in explaining the prospects for children.

These propositions may be wrong but, as a practical guide, I suggest that large changes in financial incentives do matter, and that work is sufficiently important that it is worthwhile for government to subsidize it. This is the case even where subsidies incur the political wrath of those conservatives who want wages to reflect relative productivity; of anti-poverty activists who prefer more generous untied transfers; and of union leaders who want to restrict employer access to low-skill labour.

The goal of ES programs is to increase participation in the paid labour force by "making work pay." Over some range of low earnings, program benefits increase as earnings increase, thereby augmenting what would otherwise be the earnings derived from employment. What goes up for the poor comes down for the middle class. Over some range of higher earnings, the ES benefit is clawed back as earnings rise.

There are difficult trade-offs in designing the clawback features of an ES program. Over the phase-out range, they add to the marginal effective tax rates faced by modest-income families. If the clawback rate is reduced, however, benefits extend into higher-earnings ranges. Program costs also rise dramatically as the clawback rate is lowered and large numbers become eligible for the benefit. In sum, lowering the clawback rate raises the benefit for a family of any given earnings level over the phase-out range, extends eligibility to higher-earning families and raises their marginal tax rates, and increases program cost.

This brings me to the complementary reform of reduced targeting for child benefit programs.

Universalizing Child Tax Benefits

The appropriate policy to address the second poverty trap is to restore a much greater measure of universality to child benefit programs such as the Canada Child Tax Benefit (CCTB).

To do so is undeniably an expensive proposition. To illustrate, Ottawa currently (spring 1999) provides a targeted annual benefit via the CCTB of approximately $1,500 per child. Were Ottawa to universalize the present benefit, it would cost an estimated additional $6 billion annually (Richards 1999, 207). A near-universalization variant is to claw back the benefit at a low rate, say 5 percent, for family earnings above $35,000. This would deny any benefit to families earning above $105,000 annually and lower Ottawa's lost tax revenue to about $4 billion annually.

Why universalize child benefit programs? There are two straightforward arguments. Based on the discussion in Part 2, poverty traps have become a significant component of any explanation for the persistence of an excluded minority with low attachment to the world of work. Second, middle- and upper-income families also have children. Currently, Canada's tax regime takes little account of the costs of good child rearing among those who are not poor (Boessenkool 1999). By construction, universalizing child benefit programs would provide no additional benefit to single individuals, families without children, or families already receiving the maximum. In the debate over the spending of Canada's new-found fiscal surplus, universalizing child benefits can be portrayed simultaneously as an appropriate amendment to the social contract underlying the welfare state and as a means to deliver significant individual tax reduction.

Conclusion
Let me summarize with three statements that belong in a contemporary social contract underlying social programs intended to help low-income families adjust to the knowledge society. Admittedly, they are general statements; hopefully, they are not mere "wasted effort."

- **Redistribute**: *Government social programs should redistribute to families with children in a manner more generous than to families (or individuals) without children.* Whatever a jurisdiction collectively decides about redistribution towards able-bodied adults without dependent children, it should be more generous to adults caring for children.
- **Make work pay**: *Government social programs should maintain a significant fiscal incentive to undertake paid employment among poor parents, even when their children are young.* Redistribution is not the only relevant goal. A concern for children's outcomes among poor families suggests that source of income matters. Hence, social policy intended to redistribute towards low-income families must address poverty traps and maintain significant incentives to undertake employment.
- **Reciprocal obligations**: *Government social programs should discourage long-term reliance on transfer programs by requiring a "co-payment" from the able-bodied poor in exchange for receipt of benefits.* Traditional social assistance is a kind of social insurance against dire poverty. As with other forms of insurance, people can abuse social assistance programs. Earnings supplement programs can be considered an element in a social contract of "reciprocal obligations" that requires the nonpoor to undertake redistributive taxation and the poor to engage in employment and/or training.

Notes

1 Portions of this chapter are taken from a chapter in a recent publication of the C.D. Howe Institute (Richards 1999).

2 Polarization refers to the number of individuals in the tails of a distribution relative to the number who are reasonably close to the middle. By definition, polarization is increasing over time when the proportion in the tails is rising.

3 See Doug Allen (1999) for a survey of the econometric evidence on alternative explanations for rising divorce in Canada and the United States.

4 Incidence refers to the proportion of persons in a family category whose incomes fell below the relevant measure defined by the Low Income Cutoff (LICO), 1992 base. The LICO methodology designates families or individuals as poor if they spend significantly more of their income (above 60 percent) on necessities than does the typical Canadian family or individual in the relevant category (who is assumed to spend 40 percent on necessities). As of the early 1990s, 44 percent of single mothers received some welfare income. Receipt of welfare is much more pronounced among single mothers under 35 (58 percent received welfare) than among older single mothers (among whom only 31 percent received welfare) (Dooley 1995, 52).

5 These paragraphs contain conclusions based on admittedly contestable evidence. For a thorough survey of the empirical literature on determinants of children's outcomes, I recommend two publications by Haveman and Wolfe (1994, 1995).

6 In this instance, Mead was writing for the Institute of Economic Affairs, a conservative British policy institute. The intent of this volume was to influence the newly elected British Labour government.

7 There is a vast literature analysing American ghettos. Perhaps the single most important source is William Julius Wilson (1987) and his colleagues at the University of Chicago.

8 As an example, between 1975 and 1995 the real value of single-parent benefits increased by 8 percent in British Columbia and by 20 percent in Ontario. Following the election of the Progressive Conservative government in Ontario, provincial welfare benefits were cut. After the cuts, 1996 benefit levels were 2 percent lower than in 1975. A comprehensive nationwide survey reported an 18 percent increase in the real value of single-parent benefits between 1981 and 1993. The statistics for Ontario and British Columbia refer to a single parent with one or two children (Brown 1995, Table 3; Canada 1997a, Table 5). The nationwide study is by Lefebvre et al. (1998, Table 5); it uses Survey of Consumer Finances data.

9 A major transfer program is the federally funded Canada Child Tax Benefit (CCTB). It is subject to clawback when annual family net income exceeds $21,000. Starting in July 2000, for a family with two children the clawback rate will be 20 percent up to $30,000. Thereafter, the clawback rate will drop to 5 percent. The CCTB is exhausted at income above $70,000 (Canada 1999a, 179-85).

10 In Saskatchewan, for example, 17 percent of caseload heads classified as employable are actually in some form of employment. (The source for this statistic consists of unpublished analyses of the provincial social assistance caseload.) Social assistance recipients earn, however, an impossible-to-quantify level of unreported income.

11 This estimate simply combines two summary statistics: the 18 percent increase between 1981 and 1993 in the real value of single-parent benefits (Lefebvre et al. 1998) and the 16 percent 1973-89 decline in earnings among the bottom fifth of Canadian male wage-earners (Morissette et al. 1995).

12 To provide a reference point, Ottawa is currently spending approximately $6 billion on the targeted Canada Child Tax Benefit. Hence, expenditures per British resident on the WFTC will by 2000 be similar to current expenditures per Canadian resident on the CCTB. Analogously defined, 1994 per capita spending on the EITC was about four-fifths of current per capita CCTB spending.

13 A well-written statement of the opponents' arguments is that by Michael Mendelson, a senior analyst with the Ottawa-based Caledon Institute. He criticizes the modest Canada-wide Working Income Supplement (WIS), arguing that it "diminished social cohesion and

promoted the politics of division" (Mendelson 1998, 26). This monograph was written to warn a British audience against such programs.

14 Prominent examples are Walter Mead, who has written extensively on workfare and is quoted above, and the Republican administration in Wisconsin, which has aggressively implemented workfare programs over the last decade.

15 The net effect of an ES program on wages and employment levels depends on the elasticity of supply of affected workers, and the elasticity of demand among potential employers. If, as is likely, the supply elasticity is high, net effect may be a sizeable increase in employment but little increase in wages. Minimum wage regulations serve as a constraint in this market dynamic.

16 For an up-to-date discussion of the relative advantage of minimum wage and ES programs in increasing employment, see the *Economic Outlook* (1998, 31-79).

References

Allen, D. 1999. "No-Fault Divorce and the Divorce Rate: Its History, Effect, and Implications." In D. Allen and J. Richards, eds., *It Takes Two: The Family in Law and Finance*, 1-32. Toronto: C.D. Howe Institute.

Barr, N. 1993. "Economic Theory and the Welfare State: A Survey and Interpretation." *Journal of Economic Literature* 30: 741-803.

Beach, C., et al. 1996. *Are We Becoming Two Societies? The Myth of the Disappearing Middle Class.* Social Policy Challenge 12. Toronto: C.D. Howe Institute.

Boessenkool, K. 1997. "Back to Work: Learning from the Alberta Welfare Experiment." *Commentary* 90. Toronto: C.D. Howe Institute.

–. 1999. "Putting Tax Policy in Its Place." In D. Allen and J. Richards, eds., *It Takes Two: The Family in Law and Finance*, 129-67. Toronto: C.D. Howe Institute.

Brown, D. 1995. "Welfare Caseload Trends in Canada." In J. Richards et al., *Helping the Poor: A Qualified Case for "Workfare."* Social Policy Challenge 5. Toronto: C.D. Howe Institute.

Canada. 1994. *Child Care and Development: A Supplementary Paper.* Ottawa: Department of Human Resources Development.

–. 1997a. *Welfare Incomes, 1996.* Cat. H68-27/1996E. Ottawa: National Council of Welfare.

–. 1997b. *Income Distribution by Size in Canada, 1996.* Cat. 13-207. Ottawa: Statistics Canada.

–. 1998. "1996 Census: Aboriginal Data." *The Daily* (13 January 1998). 11-001E. Ottawa: Statistics Canada.

–. 1999a. *The Budget Plan 1999.* Ottawa: Department of Finance.

–. 1999b. *Canada's Tax and Income Security Systems: Issues and Challenges.* Conference presentation. Ottawa: Statistics Canada.

Dooley, M. 1995. "Lone Mother Families and Social Assistance Policy in Canada." In M. Dooley et al., *Family Matters: New Policies for Divorce, Lone Mothers, and Child Poverty.* Social Policy Challenge 8. Toronto: C.D. Howe Institute.

Harris, J. 1998. *The Nurture Assumption: Why Children Turn Out the Way They Do.* New York: Simon and Schuster.

Hatfield, M. 1997. *Concentrations of Poverty and Distressed Neighbourhoods in Canada.* Working Papers, W-97-1E. Ottawa: Department of Human Resources Development.

Haveman, R., and B. Wolfe. 1994. *Succeeding Generations: On the Effects of Investments in Children.* New York: Russell Sage Foundation.

–. 1995. "The Determinants of Children's Attainments: A Review of Methods and Findings." *Journal of Economic Literature* 33,4 (December).

Lefebvre, P., P. Merrigan, and M. Dooley. 1998. *Lone Female Headship and Welfare Policy in Canada.* Department of Economics Working Paper No. 98-02. Hamilton, ON: McMaster University.

Mead, W., et al. 1997. *From Welfare to Work: Lessons from America.* Choice in Welfare 39. London: Institute of Economic Affairs.

Mendelson, M. 1998. *The WIS that Was: Replacing the Canadian Working Income Supplement.* Layerthorpe, UK: Joseph Rowntree Foundation.

Morissette, R., J. Myles, and G. Picot. 1995. "Earnings Polarization in Canada, 1969-1991." In K. Banting and C. Beach, eds., *Labour Market Polarization and Social Policy Reform*. School of Policy Studies. Kingston, ON: Queen's University.

OECD (Organization for Economic Cooperation and Development). 1994. "The OECD Jobs Study: Summary." *OECD Economic Outlook* 55 (June): 1-4.

–. 1997. *Making Work Pay: Taxation, Benefits, Employment and Unemployment*. The OECD Jobs Strategy. Paris: OECD.

–. 1998. *Employment Outlook*. Paris: OECD.

Picot, G., and J. Myles. 1995. *Social Transfers, Changing Family Structure, and Low Income Among Children*. Research Paper No. 82, Analytical Studies Branch. Ottawa: Statistics Canada.

Richards, J. 1997. *Retooling the Welfare State: What's Right, What's Wrong, What's to Be Done*. Policy Study 31. Toronto: C.D. Howe Institute.

–. 1999. "The Case for Earnings Supplements: The Devil's in the Detail." In D. Allen and J. Richards, eds., *It Takes Two: The Family in Law and Economics*, 170-209. Toronto: C.D. Howe Institute.

Saskatchewan. 1998. *Building Independence: Investing in Families*. Regina: Department of Social Services.

United Kingdom. 1998. "The Modernisation of Britain's Tax and Benefit System: The Working Families Tax Credit and Work Incentives." *Budget 98*. Supplementary document to budget. London: HM Treasury.

Wilson, W. 1987. *The Truly Disadvantaged*. Chicago: University of Chicago Press.

4

Transition to the Knowledge Economy: Economic and Social Disparities in the New Economy

Tom Wall

Introduction

We are living through a period of change, historic in its speed and impact. This is occurring as a result of the technological advance and widening application of information and communication technologies (ICTs). The ICT revolution may have an impact on the power and income relationships within society as profound as the industrial revolution. While the impact of the industrial revolution was experienced over two centuries, sequentially affecting countries and continents, the impact of ICTs is occurring on a global scale within the life span of a single generation.

The social and economic impact is not predetermined by the technology. It is, however, influenced by political and business actions and philosophies. In many countries expert committees are examining the impact of the information society for their economy. The focus is generally on problems associated with competitiveness, adaptation to change, spending on science and technology, and education. This chapter examines the impact of change on employment, income disparities, social cohesion, and democracy, and highlights the role social dialogue plays in the process of change and readjustment within the European Union (EU). Social contracts, accords, or partnership agreements have contributed greatly to the transformation of some European economies. The chapter concludes with a call for measures to protect fundamental consumer and labour rights, within a global economy driven by the commercial exploitation of information and knowledge.

An Ill-Defined Future

Former US President Gerald Ford is credited with the observation that "predictions can be difficult, especially about the future." J. Robert Oppenheimer, the nuclear physicist, defied the odds when he predicted back in 1953 that "the open society, the unrestricted access to knowledge, the unplanned and uninhibited association of men for its furtherance – these are what may make a vast, complex, ever growing, ever changing, ever more specialized and expert technological world, nevertheless a world of human community" (Oppenheimer 1953). This statement was remarkable, as much for its optimism – Oppenheimer is known as the father of the atomic bomb – as for its foresightedness. Today the information society is a reality, to some degree at least, in most developing countries, and it is therefore possible to assess its impact more accurately. The information society does work, and in many respects wonderfully so, but for whom? Is the process leading to the inclusive community Oppenheimer dreamed of? Or is it further marginalizing the most disadvantaged social and regional groups? Is the knowledge society likely to strengthen participation and democracy, or will it consolidate the power of already powerful individuals and corporations? These questions are of vital importance for the future of our societies, whatever label we choose to apply to them in the future.

Defining the Information and Knowledge Society

Before assessing the social impact of change, definitions are called for. What is meant by the terms *information society* and *knowledge society*? A high-level expert group established by the European Commission described the information society in the following way: "The information society is the society currently being put in place, where low cost information and data storage and transmission technologies are in general use. This generalisation of the information and data use is being accompanied by organisational, commercial, social and legal innovations that will profoundly change life both in the world of work and in society generally" (European Commission 1997).

The expert group report states that there can be different information society models, reflecting the different models of industrialized society. The principal difference is the degree to which social exclusion is avoided or reinforced.

Information is not the same as knowledge or learning, however. To move from an information society to a knowledge or learning society, the increasing volume and accessibility of information needs to be used to inform and empower individuals, companies, and communities. The contrast between the information society and what is referred to as the "learning economy" is described in another European Commission report: "The two concepts differ because the outcome of learning, i.e., knowledge, is a much wider concept than information. Information is the part of knowledge which can be transformed into 'bits' and easily transmitted through a computer network while learning gives rise to know-how, skills and competencies which are often tacit rather than explicit and which cannot easily be transmitted through telecommunication networks" (Lundvall and Johnson 1994, quoted in European Commission 1998). Information and information technology, therefore, are means to an end – the objective being to utilize the flow of information to increase the stock of knowledge in ways that contribute to individual and collective progress.

In reality, however, ICTs are products as well as processes, their ownership and control prized as much for the ability to bestow influence as to generate wealth. Conflict between the interests of the emerging monopolies and oligopolies within the ICT sector and society's need to protect freedom and diversity will be addressed later. For now, let us review the extent of change occurring and the impact on employment, working conditions, and social cohesion within the developing information economies.

Where Is It Happening?

While the ICT revolution is global, the speed of application and diffusion varies widely. It is difficult to quantify the flow of information and the extent of knowledge within society. Comparing usage of the Internet as one indicator of the growth of the information society, figures show the United States, Canada, and the Scandinavian countries far ahead in achieving density levels of more than 30 percent of the total population. The rest of Europe lags behind, although in all countries growth rates are very high, with rates of expansion of 50 percent per annum being common.[1]

The extent of computer and Internet use will depend not just on computer literacy but also on basic literacy. Some leading information-society countries have disappointingly poor levels of literacy, if one considers the percentage of people between the ages of 16 and 65 who have the knowledge and skills to locate and use information contained in documentary form, and the ability to do arithmetic calculations. In the United States, more than 40 percent of the adult population under 65 were adjudged in the Organization for Economic Cooperation and Development (OECD) International Adult Literacy Survey to be at levels suggesting poor or very poor skills under these headings. The United States is not alone. Most European countries and Canada are only marginally better, and literacy levels in Ireland and the United Kingdom are even lower. Sweden is the only country among those surveyed to have relatively good scores. These findings are clear evidence that the primary means of access – basic literacy – is denied to a significant proportion of the population, even in those countries most advanced in terms of information technology. Unless basic educational standards are improved, a large proportion of the population will be left behind in the knowledge society.

Relevant educational systems that allow all to participate in a process of lifelong learning are vital to the establishment of a knowledge society. Even in respect of formal education, there are wide differences in participation rates. While developed countries have similar participation rates at the primary level, enrollment rates vary for the 15 to 29 age group from 45.9 percent in Finland to 29.2 percent in Japan (OECD 1998b).

The value put on learning is as important as the formal educational infrastructure. The son of a member of Ireland's Jewish community who settled in Dublin in the early 1900s recalled his father's unhappiness with the value the West placed on wealth compared with knowledge: "For in the communities of Lithuania there was one common characteristic never seen in the west. Scholarship had the highest value of all things in the community. A man might be wealthy but that mattered little. If a man were a scholar, the congregation would rise as he entered the Synagogue. The degrees of Knowledge were the degrees of honour ... and he could never assimilate the value which the west placed upon money" (Keogh 1998).

While it would be foolish to think that we can imbue all with such respect for learning, we should try to ensure that knowledge is valued for more than its functional uses in the future.

Employment in the New Era

Fears of jobless growth occurring as a result of rapid technological change appear to have been misplaced. Commentators such as Charles Handy and Jeremy Rifkin predicted the *end of work*. The latter (Rifkin 1995) stated:

> Short of a long-term global depression, chances are that the Third Industrial Revolution will continue to run its course, elevating productivity and displacing growing numbers of workers, all the while providing some new job opportunities but not nearly enough to absorb the millions made redundant by the new technologies. Global markets are also likely to continue to expand, but not nearly fast enough to absorb the overproduction of goods and services. Rising technological unemployment and declining purchasing power will continue to plague the global economy, undermining the capacity of governments to effectively manage their own domestic affairs.

Were such predictions to be borne out, the social consequence would be catastrophic. The actual outcome to date in terms of overall employment is less dramatic and, not ignoring recent problems in Europe and Asia, altogether more hopeful. Most countries have experienced the predicted shift in employment from industry to services. In the United States, about three-quarters of workers are employed in services. The proportion in Europe is lower, at about two-thirds. Despite the shift in employment towards services, however, the net effect on employment has been positive so far.

Part of the reason is that productivity growth has not been as high as envisaged and, apart from the recession of 1992-94, employment growth has been sustained at about 2 percent per annum in the United States, and at 0.3 percent in Europe. If anything, economic growth has tended to be more, not less, employment-intensive in recent decades. Additional jobs have been created in the United States as soon as growth exceeded 0.6 percent, and in Europe after growth of 2 percent. This compares with job-intensive growth being achieved after growth rates of 2 percent and 4 percent, respectively, during the 1960s and 1970s (European Commission 1996). Overall, in the decade 1986-96 approximately 50 million net additional jobs were created in OECD countries, despite a decline in employment in manufacturing in almost all member countries in this period, with Ireland being a rare exception.

There is no reason why employment should not continue to grow in the future. Investment in knowledge and learning is becoming the principal driver of economic progress. Unlike data processing and distribution, which is highly automated, the process of acquiring and applying knowledge will continue to be labour-intensive. The application of increased knowledge is likely to stimulate growth further, hopefully in directions that are sustainable.

Types of Jobs Created

While technological displacement has not led to an unemployment crisis, and is unlikely to do so in the near future, its impact on the quality of work may be less benign. As already indicated, services have accounted for virtually all of the net growth in employment in recent years. The gains have mainly been in sectors such as finance, insurance, real estate, and community and social services. Some of the expanded occupations are of the professional variety, but many more are low-skill, low-paying jobs. Close to half (45 percent) of the employment increase was in part-time jobs, which represents almost 1 in 5 jobs within the OECD area. While much of the increase in part-time work is voluntary in the sense that workers, principally women, are attempting to balance child rearing with work commitments, a significant proportion is involuntary. A European study suggests that 37 percent of part-time workers would prefer a full-time job. This statistic hides significant national differences, however. While the vast majority (89 percent) of part-time workers in France would prefer a full-time job, only 6 percent of part-time workers in Denmark share this preference (European Foundation for the Improvement of Living and Working Conditions 1995). The growth in part-time work has facilitated, however, an acceleration of female participation in the workforce: between 1986 and 1996 it went from 51 percent to 57 percent in the European Union, from 65 percent to 71 percent in the United States, and from 66 percent to 68 percent in Canada (OECD 1998).

Contrary to the expectations of some, self-employment has not increased overall as a percentage of total employment. OECD figures show that between 1986 and 1996 the proportion of self-employed people fell overall both in the European Union and in G-7 countries. Nevertheless, work has become more insecure. The effect of global competition and a greater reliance on temporary and fixed-term contracts has meant that workers have become more mobile within their careers, may change careers throughout life, and are more likely to experience periods of at least short-term unemployment. Increases in telework have isolated a growing proportion of the workforce from traditional social contact and legal and union protection.

Besides becoming less secure, work is also becoming more pressured and stressful. A Europe-wide survey has shown a sharp increase in the pace of work experienced by workers between 1991 and 1996. Some 54 percent of workers are now exposed to "high-speed work" and 56 percent are required to work to tight deadlines, reflecting an increase of six percentage points over a similar survey five years earlier. The principal reason given for the increasing pace of work is pressure from clients. On average, 28 percent of European workers consider their work to be stressful. (European Foundation 1996).

Income and Economic Growth

Since the 1960s, average per capita income has increased during most years in both Europe and North America. The gap between Europe and the United States narrowed between 1960 and 1980 but has since stabilized at around 40 percent. The contrast between Europe and the United States with respect to economic growth and earnings is interesting. In Europe, average real earnings and living standards have tended to track economic growth. In the United States, however, economic growth has not led to an improvement in workers' average living standards. It seems that US economic growth has contributed to increased employment at the expense of earnings growth. Whereas in parts of Europe, as we will see, social pacts have allowed some dampening of wage growth in the interests of job retention and creation, in the United States the process seems to be entirely driven by market forces.

A long-term divergence of income from economic growth in a developed democracy has few if any parallels. What factors have led to this development?

The neoclassical school of economic theory sees wage levels as being a function of supply and demand factors. For them, the US demonstrates the positive employment returns to be achieved from a relatively free labour market untrammelled by undue regulation. Unfortunately for such purists, there is an abundance of evidence of economies where growth in both employment and income have been sustained and accompanied by labour market regulation. In the European Union, the Netherlands, Ireland, Denmark, and Austria have all enjoyed relatively strong growth in earnings, living standards, and employment during the 1990s without any weakening of social protection. Their economic success is not unconnected to the existence of social accords involving the social partners – a subject to be dealt with later.

The American experience may be more the outcome of structural employment shifts rather then market forces. The drift from *mill to mall* is more pronounced in the US. The decline in density of trade union membership is also likely to have played a role in declining incomes. It is tempting to point to the relatively greater diffusion of the information society in the US as the underlying cause of both these changes. There is certainly a relationship. The propensity of the new American ICT companies to be non-union is a case in point. Falling incomes and/or a dismantling of social protection are not prerequisites for employment growth in the information society, however.

Income Disparities

There is evidence of significantly increased inequality in the US and the UK in particular. In Britain income disparity widened significantly in the 1980s, with the percentage of households below 50 percent of average income increasing from 9 percent to 24 percent between 1979 and 1994 (UK 1996).

Average real earnings declined in the US between 1985 and 1995. The principal losers were the middle and lower income groups. Between 1989 and 1996, the richest 20 percent of the American population increased their share of national income from 42.5 percent to 44.4 percent, to the detriment of all other income quintiles (US Economic Policy Institute 1998). As a result, the income differential between the poorest and the richest 20 percent moved from 8.3 times to 9.1 times. Canada is one of a few countries to show a progressive trend. The gap between poorest and richest, already lower than the United States, has continued to shrink. In 1984, the share of income enjoyed by the richest 20 percent was 7.3 times that of the poorest, falling to 6 times by 1994.[2]

Increasing income disparity in the United States is a consequence of the widening of wage differentials over the last quarter-century. Based on constant-dollar values, average earnings in the United States have been falling and the decline has been felt particularly among those who have only high school (or below) educational qualifications.[3] This growing divergence in income and career expectations between college graduates and those less qualified seems to be common to most countries.

The decline in earnings experienced by early school-leavers is in large part a result of the reduction in the availability of traditional unionized blue-collar jobs.

An Unequal World

Disparities between north and south are widening as a result of the inability of many countries to participate, other than marginally, in the knowledge revolution. As a World Bank (1995) report notes: "There is no worldwide trend toward convergence between rich and poor workers. Indeed, there are risks that workers in poorer countries will fall further behind, as lower investment and educational attainment widen disparities. Some workers, especially in Sub-Saharan Africa, could become increasingly marginalized. And those left out of the general prosperity in countries that are enjoying growth could suffer permanent losses, setting in motion intergenerational cycles of neglect."

If the information society is to be globally sustainable, developing countries need assistance in developing the educational and technological infrastructure.

Political Choices and Challenges in the Information Society

Inequality and growing income disparities are not a direct result of changing information and communication technologies. They result primarily from the social and economic policies pursued by governments. Growth in income disparities in the United States and Great Britain in particular was the outcome of conscious strategies adopted by both the Thatcher and Reagan governments. The relative stability of income distribution within some European countries and Canada have reflected different political priorities. Technology will always operate within differing political and economic climates, however. Greater availability of information is of benefit, but if, because of inequalities in education or income, access is limited to a privileged minority, it will reinforce disparities. If, on the other hand, measures are taken to overcome social exclusion and disadvantage, the information society will prove to be more egalitarian and sustainable.

Many opportunities are opened up as a result of greatly increased and unfettered information availability worldwide. Our democratic systems may be enhanced through the use of communication systems that provide unrestricted access for individuals and communities to information vital to making informed decisions about their future. The standard of social services can be improved as ICTs reduce costs and improve accessibility, especially in remote communities. What has been referred to as the "death of distance" (Cairncross 1997) can reduce social and regional disparities as disadvantaged communities become empowered through knowledge. Workers have the potential for greater autonomy and reward in a society where their knowledge and skills are valued. The net effect may be improved living standards achieved through higher levels of growth, employment, leisure opportunities, and individual choice.

What are the potential roadblocks to this idyllic future? The most important thing is to avoid installing corporate culture with the equipment.

Through the control of satellite television and other media interests, powerful individuals are in a strong position to influence the type and content of the information we receive. The emergence of digital television and the likely merging of computer and television technologies present greater opportunities than ever for the transmission of cultural and political values through information and entertainment outlets. This is particularly so where a few powerful individuals control vast slices of the information and communications industry.

Developments in ICTs are providing greater choice, but having more products does not necessarily mean having more real choice. This is particularly true in the film and TV industry. In Europe, there is a noticeable "dumbing down" in standards in television as competition intensifies. The tendency of public broadcasting companies faced with competition is to scrap all programs that do not appeal to mass audiences.

Winning Workers to Corporate Ways

As consumers we have at least the option of "turning off and switching on." For many workers the choices are more restricted. Corporations, particularly those in the ICT sector, aim to motivate their workforce by imbuing them with a sense of commitment and loyalty to the corporation. This is not necessarily a bad thing. Workers have a common interest with the employer in ensuring the viability and profitability of the business – if only to ensure that their jobs remain secure. Sometimes, however, staff are required to buy into a value system quite different from that traditionally adopted by the host community. Most American high-tech corporations, for example, are hostile to trade unionism, ignoring the fact that within many European countries trade union organizations are seen as vital to the preservation of a participative democracy. In the past, multinational corporations tended to adapt to different environments. Now they tend to use the threat of relocation to ensure that it is *their* value system that dominates.

Peter Drucker (1993) heralded a "post-capitalist society" in the sense that knowledge, not capital, would be the key asset for companies. As this "means of production" is owned by the workers, he predicted a fundamental change in their favour in the power relationships within organizations. Highly knowledgeable and skilled employees often have the power to choose their employment and dictate pay and conditions in a manner undreamed of by most workers past and present. This is not, however, the start of a social revolution on the shop or office floor. It is simply evidence of the labour market continuing to benefit those whose skills are in short supply relative to demand. For most workers, a "free" labour market threatens their rights and privileges, so they will continue to rely on their collective strength.

Balancing Freedom and Protection

Workers need protection with respect to trade union rights, rights to information and consultation, and health and safety protection. The growth of telework has complicated contractual relationships, often to the detriment of the workers involved. Incidences of work-related upper-limb disorders and stress are on the increase. There is a need to ensure adequate social protections to people who work outside traditional systems.

The possibility of cultural encroachments, occurring as information is diffused, creates risks to broader cultural diversity, including language. English is the lingua franca of business, entertainment, and the Internet. Cultural and linguistic diversity needs to be protected in the global information market.

There is also a threat to consumers in a global economy in which electronic commerce, or e-commerce, will take an increasing share of the market. There are sharp differences between the United States and the European Union and Canada over whether governments or industry should take responsibility for consumer protection and data privacy. The United States believes that these issues should be the subject of voluntary regulation by business. The European Union and Canada support uniform legislation designed to give minimum protection. Unions in Europe strongly support the need for regulations on privacy, intellectual property rights, and consumer protection, as well as rights for workers. Unregulated e-commerce will be hugely attractive to the most unscrupulous traders. Unless regulatory arrangements are in place worldwide, buttressed by effective monitoring and enforcement, consumers will have no confidence in doing business over the Internet.

The knowledge society must have breadth as well as depth. It must be accessible to all regardless of region, language, income, gender, and age. This will happen only if politicians, the business community, trade unions, and other interest groups come together to ensure that rapid technological change does not undermine social cohesion or marginalize the disadvantaged even further. This requires social dialogue among all interests with a view to gaining a consensual framework for the future knowledge society. The challenge is to regulate worker, consumer, and environmental protection in a manner that does not stifle individual and commercial freedom and enterprise.

Europe and the Social Contract

There is a consensus in Europe that although market forces make the information society inevitable, the shape it takes will be determined by political choices. The concept of a social contract imbued with aspirations of equity and consensus building is strongly felt, if only vaguely defined. Social dialogue is a key feature of the way the European Union deals with change affecting workers. Treaties provide an institutional framework for dialogue between the social partners at European and national levels. They contain commitments to fundamental rights for workers and the achievement of a high level of employment. Consensus between the social partners offers the best opportunity for coping with rapid change with a minimum of social upheaval.

Trade unions in most European Community countries support the concept of social partnership at European, national, and enterprise levels. Social contracts have for some time been a feature of the Scandinavian countries in particular. In a number of countries, social partnership has helped transform economies to meet the challenge of global competition and the information society. The following examples illustrate this approach.

Social Consensus in the Netherlands
There are no formal agreements or social pacts in the Netherlands, but a form of social consensus has emerged between the social partners that has helped transform the Netherlands into one of the most successful European economies. In the early 1980s, unemployment had reached a record level, equivalent to 14 percent of the labour force. It was estimated that when work schemes, early retirement, training schemes, and other forms of assistance were considered, the real unemployment rate was close to 28 percent. An accord between unions and employers at a central level in 1982 recommended a "new direction." It advised union negotiators to forego nominal wage increases and suspend the payment of contractual cost-of-living adjustments due under existing agreements, in order to create a basis for discussions about employment-creation measures, including the possibility of reductions in working hours. The recommendations were widely followed: wage rates were restrained, unit labour costs fell, new flexible work practices and shorter working hours were agreed to. There was a surge in employment, particularly in part-time jobs.

The success of this consensus encouraged a continuation of the general approach. In recent pacts, wage moderation is traded for lower taxes, thereby sustaining low inflation, permitting reform of public finances, achieving competitiveness, and producing economic and employment growth. The outcome has been what is sometimes referred to as the "Dutch miracle" – impressive rates of job creation assisted by continued wage moderation and reductions in taxes on labour. In effect, a virtuous economic cycle has been established. The process is monitored and developed through bipartite meetings (employers and unions) and biannual meetings between the government and the social partners in a Social and Economic Council.[4]

Social Partnership in Ireland

In the mid-1980s Ireland suffered from economic problems comparable to those of the Netherlands. Public finances were out of control, with the national debt at about 140 percent of gross national product. Falling growth rates were leading to record levels of unemployment. The Irish Congress of Trade Unions proposed a way forward based on agreement between the government and the other social partners. The aim was, through a national consensus, to plot a way out of the economic mire. A "Program for National Recovery" was agreed upon. It was a three-year agreement that provided for wage increases limited to 2 percent per annum. In return for wage moderation, there were a series of measures to stimulate employment and broaden the tax base to permit lower taxation of workers' earnings, and a commitment to improve social protections.

The pact was highly successful and achieved virtually all of its objectives. It is credited with being the major factor in the transformation of the Irish economy, which is now the fastest-growing economy in the OECD, with growth of 8 to 9 percent annually. To date, four three-year pacts have been agreed to, each building on the success of the previous one and attempting more ambitious targets for economic growth, investment in education and health care, social inclusion, and action to promote enterprise and employment through the maintenance of an innovative and competitive business environment. The most recent agreement (Partnership 2000 – for Inclusion, Employment and Competitiveness) has extended the partnership in two directions. For the first time, the voluntary sector, representing the disadvantaged groups in society, are full partners in the process. The second novel aspect is an agreement between employers and unions to jointly work towards the institution of a partnership process within individual companies. The agreement includes provisions to make the information society more accessible and to foster lifelong learning.

The partnership process is supported by all the political parties represented in parliament, so changes of government do not threaten it. The agreements are voluntary and have no status in law. While all unions operate within the process, some non-union companies regulate their affairs independently. Perhaps because of their voluntary nature, the pacts hold great moral force. Employers, initially somewhat skeptical, see these agreements as highly beneficial. They are able to plan in a stable social, political, and industrial relations environment knowing in advance future wage adjustments. Perhaps the greatest benefit is that it takes conflict out of not just industrial relations but also the whole process of dealing with economic and social development. Effectively, the involvement of all the major social actors means that conflicting interests and disputes are resolved through problem solving rather than confrontation.

Figure 1

Increases in disposable household income in Ireland, 1987-95

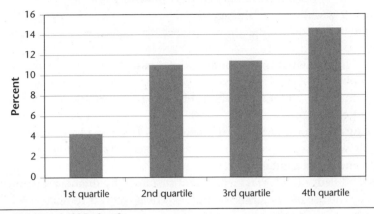

Source: CSO Household Budget Surveys.

Figure 1 charts the rise in disposable household income during the first half of the period of social partnership. Average income increased by about 10 percent in real terms during the period. Despite the fact that social equity was a declared objective of the process, however, the increase in living standards of the lowest income quartile was less than half the average. In the period since 1995, average income growth has been higher, running at about 3 percent per annum. No figures are yet available to assess income disparities in the more recent period, but there is reason to believe that they have stabilized, if not narrowed. Recent tax changes have favoured the lower-paid, and a halving of the unemployment rate since 1994 is likely to have contributed. Nevertheless, in the context of preparations for a possible future agreement, consideration is being given to further measures to reduce disparities, such as flat rate rather than percentage wage adjustments.

The Need for a Global "Social Market"
It will prove difficult for Europe and other economies pursuing policies aimed at social cohesion to sustain competitiveness in a largely unregulated global market. Corporations will continue to seek out locations for reinvestment where they are unhindered by labour unions or state-imposed restrictions. A balance needs to be achieved between the interests of reducing inequality and exclusion and maintaining economic growth and competitiveness. Without returning to protected markets, ways must be found to ensure that globalization does not lead to a lowering of standards. In 1998, the International Labour Conference approved a declaration on fundamental principles and rights at work. These fundamental rights refer to:

- freedom of association and effective recognition of the right to collective bargaining
- elimination of all forms of forced or compulsory labour
- effective abolition of child labour
- elimination of discrimination with respect to employment and occupation.

These fundamental rights should be the basis for future unhindered access to world markets. The refusal of the World Trade Organization to accept that such fundamental rights should be a criterion in regulating trade is a cause of concern.

The turmoil in world financial markets that threatened a global recession in 1998 was caused in part by the advantage taken by individual companies of the ending of capital controls. A huge artificial market in futures, options, and hedge funds was created and sustained by financial institutions, aided by the use of advanced computers. The effect was to make a few people enormously wealthy and endanger the world economic system. This near-disaster provides us with a timely warning of the need for effective international controls to protect the many from the greed of the few.

Conclusion

Despite evidence to the contrary, the information society has the potential to facilitate greater levels of social, political, and financial participation. This can be realized through a strategy that harnesses knowledge in the interest of all in society. We must ensure that democracy and social cohesion are strengthened, not threatened, in the new knowledge society. This can best be achieved by dialogue involving all the social partners. Social dialogue allows commercial interests to be made more compatible with social needs. The knowledge society will prove illusory unless it is accessible to all.

Notes

1 Nua Internet Surveys: <http://www.nua.net/surveys/how_many_online/europe.html>
2 Data secured online from the Centre for International Statistics at the Canadian Council for Social Development: <http://www.ccsd.ca/facts.html>.
3 Economic Policy Institute analysis of US Bureau of the Census Current Population Survey data (1998).
4 This synopsis is based on a paper by Jelle Visser on the "Dutch miracle" delivered at a 1998 seminar organized by the Research and Policy Unit "Notre Europe" and the European Trade Union Institute in Brussels.

References

Cairncross, F. 1997. *The Death of Distance: How the Communications Revolution Will Change Our Lives.* Cambridge, MA: Harvard Business School Press.
Drucker, Peter. 1993. *Post-Capitalist Society.* New York: Harper Business.
European Commission. 1996. "Living and Working in the Information Society – People First." *Bulletin of the EU,* Supplement 3/96.

–. 1997. *Building the European Information Society for Us All – Final Policy Report of the High Level Expert Group*. Luxembourg: Office for Official Publications of the European Communities.

–. 1998. *Society, the Endless Frontier*. Luxembourg: Office for Official Publications of the European Communities.

European Foundation for the Improvement of Living and Working Conditions. 1995. *BEST, Bulletin on Working Time*, no. 8.

–. 1996. *Second European Survey on Working Conditions*. Luxembourg: Office for Official Publications of the European Communities.

Keogh, Dermot. 1998. *Jews in Twentieth Century Ireland*. Cork: Cork University Press.

Lundvall, B.Å., and B. Johnson. 1994. "The Learning Economy." *Journal of Industry Studies* 1: 23-42.

OECD (Organization for Economic Cooperation and Development). 1998a. *Labour Force Statistics 1977-1997*. Paris: OECD.

–. 1998b. International Literacy Survey (ILS) Database. Web site: <http://www.oecd.org>

Oppenheimer, J. Robert. 1953. *Science and the Common Understanding*. New York: Simon and Schuster.

Rifkin, Jeremy. 1995. *The End of Work: The Decline of the Global Labour Force and the Dawn of a Post-Market Economy*. New York: Putnam.

UK. 1996. *Households Below Average Income 1979-1993/94*. London: Department of Social Security.

US Economic Policy Institute. 1998. Online data under "Living Standards & Labor Markets," available at <http://www.epinet.org>.

World Bank (International Bank for Reconstruction and Development). 1995. *World Development Report 1995*. Washington, DC: The World Bank.

Part 2
The Global Market, Regions, and Communities

5

The Nexus of the Information Revolution and Globalization

Someshwar Rao and Ron Hirshhorn[1]

Introduction

Profound changes are under way in the global economic system that present major new opportunities as well as significant new challenges for workers, firms, and economies. The revolution in information and communication technologies (ICTs) has been a central force underlying these developments. This chapter explores the links between ICTs and globalization and examines the relevance and importance of these relationships for Canada. Three main questions are addressed. First, how has the development of increasingly sophisticated ICTs contributed to globalization? Second, to what extent has Canada participated in the identified processes of globalization? And third, what can we say about Canada's experience with what we term "ICT-related globalization"?

In the next section ("ICTs and Globalization") we examine the role ICTs have played in the growth of international commerce and the increased global flow of information. This section also briefly considers the implications of these developments and how, in particular, they affect countries' ability to achieve high rates of economic growth. The third section ("Canadian Participation in ICT-Related Globalization") focuses on Canada's participation in those processes through which the information revolution has promoted globalization. We review a variety of evidence that shed light on the extent to which the relevant global forces have impacted on Canada. Important aspects of this experience are examined in the fourth section ("Canada's Experience with ICT-Related Globalization"). In the fifth section ("Canada's Progress in the Use of ICTs"), we briefly review evidence on the effects of Canada's involvement in the growing internationalization of business. We also look at concerns pertaining to the adoption of ICTs in Canada and, in particular, the concern that ICT may lead to higher levels of unemployment. The conclusion identifies some important implications of these developments.

ICTs and Globalization

Over the past two decades, we have witnessed a proliferation of new, increasingly powerful ICT products. These are the result of dramatic advances in basic technology, including exponential increases in computing power, progress in digitalization, and developments that have greatly expanded communications capacity. It is now possible to transform virtually all forms of information into a digital stew of 1's and 0's that can be manipulated, processed, stored, and transmitted at very high speed and very low cost.

In this section we examine the connection between these developments and the trend towards global economic integration. We also briefly consider the implications of developments that are strengthening economic and information links among world economies. Countries have participated to varying degrees in these developments. In the second part of this section, we argue that countries that have progressed in their evolution as information societies, and whose citizens have good access to worldwide information flows, are well positioned for growth in the new global economic order.

The Impact of ICT Development on Globalization

Three points of connection between developments in the ICT sector and developments in the global economy deserve particular attention. The first

Figure 1

Growth of world foreign direct investment (FDI) flows, gross domestic product (GDP), and exports

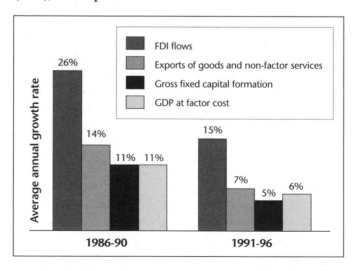

Source: World Investment Report 1997, United Nations.

is the link between advances in information and communication technology and the increasing internationalization of business. Global foreign direct investment (FDI) has grown strongly over the past decade, outpacing the growth of both world output and world trade by a wide margin (Figure 1). FDI flows have also become more diversified internationally, and in 1996 developing countries accounted for 40 percent of inflows, more than twice their share over the 1985-90 period. Through this foreign investment, the world's 45,000 multinational enterprises (MNEs) have established approximately 280,000 affiliates and created jobs for about 75 million workers. The growth in global FDI is the result of a number of factors, including the relaxation of investment restrictions worldwide and the privatization of many state enterprises. Arguably, however, the most important influence has been the development of advanced information and communications systems that allow firms to effectively coordinate activities spread around the globe and monitor the activities of foreign suppliers and the demands of foreign consumers.

It is interesting to compare recent globalization with that which occurred in the late 19th and early 20th centuries. Driven largely by the growing demand for food and raw materials in North America and Europe, foreign trade and investment grew to account for a high share of global economic activity in the decades prior to 1913. Most of the international investment was in the form of portfolio investment, but FDI is estimated to have accounted for one-third of the total stock of overseas investment by 1913 (UNCTAD 1997). This period saw the introduction of significant new transport and communications technologies (i.e., the telegraph and telephone) and the emergence of the multinational enterprise. Business, however, was not integrated across national boundaries. Information and communication technologies were not adequately developed to allow the true internationalization of business.

In the recent period, advanced technologies have helped MNEs rationalize production on a global basis. By situating discrete segments of the value-added chain around the globe to take advantage of country-specific strengths, improve sales prospects, and manage corporate risks, MNEs are contributing to a process of deepening economic integration. As a consequence of the increased flows of goods, services, and technology among MNE parents and their affiliates, it is estimated that about one-third of world trade now occurs within firms.

ICTs have also facilitated the coordination of activities among firms and supported the increase in interfirm collaboration. Between 1980 and 1993, for example, the number of technology alliances worldwide is estimated to have increased ninefold (Figure 2). Taking advantage of the increased efficiency of international communications and transactions, firms have actively pursued the opportunities offered by international agreements,

Figure 2

Global alliances (cumulative) in new technologies

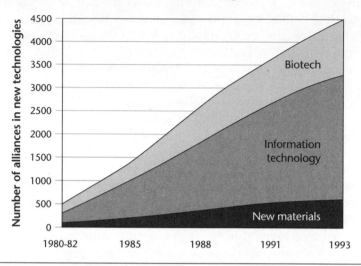

Source: UNCTAD, based on MERIT-CATI Databank, Maastricht, Netherlands.

including alliances, partnerships, and joint ventures, to gain entry to new markets, acquire technologies, and reduce R&D costs and risks.

The second connection of interest is the link between the development of ICTs and the growth in global trade. ICT industries constitute one of the most dynamic segments of the global economy, and they have themselves become an important focus of global commerce. Between 1990 and 1995, global ICT revenues increased by nearly 60 percent, about two-thirds faster than world gross domestic product (GDP). Worldwide ICT revenues in 1995 were close to $1.4 trillion (all monetary amounts shown here are in US dollars), more than 5 percent of world GDP. These trends reflect the growing world demand for increasingly flexible and less costly computer and telecommunications products. World trade in ICT goods amounted to more than $470 billion in 1994, representing over a tenth of all global merchandise trade.

Data on trade in ICT services are not available, but the World Trade Organization (WTO) estimates that it could be as high as $500 billion. Moreover, available evidence on individual ICT services indicate that this area of trade is also growing rapidly. International telephone calls, for example, rose from less than 4 billion minutes in 1975 to more than 60 billion in 1995, an annual average growth rate of 15 percent.[2] Software exports from the United States, the leading world producer, grew by more than 20 percent per year over the first half of the 1990s (OECD 1997b).

The growth in ICT trade has been supported by major changes in the policy environment. ICT has traditionally been among the most heavily regulated and protected sectors, but this is no longer the case in most industrial economies. There is a growing appreciation that competitive markets provide the most reliable mechanism for ensuring that citizens participate in the fruits of the ICT revolution. Competition has been, or is being, introduced into most telecommunications services; longer-term contracts and preferred supplier arrangements protecting major telecommunications equipment firms are being terminated, and governments themselves are getting out of the telecommunications business. New trade opportunities have also been created by two recent important international initiatives: the WTO agreement liberalizing global trade in information technology products and the 1997 WTO agreement to liberalize trade in basic telecommunications services.

The development of ICTs has, at the same time, facilitated growing trade in non-ICT services. Information-intensive services have become more transportable and tradeable as a result of advances in information and communication technology. International competition is becoming a significant factor in markets for such services as accounting, banking, consulting, marketing, advertising, and design.

The third important link between the ICT sector and the global economy arises from the use of ICTs by households and business to become a part of expanding global networks for information exchange, data transfer, and electronic transactions. While there has been significant growth globally in traditional communications channels, such as wireline telephone and broadcast TV, the most rapid expansion has occurred in newer options, such as cellular telephone, direct to home (DTH) satellite service, and the Internet.

The rapidly growing popularity of the Internet has been the most significant development. Over the 1990s, the number of Internet users has almost doubled every year. There has also been an explosive growth in content and services available on the Net. The World Wide Web has evolved into one of the primary vehicles through which organizations distribute information and create public awareness about their products and services.

The Internet is only a precursor of the high-bandwidth information highway that is expected to provide seamless information links between nations in coming years. Individuals, however, have already experienced some of the effects of a decline in the barriers of time and space. The Internet has been a factor in the growing international trade in services discussed above. It has also helped firms keep abreast of new technologies, provided new opportunities for learning, and facilitated collaboration among researchers in different organizations and different countries. A wide range of virtual communities has been created, linking individuals in different parts of the world with common concerns or interests.

Electronic commerce, or e-commerce, comprising both business-to-business and business-to-consumer activities, is becoming more important internationally. Estimates of e-commerce vary widely, and it is not known how much of the estimated $10-25 billion (in 1997) in world e-commerce involves international transactions. There is wide agreement, however, that e-commerce, and especially the business-to-business transactions that account for about 80 percent of the total, will grow rapidly in coming years and that e-commerce will become an increasingly important form of international, as well as domestic, business activity.

While the use of ICTs has contributed to global integration, globalization has, in turn, encouraged the use of ICTs. With the intensification of international competition, firms have come under increased pressure to improve efficiency and develop new products and processes. This has increased the demand for advanced technologies such as computer-aided design, computer-aided engineering, and automated materials handling systems. It has contributed to the appeal of, for example, electronic barcoding and related computerized systems that allow manufacturers to track changes in consumer demand and tailor their production and material purchases accordingly. In a highly competitive global environment, firms may pay a high price if they fail to acquire efficient computer-based systems and to utilize ICT applications in their efforts to keep abreast of available technologies, build their human capital, identify market opportunities, and develop new ways of satisfying consumer demands.

Implications

The economic contribution of ICTs has been examined through case studies focusing on the experience of firms with particular technologies and through broader empirical studies of country experience. In this work, ICTs are typically defined to include advanced manufacturing technologies as well as the telecommunications, computer, and related goods and services produced by firms generally considered to fall within the ICT sector.[3] Due to measurement problems, as well as the significant time it takes producers to fully integrate information and communication technologies, economists have had difficulty documenting the productivity impacts of ICTs (Griliches 1994).[4] Evidence of their significant economic contribution, however, including their positive influence on labour productivity in Canadian industries, is beginning to appear (e.g., Brynjolfsson and Hitt 1995; Gera et al. 1998a).

The above discussion suggests the need for an additional perspective on the contribution of ICTs – a broader and longer-term perspective that recognizes the role of ICTs in helping countries develop the mechanisms to acquire information originating outside their borders. The critical role of information has long been recognized by economists. In the neoclassical growth models of the mid-1950s, it was shown that sustained economic growth depends on technological progress, which involves the reorganization of existing information into new forms and patterns (invention) and subsequently the incorporation of the new idea or knowledge in a technology. More recently, new growth theorists such as Paul Romer (1990) and Robert Lucas (1988) have highlighted the special characteristics of knowledge. Because of its unique ability to be consumed without losing its usefulness, and because it can be passed from user to user at close to zero cost, knowledge has been shown to be a particularly valuable factor of production.

Other strands of economic research, including studies of the innovation process (e.g., Mowery and Rosenberg 1989) and historical studies into the determinants of long-run growth (e.g., Maddison 1994) shed additional light on the role of knowledge development as an engine of economic growth. This substantial literature points to the importance of investment in research, education, and other knowledge-enhancing activities and the development of efficient mechanisms for transferring information to those who can benefit from it. It also provides a context for understanding the important contribution of mechanisms that enable countries to benefit from international knowledge transfers.

ICTs such as the Internet are themselves an important mechanism for the acquisition of information developed outside a country's borders. They help organizations and households tap into the vast stock of global information that is widely and freely available. In addition, the development of ICTs has facilitated the growth of FDI, one of the major vehicles for international technology transfer, and supported the operation of a range of formal and informal information mechanisms. As Orsenigo points out in his chapter in this volume, the latter include international alliances and joint ventures, international consulting contracts, and international networking arrangements among academics and members of professional bodies.

There is evidence that the development of global trade, investment, and communications links has benefited countries with lagging performance, although the evidence also indicates that openness does not automatically lead to stronger productivity increases and improved growth. A country's ability to take advantage of technology transfers and knowledge inflows will be influenced by factors such as workers' education and training, the investment environment, and the adequacy of the physical infrastructure. Disparities in these factors have complicated efforts to test the influence of openness on the performance of developing countries. It is significant, however, that among countries belonging to the Organization for Economic Cooperation and Development (OECD), significant economic convergence has occurred over the postwar period. During the postwar boom stretching from 1950 to 1992, the bottom half of OECD countries in terms of per capita income grew on average 1.4 percentage points faster per year than the top half (UNCTAD 1997). Especially notable is the rapid progress of the poorest 25 percent of OECD countries, which grew on average 2.4 percentage points faster than the richest 25 percent.

By contributing to the strengthening of international economic links, ICTs are also associated with some of the more problematic aspects of globalization. A major concern, highlighted by recent developments, is the increase in international financial instability. The efficiency of international communications and the ease of international transactions have facilitated large-scale flows of liquid capital between countries. Unlike foreign direct investment, these flows are generally not associated with the transfer of real resources. Recent experience shows how these volatile speculative flows can cause large swings in exchange rates, create considerable uncertainty, and impede the efforts of countries to encourage productive investment and promote growth.

Globalization and the development of ICTs are complex phenomena. On balance, however, both are likely to be a positive force for increasing productivity growth and improving living standards.[5] Countries that can take advantage of the expansion in trade and investment opportunities and the increased possibilities for knowledge acquisition should be well positioned for growth in the new global economic environment.

In coming years, one of the main characteristics of successful economies is likely to be their progress as information societies. Dynamic economies can be expected to have well-developed information links that supplement their trade and investment links with the rest of the world. ICTs will be utilized to facilitate the rapid diffusion of new information within the economy. In successful economies, ICTs would also be used to build human capital and help establish the skill base that countries need in order to benefit fully from increased global flows of information.

Canadian Participation in ICT-Related Globalization

Of what relevance to Canada are the globalization trends just discussed? In this section, we address this question by examining Canada's participation in the growth of FDI and the increasing internationalization of business; in the growing international trade in ICT products; and in the growing global use of ICTs.

Trends in Foreign Direct Investment

The growth of direct investment by foreigners in Canada and Canadian FDI abroad is shown in Figure 3. Foreign investment has become a much more important element within Canada over the past decade. Over the 1985-96 period, the stock of inward FDI, resulting from investment inflows and the reinvestment of earnings by foreign enterprises in Canada, grew both in absolute terms and as a percentage of GDP. Over the same period, Canada's

Figure 3

Canada's inward and outward foreign direct investment stock
as percentages of GDP

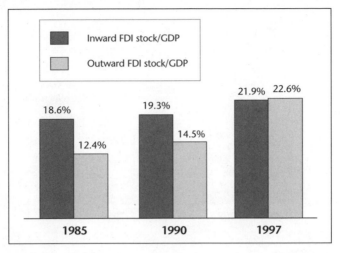

Source: Statistics Canada.

outward FDI stock grew still more rapidly as Canadian firms became more
internationally oriented. For the first time in its history, Canada has recently become a net exporter of investment capital.[6]

Partly because of the growth of inward and outward FDI, Canadian exports and imports have also increased relative to GDP over the past decade
(Figure 4). Canada's export orientation has increased in all provinces and
all manufacturing industries. The 50 largest Canadian-owned multinationals in the US and American-owned enterprises in Canada, which account
for most two-way FDI, are also responsible for more than 70 percent of all
bilateral trade. Much of this trade occurs within MNEs.

Canada has clearly participated in the growing internationalization of
business. Canada's importance as a host economy, however, has declined
since 1985, indicating that, in this respect, Canada has not participated as
fully in the growth of global investment as a number of other countries.
There has been a substantial decline since the mid-1980s in Canada's share
of both G-7 and global inward FDI stocks. Between 1985 and 1996, Canada's share of North American inward FDI stock fell by more than 40 percent, to 15 percent.

There has also been some slippage over the past decade in Canada's share
of world and G-7 outward FDI stocks. While Canadian firms have been
actively pursuing foreign investment opportunities, the emergence of certain countries (including Japan and other Southeast Asian countries) as

Figure 4

Canada's exports and imports as percentages of GDP

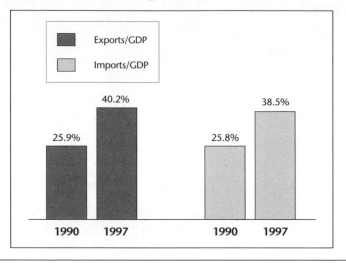

Source: Statistics Canada.

important sources of outward investment has had the effect of reducing Canada's relative standing as an investing nation.

Advances in information and communication technology have supported the influence of other factors fuelling the growth of investment in Canada and Canadian investment abroad. One of these important influences on the inward investment side has been the Canada-US Free Trade Agreement (FTA). Since the implementation of the FTA in 1989, the US has become a much more important source of inward investment. Almost three-quarters of the cumulative net FDI inflows to Canada over the period 1991-96 originated from across the border, compared with one-third in the previous five-year period. The US share of Canada's inward FDI stock, which had declined significantly in the late 1980s, rose from 64 percent in 1990 to 68 percent in 1996.

The growth in the importance of US inward investment partly reflects the efforts of US multinationals to rationalize production on a North American basis. Canadian affiliates of American MNEs now tend to manufacture a narrower range of products, but they often supply the entire North American market. Some Canadian affiliates have world product mandates. Consistent with these developments, Canadian manufacturing plants have generally become much more export-oriented. Between 1990 and 1995, for example, the number of Canadian manufacturing industries depending on foreign markets for at least 50 percent of their sales doubled.

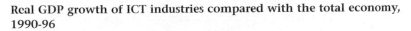

Figure 5

Real GDP growth of ICT industries compared with the total economy, 1990-96

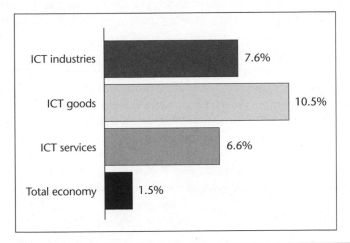

Sources: Industry Canada; Statistics Canada.

These developments are in keeping with the general internationalization of production that is under way globally. They suggest that Canada has participated not only in the growth of global foreign investment but also in the deepening economic integration made possible by the development of ICTs.

The Development of an Internationally Competitive ICT Sector
The ICT sector is one of the most dynamic segments of the Canadian economy. Over the 1990-96 period, the sector's real output grew more than five times as fast as the total economy's GDP. Growth in the goods subsector has been particularly strong, exceeding 10 percent per year (Figure 5). Labour productivity in the ICT sector grew by more than 5 percent per year over the first half of the 1990s, almost four times the rate for the overall economy. The rapid pace of technological change in ICTs has been an important factor underlying the sector's dynamism. The Canadian sector's recent growth experience, however, has also been strongly influenced by trade and regulatory reforms that have created new opportunities for Canadian firms in foreign markets while increasing competition within Canada.

Canada is a small player in the context of global ICT activities. Telecommunications service revenues in Canada comprised only 1.7 percent of the world total in 1995. Canada's share of world ICT goods production is even lower – about 1 percent in 1994 (OECD 1997b). As a component of the

Canadian economy, however, the ICT sector is highly significant. In 1996, ICT industries employed 418,000 workers, just over 3 percent of all Canadian employees, and accounted for 7 percent of Canadian GDP. Canada's ICT manufacturing exports comprised 7.5 percent of all manufacturing exports in 1996. Moreover, the sector is the most research-intensive segment of the Canadian economy, accounting, in 1996, for 37 percent of total private sector R&D spending.

The ICT sector encompasses a diverse range of industries of various sizes. Both Canadian ICT manufacturers and ICT service providers have been affected by the opening up of world markets for ICT products, but the increase in international competition has affected goods producers, such as manufacturers of telecommunications and computer equipment, and service providers, notably telecommunications carriers, in different ways.

Although Canada has a substantial deficit in its overall ICT goods trade, Canadian manufacturers have had considerable success selling in foreign markets. Over the 1990-96 period, Canada's ICT manufacturing exports increased (in current dollars) by 13.6 percent per year, which is faster than the growth achieved by the world's leading exporters, the US and Japan, as well as major exporting nations such as the United Kingdom and Germany. In the case of telecommunications equipment, Canada's most important ICT manufacturing industry, exports more than tripled, contributing to a substantial increase in the surplus Canada enjoys in this product category.[7]

Canada's success as an exporter of ICT goods owes much to the technological strengths of Nortel, Canada's major vertically integrated producer of telecommunications equipment, and of smaller telecom manufacturers, such as Newbridge and Mitel, who have become world leaders in specialized market niches. It is also a result of the strong export performance of Canadian computer firms. Through the presence of MNEs such as IBM, DEC, and Hewlett Packard, Canada has been able to capture a significant share of the rapidly growing North American computer market.

In recent years, software too has become a much more important ICT export. Although software exports are small relative to hardware exports, Canadian firms have managed to build a reputation in a number of niche markets and strongly increase foreign sales.

In ICT services generally, however, the main impact of market reforms to liberalize trade and promote competition has been on the domestic market. The structure of the Canadian telecommunications services industry has changed significantly and is continuing to evolve with the relaxation of regulatory controls limiting competition.[8] A main beneficiary of recent reforms has been the "alternative service providers" that compete with Bell Canada, the other telephone companies that are members or associate members of the Stentor Alliance, and the independent telephone companies operating in Ontario and Quebec.[9] Between 1993, when competition began to take hold, and 1996, alternative service providers more than doubled their share of long distance market revenues, while the share of Stentor members declined substantially.

In ICT services, as in ICT goods, Canada has participated in the growth in international commerce. In the case of services, however, most of the changes have occurred in the domestic market, where service providers have come under strong pressure to streamline their operations, improve operating efficiencies, and present customers with attractive product offerings.

Growth in the Use of ICTs

Canada has also been a major participant in the third identified aspect of ICT-related globalization. In recent years, there has been substantial growth in the use of ICTs by Canadian households and firms. Moreover, insofar as international comparisons can be made of ICT availability and use – or what has been dubbed "connectedness"[10] – Canada's performance compares well with that of other major industrial countries.

Increasing numbers of households in all regions of the country have been acquiring computers and modems, the prerequisites for online connectivity. Internet usage has grown dramatically, with the percentage of connected households almost doubling between 1996 and 1997. Internet usage has increased strongly in all parts of the country, but there are significant regional differences, with, for example, BC's household penetration rate being more than twice those of Prince Edward Island and Quebec, the provinces with the lowest penetration rates. A recent AC Nielsen survey suggests that about half of Canadian households with Internet connections fall into the category of "heavy users" who go online at least once a day on average (AC Nielsen 1997).

Data on the connectedness of Canadian businesses are limited, but a recent Industry Canada (1996) survey of service industries suggests that at least large and medium-sized enterprises are making significant use of the main information and communication technologies. Small firms in Canada have been relatively slow – compared with larger firms as well as with small firms in the US – to adopt advanced manufacturing technologies (Baldwin and Sabourin 1995).

Additional information on Internet use by business is provided by the member surveys of the Canadian Federation of Independent Business (CFIB). In the first quarter of 1998, 43 percent of the small and medium-sized enterprises (SMEs) surveyed by the CFIB indicated that they used the Internet. Usage rates were highest among SMEs in business services, finance, and insurance, and lowest among firms in construction, retail trade, and the hospitality sector.

It is useful to put Canada's ICT use into an international context, although this must be done on the basis of a limited amount of published data and in the absence of an analytical framework that can tell us what importance to assign to individual indicators of country connectedness. In relation to other major industrial countries, Canada ranks particularly high in terms of residents' access to and use of core technologies such as wired telephone and broadcast and cable television. Especially notable is Canadians' relatively heavy use of the telephone to connect with residents of other countries and their comparatively high subscription to cable TV. The latter is significant because coaxial cables, which have a wider bandwidth than copper telephone wires, are a potentially important on-ramp for households to a range of information highway services.

In the case of newer technologies, Canada's performance is more mixed. The use of cellular phones has not grown as rapidly in Canada as in many other industrial countries. Canada's personal computer use is comparatively high (with this country ranking third out of the 10 selected countries in personal computers per capita), but our Internet penetration rate is well below that of the leading countries. With 67 Internet users per 1,000 inhabitants in 1996, Canada nonetheless ranked ahead of Japan and most major European nations.

In a recent Industry Canada (1998) report, there is an attempt to summarize the results of these country comparisons in two composite indicators. The first composite, a measure of infrastructure availability, was constructed by simply averaging countries' rankings on five network indicators: telephone mainlines per capita, proportion of cable TV subscribers, cellular mobile telephones per capita, extent of digitalization, and Internet hosts per capita. Canada ranks fourth out of the 10 selected countries on this measure. The second composite, an indicator of ICT use, is based on four measures of ICT activity: TV receivers per capita, personal computers per capita, Internet users per capita, and outgoing telephone traffic per inhabitant. Canada ranks fourth on this composite indicator as well. On both measures, Canada's performance is behind that of the US and the two leading countries (Finland and Sweden, and Finland and Australia, respectively) but ahead of the other major industrial countries selected for comparison.

Conclusion

Canada has been very much involved in those globalization processes that stem from or have been shaped by the development of ICTs. Canada has been a significant participant in the growing internationalization of business, the increasing global trade in ICT products, and the expanding business and household use of ICTs. There are countries that have been more strongly affected than Canada by each of these trends. The forces unleashed by the information technology revolution, however, have led to a significant strengthening of Canada's investment, trade, and information links with the rest of the world. Perhaps most significantly, Canadians' access to and use of ICTs has increased substantially in recent years. Based on its level of connectedness, Canada is well positioned relative to other industrial nations to take advantage of global information flows.

Canada's Experience with ICT-Related Globalization

In this section we draw on available evidence to shed light on Canada's experience with ICT-related globalization. The discussion focuses on the three developments identified above, but with a recognition that these represent different aspects of globalization. In examining the emergence of an internationally competitive ICT sector, we are focusing on globalization in one segment of the Canadian economy, albeit one that is of particular importance to Canada's development as an information society. In examining the growth in Canada's inward and outward FDI and Canada's progress in the use of ICTs, we are looking at trends affecting the economy as a whole.

Our discussion also recognizes differences in the nature of our understanding of these latter developments. Canada's experience with inward and outward FDI has been reasonably well documented, analysed, and assessed. Much less is known about household and business experience in using advanced ICTs to become a part of global information networks. The effects of improved information flows on the economy are likely to become evident only long after new technologies have been widely adopted. In the meantime, however, we can ask whether developments are unfolding as one would hope. Are ICTs being widely and effectively adopted? Are concerns about the negative impact of new technology on employment justified?

Impacts of Growing Foreign Investment

Notwithstanding its declining share of global investment stocks, Canada remains much more dependent on foreign investment than most other industrial countries. In 1996, for example, the ratio of Canada's inward FDI stock to GDP was about 21 percent – close to three times the average ratio for all G-7 countries. The implications of Canada's heavy investment orientation have been the subject of a significant body of literature, including a number of recent research volumes published by Industry Canada.

Studies of inward FDI indicate that, consistent with theory and with the evidence for other countries, this investment has played an important role in helping Canada gain access to new technologies and skills. The technologies and skills that MNEs transfer directly to their Canadian subsidiaries have provided important spillover benefits for other Canadian firms, including those in other industries.

Studies have shown that foreign affiliates tend to have higher productivity than their domestic-owned counterparts and can thus serve as a model as well as a competitive stimulus for Canadian firms.[11] Over the past decade, there has been a substantial gap in both the labour productivity and

Figure 6

Labour productivity of Canadian-controlled firms relative to foreign-controlled firms by sectors, 1993-95

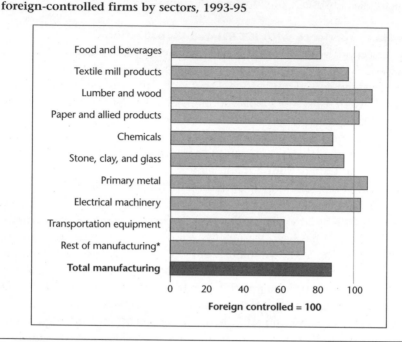

Source: Tang and Rao (1998).
* Includes tobacco; furniture and fixtures; printing and publishing; leather industries; and other manufacturing.

total factor productivity of foreign and Canadian-controlled firms (Figure 6). Studies (e.g., DeBresson et al. 1991) have demonstrated how the entry of foreign firms in particular sectors has stimulated improved performance by Canadian suppliers. They have pointed to the favourable consequences of takeovers that lead ultimately to the integration of Canadian activities into the global operations of foreign-based MNEs (e.g., McDougall 1995). And they have documented the role of FDI as a vehicle for the import of modern technologies that MNEs are reluctant to transfer through licensing and other arrangements with non-affiliated entities (e.g., McFetridge 1987).

One recent study (Gera et al., forthcoming) provides evidence that inward FDI contributed to productivity growth across Canadian industries over the 1973-92 period. Another study (Bernstein 1994) finds that R&D spillovers from the US have exerted a greater influence on Canadian industries than domestic spillovers and were a major contributor to total factor productivity growth rates. Inward FDI is one important route by which Canada has captured the benefits of such R&D spillovers.

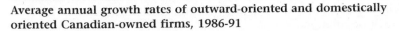

Figure 7

Average annual growth rates of outward-oriented and domestically oriented Canadian-owned firms, 1986-91

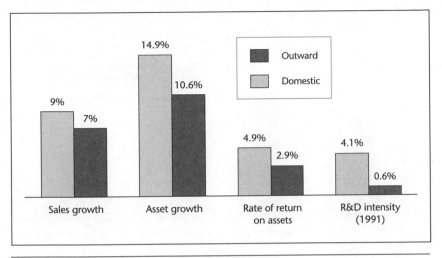

Source: Rao et al. (1994).

Outward FDI has also been found to provide Canada with important benefits. Through such investment, Canadian firms have been able to take advantage of the opportunities for efficient rationalization of their activities on a global basis. For some firms, outward FDI has become a means of gaining market access and achieving the market growth needed to support product development and more efficient scale operations.

Studies (Rao et al. 1994) have found that the growth, productivity, and profit performance of outward-oriented Canadian firms has on average been superior to the performance of domestically oriented firms (Figure 7). These results also apply to small and medium-sized enterprises: evidence indicates that the performance of outward-oriented Canadian SMEs exceeds that of their domestically oriented counterparts across a range of performance measures (Figure 8). It has been shown (Rao et al. 1994) that income receipts from Canada's growing outward stock of FDI in the 1980s made a contribution to income growth and to Canada's current account balance.

Suggestive evidence (Rao et al. 1994) has also been gathered pointing to the trade-enhancing effect of outward direct investment. Canada's experience suggests, contrary to the traditional view, that outward FDI and exports are complements rather than substitutes. This is important because evidence indicates that increased trade orientation is in itself a route to improved performance. Export industries tend to have significantly higher labour productivity and to generate better returns to labour than the overall business sector.

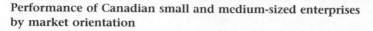

Figure 8

Performance of Canadian small and medium-sized enterprises by market orientation

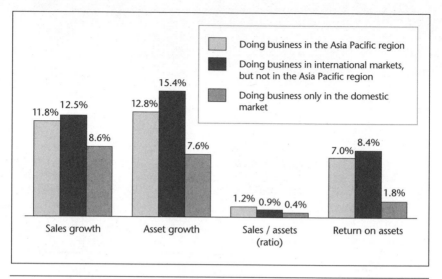

Source: Rao and Ahmad.

In general, the evidence suggests that, by facilitating the growth in Canada's inward and outward FDI, ICTs have contributed to a process that has provided significant economic benefits to Canada. For many countries, FDI is one of the major economic links to the outside world. Such investment plays a particularly important role for countries like Canada that require strong global connections to overcome the constraints of a small domestic market and a limited domestic capacity to develop new technology.

The Emergence of an Internationally Competitive ICT Sector
The ICT sector provides an interesting case study of a segment of the economy that, in recent years, has become much more fully integrated in the world trading and investment system. The ICT sector merits attention, however, not simply because it is an instructive case study of globalization but because ICT industries provide the infrastructure that is important to Canada's development as an information society. Below, we highlight three outcomes that we believe are among the more important consequences of the development of an internationally competitive ICT sector.

First, the ICT sector has become an important source of new jobs. Over the 1990-96 period, employment in the ICT sector grew at almost a 16 percent annual rate, about four times the pace of employment growth in the overall economy (Figure 9). This occurred despite the significant pressure

Figure 9

Average annual growth of employment in the ICT sector compared with the total economy, 1990-96

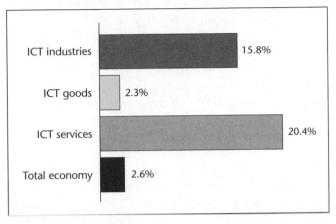

Source: Industry Canada; Statistics Canada.

on firms in major ICT industries to streamline their operations and improve operating efficiencies. In the telecommunications equipment industry, for example, employment increased at a 5 percent annual rate over the 1990-96 period although Northern Telecom consolidated its Canadian operation from 20 to four manufacturing facilities during this period. Labour productivity in the overall ICT sector grew by 5.2 percent per year over the first half of the 1990s, with productivity in the ICT goods subcomponent rising at a rate of more than 12 percent per year. With rapid output growth, including especially strong growth in the relatively labour intensive software and computer services industry group, the sector was able to implement major productivity improvements and still become an important source of new, relatively high-paying job opportunities.[12]

Second, the ICT sector has become an increasingly important source of industrial R&D. As noted above, the ICT sector was responsible for 37 percent of all of Canada's private sector R&D in 1996. About half of this $3 billion (1996) in R&D is accounted for by the telecommunications equipment industry. The sector's R&D contribution has continued to rise in recent years, due to the strong increases in R&D investment by telecommunications equipment firms as well as other ICT producers, most notably members of the research-intensive software development industry.

In both telecommunications equipment and software development, these trends have largely been driven by external developments. The prospective high returns from selling in global markets have encouraged heavy expenditures on new product development. At the same time, with intensified international competition, telecommunications equipment and software firms that are not innovative face an increased risk of market failure. In the case of Northern Telecom, outward FDI helped the firm penetrate new markets, thereby supporting the role of exports in creating conditions favourable to the growth of its Canadian research facility.[13]

A recent study (Bernstein 1996) finds that spillovers from R&D in telecommunications equipment contribute significantly to productivity gains in Canadian manufacturing as a whole. The social rate of return on R&D investment by Canadian telecommunications equipment firms from 1966 to 1991 has been estimated at 55 percent, more than three times the private rate of return (17 percent).

Third, the sector has progressed in building an advanced information infrastructure that makes high-quality information and communications services available to consumers at attractive prices. Digital switches, which permit high-speed computer communications, comprised 95 percent of all telephone switches in 1996, up from 60 percent in 1990. With their advanced switching systems and high-capacity intercity fibre-optic links, the telephone companies are reasonably well positioned to meet the demands arising from rapidly growing Internet traffic. Meanwhile, new technological alternatives are becoming available. These include information systems that make use of the relatively high-capacity coaxial links owned by cable companies; new wireless systems, such as Local Multipoint Communications Systems (LMCS); and systems based on advanced satellite technologies.

In addition, Canadians benefit from telecommunications charges that are among the lowest in industrialized countries. A recent OECD (1997) analysis found that Canada's annual residential charges are the lowest of all G-7 countries, while Canada's annual business charges are below those of all G-7 countries except the UK. Internet access charges in Canada are significantly lower than those in the US and substantially below the charges in all other G-7 countries. While these results are partly due to differences in regulatory policy – a factor that is becoming less important as market-based pricing becomes the norm[14] – they also reflect the impact of the strong competitive pressures that have encouraged Canadian telecommunications service firms to increase productivity and offer more attractive long distance rate packages.

In short, the development of a more outward-looking, internationally competitive ICT sector has produced important benefits for Canada. The infrastructure the ICT sector has put in place has supported efforts to make Canada a highly connected nation, while also facilitating the growth of FDI and the strengthening of commercial and other links between Canada and the rest of the world. At the same time, the ICT sector's development has resulted in significant new job opportunities for skilled Canadian workers and the creation of a strong research base that generates important spillovers for other Canadian industries.

Canada's Progress in the Use of ICTs

Notwithstanding Canada's relatively favourable performance on the basis of available international data on country connectedness, certain questions have been raised about Canada's progress in the adoption and use of ICTs. In this section we address three issues. The first two pertain to perceived deficiencies in the process of ICT adoption and use in Canada. The third relates to the broader concern that Canada's progress in ICT use is being achieved at a significant cost in the form of job losses and reduced employment opportunities.

Evidence supports the view that there is ample room to improve the process of ICT adoption and use in Canada. It is evident, first, that there are significant disparities in the use of advanced technologies. Among households, ICT use increases significantly with household income and education. The penetration rates for computers, modems, cellular phones, and, to a lesser extent, cable TV, are all lower among lower-income households and households headed by an adult with less education. In addition, computer and Internet use tends to be lower among older households (in which the household head is 55 years or more) and among households without children.

Among businesses, it has already been noted that there are significant differences in ICT use between small and large firms and between firms in different sectors. These gaps can be partly explained by the differences among various types of firms in terms of their capacity to productively employ advanced information and communication technologies. However, gaps between Canadian and American firms in the same size categories and industry groups suggest that, in addition, some Canadian firms have been relatively slow to seize upon opportunities presented by ICTs.

While comparative data are available only for the use of advanced manufacturing technologies (AMTs), the results are nonetheless instructive. They show that as of 1993 small and medium-sized Canadian establishments still lagged well behind their US counterparts in the use of AMTs. The most marked gap was seen in the medium-sized category (100 to 499 employees), where Canadian firms trailed significantly both in the application of at least one technology and in the use of multiple technologies (Figure 10). By contrast, Canadian firms in the largest establishment-size category surpassed their US counterparts in the adoption of five or more AMTs.

Large establishments, which have been by far the most responsive to advanced technologies, account for the major share of Canadian manufacturing shipments. Still, it is significant that in all industry categories firms in

Figure 10

Use of advanced manufacturing technologies in Canada and the US, 1993

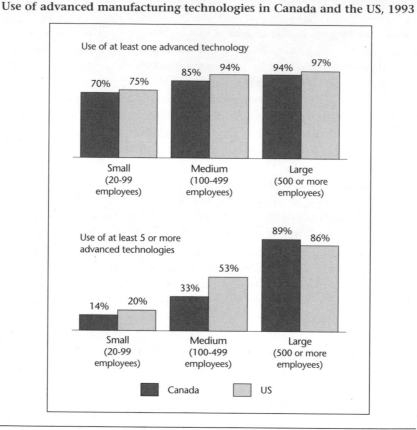

Use of at least one advanced technology

	Small (20-99 employees)	Medium (100-499 employees)	Large (500 or more employees)
Canada	70%	85%	94%
US	75%	94%	97%

Use of at least 5 or more advanced technologies

	Small (20-99 employees)	Medium (100-499 employees)	Large (500 or more employees)
Canada	14%	33%	89%
US	20%	53%	86%

Canada   US

Source: Statistics Canada.

Canada lag behind those in the US in the use of AMTs. It is also of concern that the major gaps are in the use of those technologies requiring the largest investment but offering potentially the greatest payoff, i.e., numerically controlled flexible manufacturing systems.

Recent studies identify a second problem relating to the adoption of ICTs, namely, the failure of many Canadian firms to introduce the organizational and human resource innovations needed to realize the full potential of advanced technologies. This issue touches on topics that are addressed in other chapters of this book. For the purpose of our interest in Canada's overall experience with the adoption and use of ICTs, it is important simply to take account of recent evidence indicating that Canadian firms have not given adequate attention to the workplace innovations needed to accompany the adoption of ICTs.

Studies (e.g., Newton 1997; Betcherman and McMullen 1998) have shown that more successful organizations are experimenting with modes of organization that encourage teamwork, network building, and continuous learning. In progressive organizations, human resource strategies reinforce the shift away from structured, hierarchical systems towards practices that support creativity and enhance flexibility. Assorted evidence suggests, however, that Canadian firms are not investing adequately in the development of new management systems and incentive arrangements. One recent survey (Betcherman et al. 1994), for example, found that most Canadian establishments were still quite "traditional" in their human resource practices; 70 percent of the respondents fell into this category because they were using very few innovative human resource practices. This result is similar to findings in other studies (e.g., Conference Board of Canada 1997) that Canadian firms' investment in so-called "soft technologies" is not keeping pace with their investment in "hard technologies." While, as noted above, there is evidence of productivity gains from the use of advanced technologies, one might expect these gains to have been more substantial if Canadian firms had attended to the workplace changes needed for the efficient absorption of these technologies.

The third concern, that the use of advanced technologies is leading to employment losses, changes the focus from the environment within individual firms to the overall environment affecting the use of ICTs. The view that recent technological advances could lead to massive "technological unemployment" poses a challenge to those who argue that it is in Canada's best interest to create conditions that promote the rapid adoption and effective use of advanced technologies (Rifkin 1995).

Concern about the employment effects of technological change is not new. In the early 1800s, for example, it was feared that the mechanization of England's textile industry would reduce employment. Similarly, the invention of the computer in the 1940s was seen as a serious threat to jobs in the United States. In both cases, these fears were unfounded; the subsequent periods were marked by higher wages and increased employment. Canada's own record suggests that, over the long term, the relationship between employment growth and technological progress has been complementary; as indicated in Figure 11, over time labour productivity and employment have risen in tandem.

While process innovations have often reduced the demand for labour per unit of output, the associated productivity gains have led to increases in income that have, in turn, given rise to increased spending and the demand for more workers. In addition, much technological change has taken the form of product innovations and resulted in the need for workers to satisfy newly created market demands. Historically, the positive direct and

Figure 11

Labour productivity and employment levels in Canada, 1926-95

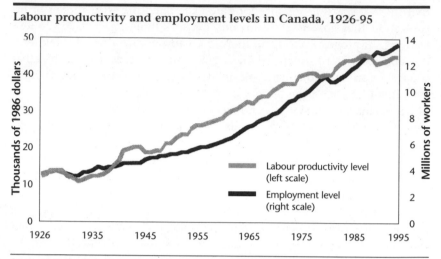

Source: Statistics Canada.

indirect impacts of technological change on employment have more than offset the negative direct effects of process innovations.

In the current environment of intense international competition, technological change is necessary if domestic firms are to establish and protect market share. The prospects for employment growth are much better in economies where advanced technologies have been effectively utilized to improve productivity and increase market responsiveness. Economies will also benefit to the extent that they can participate in the production of goods and services based on new technologies and subject to rapidly growing global demand. Employment growth will be greater in those economies in which structural changes result in the shift of resources towards technologically advanced and more dynamic economic sectors.

Evidence supports the expectation that technological change within an economy will have a positive overall impact on employment, and that firms that innovate are likely be an important source of new job opportunities. In the US, a panel study (Brynjolfsson and Hitt 1996) of Fortune 1000 firms found that employment at the firm level is positively and significantly related to computer capital and R&D spending. Similarly, in Canada there is a significant link between technology intensity and employment growth. As can be seen in Figure 12, high ICT-intensive industries have accounted for most of the net growth in employment over the past decade. There has been an accompanying shift towards high-wage jobs; the vast majority of jobs created from 1985 to 1997 consisted of high ICT-intensive, high-wage positions.

Figure 12

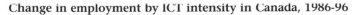

Change in employment by ICT intensity in Canada, 1986-96

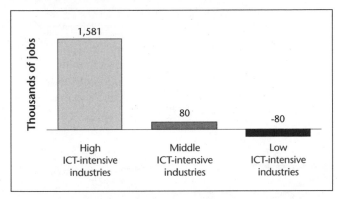

Source: Industry Canada compilations based on Statistics Canada and Conference Board of Canada data.

Another interesting piece of evidence comes from OECD data indicating that Canada had one of the strongest rates of employment growth over the 1980s although its ICT intensity was also among the highest within the OECD. More strikingly, the US, which had by far the largest average annual rate of employment growth, had a ratio of ICT investment to total investment far in excess of that for other OECD nations.

The use of ICTs has been a factor in broad structural changes that have resulted in job losses in low-technology, labour-intensive manufacturing industries and in low-skill, low-wage occupations. A recent study finds that since 1981 both knowledge workers and data workers have come to account for a significantly higher share of Canada's industrial employment at the expense of non-information workers.[15] A related disparity exists between those with postsecondary education, who have enjoyed significant growth in employment over the 1990s, and those with less than a high school education, who have experienced a reduction in job opportunities (Figure 13).

The impact of the significant economic adjustments necessitated by technological change and increasing global competition is reflected in other indicators. Since the mid-1980s, for example, there has been a strong rise in the incidence of consumer bankruptcy, along with an increase in business bankruptcies. But while ICTs have contributed to structural shifts that have disadvantaged particular sectors and specific groups of workers, they have not resulted in the large-scale job losses some predicted, and they are not responsible for Canada's current relatively high level of unemployment.

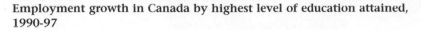

Figure 13

Employment growth in Canada by highest level of education attained, 1990-97

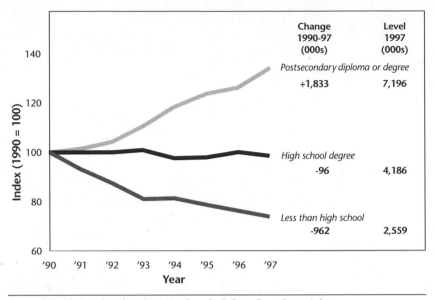

Source: Compilations based on Statistics Canada (Labour Force Survey) data.

Summary

Canada's experience with ICT-related globalization has largely been positive. While the full implications of the three identified globalization processes have not been examined, the evidence suggests that Canada has benefited significantly from the increased opportunities for international trade, investment, and communications made possible by ICTs.

Through its participation in growing global FDI, Canada has gained access to foreign technology and foreign know-how and overcome some of the constraints imposed by its small market and limited technological capacity. Canada's participation in the expanding world trade in ICT products has contributed to the development of a strong sectoral base of R&D that generates significant spillover benefits for other Canadian industries. It has also been important in helping Canadians gain access to high-quality, well-priced telecommunications services. While questions have been raised about the third major development, the participation of Canadians in the growing global use of ICTs, there is no evidence to support the major concern voiced about this development. Advanced technologies could be more broadly and effectively applied by Canadian businesses, but they are contributing to improved performance without having the undesirable employment consequences that some feared.

Conclusions

The development of increasingly sophisticated information and communication technologies has been a central force driving the transformation towards a knowledge-based global economy. Canada has been very much involved in those globalization processes associated with the development of ICTs: (1) Over the past decade Canada's inward and outward investments have increased significantly in importance. Notwithstanding its declining share of world inward and outward FDI stocks, Canada has been a significant beneficiary of the increasing internationalization of business activities. (2) Canada's trade in ICT products has grown and the output of the country's ICT sector has increased strongly. (3) In recent years, the use of ICTs, especially newer technologies, by Canadian households and businesses has grown considerably. While there is scope to improve the process of ICT adoption and use in this country, Canada's development as an information society compares favourably with that of other major industrial countries.

There is no indication that globalization forces are abating. Although recent efforts among OECD countries to conclude a Multilateral Agreement on Investment (MAI) were unsuccessful, bilateral investment treaties have proliferated. From 1990 to 1996, 1,330 bilateral treaties were negotiated worldwide, almost four times the number concluded during all of the 1980s,[16] as both industrialized and developing countries attempted to better position themselves to benefit from the growing internationalization of business activities. At the same time that business activities are becoming increasingly footloose, skilled workers are becoming more mobile. Over the 1990s, for example, there has been a sharp increase in skilled workers who have migrated from Canada to the US on temporary permits. Meanwhile, the rapid expansion in the global use of ICTs is continuing to erode the physical barriers separating individuals, producers, and consumers in different parts of the world.

Available evidence suggests that these developments are providing important benefits for Canadians. As a small country, Canada has much to gain from strengthened commercial and information links to the rest of the world. Globalization is, at the same time, however, fundamentally changing the rules of the game for firms and for governments.

A highly competitive, adaptable, and flexible economy is a prerequisite for success in an era of increasing globalization and rapid technological change. Canadian firms face pressures to identify areas where they can excel and to build their capacity to compete internationally. Managers are being pushed to find new ways to improve productivity and cut costs, to come up with innovations that will provide them with a competitive edge, and to pursue opportunities for strengthening competitiveness through foreign alliances and foreign investments. A key part of strengthening competitiveness is improving human resources. There is a need for increased investments in skill development, training, and retraining, and for mechanisms that will enhance labour market flexibility and adaptability.

As part of their response to the challenges of globalization, Canadian governments must continue to push for more open and secure access to international markets for Canadian exports and investment. They must similarly work to aggressively promote Canada as an investment location. Canadian governments are also having to adapt to the fact that, in an environment of highly mobile capital and footloose corporations, policymaking is itself, to some extent, a competitive activity; policies cannot be made in isolation from developments in other countries and without considering their influence on Canada's relative appeal as a base of business activity.

There is a growing appreciation that ICTs, which have contributed to the unleashing of the underlying global forces, are at the same time an important part of the response to globalization. As Canada progresses in its development as an information society, Canadian corporations and governments will be able to respond more effectively to the challenges of an increasingly integrated world economy.

Notes

1 The authors are grateful for the comments and assistance provided by Ashfaq Ahmad and Aaron Sydor, Industry Canada.
2 International telephone calls generated $53 billion in revenue in 1995, but because of the peculiarities of telecommunications settlement arrangements, this translated into only $28 billion in international payments.
3 The Organization for Economic Cooperation and Development (OECD) defines the ICT sector to include manufacturing and service activities associated with the capture, transmission, and display, by electronic means, of data and other information.
4 Zvi Griliches points out, for example, that in the US, although investment in information equipment grew from 17 percent to 36 percent of producer durable equipment investment between 1960 and 1992, much of this went into "unmeasurable" or poorly measured service sector activities.
5 ICTs, along with the content transmitted through advanced technologies, also expand our choices and enrich our lives in ways that are not captured by the National Accounts data used to measure changes in living standards.
6 Over the period 1990-1996, net outward FDI flows from Canada averaged $9 billion per year, exceeding FDI inflows, which averaged $8.4 billion per year.
7 The reference here is to telecommunications equipment producers (SIC 3341), rather than the telecommunications and other communications and electronic equipment industry group (SIC 3351 and SIC 3359) depicted in Figure 10.
8 A landmark development in this regard was the 1992 decision of the Canadian Radio-Television and Telecommunications Commission (CRTC) to allow competition in long distance telephone service. More recently, the market for local telephone service has been opened to competition and a policy framework has been established to foster competition and facilitate convergence between cable television and telephone companies. As well, Canada has made further commitments for market liberalization under the WTO Agreement on Basic Telecommunications Services.
9 Besides Bell Canada, the Stentor Alliance consists of: BC TEL, TCI & TCE, SaskTel, MTS, Maritime Tel & Tel, NBTel, NewTel, and Island Tel. The three associate members of the Stentor Alliance are Québec-Téléphone, NorthwesTel, and Telesat.

10 This term was developed following the last Throne Speech, in which the government indicated its intention to make Canada "the most connected nation in the world." In June
1998, the federal government organized a workshop on "Connectedness Metrics."
11 It has been found that these differences cannot be attributed to the concentration of foreign affiliates in sectors with higher productivity (Globerman et al. 1994; Tang and Rao
1998).
12 In 1995 average weekly earnings in the ICT sector were highest among telephone carriers,
where they were almost 50 percent above the all-industry average.
13 The role of outward FDI is discussed in Amesse et al. (1994).
14 With a view to achieving more economically efficient pricing, Canadian telephone companies are being permitted to increase the price of local service and reduce the long-
standing subsidies that have kept local telephone service prices well below cost. At the
same time, the CRTC is ending its regulation of the toll rates offered by major telephone
companies.
15 In a study by Gera et al. (1998b), non-information workers are distinguished from two
categories of knowledge-based workers: those in "knowledge occupations," such as pure or
applied scientific research, engineering, or professional activities in the social sciences or
humanities, which involve the manipulation of concepts and generation of ideas or expert
opinions; and those, including clerical workers, in "data occupations," which involve the
use, transmission, or manipulation of knowledge.
16 Industry Canada tabulations based on data from the United Nations *World Investment Report* (1997).

References
AC Nielsen. 1997. Canadian Internet Survey.
Amesse, F., L. Séguin-Dulude, and G. Stanley. 1994. "Northern Telecom: A Case Study in
the Management of Technology." In S. Globerman, ed., *Canadian-based Multinationals*,
421-55. Industry Canada Research Series. Calgary: University of Calgary Press.
Baldwin, J., and D. Sabourin. 1995. *Technology Adoption in Canadian Manufacturing*. Ottawa:
Statistics Canada.
Bernstein, J. 1994. *International R and D Spillovers Between Industries in Canada and the United
States*. Industry Canada Working Paper No. 3.
–. 1996. *R and D Productivity Growth in Canadian Communications Equipment and Manufactur-
ing*. Industry Canada Working Paper No. 10.
Betcherman, G., and K. McMullen. 1998. *Impact of Information and Communication Tech-
nologies on Work and Employment in Canada*. CPRN Discussion Paper No. W/01.
Betcherman, G., et al. 1994. *The Canadian Workplace in Transition*. Kingston: Queen's Uni-
versity Press.
Brynjolfsson, E., and L. Hitt. 1995. "Information Technology as a Factor of Production: The
Role of Differences Among Firms." *Economics of Innovation and New Technology* 3.
–. 1996. "Computers and Productivity Growth: Firm-Level Evidence." Mimeo. Cambridge,
MA: Sloan School of Management, Massachusetts Institute of Technology.
Conference Board of Canada. 1997. *Micro Level Investigation of the Process of Innovation*.
Ottawa: Conference Board of Canada.
DeBresson, C., J. Niosi, R. Dalpé, and D. Winer. 1991. "Technological Linkages and Foreign
Ownership in the Canadian Aircraft Industry." In D. McFetridge, ed., *Foreign Investment,
Technology and Economic Growth*, 317-60. Investment Canada Research Series. Calgary:
University of Calgary Press.
Gera, S., W. Gu, and F.C. Lee. 1998a. *Information Technology and Labour Productivity Growth:
An Empirical Analysis for Canada and the United States*. Industry Canada Working Paper
No. 20.
–. 1998b. "Technology and Demand for Skills: An Industry-Level Analysis." Paper presented
at the European Union–Industry Canada conference Transition to the Knowledge
Economy, November 1998, Vancouver, Canada.
–. Forthcoming. *Foreign Direct Investment and Productivity Growth: The Canadian Host-Country
Experience*. Industry Canada Working Paper.

Globerman, S., J.C. Ries, and I. Vertinsky. 1994. "The Economic Performance of Foreign Affiliates in Canada." *Canadian Journal of Economics* 27,1: 143-56.

Griliches, Zvi. 1994. "Productivity, R&D, and the Data Constraint." *American Economic Review* 84: 1-23.

Industry Canada. 1996. "Survey of Technology Diffusion in Service Industries." Ottawa: Industry Canada.

–. 1998. "A Report Card on the State of Canada's Connectedness." Mimeo.

Lucas, R.E. 1988. "On the Mechanisms of Economic Development." *Journal of Monetary Economics* 22,1: 3-42.

Maddison, A. 1994. "Explaining the Economic Performance of Nations 1820-1989." In W.J. Baumol, R.J. Nelson, and E.N. Wolff, eds., *Convergence of Productivity: Cross-National Studies and Historical Evidence*, 20-61. New York: Oxford University Press.

McDougall, G. 1995. *The Economic Impact of Mergers and Acquisitions on Corporations*. Industry Canada Working Paper No. 4.

McFetridge, D.G. 1987. "The Timing, Mode and Terms of Technology Transfer: Some Recent Findings." In A.E. Safarian and G.Y. Bertin, eds., *Multinationals, Governments and International Technology Transfer*. London: Croon Helm.

Mowery, D., and N. Rosenberg. 1989. *Technology and the Pursuit of Economic Growth*. New York: Cambridge University Press.

Newton, K. 1997. *Management Strategies in the Knowledge-Based Economy*. Industry Canada Occasional Paper No. 14.

OECD (Organization for Economic Cooperation and Development). 1997a. *Communications Outlook*. Paris: OECD.

–. 1997b. *Information Technology Outlook, 1997*. Paris: OECD.

Rao, S., and A. Ahmad. 1996. "Canadian Small and Medium-Sized Enterprises: Opportunities and Challenges in the Asia Pacific." In Richard D. Harris, ed., *The Asia Pacific Region in the Global Economy: A Canadian Perspective*, 395-451. Calgary: University of Calgary Press.

Rao, S., M. Legault, and A. Ahmad. 1994. "Canadian-Based Multinationals: An Analysis of Activities and Performance." In S. Globerman, ed., *Canadian-Based Multinationals*, 63-125. Industry Canada Research Series. Calgary: University of Calgary Press.

Rifkin, Jeremy. 1995. *The End of Work: The Decline of the Global Labour Force and the Dawn of a Post-Market Economy*. New York: Putnam.

Romer, P.M. 1990. "Endogenous Technical Change." *Journal of Political Economy* 98,5 (Part 2): S71-S102.

Tang, J., and S. Rao. 1998. "Productivity Gap Between Canadian-Controlled and Foreign-Controlled Corporations in Canadian Manufacturing." Mimeo. Micro-economic Policy Analysis Branch. Ottawa: Industry Canada.

UNCTAD (United Nations Conference on Trade and Development). 1997. *Trade and Development Report, 1997*.

United Nations. 1997. *World Investment Report*.

6
European Regional Development Policy and Innovation

Nicola De Michelis[1]

1

In spring 1999, the European Council of Ministers agreed on the financial perspective for the European Union (EU) for the 2000-2006 period. About 213 billion euro (i.e., about 32 percent of the Union's budget) were earmarked over the period for structural operations aimed at reducing the socio-economic differences among the regions of the EU.

Significant changes in the macroeconomic environment are imposing new constraints on, and presenting new challenges to, those responsible for the effective use of these financial resources. Accordingly, European regional policy needs – in advance of the new programming period 2000-2006 – to reconsider its strategic priorities and delivery mechanisms in the light of these changes.

First, the combination of an accelerated rate of technological innovation with changes in international trade and markets is confronting firms, institutions, and territories with enormous pressures to adjust and adapt. On the one hand, failure to exploit the technological opportunities inherent in new and fast-growing technologies, especially information and communication technologies (ICTs), contributes to a slowdown in structural adjustment in European regions, thereby worsening their competitive position in European and world markets. This is further aggravated by the fact that, once a region is left behind, catching up is increasingly difficult and costly. On the other hand, market globalization and diffusion of ICTs are reducing the importance of spatial barriers, thereby increasing the sensitivity of capital to variations of place within space. Small differences between territories in terms of labour supply, resources, infrastructure, institutional capacities, and the like assume increased importance in determining development opportunities. Regions, especially the less favoured ones, need to rapidly modernize and diversify their economic structure in order to retain and increase wealth and employment.

Second, technological catch-up and structural adjustment are intimately related to trade performance. Successful catch-up is associated with both a general improvement in trade performance and a radical modification in the composition of trade. It is clear, for example, that Europe's catch-up in scale and capital-intensive technologies from the 1950s on was associated with a rapidly increasing export market share for products embodying these technologies. The drive towards economies of scale through enlargement and homogenization of markets is a main element of the European economic integration process. The Single Market Program was partly based on the idea that large unexploited economies of scale existed in European industry, the exploitation of which had been prevented by the existence of "non-tariff barriers" to trade, commonly associated, in one way or another, with discriminatory action by governments.

Since the 1980s, however, the locus of growth within manufacturing has changed to knowledge-based industries. Europe has experienced a steady

Table 1

Market share (ratio of national exports to world exports in %), 1970-95

	Agricultural products and raw materials	Traditional industries	Scale-intensive	Specialized suppliers	Science-based	Total
EU						
1970	24.1	57.0	55.7	61.2	48.6	44.6
1988	30.3	47.6	51.2	56.0	41.3	44.0
1995	31.6	40.1	47.3	47.6	33.8	39.6
Change	*7.5*	*−16.9*	*−8.4*	*−13.6*	*−14.8*	*−5.0*
US						
1970	13.1	7.4	14.5	22.3	29.5	14.8
1988	13.4	5.2	9.4	12.2	19.8	11.6
1995	11.0	6.7	10.3	13.7	17.9	11.8
Change	*−2.1*	*−0.7*	*−4.2*	*−8.6*	*−11.6*	*−3.0*
Japan						
1970	1.2	9.3	13.8	6.4	7.7	6.7
1988	1.1	4.1	17.1	15.6	16.7	10.1
1995	1.4	3.2	12.8	15.7	14.3	9.0
Change	*0.2*	*−6.1*	*−1.0*	*9.3*	*6.6*	*2.3*
Asian NICs[1]						
1970	2.0	6.1	1.0	0.8	1.0	2.1
1988	2.6	14.5	5.6	4.0	9.1	6.7
1995	3.4	16.2	8.7	8.8	17.8	10.8
Change	*1.4*	*10.1*	*7.7*	*8.0*	*16.8*	*8.7*

Source: Fagerberg (1999).
1 NICs = newly industrialized countries

erosion of its specialization (i.e., above-average market share) in these industries, while gaining market shares in agricultural products and raw materials (see Table 1). What matters for growth and competitiveness is not so much the increasing degree of specialization in general as the ability to exploit areas of high technological opportunity, which have been dominated in recent years by ICTs. It seems relevant therefore, to ask whether Europe's deteriorating position in technologically advanced, fast-growing parts of the manufacturing sector may pose a problem for its future growth and welfare.

Third, there is a distinct geographical pattern in the localization of industries across the EU. Preliminary results from a study financed by the European Commission suggests that high-technology, high/increasing returns-to-scale industries are increasingly concentrated in central and high-wage locations in the EU. Lower-technology and lower returns-to-scale industries are more dispersed, but a process of clustering of these industries in peripheral lower-wage economies is under way. It is worth asking whether this dual development pattern is (1) sustainable, given that "... competitive advantage based on factor costs ... is rapidly undone ... [and] a low-wage country today is quickly replaced by another tomorrow" (Porter 1990), and (2) is politically and socially acceptable as the European project – particularly its social dimension – is increasingly questioned.

Finally, fast economic integration both at the international level (via multilateral trade agreements) and at the European level (through the Single Market and the Economic Monetary Union programs) is reducing the ability of member states to use traditional macroeconomic instruments (such as interest and exchange rates) to help the economy adjust to external shocks.

All these changes reflect a more intense transformation pressure calling for a stronger capability to innovate. This chapter argues that (1) supply-side policies of an industrial and regional nature are today the only policies remaining in the hands of governments for economic regulation and, accordingly, (2) the European regional policy should increasingly focus on innovation promotion as the most effective way to help territories face the challenges of globalization and technological change, through the modernization and diversification of their economic structure.

2

The European Commission defines innovation as "the renewal and enlargement of the range of products and services and the associated markets; the establishment of new methods of production, supply and distribution; the introduction of changes in management, work organization, and the working conditions and skill of the workforce" (CEC 1995).

The term is somewhat ambiguous in that it denotes both a process and its result. In the latter sense (result of innovation), the emphasis is on the new product, process, or service. In the former (innovation process), the emphasis is on the manner in which the innovation is designed and produced at the different stages leading up to it (creativity, marketing, research and development, design, production, and distribution). This is not a linear process, with clearly delimited sequences and automatic follow-on, but rather a system of interactions: comings and goings between different functions and different players whose experience, knowledge, and know-how are mutually reinforcing and cumulative.

At the regional level, the process of innovation can be defined as a systemic phenomenon based on the accumulation of learning processes through networks of cooperation (mainly public/private and between firms) that encourage interaction between those engaged locally in the economic and technological life of the region. From the standpoint of development economics, it is the process of continuous adaptation to technical change within a particular regional economy.

In the EU today, the capacity to innovate varies significantly from one region to another. This gap has different dimensions of a quantitative and a qualitative nature. Some can be quantified through standard research and technology development input indicators (see Table 2),[2] but others are of a more qualitative nature. They relate to specific structural factors in the less favoured regions in terms of productive structure, institutional framework, and demand features for innovation.

Statistical analysis confirms that there is a "technology gap" (interregional disparities in RTD input indicators) twice as great as the so-called cohesion gap (interregional disparities in income per capita, productivity, and unemployment rates) between the developed and less developed regions of the European Union.

In terms of GERD as a percentage of gross domestic product (GDP), the "cohesion" countries in Europe are below half the European Union average (less than 1 percent compared with an EU average of 2 percent). In 1995, government financing for RTD as a percentage of total budget was below 1 percent in Greece and just above 1 percent in Ireland, compared with an EU average of 2.9 percent. Moreover, BERD as a percentage of GDP in Greece and Portugal was one-tenth the EU average (0.1 percent compared with 1.30 percent).

The technology gap is a particular cause for concern with regard to the human resources for RTD, since human capital is increasingly a source of the dynamic comparative advantages that govern regional potential for innovation in an increasingly knowledge-based economy. At present, the differential between advanced and less developed regions is one to two and growing in terms of research staff as narrowly defined, mainly by reference to research workers in firms.

Table 2

Technology gap: selected indicators (1995)

	EUR11[1]	EU 4[2]	Greece	Spain	Ireland	Portugal
Basic data						
GDP/capita	18,733	10,192	8,362	10,918	13,677	7,983
GERD (Mio Euro)						
per habitants	384	83	40	87	192	47
as % of GDP	2.05	0.82	0.48	0.80	1.41	0.61
R&D personnel						
as % of labour force	1.37	0.73	0.83	0.73	1.14	0.53
RTD in public sector						
GBAORD as %						
of total budget	2.93	1.62	0.67	1.96	1.09	1.61
GOVERD as % of GDP	0.33	0.16	0.13	0.17	0.14	0.16
HERD as % of GDP	0.41	0.24	0.22	0.25	0.27	0.21
R&D personnel in GOV						
and HEI as % of total						
R&D personnel	49.0	73.0	89.0	71.0	54.0	69.0
RTD in private sector						
BERD (Mio Euro)						
as % of GDP	1.30	0.35	0.11	0.37	0.99	0.12
as % of GERDF	64.0	45.0	24.0	46.0	70.0	20.0
R&D personnel						
as % of labour force	0.69	0.20	0.09	0.21	0.53	0.16
as % of total R&D						
personnel	51.0	27.0	11.0	29.0	46.0	31.0
No. of patent applications						
per Mio population	108	11	4	12	37	2

Source: CEC (1998b).
1 Member states of the EU except Greece, Spain, Ireland, and Portugal.
2 The four "cohesion" countries: Greece, Spain, Ireland, and Portugal.

In 1995, for example, the Netherlands had about twice the number of RTD scientists and engineers as Greece and Portugal taken together. Denmark, with a labour force of 2.8 million, had the same number of RTD personnel as Portugal and Greece together, with a combined labour force of nearly 9 million. Germany, with approximately the same number of RTD personnel per thousand labour force as Japan, had more than two times the Spanish and Portuguese rates and about three times the Greek rate.

Coverage ratios of the technology balance of payments (licences, patents, know-how, and technical assistance) vary widely across Europe. In Greece and Portugal, for example, foreign patent applications were nearly 38 times domestic applications, compared with Italy, France, and Germany, where the figure was less than 5 times. In 1995, the rate of domestic patent application – possibly the best proxy for innovation – in the poorest countries was 10 times smaller than in the most developed ones.

Since technology is largely an international phenomenon (technology trends, research breakthroughs, and their associated competitive advantages are not constrained by national borders), the problem for less advanced regions is not only how to generate and develop their own indigenous RTD activities but also, most importantly, to adapt (and adopt) technological developments from elsewhere into a specific regional context. Recent empirical evidence seems to suggest that technology gaps, conventionally measured, between the strongest and weakest member states are narrowing at the national level. No such signs can be observed at the regional level, however, where disparities between advanced and less favoured regions tend to widen or, at best, remain stable.

A second important dimension of the technology gap is represented by the spatial concentration of RTD resources both at the EU and national levels.

A few centres of RTD "excellence" or "islands of innovation" – comprising technology-intensive firms and R&D laboratories that cooperate almost exclusively among themselves – are geographically concentrated in the advanced regions of the Union. "Almost half of the total amount of contracts under the RTD Framework Programmes goes to nine regions which together account for only 28% of population ... Nearly half of the partnerships under the second and third Framework Programmes were with the UK, France and Germany" (CEC 1996).

This concentration leads to the creation of "elite" networks in which the rare partners from less advanced regions are usually accepted only as subcontractors rather than main players. Those engaged in innovation in the less developed regions scarcely participate in these networks of cooperation. Firms and RTD centres from these regions participate in only 5 to 8 percent of international R&D cooperation networks. They encounter severe problems in forming links with external sources and technological partners, whether at the international level or interregionally within their own countries.

Although diffusion of ICTs has accelerated the diffusion of codifiable knowledge, thereby lowering costs and favouring access to it, tacit and imperfectly codified elements of technology still require close human and organizational interactions that are not cost-free and are highly localized.

A self-sustaining process of increased technological demand is thus followed by the development and upgrading of regional RTD capacities, which in turn drives economic development, and so on. In fact, technology, in its broadest sense, could be considered a cumulative learning process by which the knowledge base is progressively deepened and widened, facilitating the acquisition of new knowledge. This process is reinforced by the regional (spatial) concentration due to economic factors such as:

- critical masses and economies of scale (e.g., R&D centres, which serve a number of firms and permit a concentration of top-class researchers)
- externalities (e.g., creation of a scientific community and technical culture between heads of firms, and new relations between and within the R&D community)
- economies of agglomeration (e.g., concentration of technological resources, which act as centres of attraction for the location of intensive investment in certain types of technologies).

If comparison at the European level shows substantial disparities in the RTD input indicators, interregional differences within member states, the poorest in particular, tend to be even greater.

In Greece, for example, over half the country's RTD expenditure takes place around Athens and over two-thirds of business RTD is located in this same region. In Portugal, two-thirds of total RTD expenditures are to be found in the Lisbon region. In Spain over three-quarters of business RTD is located in three of the 17 regions (more than 40 percent concentrated in Madrid).

A third dimension of the technology gap is represented by differences in the quality and quantity of existing schemes for public assistance. In Europe these tend to further increase the gap between the most advanced countries of the Union and the less favoured regions (see Table 3).

In the case of public assistance for innovation, the most developed countries in the Union provided over 10 times more public aid per person employed in manufacturing than the less developed regions during the period 1994-96, particularly through horizontal measures (mainly directed at small firms), thereby offsetting the tendency of firms to underinvest in innovation.

Denmark, Finland, France, and Ireland are over the 150 index (EUR15 = 100), while less advanced countries are under the 60 index (Spain = 37, Greece and Portugal = 8). That is, advanced regions normally have bigger, more sophisticated, and better-adapted public support schemes for the promotion of innovation than less favoured regions. Paradoxically, the RTD and innovation needs of the latter are much greater than those of the former.

The Irish case is particularly interesting in that Ireland had an index of 47 (EUR12 = 100) in 1988 but 307 in 1994-96. A fundamental change in the direction of state aid towards support to innovation and RTD may help explain the exceptional performance of the Irish economy over the past decade.

Table 3

State aid to innovation in the European Union (annual average, 1994-96)

Country	Overall state aid to manufacturing (in MEuro)	Aid to manufacturing per person employed in this sector (in euro)	Total aid to innovation (in MEuro)		Aid to innovation / R&D per person employed (in euro)		Aid to innovation / R&D per person employed in manufacturing (in euro)	Index (EUR 15 = 100)
			'90	'96	'90	'96		
Austria	448	626	–	86	–	25	120	69
Belgium	1,149	1,678	155	115	43	31	168	107
Denmark	671	1,383	117	196	45	78	404	257
Germany	16,639	1,888	962	1,166	35	34	132	84
Greece	662	863	12	10	3	3	13	8
Finland	365	911	–	128	–	66	319	203
France	3,740	927	1,026	1,037	47	47	257	164
Ireland	215	838	14	124	12	98	482	307
Italy	9,760	2,151	440	271	19	12	60	38
Luxembourg	46	1,375	4	3	21	14	100	64
Netherlands	686	788	429	135	89	25	155	99
Portugal	382	371	7	13	2	3	13	8
Spain	2,101	837	216	146	18	11	58	37
Sweden	318	406	–	34	–	8	43	27
UK	1,513	263	245	176	10	7	31	20
EUR15	38,695	1,020	3,627	3,640	23	31	157	100

Source: European Commission.

3

These structural differences in technology and science systems cannot, on their own, explain the structural weakness of the economy in less favoured regions of Europe. Technology cannot be expected to assist in resolving the problems of competitiveness unless it functions as part of a system that is institutionally and organizationally capable of continuously adapting to changing demands.

The contribution of the European Structural Funds to closing the technology gap confirmed that continuous support to the existing scientific and technological systems of less favoured regions risks perpetuating and eventually reinforcing the structural problems besetting the regional innovation system. There is increasing consensus that the failure of firms or regional economies to innovate is primarily due not to scientific or technological problems but to shortcomings in the social and organizational framework within which the scientific and technological factors operate. In less favoured regions in particular, the innovation capacity of small and medium-sized enterprises (SMEs) is directly linked to cooperation with other firms (firms learn better from other firms), the public sector, and RTD and innovation intermediaries and infrastructure (technology centres, universities, laboratories, business services).

In other words, the innovative capacity of the firm is a function of the innovative capacity of the region. In less favoured regions, the organizational and institutional environment in which firms operate is often characterized by a combination of the following structural weaknesses:

- lack of technical knowledge to help firms identify and assess their needs for innovation, and lack of a structured expression of the latent demand for innovation
- lack of a dynamic business-services sector enabling firms to increase their technological profile in areas where they have, as a rule, only weak internal resources for the independent development of technological innovation
- poorly developed financial systems (traditional banking practices), with few funds available for risk or seed capital to finance innovation. Available funds are poorly adapted to the terms and risks of the process of innovation in firms.
- few technological intermediaries capable of identifying and federating local business demand for innovation and RTD, and channelling it towards regional/national/international sources of innovation and RTD that may respond to these demands
- weak cooperation links between the public and private sectors, and lack of an entrepreneurial culture prone to interfirm cooperation; hence, absence of economies of scale and critical mass in business, which may make profitable certain local innovation efforts

- sectoral specialization in traditional industries with little inclination for innovation, and predominance of small family firms with weak links to the international market
- little participation in international networks, poorly developed communications and telecommunications networks, difficulties in attracting skilled labour and integrated know-how
- few large, multinational firms undertaking R&D on the frontiers of technology, and poor links with the local economy
- lower level of public assistance for innovation; aid-intensity and number of schemes poorly adapted to the innovation needs of local SMEs
- lower quality and quantity of scientific infrastructure, and science/technology systems less well integrated into the needs and capacities of the regional productive system.

In summary, the quality of the institutional setting in these regions is often the main obstacle to an efficient regional innovation system. It seems that an increase in the innovative capacity of the regional economy inevitably requires new forms of organization and institutional cooperation if the structural competitiveness of firms in less favoured regions is to be improved.

4

Development processes in the regions depend basically on the combination of two types of microeconomic conditions. First, basic physical infrastructure and a human capital with a minimum training level must exist. In their absence and below a minimum threshold, regional development efforts are condemned to fail.

Second, intangible capital must be improved. This assumes the existence of regional strengths, including capacity to innovate, quality of management, existence of an industrial and entrepreneurial culture, an institutional environment favourable to public-private cooperation, a dynamic services sector and technology transfer to firms, availability of appropriate interfaces between innovation demand and supply, existence of a financial environment conducive to innovation, and new economic activities.

These conditions are closely connected to the relations between firms and their economic environment (relations with other companies, subcontractors, suppliers, and customers) and institutional environment (regional and industrial policies, cooperation with universities, consultants, centres of expertise, and so on). The improvement of this second set of conditions is particularly important, since the competitiveness of firms relies not only on their internal capabilities but also on the quality of the environment in which they operate.

Small and micro-enterprises, in particular, rely heavily on their business environment for the production of innovation. Because of their size, they cannot internalize all phases of production. They are thus dependent on external sources of equipment, product design, training, and services such as marketing and technological information. Although this problem is faced by SMEs in general, the situation is more critical in nonmetropolitan areas, where the local enterprise base is thinner and services are less accessible. In other words, the difficulties these businesses face are related less to their size than to their isolation. Given that SMEs constitute the predominant part of the economy in such areas, their competitive disadvantage can be an important hindrance to regional development.

The precise combination of these two types of conditions is a function of the level of development of each region. The higher the region's level of development, the more important the intangible factors are. Public policies must continuously evolve to remain effective.

Over the past decade, the Structural Funds – in particular the European Regional Development Fund (ERDF) – have concentrated on upgrading the first set of conditions, particularly the basic physical infrastructure. In the field of innovation promotion and technological development, a recent evaluation of the RTD and innovation dimension of the operations of the Structural Funds (Circa Group et al. 1999) outlines the following:

- Capacity enhancement has been overemphasized, to the point that the Structural Funds are "strengthening public RTD capabilities for which there is little use and which are of little relevance to the actual needs of industry in the less favored regions." In so doing, they are creating a future obligation to underwrite the running costs of these public facilities. Moreover, they contribute to widening the RTD supply/demand gap, making technology transfer more difficult.
- The link between technology and production continues to be a major, if not the most important, problem. There is little point in providing additional resources for innovation unless the absorption capacity of firms can be significantly improved. Particular attention needs to be paid to mobilizing and increasing the demand for innovation.
- Policy design needs to be improved. Regional governments in less favoured regions have limited experience in designing and managing innovation-oriented programs. The medium to long-term perspective is lacking; priorities are not always clear and are often dispersed over too many areas.

A number of considerations may help explain the difficulties that the Structural Funds face in this area. First, it seems that most of the programs assume a linear relationship between science and economic development, whereby injection of RTD into the system will automatically translate into economic success in the market. They therefore ignore the limitations of this model and its shortcomings, pointed out by Luigi Orsenigo in his chapter in this volume. For example, the interrelation between different stages of the innovation process and their retroactive nature, and the importance of identification and structured expression of demand by small firms, is often overlooked, as is the existence of bottlenecks and the need for interfaces between the scientific subsystem and the productive context. RTD work does not necessarily generate technological innovation, nor is it the only precursor of such innovation, particularly when the regional productive structure of less favoured regions is the reference point.

The latter is normally based on SMEs. For these enterprises, innovation is often derived from the process of adaptation/adoption of technologies that are already well established in international markets. Small firms in these regions not only are badly equipped to develop substantial RTD efforts by themselves but also find it difficult to adequately "search" and "assess" existing technologies elsewhere that best fit their productive activities.

The basic R&D effort is less relevant as a source of innovation in less developed regions because of the specific features of the productive structure in these regions (lack of intermediaries) and, in particular, the weaker links among the various layers and the lack of complementarity and coherence between the different stages and activities within the system.

Understanding the actual sources of innovation for small firms is critical. Empirical evidence now demonstrates that customers, competing small firms, and suppliers are the main sources of ideas for innovation for small firms, followed only latterly by universities and public research labs. Similarly, sources of technology depend critically on access to qualified staff and training and to cooperative research by firms, followed only afterwards by access to R&D institutions.

Second, administrations normally have little experience of this field's key strategic approaches, which inevitably require multidisciplinary links to both the RTD community and the private sector. In general, for reasons of efficiency, term, and available resources, administrations tend to favour large infrastructure projects. These are easier to manage than a large number of smaller projects, which tend to be less easy to pin down, more indirect in nature, and adapted to differing socioeconomic situations.

Third, one of the key lessons of past evaluations is that technology support for small firms has generally failed to understand their specific business structures and management practices. Many initiatives were grafted onto models and strategies for large firms; they failed to take into account the lack of organizational and managerial structures in small firms necessary to adapt internal operations and skills to the requirements of the new technology. Much emphasis was placed on the technological dimension of business improvements, while the behavioural dimension tended to be overlooked. Importantly, the link with provision of training and education was rarely made, in terms of either identifying skills shortages or providing the training courses needed to make particular technologies operational in a timely manner.

We can conclude that, in the less developed regions, factors related to firms' demand and absorption capacity are more important than those relating to the supply of R&D and scientific infrastructure. In these regions, the innovative environment or "regional productive context" is more important than elsewhere, as are relationships between firms, flows of technology, and the institutional support associated with them, which provide a means of access to the sources and media required to promote innovation.

5

Under Article 10 of the European Regional Development Fund (ERDF) Regulation, the ERDF may contribute to innovative actions in regional development through pilot schemes that encourage pooling of experience, development of innovative measures, and cooperation between different regions of the EU. Article 10 thus provides a basis on which to contribute to innovative actions promoting regional economic development and new policy experiments at the regional and European level. In line with the Article 10 priorities approved for the 1995-99 period, some of these measures aim at developing new ways of introducing innovation in the regional development agenda of the EU's less favoured regions.

Regional Innovation Strategies (RIS) are pilot actions financed under Article 10 (CEC 1999b). They last 18 months, cost half a million euro, and are 50 percent co-financed by the European Commission. Today, nearly 100 regions in Europe are involved in the process. As a pilot action, the RIS are intended to prepare the ground for future policy action – that is, they constitute a laboratory to explore, test, and validate new, more strategic ways to allocate financial resources for regional development.

The RIS provide regions with a methodology for developing strategies and action plans to promote innovation. They are first and foremost a process for stimulating social and institutional dynamism in policies supporting innovation, in a way that takes into account the actual needs of the regional productive structure.

The RIS are designed to respond to the question of how to promote cooperation between SMEs, the research community, and public administration, and how to assess and audit local technology requirements, needs, capabilities, and potential with a view to improving the innovative capacity of a region. The general objectives of RIS are to:

- establish a regional innovation system as an actively learning regional economy

- promote public/private and interfirm cooperation, and create the institutional setting for more efficient use of scarce resources to promote innovation
- develop new ways of introducing technological innovation in the regional economic development agenda of less favoured regions.

The specific objectives of RIS are to:

- foster internal coherence of the regional innovation system by connecting RTD and innovation supply with well-defined demand and business needs, of SMEs in particular
- create and/or strengthen inter- and intra-regional cooperation networks, particularly between the public and private sectors and among firms
- rationalize the regional innovation support system by raising awareness, eliminating duplication, filling gaps, and promoting synergies.

The priorities of the RIS are based mainly on lessons drawn from previous experience of the ERDF in the promotion of innovation. The first is to make innovation part of the regional development policy agenda and to do so in an appropriate way. Accordingly, the concept of innovation in the RIS is not restricted simply to R&D, nor even technology, narrowly defined, even though these are often vital components of innovation. Innovation also affects a variety of other functions, both within firms (e.g., management, marketing, and training) and outside them (e.g., finance, administrative restrictions, relations between firms, and relations with innovation infrastructure). The latter group forms part of the quality of the productive environment, the institutional climate, and the density of networks of cooperation among firms and with RTD institutional agents. Ultimately, RIS is intended to facilitate access to knowledge and the economic use of knowledge for productive purposes. Thus the RIS adopt a multidisciplinary and integrated approach to regional development.

Establishment of RIS requires a strategic and bottom-up approach based on genuine demand from firms, particularly small ones. This entails identifying the most appropriate measures for linking demand for innovation – which in small firms may be hidden or badly expressed – with the knowledge resources available at regional, national, and international levels.

The RIS have led to the emergence of new, better coordinated, and more efficient regional networks for RTD and innovation in regions such as Leipzig-Halle-Dessau (Germany), Lorraine (France), and Castilla y Léon (Spain). In the latter region, a total of 447 million euro has been pledged for the first four years of implementation (1997-2000). The objective is to increase the regional technological effort (R&D expenditure over GDP at factor costs) to 1 percent in the year 2000, from the initial 0.8 percent.

The regions are the most appropriate level for action on innovation. A policy of stimulating innovation in small firms is regarded primarily as a proximity policy, and so a prime concern for regional development policy. For example, the Limburg regional government (Netherlands) and the Welsh Development Agency (United Kingdom) adjusted their regional economic development strategies in light of the RIS results.

Finally, the RIS depend on a broad public-private partnership for one very good reason: cooperation among firms, and between firms and the public sector, is the main force for innovation in a region. In this respect, note that virtually all the RIS regions work to create clusters and networks in the broadest sense. For example, in Yorkshire and Humberside (UK), 11 Business Sector Networks, each with what is called an "Innovation Board" headed by a local business person, have been set up. The same goes for the RIS in the Basque Country (Spain), which is one of the pioneering regions in Europe to develop a comprehensive cluster approach, significantly contributing to the revitalization of regional industry.

One aim of the RIS is to secure a better use of financial resources allocated to the Structural Funds. RIS projects are pilot projects intended to feed into the mainstream operational programs. Most RIS projects are having some impact on the regional programs of the Structural Funds, and are increasing the number of projects concerned with innovation. For example, programs for the Basque Country (Spain), West Midlands (UK), and Weser Ems (Germany) will dedicate substantial budgets to projects in the RIS action plan.

The RIS recognize the past difficulties in RTD and innovation support interventions: lack of a strategic approach to linking supply and demand, overemphasis on infrastructure, and linear thinking. The RIS propose a different policy, one that is more sophisticated and thus more complex to design and implement. Intangible investment and provision of real services to businesses are more difficult to organize and finance than investments in infrastructure, although they are just as important.

In the next programming period (2000-2006), the promotion of innovation will be one of the Commission's priorities (CEC 1999a). The RIS may have helped to prepare the ground, so that those responsible for structural policies at regional and national levels can respond in the most effective way, particularly by focusing on strategic planning, partnership, and consensus building.

Notes

1 The opinions expressed in this chapter are those of the author alone and not necessarily those of the European Commission. The author would like to thank Mikel Landabaso, who, like the author, works at the European Commission and on whose work this chapter (particularly section 5) is largely based.

2 Traditionally the technology gap has been measured by standard RTD input data. Although it is increasingly recognized that these indicators are of limited value in determining the

performance of innovation systems, they nevertheless provide an indication of the endogenous capacity of the system to produce knowledge and provide technologically skilled labour.

References

CEC. (Commission of the European Communities). 1995. *Green Paper on Innovation.* Luxembourg: European Commission.

–. 1996. *First Report on Economic and Social Cohesion.* Luxembourg: European Commission.

–. 1999a. *Draft Guidance for Programmes in the Period 2000-2006.* Working Paper of the Commission. Brussels: European Commission.

–. 1999b. *Article 10 ERDF: Innovative Actions – Innovation Promotion.* Brussels: European Commission.

Circa Group et al. 1999. *Thematic Evaluation – Impact of Structural Funds on RTDI in Objective 1 and 6 Regions 1994-1999.* European Commission draft report. Brussels.

Fagerberg, J. 1999. "The Economic Challenge for Europe: Adapting to Innovation-Based Growth." Paper presented at the European Socio-Economic Research Conference, Brussels.

Landabaso, M. 1998. "Regional Policies and the Conditions for Economic Development." Paper presented at the Interregional Conference *Eurotraining for Regional and Local Authorities in Europe,* Barcelona.

Porter, M. 1990. *The Competitive Advantage of Nations.* New York: Free Press.

Internet sites

<http://europa.eu.int>
<http://www.inforegio.cec.eu.int>

7
Globalization, Information and Communication Technologies, and Local and Regional Systems of Innovation

David A. Wolfe

Introduction: Globalization and the ICT Paradigm

The current era of economic and technological change is marked by a profound degree of social dislocation and uncertainty. A recent cover story in *Business Week* ascribed the emergence of this "New Economy" to two key factors. The first is the growing trend towards globalization, which is increasing the linkages and interdependence between the economies of Europe, North America, and East Asia in terms of investment, trade, research and development, and even product identification and marketing. The second factor is the emergence of a new integrated set of information technologies that integrate computers, telecommunications, and media together in digital form and dramatically alter the economic calculus of production and distribution throughout the industrial economies. Together these key factors are reshaping the economies of both industrial and industrializing economies and changing much of the accepted wisdom about how they operate.

The resulting process of social dislocation and exclusion reduces the opportunity for growing numbers of people to participate effectively in the newly emerging economy, and undermines the economic viability of traditional communities and other social relationships. It is a challenge for regions and local communities to cope with the competitive realities of the global economy while learning to take advantage of the opportunities afforded by the new information and communication technologies (ICTs). While these challenges may seem daunting, particularly for the less favoured regions of Europe and North America, a number of recent examples suggest that the obstacles can be overcome by these regions "bootstrapping" themselves into the new economy. The effectiveness of such an effort depends, however, upon the ability of regions and local communities to marshal the resources that are critical to success in the new economy.

At the heart of the emerging techno-economic paradigm is the convergence of an integrated set of computer, communications, and video technologies based on semiconductors, which share the capacity to process and transmit data in digital form. The current diffusion of these technologies throughout the industrial economies exerts effects as vast and sweeping as those that accompanied the Second Industrial Revolution at the turn of the century (Tapscott 1996). The new information and communication technologies dramatically reduce the cost of generating, storing, transmitting, and processing information throughout all sectors of the economy. Thus they have increased the information-processing capacity of the economy at an exponential rate, while simultaneously enhancing the salience of knowledge-based inputs in every aspect of production. The dual character of ICTs makes it imperative to distinguish between the purely technical aspects of the technology and the accompanying organizational and intellectual ones – i.e., between the "hardware" and the "wetware."

The resulting economic paradigm is increasingly referred to as a "knowledge-based economy." This follows from the central role that knowledge-based activities have come to play in the production process, as well the rising proportion of the labour force that deals with the production, distribution, and processing of information and knowledge compared with the proportion handling tangible goods. The dynamic effect of the new paradigm results from the way it mobilizes knowledge, social intelligence, and innovative capacity. If knowledge is understood to include not just R&D but also design, engineering, advertising, marketing, and management, then knowledge-based inputs are becoming the defining feature of both manufacturing and service industries in the new economy. Together, the ability to deploy knowledge to create value and a sustained capacity for innovation are the keys to success for nations, regions, communities, and firms in the emerging global economy.

It may be more appropriate, however, to describe the emerging paradigm as a "learning economy" rather than a "knowledge-based" one. "Learning" in this respect refers to the building of new competencies and the acquisition of new skills, not just gaining access to information. The rapid pace of change associated with the frontiers of economically relevant knowledge means that its economic value tends to diminish the more widely it is disseminated. The easier and more inexpensive access to information tends to reduce the economic value of more codified forms of knowledge and information. In tandem with this, forms of knowledge that cannot be codified and transmitted electronically (tacit knowledge) increase in value, along with the ability to acquire and assess both codified and tacit forms of knowledge – in other words, the capability to learn. In this sense, the dramatic effect of ICTs on the rapid diffusion and availability of information and the emphasis on a "learning economy" are integrally linked. For individuals, firms, regions, and nations, it is the capacity to learn and adapt to rapidly changing economic circumstances that is more likely to determine their future economic success in the global economy (Lundvall and Borras 1998).

The impact of the ICT paradigm is intensified by the parallel emergence of new economic relations at the global level, subsumed under the concept of globalization. This concept implies that individual economies are becoming more transnationalized, or integrated into the international economy, and losing an important degree of national sovereignty and autonomy. The extent and nature of globalization, a subject of great dispute, can be gauged in several ways. One dimension refers to the growing integration of markets and production strategies, which facilitates the design and production of goods for global, rather than simply national, markets. Similarly, the sourcing of components on a global basis – and increasing reliance on the negotiation of strategic alliances with other firms for R&D, production, or marketing of goods – further contributes to the integration of national production strategies into a global strategy. The globalization of world markets is no longer limited to financing, production, or sales, but extends as well to the ever greater internationalization of research and the acquisition of knowledge. The globalization of technology is linked to the increasing importance of R&D and knowledge in the new paradigm.

Despite the several aspects of globalization mentioned above, there remains a serious debate over the degree to which it has displaced the national economy as the dominant mechanism for coordinating economic affairs. The central issues in this debate concern both the proportion of economic activity that transpires in the global – as opposed to national – economy and the extent to which multinational firms retain distinctive national characteristics and a primary allegiance to their home economy. According to Ostry and Nelson (1995, 24), techno-globalism refers to the fact that more and more, multinational corporations are exploiting technology globally and gaining access to new technology around the world through the diffusion of R&D and increased collaboration. The rise of information technology and global telecommunication networks enables firms to organize and coordinate their R&D and acquisition of technical knowledge on a global basis. It reflects one element of the growing reliance on strategic alliances by multinational firms. Companies that compete on a global basis are establishing research activities in key R&D centres and building strategic alliances with both university research centres and other firms deemed to possess complementary knowledge and skills. One illustration of this trend is the growing investment by foreign multinationals in offshore – especially US-based – research institutes. Their efforts reflect the desire to benefit from the intellectual output of the US research system, by harnessing its scientific and technological capabilities and generating new technological assets. The key issue in dispute concerns the extent to which techno-globalism is generating a convergence in the patterns of technological activity. Available evidence suggests that despite the increasingly global nature of technological activities, national differences among the leading industrial countries, and regional specificities within them, remain significant; the specific character of the home base is crucial to the innovativeness of domestic firms (Pavitt and Patel 1999).

The Global and the Local in the New Paradigm

The rise of techno-globalism and the relatively easy transmission of data and information among firms has fostered the view that national and regional differences count for little in the emerging ICT paradigm – summarized in the familiar phrase about the "death of distance" (Cairncross 1997). This perspective underlies a great deal of the thinking subsumed under the banner of the Information Society, with its emphasis on speeding the rapid adoption and diffusion of new ICTs, particularly in the telecommunications arena. Its bias is towards the liberalization of telecommunications regulatory regimes, to reduce barriers to the adoption of new technologies, and ensuring equal access to the global information infrastructure. In this perspective, which focuses on the technological hardware rather than the organizational and learning dimensions of the new ICTs, the levelling effect of telecommunications technologies accentuates the trend towards convergence, reducing the significance of national and regional differences in locational decisions. Thus the precise location of specific economic activities depends on purely economic factors, as opposed to spatial or cultural ones.

This perspective contrasts with an alternative view in the disciplines of regional science and economic geography. Despite the growing integration of individual economies into a global economy, the alternative view perceives the new as marked by a "paradoxical consequence of globalization" – the simultaneous growth in importance of the locality as a site for innovation (Acs et al. 1996). As the information and communication networks created by digital technologies integrate the economies of the globe ever more tightly, they simultaneously increase the importance of space and proximity. The production paradigm of the new economy, with its emphasis on knowledge and creativity, is highly dependent on localized, or regionally based, innovation. Innovative capabilities are often sustained through regional communities that share a common base of knowledge, and the additions to that knowledge base.

Economic geographers have long observed that patterns of production tend to concentrate over time among networks of firms drawing upon the distinctive skills and characteristics of local labour markets. They use the term *territorialization* to describe the range of economic activity that depends on resources that are territorially specific. The types of resources involved include specific assets that are available only in a certain place, or assets whose real value emerges out of the context of particular interfirm relations that are grounded in the geography of a particular region or community. These relations become an asset when they create positive spillover effects among the firms in a region: that is, when the knowledge of how to do certain things is shared effectively among networks of firms and their employees in a regional economy. The more the economic activities of a region are rooted in the specific assets of that region, the more fully territorialized its activities become (Storper 1997). The globalization perspective tends to emphasize the levelling effect of new ICT "hardware" in the rapid transmission and use of information or more codified forms of knowledge. The regional perspective emphasizes the significance of space and proximity in creating the conditions under which more tacit forms of knowledge – the "wetware" of the innovation process – are generated and shared among communities of researchers, firms, and workers to confer distinctive regional advantages.

These contrasting perspectives lead to radically different conclusions about the prospects for economic development at the local and regional level, and significantly different policy prescriptions. The perspective associated with the ICT/IS (information society) approach emphasizes the economic significance of the information and communications hardware. The quality of telecommunications access is a critical variable in determining the economic success of regions and localities in the emerging paradigm. This approach focuses on the competitive benefits conferred by state-of-the-art telecommunications linkages and their impact on leveraging local and regional economic development, by:

- providing broad access to the global information infrastructure through programs such as Canada's School-Net program, which has as its objective the linking of every elementary and secondary school in the country to the Internet
- affording local firms new growth opportunities by providing them with better access to global markets and ensuring that the local communications infrastructure is competitive with that available in the more developed and advantaged regions and localities, thus allowing them to fully participate in emerging service trends, such as electronic commerce
- reducing the previous barriers to inward investment by multinational corporations
- creating new locational and/or niche market opportunities for less favoured regions by attracting new telecommunications-based services, such as the call centres in New Brunswick
- exploring new approaches to social integration for communities in distant and disadvantaged regions, such as Canada's northern aboriginal communities

- providing public services better and more economically through the development and implementation of new forms of telecommunication services, such as distance learning and tele-health.

Considerable doubt has been expressed, however, about the viability of this approach as a strategy for promoting economic development in less favoured regions. This approach accepts much of the promotional hype about the "death of distance" at face value, without examining the extent to which access to the hardware and infrastructure provides both necessary and sufficient conditions to leverage economic development and innovation. As noted earlier, when access to information becomes a common feature of virtually all regions with the necessary telecommunications infrastructure, it is the local features that generate the distinctive advantages that remain significant.

Furthermore, providing the necessary access to telecommunications infrastructure is unlikely alone to generate an adequate level of demand for the services. As numerous studies have demonstrated, it is highly skilled and demanding end-users that create the market for the most sophisticated of the new ICTs. It is not by accident that the greatest geographic concentrations of new digital media in North America (and Europe) are located in cities such as San Francisco, New York, and Toronto that already constitute the important centres of cultural production and/or provide strong concentrations of end-users in industries such as financial services (Brail 1998). Furthermore, the exclusive focus on the hard technologies as the source of regional economic inequalities (and the solution to these problems) overlooks the extent to which organizational and cultural factors figure prominently in the ability of firms to adopt and use the latest technologies. The assumption that infrastructure access will be the determining criterion in the ability of regions to attract or develop successful firms in the new digital forms of electronic commerce is belied by the results of recent studies on the adoption of e-commerce practices, such as those by Shop.org and the Boston Consulting Group (1998) and IBM and the Retail Council of Canada (1999). Finally, many of the jobs generated in the new telecommunication services, such as call centres, do not conform to the image of highly skilled labour usually associated with employment in the high-tech industries. As the case of New Brunswick has demonstrated, many of the jobs tend to be of the lower-wage/lower value-added type, where the working conditions look more like those in traditional sweatshops than research laboratories. For these and related reasons, a number of analysts have concluded that the Information Society approach – with its emphasis on the information infrastructure hardware – fails to provide an adequate paradigm for responding to the issues of regional development.

Local and Regional Systems of Innovation

As a consequence, both academics and policy analysts are focusing attention on the concept of the regional innovation system. This is seen as a more adequate basis for understanding the problems of regional innovation and development in the new paradigm, and prescribing appropriate policy responses. The application of this concept at the regional level grows out of similar work at the national level. At base is the understanding that innovation and technical progress are sustained by a complex set of relationships among the institutions that produce, distribute, and apply various kinds of knowledge. The innovative performance of individual countries is influenced by the way elements of this institutional system interact in the creation and application of knowledge. Original contributors to the development of the concept were Christopher Freeman, Bengt-Åke Lundvall, and Richard Nelson. A synthetic definition of the national system of innovation is provided by Stan Metcalfe (1997, 285): "A national system of innovation is that set of distinct institutions which jointly and individually contribute to the development and diffusion of new technologies and which provides the framework within which governments form and implement policies to influence the innovation process. As such it is a system of interconnected institutions to create, store and transfer the knowledge, skills and artifacts which define new technologies."

While the original work within this approach focused attention on the national or sectoral level, recent efforts have shifted to an analysis of the way in which innovation systems operate at the regional and local levels as well. Although there has been some disagreement over the appropriate definition of a region, an important distinction is drawn between two types of regions: "cultural" and "administrative." According to Cooke et al. (1997), cultural regions share certain features in common with "the classical definition of nation as a people sharing a common culture, language and territory but which either have not become states (e.g., the Basque Country) or forfeited that status (e.g., Scotland)." Administrative regions include subnational areas of jurisdiction within larger federal systems, such as the German Länder or US states, or newer forms of regional government within traditionally centralized democracies such as France or Italy. All such regions are defined as "territories smaller than their state possessing significant supralocal governance capacity and cohesiveness differentiating them from their state and other regions" (Cooke et al. 1997). Within this context, regional innovation systems include the notion of how the institutional and cultural environment of a region either supports or retards the innovation process. This is defined as "the set of economic, political and institutional relationships occurring in a given geographical area which generates a collective learning process leading to the rapid diffusion of knowledge and best practice" (Nauwelaers and Reid 1995).

A critical component of the regional innovation system (RIS) is the infrastructure of R&D institutions located within it, as well as the internal and external networks of relationships within and between public agencies and private actors. A number of recent schematics have been proposed to describe this system. One of these suggests that the RIS should be conceptualized in terms of both the demand and supply sides of innovation. On the supply side are located the institutional sources of knowledge creation in the regional economy. Closely linked to these are institutions responsible for the training and preparation of highly qualified labour power. The demand side of the system subsumes the productive sector – firms that develop and apply the scientific and technological output of the supply side, in the creation and marketing of innovative products and processes. Bridging the gap between the two are a wide range of innovation support organizations that play a role in the acquisition and diffusion of technological ideas and know-how throughout the RIS. These may include technology centres, technology brokers, business innovation centres, industry liaison and similar organizations in the higher-education sector that facilitate the interface with the private sector, and mechanisms of financing innovation, such as venture capital firms (Nauwelaers and Reid 1995).

This approach to local and regional economic development leads to a corresponding emphasis on how the unique cultural and institutional characteristics of individual regions and communities either stimulate or retard the innovation process within the new ICT paradigm. The importance of these cultural and institutional features derives from the difference between codified forms of knowledge and dynamic forms of learning. As noted earlier, the increased availability of data and information places a premium on unique forms of knowledge. The new ICTs tend to devalue previously localized knowledge assets by making them more ubiquitously available, through communication networks. However, this process in turn places a higher premium on kinds of knowledge and learning that resist transmission through these networks. Some types of knowledge are more effectively exchanged through direct face-to-face contact. The more tacit the knowledge involved (i.e., the less explicit or codified it is), the more important the spatial proximity between the actors taking part in the exchange.

The reason is twofold. First, it is partly a function of the economics of time and distance – normally it is less costly and easier to interact with others who are close at hand, despite the convenience of electronic forms of communication. Second, it involves the question of trust and understanding – the transfer of tacit knowledge is facilitated by an environment or context in which the participants share a common set of values and culture. Both these factors are facilitated by proximity (Maskell and Malmberg 1999). The value of face-to-face interaction is great, particularly in the context of an abundant technical and professional labour force and a supportive regional infrastructure.

The importance of cultural and institutional features in facilitating knowledge flows within regional and local economies is closely related to the acceleration in learning processes, especially social/organizational learning. In a period of significant social and economic disruption, learning is a critical ability if regions and localities are to adjust to the reality of the new economic paradigm. According to Lundvall and Johnson (1994), the stock of knowledge is affected by two flows: learning, which increases knowledge, and forgetting, which reduces it. However, the ability to acquire and retain new knowledge depends directly on individual and collective investments in its acquisition. This ability, in turn, depends on the absorptive capacity of firms and institutions – their ability to understand and absorb new forms of knowledge – which is largely determined by their prior level of knowledge investment. This concept emphasizes the organizational and social dimensions of learning and the contribution to the learning process made by shared cognitive frameworks (Cohen and Levinthal 1990).

Investment in both individual and organizational learning is necessary, but not sufficient, to sustain a dynamic local or regional innovation system. There must also be a recognition of the broader spatial dimensions of learning within a network or community in the geographic locale. By extension, the processes of learning and knowledge acquisition are applicable not just at the level of the firm but also at the level of the locality and the region. According to Richard Florida (1995, 532), "regions are increasingly defined by the same criteria and elements which comprise a knowledge-intensive firm – continuous improvement, new ideas, knowledge creation and organizational learning. Regions must adopt the principles of knowledge creation and continuous learning; they must in effect become *learning regions.* Learning regions provide a series of related infrastructures which can facilitate the flow of knowledge, ideas and learning."

Regions that exhibit these features also tend to adopt more associative forms of governance, based on high levels of trust and social capital. The "learning regions" signify the growing shift from hierarchical forms of organization, in both public and private institutions, to more heterarchical ones in which network relations are based on conditions of trust, reciprocity, reputation, openness to learning, and an inclusive and empowering disposition. According to a number of authors (Amin 1996; Cooke and Morgan 1998), this shift requires moving from reliance upon public authorities to regulate economic affairs, to a greater degree of self-regulation by autonomous groups in the economy and society. This, in turn, involves the transfer of authority and responsibility for some critical aspects of economic policy to a range of local organizations capable of providing the required services or programs (such as vocational training or technology transfer). It also necessarily involves a more decentralized, open, and consultative form of governing, and it is closely associated with the process of institutional learning and adaptation within the region (Cooke 1997).

The appeal of the associative model of governance – especially at the level of the more dynamic regional economies – derives from the insights afforded by this analysis. For the exclusive role of the public bureaucracy, the associative model substitutes a mix of public and private roles and emphasizes the context of institutional structures and learning. It involves devolution of greater degrees of autonomy and responsibility for policy outcomes to organizations that will either enjoy the fruits of policy success or live with the consequences of failure. According to Amin (1996), the adoption of an associative model implies not an abandonment of a central role for the state but rather a rethinking of its role. At the relevant level, the state has to become one of the institutions of the collective order, working in relationship with other organizations, rather than a traditional command-and-control operation. In this model, the state continues to establish the basic rules governing the economy but it places much greater emphasis on the devolution of responsibility to a wide range of associative partners through the mechanisms of "voice" and consultation (Amin 1996). For many of the reasons suggested earlier, this approach to governance seems to work most effectively at the regional and local levels.

Over the past two decades, the most dynamic regional levels of government have experimented with a wide range of policies to generate and diffuse new ideas and promote innovation – in other words, to create the learning region climate described earlier. Differences in economic performance between the relatively successful regions have prompted a corresponding interest in the mix of regional innovation policies and institutions that foster this dynamism. While these studies are still in their infancy, their conclusions have begun to coalesce into a new heterodox policy framework. The conclusions suggest that while dynamic local and regional innovation systems can be constructed, there is no single blueprint or model for success. The framework has many different variants, reflecting the prescription that regional innovation policies must be context-sensitive, i.e., they must reflect the multiple realities created by different industrial cultures and institutional milieu in different regions (Storper 1996).

Dynamic Local and Regional Economies

The construction of a dynamic local or regional innovation system depends in part on the past history of the region, its industrial culture, and its endowment of infrastructural supports. In other words, it is path-dependent – history matters. Yet examples abound of localities and regions that have altered their development trajectory through collective efforts to improve their endowment of institutional and cultural factors. A growing number of cases, diverse in both their geographic location and institutional framework, suggest that a combination of these factors can contribute to success in the emerging global information economy. Almost all confirm the underlying importance of geographic concentrations of technical skills as a factor critical to competitive success. Localities and regions, however, may differ in terms of the industrial structure that characterizes the region, the relative mix of industries on which success is based, the underlying infrastructure of research and other institutions that support local firms, and the social or civic culture that creates cohesion in the region or locality.

History still matters – localities and regions must start from the point of their current assets and collective experiences. As such, they must confront the danger of being locked into a path of development rooted in their past economic trajectory. But there are also examples where communities and regions have deliberately altered that trajectory. Many instances are documented in the literature of dynamic regional economies that have accomplished this through a collective process of social learning and institutional adaptation. Similar stories can be found at the local and community level. The challenges at the local level are greater in some respects, because many of the factors that affect the chances of success are determined at the regional, national, or supranational levels. Local developmental paths are thus influenced by the multiple levels of governance to which they are subject. What follows are three examples of successful developmental trajectories, deliberately selected from North America and chosen from the experience of local communities.

Austin, Texas

Traditionally a government/university town, Austin is noteworthy for the rapid pace at which it has attracted a critical number of firms and national consortia in the high-technology field, through a coordinated planning and marketing effort. Its coordinated planning strategy was led by the IC^2 Institute at the University of Texas in Austin and by the state government. Under the leadership of the IC^2 Institute, key leaders in the local chamber of commerce and key faculty and administrators at the university launched a concerted effort to promote the growth of high-tech entrepreneurship in the Austin area. The strategy achieved a significant number of successes in the form of new entrants to the industry (such as Dell) that were able to build upon the electronics base created by the technical branch plants located there in 1960 (such as Texas Instruments and Motorola); a number of government installations; and a heavy investment by the university in the field. The university's $4 billion endowment was especially important, allowing it to invest in regional economic development and leverage even larger sums of private and federal investment.

Critical achievements of Austin's strategy were attracting two national high-technology consortia established in the 1980s – the Microelectronics and Computer Consortium and Sematech – by providing land and buildings for their location, and the university's expansion of its computer science and electrical engineering units. The strategy was led by a coalition that included the chamber of commerce, the chancellor's office at the university, a number of key faculty, and state government officials. While these initial successes generated an aura of growth and development for the region, the rapid pace at which they occurred brought other problems (Gibson and Rogers 1994), which will not be explored here. Austin is far from the ranks of a Silicon Valley, yet today it is widely recognized as one of the dynamic growth poles in the US economy. The key here is that Austin was able to shift its economic base through a deliberate, cohesive approach based on the mobilization of collective community (i.e., government/university/business) efforts and expansion of its infrastructural assets.

Spartanburg-Greenville, South Carolina

Traditionally a region with low education and a poor manufacturing base, the area adopted a strategy in the 1960s of attracting textile companies from other areas. By the 1980s, this had evolved to include automotive parts and manufacturing. The key here was twofold. Initially, a more open, global culture was promoted to make the area more attractive and accessible to foreign companies such as Michelin. Then the regional technical training infrastructure was systematically upgraded to include specialized and customized training programs for firms that located in the region. This strategy culminated in BMW's 1992 decision to locate its US manufacturing plant in the area, leading other firms to locate there as well (Kanter 1995).

Toronto, Ontario

This example clearly does not involve a less favoured region or locality, yet Toronto has experienced considerable economic change and adjustment over the past two decades. The traditional financial and manufacturing centre of Canada saw considerable erosion of its core industries through the recessions of the early 1980s and 1990s. The effects of the latter were intensified by the impact of the Canada-US Free Trade Agreement (FTA) and the subsequent North American Free Trade Agreement (NAFTA). Although the Greater Toronto Area (GTA) remains the second largest automotive production centre in North America, it also witnessed the rapid decline of its traditional manufacturing base and the loss of a host of lower value-added firms. At the same time, however, it began to emerge as one of the core centres for software and animation as well as one of the three major North American localities (with Silicon Valley and New York) for multimedia production and services.

Two preconditions were critical in spurring this development: (1) the presence and strong value of key software capabilities at the university level (University of Toronto and University of Waterloo), created through substantial investment by the federal and provincial governments in educational and research infrastructure during the 1960s; and (2) the centrality of Toronto as a broadcasting, entertainment, and cultural production centre within Canada. Many of these industries grew or located in Toronto as a result of federal policies in the 1970s that promoted the development of Canada's cultural industries. The unintended and indirect effects of these policies were the growth of a multimedia software sector because the cultural industries skills base was already present. The dynamism of this sector continues to depend primarily on the ready supply of highly qualified labour. This supply has been assured by the judicious investments of governments (of all three political parties) in continuous upgrading and expansion of the training infrastructure, including the establishment of highly specialized training and research institutes. The result has been an agglomeration of companies in the Toronto area that not only supply but also demand various multimedia-related services and products (Gertler and Brail 1999).

Conclusions

Despite variations, most studies agree that successful local and regional innovation systems have a number of key factors in common. Chief among these is the role played by leadership and vision in promoting the environment of innovation and entrepreneurship that is critical to their success. Almost all studies of successful development strategies point to the instrumental role played by a champion in promoting the growth of local industrial clusters. The source of this leadership may vary. In some regions, it comes from political institutions or industry associations. In others, it originates from an inspirational figure in a university setting or anchor firm that attracts or spins off likeminded individuals. In the end, the leader's role is to mobilize those in the community with an interest in altering its development trajectory.

Closely related is the role played by a strong degree of civic-mindedness in the region. This civic culture is important in building shared visions and goals for the region and in promoting the kind of networking and interaction that contributes to innovation through creation of "untraded interdependencies." In some instances, especially in Europe, this tradition is the product of decades of historical development, mostly unplanned and uncoordinated, that worked to create the right environment for innovation. In others, more recently in the US, it has emerged from conscious efforts by civic and business leaders to chart a new strategy for the locality or region. This civic culture contributes to the growth of social capital in the region and forms the bedrock on which networking and interfirm interaction can occur to create further innovation.

Another factor is the critical role played by a region's science and technology infrastructure – usually institutions of higher education and training, but also corporate research laboratories, national or regional R&D consortia, or local innovation centres geared to the needs of specific industries. It is not merely the presence of these institutions that contributes to the growth and development of the region. Rather, it is their success in generating a high degree of interaction with the region's industry and business, and their ability to promote a culture of innovation and entrepreneurship among their graduates and trainees. When institutions are successful in creating this kind of climate, they also contribute to the formation of informal linkages and networking among the region's innovative firms. The exact nature of these linkages can vary considerably. In some instances, they take the form of tight buyer-supplier relationships that contribute to a process of interactive learning. In other localities, knowledge sharing and exchange occur through joint participation in local research and innovation centres. A third model involves the kind of informal networking that occurs through the existence of a dynamic labour market and a high degree of labour mobility between firms. Whatever the exact form, all these types of interaction contribute to the spreading of tacit knowledge through the local economy and, in turn, sustains its capacity for innovation.

Another important factor is the availability of local finance to support innovative firms in the region or locale. Once again, this takes a variety of forms. In the successful Italian regions, the decentralized nature of the banking system has provided an important source of capital for local firms. In the entrepreneurial climate of the US economy, knowledgeable and flexible venture capitalists provide an important source of risk capital. In the rather atypical case of Austin, even a university endowment fund has played this role. What matters most is the presence of local individuals and/or institutions with a knowledgeable background in financing innovation and a commitment to supporting local firms.

The final factor is the role played by government. In some instances, regional governments have been central to the creation of the development model. In the US, although development has been led more by the private sector, government agencies and programs have played an important role. Government involvement seems to work best when it is undertaken in partnership with private sector leaders or champions, as part of a community-based coalition. This usually involves a new form of associative governance, where the political leaders share some of their traditional authority with local business and community leaders. While this is not a determining factor in the success of local development, it is usually a contributing one.

The lesson provided by successful regional development models is that a dynamic innovative capacity does not emerge merely by accident; it is created. The conditions under which this occurs may vary from locality to locality, and the successful basis of one is not easy to reproduce in another. The key, however, is the creation of a shared vision and the launching of a coordinated effort within the community, based on a realistic assessment of existing strengths and opportunities for growth.

References

Acs, Z., J. de la Mothe, and G. Paquet. 1996. "Local Systems of Innovation: In Search of an Enabling Strategy." In Peter Howitt, ed., *The Implications of Knowledge-Based Growth for Micro-Economic Policies,* 339-60. Calgary: University of Calgary Press.

Amin, A. 1996. "Beyond Associative Democracy." *New Political Economy* 1,3.

Brail, S.G. 1998. "The Paradox of Technological Change: New Media in Old Urban Areas." Toronto: Department of Geography, University of Toronto. (http://www.geog.utoronto.ca/deptinfo/BRAIL2.html)

Cairncross, F. 1997. *The Death of Distance: How the Communications Revolution Will Change Our Lives.* Cambridge, MA: Harvard Business School Press.

Cohen, W., and D. Levinthal. 1990. "Innovation and Learning: The Two Faces of R&D." *Economic Journal* 99,397: 569-96.

Cooke, P. 1997. "Institutional Reflexivity and the Rise of the Region State." In G. Benko and U. Strohmayer, eds., *Space and Social Theory: Interpreting Modernity and Post-Modernity.* Oxford: Blackwell.

Cooke, P., and K. Morgan. 1998. *The Associative Economy.* Oxford: Oxford University Press.

Cooke, P., M. Gomez Uranga, and G. Etxebarria. 1997. "Regional Innovation Systems: Institutional and Organizational Dimensions." *Research Policy* 26: 475-91.

Florida, R. 1995. "Toward the Learning Region." *Futures* 27: 527-36.

Gertler, M.S., and S. Brail. 1999. "The Digital Regional Economy: Emergence and Evolution of Toronto's Multimedia Cluster." In H.J. Braczyk, G. Fuchs, and H.-G. Wolf, eds., *Multimedia and Regional Economic Restructuring.* London: Routledge.

Gibson, D.V., and E.M. Rogers. 1994. *R&D Collaboration on Trial: The Microelectronics and Computer Corporation.* Boston: Harvard Business School Press.

IBM and Retail Council of Canada. 1999. *The Race Is On: Who Will Win Canada's Internet Shoppers?* Toronto.

Kanter, R.M. 1995. "Thriving Locally in the Global Economy." *Harvard Business Review* (Sept.-Oct.): 151-60.

Lundvall, B.Å., and S. Borras. 1998. *The Globalising Learning Economy: Implications for Innovation Policy.* Report prepared under the TSER Programme, DG XII, Commission of the European Union. Luxembourg: Office for Official Publications of the European Communities.

Lundvall, B.Å., and B. Johnson. 1994. "The Learning Economy." *Journal of Industry Studies* 1: 23-42.

Maskell, P., and A. Malmberg. 1999. "Localised learning and industrial competitiveness." *Cambridge Journal of Economics* 23: 167-86.

Metcalfe, J.S. 1997. "Technology Systems and Technology Policy in an Evolutionary Framework." In D. Archibugi and J. Michie, eds., *Technology, Globalization and Economic Performance,* 268-96. Cambridge, UK: Cambridge University Press.

Nauwelaers, C., and A. Reid. 1995. *Innovative Regions? A Comparative Review of Methods of Evaluating Regional Innovation Potential.* European Innovation Monitoring System (EIMS) Publication No. 21. Luxembourg: European Commission, DG XIII.

Ostry, S., and R.R. Nelson. 1995. *Techno-Nationalism and Techno-Globalism: Conflict and Cooperation.* Washington, DC: Brookings Institution.

Pavitt, K., and P. Patel. 1999. "Global Corporations and National Systems of Innovation: Who Dominates Whom?" In D. Archibugi, J. Howells, and J. Michie, eds., *Innovation Policy in a Global Economy*, 94-119. Cambridge, UK: Cambridge University Press.

Shop.org and Boston Consulting Group. 1998. *The State of Online Retailing*. Boston and Toronto.

Storper, M. 1996. "Institutions of the Knowledge-Based Economy." In *Employment and Growth in the Knowledge-Based Economy*, 255-83. Paris: OECD.

–. 1997. *The Regional World: Territorial Development in a Global Economy*. New York and London: The Guilford Press.

Tapscott, D. 1996. *The Digital Economy: Promise and Peril in the Age of Networked Intelligence*. New York: McGraw-Hill.

8

Innovation, Organizational Capabilities, and Competitiveness in a Global Economy[1]

Luigi Orsenigo

Introduction

This chapter discusses some issues concerning the relations between innovation and competitiveness in a global economy. In particular, it focuses on a set of related questions about the nature of knowledge and innovation, the sources and the loci of competitiveness, and the globalization of innovative activities.

It is now widely recognized that innovation is a major source of competitiveness and economic growth. Yet one still observes, both in the theoretical literature and in the current political debate, widely different conceptualizations of the process of innovation and of the nature of the knowledge that is produced through innovations. In particular, while in principle everybody recognizes that technical knowledge embodies elements of both codified (at least potentially), public knowledge and tacit, firm-specific knowledge, different theoretical models tend to put their emphasis on just one extreme representation. This simplification is necessary in the process of theory making and model building, but it might become dangerous, for more practical purposes, if it is then forgotten that a drastic simplification was assumed.

After a brief discussion of the notion of competitiveness and its determinants as they appear in the literature, I shall briefly discuss the models of the innovative process that underlie alternative approaches. In particular, I shall put forward the proposition that a large fraction of the current literature is still ultimately based on some version of the so-called linear model, and on an extreme distinction between processes of knowledge creation and knowledge diffusion. This distinction is indeed extremely important, but it captures only a part of what is necessary to understand the relationships between innovation and competitiveness. Thus, I shall try to emphasize that the nature of the specific technological regime characterizing different industries and technologies generates important differences in the patterns of innovative activities, and hence different conceptual and policy implications.

This discussion is directly relevant to two issues that have both a long theoretical pedigree and an immediate relevance in terms of policy: (1) What are the sources of (technological) competitiveness and where are they located: in firms, regions, industries, countries? (2) Are innovative activities becoming more "globalized," and if so, in what sense? I shall argue that sectoral differences play a major role here and that there are, indeed, complex interactions between firms, industries, regions, and countries. However, the key to competitiveness resides in the ability to identify and manage specific complementarities between different pieces of knowledge and agents.

As an example of this line of reasoning, I conclude by discussing the role of organizational innovations in explaining the deterioration of European competitiveness. Two different levels are addressed: the diffusion of new management and production practices within European firms, and the evolution of industry-university relationships.

Innovation, Competitiveness, and Growth

The concept of competitiveness is notoriously hard to define, and one finds in the literature very different uses of the term. Competitiveness has a relatively clear meaning at the level of individual firms, where it may stand for profitability, firms' growth, market share, or any other measure of performance against competitors one wishes to use. Even at this level, though, the notion is certainly not unidimensional or entirely transparent. In any case, what is clear is that competitiveness is – by definition – a relative concept. That is, it measures performance compared with others, not in absolute terms. Moving from the firm to the region or country, competitiveness is often taken to mean the foreign trade performance of an economy in relation to its trading partners and its change over time. In this sense, relative unit wage costs are the most widely accepted indicator of competitiveness, under the assumption that the evolution of costs (particularly wage costs) determines foreign trade performance. In this interpretation, it is also assumed that an inverse relationship exists between costs so defined and competitiveness.[2]

In this definition, competitiveness is not necessarily the primary focus of concern. Indeed, traditional neoclassical theory does not attribute any particular significance to trade as a factor accelerating growth and increasing employment. This definition is fairly widespread (e.g., it is used by the Organization for Economic Cooperation and Development [OECD]) and has been dominant until quite recent times. A series of empirical results and theoretical developments have cast serious doubts on its significance, however. Several studies have shown, for instance, that the hypothesized inverse relationship between changes in unit wage costs and trade performance does not hold, even over long periods of time (Fagerberg 1988; Amendola et al. 1994). Rather, several countries that experienced increases in their relative unit wage costs simultaneously increased their market share in foreign markets.

These findings have sparked research on the role of "non-cost" factors in international competitiveness, similar to the recognition of non-price competition at the firm level. In particular, it has now become relatively uncontroversial to attribute a fundamental role to technological factors in explaining the patterns of foreign trade, as opposed to factor endowments as in the standard trade theory.

The key issue here is that technology is not given; it is endogenously generated by diverse forces. These include innovative activities in the company sector and research conducted in universities and other public and private research institutions. Moreover, technology is not universally accessible, costless, and immediate. If anything, standard economic theory maintains that innovation needs economic incentives – such as patents – that inhibit imitation and provide temporary monopoly power. As a consequence, firms and countries will not normally operate on the same "production function" but will exhibit different technological levels. Thus, countries will tend to specialize and gain market shares in those products and industries where they enjoy superior technological and innovative capabilities. These advantages may be eroded over time, according to how long it takes others to imitate and/or acquire the new technological capabilities. The life-cycle approach to international trade (Posner 1961; Vernon 1966; Krugman 1990; Grossman and Helpman 1991) and the whole series of so-called North-South models held that the patterns of international specialization tend to shift over time from innovative countries to imitators.

Parallel to the recognition of the role of technological change in international trade, endogenous innovation has taken a key role in the development of the theory of endogenous growth (Romer 1990) and an integrated theory of trade and growth. Within this context, innovation and patterns of trade and growth are tightly linked, although the specific nature of these linkages may differ according to the specific hypotheses made. Thus, it has become increasingly recognized that trade performance and patterns of specialization can affect growth, and that public policies supporting trade performance and/or aimed at changing the patterns of specialization may well improve growth and wage levels in one country at the expense of others.

These developments explain much of the renewed interest in the concept of competitiveness observed in the last decade. As a consequence, new and wider definitions of competitiveness have been proposed. Trade performance is no longer considered the only measure of competitiveness. The definition now includes economic growth and other indicators of the levels of welfare in an economy. For instance, the United States Council on Competitiveness (1992) defines competitiveness as "the capacity to produce goods or services which respond to the demand of international markets whilst at the same time enabling American citizens to enjoy a steadily rising standard of living over the long term." In similar vein, a series of studies on European competitiveness (Andreasen et al. 1995; Coriat 1997) converge on the following definition: "an economy is considered as competitive if its exports are able to finance the imports needed to secure its economic growth and standard of living, without creating any risk of imbalances or bottlenecks."

These definitions are interesting precisely because they explicitly couple foreign trade, growth, and standards of living (including employment and its quality). In doing so, they direct attention to sources of competitiveness other than costs, and suggest policies that avoid compromising domestic growth and social progress for the sake of external performance.

Alternative Conceptualization of the Process of Innovation

As innovation is now commonly recognized to be a prime determinant of competitiveness and growth, it is important to ask how innovations are generated and what consequences follow. The literature on endogenous innovation, trade, and growth offers a number of basic, admittedly simplified, representations of the process of technological change. In all cases, though, innovation is essentially conceptualized as information. Two fundamental properties follow: (1) technology has (at least potentially) the characteristics of a public good, and (2) there are nonconvexities in the production and diffusion of new technology.

In the model, firms basically invest in R&D in expectation of the temporary monopoly profits that will accrue from success; innovation can be described as a patent race, which rewards only the first. But these profits are only temporary; after the patent has expired, other firms will start to imitate and/or will introduce new innovations. The present value of net expected returns from innovation is thus driven to zero for each firm. If the resources necessary to develop an innovation are given, the rate of innovation will gradually decrease. In order to generate permanent growth, it has to be assumed that the costs of innovation decrease with the number of innovations already produced, that is, with the stock of knowledge available in the economy. Innovation thus acts as an externality, making it easier to generate new additions to the general stock of knowledge. In this framework, long-run growth and patterns of trade specialization in any one country are explained by (1) the private incentives to investments in innovative activities, and (2) the spillover effects of current innovative activities on other countries and on future technological change.

Not surprisingly, then, much of the recent policy debate has focused on problems, such as the definition of intellectual property rights, that regulate the incentives to invest in innovative activities and the terms under which technology can diffuse throughout the world. In fact, these variables are the main determinants of the patterns of trade specialization across countries (or regions). If the diffusion of knowledge is not instantaneous or perfect, a country which has, by chance, acquired a technological advantage in a particular industry will maintain this advantage for some time – until other countries are able to get access to the new technology. As in product life-cycle theory and the new breed of North-South models, the patterns of specialization shift over time from innovators to imitators.

This characterization resembles what has become known in the literature as the "Schumpeter Mark I" model of innovation. In its extreme form, Schumpeter Mark I is characterized by "creative destruction," with technological ease of entry and major roles played by entrepreneurs and new firms in innovative activities. The innovative base continuously enlarges through the entry of new innovators and the erosion of the competitive and technological advantages of established firms. Moreover, this model implicitly embodies a linear representation of the process of innovation. According to the linear model, innovative activities start from the public and fundamental stock of knowledge generated by universities and the public research system. Firms then proceed to transform this general and generic knowledge into new processes and products, through R&D, design, marketing, and so on.

This representation has proved useful for dealing – in a simplified and analytically tractable way – with many important issues concerning the relationships between technological change, trade, and growth. Over the past two decades, however, research on innovation has cast increasingly serious doubts on the general validity of this conceptualization.

A compact and simplified way to introduce this discussion is to note that the economics of innovation supplies another, opposite model of the innovation process. "Schumpeter Mark II" is characterized by "creative accumulation": the prevalence of a few large, established firms made continuously innovative through the accumulation over time of technological and innovative capabilities (Malerba and Orsenigo 1997; Breschi et al. 1999), and the presence of relevant barriers to entry for new innovators. There may be different explanations for these patterns.

First, it has to be recognized that knowledge is different from information, in that it is partly tacit and unarticulated, i.e., not codified in blueprints, instructions, and so on. In consequence, knowledge generally cannot be acquired without exposure to practice and accumulated experience, typically specific to particular firms, regions, and countries as well as to specific applications. This property of knowledge implies that diffusion may be more difficult than the previous models assume. For example, the very process of absorbing new knowledge from outside sources may require the firm (or region, or country) to have already accumulated and internalized relevant knowledge; otherwise, it will not be able to understand and effectively absorb what has been done by others (Cohen and Levinthal 1989).

Second, in these conditions, innovation is better conceptualized as a process of learning rather than the acquisition of information, and it is likely to exhibit properties of cumulativeness. Precisely because learning occurs on the basis of what has been previously learned, both the probability of innovating again in the future and the direction of research are likely to depend on what has been done in the past. One would thus expect to observe relatively stable hierarchies of innovators and trajectories of technological progress, at least for prolonged periods and in the absence of drastic changes in the relevant knowledge base. Indeed, the explicit inclusion of aspects of cumulativeness – more generally, increasing returns – quite drastically changes the dynamics of patterns of specialization. In these conditions, when technological advantages emerge – for any reason, including pure chance – in a specific industry, in a specific country, firms of the "leading countries" will find it profitable to invest resources in that industry rather than in firms located elsewhere. Thus, technological advantages will tend to reproduce over time, and even increase, through a self-reinforcing mechanism, generating persistent patterns of specialization (Dosi et al. 1990; Krugman 1990; Grossman and Helpman 1991).

Third, in questioning the explanatory power of the linear model, it has been suggested that the process of innovation is better represented by the so-called chain-linked model (Kline and Rosenberg 1986), characterized by continuous and dense interactions between the various stages and agents involved in the process. More generally, this approach tends to emphasize that innovation cannot simply be represented as an addition of new information to an existing stock; on the contrary, it requires the integration of different fragments of (new and old) knowledge through the continuous construction and reformulation of specific ways of looking at problems.

Taken together, these assumptions form the basis of the notion that innovative agents are characterized by specific competencies: ways of looking at problems, heuristics to solve them, methods and ways for integrating knowledge. These competencies are likely to be agent-specific, difficult to imitate, and persistent over time. Competencies therefore explain why firms differ and why regions and countries show relatively stable differentials in performance in some activities but not in others.

A substantial body of empirical evidence derived from different sources and methodologies (case studies; econometric and statistical analyses of technologies, firms, industries, regions and countries) now supports this view. As well, there are theoretical models that explore the robustness and the implications of these hypotheses. Overwhelming evidence supports the view that patterns of technological specialization (of firms and countries) tend to remain stable over long periods of time (Cantwell 1989; Dosi et al. 1990). Similarly, innovative activities at the firm level tend to show high degrees of persistence: a large fraction of innovations is generated by firms that innovate continuously over time (Cefis 1996; Cefis and Orsenigo 1998; Malerba et al. 1997).[3] However, one also observes marked differences across technologies and industries (and partly across countries) in the ways technological change occurs. Malerba and Orsenigo (1997) and Breschi (1999) have shown that in some industries/technologies, the patterns of innovation resemble the Schumpeter Mark I model, whereas in others the Schumpeter Mark II model seems to prevail. Interestingly, these inter-sectoral differences are remarkably stable across countries. A given industry will almost always exhibit the Schumpeter Mark I (or Mark II) properties in countries as different as the USA, Japan, the UK, Germany, France, and Italy. This suggests that the patterns of technological change are strongly influenced by the specific properties of the technology, which are relatively invariant across countries. Specifically, Breschi et al. (1999) show that patterns of innovation are closely related to the nature of the relevant "technological regime," defined as a combination of:

- *conditions of opportunity* – how much is there to be discovered?
- *appropriability* – how difficult is it to protect the profits stemming from innovation from imitators, and what are the most relevant instruments: patents, secrecy, lead-times, etc. (Levin et al. 1987; Klevorick et al. 1993)?
- *cumulative nature of the knowledge base* – is the relevant knowledge base strongly tacit? Does it require the integration of various differentiated scientific and technical disciplines, methodologies, etc.? What are the main sources of technical knowledge?

The Sources and Loci of Competitiveness

Recognizing the complex and differentiated features of innovation processes and the knowledge they generate is extremely important in the search for the origins of competitiveness and the design of appropriate policies – if any – to improve the competitive position of countries or regions.

One of the first and obvious implications of the aforementioned evidence is that these features are likely to differ substantially across industries, according to the nature of the technological regime. Thus, general-purpose policies may have a very different impact in different sectors.

Second, and more generally, in order to understand the evolution of competitiveness (in specific industries and in specific countries), one has to examine the nature of the competencies underlying such advantages or disadvantages and identify where they are located, stored, and generated. In recent years, several such studies have been undertaken in various nations, for example, *Made in America* (Dertouzos et al. 1989), *Made in France*

(Taddei and Coriat 1993), *Made in Japan* (Yochikawa 1994), and so on. In Europe, the *White Paper on Growth, Competitiveness and Employment* (CEC 1994) and *The Innovation Green Paper* (CEC 1995) also fall into this category. More recently, a comparative study has been completed on the evolution and the performance of seven industries – chemical products, computers, software, semiconductors, pharmaceuticals and biotechnology, medical devices, machine tools – in the United States, Europe, and Japan (Mowery and Nelson 1999).

I cannot survey the results of these studies here. I shall concentrate instead on two related issues. The first concerns the proper unit of analysis. Are competencies located in firms, industries, regions, or countries? Where do other organizational levels, such as networks of individuals or firms, fit in? What is the role of specific institutions in determining competitiveness? The second question concerns the nature of such competencies. Are they essentially linked to technology or are other dimensions important? Is it possible to identify "meta-competencies" that emerge – despite the enormous variation existing across firms, industries, and countries – as key and general determinants of competitiveness?

The issue of the locus of competencies is old and obviously related to the characterization of the nature of the relevant knowledge and competencies used. Starting with Alfred Chandler's work (Chandler 1992), one strand of interpretation considers firms as the main repository of competencies and the main source of competitiveness. Specific firms are instrumental in generating new industries, through particular technological and organizational innovations. Such firms often remain leaders for long periods of time through continuing technological and organizational change. An industry develops around these core firms, creating supporting institutions and networks of relationships with customers, suppliers, and public institutions such as research centres and regulatory bodies. A somewhat similar account can be found in various theories of product or industry life cycles, at least in the sense that firms are the primary unit of analysis and that industry evolution is characterized by strong first-mover advantages (Utterback and Abernathy 1975; Klepper 1996).

In other interpretations, it is not firms per se that matter but groups of firms located in specific geographical areas, whether regions or nations. Here, competitiveness arises from the network of relationships and institutions that links agents together. In its simplest versions, the network is defined essentially on a geographical basis, on the assumptions that transportation costs are relevant. In more sophisticated interpretations, the spatial nature of the network derives from the observation that knowledge spillovers occur more easily at the local level, due to physical proximity that facilitates continuous interactions among agents, prompting shared experiences and cultures and the emergence of trust. This interpretation finds its origins in the Marshallian concept of industrial district and emphasizes the role of local externalities that derive from the processes of accumulation of knowledge. In its extreme forms, one finds this idea at the basis of the so-called "alternative approaches to industrialization" (Piore and Sabel 1984; Sabel and Zeitlin 1997) and in the literature on industrial districts in Italy and elsewhere (Becattini 1993; Saxenian 1994). More generally, this conceptualization is at the root of most of modern "regional economics," including Krugman (1990). There is indeed overwhelming evidence that spillovers have a strong local character (Jaffe 1989; Jaffe et al. 1993; Feldman 1994; Saxenian 1994) and that the local dimension is often crucial in the formation and reproduction of specific competencies and competitive advantages.

A third interpretation emphasizes the national level. Here, the role of specific institutions like the educational system, the financial system, national cultural traits, and specific styles of public policy are stressed. The literature on "national systems of innovation" (Nelson 1992) constitutes one well-known version of this approach, in which certain industries in certain countries are strong because they benefit from country-specific institutional arrangements. The competitiveness of the American computer and pharmaceutical industries, for example, originates not in the history of specific firms but in a general institutional environment that facilitates the emergence and development of "high-tech" industries: the existence of a strong academic research base, the research system's flexibility and readiness to collaborate with industry, the availability of venture capital, and so on. In the same vein, one would emphasize the role played by vocational training in explaining the persistent competitiveness of the German mechanical and chemical industries.

The question about the locus of competencies might appear, at first sight, as an idle academic exercise. One finds in the literature, however, evidence and cases supporting each of these approaches. For example, the comparative study mentioned earlier (Mowery and Nelson 1999) suggests that, in industries such as chemical products and pharmaceuticals, much of what makes for competitiveness is located substantially in the firms. In these industries, virtually all of the leading firms are long established: they have built and solidified their advantages over time through their own investment and learning. In other sectors, such as computer software and hardware and medical devices, higher rates of turnover among dominant firms are observed, but the shifting collection of leaders consists mainly of those headquartered in the US, suggesting that competitiveness factors in these industries reside at the level of the nation state. In machine tools, firms from a single nation have dominated different segments at various points in time, but in recent years neither the firm-level nor national locus has endured. German and American dominance during the 1950s and 1960s was challenged and largely overturned by firms from Japan and Taiwan.

Moreover, the importance of national (or local) institutions is often highly specific to particular sectors. Although they are embedded in and supported by broader national institutions, in many cases the key sectoral institutions have a structure and life of their own. The academic research and training infrastructure supporting the pharmaceutical and medical devices sectors is profoundly different from the one behind the computer, semiconductor, and software sectors. Similarly, the venture capital firms operating in these industries are quite different from those focusing on pharmaceutical bio-technology. In each sector, the specialized venture capital firms are knit into the complex networks that link firms, universities, and professional societies. In some cases, these sectoral innovation systems are concentrated in particular regions. In other cases, they are not.

One might simply conclude that all these levels are important, and that it is necessary to consider them all, perhaps judging their relative role on a case-by-case basis. Each, however, bears important implications in terms of both interpretation and policymaking. At the heart of the matter are pro-foundly different views of what defines competencies and how the process of construction-reproduction-diffusion of such competencies occurs. At the cost of drastic oversimplification, these approaches assign, first of all, a rela-tively different emphasis on the construction of competencies vis-à-vis the processes of diffusion of knowledge – or, putting it another way, on dy-namic increasing returns as opposed to externalities. Second, they imply profoundly different characterizations of agents' behaviour. Both processes are important.

In the first interpretation (the firm level), for instance, competencies are viewed essentially as deriving from processes of new knowledge creation and from the integration of such knowledge into a relatively coherent or-ganizational structure. Such processes are typically characterized by some form of static and dynamic increasing returns. Firms here are characterized as "boundedly rational" and with limited capabilities, but are nevertheless able to learn and produce novelty in a less than purely random fashion. Their behaviour, their "successes" and failures, are thus important in ex-plaining the evolution of competitiveness. Conversely, the second interpre-tation (the regional level) focuses more on processes of diffusion. Externalities matter most, and increasing returns are important mainly when they de-rive from network externalities, i.e., from interactions among agents, often independent of a detailed reconstruction or description of their actions. At the same time, agents are usually conceived as rational, at least in the sense that they are able to calculate the results of their actions and to strategize (even if in relatively simple contexts) about the behaviour of others.[4] Fi-nally, in the third interpretation (the national level), individual actions may well be irrelevant: microbehaviours are essentially determined by macro constraints/incentives, embodied in the institutional environment.

One way to start dealing with these issues is to recognize first that competencies are inherently embedded in social relationships and institutional environments, which define the incentives and constraints for individual actors, and the general logics of their behaviour. Moreover, one observes a complex interaction between the performance of firms and the nature of the institutional environment in which they operate. In pharmaceuticals, the support provided by the National Institutes of Health (NIH) for research and training in the biomedical sciences created considerable opportunities for US-based firms. Nevertheless, many of these firms displayed considerable skill in exploiting such opportunities. American companies have long supported growth in the NIH budget for biomedical research and training. American biotechnology firms have been involved in the formulation of policies on intellectual property rights and federal funding of academic research.

In a less Panglossian approach, therefore, micro-level entities learn, but sector-specific knowledge bases, local institutions, and patterns of social relations restrict and channel the possible evolutionary trajectories. Moreover, microbehaviours influence, change, and sometimes generate entirely new macro-level entities, such as sectoral systems and institutions. In other words, organizational forms, technologies, and institutions co-evolve. While this does not amount to the full development of a theory of the co-evolution of these different levels, these perspectives look rich and challenging, and early attempts in this direction have begun to yield promising preliminary results (Coriat and Dosi 1995; Dosi and Fagiolo 1998; Malerba et al. 1999).

The Locus of Competitiveness in a Globalized Arena

This discussion links naturally with another strand of the debate about the sources and effects of globalization. It is often remarked that the process of globalization is characterized by an increased ease of diffusion of innovations and knowledge through different countries. In part, this is because the diffusion of information technology makes knowledge easy and cheap to codify and transmit. A related assumption is that innovative activities are becoming increasingly globalized, with firms conducting their R&D efforts simultaneously in different countries and/or participating in international networks of collaborative research. In this context, the codification and growing accessibility of knowledge stimulates an increasing vertical division of labour in the innovative process. Some firms specialize in the generation of (codified) and general-purpose knowledge that is then transferred to other companies specialized in the development of new, specific products and processes. More generally, does globalization imply a redefinition of the sources and loci of innovation? In this respect, both the theoretical debate and the empirical evidence are mixed and sometimes confused.

There are at least three different aspects to the process of globalization of innovation (Archibugi and Michie 1995).

A first dimension relates to the international exploitation of national technology. This is certainly not a new phenomenon, but there is strong evidence that it has significantly increased in recent times. A second dimension concerns international collaboration. As Rao and Hirshhorn point out in their chapter in this volume, know-how is increasingly shared with competitors from different countries as well as between government research agencies and the academic community. This category is also less novel than is usually considered, but again data suggest that collaboration between companies has experienced a boost during the 1980s (Hagedoorn and Soete 1991). This phenomenon, however, appears to be largely confined to a few, albeit crucial, new expanding technological fields, such as information technologies, biotechnology, and new materials (and, to a lesser extent, chemicals). These fields are particularly technology-intensive, and successful innovative performance relies heavily on the ability to monitor and acquire knowledge, which is expanding at an accelerated rate. In these circumstances, no individual firm may hope to be able to control new technological developments on its own. The increase in international technological collaboration thus reflects, at least partly, the growing role of these technological fields, rather than a radical change in the possibilities and propensity to collaborate.

A related factor has to do with a process of widening, rather than deepening, of the knowledge base required to generate new products and processes. Not only do opportunities for innovation increase rapidly in some fields but their exploitation also requires the mastery of vastly differentiated scientific and technical disciplines that have to be integrated and made complementary. Ample evidence of these phenomena can be found, both for specific industries and for large companies worldwide. Grandstand et al. (1997), Cantwell (1995), and Cantwell and Fai (1998) have produced convincing evidence that while the degree of technological diversification (as opposed to product diversification) in large firms was already significant in the 1930s, it has increased again in recent years. These results suggest a growing interrelatedness between formerly distinct fields of technology and types of products that are increasingly multi-technology. In the period 1930-60, technological diversification was mainly the result of processes of product diversification. In the period 1960-99, on the other hand, technological diversification is perceived by firms as a purposeful tool used to enhance growth in a narrower range of products, by identifying and exploiting the complementarities that technological interrelatedness supplies (Cantwell and Fai 1998).

A third dimension of the processes of technological globalization relates to what has been called the global generation of technologies by firms:

strategies for generating innovations, through the development of global research networks, made feasible by the new information networks. This dimension is the technological equivalent of foreign direct investment (Archibugi and Michie 1995). In this case, the evidence is far less robust than in the two previous instances. If anything, this trend seems to be confined to a relatively small number of large multinational corporations operating in a small number of countries. Even here, the technological links between firms and their home country remain strong, while the evidence for an inherent tendency to spread technological activities around the globe is scanty and restricted to a small number of technological fields (such as pharmaceuticals) (Pavitt and Patel 1991). Finally, processes of "global generation of technologies" appear to have had little impact on the patterns of national technological specialization. If anything, nations are becoming increasingly differentiated and multinational corporations are exploiting and developing this diversity (Archibugi and Michie 1995). In sum, the evidence does not seem to support the thesis of an increasing globalization of technology.

One way of interpreting these results relates to the question raised earlier about the nature of the competencies on which competitiveness is based. The evidence discussed so far seems to question any sharp distinction between processes of creation and processes of diffusion of knowledge. The two appear to be strongly related and governed by similar cognitive and organizational principles. In particular, the processes of innovation-diffusion appear to be linked to the ability to identify and exploit, through specific organizational devices, the complementarities among differentiated fragments of knowledge, i.e., what might be loosely defined as "organizational capabilities" (Nelson 1991; Chandler 1997). Certainly, codification makes it easier to access some knowledge. But any act of codification generates new opportunities for innovation, new complementarities, new possibilities for division of labour, and new tacit knowledge. Codified and tacit knowledge still need to be integrated, but one is tempted to conjecture that organizational capabilities provide one of the main ingredients of competencies and one source of innovative capabilities and technological competitiveness.

Organizational and Integrative Capabilities: The European Paradox

An illustration of what organizational capabilities might mean at the "macro" level is offered by the recent debate on the so-called European paradox. Recent research shows that Europe, taken as a whole, does not really lag behind in basic research or R&D. Rather, the specific European weakness (as measured by the dynamics of growth of GDP, foreign trade, investment rates, and employment) appears to lie in the transformation of research into innovation and ultimately into marketable products (Coriat 1995).

Moreover, the competitive gap between Europe on the one hand and Japan and the United States on the other appears to be relatively recent, roughly coinciding with the exhaustion of the process of technological catch-up with the US and the diffusion of new organizational practices at the firm level. This is not a new suggestion. In many cases, however, the main solution recommended is to increase R&D expenditures.

While it is unlikely that increased rates of R&D expenditures would hurt European competitiveness, the European paradox suggests that the bulk of the problem lies in organizational aspects of the process of innovation, more precisely in a deficit of organizational capabilities at different levels of analysis. I shall limit my discussion to two examples.

The first concerns the observed gap in the rate of adoption and successful adaptation of organizational innovations in R&D, production, and human resources management, following the emergence of post-Fordism. The study by Andreasen et al. (1995) constitutes an important first step in documenting this gap, assessing its impact on competitiveness, and articulating a conceptual framework for analysing these issues. In particular, this study emphasizes the critical importance in organizational change of integration at different levels: between the different functions within each of the three spheres mentioned above (R&D, production, and human resources management); between different organizational practices in each of the three spheres (for example, design and production); and between the firm and its external environment.

This study provides a new perspective on the sources of competitiveness and on the possible reasons for the deterioration of European competitiveness. It also emphasizes the role played by processes of integration and integrative capabilities in determining innovative performance. As well, it points to new policy interventions that do not necessarily imply exclusive government support or that such support should take the form of financial subsidies. Rather, the experiences documented in the study suggest extensive scope for joint public/private initiatives, involving the services sector and educational institutions, and multiple levels of public agencies. It stresses also that the emphasis on organizational innovation is strictly linked to a definition of competitiveness that explicitly includes dimensions such as employment and social issues. The Andreasen et al. (1995) study shows quite clearly that successful organizational innovation involves and requires improvements in social relations, the quality of work, and investment in infrastructures and human resources. The quest for increased competitiveness not only does not necessarily conflict with objectives such as employment, wage levels, and quality of work but also tends to promote them.

This study is focused at the level of the firm. While it emphasizes the systemic nature of the required organizational change, it offers neither a complete explanation of the reasons for the unsuccessful performance of European firms in this respect nor a fully fledged analysis of the interactions between the company sector and other institutions. Clearly, much challenging work remains to be done in this area.

The second example tries to partially fill these gaps; it concerns industry-university relations. In recent years, universities in Europe have faced increasing demands to make a more direct contribution to industrial innovation and economic development. To a large extent, these demands result from observation of the American experience. Over the past 15 years, the US academic system has developed a remarkable entrepreneurial attitude. In many cases, universities have been fundamental engines of innovation and economic growth, directly contributing to the birth of new firms and industries. In other cases, they have been key agents in the process of restructuring old industrialized areas undergoing economic decline. In the US these trends have sparked debate about the appropriateness of increasing university involvement in commercial activities. In Europe, however – especially continental Europe – it is widely recognized that a significant gap exists between industry and the academic system. One thus observes a mushrooming of initiatives aimed at establishing stronger links between industry and universities and to encourage a more entrepreneurial attitude on the part of the universities.

Often, pressures favouring a more applied orientation of academic research are voiced, jointly with generic encouragement to scientists to go out into the "real world" and take a more entrepreneurial approach. While the juridical and legal structure regulating the duties of university professors discourages them from engaging in economic activity, in practice policies have been targeted towards the set-up of specific organizational devices to manage technology transfer. These include science and technology parks; diffusion of information about academic research, licensing, and liaison offices; and so on. The initiatives have taken a wide variety of forms and show a mixed performance record. The outcome of science park initiatives, for example, is usually considered to be small compared with expectations, even in successful cases.

These actions often reflect some form of the previously mentioned "linear model" of the innovation process.[5] There is now substantial evidence, though, that both the role of universities in industry and the mechanisms through which spillovers occur are much more complex across scientific disciplines and technologies, across countries, and over time than this description allows. Universities perform different functions for industry that have continuously increased over this century. Teaching, technical assistance to local industries, and the production of scientific knowledge are the traditional functions. More recently, and mainly in the US, universities have become direct promoters of economic activities through the commercialization of their research results, the generation of spin-offs, and closer collaboration with industry.

Also, the mechanisms through which scientific knowledge flows to industry are differentiated and complex, and certainly far from automatic. First, the relevance of academic research and the mechanisms through which such knowledge is transmitted vary greatly across scientific disciplines, technologies, and industries (Rosenberg and Nelson 1994). Second, spillovers from university to industry are often local and geographically bounded (Jaffe 1989). Third, the cognitive processes through which science influences the processes of innovation within firms are extremely complex and specific to different sciences. They require, on the firms' side, at least three types of competencies and capabilities: absorbing the new knowledge created outside the industry (Cohen and Levinthal 1989), exploring an expanding set of opportunities (through close links with the scientific community), and integrating different new and old scientific disciplines (Henderson 1994). More generally, the processes of interaction between industry and universities (and other research institutions) can hardly be conceptualized as a "simple" process of "knowledge transfer." Rather, it is a process of collective learning, which involves the development of specific organizational and integrative capabilities to manage the complementarities between the various types and fragments of knowledge.

The process of constructing such capabilities entails, at the same time, a cognitive aspect in the development of specific organizational competencies, and the design of specific incentive and power structures within firms: in short, organizational capabilities. Again, at stake here is the ability to integrate different spheres that are not necessarily consistent at the outset, and that are likely to evolve along diverging trajectories.

The emphasis on the organizational capabilities required to manage industry-university interactions applies not only to industrial firms but also to academic institutions. In Europe, many consider that the lack of flexibility and managerial capabilities of universities and academic researchers constitutes a major hindrance to the development of stronger industry-university ties. Simplification of the bureaucratic rules constraining researchers, introduction of increasing degrees of autonomy within the national academic systems, and the infusion of appropriate incentives to researchers to engage in activities closer to industrial needs and to acquire managerial attitudes are often (but not uncontroversially) claimed to be necessary and urgent steps.

But why does such a gap exist between academic institutions and industry in continental Europe compared with the US? And why is it so difficult to fill this gap? Comparative history and sociology of academic systems suggests that deeper changes than bureaucratic simplification and the introduction of incentives may be required in the structure and organization of universities if the situation is to improve. This literature suggests that one important determinant of the divergence between the continental European and Anglo-Saxon academic research systems in their attitude towards collaboration with industry is to be found in their different deep structures and organization – particularly concerning the degree of integration of teaching and learning (Ben-David 1977; Clarke 1983; Braun 1994).

Indeed, one of the main differences between the two academic systems is the higher degree of integration of teaching and research that has characterized the American (and, to some extent, the British) system since the end of the last century, together with their higher degree of professional orientation towards advanced scientific training.

These differences are expressed not only in the structure of curricula but also in the organization of the universities. Specifically, in the US and Great Britain departments have long been the main organizational entities. In contrast, the European institutes, dominated by a single professor, are far less interdisciplinary in nature. Moreover, integration of teaching and learning has been achieved to a much larger extent in the US than in continental Europe, through the sharp separation between undergraduate and postgraduate levels. The creation of research-oriented, postgraduate studies entailed a number of important consequences. In particular, postgraduate students are typically exposed to and trained in the practice of scientific research in research teams of students and professors within departmental organizations. This arrangement not only tends to free resources for scientific research but also provides a fundamental experience in participating in and managing relatively complex organizations. In other words, it constitutes an essential source for the development of organizational capabilities. Moreover, graduate students joining the industrial world after completing their studies constitute an essential source of skilled demand for academic research.

The coupling between scientific and organizational capabilities constitutes, in my view, an essential precondition for subsequent developments in industry-university relations. The development of an entrepreneurial function within universities has not subordinated the other, more traditional functions. Rather, as with teaching, it appears to be strongly complementary to and integrated with them. The US experience would seem to suggest that linkages with industry cannot develop without the constant mediation of teaching. Teaching produces demand for relationships and is an important source of absorptive capabilities within firms.

In continental Europe, the integration of teaching with research is less advanced than in the US (and, to some extent, in Britain). Clearly, enormous differences in educational systems, especially in higher education, exist across continental European countries, and these certainly should not be overlooked. For example, in France universities have never been the main centres of scientific research, which is essentially conducted within the national laboratories and coordinated by the CNRS (National Centre for Scientific Research). Nor have they been centres for the education of the elites, which is monopolized by the system of the *grandes écoles*. In Germany the "institute" – dominated by an individual professor – has been the main organizational unit coordinating teaching and research. Moreover, while Germany has developed an extremely efficient intermediate level of integrated teaching and practice in applied disciplines such as engineering (the "Fachhochschulen"), these largely overlook fundamental research.

Despite differences, however, academic systems in many European countries share some important common structural features when compared with the Anglo-Saxon systems. Ph.D.s are a relatively recent innovation in many continental European countries, and they remain far less professionally oriented than in the US. Departmental structures are also relatively new, and in many cases institutes continue to be a very important organizational entity. In general, research has tended to be far more removed from teaching than in the US. And in many continental European countries, research has to a large extent been separated from universities and concentrated in specialized institutions. At the cost of oversimplification, the emerging European model is based on high degrees of division of labour and specialization between teaching and research institutions, whereas in the US the dominant model integrates teaching and research.

This separation in the European system might have had negative effects on both the quality of research and, importantly, the ability of academic institutions to interact with industry. Integration of research and teaching, and collaboration with industry, was relatively more developed and frequent in engineering schools (the continental European polytechnics) and in selected disciplines in particular countries (e.g., chemistry in Germany). Events in the 1960s and 1970s, however, further weakened university-industry interaction: the development of mass academic education, the scientific revolutions linked mainly to microelectronics and molecular biology, and the crisis of the traditional industries mainly connected with the polytechnics. To remedy this gap, the "specialized model" has in more recent years again been widely proposed for managing interactions between research and industry, and technology transfer. In contrast to the situation in the US, where universities have gradually extended their functions (an integrated model centred on universities), in continental Europe various types of specialized institutions for technology transfer have been developed, which act as intermediaries between research and industry (the institutional specialization model).

Paradoxically, however, the presence of large-scale intermediary institutions may have increased the distance between university and industry –

introducing an additional layer in the relationship instead of favouring the direct development of necessary organizational and integrative capabilities within firms and academic institutions.

Conclusion

The basic argument of this chapter is that competitiveness ultimately resides in organizational competencies within firms, sectors, regions, and countries. Even if the diffusion of technological knowledge becomes easier and faster in globalized markets, the ability to exploit it requires the development of specific capabilities to integrate increasingly differentiated and heterogeneous fragments of knowledge, spheres of action, incentives, and power structures. These processes take place simultaneously at different levels of analysis (firms, sectors, regions, and countries), are highly specific, and are intrinsically tacit in nature.

The focus on organizational capabilities at different levels of analysis might contribute to our understanding of what the loci of competitiveness are, and what level of policymaking might be appropriate in any specific circumstance. An explicit recognition of the need to incorporate such diversity between levels of analysis and relevant agents is a crucial element of these policies. The emphasis on organizational capabilities contributes also to the development of a wider notion of competitiveness, extending beyond cost factors and R&D strictly defined, as well as trade performance and perhaps growth. Rather, it suggests that a satisfactory definition of competitiveness also includes employment and social relations.

Notes

1 This chapter is based on a paper prepared for the EU/Canada Conference on "Transition to the Knowledge Society – Policies and Strategies for Individual Participation and Learning," Vancouver, 4-6 November 1998. The author wishes to thank Felicia Fai for her support. The usual disclaimers apply.
2 Instead of cost competitiveness, it is also possible to use a notion based on price competitiveness, using the concept of real exchange rates.
3 Geroski et al. (1996), using a somewhat different data set and different econometric procedures, arrive at different conclusions. They show that only a very small percentage of firms innovate persistently over time. However, these few firms account for a very large fraction of total innovations.
4 Note that these assumptions are shared even in radically different approaches, as in the more formally oriented literature on local interactions and percolation models (David and Foray 1994; Cowan and Foray 1995) and in the Sabel and Zeitlin (1997) approach.
5 What follows rests heavily on Orsenigo (1998).

References

Amendola, G., G. Dosi, and E. Papagni. 1994. *The Dynamics of International Competitiveness.* Weltwirtshaftliches Archiv.
Andreasen, L.A., B. Coriat, F. den Hartog, and R. Kaplinsky, eds. 1995. *Europe's Next Step: Organisational Innovation, Competition and Employment.* London: Frank Cass.
Archibugi, D., and J. Michie. 1995. "The Globalisation of Technology: A New Taxonomy." *Cambridge Journal of Economics* 19,1: 121-40.

Archibugi, D., and M. Pianta. 1992. *The Technological Specialization of Advanced Countries.* Boston: Kluwer Academic Publishers.

Becattini, G., ed. 1993. *Prato: Storia di una città, vol. IV: Il distretto industriale (1943-1993).* Firenze: Le Monnier.

Ben-David, J. 1977. *Centers of Learning – Britain, France, Germany, United States.* New York: McGraw-Hill.

Braun, Dietmar. 1994. *Structure and Dynamics of Health Research and Public Funding.* Dordrecht, Netherlands: Kluwer.

Breschi, S., F. Malerba, and L. Orsenigo. Forthcoming. "Technological Regimes and Schumpeterian Patterns of Innovation." *Economic Journal.*

Cantwell, J. 1989. *Technological Innovation and Multinational Corporations.* Oxford: Basil Blackwell.

–. 1995. "The Globalisation of Technology: What Remains of the Product Cycle Model?" *Cambridge Journal of Economics* 19,1: 155-74.

Cantwell, J., and F. Fai. 1997. *The Changing Nature of Corporate Technological Diversification and the Importance of Organisational Capability.* Discussion Paper in Economics and Management, Series A, Vol. 10, No. 376. Reading, UK: University of Reading, Department of Economics.

CEC (Commission of the European Communities). 1994. *White Paper on Growth, Competitiveness and Employment.* Luxembourg.

–. 1995. *The Innovation Green Paper.* Luxembourg.

Cefis, E. 1996. *Is There Any Persistence in Innovative Activities?* Discussion Paper No. 6, University of Trento, Department of Economics.

Cefis, E., and L. Orsenigo. 1998. *The Persistence of Innovative Activities: A Cross-Countries and Cross-Sectors Comparative Analysis.* Discussion Paper No. 4, University of Trento, Department of Economics.

Chandler, A.D. 1992. "Organisational Capabilities and the Economic History of the Industrial Enterprise." *Journal of Economic Perspectives* 6,3: 79-100.

Clark, B.R. 1983. *The Higher Education System and Organization in Cross-National Perspective.* Berkeley, CA: University of California Press.

–. 1995. *Places of Inquiry – Research and Advanced Education in Modern Universities.* Berkeley, CA: University of California Press.

Cohen, W., and D. Levinthal. 1989. "Innovation and Learning: The Two Faces of R&D." *Economic Journal* 99,397: 569-96.

Coriat, B. 1997. "The New Dimensions of Competitiveness." *The IPTS Report,* Seville, No. 15.

Coriat, B., and G. Dosi. 1995. *Learning How to Govern and Learning How to Solve Problems: On the Co-Evolution of Competencies, Conflicts and Organizational Routines.* IIASA Working Paper No. 95-06. Laxenburg, Austria.

Council on Competitiveness of the United States. 1992. *Annual Report.* Washington, DC.

Cowan, R., and D. Foray. 1995. "The Economics of Codification and the Diffusion of Knowledge." *Industrial and Corporate Change* 6,3: 595-622.

David, P., and D. Foray. 1994. "Dynamics of Competitive Technology Diffusion Through Local Network Structures." In L.A. Leydesdorff and P. Van den Besselaar, eds., *Evolutionary Economics and Chaos Theory.* London: Pinter.

Dertouzos, M., R. Lester, and R. Solow. 1989. *Made in America. Regaining the Productive Edge.* Cambridge, MA: MIT Press.

Dosi, G., and G. Fagiolo. 1998. "Exploring the Unknown. On Entrepreneurship, Coordination and Innovation-Driven Growth." In J. Lesourne and A. Orlean, eds., *Advances in Self-Organization and Evolutionary Economics.* Paris: Economica.

Dosi, G., K. Pavitt, and L. Soete. 1990. *The Economics of Technical Change and International Trade.* New York: Harvester Wheatsheaf.

Fagerberg, J. 1988. "International Competitiveness." *Economic Journal* 98 (June): 355-74.

Feldman, M. 1994. *The Geography of Innovation.* Boston: Kluwer Academic Publishers.

Geroski, P.A., J. Van Reenen, and C.F. Walters. 1996. "How Persistently Do Firms Innovate?" *Research Policy* 25.

Granstand, O., P. Patel, and K. Pavitt. 1997. "Multi-Technology Corporations: Why They Have 'Distributed' Rather than 'Distinctive Core' Competencies." *California Management Review* 39: 8-25.

Grossman, G., and E. Helpman. 1991. *Innovation and Growth in the Global Economy*. Cambridge, MA: MIT Press.

Hagedoorn, J., and L. Soete. 1991. "The Internationalisation of Science and Technology Policy: How Do National Systems Cope?" In National Institute for Science and Technology Policy, *Science and Technology Policy Research*. Tokyo: Mita Press.

Henderson, R. 1994. "The Evolution of Integrative Capability: Innovation in Cardiovascular Drug Discovery." *Industrial and Corporate Change* 3,3: 607-31.

Jaffe, A. 1989. "Real Effects of Academic Research." *American Economic Review* 79,5: 957-70.

Jaffe, A., R. Henderson, and M. Trajtenberg. 1993. "Geographic Localization of Knowledge Spillovers as Evidenced by Patent Citations." *Quarterly Journal of Economics* 63,3: 577-98.

Klepper, S. 1996. "Entry, Exit and Innovation over the Product Life Cycle." *American Economic Review* 86,3: 562-82.

Klevorick, A., R. Levin, R. Nelson, and S. Winter. 1993. *On the Sources and Significance of Interindustry Differences in Technological Opportunity*. Cowles Foundation Discussion Paper No. 1052. New Haven, CT: Cowles Foundation for Research in Economics at Yale University.

Kline, S.J., and N. Rosenberg. 1986. "An Overview of Innovation." In R. Landau and N. Rosenberg, eds., *The Positive Sum Strategy*. Washington, DC: National Academy Press.

Krugman, P. 1990. *Rethinking International Trade*. Cambridge, MA: MIT Press.

Levin, R., A. Klevorick, R. Nelson, and S. Winter. 1987. "Appropriating the Returns from Industrial R&D." *Brookings Papers on Economic Activities*. Washington, DC: Brookings Institution.

Malerba, F., R. Nelson, L. Orsenigo, and S. Winter. Forthcoming. "'History-Friendly' Models of Industry Evolution: The Computer Industry." *Industrial and Corporate Change*.

Malerba, F., and L. Orsenigo. 1997. "Technological Regimes and Sectoral Patterns of Innovative Activities." In G. Dosi, F. Malerba, and L. Orsenigo, eds., *Industrial and Corporate Change, Special Issue on Technological Regimes and the Evolution of Industrial Structures*. London: Macmillan.

Malerba, F., L. Orsenigo, and P. Peretto. 1997. "Persistence and Heterogeneity of Innovative Activities, Sectoral Patterns of Innovation and International Technological Specialization." *The International Journal of Industrial Organization* 15.

Mowery, D., and R. Nelson, eds. Forthcoming. *The Sources of Industrial Leadership*. Cambridge, UK: Cambridge University Press.

Nelson, R. 1991. "Why Do Firms Differ and How Does It Matter?" *Strategic Management Journal* 12: 61-74.

–, ed. 1992. *National Systems of Innovation*. Oxford: Oxford University Press.

Orsenigo, L. 1998. "I Rapporti Università-Industria in Italia." *Quaderni della Fondazione Agnelli*. Torino.

Orsenigo, L., F. Pammolli, A. Bonaccorsi, M. Riccaboni, and G. Turchetti. 1988. "The Dynamics of Knowledge and the Evolution of an Industry Network." *Journal of Management and Governance*.

Patel, P., and K. Pavitt. 1991. "Large Firms in the Production of World's Technology: An Important Case of Non-Globalisation." *Journal of International Business Studies* 22,1.

Piore, M., and C. Sabel. 1984. *The Second Industrial Divide: Possibilities for Prosperity*. New York: Basic Books.

Posner, M. 1961. "International Trade and Technical Change." *Oxford Economic Papers* 13: 531-56.

Romer, P. 1990. "Endogenous Technological Change." *Journal of Political Economy* 98: S71-S102.

Rosenberg, N., and R. Nelson. 1994. "American Universities and Technical Advance in Industry." *Research Policy* 23: 323-48.

Sabel, C., and J. Zeitlin. 1997. *World of Possibilities: Flexibility and Mass Production in Western Industrialization*. Cambridge, UK: Cambridge University Press.

Saxenian, A. 1994. *Regional Advantage: Culture and Competition in Silicon Valley and Route 128*. Cambridge, MA: Harvard University Press.

Taddei, D., and B. Coriat, eds. 1993. *Made in France. L'industrie française dans la competition mondiale*. Paris: Hachette, Le livre de Poche.

Utterback, J., and W.J. Abernathy. 1975. "A Dynamic Model of Product and Process Innovation." *Omega* 3: 639-56.

Vernon, R. 1966. "International Investment and International Trade in the Product Cycle." *Quarterly Journal of Economics* 80,2: 190-207.

Yochikawa, ed. 1994. *Made in Japan*. Tokyo: The Japan Techno-Economic Society.

Part 3
Work in the Knowledge Economy

9
Employment in a Knowledge-Based Economy
Pascal Petit[1]

How does employment change in economies where information and knowledge play an increasing role? The growing importance of skilled labour in contemporary technological change constitutes a major shift from the previous phase, in which mechanical automation increased demands for unskilled work. This chapter analyses the underlying causes of the shift from both the demand-side and supply-side perspectives of labour. Such an analysis will enable us to appreciate both the transitory and the durable aspects of these contemporary evolutions, as well as the policy implications of both perspectives.

Technological Change and Employment: Challenging the Past Virtuous Cycle of Cumulative Causation
Taking accurate stock of the effects of technological change on employment is always a complex matter. Doing so makes little sense in the short term, precisely because technological change alters the structure of employment as time passes. In the longer term, the context changes so much, multiplying the interdependencies, that it becomes impossible to pinpoint the causal links. This is the first conclusion one must draw from the grand debate of the 19th century concerning the destructive impact of machines on employment (and on the compensation theory). Further, in the second half of the 20th century, we have seen that lasting technological change can be accompanied by general growth in employment, and therefore drawing up a balance sheet of the effects has become less pressing. The last decade, however, has made the issue somewhat more topical, less in terms of employment volume than in job structure and quality. Consider the diverse employment paths followed by different countries. Although the overall levels of technological development are similar, some countries developed mass unemployment while others increased the number of low-paying jobs (as in the United States). This suggests that it is the level of employment, rather than its structure, that is affected.

This may relate to the nature of technological change today, which mobilizes common knowledge and individual skills in a new way. The central role played by information and communication technologies (ICTs) perhaps signals the advent of a new relationship between people and machines both at work and elsewhere. Some economists may view this in terms of a new complementarity between technological change and vocational skills, in contrast to past perceptions of technology as a replacement for skilled labour (cf. the 1950s debates on deskilling and increasing mechanization of productive processes).

The changes under way today are not that simple, but there is no denying that technological change is interacting with the process of economic growth in a new way. The chain reaction of technological change → productivity → growth → employment that had a positive impact in the period of strong growth after the Second World War has now been interrupted. While the positive chain reaction led people to associate technological change with an increase in the number of jobs, this relationship may no longer hold. To begin with, as the Solow paradox suggests, the link between technological change and increasing productivity is not as perceptible as it was, weakening the link between productivity increases and economic growth. There has been no more than a faint correlation between these variables in the 1990s. More sophisticated estimations from simulations of interdependent macroeconomic models (such as the Organization for Economic Cooperation and Development's Interlink) indicate that productivity increases have only a weak impact on economic growth[2] and the reduction of unemployment. Beyond this mixed outcome for OECD countries, international comparisons clearly show that the job content of growth differs markedly between the United States, where it is large, and the European countries, where it is rather small.

This takes us back to the old debate about the quality of the jobs created (differences in the job content of growth) and to the organizational problems created by the paradox of low increases in productivity. Added to this are the problems that can arise when measuring different variables in real terms. Productivity indicators need to be based on real-term measurements of production volumes and other factors, something difficult to establish, by definition, in times of major product innovation; the upheavals hamper comparison because many products are no longer of the same kind.[3]

Such questions of organizational and structural change invite us to turn away from the blurred image we see at macroeconomic level and focus instead on the intermediate meso-economic level. Here we may find ways of explaining the employment dynamics of technological change today. At this level, the sectoral dimension appears to be crucial in all developed countries. The employment dynamics of industrial activity and services differ to such an extent that we must take the sectoral dimension into account as a matter of course. On this basis, one can examine and question several major features of current job market trends, in particular the trend towards more-skilled jobs.

Employment Growth Varies Markedly from One Sector to Another

There is a marked contrast between industrial activities and services. In the former, the overall number of jobs has dropped or at best stagnated over the past two decades. In the services sector, however, the same period has seen a clear rise in overall employment, despite the slow pace of economic growth compared with previous decades. The phenomenon is well known. It stands out not so much on account of its universal nature (it occurs in every country) but mainly because of the visible differences that develop between industrial activities and services.

Not all industrial activities have experienced a decline or stagnation in jobs. In the sectors producing new technologies (electronics, biotechnology, pharmaceuticals, and new materials), employment has shown a slight tendency to rise, whereas in the traditional industries (shipbuilding, textiles, and iron and steel) the downward path has prevailed. Similarly, in services employment growth has been comparatively modest in the spheres of transport and communications and even in commerce or government services.[4] By contrast, between 1970 and 1993 the number of jobs more than doubled in the financial, hotel and catering, social services, and business

Figure 1

Sectoral differences in employment changes in Europe, 1986-96 (variations in %)

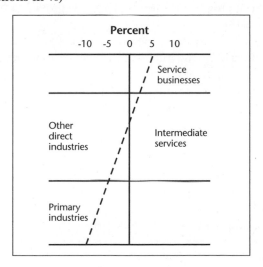

Source: European Commission (1997).

services sectors. A short summary of the sectoral structure of employment changes[5] can be found in Figure 1.

These variations are as interesting as they are novel and relate to the last two decades. In the 1950s and 1960s, industrial employment increased overall, with expanding sectors more than compensating for job losses in declining fields; now the situation is reversed. In the services sector, overall employment growth has been maintained, but not in quite the same sectors. In the major service networks, such as transportation, communications, or commerce, employment growth has remained modest overall, while in social and business services growth has been sustained (a new trend, particularly for the latter). These differences in employment trends in the services sector stem from major structural changes during the period in question. In particular, outsourcing of tertiary tasks (peripheral tasks or new specialized services) has increased, stimulating the development of business services.[6]

All the services in question are affected by the new technologies, whether the sector is expanding or declining. Of course, some specialized business services go hand in hand with the spread of new technologies and the intangible investment needed to harness them (computer services, training consultancies), but all the large service networks are directly affected by the spread of ICTs as well. The financial sector is one of the main markets for the industries producing ICTs (Baily and Gordon 1988; Oliner and Sichel 1994; Griliches 1998). All these activities can be radically transformed by such technologies, in terms of both what they produce and the way they produce it. Thus, while they are users of such technologies, the special nature of their needs means that they also play an active role in developing what they use (ranging from software design to provision of major airline reservation services).

Over and above this relative ignorance of the way sectoral employment dynamics are affected by the intensity with which new technology is used, it is no less interesting to observe that for a given service activity, the countries generating the most employment are those using the new technologies. These statistics need to be interpreted with care, if only because they are difficult to compare from one country to the other.[7] They are interesting nevertheless, and their explanation should help us to better grasp the systemic nature of technology. The intensity of ICT use in the 1980s was strong precisely in countries where the dynamics of employment were quite extensive. It is difficult to see one as an effect of the other. Rather than implying conclusions about the efficiency of ICT use, these effects suggest that transition and learning periods are strongly influenced by the way human resources are used, particularly in service activities with a high labour content.

We will summarize these hypotheses on the sectoral dimension of employment dynamics while considering a major characteristic of contemporary change – the trend towards jobs requiring greater skills.

Is the Supply of Employment Biased Towards Skilled Labour?
Whether technological change requires a more qualified workforce is a question of cardinal importance for economic and education policies today. The question is complex, given the degree to which the trend in skilled job supply can be influenced by factors other than technological change, such as industrial specialization in an economy open to trade with low-wage countries or an abundance of people with the requisite skills stemming, in the developed countries, from the long-term trend towards increased education. Before trying to sort out these causal factors, it might be desirable to quickly measure the phenomenon directly (all causes taken together).

The "skill bias" can involve different aspects and may persist in several forms:

- a drop in the proportion of unskilled work in the job supply
- a drop in the relative pay rates for such types of work
- some insecurity in employment conditions.

Effects on the employment structure and on pay rates or employment conditions are not mutually exclusive. They may combine to different degrees depending on country and sector. The first aspect (drop in the proportion of unskilled work) is somewhat universal, and can be found in most countries and sectors. This is not the case with the drop in relative wage rates, which concerns only countries where the management of labour markets was previously qualified if extensive (the Anglo-Saxon countries). These statements are reported in Table 1.

Table 1

Is technological change biased towards skilled labour?

	Characteristics of the Evolution of Employment		
	Labour demand	Wages	Insecurity
Skilled labour	+	+	−
Unskilled labour	−	−	−
	Observed		
	In all countries	In some countries: US, UK, Canada	In all countries

Furthermore, it should be noted that even the definition of a qualification or skill – a subject in its own right – is rarely dissociated from pay levels, especially when a dichotomous classification of skilled/unskilled is used. After all, the qualification needed for a particular job can be viewed from various angles. To start with, it constitutes a strategic variable (whose definition is debated between the social partners) within a given industry and takes into account not only the levels of initial training required but also the complexity of the task and the possibilities of learning on the job. For the sake of convenience, in statistics it is often reduced to data on the training undergone by those occupying the post in question; this tends to mix the effects of a larger supply of educated people with the effects of an increased demand for skilled labour by firms. It is more revealing to distinguish jobs by their task content, as a function of not two but three types of skills: cognitive abilities, motor functions, and the interrelational skills required in any job. Howell and Wolff (1992) thus define the change in qualification structure trends in the 1980s as an expansion in the demand for cognitive and interrelational aptitudes to the detriment of physical motor abilities. This differentiation should be kept in mind when looking at standard statistics based on a broad dichotomy between skilled and unskilled.

The trend towards skilled jobs is first and foremost manifest at the industrial level.[8] Thus, for all the OECD countries, the approximately 10 percent decrease in employment in industry between 1970 and 1992 can be attributed entirely to the fall in demand for unskilled workers (-20 percent), with skilled employment staying at the same level throughout that period (OECD 1996a, 63). This evolution in the structure of employment can be found in nearly all countries, although not to the same degree.[9] In the services sector, one trend towards skilled jobs is not so clear-cut. Mainly this is because in those sectors where employment is on the rise, unskilled jobs have continued to grow while their relative share has decreased, thus confirming the general character of the shift towards jobs requiring higher qualifications. What is more, this trend is not due to any composite effect in which the service or industry subsectors with the highest percentage of skilled staff might have grown more quickly than the average. The increase in skilled jobs is occurring within each subsector[10] and is not an artifact resulting from aggregation in different fields. The distortion in the skill structure is therefore quite clear-cut and across the board, although it is particularly glaring in industrial sectors where employment of unskilled workers is decreasing.

In some countries, this distortion in the job structure goes hand in hand with distortion in the pay structure. In terms of the overall economy, such a double deterioration in the situation of the unskilled is particularly evident in the US, Canada, and the United Kingdom. In countries such as

Japan, Germany, France, and Italy, the pay set-up – at this global level – does not appear to be affected (cf. OECD 1997a, chart 4.2a).[11]

One could extend this assessment to job instability, which, although generally increasing, is likely to impact unskilled jobs first and foremost. There are many indicators of job insecurity: the frequency of insecure forms of work,[12] how long a company remains in business, or the difficulties encountered in finding a job evidenced by the level of unemployment. Some surveys give as a common indicator the feeling of insecurity voiced by workers who still have a job to go to, which rose considerably from 1982 to 1996 in the major OECD countries (OECD 1997a, chart 5.1). This indicator varies considerably from one country to another, and correlates closely with the age of the worker surveyed. And while the feeling of insecurity is greater among those with less training, such as manual workers,[13] the difference is quite small. The gap did not increase even during the 1980s and 1990s, when the feeling of insecurity rose.[14] However, another indicator – the rate of unemployment by level of education – shows wide differences among countries, as the position of unskilled workers has deteriorated in countries such as Denmark, Finland, France, Ireland, Spain, and Sweden.

In summary, the feeling of job insecurity has increased and affects all workers alike. A distortion in the demand for skilled labour can be observed more or less across the board, in all sectors and countries. And while the wage structure is affected in only a small number of (mainly Anglo-Saxon) countries, the feeling of insecurity seems to affect workers in all countries. An analysis of the causes of such distortions will help clarify this issue.

Multiple Causes Relating to Firms
The relative change in the position of unskilled jobs may be due to several reasons that are more or less connected with the nature of technological change. Three sets of causes are discussed below:

- those linked to specialization within economies open to trade with countries possessing an excess of unskilled and low-paid labour
- those that have to do with corporate restructuring arrangements
- those more directly involved with the reorganization of tasks dictated by technological change.

Causes Linked to Foreign Trade
The debate about distortions in the structure of qualifications or skills has been unable to distinguish between effects due to foreign trade and those linked to technical progress. Most authors believe that the two are too closely intertwined to be separated, at least in econometric terms (cf. Cotis et al. 1997; OECD 1996a, Chapter 4). Strictly speaking, by injecting new factors

into the globalization process that reduce business costs and increase the international division of production (cf. Petit and Soete 1999), the new information technologies have played a role in transforming trade and investment flows. But over and above such real interaction, several factors act to limit the probable direct impact of trade on employment structure. The argument is that competition from low-wage countries forces countries with high wage levels to opt for activities requiring higher qualifications (in line with Hechser-Ohlin and Samuelson's comparative-advantage theory).

It is necessary to understand the scope and contemporary nature of this effect. While it is true that the developed countries have been competing with the low-wage countries for a long time now, at least with regard to trade in manufactured goods, the pay differentials bear no relation to the scale of the shifts observed in the employment structure. If price competition mechanisms were the only factor at work, several industries should have disappeared. To escape from this iron law of costs, every industry has had to diversify production (horizontally through innovative products; vertically by concentrating on quality). Here again, the new technologies that made inroads in the 1980s and 1990s have facilitated such changes, thus easing the pressure from low-wage countries.

It is also true that there is no dichotomy between the two types of competition. The impact of European integration demonstrates very clearly the narrow limits of specialization. In the 1980s and 1990s it was not competition from low-wage countries that pressured developed countries into specializing, so much as the growing might of the economies of Southeast Asia, where wage costs, while low, were still fairly comparable with the corresponding costs in southern Europe. The comparative threat came from the productive capacities these countries developed in the high- and intermediate-technology fields. Because services as well as industrial activities are affected by this distortion in the qualifications structure – although they are by no means exposed to outside competition to the same degree – we need to put the impact of foreign trade in its proper context.

Causes Related to Corporate Restructuring

The second set of reasons behind the general shift in the skills structure is directly related to organizational changes in production processes and, in particular, to relations between companies. As such, these reasons involve the very nature of contemporary technological change. A major component in the organizational changes undertaken by companies may have contributed to altering the qualifications structure. In order to stay on top as competition has changed in form, and to meet the ever increasing need to stay competitive in both domestic and foreign markets, companies in recent times have switched to widespread outsourcing of certain tasks. Tasks deemed peripheral to the company's core business were the first to be affected. This factor was not without impact on the changing qualifications structure being reviewed here. This "transfer" is said to cause changes tending in the opposite direction in the sectors involved, mainly those engaged in providing business services. Shifts in the skills structure, however, are also noticeable in service activities. This may be due mainly to the dual role played by providers of business services. On the one hand, low-skilled activities abound in this sector, thus facilitating outsourcing of routine and peripheral tasks. On the other hand, the transfer is also engendering highly skilled activities[15] connected, in particular, to the development and spread of new technologies, thus providing other companies with access to new technologies and know-how.[16] This dual role played by business services, and the new relationships they foster among firms, certainly contributes to the changes observed, although it is quite difficult to estimate the real extent of the impact of such reorganization. The development of business-to-business networks and cooperation arrangements, and the reduction in average company size, all form part of the same restructuring thrust. This spread of new types of work organization among companies should not be seen as the sole factor explaining changes in the job structure, however. A final set of causes relates directly to the way companies react to technological change proper, when reorganizing their activities internally.

Causes Related to Internal Reorganization
The third set of reasons therefore concerns changes in the choices made regarding the in-house (firm) organization of the new technology situation, assuming that one can separate this issue from the preceding ones. A company's need to be competitive in its various markets, as well as the uncertainties arising from any change in technical systems on the huge scale involved in the spread of ICTs,[17] leads it to opt for a more highly skilled employment structure. Given the market risks (coming to grips with the hazards of product innovation) and those connected with paid employment (making sure employees can keep up with process innovations), a company will endeavour to concentrate on what it does best so as to react as efficiently as possible to changes in the outside world. The features inherent in contemporary technological change accentuate this trend towards "overqualifying" jobs as a precaution.

The fact is that ICTs tend to be complementary to, or to interlink with, intangible investment at various levels. The previous phase of automation involved a fairly rigid (irreversible) link-up between intangible investment (a scientific work organization program centred on mechanization of certain parts of the production process) and tangible investment in equipment, which was much more substantial in financial terms. The current phase dovetails intangible investments – often long and costly in their gestation and requiring computer juggling with the number and purpose of compatibilities

– with not so costly tangible investments. Some see the fact that tangible investment is now taking the back seat as an automatic cause of the slowdown in productivity increases. In defence of this hypothesis, Oliner and Sichel (1994) and Sichel (1997) stress that, strictly speaking, the total tangible investments in ICTs accounts for no more than a minimal proportion of productive investment (4.7 percent of net capital stock in 1993 in the US), but if all peripheral expenditure is included, up to and including investment in software, the figure increases to some 10 percent of total investment. The benefit of this approach is that it brings out the extent of intangible investments in a particular case, and how badly handled or coordinated they are by the players, even if such estimates are still far from able to cover all the intangible investments that trial and error in management issues represent. One can make a global estimate of intangible investment in summing all the monetary equivalents of investments in education and training realized in an economy, as done by Kendrick (1994) for the US (figures are shown in Table 2). This gives us an upper limit of the intangible investment required by the new technologies, but it also shows that the 1980s and 1990s constituted the first decades where the investment in intangibles overtook the traditional formation of standard fixed capital.

This brings us to the very essence of technological change linked to ICTs. Such technologies bring together, interlink, preserve, and complement human knowledge. Doing so, they help automate old routinized tasks and develop new tasks. Some of these new tasks echo the past automation of production processes, going one step further with automated controls of production flows and breakdowns. As such, they constitute a phase largely foreseen and developed by the specialists in organization in each (large) firm. Other tasks correspond to more innovative uses, leading to new practices and elaboration of new knowledge, both tacit and codified. The exploration of this new frontier is left much more to individual initiatives. It may

Table 2

Structure of tangible and intangible investments in the US (billions of 1987 dollars, with ratios to GDP in parentheses)

	1948	1973	1990
Fixed capital stock (standard)	8,120 (6.2)	17,490 (5.4)	28,525 (5.9)
Stock of intangible capital	5,940 (4.6)	17,349 (5.3)	32,819 (6.9)
Education and training	4,879 (3.7)	13,564 (4.1)	25,359 (5.3)
Health, security and mobility	892 (0.69)	2,527 (0.77)	5,133 (1.1)
R&D	169 (0.13)	1,249 (0.38)	2,327 (0.48)
GDP (standard)	1,300	3,269	4,778

Source: Kendrick (1994).

concern the external relations of the firms or their internal organization of work. This change has been rightly described by some authors (Zarifian 1995; Laurent et al. 1998, Chapter 4) as a progressive shift. From an organization of work based on "qualifications," defined by the operating abilities of workers, we are moving to an organization of work based on "competencies," defined by the abilities of workers to react relevantly to events and develop new modes of operation. This raises important problems of organization and of compatibility between the various local or individual initiatives. The new technologies enlarge the scope for external relations, not only between firms but also between producers and consumers.

There is a risk of congestion and confusion between all these dispersed initiatives. The lack of common methods and rules reinforces the need for firms to rely on individual "competencies" in their organization of work. The design of equipment (of which personal computers are emblematic) tends to emphasize this trend. One can think of it as a first phase in a macro process of reorganization. This will be followed by a second phase with more methods available and therefore a more collective basis for work organization. In turn, these will favour more collective types of equipment. Transitions in such cases are rather long, however, and their paths are hazardous and influential, all of which makes a laissez faire policy rather risky. In particular, in the present phase of collective learning, choices may be influenced for the foreseeable future by a strong and steady growth in the supply of skilled labour.

From this brief outlook it may be concluded that the three causes evoked combine their effects, in specific ways, to fuel a certain devaluation of unskilled labour. This can manifest itself in three possible (and concomitant) forms: a distortion in the structure of employment, of wages, or in overall employment conditions. Distortions like these help us understand why the feeling of job insecurity has risen for all kinds of workers. It is the result of uncertainty about work organization, and an increased level of risk in product and financial markets. Table 3 synthesizes the various linkages underpinning generalized feelings of job insecurity, and illustrates why distortions in wage structure are more obvious in countries where individualization of wages is more widespread and most influenced by task organization. The effects on employment of structural changes in production patterns and the labour supply are magnified as increasing numbers of educated people enter the labour market.

An Expanding Skilled Labour Force

Already marked in the period of robust growth, the trend towards spending more time in education maintained its momentum during the slow growth period of the last two decades. For example, between 1985 and 1995 the percentage of 19- to 21-year-olds in education increased by more than

Table 3

Nature and causes of the depreciation of unskilled labour

	Types of bias		
Types of causes	Distortion of the employment structure	Distortion of the wage structure	Increased fear of job insecurity
Trade relations	Driven by the decline of some industries and relocation of others	Great differences ex ante between wage costs of trade partners, little effect ex post on local wages	Felt only in exposed industries
Externalization/ interfirm relations	Fuelled by the externalization of peripheral jobs	Fuelled by differences in conditions of collective bargaining among sectors	Felt chiefly in activities of firms engaged in subcontracting
Precautionary principle in work organization	–	Particularly in countries where individual wage incentives play a large role	General sense of job insecurity
Increase of skilled labour supply	Influences directly the skill structure of employment	Should favour an increase in the wage of nonqualified labour	Increased by the rise of unemployment among qualified labour

10 points, to between 40 and 50 percent of the age group. (There are some notable exceptions, such as the United Kingdom, where this figure is halved [EC 1996, section 5].) A similar if less pronounced trend can be seen in the 22- to 25-year-old age group, with actual figures varying greatly from one country to another (e.g., 40 percent in Denmark and the Netherlands, 30 percent in Spain and France, and 20 percent in the UK).

This increase is reflected in the changing skill structure of the active population as a whole. Between 1970 and 1990, the percentage of the active population receiving a higher education (two years or more at university) more than doubled in the US, Japan, the UK, and Italy (from about 15 percent to some 30 percent [OECD 1996, Table 10.4]). There are some major differences on this score. In countries like France or Germany, the percentages in higher education are half those of the countries just mentioned. Although these disparities are no doubt due in part to the lack of comparability between national criteria, the skill structure of the workforce does vary considerably from country to country and from period to period. The biggest differences between the various countries can be found in the overall employment rate of those aged 15 to 64 years. In Japan, the participation rate during the 1972-94 period increased from 75 percent to almost 80 percent. In the US, the corresponding figure rose from 60 percent to 70 percent. In Europe, meanwhile, the active policy of encouraging early retirement caused the figure to fall from 65 percent to 60 percent.

The inflow of highly trained people to the job market no doubt influenced the choices made in favour of skilled work, as Goux and Maurin (1995) suggest to partly explain the strong shift in the job skills structure in France. The effect of surplus skilled workers on employment structures varies, of course, from one country to another, reflecting the different ways labour markets operate and their different participation rates.[18] One should not conclude, however, that the excess of skilled labour plays a predominant role in the priority in employment that skilled labour enjoys, since unemployment rates rose for all categories. Certainly the unemployment rates of the 25- to 49-year-old age group show an advantage for workers with high education levels relative to those with a basic level (5 percent versus 12 percent for the men; 7.5 percent versus 15 percent for women) (see Table 4), but their rate of unemployment seems no less negligible than would have been the case some 20 years ago.

Labour market mobility is not a factor in this phenomenon, as we can make similar observations about long-term unemployment (unemployed for more than a year). Of highly educated unemployed men aged between 25 and 49 years, an average of 43 percent are unemployed for more than a year. For those with only basic levels of education, the corresponding figure is only 53 percent. Figures are similar for women in the same age group.

Table 4

European Community unemployment rates by level of education for persons aged 25-49 years in 1995

	First level of education	High school education level	Upper education level
Men	12	6.5	5
Women	15	10	7.5

Source: European Commission (1996).

While this distribution of unemployment underlines the advantages possessed by those with a high level of education, it also expresses a deep change in their status. Taking into account what unemployment can mean in terms of dequalification or of early involuntary retirement, a significant level of unemployment appears symptomatic of some challenge to the role of initial training. The reasons for such a challenge can be analysed on the basis of new requirements by workers or firms. One must acknowledge first, however, that not all countries are affected in the same way.

In Spain, Italy, and to a lesser extent Finland, the relative labour market position of people with a higher level of education is sensibly worse than elsewhere. By contrast, the general rise of unemployment does not seem to have led to an homothetic increase in the unemployment rate of these workers in Belgium, Austria, and Sweden. It may be that a relatively uniform rise in unemployment rates by level of education is a rather European phenomenon. Nickell and Bell (1995, quoted in OECD 1996a) report a relatively homothetic rise in unemployment rates for France, the UK, and Germany over the 1980s and 1990s, unlike in the US and Japan (see Table 5).

Moreover, our approach restrictively compares high and low levels of education while eliding the potentially major role played by professional training.[19] The effects of an increase in the average level of education in the workforce are complex. They may imply substitution effects of various kinds, not only in the levels of education required on the job but also in the choices of technologies and work organization. The relative importance of experience over recent training on new technologies could also be affected. The studies of Katz and Murphy (1992) on wage differentials in the US during the 1980s show effects such as accelerated obsolescence in college training. Abramovitz and David (1996) underline the interest of Katz and Murphy's work, but warn against the ready extrapolation of fluctuations that may relate more to the inertia of school systems than to any long-term effects. The part played by the school system definitively needs to be appreciated in a historical perspective. This is why we now turn our attention to how these educational systems fulfill employment needs and expectations at present compared with the 1950s and 1960s.

Towards a New Education/Employment Relationship

In a knowledge-based economy – one in which new technologies are used to take advantage of all the information and knowledge accumulated – education and professional training are assumed to increasingly determine access to jobs and the structure of wages. Such evolution is difficult to assess across countries when specific educational systems prepare students for future jobs in such different ways. These systems have especially diverse outcomes when one looks at the efficiency of short professional training, or at the status conferred on higher-education degrees (Boyer and Caroli 1993).

Table 5

Unemployment rates for men by high and low levels of education (%)

		1979-82	Early 1990s
France	High	2.1	5.9
	Low	6.5	13.6
	Total	5.2	9.4
Germany	High	1.6	2.4
	Low	4.5	6.2
	Total	3.8	5.4
Italy	High	12.2	12.8
	Low	4.8	7.7
	Total	8.2	11.5
Japan	High	1.6	1.2
	Low	2.9	2.6
	Total	2.4	2.2
United Kingdom	High	3.9	6.6
	Low	12.2	16.9
	Total	7.7	11.5
United States	High	2.1	2.8
	Low	8.6	11.0
	Total	5.5	5.8

Source: OECD (1996a) – p. 83 for definitions of the high and low levels of education for each country; p. 86 for the data drawn from Nickell and Bell (1995).

Still, the rise in the unemployment rates of educated people (discussed above) suggests that systems have not increased their "meritocratic" trend (where education plays an ever increasing role in the labour market) as extensively as could have been expected. The unemployment rates of educated workers are not the only signs justifying such concerns. The extension of schooling has been directly caused, in part, by the degradation of labour markets in most countries during the 1970s and 1980s. There has also been a relative decline in professional training, which appears to have lost, to a greater extent, its comparative advantage.

However, the cyclical nature of markets in professional training, such as computer expertise, shows that the issue does not end there. We still know little about how individual specific knowledge gets priced on the new labour market, or about the laws governing the obsolescence of this knowledge. Some studies look at the value added, if only in terms of wages, by the use of the new technologies. Thus, Krueger (1993) has estimated at 10 percent the premium on wages brought about by the use of computers in industry jobs in the US. More recent studies in the debate, taking advantage of individual longitudinal data, underline that those in charge of new equipment often have personal qualities that would have entitled them to wage premiums in any case (Entorf and Kramarz 1994; Entorf et al. 1995). Interestingly, these studies also show that the efficient use of new technologies relies on networks of personal relationships built up in the course of past experiences, whether at school, during leisure times, or in previous jobs (Gollac 1996; Goodman et al. 1994). This is one way to compensate for the lack of new methods in task organization in a context where the capacity and quality of new ICTs are improving rapidly. It stresses the hazards, the possibility of lock-in, and errors that can be met in the course of the broad learning processes under way. This is all the more crucial since our economies now need to install complementarities and complex organizational synergies in order to take advantage of the growth potential of a knowledge-based economy (Harris 1994).

Recall that we do not know much about the laws of knowledge obsolescence in these economies. Studies on the effective intellectual capabilities of individuals by age and level of education emphasize important gaps between level of education attained and actual competencies (OECD and Statistics Canada 1995; OECD 1997a).[20] This suggests that obsolescence can occur rapidly and rather differently from one country to another. Furthermore, the fact that job insecurity is just as widespread among workers with a relatively high level of training[21] points not only to the market risks that every company bears but also to the doubts of most workers about their own knowledge and capacity to cope with new challenges. The difficulty bedevilling middle managers in several countries – that of finding a job in mid-career – is symptomatic of the general nature of this malaise.

The new linkage between the accumulation of know-how and knowledge and the new ICTs leaves individuals feeling just as vulnerable, helpless, and left to their own devices as in the past, at least with respect to their cognitive capacities to communicate, understand, and make decisions (Favereau 1998). The challenge for today's policies is to lay down foundations for the best possible coordination of all such individual learning efforts.

Ambitious Policies to Coordinate Learning

We can do a first balance sheet of the various stylized facts presented here in connection with trends in labour supply and demand. In an economy more capable of harnessing the scattered mass of accumulated knowledge, the spread of new technologies and the increased internationalization of economies have paved the way for a new phase in the division of labour, involving new specializations and increased competitiveness in most product markets. Reorganization of work both within and among companies has taken place, to the relative detriment of unskilled jobs. This has also sometimes manifested itself – especially in the service sector – in the form of a concentration of unskilled jobs in specialized businesses.

Such outsourcing is not only a cause of the drop in the relative position of unskilled jobs but also one of the ways whereby the business sector can face up to the technological change now under way, with all its uncertainties, rapid changes, and demands to adapt. The complementarity between new technologies and skilled labour is in stark contrast to the replacement of skilled workers by machines that hitherto typified the automation of work. This means that human capital will play a major role in harnessing the potential of new technologies, at least in a long transition phase. The conditions required for this to happen include not only the codification of existing knowledge but also the development of new implicit knowledge. While still fairly hazy, they will simultaneously involve initial training for workers (who risk becoming obsolete quickly), occupational experience, and relationships and activities outside work. In a world where the interdependence of the economies has increased, these learning processes are likely to be strongly influenced by the experience of the most advanced countries in this process of restructuring.

It seems, in that respect, a common fact that this process has widened the gap between skilled and unskilled workers, at least for a long transition period. This evolution is all the more important to the extent that it affects all major fields – such as education, health, consumption, and leisure. Here, a difference among social groups in capacity to take advantage of contemporary (technological) changes increases the risk of fuelling a "dualism" that would limit the growth potential of knowledge-based economies (Petit and Soete 1997). The trends in the distribution of individual or family incomes confirm that such a move towards greater inequality is happening. It is important to stress that a number of changes are interacting to drive this two-tier process forward, indicating the extent to which questions of effectiveness (getting the most out of the new technologies) and questions of social justice are linked in the mid to long term. This makes it all the more necessary to coordinate policies in every field if the aim is to make sure they are effective.

There are three areas in which measures should be given first priority: (1) *distribution* to regulate the share-outs between different income categories; (2) the *job market* to encourage sound linkages between training (initial or lifelong) and experience gained in working life; and (3) *infrastructures* – in the broad sense, implying both tangibles and intangibles – to ensure that a solid structure underpins the various communication, information, and knowledge networks.

The first classic problem encountered is that of maintaining societal cohesion and economic dynamism when there is extreme inequality in terms of income. Wage inequalities are reinforced by inequalities in patrimonial assets, which benefit from the better returns to financial capital. Wealth inequalities are in turn both undermined and emphasized when compounded by differing "cultural" capacities to benefit from the advantages that the new technologies bring, in terms of consumer goods and recreation. These last difficulties are not unavoidable if intermediations (whether market or nonmarket) facilitate access to a wider range of users, or a widening of the range of products. Such widenings have obvious beneficial impacts on welfare, if only by increasing the potential of networked technologies, and can therefore be taken as policy objectives.

The second problem is how to arrange wage relationships so as to allow every individual to update their knowledge base, understand the knowledge packages that apply to their environment, and thus boost their own creative ability. This means finding an answer – suitably adapted to a knowledge-based economy – to the age-old problem of full employment and the part played by education and training (initial and lifelong) in its achievement. The coordination of individual learning processes that this implies must both avoid too rapid an obsolescence of knowledge and facilitate its renewal. This can lead to a marked segmentation between skilled and unskilled labour, between jobs requiring the upkeep of knowledge and those without any prospect. A short-term adjustment risks neglecting or excluding the possibilities that a closer involvement of workers might bring in the development of some networked technologies. The growth potential of a knowledge-based economy lies in its ability to radically rethink work patterns and bring them into line with individual learning processes in a more satisfying manner.

Finally, the third problem is raised by the need to implement the infrastructures (tangible and intangible; codes, rules, and conventions) required by the development of information networks. Whether for exchanging or processing information or accessing knowledge, this involves not only the right equipment (relatively less costly than those required for the earlier diffusion of electrical power) but also a whole set of codes, norms, and regulations in fields as varied as intellectual property rights, transactions security, or protection of privacy. Any action in these fields is highly strategic, and regulating bodies can neither overlegislate, as this would block creative development, nor underlegislate, to avoid locking in limited practices.

These regulative interventions are all the more difficult in that they involve both strictly national and transnational transactions. Countries are in very different positions to solve these problems. For some, the current level of income inequality and labour market flexibility seem to facilitate structural changes and the development of relevant infrastructure. Anglo-Saxon countries are a typical example. Being leaders in this first phase of diffusion gives them a real comparative advantage in monitoring the development of codes and norms. By contrast, follower countries in this first phase of structural change seem to be faced with two alternatives: (1) try to reproduce the experience of the "leaders" and engage in a strategy of radical structural adjustment to their growth pattern, based on more labour market flexibility and income inequality, expecting to have the advantages of latecomers in a catching-up process; or (2) explore growth paths more in synergy with their past growth pattern, which may carry a bigger risk of permanently lagging behind. For countries like Japan and Germany, where income inequalities are relatively small and where the labour markets are more institutionalized, such a strategy could mean a greater involvement of workers in new forms of organization, whether at work or in the development of new norms of consumption.

The ambition of such alternative options would be to stimulate the emergence, in a second phase of structural change, of new modes of development that take advantage of all the potential of a knowledge-based economy. Such schematic opposition between short-term adjustments and long-term modes of development better suited to economic growth and employment illustrates the dilemmas all economies face in trying to maximize the ability to gather, process, and communicate information and knowledge. The issue is made more uncertain by the complexity of the organizational issues it raises. On the one hand, the possibilities of improving the short-term adjustment realized by the "leaders" may be less hampered by social inequalities than assumed above. On the other hand, the possibility of developing alternative strategies may already be strongly limited by the extent of the diffusion of the first model in a world where interdependence between nations has consistently increased.

Notes
1 CEPREMAP/CNRS, 142 rue du Chevaleret, Paris 75013; tel. 33 (0) 1 40.77.84.27; fax 33 (0) 44.24.38.57; e-mail: <pascal.Petit@cepremap.cnrs.Fr>
2 Half a point more productivity over 10 years has the end effect of increasing growth by only 3.6 percent, which reduces the unemployment rate by 0.6 of a point (if the productivity increase is maintained for only 4 years, the cumulative growth rate over 10 years goes up 1.7 points and unemployment goes down by 0.2 of a point [OECD 1996, 52]).
3 The whole debate about measuring the inflation rate hinges on this question of measuring in real terms production whose nature has been profoundly changed by various innovations in the intrinsic quality of products and the way they are made available and used; on this debate, see the Boskin report (1996).
4 The employment growth rates in these services between 1970 and 1993 are fairly comparable for all the OECD countries, with those of the aforementioned industries generating modern-day technological change (OECD 1996a, 56).
5 Starting from the more detailed figure given in "L'emploi en Europe" (European Commission 1977).
6 The growth of employment in social services, particularly education and health, has more to do with the prolonged long-term trend towards improving our societies' living standards, which first appeared back in the 1950s and 1960s.
7 Such correlations between the proportion of investment in computer equipment and employment growth in the 1980s are more or less clear from the charts presented in OECD

(1996, 74), covering eight major OECD countries with regard to all commercial services, financial services, business services, and the trade sector.

8 Based on the classification of occupations proposed by the International Labour Office.

9 In particular in Japan, where over the period 1980-90 industrial employment is reported to have decreased only in terms of skilled worker jobs!

10 Using the formula of Berman et al. (1995), the OECD (OECD 1996, Table 4.5) was able to estimate that over three-quarters of the shift in the job structure was due to changes specific to each industry.

11 It should be noted that in no country is there any distortion in the pay set-up without a change in the job structure.

12 Even if the similarity is not convincing, part-time work is often deemed to be an insecure form of employment, but it is one that developed noticeably in Europe in the 1990s, increasing between 1990 and 1996 from 4 percent to 5.5 percent of male employment and from 27.5 percent to 31.5 percent of female employment, accounting for almost all of net job creation (European Commission 1997, Section 3).

13 Seventy-four percent of manual workers were aware of the instability of their job in 1996 in the OECD countries, compared with 65 percent of nonmanual workers (OECD 1997a, Table 5.2).

14 As it stems from two surveys (one on the UK, the other on Germany), both comparing changes in the feeling of insecurity according to personal characteristics (see OECD 1997a, 150).

15 The incidence of skilled jobs in the sector providing business services is particularly large, exceeding 50 percent of all jobs created in the 1980s and 1990s (OECD 1996a, Chart 4.5). Also, to underscore the very contemporary nature of this phenomenon, it should be remembered that it is in service activities that employment has risen fastest of all in most developed countries (a new phenomenon).

16 The development of interfirm networks, joint ventures, and other accords is part of this same logic of reorganization.

17 Not to mention the biotechnology-driven changes now in the pipeline.

18 In 1997 the percentage of those in the 15-64 age group in a job, all sectors taken together, varied in the European Community countries between about 50 percent in Italy and Spain and nearly 70 percent in Denmark, Austria, Portugal, Sweden, and the UK. The European average was 60 percent (i.e., the rates observed in France and Germany) (EC 1997, 97).

19 In France, for instance, the situation of people with a short professional training in the labour market did not deteriorate over the 1990s, whereas the situation of people without any real initial training deteriorated remarkably (Cereq 1998).

20 Half the adults in several countries are below the first two levels of literacy, including between 10 and 20 percent of those who have had an extended education (OECD and Statistics Canada 1995, 146ff).

21 Sixty-eight percent positive replies for those continuing their studies beyond the age of 19 versus 72 percent for those who discontinued their studies before the age of 16 (OECD 1997a, Table 5.2).

References

Abramovitz, M., and P. David. 1996. "Technological Change and the Rise of Intangible Investment: The US Economy's Growth Path in the Twentieth Century." In OECD, *Technology, Productivity and Job Creation*. Paris: OECD.

Baily, M., and R. Gordon. 1988. "The Productivity Slowdown, Measurement Issues, and the Explosion of Computer Power." *Brookings Papers on Economic Activity* 2: 347-420.

Bell, B.D. 1996. "Skill Biased Technical Change and Wages: Evidence from a Longitudinal Data Set." Mimeo. Oxford: Institute of Economics and Statistics, Oxford University.

Berman, E., J. Bound, and Z. Griliches. 1994. "Changes in the Demand for Skilled Labor within US Manufacturing: Evidence from the Annual Survey of Manufactures." *Quarterly Journal of Economics* 109,E2: 367-97.

Berman, E., J. Bound, and S. Machin. 1995. "Implications of Skill Biased Technological Change: International Evidence." Expert Workshop on Technology, Productivity and Employment: Macroeconomic and Sectoral Evidences. Paris: OECD.

Boskin, M., ed. 1996. "Towards a More Accurate Measure of the Cost of Living." Final Report to the US Senate Finance Committee.

Boyer, R., and E. Caroli. 1993. "Production Regimes, Education and Training Systems: From Complementarity to Mismatch?" Mimeo. Paris: CEPREMAP.

Cereq. 1998. *Les diplômes de niveau V. Au-delà d'un déclin annoncé, des diplômes qui restent pertinents*. Bref, n°144.

Cotis, J.P., J.M. Germain, and A. Quinet. 1997. "Les effets du progrés technique sur le travail peu qualifié sont indirects et limités." *Economie et Statistique* 301-302.

Entorf, H., and F. Kramarz. 1994. *The Impact of New Technologies on Wages: Lessons from Matching Panels on Employees and on Their Firms*. CREST Working Paper No. 9407. Paris: ENSAE/INSEE.

Entorf, H., M. Gollac, and F. Kramarz. 1995. "New Technologies, Wages and Worker Selection." Conference on Innovation, Washington, DC.

European Commission. 1996. "L'emploi en Europe." Commission Européenne, division Emploi et Affaires Sociales. Luxembourg: Office for Official Publications of the European Communities.

–. 1997. "L'emploi en Europe." Commission Européenne, division Emploi et Affaires Sociales. Luxembourg: Office for Official Publications of the European Communities.

Favereau, O. 1998. "Notes sur la théorie de l'information à laquelle pourrait conduire l'économie des conventions." In P. Petit, ed., *L'économie de l'information: les enseignements des théories économiques*. Paris: La Découverte.

Gollac, M. 1996. "Le capital est dans le réseau: la coopération dans l'usage de l'informatique." *Travail et Emploi* n°68.

Goodman, P., J. Lerch, and T. Mukhopakhyay. 1994. "Individual and Organizational Productivity: Linkages and Processes." In D. Harris, ed., *Organizational Linkages: Understanding the Productivity Paradox*. Washington, DC: National Research Council, National Academy Press.

Goux, D., and E. Maurin. 1995. "Changes in the Demand for Labour in France: a Study for the Period 1970-93." Presented at Expert Workshop on Technology, Productivity and Employment: Macroeconomic and Sectoral Evidences," 19-20 June 1995. Paris: OECD.

Griliches, Z. 1969. "Capital-Skill Complementary." *The Review of Economics and Statistics* 51: 465-68.

–. 1998. "Productivity, R&D, and the Data Constraint." In D. Neef, A. Siesfeld, and J. Cefola, eds., *The Economic Impact of Knowledge*. Boston: Butterworth-Heinemann.

Harris, D.H., ed. 1994. *Organizational Linkages: Understanding the Productivity Paradox*. Washington, DC: National Research Council, National Academy Press.

Howell, D., and E. Wolff. 1992. "Technical Change and the Demand for Skills by US Industries." *Cambridge Journal of Economics* 16: 128-46.

Katz, L.F., and K.M. Murphy. 1992. "Changes in Relative Wages, 1963-1987: Supply and Demand Factors." *Quarterly Journal of Economics* 107,1: 35-78.

Kendrick, J.W. 1994. "Total Capital and Economic Growth." *Atlantic Economic Journal* 22,1: 1-18.

Kiesler, S., D. Wholey, and K. Carley. 1994. "Coordination as Linkage: The Case of Software Development Teams." In D. Harris, ed., *Organizational Linkages: Understanding the Productivity Paradox*. Washington, DC: National Research Council, National Academy Press.

Krueger, A. 1993. "How Computers Have Changed the Wage Structure: Evidence from Micro Data 1984-1989." *Quarterly Journal of Economics* 108: 33-60.

Laurent, M., H. Raimond, G. Valendue, P. Vendramin. 1998. "Technologies avancées de communication, transformations industrielles et qualifications." Mimeo. Namur, Belgium: Fondation Travail-Université.

Nickell, S., and B. Bell. 1995. "The Collapse in the Demand for the Unskilled and Unemployment across the OECD." *Oxford Review of Economic Policy* 11: 40-62.

OECD (Organization for Economic Cooperation and Development). 1996a. *Technology, Productivity and Job Creation*. Paris: OECD.

–. 1996b. *Employment and Growth in the Knowledge-Based Economy*. Paris: OECD.

–. 1997a. *Perspectives de l'emploi, juillet*. Paris: OECD.

–. 1997b. *Littératie et société du savoir*. Paris: OECD.

OECD and Statistics Canada. 1995. *Literacy, Economy and Society: Results of the First International Adult Literacy Survey.* Paris and Ottawa: OECD and Statistics Canada.

Oliner, S., and D. Sichel. 1994. "Computers and Output Growth Revisited: How Big Is the Puzzle?" *Brookings Papers on Economic Activity* 2: 273-317.

Petit, P., ed. 1998. *L'économie de l'information: les enseignements des théories économiques.* Paris: La Découverte.

Petit, P., and L. Soete. 1997. "Is Technological Change Fueling Dualism?" Mimeo. Paris: CEPREMAP.

–. 1999. "Globalization in Search of a Future." A paraître n°160, *Revue Internationale des Sciences Sociales.* Paris: UNESCO.

Sichel, D. 1997. *The Computer Revolution: An Economic Perspective.* Washington, DC: Brookings Institution Press.

Zarifian, P. 1995. *Le travail et l'événement: Dynamiques d'entreprises.* Paris: L'Harmattan.

10

Work Organization and Information and Communication Technologies

Henri Rouilleault

Information and communication technologies (ICTs) are the engine of a "Third Industrial Revolution" – the shift from mass production to customized services variously referred to as the "post-industrial society," "quality and variety economy," "knowledge society," "information society," and "network society" (Castells 1996; Lasfargue 1998; Reich 1991; Touraine 1969; Streeck 1992). A deep process of technical, economic, and social change is at work. Although proceeding at different paces, this revolution concerns all countries, industries, and human activities.

Using mostly French examples, this chapter deals with the changes in work organization, job content, and industrial relations related to ICTs – changes that represent both new opportunities and new risks for enterprises and their employees. The first part of the chapter underlines the multidimensional stakes of the shift to a "service and information society." The second part analyses the organizational and social changes occurring with ICT development, focusing on three sectors: process industries, manufacturing industries, and services. The third part addresses several activities – such as design, marketing, trade, and training – that are dramatically changing, and the development of new services, occupations, and professions that the information society generates. The conclusion underlines the idea that the rapid pace of change, and the variety of organizational designs feasible with ICTs, enforces the need for "partnership for a new organization" (European Commission 1997).

A Global Approach to ICTs in the Context of a Service Economy

(1) *ICTs have spread worldwide.* It is estimated that by the year 2000 the number of Internet users in Europe will reach 27.5 million. More than 25 percent of the population in Scandinavian countries use mobile telecommunications. ICT investment comprises 11 percent of the net capital stock in the United States, and, at 5 percent of GDP, ICT industries have overtaken the automobile industry as the first manufacturing sector in the US (Petit 1998).

The development of ICTs in the 1990s extends the automation and computerization that began in the 1960s. It results from the growing convergence of three formerly separate industrial sectors: informatics, telecommunications, and broadcasting (Bangemann Group 1994; European Commission 1996, 1997; Conseil d'Etat 1998). This convergence enables cheaper prices and information storage, and fast, interactive just-in-time or postponed communication. It involves both the growing substitutability of networks allowed by microelectronics and their possible federation with the Internet; the coming substitutability of terminals such as microcomputers, TV sets, and telephones; numerous mergers and alliances between complementary businesses, large companies, and brilliant start-ups; new types of traditional services such as electronic marketing and trade; and new services such as electronic mail, netfinders, and virtual teamwork. Castells (1996) adds fast-growing and closely linked biological technologies to ICTs.

(2) *In the 1990s technological change with ICTs has been closely linked to a dramatic economic change in most industries.* After years of mass production based on scale returns, there has been a shift to customized production of a mix of goods and services. Boundaries between the manufacturing and service industries have become more and more blurred (Davis and Meyer 1998). Interactive communication between producers and customers is then crucial in a knowledge-based economy.

At the same time, the economy becomes more unstable. The link between supply and demand is shorter and more global. Stocks have to be minimized. Firms must become more adaptable and innovative.

The economy also becomes more efficient, despite the Solow paradox (1987), namely, the coexistence of the information revolution and the decline in productivity growth. The paradox can be explained by measurement errors relating to volumes, quality effects, and growth or a temporary disequilibrium between process innovation and product innovation related to ICTs (Boyer 1998; Bourlés 1998).

ICTs facilitate other important changes, such as the shift from hierarchical to decentralized companies and the evolution of the borders of the firm that occurs with outsourcing (Brunhes Bernard Consultants 1994). Electronic networks allow a new intermediate form of coordination, somewhere between coordination inside the organization and coordination by the market (Williamson 1990).

(3) *Technological change – driven first by ITs and now by ICTs – has also significantly influenced changes in the organizational and employment structure.* According to the latest available French Labour Ministry surveys and Institut National de la Statistique et des Études Économiques (INSEE) census:

- One-third of employees used computers in 1993, compared with 14 percent in 1987.
- In 1991, the workplace of 40 percent of employees was directly dependent on customer demand, compared with 25 percent in 1984.
- The number of unskilled workers diminished from 3 million in 1982 to 2 million in 1991. Management and professionals grew from 1.8 million to 2.9 million. The number of skilled workers remained stable, and white-collar positions grew slowly.

The impact of ICTs on employment volume and structure at the macro level is beyond the scope of this discussion. Let me simply mention that, first, there is nothing like an "end of work" in the long run, but, because of ICTs, the balance between jobs created by product innovation and those created by process innovation may be temporarily disturbed. Second, there is a big discussion on both sides of the Atlantic about "technological bias." ICTs seem to explain part of the decrease in unskilled relative wages in North America and part of the increase in unskilled relative unemployment (Van Reenen, this volume; Bouabdallah and Villeval 1997). ICT development is also consistent with the evolution of employment status, including the development of independent self-employment and the shift from lifelong employment in a single job or company to diversified careers (Boisonnat 1995).

ICTs support a deep mutation of human work: the unity of work time, workplace, and work team is being fragmented by the development of virtual teams. Firms must be more responsive to changing demand in quality and quantity, and more innovative on the supply side. They must become both flexible and learning organizations and cope with the potential contradictions between both qualities. Employee skills (Zarifian 1996), human capital (Reich 1991), and organizational learning (Argyris and Schön 1978) become key specific assets, crucial for company and national development.

(4) *Although the next section analyses the link between technological, economic, organizational, and social mutations in more detail, it should be noted that ICTs must also be studied more systemically, beyond the questions dealt with here (Lasfargue 1993, 1998).*

Technological, economic, organizational, and social changes are embedded in a global context, involving cultural, political, ecological, moral, and military stakes. Five important aspects should be mentioned:

- With personal computers and mobile phones, the connection between working life and family and social life is closer than at any time since the First Industrial Revolution. Individual learning (on the World Wide Web, for instance) carries both personal and work-related attributes. There are risks of exclusion for older and less-skilled workers, opportunities for personal development, and risks for personal life. These risks and opportunities call for individual and collective regulations.

- Electronic trade, e-mail, and other ICT uses raise questions of confidentiality; payment viability and signature certification; and customer, author, person, employee, and citizen protection.
- All human activities are involved, including initial and vocational training, and health (e.g., through medical diagnosis and surgery at a distance).
- There is a cultural mutation to a network culture – at once both local and more global – in a world where managers no longer have a monopoly on legitimate expertise (the main characteristic of power, according to Bauer and Cohen [1981]).
- State regulation is less effective and has to make way for a growing combination of private, national, European, and international regulations.

ICTs and Work Organization in Three Socio-Productive Contexts

Information and communication technologies in the 1990s represent a new wave of technological innovations that extends the previous wave of automation and computerization that began in the 1960s. ICTs encompass many existing technologies (d'Iribarne 1997).

This section examines the case of three socioproductive configurations: process industries, manufacturing industries, and services. It shows various situations according to the enterprise performance, the work organization, and the employment structure, both between and inside those configurations. Finally, in each case it shows there is room for participative work organization design.

Process Industries

The development of automation in the process industries in the 1970s induced several characteristics. First, there has been a growing dematerialization of work. This, however, varies between industries – from nuclear plants to refining, petrochemicals, cement, steel, and aluminum. Second, a growing diversity of products according to customer demand is made possible by automation. Third, process industries have become increasingly capital-intensive. Nevertheless, "the factory of the future" will not be humanless. On the contrary, control, supervision, and maintenance will remain crucial for viability, profitability, and equipment safety. Fourth, organizational change, but without technological determinism, has produced multi-skilling, maintenance sharing, and changing middle management roles (Du Roy and Mahieu 1998; Letondal 1997). Finally, we can observe a diminution of physical load but increase in cognitive burdens and stress due to work dematerialization, to vigilance problems, and sometimes to isolated work.

These characteristics influenced the development of the sociotechnical approach (e.g., Du Roy 1985) and the ergonomic approach (Daniellou 1986; Guérin et al. 1997). These approaches aim at a participative design with users, taking into account observed real work and simulations of future work, and emphasizing human/machine interfaces, integrated training, and collective learning.

From the 1970s information technologies played a very important role in process industries. While the communication dimension added by ICTs produced less drastic change, process industries foreshadowed many of the common problems experienced by information society organizations.

Manufacturing Industries
Because of increasing European and worldwide competition, manufacturing industries (such as the automotive, domestic durable goods, and food industries) are undergoing deep transformations. They must respond, for example, to consumer demands for variety and quality, and react to quantitative and qualitative variations. New, mainly Japanese, management methods have been adopted, such as quality certification and/or total quality management (TQM), Kaïzen, Kanban, and just-in-time.

Also, the search is on for more flexibility – industrial, working time, and numerical flexibility, as well as multi-skilling. New work layout, such as work in line or by production islands, and job rotation are often accompanied by enrichment of job content, integration of quality control, production-flow management, and stock administration. More rarely, first-level maintenance and human resources or working time management are included, although there are very few post-Taylorist Scandinavian-like experiments. Manufacturing is now characterized by the development of teamwork, management by objectives at the shop-floor level, and direct links from the shop floor with internal and even external customers. Because of robotization, jobs have become less difficult physically, but there are fewer "soft" jobs, the result of downsizing and an increased cognitive burden due to growing variety, which some researchers describe as computerized Taylorism. Increased musculoskeletal disorders have been observed in workers, mainly among subcontractor companies subject to strong cost-reduction policies, and in jobs where there is little room to manoeuvre. Finally, workforce reductions and an ageing workforce are resulting in problems for large companies.

Since the 1980s, besides assisting the development of teamwork, the adoption of information technologies on the shop floor – mainly computer-assisted production tools – strongly supported organizational changes, allowing processes to be marked out and enabling the management of growing variety on the assembly lines. These changes nevertheless raise important questions about work organization and design, if performance is to be improved while avoiding both exclusion and health problems. For instance, what is the best level of automation? How can learning organizations be built in these contexts? What work pace and engagement level is consistent with individual and collective regulations?

In the 1990s ICTs have generated sharply accelerating organizational change in manufacturing industries (Betbeder 1996; Moati et al. 1997). Previous trends have been extended with the adoption of electronic data interchange, or EDI (direct transfer of electronic data between companies, to professional standards). This has provided a technological basis for just-in-time practices in a variety-based economy, and is consistent with network development between large firms and subcontractors. Integrated software (Enterprise Resources Planning) has also been introduced to link and disseminate data on production, purchasing, sales, maintenance, inventory control, analytic accounting, and human resources management.

New questions then arise to complement the earlier ones. For example, what criteria will be adopted for outsourcing, given its indirect costs and the loss of skills and information that can result? How can software be standardized while at the same time taking into account the specific needs of each organization?

In the contexts where ICTs control the physical room to manoeuvre, we see less technological determinism than in former technologies. A large field is opening for sociotechnical design to link technology, organization, human resources, and management instruments.

Services

As far as the service sectors are concerned, we have to distinguish between commerce, services to enterprises from consultancy to industrial cleaning, and services to individuals from travel agencies to social security. Our focus here is the decentralized financial and nonfinancial services supplied to customers and users that are supported by a centralized information and decision-assistance system. The main feature in these systems is that production is a co-production of employee and customer (Gadrey 1994) involving, in a crucial way, ICT and organizational choices.

Extending the trends that have appeared in these sectors since the computerization of the 1970s, we can observe several characteristics at work with ICTs in the 1990s. There has been a strong increase in back-office labour productivity, for example, with workflow (circulation of documents in progress among computerized workstations) often coherent with business process re-engineering. The latter enables task division and the spread of Taylorization in service activities, with the risk inherent in dialogue standardization (Martin 1996). Low-content tasks have been automated and there has been customer-oriented job enrichment in the front office, often with upskilling. The development of distance banking, insurance, and other services has been notable. Call centres and hotlines have been established, and there is a large variety of organizational choices with regard to horizontal and vertical multi-skilling and on-flow and by-appointment activities. Worker stress has increased, however, particularly in call centres (due to time pressures and the contradictions between productivity indexes and quality demands) and in employees working with populations in depressed areas. Great importance is attached to "dialogue ergonomy," which requires a broader sociotechnical design concept that involves all sides – future users, customers, and employees (Eksl and Rolloy 1995).

ICTs and Occupational Structure

Without any determinism, ICT development is linked with tremendous changes in occupational structure. Besides those related to the previous socioproductive configurations, these changes are consistent with the transversal reconfiguration of occupations and professions, and with the development of new jobs.

Many occupations across several industries are changing deeply because of ICTs, particularly because of the low cost of transmission and stocking of information. Changing occupations are found in: transport and logistics (with EDI); library services (to collect, scan, stock, and disseminate formerly scarce, now abundant documentation); trade (by Internet or from call centres); and training (with open and distance learning and interactive multimedia). At the same time, call centres are developing for public or private information services, marketing and sales, technical assistance, banking and insurance, ticketing, and market research. Mobile technologies allow expert maintenance at a distance, to supplement general maintenance (Bossard 1999). Borders between occupations and professions – such as between journalists and printers (ANACT 1990) or between managers and assistants (d'Iribarne et al. 1997) – become blurred and may be transformed in several ways.

Technological and organizational design are especially affected by ICT development. With growing competition in goods and services, variety and time-to-market are crucial. Simultaneous and concurrent engineering of new products and new processes are developing (Midler and Charue 1993; AFITEP 1997). These methods suppose:

- close cooperation between professionals in different disciplines (Akrich et al. 1990)
- close cooperation between the project team and future users, in order to strengthen the latter

- cooperation around simulation tools of future work (Maline 1994)
- project management as a key for organizational learning (Rouilleault and Villeval 1995) and employee training (de Nanteuil 1998).

ICTs offer strong support to product and process innovation, through groupware, Extranet, and multimedia conferences. They facilitate the creation of virtual teams and the exchange of ideas and data without constraints of place and schedules. As noticed by Guitaut (1998), we cannot explore 100 percent virtuality in the short term. Electronic networks may relieve but also constrain individual and collective human work. Some kind of semi-virtual work requires easy interfaces with information systems, to facilitate everyone's representations. New rules must also be negotiated (Lasfargue 1998) in order to organize mixed telework between offices and home, and to avoid the growing sapping of management (Ettinghoffer and Blanc 1998) already observed by Henry Mintzberg, if we are to master the real-time pressure and the blur between working and nonworking time.

Finally, ICT development allows the growing development of new activities and new jobs in all industries. Particularly affected are informational professionals and knowledge workers: information systems architects (Betbeder 1996), Webmasters and Web watchers, multimedia librarians, and multimedia booksellers (Council of Europe 1998).

Conclusion

As we have seen, ICT effects on job content, health, employment volume, skills development, and the exclusion of unskilled older people differ according to the different technologies, the organizations in which they are embedded, and the socioproductive contexts. Their objectives and effects on enterprise performance are also varied: groupware aims mainly at new value-added creation, EDI at flexibility, workflow at cost reduction, call centres at growing turnover – and the results of their implementation vary. As is often the case, organizational change results not only from the target but also from the implementation process.

For these reasons, and because ICTs are more flexible to organizational design than before, "partnership for a new organization" is essential, both within companies and between employers and employee representatives (European Commission 1997). This may be reinforced by cluster partnerships with research, consultancy, or tripartite intermediate institutions, and by network partnerships on a European or international basis.

Partnership development is all the more important because the ICT revolution is deepening and expanding, altering at the same time work organizations, employment and working conditions, and enterprise durability and performance. Think forward to computer voice recognition, cars assembled directly from the customer's orders, and entirely electronic cash desks.

References
AFITEP. 1997. *La Cible*. Journal du management du projet. Paris.
Akrich, M., M. Callon, and B. Latour. 1990. Paris: Annales de Mines: Gérer et Comprendre.
Argyris, Chris, and A. Schön David. 1978. "Organizational Learning." Reading, MA: Addison-Wesley.
Bangemann Group. 1994. "Europe and the Global Information Society." Report for the European Council.
Bauer, Michel, and Elie Cohen. 1981. *Le Pouvoir dans les groupes industriels*. Paris: Seuil.
Brunhes Bernard Consultants. 1994. "L'Europe de l'emploi." Paris: Éditions d'organisation.
Betbeder, Guillaume. (1996). *Vers un diplome de troisième cycle d'architecte en systèmes d'information*. Lyon: IAE.
Boisonnat, Jean. 1995. *Le Travail dans 20 ans*. Paris: Odile Jacob.
Bossard, Pascale. 1999. *Nouvelles technologies de l'information et de la communication et travail*. Lyon: ANACT.
Bouabdallah, Khaled, and Marie-Claire Villeval. 1997. "Innovation et croissance des inégalités sur le marche du travail." *Revue d'Economie-Politique* 107,5: 567-605.
Bourlés, Jean, and Jean-Henri Lorenzi. 1998. "L'Innovation, moteur de la croissance: application à la périodeactuelle." In J.D. Léonard, ed., *Innovation, croissance et travail*. Grenoble: Pug.
Boyer, Robert, and Michel Didier. 1998. *Innovation et croissance*. Conseil d'Analyse Economique. Paris: La Documentation Française.
Castells, Manuel. 1996. *The Rise of the Network Society*. Oxford: Blackwell Publishers.
Conseil d'Etat. 1998. *Internet et les réseaux numériques*. Paris: La Documentation Française.
Council of Europe. 1998. "Draft Recommendation on Cultural Work within the Information Society." Culture Committee meeting, Strasbourg.
Daniellou, François. 1986. *L'Opérateur, la vanne, l'ecran*. Lyon: ANACT.
Davis, Stan, and Christopher Meyer. 1998. *Blur*. Reading, MA: Addison-Wesley.
Du Roy, Olivier. 1985. *Réussir l'investissement industriel*. Paris: Editions d'Organisation.
Du Roy, Olivier, and Mahieu Christian. 1998. *L'Usine qui n'existait pas*. Paris: Editions d'Organisation.
Eksl, René, and Gérard Rolloy. 1995. *Évaluation du projet Socrate*. Cahiers de l'ANACT n°4. Lyon.
Ettinghoffer, D., and G. Blanc. 1998. *Le Syndrome de chronos*. Paris: Dunod.
European Commission. 1996. "Living and Working in the Information Society: People First." Green Paper. Brussels: European Commission, DG V.
–. 1997. "Partnership for a New Organization." Green Paper. Brussels: European Commission, DG V.
Gadrey, Jean. 1994. *Relations de service, marchés de service*. Paris: CNRS Editions.
Guérin, F., et al. 1997 réédition. *Comprendre le travail pour le transformer*. Lyon: ANACT.
Guitaut, G. 1998. "NTIC et nouvelles compétences." Assises CNPF de Deauville.
d'Iribarne, A., M. Gadille, R. Tcobanian. 1997. *Technologies nouvelles et organisation des entreprises*. Aix-en-Provence: LEST-CNRS.
Lasfargue, Yves. 1993. *Robotisés, rebelles, rejetés – maitriser les changements technologiques*. Paris: Editions de l'atelier.
–. 1998. "Les Enjeux de la société de l'information." Crefac, communication au séminaire ANACT, Lyon.
Letondal, Anne-Marie. 1997. *L'Encadrement de proximité*. Lyon: ANACT.
Maline, Joel. 1994. *Simuler le travail*. Lyon: ANACT.
Martin, F. 1996. "Evaluation d'un workflow à finalité commerciale en entreprise." Congrès national des sciences de l'information et de la communication, Grenoble.
Midler, Christophe, and F. Charue. 1993. "A French-Style Sociotechnological Learning Process: The Robotization of Automobile Body Shops." In B. Kogut, ed., *Country Competitiveness: Technology and the Organizing of Work*, 156-75. Oxford: Oxford University Press.
Moati, P., L. Pouquet, and M. Leborgne. 1997. "Les Nouvelles logiques productives dans les PMI." In J. Léonard, ed., *Innovation, croissance et travail*. Grenoble: Pug.
de Nanteuil, Matthieu. 1998. *Agir sur la participation des salariés à la conduite des projets*. Lyon: ANACT.

Petit, Pascal. 1998. *L'Economie de l'information*. Paris: La Découverte.

Reich, Robert B. 1991. *The Work of Nations*. New York: Alfred A. Knopf.

Rouilleault, Henri, and Marie-Claire Villeval. 1995. *L'Entreprise et les projets*. Paris: Gérer et Comprendre.

Solow, Robert. 1987. Nobel Prize acceptance speech.

Streeck, Wolfgang. 1992. *Social Institutions and Economic Performance*. London: Sage Publications.

Touraine, Alain. 1969. *La Société post-industrielle*. Paris: Denoel.

Williamson, O. 1990. *Organization Theory*. New York, NY: Oxford University Press.

Zarifian, Philippe. 1996. *Travail et communication*. Grenoble: Pug.

11
Human Resource Practices and Information Technology in Canada: Results from the WES Pilot Data[1]
Caroline L. Weber

Introduction

While Canada and other industrialized countries are experiencing rapid changes in technology and are moving quickly towards a "knowledge economy," we have yet to fully grasp the impact of these transitions on individuals, firms, communities, or society as a whole. There is little agreement among researchers about the effects of technology on organizational structure, the nature or level of labour market skills required, or the nature of work itself (for a summary, see Thomas 1994).

What do we know about the organizational or employment effects of new technology? While there is little consensus across the literature, some agreement can be found on a few aspects. For example, in examining new technology implementation, researchers have identified increased levels of employee involvement, participation, and training as "critical success factors" (Wilkinson 1983).

There is much less agreement about the employment and skill-level effects of new technologies. Some argue that new technologies increase the demand for both the amounts and skills of labour required (Woodward 1965). Snell and Dean (1992) found that advanced manufacturing technologies were associated with more investment in human resources through more sophisticated selection processes, more training and development, and higher wages. In their cross-sectional study of the Canadian manufacturing sector, Baldwin and Johnson (1996) report that innovators tend to implement new technology, place more emphasis on recruiting skilled labour, and invest more in training.

This evidence is consistent with Peters's (1997) prescriptive argument that if firms are to be successful in the knowledge economy, they must be innovative. To be innovative, firms must increase rather than decrease their investments in human resources. If these arguments are correct, we would expect technology implementers to exhibit higher levels of education and training, more employment (people, hours), and higher wages if those employed are truly talented or possess scarce skills.

Others argue that new technologies are capital substitutes that reduce the amount of labour required (Noble 1984), and that new technologies essentially deskill labour, thus reducing its importance and power in the production process (Aronowitz and DiFazio 1994; Braverman 1974; Shaiken 1984). If these perspectives are correct, we would expect technology implementers to exhibit lower levels of education and training, less employment (people and hours), and lower wages.

A third group argues that the effects of technology on employment and skill levels are not predetermined; it is the way technology is used that determines the effects on labour (Barley 1986; Hill 1981; Piore 1985; Wilkinson 1983). If this perception is accurate, then we should find no consistent patterns of technology effects on labour. This sort of "no effect" hypothesis (beyond the statistical) is difficult to test. If the way we use technology is socially defined, then patterns of usage may diffuse over time. We might have to look cross-culturally to verify this hypothesis, although Barley (1986) was able to identify differences in use and implementation of new technology (CT scanners in hospitals) within one US state.[2]

The purpose of this chapter is to examine the relationships in Canadian establishments among organizational and human resource practices, establishment-level performance, and new technology. I use the Workplace and Employee Survey (WES) pilot data, collected in the winter of 1996, to explore these questions.

Data and Methodology

The WES pilot data were collected to test a new survey instrument designed to measure workplace practices in Canadian establishments and assess the effects of these practices on establishments and employees alike. As an early attempt to construct and administer a survey that collects data from both employers and employees in the same establishments, the WES pilot data represent an innovation in sampling methodologies, and an innovation in Canada. The pilot data have some limitations. They cannot provide any causal insights due to their cross-sectional nature. Nevertheless, they can provide preliminary indications of likely relationships and suggest avenues for future research.

The pilot sampled establishments based on the Business Register of Statistical Establishments, and data were collected in the winter of 1996. From the 994 eligible establishments in the sample, 747 responses were received (a 75 percent response rate), 648 of which were complete responses. On the employee side, completed surveys were received from 1,943 employees working in these establishments, thus representing an average of three employee survey responses per establishment.

The pilot survey contained questions about three types of technological change in the three prior years; earlier changes were not captured. The three categories were: major new software and/or hardware installations (New SOHA); computer-controlled or computer-assisted technology implementations (New NCC); and implementation of other major new technology or machinery (New MACH).

Generally, New SOHA represent the types of technology conceptually associated with the knowledge economy – "new computer" installations. However, microelectronic miniaturization increasingly allows computer technology to be embedded in many different types of instruments, making it more difficult to draw the line on this technology.[3] Since definitions of information technology vary and the purpose of this paper is to identify trends in the relationship between technology and work organization, the first two measures (SOHA and NCC) of what are essentially different types of computer technology implementation were both used in the analyses that follow. It cannot as easily be argued that the third category (New MACH) is part of the knowledge economy. The category was preserved and carried through the investigation, however, for purposes of comparison and as a validity check on the results and conclusions. Furthermore, in order to explore differences between establishments that implement only one type of technology and those that implement several types, eight technology-change categories were created.[4]

Because organizational and human resource practices are the focus of the WES, most of the measures available for use in this study fell into this category. Numerical flexibility practices – such as the use of various separations and new hires as percentages of the establishment's total permanent workforce – were measured, as were functional flexibility practices. The latter include the number of employee participation programs; the extent of decentralization of decision making (measured on a scale ranging from 1 to 11); the number of different types of vocational, nonvocational, and total training offered to employees; and percentage of employees participating in training programs at work. Variables such as gender, years of education, hourly wages, and hours worked are also available.

Difference-of-means tests (analysis of variance) were used to investigate whether workplace practices and employment contracts differ significantly across the different combinations of new-technology implementation. Only significant differences are reported, with one exception, which is noted (see Figure 3).

Results

Table 1 provides descriptive statistics for selected variables and Figure 1 graphically depicts the incidence of technological change by type of technology implemented. Almost 40 percent of the sample reported no new implementations of technology in the prior three years. Some 37 percent reported major implementations of new software and/or hardware (New

SOHA). Implementation rates drop off drastically – lower than 10 percent – for all other combinations.

The sample average for the percentage of employees using computers is 49 percent. Figure 2 shows, however, that the average is much higher for establishments with a major New SOHA installation in the prior three years (62 percent, compared with 41 percent in establishments with no such

Table 1

Selected descriptive statistics

Variable name	Range (minimum to maximum)	Mean or % (standard deviation)
New software and/or hardware (New SOHA)	0 to 1	53%
New computer-controlled or computer-assisted technology (New NCC)	0 to1	19%
Other new technology or machinery (New MACH)	0 to 1	17%
Total permanent employees	1 to 25,000	513 (1,518)
Percentage of establishments unionized	0 to 1	36%
Proportion of total permanent workforce unionized	0 to 100	26 (37)

Figure 1

Incidence of technological changes during the last three years

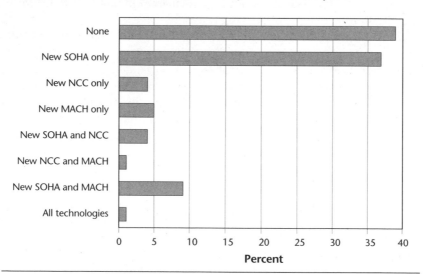

Note: Results are weighted for sample establishments. See text for explanation of types of technological changes.

installation). At 27 percent, the percentage is significantly lower for establishments that only implemented New MACH. The highest computer usage rates are found in New SOHA establishments, as might be expected. While not especially interesting, this result provides some evidence of the validity of the survey questions about new technology implementation.

Figure 3 presents the average number of employees per establishment, by size category. These differences are not significant, and the data are presented for information purposes only. Figure 4 demonstrates the relationship between numerical flexibility practices, measured by workforce separations and new hires as a percentage of the workforce, and the new types of technology implemented. Separation and new-hire rates were generally highest in establishments that implemented no new technologies or in those that implemented New MACH changes only. Overall, Figures 3 and 4 show a pattern of reduced use of numerical flexibility practices – whether "shrinking" (separations or turnover) or expanding (new hires) in establishments implementing new computer technologies.

Different approaches to flexibility are captured in the business strategy questions asked in the establishment portion of the WES. Fourteen questions were used to create four scales representing the different approaches to flexibility: internal, external, numerical, and functional. The different combinations of new technology implementations show significantly different scores on the various approaches to business strategy (Figure 5). Most

Figure 2

Percentage of employees in establishments using computers, by type of technological change during the last three years

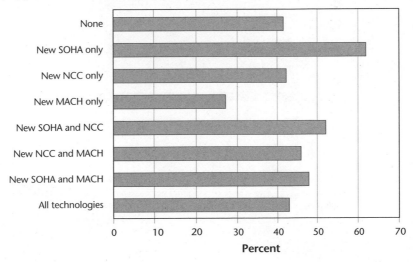

Figure 3

Average number of employees per establishment, by type of technological change during the last three years

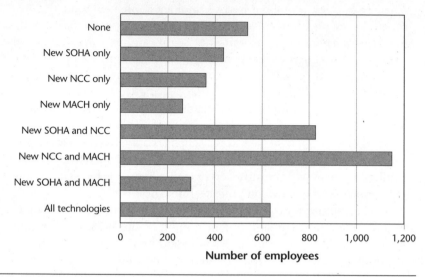

Note: There were no significant differences across technology change categories.

Figure 4

Numerical flexibility practices: all separations and new hires as percentages of current total employees in establishments, by type of technological change during the last three years

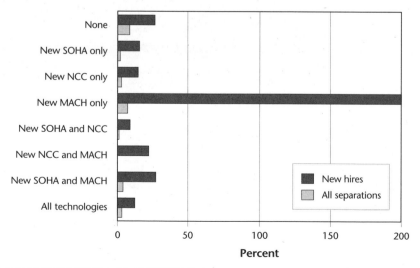

notably, those establishments implementing no new technology scored the lowest on all of the business strategy measures, suggesting that they might not engage in strategic business planning, whereas establishments implementing all three types of new technology scored the highest on internal, external, and functional flexibility, but not on numerical flexibility.

Functional flexibility practices are often represented by training activities in establishments. As Figure 6 shows, the establishments that implement more types of new technology also offer more types of training.

Functional flexibility also includes such practices as employee participation in decision making. Figures 7 and 8 show that technology implementers use formal participation programs, such as suggestion programs, quality circles, information sharing, and so on more often, and are also more decentralized in their decision making. These results are reassuring, since the

Figure 5

Business strategies and flexibility of establishments, by type of technological change during the last three years

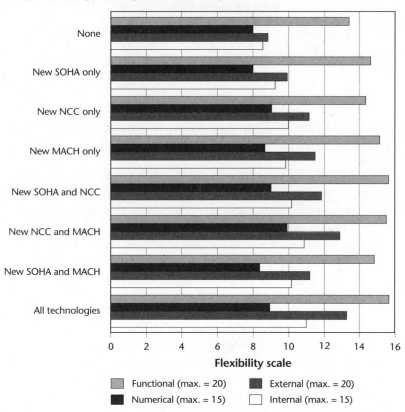

Figure 6

Functional flexibility practices: number of types of training offered in establishments, by type of technological change during the last three years

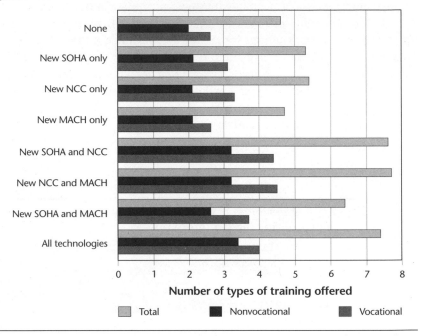

literature indicates that the successful implementation of new technologies requires increased employee participation in decision making and access to training.

Figure 9 shows rates of product and process innovations by types of technological changes. Again, we observe that technology implementers show higher rates of innovation. In general, the more types of technology implemented, the higher the rates of innovation.

The last set of charts shows the relationship between different combinations of new technology implementation, employee demographics (gender and education), and work outcomes (hours of work and wages). Figure 10 shows that establishments installing new software and/or hardware have proportionately more females in the workforce, while establishments installing new machinery have proportionately fewer females in the workforce. Figure 11 shows the average years of education by types of technology implemented. Lower levels of average education appear with different combinations of numerical- or computer-controlled technologies and new machinery implementations, while the highest levels of education are found in combination with new software and/or hardware implementations.

Figure 7

Functional flexibility practices: number of types of participation programs in establishments, by type of technological change during the last three years

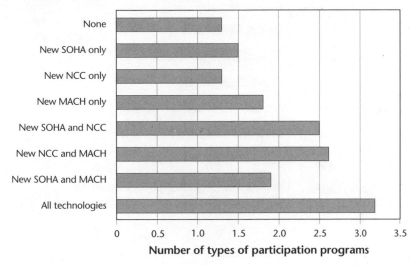

Number of types of participation programs

Figure 8

Functional flexibility practices: decentralization index of establishments, by type of technological change during the last three years

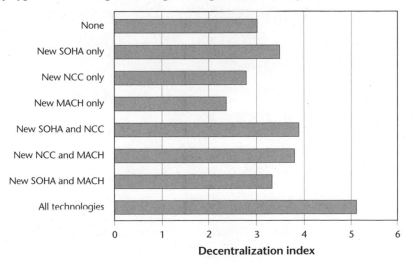

Decentralization index

Figure 9

Product and process innovations in establishments, by type of technological change during the last three years

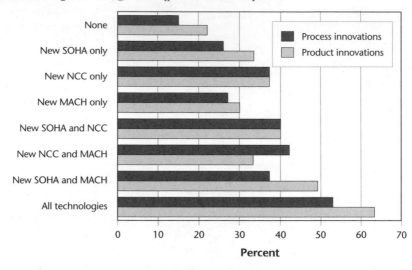

Figure 10

Percentage of female employees in establishments, by type of technological change during the last three years

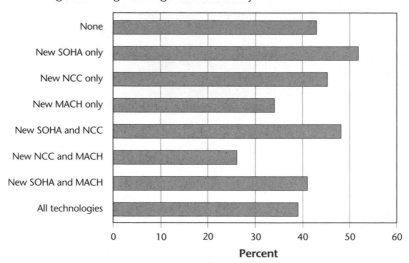

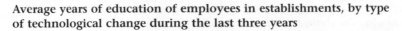

Figure 11

Average years of education of employees in establishments, by type of technological change during the last three years

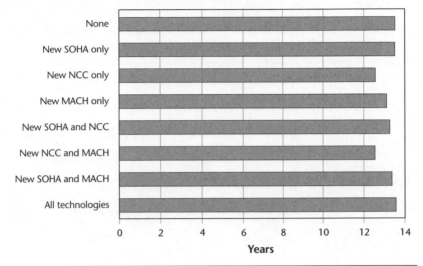

Average weekly hours of work, shown in Figure 12, are highest in establishments implementing new machinery. Wages (Figure 13) are generally higher in these establishments as well, although it appears that both no new technology and more combinations of new technology are also associated with higher average hourly wages. There is little evidence in this sample of a relationship between implementation of new computer technologies and higher hours of work or hourly wages.

Conclusions

Overall, these results suggest that establishments that implement new computer technologies are less tumultuous places in which to work, with lower turnover and fewer new hires, proportionately speaking. Yet on an intellectual or learning dimension, these establishments are more dynamic, in that they demonstrate higher levels of training and employee involvement in decision making. These results are consistent with the "optimistic" view of new technology (Woodward 1965; Peters 1997), which predicts higher levels of education and training in the presence of new technology implementation.

There is no evidence in this sample that the implementation of computer technology has adverse effects on individual employee labour market

Figure 12

Average weekly hours of work in establishments, by type of technological change during the last three years

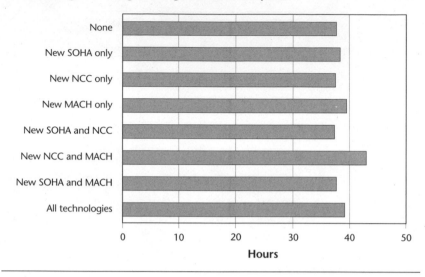

Figure 13

Average hourly wages in establishments, by type of technological change during the last three years

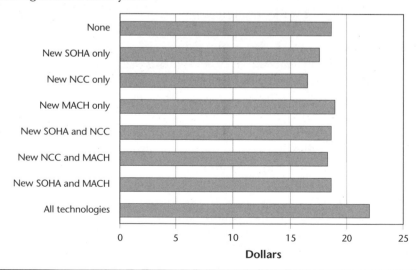

outcomes in the cross-section, either in terms of increasing hours of work or decreasing wages. There is a slight suggestion that the implementation of computer technology may increase gender segregation (non-implementers have 43 percent female employees, while New SOHA implementers have 52 percent female employees). However, the implementation of new computer technology appears to improve the economic *integration* of women at work. The results suggest that if we are concerned with the tendency of new technology to increase income inequality or segregation, we should focus attention on the effects of the installation of new machinery and other types of noncomputer technology. Gender differences are more pronounced in these establishments, where fewer women work *and* average hourly wages and hours of work are significantly higher.

The employment effects of computer technology at the establishment level appear to be neutral. Employment is neither expanding nor shrinking in computer implementers. There was no significant difference in establishment size between implementers and non-implementers of the different types and combinations of technology.

It is important to sound a note of caution in the interpretation of these results. The WES pilot data provide only a picture of the cross-section, and hence causality cannot be inferred. We should wait for future WES production data and examine changes over time before drawing any strong conclusions about the relationships between computer technologies, organizational practices, employment contracts, and firm performance in Canadian establishments.

Rather, the pilot results highlight areas that require further research. The issue of possible variation in the labour effects of different implementations of the same or similar technologies has not been explored. Additionally, little research has focused on the effects of new technology on occupational segregation or gender differences in labour market outcomes. The results presented here suggest either no effect or a small positive effect in the sense of increasing gender integration at the establishment level. This result contradicts earlier case studies on gender and technology (Crewe 1991; Edvardsson 1994; Roos 1990; Truman and Keating 1988; Walsh 1991), but is more consistent with recent quantitative studies in Canada using larger datasets (see Chaykowski and Powell, forthcoming). Again, the longitudinal WES production data will provide a resource with which to improve our understanding of these relationships.

Notes

1 I would like to thank Jean-Pierre Voyer, Strategic Policy, Applied Research Branch, Human Resources Development Canada, for suggesting the topic of this chapter, which was written while I was working at Statistics Canada. Words are inadequate to express my gratitude to Garnett Picot, Director of the Business and Labour Market Analysis Division, for providing me with the resources to complete it. I would also like to thank Ted Wannell and Marie

Drolet, both of Statistics Canada, for their assistance, and Liann Joanette for contributing her graphical presentation skills. While I have benefited from the support of these individuals and institutions, the opinions in this paper are my own, and should in no way be interpreted as representative of the opinions of anyone at HRDC or Statistics Canada.

2 Alternatively, if the way we use technology drives the effects on labour, then perhaps we can observe a relationship between the motivation for the implementation of new technology and human resource practices. Unfortunately, this question is not available on the Workplace and Employee Survey (WES) – but no survey captures all of the variables that might be desired by any given researcher.

3 For example, what if my wristwatch now contains a calculator and memory, and therefore allows me to download data from a machine that I use to monitor temperature and flow in a chemical manufacturing facility? And what if I use my wristwatch to store the information I need to write up my daily reports at my desk? Have I now become a knowledge worker even though I am officially classified as "unskilled" or "semi-skilled"? The WES does not capture this level of detail, but the illustration is provided to show how the miniaturization of microelectronics can convert what were formerly and unarguably mechanical or simple electrical devices into "computers," or knowledge devices.

4 These are: no new technology; new software and/or hardware only; new numerical- or computer-controlled technology only; new machinery only; new software and/or hardware AND new numerical- or computer-controlled technology; new numerical- or computer-controlled technology AND new machinery; new software and/or hardware AND new machinery; and all technologies implemented.

References

Aronowitz, Stanley, and William DiFazio. 1994. *The Jobless Future: Sci-Tech and the Dogma of Work*. Minneapolis, MN: University of Minnesota Press.

Baldwin, John, and Joanne Johnson. 1996. "Business Strategies in More- and Less-Innovative Firms in Canada." *Research Policy* 25: 785-804.

Barley, Stephen R. 1986. "Technology as an Occasion for Structuring: Evidence from Observations of CT Scanners and the Social Order of Radiology Departments." *Administrative Science Quarterly* 31,1: 78-108.

Braverman, Harry. 1974. *Labor and Monopoly Capital: The Degradation of Work in the Twentieth Century*. New York: Monthly Review Press.

Chaykowski, Richard, and Lisa Powell, eds. Forthcoming. *Women and Work*. Kingston, ON: John Deutsch Institute.

Crewe, Louise. 1991. "New Technologies, Employment Shifts and Gender Divisions within the Textile Industry." *New Technology, Work and Employment* 6,1: 43-53.

Edvardsson, Ingi Rúnar. 1994. "Skill, Gender and Technical Change in a Nordic Environment: Typesetting in Iceland and Sweden." *New Technology, Work and Employment* 9,1: 30-42.

Hill, Stephen. 1981. *Competition and Control at Work: The New Industrial Sociology*. Cambridge, MA: MIT Press.

Noble, David F. 1984. *Forces of Production: A Social History of Industrial Automation*. New York: Alfred A. Knopf.

Peters, Thomas J. 1997. *The Circle of Innovation: You Can't Shrink Your Way to Greatness*. NY: Alfred A. Knopf.

Piore, Michael J. 1985. "Computer Technologies, Market Structure, and Strategic Union Choices." In Thomas A. Kochan, ed., *Challenges and Choices Facing American Labor*, 175-92. Cambridge, MA: MIT Press.

Roos, Patricia A. 1990. "Hot-Metal to Electronic Composition: Gender, Technology, and Social Change." In Barbara F. Reskin and Patricia A. Roos, eds., *Job Queues, Gender Queues: Explaining Women's Inroads into Male Occupations*, 275-98. Philadelphia: Temple University Press.

Shaiken, Harley. 1984. *Work Transformed*. New York: Holt, Rinehart and Winston.

Snell, Scott, and James Dean. 1992. "Integrated Manufacturing and Human Resource Management: A Human Capital Perspective." *Academy of Management Journal* 35,3: 467-504.

Thomas, Robert J. 1994. *What Machines Can't Do: Politics and Technology in the Industrial Enterprise*. Berkeley, CA: University of California Press.

Truman, Carole, and Joan Keating. 1988. "Technology, Markets, and the Design of Women's Jobs: The Case of the Clothing Industry." *New Technology, Work and Employment* 3,1: 21-29.

Walsh, Janet. 1991. "Restructuring, Productivity and Workplace Relations: Evidence from the Textile Industry." *New Technology, Work and Employment* 6,2: 124-37.

Wilkinson, Barry. 1983. *The Shopfloor Politics of New Technology*. London: Heinemann Educational Books.

Woodward, Joan. 1965. *Industrial Organization: Theory and Practice*. New York: Oxford University Press.

12

The Changing Skill Structure of Employment in Canada[1]

Yves Gingras, Philippe Massé, and Richard Roy

Introduction

The view that industrialized economies are experiencing a new period of economic development in which knowledge plays an increasing role in the organization and development of economic activities has gained currency in recent decades. While one can claim that all modern economies have been founded on knowledge, some argue that we are now entering an era in which the capacity to accumulate knowledge becomes a *sine qua non* for individuals to access employment and adapt to changing circumstances, and for an economy to achieve growth (Lavoie and Roy 1998). In this context, understanding changes in employment patterns, particularly as they relate to changes in skills requirements, has become increasingly central to a better understanding of the labour market implications of the trend towards a more "knowledge-based economy" (KBE).

Technological change in general, and information and communication technologies (ICTs) in particular, are often considered the main sources of significant labour market change. Like electricity and steam power, ICTs are general-purpose technologies (GPTs) that are very pervasive and, according to Lipsey (1996), bring with them deep structural adjustments (DSAs).

While these new technologies are a catalyst of change in employment patterns, they are only one of the myriad interconnected factors that are contributing to the labour market reality we are presently witnessing. Suffice it to mention the recent intensification of international competition, which has led to changes in trading patterns and important employment adjustments, institutional change in the labour market, changes in organizational behaviour, government policies, and so on. All of these elements contribute to modify employment patterns (OECD 1996).

The purpose of this chapter is to present a short synthesis of recent findings on the changing skill structure of employment and on some of the sources of change emerging from Human Resources Development Canada's (HRDC) research program on the theme of *Skills Requirements in the Knowledge-Based Economy.* It will address three main questions:

- How has the skill structure of employment evolved in Canada?
- What has been the role of technological change in the changing structure of employment?
- Do the skills of the Canadian workforce meet the requirements of the knowledge-based economy?

The bulk of the chapter examines the changing structure of employment using an occupational classification scheme that categorizes occupations on the basis of the tasks performed by workers. This approach was originally developed by Wolff and Baumol (1989) and adapted for Canada by Lavoie and Roy (1998).

The section that follows, "A Knowledge-Based Occupational Classification Scheme," presents the rationale for examining the occupational structure rather than the industrial structure in order to understand the employment implications of a KBE, and describes the classification scheme. "Occupational Employment Trends and the Skill Requirements of Knowledge Occupations" examines the broad employment trends by type of worker over the period 1971-91 and the skills required of these occupations along several dimensions. "Sources of Employment Changes" presents some evidence on the possible sources of employment changes, particularly the impact of computerization on the demand for the different types of workers. In "Skills Requirements and the Skills of the Canadian Workforce" we examine several indicators to assess whether Canada's population possesses the skills to meet the requirements of the new economy. Finally, the conclusion summarizes briefly some of the main findings, identifies knowledge gaps, and outlines plans for future research.

A Knowledge-Based Occupational Classification Scheme
In a recent study, Marie Lavoie and Richard Roy (1998) presented some of the basic facts regarding the broad employment trends in the knowledge-based economy. The study provides a sense of the magnitude of the trend towards a KBE and its significance in terms of labour force composition. This section discusses the advantages of using occupations as opposed to industrial sectors for analysing employment trends, and describes Lavoie and Roy's (1998) classification of occupations and its rationale in the context of a KBE.

Contrary to what has been done in most Canadian studies, Lavoie and Roy (1998) do not define the KBE on the basis of industrial activities. Instead, the authors argue that the basic tasks performed by workers are more useful for understanding the skills required by the KBE and the evolving structure of employment. In particular, an industrial classification approach cannot properly capture the effects of workers' displacement due to organizational changes within firms.

The increasing rate of "contracting out" since the mid-1970s provides a good example of the potential impact organizational changes in production may have on employment. Taking the business services industry as an example, it has been argued that a significant portion of the employment growth in this sector simply reflects a shift of former internal production activities from other industries. In other words, according to this perspective, the overall composition of production in the economy, and hence total labour requirements, may not have changed much over time. Based on a classification by industry, however, one could wrongly conclude that a tremendous growth in business services activity in the economy has occurred and that an increase in the supply of workers appropriate to that industry is needed.[2] Organizational changes in production therefore cannot be entirely understood or identified on the basis of an industrial classification of activities; thus an occupational approach allows for a better understanding of the employment effects of the restructuring within establishments and firms.

The Classification Scheme

It is increasingly recognized that knowledge, as an asset, plays a critical role in the economy, and countries endowed with more knowledge are expected to be more productive. Moreover, there is growing evidence across countries to indicate important employment trends emphasizing highly skilled workers. While most studies examining employment trends combine various types of knowledge, Lavoie and Roy (1998) take into account the differentiated nature of knowledge and assume that there is some heterogeneity in the potential contribution and productivity level among categories of workers, especially among categories of highly skilled workers.

The classification scheme follows the approach developed by Wolff and Baumol (1989) and is based on the reasoning that human production tasks involve dealing with objects, with people, or with symbols, and are directed at producing goods, providing personal services, or generating information. Under this scheme, the labour force is divided into two main categories of workers: information and non-information occupations. Information occupations are further divided into two groups: data and knowledge occupations. The distinction between these two categories of occupations is meaningful in a context where ICTs affect these groups of occupations quite differently.

Data occupations involve the manipulation of symbolic information, whereas knowledge occupations involve mainly the generation of ideas or the provision of expert opinions. In other words, data workers – such as most clerical workers and technicians – use, transmit, or manipulate information, whereas knowledge workers – such as engineers, scientists, or economists – produce knowledge. The broad distinction between these two categories of occupations in a context in which ICTs are highly pervasive is that data occupations involve a relatively large portion of routinized tasks that could be fairly easily replaced or supported by electronic devices, whereas the knowledge category of occupations involves the production of new ideas and requires some level of creativity for which the computer and other technologies can hardly serve as a substitute.

Looking at the non-information category of occupations – services and goods occupations – the same logic can apply in relation to the diffusion of ICTs. Goods occupations are amenable to technological change, given the more routinized and therefore codifiable nature of the tasks these occupations entail. Conversely, services occupations, which include personal services, are not really codifiable since the tasks are highly tacit. That is, they constitute a group of occupations for which the expertise is mainly built on experience (learning by doing) instead of routinized tasks. These distinctions are likely important in the context of technological change, as will be discussed in the section "Sources of Employment Changes" below.[3]

The knowledge category of workers has been further divided into five subcategories: pure science, applied science, computer science, engineering, and social sciences and humanities (SSH). This division reflects the fact that the knowledge category is not homogeneous in terms of tacit/codified content of tasks as well as in terms of the nature of the know-how involved. Moreover, in relation to technological change, science and technology expertise is at the core of the innovation process and is therefore the driving force in the KBE. Disaggregating the knowledge category is thus necessary to better understand the way in which these different bodies of knowledge are linked with scientific and technological change.

The final category of occupations to consider is the management category. Whereas Wolff and Baumol (1989) considered this category as a hybrid of the knowledge/data occupations, Lavoie and Roy (1998) argue that managing requires different skills from those required to perform a knowledge occupation and from the ones on which data occupations rely. In other words, managerial complexity is different from scientific, technological, or social complexity. As a result, the management category is treated separately and is split into two categories – science and technology (S&T) management and other management. The classification scheme is shown in Figure 1.[4]

Occupational Employment Trends and the Skill Requirements of Knowledge Occupations

We now examine growth and changes in the composition of employment for each category of workers over the 1971-96 period based on the classification scheme described above. We also provide some evidence on the skill requirements for the knowledge category of occupations.

Figure 1

Occupational classification. Occupational titles included are examples only.

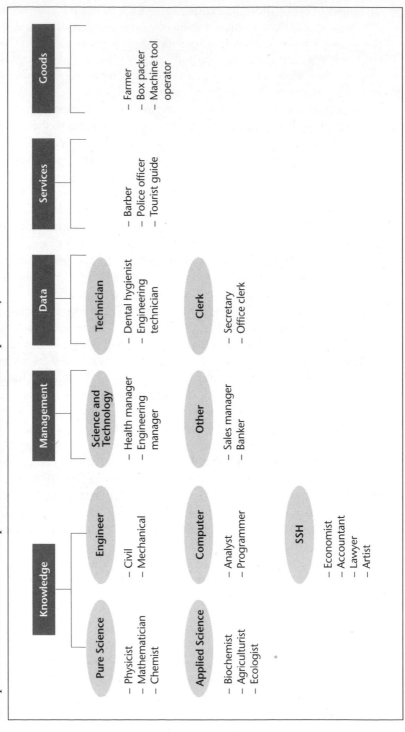

Source: Lavoie and Roy (1998).

Employment Trends by Occupational Skills

Table 1 shows employment growth and employment share by type of worker over the 1971-96 period. Growth in total employment averaged 2.1 percent per year over this period, with major recessions in the early 1980s and 1990s contributing to slower overall employment growth in more recent decades compared with the 1970s. The management category outpaced all other groups of occupations over this period with spectacular growth during the

Table 1

Employment by category of occupations, 1971-96

Categories	Total Employment (in thousands)				
	1971	1981	1986	1991	1996
Knowledge	428	677	827	1,038	1,172
Pure Science	25	30	37	45	51
Applied Science	58	77	89	106	112
Engineering	96	137	148	185	198
Computer	24	59	97	144	177
SSH	226	373	456	558	634
Management	219	747	966	1,260	1,383
Science & Technology	18	87	96	123	135
Other	201	660	870	1,137	1,248
Data	2,935	3,953	4,299	4,874	5,075
Services	1,175	1,485	1,795	2,047	2,213
Goods	3,346	3,805	3,815	3,786	3,927
Total Employment	**8,103**	**10,667**	**11,702**	**13,005**	**13,769**

Categories	Average Annual Rate of Growth (%)			
	1971-81	1981-91	1991-96	1971-96
Knowledge	4.7	4.4	2.5	4.1
Pure Science	1.9	4.1	2.5	2.9
Applied Science	3.0	3.2	1.1	2.7
Engineering	3.6	3.1	1.4	3.0
Computer	9.5	9.3	4.2	8.3
SSH	5.2	4.1	2.6	4.2
Management	13.0	5.4	1.9	7.6
Science & Technology	17.0	3.5	1.9	8.4
Other	12.6	5.6	1.9	7.6
Data	3.0	2.1	0.8	2.2
Services	2.4	3.3	1.6	2.6
Goods	1.3	-0.1	0.7	0.6
Total Employment	**2.8**	**2.0**	**1.1**	**2.1**

Source: Lavoie and Roy (1998).
Note: Census data used for 1971, 1981, 1986, and 1991. Figures for 1996 are based on the Labour Force Survey data.

first decade. At 7.6 percent per year, the management category had by far the highest rate of growth over the 1971-96 period, expanding at nearly four times the pace of total employment and close to twice that of total knowledge occupations (4.1 percent). Knowledge occupations grew the fastest in the 1990s, however, at more than twice the rate of total employment (2.5 versus 1.1 percent per year).

At a disaggregated level, computer science occupations outpaced all other groups of occupations (8.3 percent) except for the S&T management category, which grew at about the same rate. While computer science occupations accounted for the same proportion as pure science occupations in 1971, the rate of growth of the former was nearly three times that of the latter during the entire period. This reflected the skill bias towards computer science workers as a result of the proliferation of computer technologies. Interestingly, the SSH group[5] experienced stronger growth than the engineering and science occupations assumed to be at the core of the knowledge-based economy, where science and technology activities are increasingly considered the engine of the economy.

While the growth of knowledge occupations has been strong, their overall share of employment remains small. In 1996, knowledge occupations accounted for only 8.5 percent of total employment in Canada, up from 5.1 percent in 1971. On the other hand, their share has generally increased in all major industry groups, including industries normally considered "low-tech." The growth in employment of knowledge workers therefore represents a widespread trend in the Canadian economy.

Skill Requirements of Knowledge Occupations

Given the pervasiveness of knowledge occupations in the economy, an important question relates to the underlying skills required in these fast-growing occupations. As shown in Figure 2, knowledge workers are highly educated. Around 50 percent have a university degree and another 28 percent have at least some postsecondary qualifications.

While education is an important measure of the skills required to perform a job, other dimensions of skills are increasingly emphasized in the context of the emerging KBE. For example, evidence from HRDC's Essential Skills Project and Sector Studies indicates that the literacy requirements of jobs are increasing in many sectors as a result of technological and organizational change.[6] Literacy skills are also essential to the development of "digital literacy" skills – that is, familiarity with computers and networks and the ability to use them. Other dimensions, such as problem-solving skills, communication skills, organizational skills, and the ability to work in teams, are also being increasingly emphasized.

The importance of literacy skills for knowledge work is revealed in a study by Boothby (forthcoming), who used the results from the International Adult

Figure 2

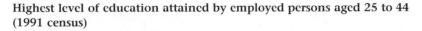

Highest level of education attained by employed persons aged 25 to 44 (1991 census)

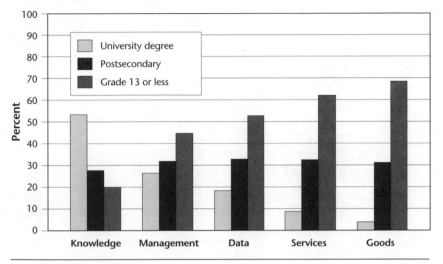

Source: Lavoie and Roy (1998).

Literacy Survey (IALS) to examine the distribution of literacy levels among the different occupational categories[7] for three types of literacy skills: prose, document, and quantitative literacy.[8] Figure 3 shows the document literacy levels by occupational category. In general, workers with the highest literacy level (level 4/5) are concentrated among knowledge, management, and data occupations. In contrast, workers with the lowest literacy levels (levels 1 and 2) make up the majority of workers in data manipulation, service, skilled goods, and other goods occupations. Similar patterns can be observed when examining prose and quantitative literacy.

With respect to other skill dimensions, a recent study by Béjaoui (forthcoming) examines the basic competencies required by occupations according to five skill types: cognitive skills, authority-management skills, communication skills, fine motor skills, and gross motor skills.[9] His analysis shows that the knowledge and management categories of occupations require significantly higher levels of cognitive, authority-management, and communication skills than most other occupations.

Sources of Employment Changes
The preceding section has shown that over the last quarter-century or so, the proportion of knowledge workers has grown substantially in the Canadian economy. This phenomenon has generally encompassed all major

Figure 3

Document literacy levels by occupational category

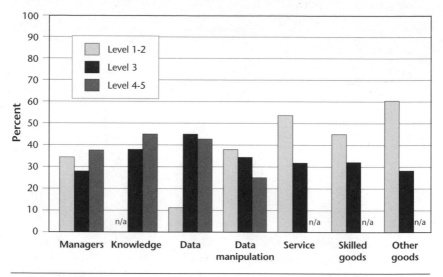

Source: Boothby (forthcoming).
Note: N/a = Percentages omitted due to insufficient sample size.

industry groups and therefore represents a widespread trend in the Canadian economy. Why is this happening?

A number of different factors have been proposed to explain the occupational employment trends we are observing. The proliferation of technological innovations and their dissemination throughout the economy is certainly a prime candidate. They may have made the organization of production more complex so that businesses may require more and more knowledge workers to operate and thrive in the new world economic order. The fact that the proportion of knowledge workers has grown in all major industry groups certainly suggests that the source of change is systemic. Institutional reforms and the globalization of markets, perhaps triggered by innovations in information technology, may also have played a key role in the growing importance of knowledge workers. Other lines of argument, however, such as changes in tastes and differences in labour productivity growth-rate trends between industries, also offer possible explanations for such variations in the labour force composition over time.

An Employment Growth Decomposition Exercise

To help delineate the broad proximate causes of the changes in the share of knowledge workers in the economy, Lavoie and Roy (1998) use a growth accounting methodology to decompose the total change in the proportion of a given group of workers in total employment over time into three different components.

The first component is a skill *substitution effect* occurring within the production technology of domestic firms or industries. That is, for given levels of industry output and employment composition, factors such as technological innovations or institutional reforms may favour a more intensive use of a given type of worker. For example, it is often claimed that the widespread diffusion of computer-based technology in the 1980s has led to a systemic substitution in the skill mix of the labour force favouring knowledge workers.

The second source of change can be attributed to differences in labour productivity growth rates among industries (the *productivity lag effect*). That is, for a fixed proportion of industry output and unchanged occupational structure, industries with stagnant labour productivity will require a growing fraction of total employment through time.

Finally, the third component – the *output effect* – occurs when, for a given occupational structure and labour productivity by industry, shifts in the composition of final output of the domestic industry give rise to proportional changes in the structure of employment. For example, an increase in domestic final spending on products requiring a relatively large proportion of knowledge workers in their production (in the finance, insurance, and real estate industries, for example) will give rise to an increase in the proportion of knowledge workers in the economy.[10]

Table 2 presents the results from the decomposition exercise. Of the three effects, the substitution effect is the most dominant. It is extremely important, especially for the knowledge and management categories of occupations, over the whole period. Both management and computer science workers, in particular, were strongly affected over time by this component, which tends to reflect their pervasive expertise throughout the economy. It is fairly obvious that computer scientists have become an important source of expertise to deal with the increased complexity of problems related to the widespread diffusion of computer technologies. The intensification of global competition – in part brought about by the introduction of ICTs – may also explain the widespread need for managerial expertise.

Moreover, the importance of the substitution effect in explaining the growth of knowledge workers seems to be increasing over time. For example, between 1971 and 1981, the substitution effect accounted for about a third of their growth compared with 60 percent over the 1981-91 period.

The productivity lag component extensively influenced the growth in data and services workers. Despite the fact that a part of their activity is readily amenable to technological change, another portion – the tacit part – cannot be transformed by technology. The output component had a modest effect compared with the other two but was larger for data workers and,

Table 2

Decomposition of the change in business sector employment composition, 1971-91

Categories		Substitution Effect	Productivity Lag Effect	Output Effect	Total Change[1]
Knowledge	1971-91	1.53	0.96	0.61	3.10
	1971-81	0.39	0.47	0.30	1.16
	1981-91	1.14	0.49	0.31	1.94
Pure Science	1971-91	0.02	0.01	0.01	0.04
	1971-81	−0.03	0.01	0.00	−0.02
	1981-91	0.05	0.00	0.00	0.05
Applied Science	1971-91	0.03	0.06	0.01	0.10
	1971-81	0.01	0.04	−0.00	0.05
	1981-91	0.02	0.02	0.01	0.05
Engineering	1971-91	0.21	0.07	0.13	0.41
	1971-81	0.08	0.06	0.07	0.21
	1981-91	0.13	0.00	0.06	0.19
Computer	1971-91	0.76	0.06	0.09	0.91
	1971-81	0.21	0.02	0.03	0.26
	1981-91	0.55	0.04	0.06	0.65
SSH	1971-91	0.51	0.76	0.37	1.64
	1971-81	0.12	0.33	0.21	0.66
	1981-91	0.39	0.42	0.17	0.98
Management	1971-91	7.81	0.37	−0.23	7.95
	1971-81	4.97	0.13	−0.06	5.04
	1981-91	2.85	0.24	−0.17	2.92
Science & Technology	1971-91	0.88	−0.05	−0.01	0.82
	1971-81	0.65	−0.03	0.01	0.63
	1981-91	0.23	−0.03	−0.02	0.18
Other	1971-91	6.93	0.43	−0.22	7.14
	1971-81	4.31	0.15	−0.07	4.39
	1981-91	2.62	0.27	−0.15	2.74
Data	1971-91	−2.29	3.56	0.77	2.04
	1971-81	−1.83	2.25	0.35	0.77
	1981-91	−0.46	1.30	0.42	1.26
Services	1971-91	−1.58	3.72	−0.33	1.81
	1971-81	−0.93	1.92	−0.04	0.95
	1981-91	−0.65	1.79	−0.29	0.85
Goods	1971-91	−5.46	−3.55	−5.87	−14.88
	1971-81	−2.59	−2.28	−3.05	−7.92
	1981-91	−2.87	−1.27	−2.83	−6.97

Source: Lavoie and Roy (1998).
[1] The total change in this table is based on total hours worked.

to a lesser extent, for knowledge workers, reflecting a shift towards data-intensive output and a weaker shift towards knowledge-intensive output.

The intensification of the substitution effect during the 1980s, particularly for knowledge workers, combined with the fact that their share has increased in all major industrial sectors, suggests that knowledge workers have now become essential in the production process of most industries. These findings suggest that technological change is a major force behind such occupational employment trends. The results are only suggestive of the role of science and technology, however, and little is actually known about its impact on the structure of employment in Canada.

HRDC has therefore embarked on a research program aimed at developing a better understanding of the relationship between various types of technology or measures of technological change and occupational employment trends. For example, the program will investigate the impact of advanced manufacturing technologies such as robots and computer-aided design on the employment structure in the manufacturing sector. Another study will examine the impact of research and development (R&D) investments (fundamental, development, and applied research) on employment in all sectors of the economy, including the public sector. The international dimensions of technological change (e.g., foreign direct investment, foreign R&D, trade) and their impact on the employment structure also will be examined. Results from a first study by Lavoie and Therrien (1999), which focuses on the impact of investment in computers on the different categories of workers, provides us with a first glance at the potential role of technology, and are described next.

Employment Effects of Computerization

Computerization – the diffusion of a combination of hardware and software – has accelerated in the last 25 years due to advances in electronic technologies, the advent of the microprocessor, and the tremendous development of the software industry. The process of codification has intensified and routinized tasks are disappearing, changing the structure of employment. The computer is increasingly associated with a number of occupations requiring highly skilled workers.

Lavoie and Therrien (1999) examine the impact of investments in computers at the industry level on the occupational structure of employment over the 1971-91 period. The authors assume that computerization complements some categories of skills and replaces others, depending on the nature of tasks – that is, tacit versus codified, and core versus complementary.[11] Three hypotheses are tested:

1   The increasing use of computers is biased in favour of certain categories of workers. That is, computerization increases the proportion of certain

categories of workers required per unit of output because it increases the complexity of certain tasks that are too tacit to be codified and that require the development of new skills (labour-using or complementarity bias).

2   The increasing use of computers reduces the demand for certain categories of workers because their core and complementary tasks are codifiable (substitution bias).

3   The computer has no effect because of the highly tacit nature of the tasks performed in certain occupations (neutral effect).[12]

In contrast to similar studies that tend to divide the workforce into two broad skill categories (e.g., skilled versus unskilled), the authors segment total employment into the nine categories of occupations described earlier under "Occupational Employment Trends and the Skill Requirements of Knowledge Occupations." This enables them to capture the diversity of possible relationships between computers and the different occupational categories. In addition, unlike most other studies, which focus exclusively on the manufacturing sector, Lavoie and Therrien (1999) provide evidence on the primary, manufacturing, and service sectors.[13] Only the results of the aggregate analysis will be presented here, however.

An examination of the magnitude of the regression coefficients presented in Table 3 reveals that in the 1970s, the impact of the computer on the employment structure was not significantly different from that of other types of physical capital. In the 1980s, however, the impact of computers outweighed the effect of other capital, reflecting the significant diffusion of computers from the mid-1980s onward.

The aggregate estimates show that there is an increasing complementarity between computer intensity and the knowledge, data, and management categories of workers. For knowledge workers, the computer is mainly a complementary tool supporting core activities. In contrast, computers are more central to the core activities of data workers but tend to change the content of their jobs, placing greater emphasis on tacit complementary tasks. Thus, for data workers there appears to be a shift in the content of their work from codifiable core tasks to tacit complementary tasks as a result of computerization.

Computerization has not had any effect on service workers, because their tasks are largely tacit and cannot yet be codified (e.g., barbers, child-care workers). On the other hand, computerized equipment and goods workers were found to be substitutes, with the strength of this relationship increasing significantly during the 1980s compared with the 1970s. As a whole, however, the authors find that computerization is more a labour-using than a labour-saving process but that computerization itself is not sufficient to account for all employment effects of technology.

Table 3

Employment effect of computerization

	Knowledge	Management	Data	Goods
Capital intensity	1.5061**	0.2412	3.3895**	-4.8594**
Computer investment intensity (1971 and 1981)	1.1608**	0.2448**	3.8560**	-6.4636**
Computer investment intensity (1986 and 1991)	2.5829**	0.5433**	5.6372**	-10.025**

** Statistically significant at the 5% level.
Notes:
Dependent variables are employment shares (× 100) for the Knowledge, Management, Data, and Goods occupations.
Capital intensity = (Capital stock)/(Value added)
Computer investment intensity = (Computer investment)/(Machinery and equipment investment)
Time and industry dummies are included. Relative wages (wages of knowledge, management, data, and goods occupations relative to the wages of the service occupations) are also included.
Coefficients are produced by SUR estimation. Standard errors are heteroscedastic-consistent.
See Lavoie and Therrien (1999) for a detailed description of the methodology and estimation results.

In answer to our second question, the evidence presented in this section suggests that technology is indeed playing a role in shaping the structure of employment in Canada. The results are also consistent with firm-level evidence, which has shown a complementarity between the introduction of computer-based technology in firms and the use of more highly skilled workers (see, for example, McMullen 1996). While computer investment captures the general technology trend, future work using other technology variables will help to more fully capture the employment effects of technology and perhaps refine the impact of computerization.

Skills Requirements and the Skills of the Canadian Workforce

The final question to be addressed in this chapter is whether, in the face of growing demand for knowledge workers, the skills of the Canadian workforce meet the requirements of the knowledge-based economy. Does the Canadian population provide a pool of skilled labour adequate to the needs of the economy? Is the Canadian labour supply comparable to that of other modern economies? Are we investing enough in the acquisition of skills? In a recent paper, Gingras and Roy (1998) examine a series of indicators to get at some of these issues.

As shown earlier under "Occupational Employment Trends and the Skill Requirements of Knowledge Occupations," university-level qualifications appear to be an important requirement for accessing knowledge occupations.

Figure 4

Demand and supply of university-trained workers (1971 = 100)

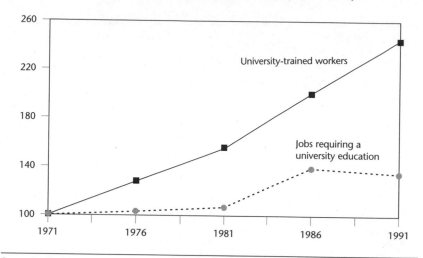

Source: Applied Research Branch, HRDC, using census data for 1971, 1981, 1986, and 1991.
Note: Jobs requiring a university education are those defined in the Canadian Classification and Dictionary of Occupations as requiring 17 or more years of education.

Figure 4 compares the growth in the number of jobs requiring a university degree with the growth in the number of university graduates between 1971 and 1991. The figure shows that the former grew by 40 percent while the latter grew by some 140 percent over that period. Thus the increase in the supply of university-educated workers has far outstripped the growth in the economy's need for these qualifications. This suggests that Canada may actually have a surplus of university-level skills.

It is possible, however, that the methodology underlying the data presented in Figure 4 overestimates the extent of the observed "oversupply" of university-educated workers. For example, the level of skills required by today's jobs may have increased, in which case the assessment of needs may fall short. Indeed, we observe from a recent review of the literature and of some sector studies performed by HRDC that skill requirements have increased over time for several occupations (upskilling). There are also examples of jobs being deskilled. While it is difficult to be categorical, it appears that overall there has been a slight increase in skill requirements within occupations.

Evidence from the National Graduates Survey also suggests that the effective growth of demand for university graduates may be greater than is suggested by Figure 4 (Gingras and Roy 1998). According to the survey, recent cohorts of university graduates are at least as satisfied with their job/education match as were earlier cohorts. For example, 84 percent of 1990 graduates at the university level reported that they were satisfied with their job/education match two years after graduation, compared with 71 percent for the 1982 cohort. Similar trends are also evident for graduates from trade/vocational and career/technical programs. If recent graduates were compelled to accept jobs for which they are overqualified, we would expect to see a deterioration in the match.

It is also possible that the number of university diplomas awarded overstates the actual level of competence possessed by graduates. While the level of education can provide some indication of a person's skill levels, we need to recognize that education varies in quality and that individuals have different aptitudes. Thus for a given level of education, the skill level of individuals may vary.

For example, the 1994 International Adult Literacy Survey indicated that 11 percent of university graduates in Canada had difficulty reading and interpreting texts. This variation in literacy skills within similarly educated groups may explain why some workers end up in jobs requiring less education than they possess. Indeed, Boothby (forthcoming) finds that around 20 percent of university graduates were in a job that required lower educational qualifications and that those with lower than average literacy levels had a much higher probability of being in such a situation. Moreover, real earnings for these university graduates were much lower than for those whose level of education matched that required by their job. To some extent, the use of educational data could result in an overestimation of skill levels, and thus the supply of skills would be lower than that shown in Figure 4.

While the apparent oversupply of skilled labour may not be as large as suggested in Figure 4, any true gap between the supply and demand for skilled labour would lead to increased differentials in labour market outcomes between high- and low-skilled individuals. In particular, an excess supply of skilled labour should lead to a fall in their relative wages. In the case of an economy-wide shortage of skilled labour, we should observe a relative rise in the wage premium paid to skilled workers. To the extent that wages are inflexible, we would expect the emergence of a gap between the supply and demand for skilled labour to be reflected in quantity adjustments (e.g., employment and participation rates).

Gingras and Boothby (1998) examine trends in access to employment and the earning ability of individuals with postsecondary education (high-skilled) relative to those with less than postsecondary education (low-skilled), and find no evidence of a deterioration in the labour market conditions of the low-skilled workforce aged 20-54 over the last 20 years. As shown in Figure 5, the overall employment rate of low-skilled workers aged 20-54 shows no deterioration relative to that of high-skilled workers between 1971

Figure 5

Employment rate and weekly earnings ratios: low- to high-skilled persons aged 25-54. (A) Employment rate ratio, 1976-97. (B) Weekly earnings ratio, 1976-95. SCF data were not collected for 1983.

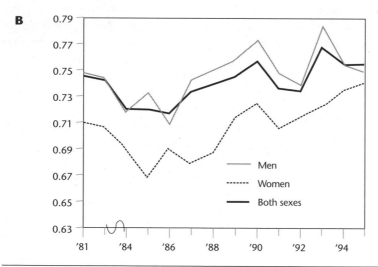

Source: Gingras and Boothby (1998).

and 1996. Access to employment for low-skilled women has actually improved, whereas it has declined slightly for low-skilled men.

An examination of trends in relative earnings leads to a similar overall conclusion. Between 1981 and 1995, the ratio of average weekly earnings of low-skilled persons to the average weekly earnings of high-skilled persons

Figure 6

Percentage of the population aged 25-64 with tertiary education, 1995

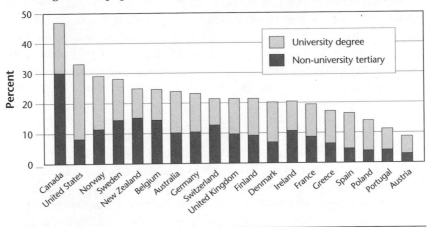

Source: OECD (1998).

actually showed a slight increase. Taken together, these trends suggest that overall there has not been a shortfall of skilled labour in Canada.[14]

How Do the Skills of the Canadian Workforce Compare with Those of Other Countries?

While the evidence indicates that, in the aggregate, the skills of the Canadian labour force largely meet the requirements of the economy, an important question is how these skills compare with those of other countries. As shown in Figure 6, Canada counts among the countries having the highest stock of human capital in terms of educational level. According to the OECD (1998), Canada led the industrialized nations in terms of the proportion of the population aged 25 to 64 having a tertiary education. In 1995, 47 percent of the Canadian population had a postsecondary education; the corresponding number for the second-place United States was 33 percent.

Canada also compares relatively well internationally in terms of average literacy attainment. For example, Canada ranked fourth behind Sweden, the Netherlands, and Germany on the document scale in 1994-95. It also ranked third and fifth on the prose and quantitative scales, respectively (OECD 1997). In general, the stock of skills of the Canadian labour force compares favourably with that of other industrialized countries.

Is There a Minimum of Skills Required to Succeed in the New Economy?

In economies where the average level of human capital is rising and production activities are becoming increasingly complex, it is possible that some share of the least skilled segment of the labour force will have difficulty finding work and will eventually quit the job market. Several studies have found that older workers with fewer than eight years of education have seen their situation deteriorate substantially in recent years. In fact, this phenomenon is not restricted to older workers. As Gingras and Boothby (1998) show, the labour market situation of the least educated (those with zero to eight years of schooling) is worsening for most age groups in Canada. Older workers are more vulnerable because the poorly educated are concentrated in this group.

The phenomenon of the least qualified workers being shut out of the labour market suggests that there is a minimum level of competence required to land a rewarding job in Canada. According to HRDC's Essential Skills Project, the literacy requirements of the lowest-skilled jobs are clustered around level 3. According to the IALS, nearly 75 percent of young Canadians between 16 and 25 possessing a high school diploma have attained level 3 or better. The rest are at levels 1 and 2 and face a reduced choice of jobs and lower earnings. Moreover, the IALS shows that persons with low levels of literacy skills are less likely to have access to adult education and training opportunities. The Canadian job market thus offers little to youths who do not have a high school diploma.

In Canada, concerns over low literacy attainment extend beyond its impact on the labour market performance of selected vulnerable groups to inequality more generally. While Canada ranks well in terms of average literacy levels, the distribution of literacy skills in Canada is much broader than in other leading countries, with relatively large numbers in both the highest and lowest literacy levels. Moreover, despite the high literacy levels recorded among youth, the literacy profile of the Canadian population is not expected to change by much in the next 30 years as a result of population ageing and increased reliance on immigration as a source of population growth – literacy proficiency tends to decline with age and is lower among immigrants. In a context where the demand for literacy skills is increasing, this finding suggests that literacy may be a source of polarization in the future.

Conclusion

This chapter has sought to provide a brief synthesis of some of the main findings of recent HRDC research on the changing skill structure of employment in Canada. Three questions were addressed:

- How has the skill structure of employment evolved in Canada?
- What has been the role of technological change in the changing structure of employment?

- Do the skills of the Canadian workforce meet the requirements of the knowledge-based economy?

With respect to the first question, we can say that on the whole the Canadian economy is becoming increasingly knowledge-based. The knowledge and management categories of occupations have been growing rapidly, and although their overall share of total employment remains small, they are increasingly essential to the production process of most industries. These occupations require high levels of education and literacy skills. They also place greater emphasis on cognitive and communication skills than most other occupations. In fact, as a general rule, employment in occupations that require high levels of cognitive and communication skills has increased faster than in other occupations. These are some of the skill dimensions that are increasingly emphasized in most definitions of a knowledge-based economy.

As for the second question, our research suggests that technological change is a major driving force behind the occupational employment trends we have been observing, particularly beginning in the second half of the 1980s. The growth decomposition analysis has shown that the substitution effect is dominant in explaining the widespread growth of knowledge and management occupations. The analysis of the employment effects of computerization shows that, in general, there is an increasing complementarity between computer intensity and the growth of the knowledge, data, and management categories of workers. It is worth emphasizing, however, that computerization has different effects depending on the occupation, complementing some categories of skills and replacing others, depending on the nature of tasks – that is, tacit versus codified, and core versus complementary.

While computer investment captures the general technology trend, future work using other technology variables will help to more fully capture the employment effects of technology and perhaps refine the impact of computerization. Further research is also required to assess the impact of other factors that may have influenced the employment structure in Canada (such as organizational change, institutional change, and international trade). One important area concerns the relationship between technological and organizational change and changes in the skill structure of employment and the nature of work. Future work in this area will focus on data from the new Workplace and Employee Survey (WES). This innovative survey links information on workplaces (such as the adoption of technology, organizational change, training, and other human resource practices) to information on employees in those workplaces (such as their wages, hours of work, job type, and skills). It is hoped that, through time, the WES will provide us with a better understanding of how technology and organizational change affect skill requirements, and how changes at the micro level are reflected in changes in the aggregate economy.

The final question addressed in this chapter is whether the Canadian labour force possesses the skills to meet the changing requirements of the economy. Our analysis of various indicators suggests that Canada is not suffering from a broad-based shortage of skilled labour. We do not observe any significant deterioration in the labour market situation of low-skilled workers relative to that of high-skilled workers. Overall, the supply of highly educated individuals appears to have more than offset increases in demand. In fact, Canada compares favourably with most of its principal trade competitors in world markets in terms of the stock of skills.

While the skills of the Canadian population appear to be adequate overall, we must recognize that they are not evenly distributed and that certain segments may be at risk of exclusion. As we have shown, the economy is increasingly demanding in terms of minimal skill requirements, and it appears that a high school diploma is now required to gain access to stable jobs and income. In this context, greater efforts to encourage youth to finish high school are warranted.

As emphasized in this chapter, however, education is but one dimension of skill. The development of new measures of skills, competencies, and aptitudes is crucial to gaining a better understanding of which attributes are important in a knowledge-based economy and how they contribute to labour market success. The International Adult Literacy Survey and the work by Boothby (forthcoming) and Béjaoui (forthcoming) summarized here have advanced the state of knowledge in this respect. Next steps in this area will focus on the OECD International Life Skills Survey (ILSS), sponsored by HRDC and Statistics Canada. This survey will build on the IALS by developing and testing a number of basic skills: numeracy, prose and document literacy, teamwork, problem solving, and information technology. In sum, establishing which skills are quantitatively important is essential if public policy is to effectively address the issue of how to foster their acquisition, development, and maintenance throughout life.

Notes

1 This chapter is an adapted version of a paper published in the Applied Research Branch, Human Resources Development Canada, publication series (Research Paper No. R-99-7E). The authors wish to thank Marie Lavoie, Ali Béjaoui, and Daniel Boothby for their significant contribution and helpful comments. The views expressed in Applied Research Branch documents are those of the authors and do not necessarily reflect the opinions of Human Resources Development Canada or of the federal government.

2 This industry is usually classified as knowledge-intensive and requires highly educated workers.

3 Distinguishing the nature of knowledge into tacit and codified is fundamental in order to understand the employment effects of technological change. While codified knowledge

essentially means that it is easy to transmit and access and is even substitutable, tacit knowledge is not easily transferred from one person to another since it requires that a learning-by-doing process be acquired.

4 Appendix A in Lavoie and Roy (1998) contains a list of four-digit occupational codes included within each occupational category.

5 The SSH category of occupations – the largest subcategory of the knowledge group – comprises a variety of knowledge expertise. If we subdivide this category, we find that, over time, accountants made up between 40 and 50 percent of the SSH category, followed by the artistic group, which accounted for a little less than a third of the SSH category. Legal occupations made up almost 10 percent. Together these three categories of expertise accounted for 80-90 percent of the SSH group between 1971 and 1991 in Canada.

6 Information on HRDC's Essential Skills Project and Sector Studies can be accessed via the Internet at <http://www.hrdc-drhc.gc.ca/hrp/index_e.html>.

7 The occupational classification used by Boothby (forthcoming) is based on the one developed by Lavoie and Roy (1998) but differs from the latter in that the data and goods categories of occupations have been further divided to reflect the fact that each of the original categories contains a wide range of occupations, some of which require a high degree of knowledge whereas the others are mostly routine in nature. As a result, the data category is divided into the "data" and "data manipulation" categories and the goods category is divided into the "skilled goods" and "other goods" categories.

8 The IALS measured three types of literacy skills. The prose scale refers to the literacy needed to understand and use information from texts, including news stories and fiction. The document scale refers to the literacy required to locate and use information contained in various formats, such as job applications, maps, and tables. The quantitative scale refers to the knowledge and skills required to apply mathematical operations to numbers contained in text, such as completing an order form or balancing a chequebook. Level 1 on these scales is the lowest level measured and level 5 is the highest. See OECD (1997) for a guide to the scales and their interpretation.

9 The author uses indexes of the basic competencies required by occupations constructed and averaged at the four-digit level (around 500 occupational groups) by Hunter and Manley (1986) using the Canadian *Classification and Dictionary of Occupations*, which provides direct measures of 43 traits/functions across 6,500 occupations (e.g., complexity of work involving data, people, or things; specific vocational preparation; intelligence; scientific work; motor skills; and so on). These features of occupations were then aggregated according to an optimization procedure (LISREL) into the five skill dimensions or basic competencies for each occupation. See Béjaoui (forthcoming) for details.

10 For complete details on the growth accounting methodology, see Lavoie and Roy (1998).

11 While the employment effects of computerization are worth assessing given their rapid diffusion, the authors acknowledge that it is only one of many factors. For example, technological change is not limited to computer technologies, which may have a small effect relative to other types of capital in a given industry. Moreover, the complementarity between skills and computer technology may also be supplemented by supply-side factors, organizational change, increasing intensity of international trade, and the speed of structural adjustment.

12 There is a fourth effect of computerization on employment that is not examined by Lavoie and Therrien (1999), namely, that the computer may not lead to a change in the number of workers in a particular occupation but may instead transform the skill content of an occupation by either "upskilling" or "deskilling" work along a number of dimensions.

13 The public sector is excluded from their analysis.

14 For workers aged 55 and over, it can be demonstrated that the slight deterioration in the employment ratio for unskilled workers is primarily attributable to an age-composition effect. In this group, the average age of unskilled workers is considerably higher than that of skilled workers, and since the probability of being retired increases with age, we expect a deterioration of the employment rate of unskilled labour. This phenomenon is not, however, related to the level of expertise. The situation described earlier is slightly different for workers aged 55 and over. It can be shown that employment and earnings outcomes for

low-skilled older workers have deteriorated somewhat relative to those of high-skilled older workers. Much of this result, however, is due to the fact that the least skilled – those with 0-8 years of education – are concentrated in this group, and is not inconsistent with the view that there has not been a deterioration in labour market conditions for low-skilled older workers in general.

References

Béjaoui, Ali. Forthcoming. "Sur la mesure des qualifications: implications pour l'émergence de l'économie du savoir."

Boothby, Daniel. Forthcoming. *Literacy Skills, the Knowledge Content of Occupations and Occupational Mismatch.* Research Paper, Applied Research Branch. Ottawa: HRDC.

Gingras, Yves, and Daniel Boothby. 1998. *Have the Labour Market Conditions of Low-Skilled Workers Worsened in Canada?* Research Paper R-99-1E, Applied Research Branch. Ottawa: HRDC.

Gingras, Yves, and Richard Roy. 1998. *Is There a Skill Gap in Canada?* Research Paper R-98-9E, Applied Research Branch. Ottawa: HRDC.

Hunter, A.A., and M.C. Manley. 1986. "On the Task Content of Work." *Canadian Review of Sociology and Anthropology* 23,1: 47-71.

Lavoie, Marie, and Pierre Therrien. 1999. *Employment Effects of Computerization.* Applied Research Branch, Working Paper W-99-2E. Ottawa: HRDC.

Lavoie, Marie, and Richard Roy. 1998. *Employment in the Knowledge-Based Economy: A Growth Accounting Exercise for Canada.* Research Paper R-98-8E, Applied Research Branch. Ottawa: HRDC.

Lipsey, R. 1996. "Economic Growth, Technological Change and Canadian Economic Policy." C.D. Howe Institute, Benefactors Lecture. Toronto: C.D. Howe Institute.

McMullen, K. 1996. *Skill and Employment Effects of Computer-Based Technology: The Results of the Working with Technology Survey III.* Ottawa: Canadian Policy Research Networks Inc.

OECD (Organization for Economic Cooperation and Development). 1996. *The Knowledge-Based Economy.* Paris: OECD.

–. 1997. *Literacy Skills for the Knowledge Society.* Paris: OECD.

–. 1998. *Human Capital Investment: An International Comparison.* Paris: OECD.

Wolff, E.N., and W.J. Baumol. 1989. "Sources of Postwar Growth of Information Activity in the United States." In L. Osberg et al., eds., *The Information Economy: The Implications of Unbalanced Growth,* 17-46. Halifax: Institute for Research on Public Policy.

13

Technology, Jobs, and Skills: Evidence from Europe[1]

John Van Reenen

Introduction

The effect of the development of tools on the evolution of human activity has long been a principal concern for students of social behaviour. Marx viewed the development of productive means as the key force in his theory of history. The identity of the dominant class was determined by their ability to best muster the developments of technology. In neoclassical economics, technological progress is also regarded as the driving force behind economic growth, a notion that is reinforced by endogenous growth theory (see the chapter by Richard Lipsey in this volume). Given its role in economic growth, technological progress leads on average to higher standards of living. But how are the benefits of such progress distributed across society? Who gets a "share of the plunder"?

In the past, many commentators have worried that technology could lead to a "deskilling" of workers. Adam Smith's pin factory symbolizes the destruction of skilled artisans and their replacement by workers required to perform only the most menial repetitive tasks (Braverman 1974; Edwards 1979). More recently, however, debates by economists have focused on whether modern technologies are generally biased towards more-skilled workers. Particularly heated is the debate over what causes the increasing inequality of wages and employment between the skilled and the unskilled. Although closely related, the existence of skill-biased technical change does not explain recent changes in the wage and employment structure. Demonstrating that technology is biased towards more-skilled labour is not sufficient (and, some would argue, not even necessary [Leamer 1994]) to establish technological change as the dominant explanation for increases in inequality. We must also consider the supply of skills, for example.

This chapter surveys evidence of the effects of technological change on employment (in total and by skill group) by examining the micro-econometric evidence.[2] Most studies considered here use direct measures of technology instead of associating technology with a residual time trend.

The following section briefly discusses some theory that implicitly or explicitly forms the background of the empirical studies. The section "Econometric Models" reviews empirical problems with implementing the theory, and "Selected Results" discusses the results of the papers explicitly. The last section draws some conclusions.

Theoretical Guide[3]

The Skill Bias of Technical Change

We start with a general framework within the context of a neoclassical model of production. For simplicity we consider the case of three variable factors (skilled labour, unskilled labour, and materials) and two quasi-fixed factors (physical capital, denoted by K, and "technological capital," denoted by R). Consider a quasi-fixed translog cost function:

$$\ln C = \alpha_0 + \sum_h \sum_{i=B,W,M} \alpha_{hi} D_h \ln w_i + \sum_{i=B,W,M} \sum_{j=B,W,M} \beta_{ij} \ln w_i \ln w_j + \beta_q \ln q +$$

$$\sum_{j=B,W,M} \beta_{iq} \ln w_i \ln q + \beta_K \ln K + \sum_{j=B,W,M} \beta_{iK} \ln w_i \ln K + \beta_R \ln R + \sum_{j=B,W,M} \beta_{iR} \ln w_i \ln R \tag{1}$$

where C are the variable costs (B is "unskilled" blue-collar labour, W is "skilled" white-collar labour, and M is materials). The α parameters reflect own price effects. We allow these to differ in different "units," indexed by D_h. ($D = 1$ if in unit h, etc). For example, we might allow the own price effects to vary in different industries or even different firms (fixed effects). The β parameters measure the effect on total cost of the other factor prices (w), the log of plant output (q), technological capital (R) and the fixed capital stock (K).

Since cost is homogeneous of degree one in prices, there are a series of restrictions as follows:

$$\sum_{j=B,W,M} \beta_{ij} = \sum_{i=B,W,M} \beta_{ij} = \sum_{i=B,W,M} \sum_{j=B,W,M} \beta_{ij} = \sum_{i=B,W,M} \beta_{iR} = \sum_{i=B,W,M} \beta_{iK} \tag{2}$$

These allow equation (1) to be normalized by one of the factors. Taking the materials price (w_M) as the unit of normalization, we obtain a normalized translog cost function where costs (relative to materials price) are a function of the relative prices, output, capital, technology, and their interactions. From Shephard's lemma, the variable cost share S_i for input i is given as:

Unskilled workers

$$S_B = \alpha_B + \sum_{i=B,W} \beta_B \ln(w_i / w_m) + \beta_{Bq} \ln q + \beta_{BK} \ln K + \beta_{BR} \ln R \tag{3a}$$

Skilled workers

$$S_W = \alpha_W + \sum_{i=B,W} \beta_W \ln(w_i / w_m) + \beta_{Wq} \ln q + \beta_{WK} \ln K + \beta_{WR} \ln R \tag{3b}$$

Note that the materials equation has been dropped because the cost shares sum to unity.

We can test for homotheticity of the structure of production (i.e., that the cost shares are independent of the levels of output and the quasi-fixed factors) by imposing the following restrictions:

$$\beta_{iq} = -(\beta_{iR} + \beta_{iK}), \quad \text{where } i = B, W$$

If these can be accepted, the cost share equations simplify to:

Unskilled workers

$$S_B = \alpha_B + \sum_{i=B,W} \beta_B \ln(w_i / w_m) + \beta_{BK} \ln(K / q) + \beta_{BR} \ln(R / q) \tag{4a}$$

Skilled workers

$$S_W = \alpha_W + \sum_{i=B,W} \beta_W \ln(w_i / w_m) + \beta_{WK} \ln(K / q) + \beta_{WR} \ln(R / q) \tag{4b}$$

The elasticities of substitution and complementarity can now be calculated. In terms of the technology variable, if the coefficients $\beta_{WR} > 0$ and $\beta_{BR} > 0$, we would say that technology is labour-biased. If $\beta_{WR} > 0$ and $\beta_{BR} < 0$, then technology is clearly skill-biased.

The formulation is often further simplified using value added (*VA*) rather than output. In this case the dependent variable is the share of skilled labour in the wage bill, and the factor demand equation is simply:

Skilled workers

$$S_W = \alpha_W + \beta_W \ln(w_W / w_B) + \beta_{WK} \ln(K / VA) + \beta_{WR} \ln(R / VA) \tag{5}$$

Again, skill-biased technical change would be indicated by a positive co-efficient on β_{WR}.

Versions of this structure are very common in the literature. It seems a natural one given the difficulties in accurately measuring a user cost of physi-cal or technological capital (especially one that varies exogenously across microeconomic units). Sometimes the physical capital factor is allowed to be variable and only the technological component is fixed (e.g., Duguet and Greenan 1997).

Many researchers have estimated equation (5) in employment shares rather than cost shares. Although less appropriate from a theoretical point of view, this clearly has the advantage of allowing a statistical decomposition of the effects of technology into a relative wage component and a relative em-ployment component.

Models other than the neoclassical framework suggest different ration-alizations for the correlation of technology with cost shares. For example, the neoclassical assumption that factor prices are exogenous is clearly ques-tionable, since wage setting is not conducted in a competitive spot market. Models of bargaining would suggest that workers may be able to "capture" some of the rents from innovation. If skilled workers are more able to do this than unskilled workers (because of higher turnover costs associated with more-skilled employees, for example), then the technology-cost share cor-relation could be driven by relative wage movements rather than relative employment movements. This underlines the importance of analysing movements in factor prices and quantities.

The literature on the effects of technology on wages has been primarily motivated by attempts to assess the productivity effects of computers on highly skilled workers. Note that a competitive labour market would have only one wage for each skill type, so the underlying model behind these correlations is not entirely clear. We offer a critique of the innovation-wage relationship elsewhere (Chennells and Van Reenen 1997).

The impact on labour demand can also be derived from the structure outlined above. One problem with this, of course, is that much of the effect of innovation might derive from increased output, which implies estimat-ing the production function directly. In fact, researchers have tended to estimate simpler equations of employment based on aggregating across all workers and estimating employment growth equations (see the subsection "Technology, Homogeneous Labour, and Employment" below).

There are, of course, serious difficulties in extrapolating results from the micro level to produce macro-level implications. We have focused on the demand side, but the equilibrium effects of technological change will also depend on what is happening in other areas of the economy, particularly to the supply of more-skilled labour. Furthermore, reallocations of output and employment will occur within and between sectors that will tend to complicate the aggregate effects. The microeconometric evidence is only a small part of the story, and researchers should resist extrapolating too much from these partial equilibrium results.

Skill Bias and Unemployment

In this section we consider the implications of our model of skill-biased technical change for unemployment and jobs. There are a great number of complex interactions between innovation and employment but we begin with what we think is the most important route.

If technology is skill-biased, an exogenous increase in the stock of technological capital (a "technology shock") will increase the demand for skilled labour relative to unskilled labour. This can be illustrated on the standard relative demand and relative supply diagram. As the relative demand curve shifts out, in equilibrium there is a rise in both the relative wages and the relative employment of the more-skilled group.

Note that there is no unemployment in this model since the labour market clears. Now consider introducing some institutional limits to how far the wages of less-skilled workers can fall. These could arise due to minimum welfare levels, minimum wages, trade unions, or efficiency wage considerations. In this case there will be less of an increase in wage inequality, but there will be some unemployment for unskilled workers.

This is not a new idea. Solow (1966), for example, discussed it in his Wiksell lectures. More recently, the basic supply-demand analysis has become the dominant view of changes in the labour markets of the industrialized countries in the last 20 years, at least in the United States. In the flexible labour market there, wage inequality has increased and unemployment has remained stable. In the relatively inflexible labour markets of Europe (outside the United Kingdom), wage inequality has been stable but unemployment has increased dramatically. Paul Krugman (1994) has christened US inequality and European unemployment as "two sides of the same coin."

The debate on these matters is fierce. As noted in the introduction, the existence of skill-biased technological change and the question of whether technology is responsible for recent labour market trends are related but quite distinct analytical issues. Explaining recent history is a far harder task than simply understanding skill bias. This is not least because of strong disagreement on the appropriate model of the labour market.

Three key questions must be addressed:

1 Has the demand for skilled workers outstripped the supply of skilled workers? Or more accurately, has the demand/supply gap become greater over time?

2   If demand has accelerated relative to supply, is this due to technological change or some other factor, such as increased trade with less developed countries?
3   If the answer to both (1) and (2) is yes, how much of the change in unemployment and inequality can be accounted for?

Has the demand for skilled workers outstripped the supply of skilled workers?
Katz and Murphy (1992) and Autor et al. (1997) try to date the timing of the increase in demand for skills in the US. They use a weighted average of the growth of relative wages and employment, assuming that the labour market is in equilibrium with no unemployment. Given an assumption over the degree of substitutability between the skilled and the unskilled, it is possible to use a CES production function to estimate the relative employment changes. It is very difficult, however, to date precisely the timing of the acceleration in demand, although both authors argue that it exists (as does Machin [1998] for the UK[4]).

More general methodologies have been proposed to take into account the unemployment in Europe and elsewhere. Nickell and Bell (1995), Jackman et al. (1996), and Manacorda and Manning (1997) argue that there has been relatively little increase in mismatch outside of the UK and US, and that most of the increase in European unemployment has other roots.

Has the demand change been due to technological change?
There is greater agreement that, to the extent that demand has shifted towards the skilled, this is due to technology rather than trade. The methodologies used to reach this conclusion are based on the fact that most of the change in skills has been a within-industry phenomenon (see Berman et al. [1994] for more discussion of this debate).

How much can technological change account for?
This question needs a full general equilibrium analysis, which has rarely been attempted (see Minford et al. [1995] for one attempt). Back-of-the-envelope calculations in Machin and Van Reenen (1998) suggest that technological factors alone can account for only a third or less of the changes in the US and UK, but far more outside these two countries.

Technology, Homogeneous Labour, and Employment
The debate of the previous subsection is a crucial one for policymakers. Yet there is another strand in the literature that asks whether technology is responsible for falls in jobs *even when it is not skill-biased*. Although a great deal has been written on this topic, the literature and the surrounding policy debate are littered with confusion.

Information and communication technologies (ICTs) have diffused rapidly in Europe over the last 20 years and unemployment has also risen. There is strong temptation to suggest a causal link between the two. Waves of technology have passed over Europe in the past, however, without creating persistent and structural unemployment. Nevertheless, the debate over technological unemployment has proved persistent. Similar arguments were being made in the 1960s over the introduction of automation, while in the 1930s Lord Kaldor (1932) commented: "Today there is scarcely any political or journalistic observer of world affairs who does not attribute to the rapid growth of technical improvements one of the major causes of the present trouble."

Yet the fact remains that an examination of long-term unemployment trends shows no upward trend, despite the presence of technological change for several hundred years. If we examine UK and US unemployment since the 19th century, the main difference is that unemployment was far more volatile before 1945 than in the postwar period. It is possible that technology has a temporary destabilizing effect on employment, but it is difficult to believe that it is the major cause of the recent rise in European unemployment levels. Only technology combined with something else – such as wage rigidity – could be part of the cause.

What can economic theory tell us about the likely effects of technological change on employment? One form of technological change to consider is labour-augmenting process innovations. This case has been explored thoroughly in the literature. There are essentially two forces at work. For a given level of output, this type of technological change means that employment must fall, since the same output can be produced with a lower level of inputs. Offsetting this, however, is the fact that output will increase as prices fall, because costs have fallen. This is the primary "compensation mechanism" of technological change. It means that examining the impact of technology on output (the production function relationship) is fundamental to understanding the effects of technology on output.

Elsewhere (Van Reenen 1997), we have considered a simple model that shows how the effects of technological change work. This model leads us to the following results:

1 *Price elasticity of product demand.* The greater the sensitivity of consumers to price changes, the more likely it is that an innovation will raise employment. The higher the price elasticity, the greater the increase in output generated by an innovation.
2 *Substitution of capital for labour.* The easier it is to substitute, the more likely there will be positive effects of labour-augmenting technological change, since labour is now relatively cheaper than capital and the firm

will substitute into labour. The opposite is true for capital-augmenting technological change.

3 *Monopoly power.* If the firm has some degree of market power, not all of the reduction in cost will be passed on in the form of lower prices. This will blunt the output expansion effect and make positive employment effects less likely.

Generalizations of the model lead to the consideration of further possible effects.

4 *Market share effects.* If the innovation does not diffuse immediately throughout the industry, the firm will have a cost advantage and so will tend to expand at the expense of its rivals. This will mean larger effects at the firm level in the short run. It also means that researchers should be careful in generalizing from the microresults to the economy level.

5 *Union effects.* If some of the efficiency gains from innovation are captured by unions in the form of higher wages (or reduced effort, etc.), this will also blunt the output expansion effects. The results are uncertain if the union also bargains over the employment level (Ulph and Ulph 1994).

6 *Product innovation.* Product innovations will tend to have stronger output expansion effects and are therefore more likely to result in employment increases (see Katsoulacos [1986] for a fuller analysis).

7 *Economies of scale.* These will tend to magnify the positive employment effects.

Econometric Models

We discuss some econometric problems focusing on fixed effects, endogeneity, and measurement. Consider the basic equation to be estimated as the stochastic form of equation (5):

$$S_W = \alpha_W + \beta_W \ln(w_W / w_B) + \beta_{WK} \ln(K / VA) + \beta_{WR} \ln(R / VA) + u \qquad (6)$$

where u represents a stochastic error term. This could be justified by allowing the α_W to be random across units, or due to measurement error or optimization mistakes. It is unlikely, however, that the error term is uncorrelated with other right-hand side variables. Some firms may have dynamic managers who employ both top-quality workers and high-quality technology. For this reason, controlling for *fixed effects* is important and researchers might estimate the equation in differences (or by including dummies if the time series is long enough):

$$\Delta S_W = \beta_W \Delta \ln(w_W / w_B) + \beta_{WK} \Delta \ln(K / VA) + \beta_{WR} \Delta \ln(R / VA) + t + e \tag{7}$$

where Δ denotes the difference operator, t denotes time dummies, and e denotes the error term. Unfortunately, estimating this type of model usually requires panel data, which is rare in firm-level work. This is one reason most research has focused until recently on the industry level.

A second fundamental problem is dealing with the issue of *endogeneity*. Even when unobserved heterogeneity is removed, firms might still change their technology in response to a change in the make-up of skills available, rather than vice versa. If the "technological" factor were truly fixed, this would not be an issue. But the factor is "quasi-fixed," meaning it will move partially towards the long-term equilibrium in the short term. Weak exogeneity (R is insensitive to current shocks this period, but may partially adjust next period) may be more plausible for research and development (R&D) than for other technology proxies (such as computer use). The use of longer differences (to mitigate such problems as measurement error) will exacerbate these problems of endogeneity. The only solution is to develop instrumental variables to deal with the fact that technology and skills decisions are being taken simultaneously. Unfortunately, such instruments are not easy to find, and researchers have been rightly reluctant to use the standard approach of using lags because of concerns that they are weak instruments.

A related issue is the interpretation of the coefficients on the relative wage terms. These terms are directly involved in the construction of the dependent variable. It is doubtful how much of the interfirm or inter-industry variation in relative wages is due to changes in the price of labour, rather than due to changes in the quality mix of labour, which is imperfectly captured by observable skill. An intellectually respectable solution would be to use credible instruments for relative wages. One commonly encountered shortcut in the literature is to argue that time dummies will capture the real variation in wages, and to include these instead of the relative wage terms.

The third and perhaps the most basic issue, however, is the problem of *measurement* of technology. This is a very serious problem, since the technology input is a far more nebulous concept than the input of, say, labour, which in itself is difficult enough to measure. The traditional approach is simply to use time trends. The problem here, of course, is that the trends are likely to be picking up a lot more than just technological change, such as unmeasured price movements, changing demand conditions, cost shocks, and so on. These criticisms are well known from the debate on how suitable total factor productivity (TFP) is as a measure of technology.

Researchers have turned to a variety of alternatives in seeking observable measures of technology. We can distinguish crudely between three types of measure, which correspond to inputs into the knowledge production function, outputs from the knowledge production function, and subsequent diffusion of these outputs around the economy.[5] Inputs are generally measured by R&D activities. R&D expenditure has the advantage that it is measured in many databases over time, across countries, and in a reasonably standard way[6] – at least by comparison with the alternatives. Also, R&D is measured in terms of a unit of currency, which provides a natural weighting, whereas other innovative measures are more qualitative. A big disadvantage of using R&D as the technology measure is the existence of spillovers. A firm might invest in large amounts of R&D without receiving any benefit from it, if the R&D does not produce any outputs (either in the form of innovation for the firm or in the form of acquiring the ability to learn from other firms' innovations). There are long and unknown variable lags between the act of investing in R&D and reaping useful output from it.[7] The transmission mechanisms for knowledge to spill over from one firm to another are also poorly understood. For example, the R&D spending of Intel has dramatically affected the development of computer technologies used by other firms all over the world, but the process by which this knowledge has been absorbed by other firms is unclear and rarely addressed in the literature.

Patents are a widely available and standard way to measure the outputs of knowledge. The problem with patents is that a large number of them appear to be of very low value and there is no obvious method of weighting them to take this into account.[8] In some countries expert innovation surveys exist, which can be viewed as a method of cutting off the lower tail of low-value patents. The UK Science Policy Research Unit (SPRU) Innovation Survey is a good example of this, since industry experts were asked to list the most important innovations in their field, in order to weed out the innovations with little value. Output measures such as patents suffer from some of the problems of R&D – such as spillovers and variable time lags – and add new problems (such as the econometric difficulties of dealing with nonlinear count data).

Diffusion measures seem to be closely related to what is usually thought of as technology. A common example would be the use of computers in a firm. Researchers are usually faced with the problem of which technologies to include: what sort of computers (word processors, mainframes); whether to also include production-based technologies (lasers, robots, NC, CAD/CAM); how to weight the usage (the proportion of people using the computer is a common form of weighting). The most satisfactory method seems to be constructing the capital stock of information technology (IT), although since IT is hardwired into more and more modern organizations, separating out this component becomes increasingly difficult. Measuring the diffusion of a particular technology is difficult in any time series context, since the passage of time changes the significance of using a particular type of technology. For example, in 1978 an indicator of whether a computer was extensively used within the firm gave a very different signal from the same indicator in 1998. Diffusion-based measures of technology are more likely to suffer more from simultaneity problems than, say, R&D. Current changes to a firm's environment will have less of an effect on something like R&D than on the decision whether or not to postpone investing in more computers. This is primarily because of the greater adjustment costs attached to restructuring or cancelling a research program than to purchasing a new piece of hardware.

The measurement of skills is a less controversial issue, and the problems associated with it are well known. There are two main methods of measuring skills. Perhaps the most common in the literature is to use an indicator of occupation, often simply by dividing the population into manual (production) and nonmanual (nonproduction) workers. Such categorizations can be criticized, since many nonmanual occupations require very low levels of skill. Education-based measures are more closely tied to ideas of levels of human capital, but face the problem that even highly educated workers may not be employed at very skilful jobs. Some authors have developed measures based on job content, where an occupation is broken down into different levels of task complexity (see Wolff 1996). In studies that have compared them, these measures all tend to be highly correlated across industries (e.g., Gera et al. 1998). Nevertheless, there are real worries that the categories chosen are not comparable over time and across countries.

Another measurement issue relates to double-counting. Innovative activities tend to be labour-intensive and involve skilled workers. R&D is a good example, since typically about half of all R&D costs is staff costs and only 10 percent capital costs. This will automatically generate a positive correlation between the level of skilled (i.e., better-paid) employees and the level of R&D. Correcting for this double-counting has been found to be important in the productivity literature. The problem reappears here in many guises.

Finally, there are issues to be grouped under "selectivity." The usual problems of sample response and survivor bias are encountered, but there are particular problems relating to the use of R&D expenditure. In most European countries, disclosure in company accounts of the amount of R&D carried out is not compulsory. This means that researchers have to be aware that excluding, or setting to zero, those companies that do not disclose any R&D is likely to introduce a selectivity bias.

Selected Results

Skills

Industry-Level Studies
Berman et al. (1994) use the United Nations General Industrial Statistics

Database to provide some basic decompositions of the changes since 1970 in skill distribution across manufacturing sectors of 14 industrialized countries. In each country there has been an upgrading in the skill structure (as measured by the employment or wage bill share of nonproduction workers). This has been accompanied by an increase in wage inequality in some (notably the US and UK), but not all, countries.

The authors then decompose the change of skilled employment share into a "within-industry" and "between-industry" component:

$$\Delta P = \sum_i \Delta S_i \bar{P}_i + \sum_i \Delta P_i \bar{S}_i$$

where P = proportion of skilled workers; S = share of industry, i, in total employment; a bar denotes a mean over time and the Δ is the difference over the same two time periods.

The between-industry contribution arises because the less-skilled industries (such as textiles) have been declining as a share of total manufacturing employment. This effect of industrial restructuring is relatively minor, however. The vast majority of skill growth has occurred within industries. It appears that the within-industry growth has occurred more in some industries than others. Chemicals, computers, non-electrical machinery, and printing and publishing are particularly large contributors to the within-industry component, and this tends to be true across all countries (the rank correlation coefficients tend to be positive across countries). Since these industries have also experienced a lot of technological change, the authors argue that technological factors may be behind the upskilling evident in the data.

An important drawback of the Berman et al. (1994) study (and the earlier studies that focused on the US[9] using a similar methodology) is that there are no direct measures of technology. Machin and Van Reenen (1998) estimate a version of equation (7). They use 15 two-digit manufacturing industries from seven Organization for Economic Cooperation and Development (OECD) countries (Denmark, France, Germany, Japan, Sweden, UK, and US) between 1973 and 1991. The data were based on the OECD STAN/ANBERD dataset combined with occupational data from the UN dataset used by Berman et al. (1994). Information on educational sources was obtained by aggregating individual datasets from the different countries.

Their measure of technology was R&D as a proportion of value added. There was a positive and significant association of skill upgrading and R&D intensity in almost every specification. This was robust to different measures of skill, conditioning on capital, and output, using employment shares as the dependent variable, including industry wage differentials as a control variable, or using either first- or four-year differences. Machin and Van Reenen (1998) conclude that direct measures of technical change are important in explaining the upgrading of the skill structure, but stress that technology accounts for different proportions of the change in different countries (for example, the proportion "explained" in the US and the UK is far smaller than elsewhere).

Goux and Maurin (1997) probe the decomposition of sectors into within and between components in more detail for France. They find that, in contrast with most other countries, most of the change in skill shares in France is due to between-industry movements, and these movements are driven by changes in domestic demand rather than import/export patterns. Part of the reason for this difference with the results from other countries is that the supply of qualifications has expanded very rapidly in the 1970-93 period in France, and was accompanied by falls in wage inequality. A second reason may be that the authors look at non-manufacturing sectors instead of just the manufacturing sector. The within-sector changes tend to be larger in manufacturing than in services (although, as Desjonqueres et al. [1999] and Autor et al. [1997] show, in the US and UK, at least, the within-sector movements also dominate).

Goux and Maurin (1997) complement their decomposition analysis with some direct measures of technological change. They estimate a version of equation (7) for higher and lower professional share of the wage bill between 1982 and 1993 for 35 sectors (aggregated from Enquête Emplois), but replace the technology variable (R/VA) with a set of industry fixed effects. They then regress these fixed effects against cross-sectional measures of technological change drawn from the TOTTO surveys. Computer utilization is found to be associated with significantly greater skill upgrading in these estimates. This is quite consistent with US and UK studies (e.g., Machin and Van Reenen [1998]). More surprisingly, however, they find that a measure of the utilization rate of industrial technologies (e.g., robots) has a negative correlation with skill upgrading. One suspects that these measures of diffusion may be subject to some sort of definitional problem. Industries with a lot of industrial technologies are likely to be more reliant on manual workers. Sectors with a growing number of white-collar workers are more likely to have computers. Although R&D intensity is less likely to be endogenous (at least in the short term, when it is relatively fixed) Machin and Van Reenen (1998) attempt to control for this problem by explicitly instrumenting R&D with government subsidies for R&D (assumed exogenous). They did not find evidence of endogeneity bias in their sample.

Fitzenberger (1996) takes a slightly different approach in his analysis of German skill patterns between 1970 and 1990. He follows Leamer (1994) in criticizing labour economists for working with an overly simplistic model that underestimates the importance of trade vis-à-vis technology. Using a three-skill group approach, he shows that, in Germany, both the more qualified and less qualified had faster wage growth than the middle group (broadly, those with only an apprenticeship training). The unemployment of the least skilled group had risen faster, however, than that of the other groups. This is consistent with a view that the demand for the most skilled has been increasing relative to the other groups as both their wage and employment relativities rose. The declining position of the least skilled is a combination of lower demand and wage increases generated by union power.

The trade approach focuses on the sector bias of technological change. If technological change is faster in the skill-intensive sectors, this "mandates" a growth in the skilled/unskilled wage differential. Fitzenberger (1996) cannot find a clear pattern in the data when he examines TFP growth across different sectors. Some work does suggest some sector bias towards the more-skilled sectors in the US, but there is no consensus.[10] Part of the difficulty is undoubtedly in estimating TFP, which, being an indirect residual from a postulated production function, is subject to a range of problems.

Another study that focuses on Germany is by Falk and Koebel (1997). They take quite an aggregate approach in dividing the economy into five sectors. Using biannual data from 1977 to 1994, they estimate factor demand equations for three groups of workers, materials, and capital. They assume that capital is variable and take technology to be simply a common time trend.[11] They too find that technology is the main factor in explaining skill upgrading. Unfortunately, the study is also subject to the criticism that there are no direct measures of technology.

Enterprise-Level Studies

Aggregation may be a serious problem for these industry studies, so we now consider analyses based at the level of the enterprise (both firm and plant).

Duguet and Greenan (1997) use an innovations survey to estimate cost share equations for a large panel of French manufacturing firms over the period 1986-91 in long differences (there are almost 5,000 companies). They jointly model the five technological change variables (product improvements, new products, product imitations, process improvements, process breakthroughs) alongside the share equations (two types of labour and capital). Capital is therefore treated as variable and innovations as quasi-fixed.

They find that skilled workers are not as easily substitutable for capital as unskilled workers. Furthermore, they find evidence for skill bias and argue that it comes primarily from the introduction of new products, although their results here are mixed. There appear to be differences in the different sorts of innovation, but with no systematic pattern.

One problem with subjective innovations surveys is the comparability of the notion of innovation across different firms. Different firms may have different ideas of what counts as "innovation." An interesting extension, given the increasing availability of this type of innovation survey (e.g., CIS), would be to use the longitudinal aspect of the panel when the question is asked of the same firms in the future. If the same individual is questioned over time, then differencing can remove the "permanent" component of the measurement error.

Greenan et al. (1998) also use a large sample of French firms (about 11,000) producing in both the manufacturing and non-manufacturing sectors (combining the Enquête Structure des Emplois with the BIC). They have information for three years (1986, 1990, and 1996) and estimate a variety of long-differenced models. They use an unusual measure of IT capital intensity derived from the firms' balance sheet expenditure on office and computing equipment. This includes computers but also less advanced equipment (such as photocopying machines). They are also careful to avoid double-counting expenditure on IT personnel. Using four skill groups and a version of equation (7), they identify significant negative effects of IT capital on the share of blue-collar workers, but only in the manufacturing sector.

Machin (1996) uses the 1984-90 British Workplace Industrial Relations Survey (WIRS) of 402 establishments, which contains information on the presence of computing technologies. He distinguishes between the employment proportions of five occupational groups. The introduction of computers has a significantly negative effect on the least skilled groups and a significant positive effect on the most skilled group.

Machin's measures of computing are rather crude (basically a binary dummy). Caroli and Van Reenen (1998) extend the UK analysis by using a more sophisticated set of variables to measure the impact of computing. They also find that establishments that use new technology more intensively reduce the proportion of the least skilled workers to a much greater extent than other plants. A further finding is that plants that introduced major organizational changes in the early 1980s were more likely to shed unskilled workers in the later 1980s than plants that did not introduce organizational innovations. They compare these results to the Enquête Reponse, the French equivalent of WIRS. Following about 1,000 of these establishments over time, they also find that the plants with the highest levels of technological and organizational innovation between 1989 and 1992 had the fastest falls in unskilled employment in the 1992-96 period.

Another paper that stresses the importance of organizational influences is Aguirregabriria and Alonso-Borrega (1997). They use rich Spanish firm-level panel data between 1986 and 1991 (more than 1,000 firms). They are able to distinguish between five types of labour and three types of capital (fixed, R&D, and "bought-in" innovations). They estimate employment (not cost share) equations along the lines of equation (7), treating the types of capital as quasi-fixed. The equations are first differenced and right-hand side variables are instrumented by their own levels in t-2 using the Arellano and Bond (1991) GMM procedure. Since some of the innovation variables are zero, they also use introduction dummies. Their most interesting result is their obtaining of strong negative impacts of the introduction of technological capital on the least skilled group. Smaller incremental changes in the stock variables do not have significant impacts on the demand for skills. This paper is admirable for its attempt to deal with endogeneity and probe the innovation relationship more deeply that most other studies. Nevertheless, difference-based GMM methods for dealing with endogeneity have come in for much recent criticism, due to the "weak instruments" problem (e.g., Blundell and Bond 1999; Griliches and Mairesse 1997). Also, the exact definition of "technological capital" is rather unclear in the paper.

Data constraints have hampered establishment-level analysis in German studies. A notable exception is Kaiser (1998). He focuses on a sample of firms in the German business-related services sector. His employment measure is the managerial forecast of what the change in net employment is expected to be for each of four different skill groups over the next two years. Using ordered probit techniques, a positive impact of current IT capital intensity is detected for employment growth of the most skilled group, and a negative and significant impact revealed for the least skilled group. The main criticism of the study is the lack of any real longitudinal element to the data and the fact that employment is measured in qualitative rather than quantitative terms.

Summary

We end this subsection with three general comments.

First, there does appear to be considerable support for the notion of skill-biased technical change. This occurs across a range of studies, and these are usually robust in controlling for fixed effects. This is bolstered by findings from other research in the US (Doms et al. 1997; Dunne et al. 1997; Berndt et al. 1992; Autor et al. 1997; Mishel and Bernstein 1996; Goldin and Katz 1997; Bartel and Lichtenberg 1987; Osterman 1986; Adams 1997; Wolff 1996) and in other countries: Sweden (Hansen 1995), Canada (Gera et al. 1998), and Finland (Vainiomaki 1998).

Second, there have been few attempts to find instrumental variables to deal with the potential endogeneity of technology. Candidates could include government-induced schemes to alter the incentives to accumulate technological capital (such as R&D tax credits, government grants, and so on).

Third, surprisingly few studies try to analyse the mechanisms by which technological change translates into higher demand for skills. One mechanism is through organizational changes such as de-layering, decentralization, and giving greater autonomy to workers. These organizational factors have been found to be important in the case study evidence and in the literature on the productivity paradox (investigating why computers have not raised measured productivity by as much as might have been expected). Some of the most interesting work discussed above suggests that this organizational restructuring could be the link between technology and labour demand (cf. Bresnahan et al. 1998).

Employment

There are fewer econometric studies of the relationship between overall employment and technology. Those that do exist tend to be mainly descriptive in character and focused on specific industries (e.g., Soete and Dosi 1983). The analysis in Blechinger et al. (1998) captures some of the salient points. An examination of the OECD STAN/ANBERD database (which covers manufacturing) reveals that the high-technology industries (those with higher R&D intensity) expanded more quickly (contracted less slowly) than the medium- or low-technology industries.

Van Reenen (1997) examined 598 firms listed on the London Stock Exchange. Companies are not required to disclose information about the skill composition of their workers. He examined a dynamic employment equation:

$$LnN_{it} = f_i + \Sigma_{k=0,\ldots6}\beta_k \, INNOV_{it-k} + \alpha_1 lnN_{it-1} + \alpha_2 lnN_{it-2} +$$
$$\gamma_1 ln(W_{it}) + \gamma_1 ln(K_{it}) + \delta' x_{it} + time \; dummies + v_{it} \qquad (8)$$

where N = total employment, $INNOV$ is a count of firm-level innovations, W = average wage, K = fixed capital, f = a fixed effect, x includes other controls such as the number of industry innovations, and i = firm.

This model is derived from the first-order conditions for a CES production function (Van Reenen 1997). The user cost of capital is proxied by the fixed effects and time dummies. The innovation measures are drawn from the SPRU Innovation Survey (see the earlier subsection "Technology, Homogeneous Labour, and Employment"). These are head counts of the first commercialization of technologically important innovations identified by expert surveys in 1983, 1980, and 1970.

Equation (8) was estimated in first differences using the same standard GMM technique of Arellano and Bond (1991) that was used in the study by Aguirregabriria and Alonso-Borrega (1997) discussed above. Lagged employment was always instrumented, and in some of the specifications firm wages and capital stocks were also treated as endogenous. The sample period runs from 1976 through 1982.

Throughout the paper, significantly positive effects of innovation were identified on firm employment. These were stronger for product innovations rather than process innovations. Over time the impact of innovations died away, presumably as other firms imitated the leading-edge firm.

Martinez-Ross (1998) estimates a similar model for Spanish firms for the period 1991-95. She also finds it important to allow for second-order dynamics in the employment equation. Her measure of innovation is drawn from a survey of Spanish firms, where firms were asked whether they had introduced new technologies and, if so, how many (similar to the Community Innovation Surveys). She criticizes the Van Reenen (1997) study for assuming that the innovation measures were weakly exogenous. Instrumenting innovations by lagged innovations leads to a far lower (and insignificant) effect compared with the OLS results.

The Van Reenen (1997) study argued that the rarity of SPRU innovations (compared, say, with the Spanish survey) would make lagged innovations an extremely poor instrument for current SPRU innovations. If patents affect employment only when they are commercialized as innovations, then past patent stocks become legitimate instruments. When using lagged patents as an instrument for innovations, no evidence was found of endogeneity bias.

Blechinger et al. (1998) use panel data from a large sample of Dutch firms in both the manufacturing (772 companies) and services sectors (836 companies). They relate employment growth over the 1988-92 period to characteristics of the firm in 1988. Essentially these controls include the size of the firm and indicators of technology. They found that office automation had a significantly positive effect in the service sector and production automation had a significantly positive effect in the manufacturing sector. The authors recognized the potential endogeneity problem. There are many unobservable reasons why firms may be growing faster in 1988-92, and these shocks could induce firms to innovate in order to capture the higher demand. The authors try to control for these by including an inverse Mills ratio in the manner of Heckman (1979). This procedure is formally close to instrumenting the endogenous variable. It is still the case that one requires a variable that will shift the probability of innovating that is uncorrelated with the residual term in the employment growth equation. Unfortunately there are no obvious identifying instruments in this study, and much then relies on the particular functional form.

The Blechinger et al. (1998) study also examines the impact of the lagged proportion of R&D personnel on employment growth. Again, a positive effect of the innovation proxy is identified. Other studies using R&D have not found the same result. Klette and Førre (1998), for example, use data from Norwegian manufacturing plants and industries to investigate whether R&D intensity is associated with above-average employment growth. The data are extremely rich and comprehensive, being essentially the population of firms with more than 20 employees. R&D is measured as firm R&D intensity in the same line of business as the plant.

The study found that R&D-intensive establishments had lower net job creation than their less R&D-intensive counterparts. This was robust to controls for size, sector, and business cycle. Furthermore, the high-tech sectors themselves fared worse in employment terms than other sectors (although not significantly so). A worry concerning this study is that the Norwegian economy suffered from a series of negative shocks arising from the oil and banking sectors. Nevertheless, the authors claim that results are not driven by a few disastrous cases associated with these shocks, but are a more general phenomenon. It is important to replicate this extremely careful study in other countries, to see whether these results are a specific feature of a small, open economy in crisis or a more general phenomenon.

A novel approach to the question of the impact of computers on employment is offered in Entorf et al. (1997). French individual workers are followed for five quarters in the Enquête Emplois. By matching these employees with other surveys (e.g., TOTTO, DMMO, EET), the authors can examine the employment profile of workers who use different forms of new technology, and compare their employment trajectories with those who did not use these devices. Using multinomial probit techniques and controlling for a host of observed (gender, education, experience, part-time, region, occupation, establishment turnover, and age) and unobserved factors, they find that computer use reduces the probability of unemployment in the very short term (one quarter) but not the long term (one year). Although the authors make extensive attempts to control for selectivity, one still wonders whether the results could be driven by the fact that employers are unlikely to give advanced tools to workers who are likely to leave in the near future. Still, this is one of the most sophisticated attempts to examine the problem in our current batch of research.

Summary

The research findings considered here are comparable with other parts of the literature on innovation and employment. Overall, there appear to be consistently positive effects of proxies for product innovations on the growth of employment (e.g., Konig et al. 1995; Entorf and Pohlmeier 1991; Smolny 1998 [for German firms]; and Leo and Steiner 1994 [for Austrian firms]). The results for process innovations are very mixed – although usually insignificant, several examples of positive effects exist (e.g., Blanchflower and Burgess 1997 [for UK and Australian plants]; Regev 1998 [for Israeli firms]). In an interesting study of French data, Greenan and Guellec (1997) found that process innovations have a strong positive effect at the firm level, but this washes out at the industry level. The story is reversed for product innovations. When measures such as R&D are used, negative correlations frequently arise (e.g., Brouwer et al. 1993 [for Dutch firms]). Hall (1987) found different effects for small US firms (positive) than large US firms (negative). The most plausible explanation for these results is that the effects of innovation depend critically on the type of innovations being produced.

In general, employment studies have rarely been conducted with as detailed an eye to the econometric problems involved as those investigating wages and skills. This perhaps reflects the greater theoretical ambiguity involved in estimating the relationship (and policy interest in the microeconomic results). The econometric problems are particularly difficult in these studies, however, and future work needs to address them more seriously.

Conclusions

In this chapter we have focused on factors that relate to the impact of technological change on employment. We discussed studies that distinguished between different types of skills and those that focused on total employment. Most studies have been microeconometric, so they relate indirectly to the macro question of the causes of aggregate unemployment.

In any survey it is difficult to reach definitive conclusions except on methodologies. Nevertheless, we hazard the following:

First, considerable evidence of a positive correlation of various measures of technology with the skill structure suggests that technology is, on average, biased towards skilled labour. Second, the evidence on total employment is more mixed, with most measures suggesting a positive association (notably product innovation) but some others (notably R&D-based) being more negative. On balance, innovation at the micro level is probably associated with employment growth.

The three main methodological problems with these results is the presence of unobserved heterogeneity, endogeneity, and measurement problems. Most of the studies mentioned here have recognized the problem of heterogeneity and have turned to panel data, where one can make attempts to control for fixed effects. While there are well-known problems in this, we feel that it is a huge improvement over earlier work examining cross-sectional correlations.

There are fewer attempts to deal with the issue of the endogeneity of technology. Some authors have relied on GMM approaches, which identify based on an assumed serial correlation structure. A more satisfactory approach would be to use some of the empirical work on the determination of innovation. The large numbers of public policies towards stimulating innovation may offer some hope for identification in this respect. These policy changes may in many cases be regarded as natural experiments that exogenously shift the innovation measure independently of shocks in current employment and skills.

Another area for future work is the theoretical framework for analysing technology effects. The basic neoclassical model needs to be supplemented by a richer understanding of technological adoption in a tractable manner. There is a plethora of theoretical models; the task is to translate them into an empirically coherent form for implementation and testing. In particular, examining the role of organizational change in translating the effects of technology into labour demands should be a key area of future research (Caroli 1999).

Finally, the links between microeconomic analysis and macroeconomic outcomes are still very crude. We reiterate that the existence of skill-biased technological change is not the same as saying that technology is responsible for unemployment. Linking the empirical results here with simple general equilibrium models must be another important avenue of future research.

Notes

1 This chapter has benefited from helpful comments by Francis Kramarz, Lucy Chennells, Bronwyn Hall, and participants in seminars in Vancouver, Nice, and Brussels. Financial support from the Economic and Social Research Council is acknowledged.
2 We focus on evidence coming out of activities associated with the TSER Network R&D, Innovation and Productivity.
3 This section owes much to the exposition in Adams (1997).
4 See Mishel and Bernstein (1996) for a dissenting view.
5 This roughly corresponds to the Schumpeterian triad of invention, innovation, and diffusion.
6 In OECD statistics most countries follow the guidelines of the Frascati Manual (1993). Within countries, accounting regulations often define how R&D is to be reported (e.g., in the US under FAS and in the UK under SSAP13 [Revised]).
7 Of course the same is true of the standard way in which the physical capital stock is measured. The main difference here is that the degree of uncertainty involved with R&D investments is much greater, and there is usually a method of benchmarking the physical capital stock in a particular year.
8 Some current ideas include renewal fees, number of countries where the patent is registered, surveys of inventors, and citations.
9 For example, Berman et al. (1994) and Bound and Johnson (1992).
10 For different conclusions, see Sachs and Shatz (1994), Lawrence and Slaughter (1993), Haskel and Slaughter (1998), and Desjonqueres et al. (forthcoming).
11 They use the normalized quadratic cost function rather than the translog, which gives rise to a slightly different functional form for the factor demand system than that represented in equation (7).

References

Adams, J. 1997. *The Structure of Firm R&D and the Factor Intensity of Production*. National Bureau of Economic Research Working Paper No. 6099. Cambridge, MA: NBER.

Aguirregabriria, V., and C. Alonso-Borrega. 1997. "Employment Occupational Structure, Technological Capital and Reorganisation of Production." Universidad Carlos III de Madrid Working Paper 97-12. Madrid.

Arellano, M., and S. Bond. 1991. "Some Tests of Specification for Panel Data: Monte Carlo Evidence and an Application to Employment Equations." *Review of Economic Studies* 58: 277-97.

Autor, D., L. Katz, and A. Krueger. 1997. *Computing Inequality: Have Computers Changed the Labor Market?* National Bureau of Economic Research Working Paper No. 5956. Cambridge, MA: NBER.

Bartel, A., and F. Lichtenberg. 1987. "The Comparative Advantage of Educated Workers in Implementing New Technology." *Review of Economics and Statistics* 69: 343-59.

Berman, E., J. Bound, and Z. Griliches. 1994. "Changes in the Demand for Skilled Labor within US Manufacturing Industries." *Quarterly Journal of Economics* 109: 367-98.

Berndt, E., C. Morrison, and L. Rosenblum. 1992. *High-Tech Capital Formation and Labor Composition in US Manufacturing Industries: An Exploratory Analysis*. National Bureau of Economic Research Working Paper No. 4010. Cambridge, MA: NBER.

Blanchflower, D., and S. Burgess. 1997. "New Technology and Jobs: Comparative Evidence from a Two-Country Study." *Economics of Innovation and New Technology* 6,1/2.

Blechinger, D., A. Kleinknecht, G. Licht, and F. Pfeiffer. 1998. "The Impact of Innovation on Employment in Europe: An Analysis Using CIS Data." ZEW Dokumentation 98-02. Mannheim, Germany.

Blundell, R., and S. Bond. 1999. "GMM Estimation with Persistent Panel Data: An Application to Production Functions." Working Paper No. W99/4. London: Institute for Fiscal Studies.

Bound, J., and G. Johnson. 1992. "Changes in the Structure of Wages in the 1980s: An Evaluation of Alternative Explanations." *American Economic Review* 82,3: 371-92.

Braverman, H. 1974. *Labor and Monopoly Capital: The Degradation of Work in the Twentieth Century.* New York: Monthly Review.

Bresnahan, T., E. Brynjolfsson, and L. Hitt. 1998. "How Do Information Technology and Work-Place Organization Affect Labor Demand? Firm Level Evidence." Mimeo. Cambridge, MA: Massachusetts Institute of Technology.

Brouwer, E., A. Kleinknecht, and J. Reijnen. 1993. "Employment Growth and Innovation at the Firm Level: An Empirical Study." *Journal of Evolutionary Economics* 3: 153-59.

Caroli, E. 1999. "New Technologies, Organisational Change and the Skill Bias: Going into the Black Triangle." In P. Petit and L. Soete, eds., *Employment and Economic Integration.* Oxford: Oxford University Press.

Caroli, E., and J. Van Reenen. 1998. "Skills and Organizational Change: Evidence from British and French Establishments in the Late 1980s and 1990s." Mimeo. London: Institute for Fiscal Studies.

Chennells, L., and J. Van Reenen. 1997. "Technical Change and Earnings in the British Establishment." *Economica* 64: 587-604.

Desjonqueres, T., S. Machin, and J. Van Reenen. 1999. "Another Nail in the Coffin?" The Labour Market Consequences of Technical and Structural Change. Discussion Paper Series 34, *Scandinavian Journal of Economics.*

Doms, M., T. Dunne, and K. Troske. 1997. "Workers, Wages and Technology." *Quarterly Journal of Economics* (February): 253-89.

Duguet, E., and N. Greenan. 1997. "Skill Biased Technological Change: An Econometric Study at the Firm Level." Working Paper. Paris: Centre de Recherche en Economie et Statistique.

Dunne, T., J. Haltiwanger, and K. Troske. 1997. "Technology and Jobs: Secular Changes and Cyclical Dynamics." *Carnegie-Rochester Conference Series on Public Policy* 46,0: 107-78.

Edwards, R. 1979. *Contested Terrain: The Transformation of the Workplace in the Twentieth Century.* New York: Basic Books.

Entorf, H., M. Gollac, and F. Kramarz. 1997. "New Technologies, Wages and Worker Selection." *Journal of Labor Economics* 15.

Entorf, H., and W. Pohlmeier. 1991. "Employment, Innovation and Export Activity." In J. Florens et al., eds., *Microeconometrics: Surveys and Applications.* Oxford: Basil Blackwell.

Falk, M., and B. Koebel. 1997. "The Demand for Heterogeneous Labour in Germany." ZEW Discussion Paper 97-28.

Fitzenberger, B. 1996. "Wages, Prices and International Trade: Trends Across Industries for an Export Champion." University of Konstanz Discussion Paper II-323.

Frascati Manual. 1993. "The Measurement of Research and Development Expenditures in the OECD." Paris: OECD.

Gera, S., W. Gu, and Z. Lin. 1998. "Technology and Demand for Skills: An Industry-Level Analysis." Paper presented at the European Union–Industry Canada conference Transition to the Knowledge Economy, November 1998, Vancouver, Canada.

Goldin, C., and L. Katz. 1997. "The Decline of Non-Competing Groups: Changes in the Premium to Education." *American Economic Review* 87.

Goux, N., and E. Maurin. 1997. "The Decline in Demand for Unskilled Labour: An Empirical Analysis Method and Its Application to France." Mimeo. Paris: Centre de Recherche en Economie et Statistique.

Greenan, N., and D. Guellec. 1997. "Technological Innovation and Employment Reallocation." Mimeo. Paris: Institut National de la Statistique et des Études Économiques.

Greenan, N., J. Mairesse, and A. Topiol-Bensaid. 1998. "Information Technology and R&D Impacts on Productivity and Skills: A Comparison on French Firm Level Data." Mimeo. Paris: Institut National de la Statistique et des Études Économiques.

Griliches, Z., and J. Mairesse. 1997. "Production Functions: The Search for Identification." In S. Strom, ed., *Essays in Honour of Rayner Frisch.* Econometric Society Monograph Series. Cambridge, UK: Cambridge University Press.

Hall, B.H. 1987. "The Size Distribution of US Manufacturing Firms." *Journal of Industrial Economics* 35,4: 583-606.

Hansen, P. 1995. "Trade, Technology and Changes in Employment of Skilled Labor in Swedish Manufacturing." Mimeo. Stockholm: Trade Union Institute for Economic Research.

Haskel, J., and L. Slaughter. 1998. "Does the Sector Bias of Skill Biased Technological Change Explain Changing Wage Inequality?" Mimeo.

Heckman, J. 1979. "Sample Selection Bias as a Specification Error." *Econometrica* 47: 153-61.

Jackman, R., R. Layard, M. Manacorda, and B. Petrongolo. 1996. "European vs. US Unemployment: Different Responses to the Same Shock?" Mimeo. London: London School of Economics.

Kaiser, U. 1998. "The Impact of New Technologies on the Demand for Heterogeneous Labour." Mimeo. Mannheim, Germany: Zentrum für Europäische Wirtschaftsforschung GmbH (ZEW).

Kaldor, N. 1932. "A Case Against Technical Progress." *Economica* (May): 180-96.

Katsoulacos, Y. 1986. *The Employment Effect of Technical Change.* Oxford: Oxford University Press.

Katz, L., and K. Murphy. 1992. "Changes in Relative Wages, 1963-1987: Supply and Demand Factors." *Quarterly Journal of Economics* 107,1: 35-78.

Klette, T.J., and S.E. Førre. 1998. "Innovation and Job Creation in a Small Open Economy: Evidence from Norwegian Manufacturing Plants 1982-92." *The Economics of Innovation and New Technology* 5: 247-72.

Konig, H., H. Buscher, and G. Licht. 1995. "Employment, Investment and Innovation at the Firm Level." In *The OECD Jobs Study: Evidence and Explanations.* Paris: OECD.

Krugman, P. 1994. "Past and Prospective Causes of High Unemployment." Mimeo. Palo Alto, CA: Stanford University.

Lawrence, Robert, and Matthew Slaughter. 1993. "International Trade and US Wages in the 1980s: Great Sucking Sound or Small Hiccup." *Brookings Papers on Economic Activity,* 161-227.

Leamer, E. 1994. "'Trade, Wages and Revolving Door Ideas." National Bureau of Economic Research Working Paper No. 4716, Cambridge, MA: NBER.

Leo, H., and V. Steiner. 1994. *Innovation and Employment at the Firm Level.* Vienna: Osterreichisches Institut fur Wirsschaftsforschung.

Machin, S. 1996. "Changes in the Relative Demand for Skills in the UK Labour Market." In A. Booth and D. Snower, eds., *Acquiring Skills,* 129-46. Cambridge, UK: Cambridge University Press.

–. 1998. "Recent Shifts in Wage Inequality and the Wage Returns to Education in Britain." *National Institute Review* 166: 87-96.

Machin, S., and J. Van Reenen. 1998. *Technology and Changes in Skill Structure: Evidence from Seven OECD Countries.* Berkeley Center for Labor Economics Working Paper No. 3. Berkeley: University of California.

Manacorda, M., and A. Manning. 1997. "Just Can't Get Enough: More on Skill Biased Change and Unemployment." Mimeo. Centre for Economic Performance. London: London School of Economics.

Martinez-Ross, E. 1998. "Wages and Innovations in Spanish Manufacturing Firms." Mimeo. Barcelona: Universitat Autonoma de Barcelona.

Minford, P., J. Riley, and E. Nowell. 1995. "The Elixir of Development: Trade, Technology and Western Labour Markets." Mimeo. Cardiff: Cardiff Business School.

Mishel, L., and J. Bernstein. 1996. "Did Technology's Impact Accelerate in the 1980s?" Mimeo. Washington, DC: Economic Policy Institute.

Nickell, S., and B. Bell. 1995. "The Collapse in the Demand for the Unskilled and Unemployment in the OECD." *Oxford Review of Economic Policy* 2,11: 40-62.

Osterman, P. 1986. "The Effect of Computers on the Employment of Clerks and Managers." *Industrial and Labour Relations Review* 39,2: 175-85.

Regev, H. 1998. "Innovation, Skilled Labour, Technology and Performance in Israeli Industrial Firms." *Economics of Innovation and New Technology* 6,1/2.

Sachs, Jeffrey, and Howard Shatz. 1994. "Trade and Jobs in US Manufacturing." *Brookings Papers on Economic Activity,* 1-84.

Smolny, W. 1998. "Innovations, Prices and Employment: A Theoretical Model and Empirical Application for West German Manufacturing Firms." *Journal of Industrial Economics* 46,3: 359-82.

Soete, L., and G. Dosi. 1983. *Technology and Employment in the Electronics Industry.* London: Francis Pinter.

Solow, R. 1966. Wiksell Lectures. Massachusetts Institute of Technology.

Ulph, A., and D. Ulph. 1994. "Labour Markets and Innovation: Ex Post Bargaining." *European Economic Review* 38: 195-210.

Vainiomaki, Y. 1998. "Technology, Skills and Wages: Results from Linked Worker-Plant Data for Finnish Manufacturing." Mimeo. Finland: Statistics Finland.

Van Reenen, J. 1997. "Technological Innovation and Employment in a Panel of British Manufacturing Firms." *Journal of Labor Economics* 15,2: 255-84.

Wolff, E.N. 1996. *OECD Economic Studies.* Paris: OECD.

Part 4
Participation and Inclusion
in the Knowledge Society

14
Learning in the Workplace: Training Patterns and Training Activities[1]

Gordon Betcherman, Norm Leckie, and Kathryn McMullen

Introduction

The workplace provides the focal point for many important activities related to the accumulation and application of "know-how" integral to the knowledge-based economy. It is here that employees bring their expertise and experience, where new learning takes place, where organizational capital further extends the sum of individual human capital, and where the benefits of knowledge and innovation are transmitted to consumers through new and better products and services.

Not surprisingly, then, considerable importance has been placed by economists and business specialists on the organizational structures and strategies that not only attract able and motivated workers but also encourage an atmosphere conducive to learning and innovation. And, indeed, while this may not be an area where public policy plays a central and direct role, governments have become increasingly interested in how they can support the diffusion of learning- and innovation-based organizational models.

While there may not be a consensus about all the components of such models, training is clearly one of the core elements. In using this term (which admittedly has become somewhat old-fashioned in the cutting-edge business literature), we mean to encompass a wide range of developmental activities, ranging from the more traditional structured training programs to flexible learning opportunities where skills acquisition is built into organizational processes. Our earlier work has emphasized that commitment on the part of management is the overriding determinant of training activity in an organization. Firms with this commitment have a solid sense of the role of human resources in their overall business strategy, and their organizational structures and processes encourage employee discretion and involvement in decision making. They make their commitment to training well known throughout the organization, and encourage the active participation of employees in their own skills development.

The empirical literature suggests that firms get a performance payoff from such strategies, yet these organizational models have been adopted by only a minority of Canadian firms. In a study of Canadian establishments conducted in the mid-1990s, we found that no more than one in five companies had committed themselves to a "learning organization" model (Betcherman et al. 1997). For the clear majority of firms, training is seen as a cost to be minimized, and, according to our surveys over the past few years, there is little evidence to suggest that this is changing. Why has the concept of human resource development not been embraced more widely? Given the firm's key role in decision making regarding human capital investment, we focus in this chapter on exploring the barriers employers face in this area.

For governments, the ultimate concern is whether disincentives may be leading to a level and composition of investment that is suboptimal (from a social returns point of view). Unfortunately, the information base is not up to the task of directly addressing this underinvestment question; as a consequence, policymakers must focus on understanding what the disincentives are and why they are important.

In the next section, "Evidence on Training Incidence Among Employers," we briefly summarize the evidence on patterns of employer-sponsored training in Canada. By describing these patterns, we are able to highlight where (in which types of firms) training investments are relatively large and, more important for our purposes here, where they are small. The context is set by identifying which segments of the employer population seem most likely to have been affected by training disincentives, as revealed in their observed investment behaviour.

Various disincentives have been discussed in the economics literature and these provide the focus of the section "Disincentives to Investing in Training." We organize the disincentives in the following categories: externalities, information barriers, employee-based obstacles, and a miscellaneous group. In each case, the theoretical arguments are discussed and then the relevant Canadian empirical evidence is reviewed. As we will see, that evidence is limited and can provide only partial insight into the importance of these disincentives.

In the section "New Evidence from the Workplace Training Survey," we supplement this literature review with a new empirical analysis of training obstacles reported by Canadian establishments. This analysis is based on the 1995-96 Ekos Workplace Training Survey, which gathered information on training experiences from more than 2,500 establishments throughout the Canadian private sector.[2] We focus on the part of the survey that questioned employers on the extent to which a number of potential obstacles to training were problems in their establishment.

Our conclusions are presented in the final section.

Evidence on Training Incidence Among Employers

One way of identifying training barriers is to examine patterns of workplace training. Where training activity is low, it is assumed that training disincentives and obstacles are high. Evidence from recent Canadian surveys of workplace training (Betcherman et al. 1997; Ekos Research Associates 1993; Canadian Labour Market and Productivity Centre 1993) indicates that the incidence of workplace training tends to be lowest in small firms and rises with firm size. For example, based on results from the Workplace Training Survey (WTS), Table 1 shows that the incidence of formal training in small establishments is less than half that in large establishments (Betcherman et al. 1997). The results also indicate that the incidence of formal training is fairly low in certain manufacturing industries and in traditional services (which includes, for example, retail trade and accommodation and food services). Low training incidences were also reported in Newfoundland, Quebec, and Manitoba; it should be noted, however, that the confidence

Table 1

Percentage of establishments with formal training, by establishment size, industry, and region, 1995[1]

Total	41.8
Employment Size	
Less than 20 employees	37.8
20-99 employees	64.5
100+ employees	85.7
Industry	
Non-farm primary	48.7
Natural-resource manufacturing	36.7
Labour-intensive manufacturing	43.6
Scale-based manufacturing	33.7
Research-based manufacturing	50.0
Distribution services	46.0
Information services	48.2
Traditional services	37.9
Non-market services	73.0
Construction	33.6
Region	
Atlantic	35.7
Quebec	30.5
Ontario	50.9
Prairies	39.0
British Columbia	45.7

Source: Betcherman et al. (1997).
1 All differences by size, industry, and region are significant at the 1% level.

levels around the estimates for the small provinces are very large because of small subsample sizes.

The low incidence of formal training in small establishments points to the possibility that training costs are a particular problem for small firms. Indeed, the WTS data indicate that training expenditures per employee are twice as high in small establishments (those with less than 20 employees) as in large ones (100 or more employees) (Betcherman et al. 1997). Larger firms are able to take advantage of economies of scale unavailable to small firms and are better able than small firms to accommodate downtime while employees are being trained. This suggests, then, that small firms face higher barriers to training than larger ones. Similarly, the fact that training activity is relatively low in some regions and some industries raises the possibility that barriers or disincentives are higher in those segments of the economy than elsewhere.

Many surveys, including the WTS and the Adult Education and Training Survey (AETS), have found a low training incidence for particular groups of employees. Youth, and workers in nonstandard work arrangements (such as part-time or self-employed), have low participation rates in workplace training. Because of weak firm attachment, employers are less likely to recoup training expenditures directed at such individuals and are therefore less likely to invest in training for them (Betcherman et al. 1998).

Disincentives to Investing in Training
Training disincentives can be organized into four categories: externalities, information barriers, employee-based obstacles, and a miscellaneous group.

The Classic Argument: Externalities and Poaching
Externalities associated with employer-based training have long been recognized by economists (e.g., Pigou 1912). These potential externalities stem from the possibility that employees may leave the firm after training. Thus, employers may be unwilling to sponsor training where they believe they will be unable to fully recoup its costs through higher employee productivity in the future, and suboptimal investment levels may result.

An important development emerging from human capital theory, however, has been the distinction between general and firm-specific training, and the implication that the externality problem might not be as serious as had traditionally been argued (Becker 1964). General training, the argument goes, is useful to employees in the external labour market; its benefits will thus accrue to the trained workers who can command higher wages elsewhere. Accordingly, employers would be disinclined to sponsor such training if they have to bear the costs. To the extent that training is general, therefore, financing should fall primarily on employees, either through direct contributions or reduced wages. Firm-specific training, on the other hand, is not transferable, and employers can capture (a share of) the benefits in the form of higher employee productivity. In this instance, the employer should be willing to finance the training. The implication of human capital theory, then, is that there is not necessarily an externality problem for employers: in the case of general training, the cost will be borne by the employee; for specific training, the employer will capture the productivity gains because there is no mobility threat.

More recently, this theoretical argument has been questioned, essentially on two counts (e.g., Stevens 1996). The first is that the distinction between general and specific training is not as clear as human capital theorists suggest, and in any event this distinction is not apparent to the parties. Most training, in fact, contains both general and specific aspects. Thus, the rational financing decisions suggested by Becker are less obvious.

The second count concerns the financing of general training, assuming that this can be identified. The human capital framework suggests that employees should fund general training, but obstacles impede such financing. First, liquidity constraints mean that workers cannot use their human capital as collateral for loans to finance such investments. Second, labour market rigidities and other institutional factors affecting wage determination (such as minimum wages, pay-equity legislation, collective bargaining arrangements) limit the potential for employees to accept lower wages to finance their training.[3]

To sum up, the training externality problem hinges critically on notions of mobility and risk. For training with a general component, employers who bear (some of) the cost run the risk of losing (some of) their investment if the trained employee leaves the firm. And in the case of employer-funded, firm-specific training, there is still the risk of employee turnover (even if that training has not changed the worker's labour market situation).

The importance of mobility and risk – and the potential importance of disincentives due to these externality problems – can vary according to the institutional framework. Where the framework encourages job stability (through employment protection legislation, collective agreements, or culture), we can expect to see more workplace training. On the other hand, more flexible labour market institutions run the risk of increasing the possible disincentives employers face in sponsoring training. To some extent, this is supported by cross-country evidence (e.g., OECD 1993). Labour market tightness, by affecting search prospects and job tenure, can also have an effect.[4]

Is there empirical support for the contention that externalities create a disincentive for employers to invest in workplace training? Various employer training surveys have included questions on training obstacles; the most relevant obstacles reported are those relating to "poaching." This tends to be articulated in terms such as "fear of losing workers once they are trained" or "trainees don't stay long enough to recoup training investment." We contend, however, that externality-based disincentives are also expressed in questions relating to cost as a training barrier. This contention is based on the argument that training costs become a disincentive for firms when they fear losing the benefits because of concerns about losing trained workers. Thus, for purposes of this discussion, barriers relating to poaching and costs have been grouped together.

There is a range of Canadian evidence on externalities as a training obstacle. The importance attached to this class of disincentives seems to vary across surveys and over time:

- According to a 1984-85 survey sponsored by Employment and Immigration Canada, cost and risk of losing trained workers were the least frequently cited reasons for not sponsoring formal training (Employment and Immigration Canada 1987).
- On the other hand, according to the 1987 Human Resource Training and Development Survey undertaken by Statistics Canada, "limited resources" was the predominant reason firms were unable to meet all their training needs (Rechnitzer 1990).
- A 1989 Ontario government survey of training in the private sector found that the cost of formal training was the most frequently mentioned factor inhibiting the provision of more training (cited by 50 percent of respondents). Downtime was also frequently mentioned (25 percent). The risk of losing trained employees, however, was cited by only a small minority (7 percent) (Ontario Ministry of Skills Development 1989).
- In 1990, the Canadian Labour Market Productivity Centre (CLMPC) surveyed 193 business and 72 union leaders about training (CLMPC 1990a). The results highlight the differences between business and labour on the issue of disincentives. Employers most frequently reported a lack of facilities and interest. Labour most frequently mentioned a lack of employer interest (to a greater degree than mentioned by employers), a preference for recruitment, a lack of government funding, and a preference for informal training (44 percent).
- In 1990, the CLMPC conducted a national survey of 822 high-tech firms and similarly found a preference for informal, on-the-job training as the reason the firms did not offer more formal training (CLMPC 1990b). The cost of training per se was cited by 15 percent of respondents as a reason for not providing formal training.
- The National Training Survey, a major survey of 17,500 organizations sponsored by the CLMPC in 1991, asked organizations wanting to do more training why their training needs were not met. The predominant reasons were related to cost, i.e., lack of funds and lack of time, both reported by more than 50 percent of respondents (CLMPC 1993).

- In a 1993 Ekos Research Associates survey of 2,500 employers, about 30 percent of respondents mentioned training costs and a lack of government assistance as problems for the provision of training (Ekos Research Associates 1993). These were among the most frequently cited problems, along with information constraints (see below). About 22 percent of respondents cited a fear of losing trained workers as an inhibiting factor.
- In the 1995-96 Ekos Workplace Training Survey, cost-related factors were the most frequently cited obstacles; none, however, were reported by more than one-quarter of the weighted sample (Betcherman et al. 1997). We will turn to these data in more detail in the section "New Evidence from the Workplace Training Survey."

Information Barriers: Empirical Evidence

Various kinds of information-related factors may create disincentives for employers to invest in training. We focus on two: firms being unable to properly account for training investments, and information shortcomings regarding the supply of training.

Measurement/Accounting Issues

For a variety of reasons, firms rarely account in any comprehensive manner for human resource development investments. This is part of a broader problem with accounting for investments in intangible assets (Government of Canada and OECD 1997).

In the area of training, Miller and O'Leary (1996) and others have documented the fact that conventional accounting frameworks cannot accurately measure the return on investments in training or in other forms of knowledge acquisition. At best, these frameworks measure the costs of training but not the associated returns.[5] Even in terms of costs, it is well known that there is great variation among firms regarding what factors are included.

The significance of these measurement and accounting problems is that an overall underinvestment by firms in training may well result. Assume that firms as investors are somewhat risk-averse. In considering investment options where some (e.g., physical capital) have explicit expected rates of return and others (e.g., human capital) do not, it can be anticipated that firms will tend to cautiously undervalue the latter, thus tilting decision making at the margin away from these intangible investments. This information problem may also play out at the level of financial markets, where investors, lacking accurate rate-of-return information, will undervalue firms investing in intangible assets (Government of Canada and OECD 1997).

Survey evidence demonstrates that measurement of training activities among Canadian firms is very partial. Results from the WTS indicate that only about one-third of Canadian employers track training expenditures and just over 40 percent formally measure the impacts of the training they support (Betcherman et al. 1997). Moreover, in-depth analysis provided by case studies of establishments participating in the survey revealed that the measurement that does occur is far from systematic and comprehensive.

Lack of Information on Training Opportunities
Over the past 15 years or so, the supply side of the training "market" has proliferated, with the emergence of providers from both the commercial and noncommercial sectors. This development has been due to a number of factors, including deregulation and new technological opportunities, such as interactive learning technologies. As Betcherman et al. (1998) argue in a recently released report on training policy, while the development of this supply side has created new options for firms and employees, a variety of information failures hinder the ability of these potential consumers to fully exploit the opportunities in the market. This situation points to the need for better information flows, including training standards, to improve the functioning of the training market.

The lack of information ranges from difficulties in identifying potential suppliers, to evaluating what course content is required to meet occupational requirements, to assessing the quality of the training offered by different suppliers. Problems are likely greatest when it comes to the private training institutions and companies that have grown so rapidly in recent years.[6]

Together, these information gaps can be expected to create reluctance on the part of some employers to tap into the training market. Problems may well be compounded for employers in small or remote communities and for small firms in general, where the costs of accumulating and evaluating information may be relatively high.

For the most part, surveys have not explored the significance of information failures as a constraint on employer investments in training. The few surveys that do offer some evidence suggest that information problems are an issue for a minority of firms. The most detailed picture probably comes from the 1993 Ekos survey, which asked about a number of potential training barriers, including several relating to information (Ekos Research Associates 1993). Lack of information was particularly notable with respect to knowledge about the availability of government training programs, as well as of training courses in general (cited by 35 and 27 percent of respondents, respectively). Other information-related barriers included lack of suitable training centres (21 percent) and lack of suitable training courses and trainers (18 percent). In the WTS, about 17 percent of respondents cited information concerns in the form of a lack of suitable training courses or trainers (Betcherman et al. 1997).

Employee-Related Obstacles
Our focus in this subsection is on how employee-related factors may create

disincentives for employers to invest in training. While employers are the primary decision-makers in the area of workplace training, employee-initiated demand is not insignificant. For example, using data from the 1994 AETS on full-time employees with at least one year tenure, Kapsalis (1996) found that employee demand for training had a significant impact on the incidence of employer-provided training. Among the evidence in support of this finding is the fact that in one-quarter of training events, the employee had suggested the training. In addition, the incidence of employer-sponsored training was much higher among employees who had expressed a need or desire to take training than among those who had not (47 and 41 percent versus 30 and 28 percent, respectively). Finally, regression analysis indicated that employee demand for training increased the likelihood of employer-sponsored training by one-third.

The AETS data indicate that more than half (55 percent) of these employees reported that they were "too busy" to take training needed for work; 29 percent found the time or location of the training inconvenient; and 12 percent reported family responsibilities as a reason for not training (Kapsalis 1996).

While employee interest is a factor, evidence from establishment surveys suggests that employers generally do not see employees as a major stumbling block in the provision of training. First, in a survey of business leaders, the CLMPC (1990a) found that "no worker interest" was least frequently (8 percent) cited as an obstacle to the improvement of training and retraining; this result was supported by a companion survey of union leaders. Also, results from the 1991 National Training Survey showed that "no employee interest" was least likely to be mentioned (2 percent) as a reason for not being able to meet training needs (CLMPC 1993). Finally, Ekos Research Associates (1993), using results from its National Survey of Employers on Employment and Training Issues, found that factors associated with employees, such as "not enough candidates" (14.2 percent) and "non-completion of courses" (7.8 percent) were among the least likely to be mentioned by employers as problems in the provision of training.

Employee factors as potential disincentives to training are unevenly distributed across the workforce. Evidence from the AETS shows very clearly that participation both in employer-sponsored training and in training undertaken by workers on their own rises significantly with education and income; it is much higher for workers in managerial, professional, and technical occupations than for those in clerical, sales, and goods-producing occupations. This conclusion is supported by evidence from the 1994 International Adult Literacy Survey (IALS) (OECD and Statistics Canada 1995), which found that the higher an individual's literacy level, the greater the likelihood that he or she had received some training in the previous year. These unequal training patterns obviously reflect employer preferences in whom they choose to invest. They also reflect, however, differences in how workers recognize the importance of training, and their interest in pursuing further training.

Other Disincentives
The literature addresses various other disincentives that firms might face in investing in training. While it can be argued that these might in some way be fitted into the preceding categories, they are interesting to briefly consider on their own. We include four below.[7] In most cases, little if any empirical evidence is available with which to test their importance.

Surplus Skilled Labour
It has been argued that in many sectors of the economy a surplus of skilled labour exists, as a result of which firms have little incentive to invest in further training (beyond very firm-specific orientation training) (e.g., Livingstone 1997). This has long been articulated as the "buy instead of make" decision. In countries like Canada, where educational attainment levels are high and high unemployment rates persist, the possibility of a surplus of skilled labour seems plausible. There is, however, essentially no up-to-date evidence with which to evaluate this disincentive.[8]

In fact, even within the overall context of high unemployment, the present debate increasingly centres on concerns about shortages of skilled labour in certain occupations, most notably in the high-technology area. There is a certain amount of disagreement about the extent and nature of these shortages, but most serious analysis has concluded that the labour market is very tight for certain skill sets (Davidman 1999). Whether this situation is leading to more employer-based training is difficult to ascertain. A 1998 study by Industry Canada found that one-half of information technology firms have increased the training they provide for high-skilled workers. It has been suggested, on the other hand, that various factors may be acting as continuing obstacles to training in these sectors, despite the apparent tightness of the labour market. For example, the concentration of contractors – which stems from the project-based nature of much high-technology work – may be a disincentive for employers, given the uncertain future tenure. Some observers have also argued that the skills in particular demand may be of a general nature and thus unlikely to be developed through employer-sponsored training.

Low Skills/Bad Job Trap
The quality of the labour force can affect the employer's likelihood of training because of the types of job designs implemented and the training then required. If a firm can draw on a highly educated and literate labour force, it is more likely to build a competitive strategy based on challenging, high-skill

job designs. In turn, this creates an incentive to make investments in job-specific training that builds on the basics. In contrast to this "high-skill equilibrium," in a "low-skill equilibrium" employers drawing on a less educated workforce will design jobs in such a way as to preclude the need for advanced skills (Finegold 1992). In such a case, there will be little incentive to invest in training. Furthermore, as the IALS results have demonstrated, literacy skills are subject to the "use it or lose it" principle – workers who spend long periods in low-skill jobs that do not require their literacy skills find that those skills deteriorate over time. As a consequence, employers who follow a low-skill strategy will find it increasingly difficult to change their skills strategy by training their existing workforce.[9]

Expectations of Government Responsibility

In a society where education has traditionally been seen as a public good, there is a potential for firms (and workers) to resist the notion of private financing of training and to expect public financing.[10] This can occur even where private returns exceed social returns, as long as the information failures discussed earlier exist. Various surveys have found that some portion of the employer population identifies a lack of government assistance as a barrier to training. For example, in the 1993 Ekos National Survey of Employers on Training and Employment Issues (NSETEI) and the 1995 Ekos Workplace Training Survey, 30 percent and 25 percent of the respondents, respectively, cited this factor (Ekos Research Associates 1993; Betcherman et al. 1997).

Tax-Related Factors

There has been very little analysis of how the tax system affects the training decisions of firms (and, indeed, of workers).[11] As economists, however, we can expect there to be behavioural responses here, as in so many other areas. Booth and Snower (1996, Chapter 15) offer some illustrations. For example, where income or profit gains from training are reduced in net terms because of personal or corporate taxes, we would expect this to result in a disincentive to train. Similarly, the tax treatment of other types of investment (e.g., on physical capital) will affect the relative attractiveness to the firm of training investments.

New Evidence from the Workplace Training Survey

To complement the literature review, we now present some new results on disincentives to employer-sponsored training based on data from the Workplace Training Survey.[12] As indicated earlier, the WTS was a national survey of employers (n = 2,584) conducted in 1995 to gather information on incidence, impacts, and other aspects of workplace training in Canada. Results from the survey were weighted to reflect the size, industrial, and provincial composition of establishments in the country. For comparative purposes, we also present some results on training obstacles from the 1993 Ekos National Survey of Employers on Training and Employment Issues (NSETEI), which asked similar questions on obstacles. It should be noted that 1,089 establishments participated in both surveys, which allows us to conduct some longitudinal analysis.

In both surveys, employers were asked to rate the importance of various potential training obstacles on a seven-point scale (from 1, representing "not a problem," to 7, representing "a major problem"). For the present analysis, these responses were aggregated into two groups to create dichotomous variables: "yes, a major problem" (6-7) and "no, not a major problem" (1-5).[13]

In Table 2 we present the aggregated results from questions on training obstacles that were (almost) identically worded in the 1993 NSETEI and 1995-96 WTS.[14] When considering the results, however, it should be kept in mind that these data relate to the complete samples and not just the common group of 1,089 establishments. Thus, differences in the two years may be due to differences in sample composition. Keeping this in mind, the incidence of reported training obstacles declined between 1993 and 1995. Note that in 1995 similar proportions (about one-fifth) of employers cited each training obstacle. In other words, no single factor stands out as a disincentive for a large proportion of employers. Each is important, however, for a significant minority of firms. In both years, the most frequently cited obstacles relate to cost and lack of government assistance. Poaching ("losing trained workers to other employers") was the least frequently cited barrier in 1995 but not in 1993.[15]

Table 2

Percentage incidence of training obstacles,[1] weighted, 1993 and 1995

Obstacle	1993	1995
Training cost the organization too much	29.5	20.2
Lost production while workers on training	18.4	16.4
Insufficient government assistance	29.9	22.7
Lose trained workers to other organizations	24.5	15.5
Lack of suitable training courses and trainers	17.5	16.7

Source: Published incidence rates based on Ekos Research Associates National Survey of Employers on Training and Employment Issues (Human Resources Development Canada) and the Workplace Training Survey (Betcherman et al. 1997).
1 Establishments responding 6 or 7 on a 7-point scale capturing the degree to which obstacle was a problem, varying from 1 (not a problem) to 7 (serious problem) for questions on obstacles that were worded the same in both surveys. Note, however, that the incidences are based on different samples of establishments in the survey years.

How persistent are reported training obstacles? To accurately answer this question, we need to examine the incidence of the obstacles among the same group of establishments in the two survey years. In Table 3, we present the results of the longitudinal analysis based on the restricted sample of employers who answered similarly worded questions on obstacles in both the 1993 and 1995 surveys. Note that results in this table (and only this table) are not weighted.

The main finding from Table 3 (middle column) is that there is a lot of "churning" among employers with respect to reported training obstacles – i.e., a lack of persistence in training obstacles. Between only one-quarter and one-third of establishments experiencing a specific training obstacle in 1993 continued to experience the same obstacle in 1995. This suggests that most establishments are able to overcome perceived obstacles to training. The third column of Table 3 indicates that only about 10 percent of establishments reported a specific training obstacle in 1995 after not having experienced it two years earlier.

Do employers who do not train overestimate the extent to which factors may be an obstacle to training? To answer this question, we compared the

Table 3

Incidence of obstacles to workplace training: longitudinal analysis,[1] unweighted, 1995

Obstacle	(1) *Persistence:* Percent of establishments that had reported obstacle in 1993 and also reported obstacle in 1995	(2) *"Newcomer":* Percent of establishments that had *not* reported obstacle in 1993 but reported obstacle in 1995
Training cost the organization too much	33.5	9.8
Lost production while workers on training	26.0	12.4
Insufficient government assistance	32.7	12.5
Lose trained workers to other organizations	29.6	8.1
Lack of suitable training courses and trainers	25.2	11.5

Source: Ekos Research Associates National Survey of Employers on Training and Employment Issues (HRDC) and estimates by the authors based on the Workplace Training Survey.
1 Based on establishments (*n* = 1,080) responding 6 or 7 on a 7-point scale capturing the degree to which obstacle was a problem, varying from 1 (not a problem) to 7 (serious problem), among establishments responding to the relevant questions in 1993 and 1995, 0 for questions on obstacles that were worded the same in both surveys.

Table 4

Percentage incidence of training obstacles[1] by whether or not establishment provided formal training to its employees, weighted, 1995

Obstacles	Provided Formal Training	No Formal Training	Total
Training cost the organization too much	16.9	22.5	20.1 ***
Lost production while workers on training	18.4	14.9	16.4 **
Insufficient government assistance	20.7	24.1	22.7 **
Lose trained workers to other organizations	12.9	17.3	15.5 ***
Lack of suitable training courses and trainers	13.9	18.7	16.7 **

Source: Estimates by the authors based on the Workplace Training Survey.
1 Establishments responding 6 or 7 (a major problem) on a 7-point scale varying from 1
   (not a problem) to 7 (a major problem).
Differences significant at: ** 5% level, *** 1% level.

incidences of cited training obstacles for firms that provided formal training with the incidences among those that did not (Table 4). The results indicate larger proportions of non-training employers than training employers citing specific obstacles. (The one exception is lost production, which presumably may be something that is learned only after the training is provided.) Further econometric analysis would be required to test whether this result reflects the fact that non-training employers overestimate training

Table 5

Percentage incidence of training obstacles[1] by workforce size of establishment, weighted, 1995

Obstacles	< 20 employees	20-99 employees	100 or more employees	Total
Training cost the organization too much	20.7	15.6	15.1	20.1
Lost production while workers on training	16.5	14.6	19.3	16.4
Insufficient government assistance	23.3	16.6	24.1	22.7*
Lose trained workers to other organizations	15.7	15.9	8.3	15.5
Lack of suitable training courses and trainers	17.0	13.1	17.0	16.7

Source: Estimates by the authors based on the Workplace Training Survey.
1 Establishments responding 6 or 7 (a major problem) on a 7-point scale varying from 1
   (not a problem) to 7 (a major problem).
* Difference significant at 10% level.

obstacles or whether it simply reflects differences in the composition of the two subsamples.

In the next series of tables, we present the results on training obstacles for various characteristics of establishments. First, looking at size, based on actual training patterns we would expect training obstacles to be greater for smaller establishments, presumably because of a lack of economies of scale compared with larger employers. Variations by size, however, seem to depend on the specific obstacle; for the most part, differences are not statistically significant across size categories (Table 5).

Still, as expected, smaller firms were generally more likely to identify the cost of training as an obstacle than larger firms, while lost production during training was somewhat more likely to be cited by larger firms. On the one hand, this is surprising since one would expect that large firms would be most able to absorb downtime; on the other hand, this result may reflect a greater flexibility in many small firms. Small employers were more likely to cite poaching as a disincentive, presumably because of their inability to match compensation offers that larger firms can make. Finally, insufficient government assistance and a lack of suitable training courses and trainers were cited most frequently by large establishments and small establishments, with medium-sized employers least likely to report these barriers.[16]

Table 6 shows reported training obstacles by region. Differences here could reflect institutional differences (due, for example, to culture or public policies), differences in the composition of the employer population, or labour market conditions. All of these can affect the training decision. The results indicate statistically significant differences across regions. For the most part,

Table 6

Percentage incidence of training obstacles[1] by region***, weighted, 1995

Obstacles	Atlantic	Quebec	Ontario	Prairies	BC	Canada
Training cost the organization too much	24.9	31.2	11.8	12.9	29.1	20.2
Lost production while workers on training	20.6	18.0	10.9	15.4	26.6	16.4
Insufficient government assistance	26.8	33.1	17.4	19.9	19.5	22.7
Lose trained workers to other organizations	18.3	20.1	16.3	10.0	11.4	15.5
Lack of suitable training courses and trainers	18.6	22.0	14.3	13.6	16.5	16.7

Source: Estimates by the authors based on the Workplace Training Survey.
1 Establishments responding 6 or 7 (a major problem) on a 7-point scale varying from 1 (not a problem) to 7 (a major problem).
*** All differences significant at 1% level.

Table 7

Percentage incidence of training obstacles[1] by whether or not in a rural community, weighted, 1995

Obstacles	Rural	Urban	Total
Training cost the organization too much	21.1	20.1	20.3
Lost production while workers on training	20.3	15.3	16.6**
Insufficient government assistance	24.4	23.3	23.5
Lose trained workers to other organizations	17.3	15.6	15.9
Lack of suitable training courses and trainers	13.1	15.7	15.3

Source: Estimates by the authors based on the Workplace Training Survey.
1 Establishments responding 6 or 7 (a major problem) on a 7-point scale varying from 1
   (not a problem) to 7 (a major problem).
** Difference significant at 5% level.

employers in Quebec were most likely to report different training barriers, consistent with the survey's finding that this region had the lowest incidence of formal training. Employers in Ontario and the Prairies were the least likely to report training obstacles.

We might expect the incidence of certain training obstacles to be higher in rural communities than in urban centres because of a thinner supply side and higher information costs. As Table 7 shows, however, any differences are very small and not statistically significant.

As the literature review indicated, labour turnover plays a big role in the perception of externalities as a disincentive to training. We would expect employers in high-turnover environments to cite potential loss of trained

Table 8

Percentage incidence of training obstacles[1] by level of turnover, weighted, 1995

Obstacles	0-4%	5-25%	26%+	Total
Training cost the organization too much	19.0	20.3	22.2	20.0
Lost production while workers on training	14.6	11.7	25.7	16.0 ***
Insufficient government assistance	15.5	13.9	18.2	15.6
Lose trained workers to other organizations	10.1	10.7	23.6	12.1 ***
Lack of suitable training courses and trainers	23.0	18.1	28.3	22.6 ***

Source: Estimates by the authors based on the Workplace Training Survey.
1 Establishments responding 6 or 7 (a major problem) on a 7-point scale varying from 1
   (not a problem) to 7 (a major problem).
*** Difference significant at 1% level.

Table 9

Mean percentage of work force that is part-time by whether or not training obstacles[1] were reported, weighted, 1995

	Mean Percentage Part-Time	
Obstacles	Obstacle	Not
Training cost the organization too much	21.5	20.4
Lost production while workers on training	20.0	20.7
Insufficient government assistance	18.7	20.8*
Lose trained workers to other organizations	20.4	20.6
Lack of suitable training courses and trainers	21.1	20.3

Source: Estimates by the authors based on the Workplace Training Survey.
1 Establishments ressponding 6 or 7 (a major problem) on a 7-point scale varying from 1 (not a problem) to 7 (a major problem).
* Difference significant at 10% level.

workers as an obstacle to the provision of workplace training. These employers might also be expected to cite costs as an impediment to training. Table 8 indicates that the incidence of each training obstacle does rise with the level of turnover. For example, the percentage of employers with more than 25 percent staff turnover that cited the threat of poaching as a training barrier was more than double the percentage of firms with less than 25 percent turnover that cited this threat. There were also appreciable differences by level of turnover for lost production time and lack of suitable training courses/trainers being identified as training barriers.

The final potential correlate of training obstacles we discuss here is the extent to which an employer relies on part-time workers. Where the employment relationship is part-time and/or of expected short tenure, there is less incentive for the employer (and, indeed, the employee) to invest in training, due to the greater risk that the investment will not be recouped because the worker is unlikely to work enough hours before the employment relationship ends.[17] Thus, we might expect employers with a large proportion of part-time workers to emphasize the importance of certain obstacles, such as losing trained workers or the high costs of training. As Table 9 indicates, however, there was very little difference in the mean percentage of employment that is part-time between employers who cited the different training obstacles and employers who did not.

Conclusion

Employer-sponsored training is of particular interest to policymakers in the current context. This is largely due to two developments. First, economic theory has placed new emphasis on the importance of intangible assets that drive knowledge generation and innovation. Ultimately, the source of these drivers of growth is people. This has placed renewed importance on human resource development – not only initial schooling but also lifelong learning in the workplace. Second, Canada, along with many other countries, is concerned about the appearance of skill shortages, especially in critical knowledge- and technology-intensive areas. Thus, makers of public policy are interested in encouraging employer investment in training, even if direct interventions are not prominent in the potential toolkit. In this environment, then, understanding disincentives to training, including how they might be overcome, is a priority for policymakers.

In theory, there are many disincentives that can influence employers in deciding whether or not to make investments in employee training. The classic externality-based concern is that, once trained, employees may leave the firm, thus precluding any possibility that the firm will recoup a (full) return on its investment. There are also various disincentives stemming from imperfect information. In some cases, employees may themselves create disincentives for employers because of a lack of interest or a lack of basic skills that provide a necessary foundation for ultimately ensuring productivity gains from training. Finally, there is a host of other potential barriers stemming from labour force conditions and public policy.

Unfortunately, the empirical base on which to evaluate these obstacles is partial. One strategy is to observe actual training patterns across the employer population, thereby identifying where investments are low and (presumably) where barriers are high. This sort of exercise does lead to the identification of certain correlates of training, most prominently firm size. A second empirical strategy is to analyse how employers rate the importance of various potential disincentives. From the current exercise, in which we have both reviewed existing evidence and undertaken new analysis, it seems fair to conclude that, for large numbers of firms, specific obstacles do not lead to real underinvestment. It is plausible that decisions not to train are often "rational" in the sense that the likely return does not warrant the investment, either because workers with the necessary skills are available or because they can learn the required skills informally.

This does not mean that disincentives do not exist. While none of the potential barriers are consistently and widely cited as important, a number do appear to be significant for a minority of firms. In these cases, investment may not occur at socially optimal levels, which is an issue for policymakers. The appropriate response for governments may be to consider how they can support the functioning of the training market by providing better information and supporting intermediaries and partnerships that pool risk and strengthen the links between industry and the learning sector.[18]

Notes

1 Prepared with the financial support of the Micro-economic Analysis Branch, Industry Canada. This research was undertaken under the auspices of the Canadian Policy Research Networks (CPRN) and was initially reported in a CPRN discussion paper (Betcherman et al. 1997).

2 The methodology and results of this survey are reported in Betcherman et al. (1997). While the survey collected detailed data from employers on the importance they attached to various training barriers, the published study did not report these in any detail.

3 Indeed, researchers have generally found no evidence of trainees financing their own general training through lower wages. For example, Barron et al. (1989) showed that employees who received training felt to be useful to other firms did not receive lower wages than workers who did not receive such training. Also, Feuer et al. (1987) showed that engineers who had (general) education financed by their employers were paid no less than those who paid for their own education. It is true that there could be various interpretations for these findings beyond the one emphasized here, that downward wage inflexibility is a constraint on employees financing their own general training. For example, these results may indicate that employers in certain circumstances may be prepared to finance general training.

4 The link between turnover and training is not empirically conclusive. On the one hand, as noted in the text, the OECD (1993) showed that the incidence of workplace training and high average tenure are broadly related across diverse economies. Betcherman et al. (1997) found a negative relationship between establishment turnover rates and the probability of formal workplace training. On the other hand, Levine (1993) found no relationship between plants reporting high levels of on-the-job training and turnover levels.

5 It should be understood that developing proper accounting frameworks is not a simple matter. Indeed, this has been evident from work coordinated by the OECD. There are a great number of "unknowns," including, for example, the expected tenure of the employee and thus the length of the payback period over which employers may recoup their investment. Using data from the US National Longitudinal Survey of Youth, Lowenstein and Spletzer (1997) found that employers would delay formal training for employees for whom there is uncertainty regarding future mobility.

6 More detail is provided in Betcherman et al. (1998).

7 For a more exhaustive list, see Booth and Snower (1996), especially Chapter 15.

8 In the 1990 CLMPC survey of business and union leaders (CLMPC 1990a), there was evidence that about one-quarter of business leaders preferred recruitment over training. The union leaders considered a preference for recruitment to be a more prevalent factor.

9 The relationships among the skills of the labour force, the job designs selected by employers, and subsequent need for further training are discussed in Betcherman et al. (1998).

10 In Canada, government traditionally has also used immigration as a policy instrument to help firms meet skill needs, especially in times of labour shortages. This augments the expectation that human resources development is a public responsibility.

11 One exception is Kitchen and Auld (1995).

12 We have already cited the survey report (Betcherman et al. 1997). This section expands upon the discussion of training obstacles contained there.

13 In addition, there were some responses to an open-ended question on training obstacles that were recoded into dichotomous variables and that we report on separately in this chapter. Tables 2 to 8, we do concentrate on the closed responses because of higher incidences reported for these obstacles compared with the responses to the open-ended question.

14 Except where indicated, all results presented in Tables 2 to 8 are weighted.

15 As we have noted, on the WTS there were some responses to an open-ended question on training obstacles. These were offered by about 25 percent of the respondents. Three of these responses – lack of suitable candidates, employees don't see a training need, and employees don't complete the training – were amalgamated into a single employee-driven obstacle, which we discussed above. Only 4 percent of employers cited this type of obstacle.

Similarly, a lack of information about what training was available was mentioned as an obstacle by only 3.2 percent. Other open-ended responses, which were of a cost-related nature, cited by more than 3 percent of employers were: too busy/loss of workers and production (6.4 percent), cost (3.3 percent), and travel distance/geographic location (3.1 percent). As can be seen, these obstacles were not of wide concern to WTS respondents, but this may have to do more with the form of the question (open-ended) than actual experience.

16   With regard to lack of government assistance and training courses and trainers, small firms may find it difficult or costly to gather information about what is available. On the other hand, large firms would have better access to information but may simply have sophisticated requirements.

17   Household surveys such as the AETS have documented the relatively low training participation rates of part-time employees.

18   These ideas are developed in some detail in Betcherman et al. (1998).

References

Barron, J.M., D.A. Black, and M.A. Lowenstein. 1989. "Job Matching and On-the-Job Training." *Journal of Labor Economics* (January): 1-19.

Becker, Gary. 1964. *Human Capital.* New York: National Bureau of Economic Research.

Betcherman, Gordon, Norm Leckie, and Kathryn McMullen. 1997. *Developing Skills in the Canadian Workplace: The Results of the Ekos Workplace Training Survey.* CPRN Study No. W/ 02. Ottawa: Canadian Policy Research Networks.

Betcherman, Gordon, Kathryn McMullen, and Katie Davidman. 1998. *Training for the New Economy: A Synthesis Report.* Ottawa: Canadian Policy Research Networks.

Booth, Alison, and Dennis J. Snower, eds. 1996. *Acquiring Skills: Market Failures, Their Symptoms and Policy Responses.* Centre for Policy Economic Research. Cambridge, UK: Cambridge University Press.

CLMPC (Canadian Labour Market and Productivity Centre). 1990a. "Business and Labour Leaders Speak Out on Training and Education," January.

–. 1990b. "High-Tech Sector a Growing Source of Skilled Jobs," June.

–. 1993. *1991 National Training Survey.* Ottawa: CLMPC.

Davidman, Katie. 1999. "The Status of Human Resource Development in the Canadian Software Sector." Discussion Paper. Ottawa: Canadian Policy Research Networks.

Ekos Research Associates. 1993. "National Survey of Employers on Training and Employment Issues." Prepared for Employment and Immigration Canada.

Employment and Immigration Canada. 1987. "An Overview of the Results of a Survey of Training in Canadian Industries." *Labour Market Bulletin,* 4,2.

Feuer, M.J., H. Glick, and A. Desai. 1987. "Is Firm Sponsored Education Viable?" *Journal of Economic Behavior and Organization* 8: 121-36.

Finegold, D. 1992. "The Changing International Economy and Its Impact on Education and Training." *Oxford Studies in Comparative Education* 2,2: 57-82.

Government of Canada and OECD. 1997. *Changing Workplace Strategies: Achieving Better Outcomes for Enterprises, Workers and Society.* Ottawa: Supply and Services Canada.

Human Resources Development Canada and Statistics Canada. 1995. *Adult Education and Training 1992.* Ottawa.

Kapsalis, Constantine. 1996. "The Motivation for Training Decisions." *Canadian Business Economics* (Fall): 71-80.

Kitchen, Harry, and Douglas Auld. 1995. *Financing Education and Training in Canada.* Toronto: Canadian Tax Foundation.

Levine, D.J. 1993. "Worth Waiting For? Delayed Compensation, Training, and Turnover in the United States and Japan." *Journal of Labor Economics* 11,4: 724-52.

Livingstone, D.W. 1997. "The Limits of Human Capital Theory: Expanding Knowledge, Informal Learning and Underemployment." *Policy Options* (July/August): 9-13.

Lowenstein, M.A., and J.R. Spletzer. 1997. "Delayed Formal On-the-Job Training." *Industrial Labour Relations Review* 51,1: 82-99.

Miller, Peter, and T. O'Leary. 1996. "The Factory as Laboratory." In M. Power, ed., *Accounting and Science: Natural Inquiry and Commercial Reason.* Cambridge Studies in Management, No. 26, 120-50. Cambridge, UK: Cambridge University Press.

OECD (Organization for Economic Cooperation and Development). 1993. *Employment Outlook.* Paris: OECD.

OECD and Statistics Canada. 1995. *Literacy, Economy and Society: Results of the First International Adult Literacy Survey.* Paris and Ottawa: OECD and Statistics Canada.

Ontario Ministry of Skills Development. 1989. *The Training Decision: Training in the Private Sector.* Toronto: Ministry of Skills Development.

Pigou, A.C. 1912. *Wealth and Welfare.* London: Macmillan.

Rechnitzer, Edith. 1990. *Human Resource Training and Development Survey Results 1987.* Ottawa: Statistics Canada.

Stevens, Margaret. 1996. "Transferable Training and Poaching Externalities." In Alison Booth and Dennis J. Snower, eds., *Acquiring Skills: Market Failure, Their Symptoms and Policy Responses,* 21-40. Centre for Policy Economic Research. Cambridge, UK: Cambridge University Press.

15
Firms and Human Resources Investment
Gerhard Bosch

Introduction

This chapter addresses, first, how firms might be encouraged to make investments in their own human capital, and second, their role in training the unemployed. In terms of what factors influence firms to invest in the human capital of their employees, we think the following closely linked factors are crucial:

1 In the countries of the Organization for Economic Cooperation and Development (OECD), firms are increasingly operating in markets that compete more on quality and less on cost.
2 Some labour market regulations promote post-Taylorist forms of work organization and investments in workforce human capital, rather than hiring and firing.
3 Small and medium-sized companies are supported by external training infrastructures.
4 The learning costs associated with the introduction of new forms of work organization and human resources strategies are reduced by high-trust industrial relations and by exchange of experience through networks of firms.

The second question relates to the role firms play in the training of the unemployed. Learning in modern work organizations is gaining importance beyond the traditional on-the-job-learning in Taylorist work places. Training of the unemployed must therefore take place not only in vocational schools or external training agencies but also in firms. Firms, however, are not always interested in training the unemployed, especially the long-term unemployed. Some incentives for training the unemployed might therefore be necessary, such as the Danish leave schemes.

In the following section, we analyse the factors that might encourage firms to invest in training. We then describe in more detail the close link between work organization and human resource strategies ("Team Work, Direct Participation, and Human Resource Investment in Europe"). Finally, we discuss the role of firms in training the unemployed.

Factors Influencing the Decisions of Firms Regarding Investments in Human Capital

At present, there are two broad trends in the evolution of work organization in Europe. Some firms that rely on specialist knowledge and competencies are trying to increase internal flexibility (multi-skilling and working time flexibility) in their core workforce, and take their employees' interests into account as much as possible in doing so. These firms are breaking with the Taylorist tradition and introducing flat hierarchies, self-responsibility, employee participation, teamwork, and stable employment. In other firms, however, particularly in labour-intensive service industries dominated by price competition, Taylorism is actually being reinforced. Competencies are concentrated in a small proportion of the workforce, and flexibility is achieved by increasing the size of the peripheral workforce. Little account is taken of employees' interests.

These remarks are intended to show that several different forms of work organization currently coexist and compete with each other. What are the reasons for these differences?

Product Markets

Firms need to make more use of employees' skills and knowledge in order to achieve higher productivity, greater flexibility, and better product quality. As the European Commission states in its Green Paper on work organization: "In traditional economic thinking, labour is a factor of production similar to land and capital – a cost to be reduced. In a knowledge based economy, however, people represent a key resource. Organizations are valued not only on the basis of their products or machines but primarily on the knowledge-creating capacity of the workforce, the people who work for them, how they work, what work means to them" (European Commission 1997, 3).

Exaggerating somewhat for the purposes of simplification, the traditional model of European and North American firms can be summed up in the key terms "complex organization" and "simple jobs." Flexibility is accomplished by designing a complex work organization, with simple jobs and short learning times, in which workers can be replaced easily. The complexity of the organization is grounded in the radical split between "thinking" and "doing." This type of organization is well suited to mass production in a stable environment. However, if products become more diverse and markets more turbulent, if quality requirements increase and the pace of technological change quickens, such organizations lack flexibility. What is required is a

Table 1

Evolution of trade prices, 1980-90 (percentage change)

	Import prices	Export prices	Trade price gap
Germany	20.2	40.4	20.2
Canada	38.0	14.0	24.0
EU (unweighted average)	20.7	31.2	10.5
Japan	-7.5	43.2	50.7
USA	0.7	30.3	29.6
OECD (unweighted average)	18.0	29.5	11.5

Source: OECD (1997).

simplified organization with more complex jobs. Flexibility can be achieved by the reintegration of tasks and the introduction of teamwork. As a result, a considerable proportion of a firm's coordination and communication problems can be resolved at lower levels of the organization, with a corresponding reduction in organizational complexity. In order to achieve such a modern flexible firm, decentralization at all levels of the organization is required. Top-down control in corporate organization has to be replaced by a continuous dialogue with business units (Bosch 1995).

It is difficult to measure quality. One indicator could be the research and development (R&D) intensity of products. In countries with a higher proportion of employees working in high-technology manufacturing (more than 8 percent of turnover spent on R&D) and a low proportion in low-technology manufacturing (less then 3 percent of turnover spent on R&D), one would expect companies to compete more on quality than on costs. A second indicator could be the development of export and import prices. Table 1 shows that export prices in the industrialized countries rose faster than import prices in the 1980s. Labor-intensive mass production and Taylorist work organization are moving to low-wage countries. As is often said, Taylorism in manufacturing does not end; it is exported.

To promote this change towards higher-quality products, most industrialized countries invest more in R&D, education, and training. In the 1980s, the Swedish government, for example, came to the conclusion that the quality of Swedish products had deteriorated. They increased R&D expenditure and tried through several government programs to promote the introduction of flexible work organizations (NUTEK 1996). As can be seen in Table 2, Sweden spends more today on R&D, education, and training than any other OECD country, and has the most proactive approach to structural change.

In countries with high spending on education, the structure of the workforce will change. Firms that traditionally had adjusted their work organization to employ unskilled labour suddenly find that labour markets

Table 2

Investments in R&D, education, and training in 1993 (% of GDP)

	R&D	Training and education	Total
USA	2.7	6.8	9.5
Canada	1.5	7.3	8.8
Germany	2.5	5.9	8.4
Sweden	3.1	6.9	10.0
Turkey	0.3	3.4	3.7

Source: Schumacher (1997).

have changed. A good example is Ireland, which now invests a high proportion of gross domestic product (GDP) in education and training (5.8 percent in 1993) (Schumacher 1997).

Labour Market Regulations

Despite arguments to the contrary in the management literature, the Taylorist era is by no means over. In those parts of the service sector where price competition is particularly strong, Taylorist practices are currently spreading again. Examples of the "re-Taylorization" of work organization can also be observed in other sectors, such as construction. One important driving force behind this "re-Taylorization" is the wage differentials between skilled and less-skilled labour, and the existence of a pool of less-skilled workers. In the European construction industry, such pools have developed in recent years as a result of transnational migration in particular. We have only to think of the Portuguese or Eastern European construction workers now active in Germany.

In Berlin, where one can find some of the biggest construction sites in Europe, the volume of construction amounts to about 35 billion DM a year. About 100,000 construction workers are needed for such a construction volume. The number of construction workers actually from Berlin fell, however, from more than 54,000 in 1993 to 28,000 in 1998. There are now 10,000 construction workers from other German states (mainly from East Germany), 30,000 seconded workers from Eastern Europe or other European Union (EU) countries, and 30,000 illegal workers, mainly foreigners; all work for lower rates than Berlin's construction workers. The work organization has changed. Since most foreign workers do not have a vocational qualification in one of the building trades, work organization is undergoing a process of "re-Taylorization," which is being driven by the ready availability of cheap labour. The skilled German workers on building sites are increasingly having to take on a coordinating and supervisory role (Bosch and Zühlke-Robinet 1998).

Women and students form the less-skilled pools in the service sector. One area typically dominated by Taylorist forms of work organization is the food retail trade. A study (Kirsch et al. 1998) carried out by our institute (Wissenschaftszentrum Nordrhein-Westfalen) in four EU member states (the Netherlands, Denmark, the United Kingdom, and France) shows that the labour supply here is increasingly being differentiated by qualification:

> In a mode of work organization based on this principle of functional differentiation, more highly qualified, and in most cases better-paid personnel are not allocated on principle to checkout work and must not therefore be allocated to a job beneath their level of qualification. Rather, the objective is to make constant use of the specific product knowledge and skills of this section of the workforce by allocating them exclusively to customer advice and sales duties (on the full-service counters). The skill requirements for shelf-stacking duties are even lower than for checkout operators, and here a Taylorist mode of work organization has efficiency advantages. All activities that are linked to the logistical cycle can be routinized to a large extent.

The incentives for such differentiation vary from country to country. In Germany, for example, skilled workers in the retail food trade are considerably better paid than less well-qualified ones. In France, the differentials are smaller, so that the wage structure exerts less pressure on managers to introduce Taylorist practices.

A second source of rationalization in the retail food trade is the precise adjustment of hours worked to customer flows, which is easier to manage with part-timers than with full-timers. The personnel manager of a French hypermarket put it in the following terms: "If I assume that I have 350 hours' work to allocate in a day, then obviously it makes a difference whether I can distribute those hours among 200 or 300 people. In the latter case, I have many more opportunities for adjusting manning levels to customer flows" (Kirsch et al. 1998).

The labour markets in various countries provide varying levels of support for such strategies, however. There are more part-time workers available in Germany, the UK, and the Netherlands than in France. In Germany, at least, this also applies to skilled workers. This availability is clearly reflected in the personnel structure of the retail food trade in the various countries. In France, the increase in the share of part-timers over the past few years has been lower than in Germany.

With the increasing division of labour and the precise scheduling of hours worked, employees in Taylorist work organizations are ever more dependent on fluctuations in demand. Employee dissatisfaction, particularly with demands to work unpredictable hours at short notice and without additional payment, cannot be overlooked.

Labour market regulations can also promote investments in human capital. Pischke (1997) found that German companies invest more than American companies in training their workforce, especially in training their unskilled workers. He gives two reasons for this difference. First, earnings are more unequally distributed in the US than in Germany. Because the wages of newly trained workers will rise less in Germany than in the US, the company profits most from the productivity gains. Second, because German workers are better protected against dismissals than American workers, it is less costly for companies to retrain than to replace workers. The OECD also found a positive relationship between job tenure and investment of companies in training (OECD 1993, 143).

The fact that firms must first seek to redeploy workers internally is viewed positively by leading members of the business community, even from the point of view of efficiency alone. The former CEO of Scandinavian Airlines System has written that protective legislation "provides a basic platform of security which allows the decentralization of responsibility and encourages risk taking. Surprisingly, in decentralizing SAS, we have met with less success in the United States than anywhere else ... Americans are actually reluctant to take risks in their daily job. I think this is because most US companies do not offer real job security" (Carlzon 1989, 84).

External Infrastructures for Small and Medium-Sized Enterprises

While big firms have enough resources to organize training themselves, small and medium-sized enterprises (SMEs) have to rely on external training centres. A German study showed that workplaces with fewer than 20 employees organized only 19 percent of further training internally, while companies with more than 1,000 employees organized 92 percent of further training internally (von Bardeleben et al. 1989).

With new technologies and increasing skill requirements, it also becomes more difficult for SMEs to provide the necessary vocational training. A good example is the case of the German construction industry. As reported by Streeck et al. (1987), during the 1960s the number of apprentices had declined sharply. In 1970 the share of apprentices in total employment in the industry was only 1.8 percent, compared with 10.2 percent in 1950. The old craft-oriented training system was clearly no longer able to provide a good supply of young tradesmen to replace an ageing workforce. In order to reverse this decline of the dual system in the construction industry, the social partners decided to adopt completely new methods. The reform of the training system had three main elements: (1) training was to take place in two stages, with the second building on the skills and knowledge acquired in the first; a vocational qualification could be acquired at the end of both stages; (2) in the first year in particular, the training was to go beyond the confines of individual trades; in order to ensure this (3) apprentices were to spend alternating blocks of time in training workshops serving a number of firms and in vocational schools.

The reform was accompanied by a significant increase in training allowances for apprenticeships in order to make the building trades more attractive to young people; the allowances are now some of the highest in any sector of the economy. So that the burden of the higher costs[1] of the much-improved vocational training system would not weigh too heavily on firms, a financing system based on levies and administered by the holiday and wage compensation fund was introduced. All firms in the construction industry pay a monthly contribution of 2.8 percent of the wage bill to a fund that is used to reimburse a considerable proportion of the costs incurred by firms that offer training places for apprentices.

The success of the reform and of the system of financing is irrefutable. The number of apprentices has risen considerably over time, with a new peak of around 100,000 trainees being reached in the 1990s, and more firms are offering training places than before. It has to be acknowledged, however, that the number of apprentices is subject to considerable cyclical fluctuations and the construction industry is often left behind in the competition with other industries for apprentices. The reform also changed the way in which training is organized. The time that apprentices spend in firms fell from 80 percent to 46 percent of their working time; the time spent in vocational schools rose from 20 to 26 percent; and the time spent in the joint training centres (Möbus, Grando) is around 20 percent.

High-Trust Industrial Relations and Reduction of Learning Costs

In management research, which is heavily influenced by the traditions of the English-speaking world, employers are generally assumed to enjoy a high degree of autonomy in implementing the personnel strategies they consider necessary. Negotiations with trade unions and works councils have no place in this literature and are frequently treated simply as disruptive factors, despite the fact that in many countries they influence styles of personnel management that have been very successful. Thus there are no universal management strategies; rather, strategies are shaped by institutions. This is acknowledged in more recent management research, and has led to a series of international comparisons of management styles (Gooderham et al. 1996; Brunstein 1995; Brewster and Hegewisch 1994). There is, therefore, no toolbox of instruments with which the same results – a highly motivated workforce, for example – can be achieved in all countries.

The institutional frameworks within which new management strategies can develop vary considerably from member state to member state within the European Union. This is evident from representative surveys of firms that have been conducted with support from the European Commission.[2] Striking differences can be observed between the various European countries in their use of certain personnel policy instruments. For reasons of space, we can mention only two of these differences here.

- Performance appraisals and individual award systems are much more common in the UK than in Germany or Scandinavia. In the latter countries, there is a greater tendency for pay structures to be determined in negotiations with works councils or trade unions. These seek to restrict the use of performance appraisals and individual award systems, since, in their view, they tilt the balance of power too much in favour of management (Gooderham et al. 1996).
- In the Scandinavian countries and Germany, trade union influence at the plant level has actually increased in recent years, whereas managers in the UK consider such influence to have declined drastically. During the introduction of direct participation in firms,[3] only 26 percent of plant-level workforce representatives were not involved in Denmark and Sweden, compared with 76 percent in Portugal and 67 percent in Ireland. The scope of the participation also varied. In more than 40 percent of firms in Denmark and Sweden, joint decisions were taken on the measures to be implemented, whereas in other countries management simply informed workforce representatives (Gooderham et al. 1996) (see Table 3).

National social structures and skill levels in the labour force are also important factors. In countries with high levels of wage inequality, the social distance between the various levels of the hierarchy is also greater. The greater earnings equality in the Scandinavian countries facilitates direct

Table 3

The extent of workforce representative involvement in firm management (% of respondents practicing direct participation)

	None	Information	Consultation	Negotiation/ joint decision
10-country average	45	20	9	26
Denmark	26	18	11	45
France	39	32	13	16
Germany	45	18	5	33
Italy	59	17	8	16
Ireland	67	11	7	15
Netherlands	57	18	9	17
Portugal	76	7	4	13
Spain	50	23	8	21
Sweden	26	23	8	43
UK	48	21	13	18

Source: Sisson (1997).

cooperation at the workplace and has contributed to the emergence of a "democratic" management style (Bosch 1996).

These results are consistent with other, more qualitative comparisons of management strategies. It is clear that the influence of trade unions has been drastically reduced in Great Britain and that firms have adopted a core-periphery strategy. At the same time, British firms have been able to exploit their regained autonomy in order to introduce individual incentive schemes. In Germany, payment systems are regulated by collective agreements, which leaves management little scope for exerting its own influence. The system of co-determination, the importance of which has actually increased in recent years,[4] is highly formalized (Wächter and Stengelhofen 1995). Works councils act as intermediaries between workers and management and are skeptical of any forms of direct communication between the two sides. In Norway, contacts between management, trade unions, and employees are much more informal. Many of the new management instruments can also be used at the workplace, since they are consistent with the tradition of Norwegian co-determination. "Direct participation appeared to be a supplement to, not a replacement for, representative participation" (Hammer et al. 1994, 30).

In countries like Norway, Sweden, Denmark, or Germany, companies have to negotiate new forms of work organization and human resource strategies. The nationwide Norwegian "Main Agreement" between the Social Partners is full of declarations of good intent and reads in part like an exposition of the philosophy of the modern, participation-oriented firm – with one difference: employees' rights are firmly enshrined in the agreement and can survive crises. The common interest of both parties in high-trust organizations is emphasized (Main Agreement, sections 9-1 and 9-2):

> LO[5] and NHO[6] agree on the need for good and trusting relationships between enterprise and employees. For individual employees and the workforce as a whole a strong feeling of unity between enterprise and employees is of the greatest importance. It is also a necessary basis for efficient production. Developing forms of co-determination and a better working environment in the enterprise will necessitate extensive decentralization and delegation of decision-making powers within the enterprise, so that those who work in each department or working group are allowed a greater right to make their own decisions in their daily work.

Not only was "productivity" written into the agreement as an objective in the early 1990s (Qvale 1995) but the social partners also agreed that enterprise development measures should be jointly financed.[7] By 1992, projects in about 500 plants had been supported through the joint funding agreement. This represents about 7.5 percent of the 6,685 Norwegian firms with more than five employees. In the metal and engineering industries, 15 percent of firms have completed such a project (Sivesind et al. 1995, 309).

In the past, the purpose of company reorganization projects tended to be the improvement of working conditions. Nowadays, the state-supported "Enterprise Development 2000 Program" leans more heavily towards encouraging improvements in competitiveness "by utilization of Norwegian traditions of cooperation." In particular, firms facing direct international competition are being targeted. The plan is for this program to provide support for projects in 80 to 100 firms between 1995 and the year 2000. Thus in this area, LO, NHO, and the state have assumed joint responsibility for stimulating the further development of company organizational structures in private industry. In doing so, they have succeeded in involving a remarkably high proportion of Norwegian firms in jointly managed projects.

Team Work, Direct Participation, and Human Resource Investment in Europe

Firms that compete on quality have to develop their employees' competencies. Their customer-specific products or services cannot be produced with a constantly changing workforce. In order to maintain product quality and increase employee motivation, the Taylorist division of labour is being weakened and tasks integrated. With centralized management structures it is no longer possible to cope with the growing range of variants required to meet individual customers' specifications. For this reason, tasks are increasingly being delegated to teams or work groups.

It is becoming increasingly clear that work organization is made up of several different elements. A change in one element has far-reaching consequences for the whole structure.

One precondition for flexible working times in a group is that workers should be able to cover for each other. In general, this requires a loosening of the division of labour within the group and the development of multi-skilling, which in turn requires training programs. The role of supervisors also changes. They give fewer direct instructions and become moderators and coordinators. In many cases, payment systems also have to be changed, with wage levels being set not in accordance with the demands of a single job but rather with those of a work system. In other words, bonuses will have to be paid according to group rather than individual performance.

In a research project for Directorate-General V (DG V) of the European Commission, we looked at the relationship between working time flexibility and work organization. In case studies we carried out in seven EU member states, we found that many companies introduced team work to manage shorter and more flexible working hours (Lehndorff et al. 1998). Many decisions were delegated to teams.

If firms increase the flexibility of their core workforce, they become increasingly reliant on their employees' active participation and motivation. The establishment of teams is also an instrument for increasing the scope for individual workers to organize their work and manage their own working time. For if working time is increasingly becoming the buffer for fluctuations in orders, individual workers in establishments with a rigid division of labour are losing their autonomy with respect to working time. The examples in Table 4 show that group work is being introduced in firms in very different industries and that one of the basic responsibilities of these groups is the management of working-time problems. The extensive management literature of recent years has almost completely ignored the importance of working-time questions and concentrated on other topics, such as the advantages of a less rigid division of labour in reintegrating production and quality control. In many of these companies, training had to take place to provide the necessary skills for the team members. This shows that if you re-engineer the firm, you cannot just change one element of work organization; changes in other areas are also necessary.

The importance of training in new forms of work organization was shown in a European survey on training (EPOC Research Group 1997). The EPOC Research Group was mainly interested in *direct participation.* This included individual consultation, group consultation, individual delegation, and group delegation, but not participation through intermediary employee representative bodies. About 5,800 managers of workplaces with more than 50 employees (in smaller countries, more than 25 employees) returned a questionnaire. Ten EU countries were involved. As the EPOC Research Group (1997, 171) reports (see Table 5):

> One quarter of all workplaces practicing direct participation reported they needed a very highly qualified workforce, whereas only about 5 per cent say that they could manage their business with unqualified employees. Taking in account the values in the other categories as well, it is obvious that qualification is a very important factor for direct participation: in 80 per cent of workplaces practicing direct participation the level of required qualification is medium or higher. The proportion with direct participation requiring high qualification is double that in workplaces without.

The Role of Firms in Training the Unemployed

To focus solely on formalized training is to ignore other forms of investment in vocational training. Particularly in periods of rapid change, a growing share of vocational training is provided at the workplace and relates to specific jobs. In 1994, in a survey on further training conducted regularly in Germany, employees were asked for the first time about "informal" further training. The results reveal the great significance of learning at the workplace.

Table 4

Group work and working time

Firm	Product	No. of employees	Groups and size of group	Competencies	Autonomous time management	Training
A	Insurance	1,400	Teams, 5-10 employees	Case processing Working time scheduling	Team responsible for organizing working time provided a certain level of service provision is maintained	Courses
B	Teaching equipment Furniture Teaching materials	360	Teams, approx. 10-15 employees	Planning Stock keeping Delivery dates Working time, holiday scheduling	Team responsible for organizing working time by arrangement with colleagues	Training on the job Courses
C	Automotive component supplier	3,169	Production platforms	Planning Stock keeping Quality control Training Maintenance, etc.	Independent responsibility for distribution of working time	Team decides Firm-specific training modules available
D	Car maker	9,000 (in plant)	Groups	Holiday scheduling	Shift plan, autonomous holiday scheduling	Training on the job Courses Master decides in cooperation with the team

Source: Lindecke/Lehndorff (1997).

Table 5

Qualification requirements in workplaces in 10 EU countries with and without direct participation

	Very high (1) %	2 %	3 %	4 %	Very low (5) %
Workplaces *with* direct participation	23	30	27	14	5
Workplaces *without* direct participation	11	29	29	20	12

Source: EPOC Research Group (1997).

One-third of the economically active population read specialist literature related to their jobs, while one-quarter attended short training programs or other events or learned by observing and testing things out at the workplace. Other forms of learning linked to a particular job or activity, such as quality circles, instruction from colleagues, etc., are also increasingly important. As a result, many firms have now become learning organizations.

These developments have far-reaching consequences for labour market policy. In the past, when work organization took a number of well-established forms, it was sufficient to provide the unemployed with vocational training. In addition to its specialist or technical content, this further training always had a hidden, nontechnical curriculum. Training providers impart to the unemployed certain ideas about the division of labour, the role of teamwork, management styles, and integration into a management hierarchy. Through the choice of subject matter and teaching methods, the unemployed are trained how to integrate themselves into traditional Taylorist organizations. When group work is introduced, firms have to expend considerable time and effort trying to modify this learned behaviour yet again. In such a situation, a certain amount of "unlearning" has to take place before workers can learn to accept more responsibility and be more willing to cooperate.

"Unlearning" of this kind can be very costly and may well constitute a further barrier to the recruitment of unemployed individuals. In consequence, there has been a change of paradigm in European labour market policy in recent years. Training for the unemployed offered by external providers is increasingly being supplemented by more "hands-on" learning, such as a period of work experience or training modules in firms. Furthermore, learning in training centres is being organized around teams and projects.

A typical example is provided by a "learning association" comprising a training centre and several small and medium-sized firms. In a town in North Rhine–Westphalia, six small and medium-sized precision engineering companies, in collaboration with a further-training centre and the local employment office, have established a learning association of this kind for unemployed people. The firms had a need for skilled workers that could not be met through the labour market. Furthermore, they had all reorganized their plants and were not keen to recruit skilled workers of the old school with outmoded ways of thinking. In Germany, unemployed people taking a course of further vocational training are entitled to a subsistence allowance of, on average, 65 percent of their former net wage for up to two years. The employment office also pays the costs of the further training.

The further-training centre put in place a two-year retraining course for 20 unemployed individuals wishing to acquire skilled-worker status. The course was based on the German national standards but the practical projects were developed in such a way as to reflect the requirements of the six companies. In the course of their retraining, the unemployed individuals spent several periods of work experience in various firms. Once they had obtained their certificate of qualifications as skilled workers, all of them were taken on by the firms. Their status as skilled workers, however, means that they can move from firm to firm within the labour market for skilled workers.

In Denmark, a further step forward has been taken with the introduction of so-called "job rotation." The basic idea is that an employee is given leave to take part in a training program or for some other reason, and is replaced during his or her absence by an unemployed person. The chances of an unemployed person finding work are improved if he or she has recent work experience. Thus paid leave arrangements (PLAs) were introduced in Denmark in 1992. They were tried for two years and then became part of Danish labour market policy. Table 6 gives an overview of the different types of

Table 6

The Danish paid leave arrangements in the labour market reform of 1994

	Education leave	Sabbatical leave	Child-minding leave
Target Group	1. Employed 2. Unemployed 3. Self-employed	1. Employed	1. Employed 2. Unemployed 3. Self-employed
Applicant must be eligible for unemployment benefits?	Yes	Yes	No
Maximum duration	1 year	1 year	26 weeks / 1 year
Right for the applicant?	No	No	Yes (up to 26 wccks)
Mandatory substitute?	No	Yes	No
Amount paid as share of unemployment benefit	100 percent	60 percent	60 percent

Source: Madsen (1998, 66).

PLAs. In the sabbatical leave scheme, employment of a substitute is mandatory. In the two other schemes, this is not a formal requirement but it is encouraged in various ways (there are agreements between firms, training centres, and employment offices) (Madsen 1998).

The leave schemes are very popular in Denmark. In 1996, 121,000 individuals took some form of leave. A total of 72,700 persons went on education or training leave, 46,999 took child-minding leave, and 1,500 took sabbaticals. Half of those taking leave are unemployed. On average, about three-quarters of the vacant jobs are filled by substitutes. The replacement rate is higher in small firms and in the public service. Forty-six percent of the substitutes have been employed before, and only 54 percent have been unemployed. It is estimated that the leave schemes reduced declared unemployment by between 60,000 and 70,000 in 1995. Two-thirds to three-quarters of this figure is accounted for by unemployed people taking leave and therefore not being counted as unemployed (Madsen 1998).

The Danish job rotation model has now been copied in a number of European countries (Schömann et al. 1998). In several German *Länder*, for example, job rotation schemes have been introduced with support from the European structural funds, initially on an experimental basis. These trial schemes are currently being evaluated. The most significant barriers to implementation are (1) the reluctance of employers to release workers for further training and (2) the difficulty of finding a suitable substitute who would also be acceptable to the employer (Schmid and Schömann 1999).

Conclusions

Firms tend to invest in human resources when they compete primarily on product and service quality rather than on price. Labour market regulations are another important factor driving such investment. When wage differentials between skilled and unskilled workers are low, investment in further training is worthwhile for firms. They reap most of the additional returns instead of seeing them swallowed up in wage increases for more highly skilled personnel. Company reorganization linked to the introduction of team work and greater autonomy for skilled workers is also made easier when the learning costs associated with such human resource strategies can be reduced for individual firms. Regional networks with joint training facilities are important for small and medium-sized firms. At the level of the economy as a whole, the diffusion of new human resource strategies is facilitated by high-trust industrial relations, which provide a framework within which the basic conditions for new personnel strategies can be negotiated and trade unions or works councils can work to gather support for their implementation.

Our analyses have shown that investment in research and training for future competition in high-quality markets, labour market regulations, industrial relations, and regional networks of small and medium-sized firms vary considerably from country to country. Thus we do not assume that standardized human resource strategies can be implemented throughout the world, but rather that there are very different national models. It is true that new forms of post-Taylorist, decentralized company organization are spreading in all industrialized countries. Differences between countries, however, are to be found primarily in the extent to which these forms of organization are diffused, and in their detailed arrangements.

We have already examined some of these differences. In the UK, where company reorganizations have been implemented by management, largely without negotiation with the trade unions, individual award systems are much more widespread than in Scandinavia, where teamwork based on equal qualifications and similar rates of pay is much more common. Only recently have academic researchers begun to take note of these various strategies and to shed light on national profiles and the combinations of conditions associated with them (e.g., Brunstein 1995). This can be put to good use in the further development of management theory, in order to demonstrate that human resource strategies are dependent on the particular conditions prevailing in each country, and to dispel the notion that there is just one (American, of course) formula for companies that can be implemented throughout the world.

At a time when firms are putting in place new forms of work organization, and a growing share of learning within firms no longer takes place in the classroom but as part of the work process in learning organizations, the reintegration of unemployed people into the labour market is becoming increasingly difficult. As a result, a paradigm shift has necessarily had to be effected in the active labour market policies that have been developed in many European countries. It is no longer sufficient to use public funds to finance the retraining of unemployed people in external further-training centres. Unemployed people must also be involved in learning processes within firms. Various instruments are currently being tested. In Denmark, attempts are being made, through the various paid leave arrangements, to create temporary vacancies that can be filled by unemployed people. The Danish example is being followed in other European countries. This process of experimentation, which in some cases has a cross-border dimension, is being supported by EU structural funds.

Notes
1 The costs rose both because of the increases in training allowances and the shorter time spent by apprentices in firms.
2 These surveys are the Price Waterhouse Cranfield Study and the investigation carried out by the EPOC Research Group (Sisson 1997).
3 The EPOC studies identify various forms of direct participation, such as individual consultation, group consultation, individual delegation, and group delegation (Sisson 1997).

4   A panel study of the implementation of the German Law on Labour Relations at the Workplace, amended in 1972, that compared the way in which the legislation was put into practice in 1974-75 and 1989-90 concluded that the participation of works councils in company decision-making processes had increased dramatically. In particular, it would seem that difficult situations, such as major reorganization and redundancy programs, tended to bring management and works councils closer together (Kotthoff 1994).

5   The blue-collar workers' union federation.

6   The national employers' federation.

7   Supplementary Agreement: Enterprise Development, which in 1992 produced the Joint Enterprise Development Program, or HF-B.

References

von Bardeleben, R., et al. 1989. "Weiterbildungsaktivitäten von Klein- und Mittelbetrieben im Vergleich zu Großbetrieben." In *Berufliche Bildung in Wissenschaft und Praxis*, Heft 6.

Bosch, G. 1995. "Flexibility and Work Organisation." In *Social Europe*, Supplement 1/95. Brussels: European Commission, DG V.

–. 1996. "Flexibility in the Norwegian Labour Market in a Comparative Perspective." In Jon Erik Dolvik and Arild H. Steen, eds., *Making Solidarity Work?* Oslo.

Bosch, G., and K. Zühlke-Robinet. 1998. *The Labour Market in the German Construction Industry.* Gelsenkirchen.

Brewster, C., and A. Hegewisch, eds. 1994. *Policy and Practice in European Human Resource Management.* London.

Brunstein, I., ed. 1995. *Human Resource Management in Europe.* Berlin.

Carlzon, J. 1989. *Moment of Truth: New Strategies for Today's Customer-Driven Economy.* New York: Harper and Row.

European Commission. 1997. "Partnership for a New Organization." Green Paper. Brussels: European Commission, DG V.

EPOC Research Group. 1997. *Survey on Employee Direct Participation in Organizational Change.* Brussels: European Commission, DG V.

Gooderham, P.N., O.A. Kvitastein, and O. Nordhaug. 1996. *Management of Human Resources in European Firms: A New Institutional Perspective.* Bergen: Department of Organizational Sciences, Norwegian School of Economics and Business Administration.

Hammer, T.H., B. Ingebritsen, J.I. Karlsen, and A. Svarva. 1994. "Organizational Renewal: Management of Large-Scale Change in Norwegian Firms." In *Center for Advanced Human Resource Studies.* Working Paper 94-21. Ithaca, NY: Cornell University.

Kirsch, J., et al. 1998. *Arbeitszeitarrangements und Beschäftigung im Dienstleistungssektor am Beispiel des Einzelhandels – ein europäischer Vergleich.* Institut Arbeit und Technik.

Kotthoff, H. 1994. *Betriebsräte und Bürgerstatus.* Wandel und Kontinuität betrieblicher Mitbestimmung. München: Mehring.

Lehndorff, S., et al. 1998. *Arbeitszeit und Arbeitsorganisation – Erfahrungen aus neun europäischen Ländern* [Research Report for the European Commission. G.D. V]. Gelsenkirchen: IAT.

Madsen, P.K. 1998. ILO Country Employment Policy Review Denmark. Geneva: International Labor Organization.

NUTEK (Swedish National Board for Industrial and Technical Development). 1996. *Towards Flexible Organizations.* Stockholm: NUTEK.

OECD (Organization for Economic Cooperation and Development). 1993. *Employment Outlook.* Paris: OECD.

–. 1996. *Technology, Productivity and Job Creation.* Analytical Report. Paris: OECD.

–. 1997. *Employment Outlook.* Paris: OECD.

Pischke, J.S. 1997. "Ausbildung und Lohnstruktur: Deutschland und die USA in den achtziger Jahren, Beitrag zum 27." Wirtschaftswissenschaftlichen Seminar Ottbeuren, 14-17 September 1997.

Qvale, T.U. 1995. "Local Development and Institutional Change: Experience from a 'Fifth Generation' National Programme for the Democratisation of Work Life." Contribution to the Royal Netherlands Academy of Arts and Sciences and Kurt Lewin Symposium in Organizational Decision-Making Under Different Economic and Political Conditions, June 1994. Mimeo. Amsterdam: Vrije Universiteit.

Schmid, G., and K. Schömann, eds. 1999. Learning from Denmark. WZB Discussion Papers FSI 99 – 201. Berlin: Wissenschaftszentrum Berlin für Sozialforschung.

Schömann, K., R. Mytzek, and S. Gülker. 1998. Institutional and Financial Framework for Job Rotation in Nine European Countries. WZB Discussion Papers FSI 98 – 207. Berlin: Wissenschaftszentrum Berlin für Sozialforschung.

Schumacher, D. 1997. "Immaterielle Investitionen in Deutschland und im internationalen Vergleich." Vierteljahreshefte zur Wirtschaftsforschung, 2.6, Berlin.

Sisson, K. 1997. *New Forms of Work Organization – Can Europe Realize Its Innovative Potential? Results of a Survey of Direct Employee Participation in Europe.* Official Publications of the European Communities No. 251. Brussels: European Foundation.

Sivesind, K.H., R. Kalleberg, S. Hovde, and A. Fennefoss. 1995. "A Social Democratic Order Under Pressure: Norwegian Employment Relations in the Eighties." In R. Locke, T. Kochan, and M. Piore, eds., *Employment Relations in a Changing World Economy.* Cambridge, MA; London: MIT Press.

Streeck, W., et al. 1987. "The Role of Social Partners in Vocational Training and Further Training in the Federal Republic of Germany." In CEDEFOP Document 1987, Luxembourg.

Wächter, H., and T. Stengelhofen. 1995. "Germany." In I. Brunstein, ed., *Human Resource Management in Europe.* De Gruyter Studies in Organization No. 68. Berlin:336 Walter de Gruyter.

16

The Impact of the Knowledge-Based Economy on Women's Participation

Brenda Lipsett

Introduction

The emergence of the knowledge-based economy and society (KBES) is changing the nature of employment and imposing adjustment challenges for individuals. This chapter examines the major issues related to the KBES from the perspective of Canadian women. I take the position that the shift to the knowledge society encompasses evolutionary change across a broad spectrum of social and economic factors.[1] These factors include:

- changes in the economic environment, in which information and communication technologies (ICTs) are seen as a catalyst for global trade and investment driving increased competition
- the increased importance of knowledge in production – ideas, innovation, and information rather than repetitive tasks – and a shift to knowledge occupations from data and goods processing (Lavoie and Roy 1998)
- firm-level impacts on productivity, source of investment, new markets, and access to technology
- firms' responses, including technological change, organizational change, new human resource and industrial relations practices, functional and numeric flexibility, and changing skill and knowledge requirements
- the subsequent impact on work and workers, including flexible work arrangements, upskilling and deskilling, insecurity, and wage inequality.[2]

Central is the need to both adapt to the new economic realities and choose a "high-road" economic development strategy. (We cannot, nor would we want to, succeed based on a low-cost, abundant-labour, competitive strategy.) At the same time, we need to ensure that women as well as men have opportunities to fully and equitably participate in the knowledge-based economy and society.

The following section sets out the labour market trends and facts associated with transition to the KBES. Economic and feminist theories are then presented in the section "A Theoretical Approach to Expanding Opportunities for Women," and reveal three main issues for women: flexible work arrangements accommodating work/life balance; education and labour market participation facilitating gender equity; and technology/workplace training and entrepreneurial support to ensure "the right stuff" for success in the KBES. These issues are more broadly related to workplace adjustment, economy-wide structural adjustment, and individual adjustment, and are discussed in greater detail in the section "Three Adjustment Issues for Women." Policy and research directions follow in the last section.

Women's Labour Market Participation Trends

Distinct labour market trends mark the transition to the knowledge society.[3] One is a gradual shift towards nonstandard work forms (part time, temporary, and self-employment) and other work arrangements (home-based, shift work, flextime) that expand working time options and flexibility as well as contribute to firm performance (Lipsett and Reesor 1997a). Another is a narrowing of the gap between male and female labour force participation rates, levels of education, and wages, signalling reduced gender-based labour market rigidity.

Women's labour force participation has changed along a number of dimensions. Along with the well-known trend towards an increase in female participation rates, labour force commitment has increased and the "m"-shaped age-specific curve has disappeared as women spend less and less time out of the labour force caring for young children. More than 70 percent of women work full time, and increasingly work part time involuntarily. Some are combining two or more part-time jobs to increase their hours of work; more women than men were multiple job holders in 1997. On average, however, women work fewer hours per week than men. An important factor in women's increased labour force participation and commitment is economic necessity. The overall lack of growth in real wages and the increase in households headed by females, both lone parents and older women, makes it essential that women work continuously. In 1997, 11 percent of the female labour force was widowed, separated, or divorced, and a further 26 percent was single, according to Statistics Canada's Labour Force Survey. Finally, the female/male pay differential has been narrowing, with rising wages for women and a drop in male wages, particularly among young men. According to the 1996 census, full-time female workers were paid 71 percent of what male earners were paid in 1995, up from 64 percent in 1980. The total income gap is greater, however, with women's income representing only 56 percent of men's in 1995 (Status of Women 1997).

Occupational segregation persists but has been declining, with women entering nontraditional occupations. In 1997, 61 percent of women worked in 5 out of 21 occupations – clerical, medicine and health, social sciences, teaching, and services – down from 70 percent in 1976. Of particular note, the proportion of women in the key KBES occupations – natural science, engineering, and mathematics – rose from 9.5 percent in 1976 to 21 percent in 1997. The index of dissimilarity (ID), the most commonly used measure of occupational segregation, fell to 0.39 in 1997, from 0.48 in 1976.[4] To interpret, an ID of 0.39 with a female labour force share of 45 percent implies that about 21 percent of women and 18 percent of men would have to change occupations in order to yield the same proportion of women in every occupation.

Along with increased paid work, women still perform the bulk of unpaid work of economic value – notably child care and housework. This is the major conclusion of Statistics Canada's Total Work Accounts System (TWAS), which identifies population groups with varying degrees of responsibility involving paid work and family and community ties (Stone and Chicha 1996). Gender and family obligations clearly influence allocations among paid work, unpaid work in business and voluntary organizations, children and ageing relatives, friends, household, and oneself. Despite the high level of women's integration into the labour market, they continue to be the principal doers of unpaid activity. The presence and age of children are associated with reduced paid work for women but not for men. The effect on women's labour market participation is seen in a higher incidence of part-time work. Family responsibilities, career interruptions due to maternity, and the difficulties in balancing paid work and family obligations contribute to the incidence that impacts, in the long run, on the incomes and career advancement of women.[5]

It is clear that women have made important labour market strides over the past two decades but a gender gap still persists. The KBES has the potential to increase productivity and thus standards of living. Will the shift to the KBES reinforce progress or act as a barrier to achieving greater gender equity? Economic and feminist theories can shed light on the factors that determine wage and employment outcomes, point to the implications of a shift to a knowledge society, and suggest adjustment actions appropriate for individuals, employers, and governments.

A Theoretical Approach to Expanding Opportunities for Women

Theoretical explanations for differential employment and wage outcomes by gender can be grouped into three categories: neoclassical and human capital theories; institutional and labour market segmentation theories; and non-economic and feminist theories.[6] Each offers a partial explanation of participation and outcomes for women. As such, they offer insight into the reasons for male/female labour market differentials and provide counsel on how to adjust equitably to a knowledge-based economy.

Neoclassical and human capital theories assume that workers seek out the best-paying jobs after taking into consideration their personal endowments (such as education and experience), constraints (such as responsibility for child care), and preferences (such as hours and location of work), and that employers maximize profits by maximizing productivity and minimizing costs. Competition and efficient labour markets ensure that employers pay workers their marginal product. Thus, these theories focus on productivity-related factors in explaining female/male pay differentials.

The labour supply factors influencing lower pay for women include less education; fewer fields of study relevant to the labour market, and less experience because of intermittent or truncated labour market participation due to marriage and/or household and child-care responsibilities. These supply-side factors can also affect women's choice of occupation, favouring those with a relatively high starting salary, relatively low returns to experience, and low penalties for temporary withdrawal from the labour force.

With skill-biased technological change, important labour demand factors relate to education, experience, and on-the-job training to enhance labour productivity. Other important factors that influence employers' preferences for male versus female workers relate to the supposedly higher indirect costs for women workers. These costs can arise from higher absenteeism rates, higher turnover rates, added pressure for day-care facilities, and lower flexibility to work late or on weekends; they are often caused by women's responsibilities to care for young children and other family members. Depending on the importance of these productivity and cost factors to various employers/occupations, the types of jobs employers offer women can be affected.

Neoclassical economics and human capital theory highlight the important role played by systematic differences in the human capital accumulated by men and women. These theories point to the need for policies to address non-labour market factors such as education, family policy, male responsibility, and the more equal sharing of child care and household work. They imply that policymakers should be concerned with increasing women's human capital, especially education and training in pure science and technology and in other nontraditional occupations. Policymakers should also be interested in improving women's ability to combine work and family responsibilities, either through the provision of day care, reorganization of working time arrangements (such as flextime and telework), or parental leave arrangements that do not indirectly discriminate against women workers.

Labour market segmentation theories stress the existence of segregated labour markets and occupations. For example, dual labour market theory divides the labour market into good jobs and bad jobs in a primary and secondary sector (alternatively, core and periphery jobs, or standard and nonstandard work arrangements).[7] The resulting two labour markets function independently, largely because firms in the primary sector have some market power, which insulates them from competition, while firms in the secondary sector face intense competition. Primary-sector jobs are characterized by relatively good pay, employer-sponsored benefits, security, and opportunity for training and advancement. Since jobs in the primary sector are more secure, firm-specific experience and low labour turnover should be more highly valued, favouring male workers with more continuous labour market experience rather than women.

In the context of a shift to the KBES, with the accompanying increase in competition from subcontracting and globalization of trade, the line between primary and secondary sectors becomes blurred, potentially expanding opportunities for women. A simple bifurcation of good jobs and bad jobs along standard and nonstandard work arrangements is less appropriate. High-skilled job opportunities involving more flexible work arrangements – part time, temporary, self-employment, and home-based work facilitated by telecommunications advances – have expanded. Along with the increase in flexibility, the value of firm-specific experience and low labour turnover is declining, potentially benefiting women who desire flexible work arrangements. A critical factor in realizing these benefits will be women's ability to acquire and maintain currently relevant skills. Income security (wages and employer-sponsored benefit plans) and control over work schedules remain important issues in flexible work arrangements for balancing the needs of workers and the needs of employers (Lipsett and Reesor 1997a). Thus, labour market segmentation theories highlight job quality and point to workplace practices and policies that can enhance good opportunities in flexible work arrangements.

Feminist theories attempt to explain the constraints and preferences that economic theories take as given. They are based on the view that women's disadvantaged position in the labour market is linked to their subordinate position in society and the family. While this may not be the case for all women, the stereotype – women responsible for housework and child care and men as breadwinners – still has an important influence on behaviour and expectations. This gender division of responsibilities helps explain why women may receive lower levels of education in fields of study less relevant to the labour market, accumulate less labour market experience upon family formation, and encounter some work environments chilly to women. Feminist theories point out that in determining women's labour market position, changes in the spousal division of labour, family labour supply, and human capital investment decisions are as critical as changes in government and firm policies.

Contributing to our understanding of current and future opportunities for women, feminist theory highlights the close correspondence between female occupations and stereotypes of women's abilities (e.g., their caring nature and manual dexterity qualify women for nursing and electronics assembly). In the context of the KBES, stereotypical strengths and weaknesses can be considered both advantages and disadvantages. Women's stereotypically strong communication skills, networking, honesty, cooperation, and flexibility are assets in an environment that values information sharing, teamwork, and consensus building. The ability to juggle multiple roles and tasks would be assets in self-employment and managing microenterprises. The stereotypical disinclination to supervise others and do math and science would negatively affect prospects in the key KBES occupations in management and pure sciences. According to the Organization for Economic Cooperation and Development (OECD 1996), new high-performance workplaces and flexible enterprises stress worker qualities such as initiative, creativity, problem solving, and openness to change, and are willing to pay for these skills. Multifaceted competencies, including the communication and social skills required for team and project organization, are becoming strategically more important. They are also linked with work requirements for greater responsibility and accountability (Vickery 1996). Women can be proactive in adjusting to new realities by honing these skills.

Male stereotypes also play a role in determining male occupations (such as physical strength and mathematical ability qualifying men for construction and engineering occupations). This impact on labour market segmentation can also work to the detriment of men, as evidenced by the fact that male occupations were particularly hard hit in the restructuring of the 1980s (particularly in manufacturing and the primary goods sectors), or be of benefit with the increased demand for engineers in the emerging KBES. Thus, the policy direction would be to change gender stereotypes in general, integrating men into female occupations and women into male occupations, to eliminate barriers to adjustment and expand (equal) opportunities for men and women.

Neoclassical, segmented labour market, and feminist theories all point to (well-paid, high-end) self-employment as a good option for women since, by definition, there is no hiring preference based on gender stereotypes, educational attainment or qualifications, or continuous labour market experience, and no preset hours of work.

Three Adjustment Issues for Women

The theories and trends presented above reveal three main issues for women in the emerging knowledge-based economy: (1) flexible work arrangements accommodating work/life balance, (2) education and labour market participation facilitating gender equity, and (3) technology/workplace training and entrepreneurial support. These three issues are more broadly related to workplace adjustment, economy-wide structural adjustment, and individual adjustment.

Workplace Adjustment:
Flexible Work Arrangements Accommodating Work/Life Balance

A number of research studies have linked the KBES to work arrangements. Betcherman et al. (1994) portrayed technology as a catalyst for change. Innovation in the product market leads to organizational change, followed by employment restructuring involving greater use of contingent workers and increased skill requirements in core jobs. Workplace flexibility in the form of contracting out, multitasking on the shop floor, contingent compensation, and joint union/employee-management initiatives is seen as the main response to technological change and increased competition. While recognizing the need for an adaptable workforce, the study concludes that increased flexibility on the management side is needed to meet family needs. The OECD (1996) found that translating technological change into productivity gains would necessitate a range of firm-level organizational changes to increase flexibility, particularly relating to work arrangements, networking, multi-skilling of the labour force, and decentralization. This expanding demand for flexibility in work arrangements can be advantageous to women. Recognizing that changing the unequal sharing of household and family responsibilities will take time, women need to work within this constraint and seek options for rewarding employment that provide the flexibility to accommodate their other responsibilities.[8]

Flexible work arrangements include temporary, home-based or telework, flextime, part time (less than 30 hours per week), long time (more than 48 hours per week), weekend work, shift work, job sharing, multiple jobs, compressed work weeks, and self-employment. These arrangements have the potential to meet the needs of employers and workers as workplaces restructure to meet the demands of a 24-hour/7-day world of production and commerce. But realization of this potential is not automatically assured. It requires high levels of commitment and trust to develop workplace mechanisms that balance employers' needs for increased flexibility in the workplace with employees' needs for employment security and personal control over their time. Based on Statistics Canada's 1995 Survey of Work Arrangements (SWA), flexible work arrangements are now the norm (Lipsett and Reesor 1997a).

To support men and women in accommodating family and other responsibilities, workplace policies such as flextime, home-based work, and family-related leave need to catch up with the reality of dual-earner families. According to hours of work preferences, as few as 5.3 percent of men and 7.5 percent of women want to reduce their hours of work if it means a proportional decrease in pay (Lipsett and Reesor 1997b). According to the SWA, low-waged women workers, many of whom work part time involuntarily, want to increase their hours of work and increase their take-home pay. Part-time workers generally would prefer to increase their hours of work, although part time is an attractive option for many whose other option may be withdrawal from the labour force. Thus, in order to maintain hours of work and income, control over work schedules, flextime, and telework is the preferred policy direction, rather than hours of work reduction. The shift-work study by Johnson (1998) and the study of Canadian small business employees by Duxbury and Higgens (1997) support this controversial conclusion.

Flextime

Flextime, a flexible work arrangement where employees can vary the beginning and end of their work day around core hours, has increased from 16.6 percent of all paid workers in 1991 to 23.6 percent in 1995, according to the SWA (Lipsett and Reesor 1997a). Although females were slightly more likely to have a flexible schedule in 1991, more males than females had control over their start and stop times in 1995.[9] Married workers are more likely to be on a flexible schedule than single workers (25.6 percent versus 19.1 percent). Furthermore, workers who are in a dual-earner family are more likely (26.6 percent) to work a flexible schedule than workers in other family types. In particular, dual-earner families with at least one child under 6 are the most likely (28.7 percent) to have flexible schedules. The higher incidence of flextime among typically time-crunched families suggests that it can be an important tool in managing work and family responsibilities.[10] For women, flextime can be a particularly important tool, given the time-use analysis by Stone and Chicha (1996), which shows that men do less than their fair share of housework and child care even if their wives work full time.

Home-Based Work

In the shift to the knowledge-based economy, more and more companies are allowing or asking their employees to work from home. Contributing factors include the rising number of information-based and service-related jobs, improvements in computers and telecommunications, corporate restructuring to reduce costs and increase productivity, and the desire of workers for a better balance between work and family life. According to a national study, the most positive impacts of home-based work for employees are on finances, family life, time pressures, and working hours, with those noting major improvements outnumbering those noting major deterioration by a margin of at least three to one (Ekos Research Associates 1998). Among the subsample that conducts work primarily from home, the perceived impacts are even more positive. Women are more likely than men to perceive positive impacts, primarily in the area of family life and working hours (Ekos 1998, preliminary results, detailed tables).[11]

According to the 1995 SWA, of those home-based employees who do not have an external office and who do virtually all their work from home, half work part time and three-quarters are female; they are predominantly aged 35 to 44 and increasingly have a university education (Lipsett and Reesor 1997a). These 100 percent home-based workers are concentrated in 9 out of 51 occupations, principally stenographic and typing, bookkeeping and account recording, and non-government managers and administrators. Personal choice is more often the main reason for employees doing all of their work from home, and a larger percentage are provided with information technology compared with home-based workers who do only some of their work at home.

Going to work without leaving home is a work/life strategy that suits many women and is not necessarily associated with low wages.[12] Table 1 compares the earnings of the 100 percent home-based employees with employees who do at least some of their work at the employer's worksite. There are clearly good *part-time* opportunities for women at home, with an average hourly wage of $17.41 compared with $11.00 an hour for part-time worksite employees in 1995. *Full-time* 100 percent home-based female employees, however, earn less on average than their worksite counterparts.

Although home-based employment can be an option in balancing work and other responsibilities, it is important that this option (along with self-employment, covered below) is not presented as de facto child-care policy.

Temporary Employment
It has been suggested that changing work arrangements in the shift to the KBES favour a core of knowledge workers, and a periphery of contingent workers performing routine tasks on short-term contracts. Contingency, however, relates not only to the economic fluctuations of firms but also to the short-term fluctuations in skill requirements that accompany technological change. Temporary workers are not a homogeneous group and have a variety of educational backgrounds, suggesting that opportunities of choice can exist in nonpermanent work arrangements for skilled workers.

Evidence from the 1995 SWA indicates that 11 percent of female workers are employed in nonpermanent employment arrangements (versus 8.5 percent of men) (Lipsett and Reesor 1997a). These arrangements are primarily used by employers for project-based work, such as the introduction of new information systems; to match staffing levels to peaks in demand, increasing numerical flexibility; to control staff costs; and for short-term cover while staff are on holiday, maternity, or sick leave. Some workers (such as

Table 1

Average hourly earnings of 100 percent home-based employees compared with worksite employees, 1995

	Both		Men		Women	
	100% home-based	Worksite	100% home-based	Worksite	100% home-based	Worksite
Part time	$15.95	$10.41	–[1]	$8.88	$17.41	$11.00
Full time	$14.71	$15.96	$21.23	$17.23	$11.64	$14.31

Source: Human Resources Devleopment Canada calculations based on the 1995 Survey of Work Arrangements, Statistics Canada.
1 Insufficient cell size for publication purposes.

students, young parents, and early retirees) use these arrangements voluntarily; others facing a weak labour market would prefer a permanent job. By enhancing firm flexibility, temporary employment arrangements can improve firm performance. For employees, however, temporary employment may involve lower and less predictable income, lower productivity as a result of low employer/employee commitment, fewer fringe benefits, less employment security, significant barriers to advancement, and fewer opportunities for employer-sponsored training, which may limit long-term skill development. The extent to which temporary employment is voluntary or acts as a bridge to a permanent job can mitigate these effects, and provide further options for women who want to work for only part of the year.

Self-Employment
Self-employment has grown as an alternative work arrangement along with the emerging KBES. The recent growth in self-employment has been strongest among those without employees (the own-account self-employed) and among women. More men than women are self-employed but women entrepreneurs are growing in numbers at twice the rate of men (Industry Canada 1998, based on the 1991 and 1996 Census of Canada). However, female employers represent only 9 percent of those self-employed in 1997 (up from 5 percent in 1976), suggesting that support to own-account businesses may be required for future growth.

According to the 1995 SWA, men are more likely than women (47 percent versus 32 percent) to choose self-employment because they enjoy the independence. Not surprisingly, given the traditional demands imposed by home and family, women were more likely than men to cite working from home (13 percent versus 2 percent) and flexibility of the work schedule (9 percent versus 4 percent) as reasons for the choice. In particular, 20 percent of women in the peak child-rearing ages of 25 to 34 chose self-employment in order to work from home (Marshall 1998). The 1996 Census of Canada reveals that many women combine work and family responsibilities through home-based self-employment: 45 percent of women self-employed and working at home have children at home, compared with 34 percent of all working women) (Industry Canada 1998).

Work Arrangements and Entitlement to Employer-Sponsored Benefits
Although nonstandard work arrangements (part time, temporary, and own-account self-employment) can help women combine work and other responsibilities, employment insecurity and lack of access to employer-sponsored benefits can make these jobs less attractive. By definition, the self-employed are not entitled to employer-sponsored benefits, such as pension, health, or dental plans. Both men and women in part-time and nonpermanent jobs have lower entitlement to workplace benefits than full-time and permanent workers. The gender dimension of the issue is that more women than men are in part-time and nonpermanent jobs. The lack of entitlement to workplace benefits has obvious long-term health and retirement security implications.

Some non-covered female (and male) workers have access to nonwage benefits through a family member.[13] This interdependence can facilitate nonstandard employment arrangements and may play a role in family labour supply decisions. Even after taking this into account, however, part-time and temporary workers (sometimes referred to as secondary earners) are still much less likely to have access to employer-sponsored benefits than full-time permanent workers (Lipsett and Reesor 1998).

The emerging KBES may be of benefit to women who want nonstandard work arrangements with the added security of employer-sponsored pension, health, and dental plans. Female part-time and temporary employees in high-skilled white-collar occupations[14] are more likely to be covered by workplace benefits. Overall, however, areas where employment has grown significantly in recent years – small firms and nonstandard employment arrangements – are generally associated with low employer-sponsored benefit coverage. (Areas where employment is declining – large unionized private sector firms and the public sector – are positively associated with employer-sponsored benefit coverage.)

As the Canadian labour market evolves, with continued trends towards more nonstandard arrangements, the advantages of a strong and comprehensive universal health care system – attached to the individual rather than the job – become more apparent. In addition, the limited coverage and portability of employer-sponsored pension plans emphasizes the importance of maintaining a strong, portable public pension system to complement private efforts.

Structural Adjustment: Education and Labour Market Participation Facilitating Gender Equity

In the KBES, the relationship between technological change and employment is being discussed within the framework of the rapid internationalization of production, liberalization of international trade and investment, and globalization of information and communications (Freeman and Soete 1997). A review of the Canadian evidence suggests that Canada has been, and continues to be, a knowledge-based economy, experiencing a continuous shift towards high-skilled workers of all types (OECD 1998).[15] At the aggregate level, the main challenges relate to: (1) the exclusion of the unskilled labour force, implying a policy priority for education and training; and (2) the distributional impact of job creation and destruction, emphasizing the importance of employment insurance policies for income redistribution and of re-employment to avoid heightened social inequality.

For women and men, differential adjustment impacts arise from persistent occupational segregation. Whereas "male" occupations were hardest hit in the industrial restructuring of the 1980s, "female" occupations in the service sector are expected to bear the brunt of restructuring in the 1990s. According to Freeman and Soete (1997), the employment impact of ICTs is expected to be in the service sector, particularly in those sectors and occupations previously protected from automation and codification.[16] The potential of ICTs to increase efficiency is high in information- and communications-dependent services such as finance, insurance, and business, and effects on employment and employment displacement could be substantial. On the job-creation side, the ability of information technologies to separate information-service production and consumption is likely to create further openings in many information-type services (such as education, health, and public services), increasing their domestic and international tradeability. At the same time, networks linking distribution and consumption generate opportunities for just-in-time production and selling. These areas potentially offer scope for women entrepreneurs in growing small businesses. The net direct and indirect employment effect is not known.

Traditional sex divisions of labour can be perpetuated in a number of ways: by choice; because few realistic alternatives are available; or because of cultural factors such as gender stereotyping and streaming in school. With the equal distribution of intelligence, if not physical strength, the emergence of the KBES has the potential to promote wage equity and gender equality. Women, however, may be limiting their access to opportunities in some aspects of the KBES. For example, the analysis of the National Graduates Survey data indicates that, despite the small proportion of women in engineering, female engineers have higher earnings than men (for the 1990 cohort). "It is especially ironic that women are the least represented in the discipline where they have the highest relative earnings" (Lavoie and Finnie 1996). Qualitative work suggests that one reason may be the chilly environment for women in engineering occupations. This same work demonstrates, however, that the majority of women express a high level of satisfaction with their choice of education program. Given the potential payoffs, women need to empower themselves and take advantage of emerging opportunities in nontraditional occupations.

The shift to the KBES poses fundamental challenges for knowledge and skill acquisition and learning processes. The recent Human Resources Development Canada (HRDC) and Statistics Canada analysis of the School Leavers' Follow-Up Surveys indicates that 18 percent of men and 10 percent of women do not complete high school. Learning disorders are higher for males than females. University enrollments and graduation rates are higher for women. The International Adult Literacy Survey (IALS) results for Canada show only one significant difference between the genders – a comparative advantage for women in prose literacy. Women are now more likely than men to be enrolled in postsecondary education, narrowing the gender education gap, although they still lag in the key KBES fields of engineering, mathematics, and pure science. Thus, in an economy in which the important jobs are increasingly characterized by knowledge and not physical power, some advantages for women are becoming apparent.

Questions remain, however. Are there differences between women and men in terms of their exposure to technological and organizational change? Do the skill impacts of technological and organizational change differ between men and women? How does access to training opportunities in the workplace differ between men and women in the wake of technological change? From preliminary evidence of an analysis of technological and organizational change and skill requirements and the impact on women in the workforce, based on data from the pilot Workplace and Employee Survey (WES) of Statistics Canada, no differential impacts between men and women are indicated (Betcherman et al. 1998). Women's equal access to sophisticated technology is still open to question (Tremblay 1998).

Individual Adjustment:
Technology/Workplace Training and Entrepreneurial Support
Defining the requirements to operate well in the KBES points to areas where some women (and men) can benefit from support. The requirements involve flexibility and working smarter, not longer. Education and literacy skills lay the foundation. Tacit knowledge acquired from experience and informal training are critical in the know-how and know-who (as well as know-what and know-why) components of the KBES, emphasizing the importance of continuous learning. The worlds of work and learning are being brought closer together in the workplace, with the increased importance of

data synthesis and interpretation and learning how to create better products and processes. Continuous learning in this context is at the core of individual and organizational adjustment. It is only indirectly related to formal training and education.

Learning in both formal and informal situations can take place either during work time or off-hours. The differences in men and women's non-market labour patterns (discussed earlier in the section "Women's Labour Market Participation Trends") may result in differing opportunities for continuous learning and adaptation to the KBES. Adding investment in human capital activities to the total work accounts reveals that many mothers in the labour force may find it very difficult to reconcile their job and family obligations with opportunities for education and training. That is, if work in the home is unevenly shared between partners, the one doing more hours of unpaid work will be left with less time to pursue learning, regardless of how convenient information and communication technologies make it. Opportunities for learning and training during working time would thus be important to time-crunched women (and men). Employers, however, would be reluctant unless they are able to appropriate the productivity gains from training, or trade off employment security provisions for employability security.

Technological change and training go hand in hand in the emerging KBES. ICTs are an important tool, with access to computer equipment and knowledge/technical ability influencing the ability of individuals to take full advantage of these technologies. Evidence indicates some gender differences (Ekos Research Associates 1998).[17] Men are more likely to access the Internet, an indicator of participation in the KBES, and are much more likely to be heavy users. Women are more likely than men to find access to equipment a barrier to getting on the information highway, and are much more likely to find lack of knowledge of how to use new technology a barrier. Both men and women see removing these barriers to access as a shared responsibility between individuals, employers, governments, and Internet service providers. And both genders put the greatest burden on individuals themselves. Women, however, are more likely than men to see a strong role for employers in removing barriers to the information highway (43 percent of women versus 36 percent of men see employers as having the most responsibility for removing barriers) (Ekos 1998, preliminary results, detailed tables). These results reinforce the importance of workplace training to the women noted above.

Support to grow own-account businesses may be required, as suggested by the fact that women employers represented only 9 percent of those self-employed in 1997. Self-employment among women has grown rapidly in the 1990s, but mainly among those without employees. The Canadian Bankers Association report (1997) found that small businesses solely owned by women are more likely to have their loan applications turned down than are firms owned by men or two-gender partnerships. The study concludes that the gender of the business applicant is not in itself a factor in loan turndowns, since the loan application is evaluated on business merit. Differences in turndown rates are due to business characteristics – prevalence of female owners in smaller businesses, start-ups, and service businesses – not the gender of the owner.

Labour market programs can assist women in gaining access to entrepreneurial training and to the business planning and support services required to succeed. As stressed in the guide of the International Labor Organization (ILO) to policy and program options following the Beijing Conference on Women (Lim 1996), the aim of these self-employment programs should be to create productive and sustainable self-employment. They should develop entrepreneurship, viable micro-enterprises, and small firms, not just generate income as a secondary activity for women. In addition, the Internet is a growing source of information for businesswomen about training courses, assistance programs, and market research (Industry Canada 1998).

Policy and Research Directions
The research to date does not permit a strong conclusion on the impact of the KBES on women. As with all dynamic developments, there are winners and losers, opportunities and endings. Nevertheless, some policy directions for governments, employers, and workers emerge from a review of theory and available evidence.

An important role for public policy will be to develop programs to help people (men and women) adapt to the KBES. Programs would include income redistribution and re-employment (employment insurance), knowledge diffusion, training and education to upgrade human capital, lifelong learning and active ageing, and promoting organizational change to increase flexibility and benefits for workers and employers. As mentioned earlier, in areas where employment has grown significantly in recent years – small firms and nonstandard employment arrangements – low benefit coverage emphasizes the importance of maintaining a strong, universal, and comprehensive health care system attached to the individual rather than the job, and a strong, portable public pension system to complement private efforts.

Policies to support and empower women in the emerging KBES include more flexible work arrangements, expanded working time options, flexible workplace practices, greater control for women over daily schedules, just-in-time services – child care, elder care, training – to complement just-in-time work arrangements, support for expanding women's own-account self-employed businesses, and erosion of the traditional division of labour according to gender both at home and at work. Measures like these would reduce labour market segmentation, increase competition for KBES professional and management jobs, and expand alternatives, offering greater choice to men and women.

Future research is required on KBES indicators. Central measures would focus on human capital indicators and employment in knowledge-based occupations. Measuring the private and social rates of return to investments in education and training will help point to the means of enhancing the learning capacity of individuals and firms. A gender-based analysis of knowledge-based occupations and occupational segregation, following up on the work begun by Lavoie and Roy (1998), would provide an indicator of women's employment participation in the KBES. The Workplace and Employee Survey has the potential to be a rich data source to develop micro-level firm indicators on human resource requirements, as well as gender employment and occupational mobility, that can be used to better match supply and demand for skills in the labour market. Better indicators of participation in the KBES also need to be developed in addition to the often-used proxy of Internet use. Further expansion of the income, work, and learning gender-equality indicators begun by the Status of Women (1997) could explore the impact of the KBES on women.

Research is also required on career progression and the dynamics of workplace benefit coverage – and, as women move between school and work, on jobs and family, work and retirement, and the extent to which part-time and lower-quality temporary jobs are stepping stones to better jobs. If workers remain in jobs of low quality (low wages and few benefits) for long periods of time, their current and future security will be compromised accordingly. Any advantage women may have in ability to cope with change, flexibility in adapting to nonstandard work arrangements, and communication skills will be lost if career progression remains based on continuous full-time employment. The study on career development in the public service, conducted by the Centre for Research and Education on Women and Work at Carleton University in Ottawa, will contribute to the knowledge base on career development strategies that work for both genders. The longitudinal Survey of Labour and Income Dynamics provides useful information on transitions between nonstandard and full-time paid employment, and includes information on employer-sponsored pension plans.

Notes

1 I also take the position that direct gender discrimination in hiring and pay practices is against the law and is a legal issue. It ignores the important fact that the definition of liberation and personal control and power varies among women by generation and cultural background, as pointed out by sociologist Janet Billson (1995).

2 A narrower view of the KBES has as its main feature an increasing need to rely on highly skilled workers whose skills are not exclusively related to science and technology but also to the control, management, and coordination of tasks (Lavoie and Roy 1998).

3 Factors outside the KBES framework continue to influence firm and worker outcomes, notably deregulation, monetary policy, and demographic changes.

4 The index of dissimilarity (ID) is calculated as one-half the sum over all occupations of the absolute difference between the proportion of all females and the proportion of all males in each occupation. It has a minimum value of 0 (no segregation) and a maximum value of 1 (complete segregation). It is interpreted as the sum of the minimum proportion of women plus the minimum proportion of men who would have to change their occupation in order for the proportion of females to be identical in all occupations. When the labour force share of women is less than 50 percent, the implied percentage shift for women is greater than for men (Anker 1998). Here, the ID is calculated using Labour Force Survey data for 21 occupational groups. The result is only suggestive of the direction and magnitude of change, since the level of occupational aggregation matters, with more disaggregated occupations yielding higher ID values. ID is a crude measure of change over time since it comprises changes due to the occupational structure of the labour force and the extent to which occupations are feminized.

5 According to results from the TWAS, women aged 20-44 working full time with a spouse and at least one preschool child spend the most time on work of economic value. Compared with their male counterparts also working full time, women spend fewer hours in paid work (4.2 hours per day for a seven-day week versus 5.9 hours for men) and considerably more hours in child-care activities (3.1 hours versus 1.4 hours) (Stone and Chicha 1996).

6 See Anker (1998) for a fuller theoretical review of occupational segregation by sex, and Dosi (1996) for a review of general equilibrium and growth theory pertaining to the KBES.

7 Dual labour market theory has been applied to occupational segmentation by sex. It implies relatively low wage rates in female occupations because many female workers crowd into a small number of female occupations. Male occupations benefit from reduced competition within this wider set of occupations, and consequently tend to have relatively high wage rates. This distinction is becoming less relevant in Canada as women move into nontraditional occupations. In addition, the study by Baker and Fortin (1998) finds that the link between female wages and gender composition is much stronger in the United States than in Canada, where it is generally small and not statistically significant. The relatively more advantageous position of women in female jobs in Canada is found to be linked to higher unionization rates and the industry wage effects of public goods sectors.

8 According to Status of Women (1997), the gap between the child-oriented work of men and women has been increasing, although the gap has been declining in paid work, work for other relatives and friends, and work for self and household, signalling better gender balance.

9 Greater flexibility for men is confirmed by the results from the 1994 General Social Survey reported by Statistics Canada (1996). These results also indicate that women are more likely than men to experience reduced stress with a flextime schedule.

10 According to the National Child Care Survey, October 1988, when asked to select only one child-related benefit their employers could provide that would best support them as parents, nearly one-quarter of working parents (23 percent) identified child-care facilities in the workplace and another one-fifth (19 percent) cited flexible work hours. These results are reported in Statistics Canada (1996).

11 Forty-seven percent of women perceive the impact on family life to be much better versus 38 percent of men, and 44 percent of women perceive the impact on working hours to be much better versus 36 percent of men. By comparison, 11 percent of men and women perceive the impact on family life and working hours to be much worse. The remainder of the sample reported little or no effect (Ekos Research Associates 1998, preliminary results, detailed tables).

12 The hourly earnings of both men and women who work long hours (more than 48 hours a week) suggests that the 100 percent home-based employees are paid substantially less than the average worksite long-hours worker, although the cell sizes are too small to report.

13 Taking access to employer-sponsored health plans as an example, the charts classify workers into one of three categories – own coverage (are entitled to their own insurance), possible coverage (no personal coverage, but at least one person in the family unit has coverage),

and no coverage (nobody in the family unit has coverage) – and find that an additional 22 percent of married female employees are possibly covered through a spousal employer-sponsored health plan. This raises the percentage of female married workers who may have extended health coverage to 80 percent, up from 58 percent. Employed married men are less likely to access workplace benefits through their spouse than employed married women. There is little difference among the self-employed.

14 Officials and administrators in government and persons working in management and administration; mathematics; statistics; systems analysis; architecture and engineering; elementary, secondary, and university education; nursing therapy; medicine and health.

15 The evidence does not support a simple skill-biased demand shift with the introduction of information and communication technology in the early 1980s.

16 The process of codification, where some knowledge is coded as information and stored electronically, allows for increased memorization and storage and the rapid manipulation and interpretation of data information. The codification process increases the importance of tacit knowledge, high-level skills, and competencies. Talent, creativity, and continuous accumulation of new knowledge thus become the main value-added activity of service activity (Freeman and Soete 1997).

17 Canadian Heritage, HRDC, Industry Canada, Rogers Cable Television, Bell Canada, Stentor Telecom Policy Inc., Treasury Board Secretariat, and Agriculture Canada sponsored this project.

References

Anker, R. 1998. *Gender and Jobs: Sex Segregation of Occupations in the World*. Geneva: International Labour Office.

Baker, Michael, and Nicole Fortin. 1998. "Gender Composition and Wages: Why Is Canada Different from the United States?" Draft paper presented at the Women and Work Conference in Kingston, Ontario, 5-7 April 1998.

Betcherman, G., et al. 1994. *The Canadian Workplace in Transition*. Kingston: Queen's University Press.

Betcherman, G., D. Lauzon, and N. Leckie. 1998. *Technological Change, Organizational Change and Skill Requirements: Impacts on Women in the Workforce*. Applied Research Branch, Technical Paper. Ottawa: HRDC.

Billson, Janet. 1995. *Keepers of the Culture: The Power of Tradition in Woman's Lives*. New York and Toronto: Lexington Books.

Dosi, Giovanni. 1996. "The Contribution of Economic Theory to the Understanding of a Knowledge-Based Economy." In *Employment and Growth in the Knowledge-Based Economy*, 81-92. Paris: OECD.

Duxbury, L., and C. Higgens. 1997. "Balancing Work and Family: A Study of Canadian Small Business Employees." Ottawa: Carleton University.

Ekos Research Associates. 1998. "Information Highway and the Canadian Communication Household." Draft Wave 1 Report.

Finnie, Ross. 1996. *Earnings Dynamics in Canada: Earnings Patterns by Age and Sex in Canada, 1982-1992*. Research Paper R-97-11E, Applied Research Branch. Ottawa: HRDC.

Freeman, C., and L. Soete. 1997. *The Economics of Industrial Innovation*, 3rd ed. Cambridge, MA: MIT Press.

Industry Canada. 1998. *Shattering the Glass Box? Women Entrepreneurs and the Knowledge-Based Economy*. Ottawa: Industry Canada.

Johnson, Karen. 1998. *Shiftwork from a Work and Family Perspective*. Research Paper R-98-**E, Applied Research Branch. Ottawa: HRDC.

Lavoie, Marie, and Richard Roy. 1998. *Employment in the Knowledge-Based Economy: A Growth Accounting Exercise for Canada*. Research Paper R-98-8E, Applied Research Branch. Ottawa: HRDC.

Lavoie, Marie, and Ross Finnie. 1996. *The Accumulation of Technology: A Cross-Cohort Longitudinal Analysis of Recent Engineering Graduates*. Applied Research Branch, Working Paper W-96-10E. Ottawa: HRDC.

Lim, L. Lean. 1996. *More and Better Jobs for Women: An Action Guide*. Geneva: International Labor Organization.

Lipsett, Brenda, and Mark Reesor. 1997a. *Flexible Work Arrangements: Evidence from the 1991 and 1995 Survey of Work Arrangements*. Research Paper R-97-10E, Applied Research Branch. Ottawa: HRDC.

–. 1997b. *Hours of Work Preferences: Evidence from the 1995 Survey of Work Arrangements*. Draft Research Paper, Applied Research Branch. Ottawa: HRDC.

–. 1998. *Women's Entitlement to Workplace Benefits: The Influence of Work Arrangements*. Kingston, ON: John Deutsch Institute.

Marshall, Katherine. 1998. "Balancing Work and Family." In *Work Arrangements in the 1990s*. Statistics Canada, Analytic Report 71-535-MPB, No. 8.

OECD (Organization for Economic Cooperation and Development). 1996. *The Knowledge-Based Economy*. Paris: OECD.

–. 1998. *EDRC Review of Canada*. Paris: OECD.

Statistics Canada. 1996. *Working Arrangements and Time Stress, Canadian Social Trends*. Ottawa: Statistics Canada.

Status of Women (Federal, Provincial, and Territorial Ministers Responsible for the Status of Women). 1997. "The Economic Gender Equality Indicators." Ottawa.

Stone, Leroy, and Marie-Therese Chicha. 1996. *The Statistics Canada Total Work Accounts System*. Catalogue number 89-549-XPE. Ottawa: Statistics Canada.

Tremblay, Diane-Gabrielle. 1998. "The 'New Division of Labour' Debate and Women's Jobs: Results from a Survey Conducted in Canada from a Gendered Perspective." Télé-université, Université du Quebec, presented at the Women and Work Conference in Kingston, Ontario, 5-7 April 1998.

Vickery, Graham. 1996. "Firm Strategies and Human Resources Development in the Knowledge-Based Economy." In *Employment and Growth in the Knowledge-Based Economy*, 135-41. Paris: OECD.

17

The Changing Gender Division of Labour in the Transition to the Knowledge Society

Ursula Huws

The term *knowledge society* begs several questions. Taking its place alongside a range of related phrases – such as *information society, virtual organization, networked economy,* and *weightless economy* – it suggests the emergence of a new sphere of human interaction untethered to any material base and largely independent of the laws of geography and Newtonian physics.[1] As the key source of value in this new cyber-economy, the notion of "knowledge" consigns all other products of human labour to a shadowy sphere of "non-knowledge" that is, by implication, backward and obsolescent.

To understand the impact of the introduction of information and communication technologies (ICTs) on the workforce as a whole (rather than on the specialist subset whose work consists exclusively of the manipulation of abstract symbols), it is necessary to subject this assumption to some critical analysis. At the risk of stating the obvious, it is useful to remind ourselves first that these technologies are not proliferating in an entirely new world. Computers, mobile telephones, modems, and the other concrete technological manifestations are being employed by real people, with physical bodies, in the same old material world into which they were born. Far from being outside the messy reality of this world, the "knowledge society" is an integral part of it. The new machines are in use in old homes, offices, shops, and banks; the workers who use them inhabit these spaces and have other, physical dimensions to their lives. They are sons, daughters, spouses, and parents of people with whom they communicate directly, and who may not use these technologies in their daily lives. They also have other physical needs – to eat, sleep, exercise, be taken to hospital, travel to work, have their hair cut, be kept warm, and so on.

However advanced its technological base, therefore, the "knowledge society" will remain a society in which a large number of human activities, both paid and unpaid, do *not* involve the use of new ICTs, although undoubtedly these technologies will play an increasingly important role in the organization and management of these physical activities. The corollary is that value will continue to be added by, and profitable industries based upon, the labour involved in these non-virtual forms of activity. The knowledge economy, therefore, will be one in which substantial portions of the workforce are employed in health care, cleaning, cooking, personal services, road building, transport, mining, the manufacture and packing of material commodities, construction, and garbage disposal. Whether these activities continue to be performed in the same geographical locations, by workers of the same ethnic and gender identities, is a more open question whose answer may depend, in part, on political decisions made in the present.

A further problem is raised by an attempt to tease out the specific impacts on the gender division of labour of the workforce restructuring accompanying the introduction of the new technologies. Given that they now constitute somewhere between a third and a half of the paid workforce in most developed countries, how are we to understand "women" as a special social category?

Obviously, the new technologies have no intrinsic features that affect men and women differently. Women constitute over half the world's inhabitants and encompass (as do men) an enormous and diverse range of social categories, with variations by class, age, ethnicity, language, religion, ability, qualification, occupation, habitation, and many other variables. No change will affect all these groups equally. Further, for any given change, the impact on a specific individual will be affected by that person's "place" in society, itself determined by the combination of these structural variables and by the personal human agency through which individuals respond to changing circumstances. Any given change, therefore, will be highly differentiated in its effects. Some men will be advantaged, others disadvantaged; some women will benefit while others will be affected adversely. If any given change potentially affects women as a group unequally, it will be only *insofar as their existing social position is unequal.*

To assess the gender impact of the introduction of the new ICTs, therefore, it is necessary to map the relative positions of men and women in existing societies, and identify the effect of each variable on their place in relation to the new threats and opportunities.

Income is one obvious variable. Although new hardware, software, and communication infrastructures continue to fall in cost in real terms, it is still relatively expensive for an individual to become a fully functioning citizen of the knowledge society; resources are needed for personal computers, Internet access, and online communication. There are significant differences between countries here, even within the European Union (EU). Globally, the differences are even more dramatic.

In 1994, for instance, the average cost of a local telephone call (in US currency) was 1 cent in the United States, 9 cents in the United Kingdom,

17 cents in Italy, and 26 cents in Nigeria. Relative to income, the differences are even greater. A telephone line subscription represents only 0.5 percent of per capita gross domestic product (GDP) in Canada, but 22 percent in Bangladesh and 26 percent in Burkina Faso. In the EU, the range is from 0.4 percent in Finland to 1.1 percent in Spain (ITU 1995). Turning to computer and Internet costs, in the words of Mike Holderness (1996), "a reasonable computer costs about one year's unemployment benefit in the UK or about the annual income of three schoolteachers in Calcutta, while the annual subscription to Ghana's only Internet host is about the same as the entire annual income of a Ghanaian journalist."

Leaving aside differences between countries, within most countries there are also great disparities of wealth, and in each case women are greatly overrepresented among the poor. There are a variety of reasons for women's poverty. They are, for example, more likely to be in part-time or low-paid employment, or employed in the informal sector. Not only are they likely to earn less during their working lives, they also receive lower pensions and are more likely to be in poverty in old age, even when they receive a pension in their own right. Women are also more likely to be sole parents than men – another group found disproportionately among the very poor. As well, in most European countries the rate of unemployment is higher for women than men. In 1996, for instance, the average EU unemployment rate was 12.5 percent for women compared with 9.6 percent for men (European Commission 1997). Here, too, an additional cause of inequality is often the nature of social protection systems. Where levels of unemployment benefits are linked to past earnings (as in Germany) benefits will tend to be lower for women because they are more likely to have been employed in low-paid occupations. Where benefits are means-tested (as in the UK), the base is often total household income rather than income of the unemployed individual. In such cases, women living with male partners are often denied benefit income in their own right. Taken together, these factors mean that women are more likely to be living in poverty than men and are less likely to be able to afford the cost of entry into the knowledge society.[2]

Leisure is a second prerequisite for full participation in the knowledge society: enough leisure to at least acquire the requisite skills, access information, and reflect upon it. Here, too, women are more likely to be at a disadvantage than men. Because they usually carry out a much higher proportion of the unpaid domestic work (including care work) than men, women typically have less free time (Gunnarsson 1997; see also the chapters by John Richards and Brenda Lipsett in this volume). Certainly fewer women than men have the freedom to spend their evenings browsing the Net.

Education is a third area where men and women are distributed unequally. Asymmetry in subject choice continues in most European educational institutions; girls are more likely to be channelled towards the arts, the humanities, and modern languages, while boys are directed towards scientific and technical subjects. As a result, as Lipsett points out in her chapter in this volume, scientific and technical occupations concerned with ICT design, development, installation, and management are heavily dominated by men. Indeed, when evaluating the impact of major EU education and programs, the EU Task Force on Human Resources, Education, Training and Youth found that "the net effect of the programs was to widen the gap between men's and women's skills. Women participated in typically female areas such as languages (81% in language subjects of ERASMUS) and in school-based exchanges such as PETRA (about 50%) but were scarcely found in the more technologically-based programs of FORCE (19%) and COMETT (15-34% depending on the action) and in engineering subjects of ERASMUS (17%)" (Rees 1994).

Finally, like those elsewhere, the labour markets of all European countries are to varying degrees strongly segregated by occupation. Women predominate in clerical work, retailing, caring work, cleaning and catering occupations, and unskilled and semi-skilled assembly and packing work in the clothing, footwear, electronics, and food processing sectors. Men dominate in virtually all other fields, especially skilled manual work and technical and managerial occupations. When information technologies are introduced, the effects differ greatly from occupation to occupation. In some cases, it is men's jobs that are adversely affected. For instance, in the developed economies, decline in the traditional "heavy" extractive and metal-based manufacturing industries has created a decline in demand for manual work requiring physical strength and endurance, in which the traditional male labour aristocracy has been found. Men made redundant in industries like mining, steel production, or shipbuilding have, by and large, been difficult to reabsorb into the new service industries, which tend to require quite different skills, including the social and keyboard skills more likely to be found among women. Indeed, it can be argued that the decline of European heavy industry has produced a crisis of masculinity for a generation brought up to believe that being a "real man" involves exercising physical strength and courage to earn a wage sufficient to support a dependent wife and children. It is certainly the case that many policymakers in Europe believe that the problem of unemployment is primarily the problem of unskilled or semi-skilled male manual workers, whether these are older men made redundant in the declining manufacturing or extractive sector or young men leaving education with insufficient or inappropriate qualifications. For other groups of men, however – those in white-collar technical and managerial occupations – the new technologies have more often presented new opportunities than threats.

Similar disparities exist among female workers. While some jobs in manufacturing have disappeared, others have been created, albeit in a more precarious global market than before. Clerical work has been at the heart of ICT-driven restructuring. Many clerical jobs have been deskilled or reskilled, and some have disappeared while others have been created. By contrast, the minority of women who have had a chance to upskill themselves have discovered unprecedented new opportunities.

The transition to the knowledge society must therefore be set against a strongly differentiated background. "Men" and "women" cannot be seen as homogeneous categories but must be studied in their specific situations, where occupational and regional variables play a major role. Nevertheless, it is already possible to see that the new forms of work emerging from the introduction of ICTs exhibit strongly gendered patterns, which not only reproduce existing patterns of segregation but in some cases add new dimensions to them.

The combination of telecommunications and computer technologies has made it possible for a wide range of tasks – previously conducted in a single, fixed location – to be delocalized in a variety of ways. Terms such as *telecommuting* and *telework* have been used to describe this shift in time and space, but they are not entirely satisfactory. The term *telecommuting* implies a direct substitution of telecommunications for transportation, which does not always take place. For instance, a programmer in India working for a client in North America or Europe is unlikely to be someone who formerly commuted to the client's premises. The term *telework* avoids this pitfall, but is often interpreted to suggest that the "teleworker" is a special kind of worker, deserving special treatment in contracts and labour law. The use of ICTs is now so pervasive, however, that probably about a third of the European workforce could be defined in one way or another as "teleworkers," rendering the term so broad as to be meaningless. It is more useful, therefore, to speak in terms of "telemediated" work in order to encompass the range of activities now carried out by this means. I focus here on some of the telemediated forms of work that are most prevalent in Europe at present.

The first is telemediated homeworking. In the UK, the Labour Force Survey has included questions since 1997 that make it possible to identify the characteristics of people who work in their own home or use it as a base. In 1997, during the reference week, around 4 percent of the workforce worked at least one full day at home in their main job and used a telephone and computer for the work done at home. Of these, around 70 percent were male (despite the fact that men form only 52 percent of the total workforce in the UK); around a third worked in the banking, finance, and insurance sector; around one in six worked in public administration, education, and health; and almost 70 percent were in three occupational groups: managers and administrators; professionals; and associate professional occupations. By 1998, telemediated homeworkers formed 5 percent of the workforce (Office of National Statistics 1998). There are no detailed statistics for other EU

Table 1

Home-based telemediated work by gender in the UK: selected occupations

Occupations	% women	% time spent in the home	Typical employment status
Data entry	96	93	Pseudo self-employed
Secretarial	94	70	Pseudo self-employed
Engineering/maintenance	1	1	Employee
Financial services	16	15	Employee
Translation	50	96	Genuine self-employed

Source: Teleworking in Britain Survey, Analytica, 1993.

countries, but it is estimated that about 10 percent of the Swedish workforce consisted of home-based teleworkers in 1997, compared with 4.2 percent in 1994-95.[3] Levels in most of the rest of Europe are much lower. A 1993 study estimated that home-based teleworkers formed 1 percent of the workforce in France and even less in Germany, Italy, and Spain (TELDET 1994).

Strong differentiations by gender lie hidden within this category. A study carried out in 1993 for the UK employment department (Huws 1993) looked at a range of variables including occupation, employment status, and the amount of time spent at home. The results are presented in Table 1.

As can be seen, the occupations in which women are concentrated – data entry and secretarial work – are also those most likely to be characterized by lack of employee status, which is, in turn, associated with precariousness, lower pay, and a lack of access to training and benefits. Occupations in which men form the majority, such as engineering/maintenance and financial services, typically carry employee status and full integration into the corporate culture and the accompanying benefits. Furthermore, in the female-dominated category work is carried out almost exclusively in the home, and is thus likely to be associated with social isolation. The male-dominated occupations, although based at home, involve visits to clients' premises and to the employer's offices, and are therefore much more gregarious in nature.

Home-based translators form an interesting intermediate group, consisting equally of men and women. Because of the equal distribution, I chose this occupational group as the sample population for a survey of teleworkers designed to explore gender differences while controlling for occupational differences; it was carried out by Analytica in 1996 with the support of the European Commission's Equal Opportunities Unit (Huws et al. 1996b). The results of this survey confirmed the view that gender differences in labour market behaviour are not intrinsic but are strongly influenced by the individual's position in that labour market. In this sample group, many of the differences between men and women found in other surveys of teleworkers all but disappeared. For instance, women were just as likely as men to have a separate room in which to work, and there were a number of men who defined themselves as the secondary earners in their households and who took on a major share of the responsibility for housework and child care. These results imply that occupational segregation is a major cause of the relative disadvantage experienced by women who are teleworkers. The survey also confirmed, however, the relative disadvantage of male translators compared with other male workers. Virtually all the translators in this Europe-wide survey suffered from stress caused by the insecurity of their employment; they experienced periods without work and therefore without income. Most also had to work long and unsocial hours in order to meet deadlines during their periods of employment, with work encroaching on family and leisure time. In other words, the results suggest that although women benefit to some extent from sharing their occupational status with men, the price paid by men for entering a mixed occupation is high in terms of precariousness and social isolation; they have, in effect, become "feminized" in their relation to the labour market.

Nomadic workers carry out another type of telemediated work, using portable technologies such as laptop computers and mobile phones to keep in touch with their base, and working on clients' premises, from the backs of cars, and in hotel rooms or wherever else they happen to find themselves. A study I carried out in 1990 again found strongly gendered patterns. This group of workers was overwhelmingly male, worked exceptionally long hours, and had a somewhat macho work culture. It seems likely that women are deterred from entering this type of work by a mixture of factors, including the difficulty of combining long and unpredictable hours with child care; risks to personal safety entailed by solitary travel; and management assumptions that some occupations, such as selling or debt collection, require stereotypically male characteristics such as assertiveness (Huws 1990).

Other types of telemediated remote work involve not moving individual workers out of the office but relocating whole fields of activity to remote sites. Work might be shifted from a city centre to a suburban site, a remote region, or even another country or continent. In this development, too, we find traditional patterns of occupational segregation being reproduced or adapted. Where relatively low-skilled activities are involved, such as data entry or responding to customer inquiries, the workforce is almost invariably female. This type of relocation also involves higher-skilled technical and professional activities, however, which are more likely to be carried out by men.

One of the most rapidly growing forms of telemediated work is call centre work, estimated to be growing at 30 percent per annum in the EU as a whole and as much as 50 percent per annum in the UK, one of the most favoured locations for call centres in the EU (along with Ireland, the Netherlands,

Belgium, and Denmark). It was estimated that in 1997 there were already 1.1 million call centre workers in the UK (half the estimated European total), and that one worker in 250 across the EU was working in a call centre, of whom 15 percent were in pan-European call centres (Fernie and Metcalf 1998; Datamonitor 1997). As one report from the London School of Economics (Fernie 1998) commented, "there are at least thirty times as many computer telephonists as coal miners in Britain today; more people work in this sector than in coal, steel and vehicle production put together."

Studies of call centre workers show that working conditions are relatively stressful. The high rate of staff turnover is attributed to a combination of comparatively low wages, poor promotion prospects, and exceptionally intensive levels of monitoring and control (Reardon 1996). Recent literature on the subject (e.g., McLouchlin 1997; Dives 1997; and IDS 1997) shows a growing concern to avoid "overheating" and "staff burnout." Employment in this sector is strongly segregated by gender. Women, generally young women, form the overwhelming majority of those working in incoming call centres (estimated at 82 percent of all call centres globally) (Call Center News 1998). They are engaged in routine tasks such as those involved in telephone banking, directory inquiries, booking maintenance calls, dealing with customer complaints, selling airline tickets or vacations, or mail-order selling. Men are more likely to be found in higher-skilled, technical types of call centre work, such as computer help lines, and in outgoing call centres, where a more proactive, if not aggressive, approach is thought to be required for such activities as selling financial services or debt collection.

It seems likely that many of the selection criteria draw on stereotypes of femininity and masculinity, with women being considered more friendly, patient, and helpful than men, and less likely to lose their tempers with rude or awkward customers. Television commercials and magazine advertisements for services such as telephone insurance generally show tele-sales operators as attractive, smiling young women, waiting only to serve the customer, in much the same manner as airline stewardesses, waitresses, or other traditionally feminine service occupations. The "masculine" call centre occupations, by contrast, refer implicitly to such attributes as technical expertise and authority. In developing countries, the patterns are similar. Studies of data entry workers in Asia, South America, and the Caribbean (Huws 1984; Soares 1991) reveal them to be overwhelmingly female, while most of the programmers in India's booming software export sector are men.

It is apparent that these new forms of division of labour within regions are accompanied by even more profound differences between regions. For an ever growing range of activities, the new technologies allow work to be relocated not just from the office to the home, or from the city centre to the suburb, but to any part of the globe where the right infrastructure is available in combination with an appropriate supply of skills. While this development has the potential for creating new opportunities for economic development in historically disadvantaged regions, it also introduces new threats. Paradoxically, the evidence seems to suggest that instead of enabling regions to become more diverse in terms of the employment opportunities offered to residents, many local labour markets are in fact becoming narrower and more specialized.

I conducted a study at the Institute for Employment Studies for the UK's Rural Development Commission, to investigate the criteria used by employers in selecting locations for telemediated work. I carried out a cluster analysis of the relevant variables at a local authority district level. This study found evidence that a new, and polarized, industrial geography is emerging in the information society. It is characterized by increasing regional specialization, where some regions become magnets for high-skilled, high value-added work such as research and development while others attract only low-skilled routine functions (Huws et al. 1996a). This pattern appears to be replicated around the globe, leading to a new international division of information-processing labour. Thus regions like New Brunswick in Canada, the northeast of England, or Dublin become call centre capitals for their time zones. Regions like California or the areas surrounding Stuttgart in Germany or Cambridge in England attract research and development. Russia, Bulgaria, and India specialize in software development. And Barbados, China, or the Philippines become favoured sites for bulk data entry.

The combined effects of this geographical segregation and the sexual division of labour mean that the life chances of women (and men) differ profoundly depending on the accident of where they live. In the new global marketplace, each region has to find unique local assets to compete for new footloose jobs. In the 1970s and early 1980s, a main selling point was often the nimble fingers of women workers, on which much of the so-called Asian economic miracle was built.[4] In the late 1990s, it is often women's smiling voices that are presented as the main attraction.[5]

If present trends are allowed to run their course with no intervention from policymakers, there is a danger that societies will become increasingly polarized along a range of dimensions. First, there is the gulf between those with and without means to access the new information networks. Next, some have secure, permanent employment and the resources to continuously develop their skills and knowledge, while others are in insecure, peripheral employment without access to training. Third, some design and control the new technologies while others merely operate them. Finally, some regions with a concentration of high-skilled, high value-added employment have entered a virtuous cycle of increasing prosperity and diversity, while others have entered a downward spiral of low-skill, low value-added work, and have effectively become industrial colonies of the former. Although men and women are to be found in each category, it is likely that men will predominate in the "haves" while women will concentrate in the "have-nots." In the long term, such a polarization will have harmful effects on economic development. The creation of an impoverished and excluded class not only brings with it a danger of increased social unrest and crime but also constitutes a drain on welfare resources and deprives industry of a potential market for new consumer goods and services.

What implications do these developments have for strategies for individual participation and learning? At the most general level, it is clear that there are no easy universal solutions. If social exclusion is to be avoided, each region will have to develop strategies appropriate to the specific regional context, building on an analysis of particular strengths and weaknesses, and its niche in the global division of labour. Sensitivity to specific local cultures and an awareness of how these cultures fit into the international picture will also be required.

It is also necessary to take account of the radical structural changes that have taken place in the labour market and its institutions and, more generally, in society as a whole – changes that have fundamentally transformed the very idea of what work is. The fracturing of the traditional unities of time and space effected by the introduction of ICTs has been accompanied by other broad social and economic changes. The postwar model of the welfare state was based on a series of assumptions. First, national economies were thought to be relatively self-contained and susceptible to regulation by national governments. Next, the "normal worker" was defined as someone who was educated once – in adolescence and early adulthood – for a lifetime career in the same occupation, employed on a continuous permanent full-time basis, and earning a wage sufficient to support a dependent spouse and children. Third, unemployment, disability, and sickness were considered exceptional misfortunes that could be protected against by means of a social insurance model. Last, society was made up of stable family units in which a stay-at-home housewife took care of the reproductive labour, supported by the wage of a male breadwinner.

In this welfare state model, work is undertaken on the employer's premises between fixed and specified hours. The time spent there by the worker belongs to the employer, while the time spent elsewhere is "leisure" or "consumption" and belongs to the worker. The rules governing behaviour at the workplace are explicit and precise; can be found in staff handbooks, labour legislation, and collective agreements; and are formally negotiated in detail, generally through the mechanisms of collective bargaining. The two worlds of work and nonwork are rigidly demarcated. Of course, this normative model never precisely matched the reality. There were always some workers who earned less than a family wage, worked irregular hours, lived outside nuclear families, were unemployed for long periods, or worked informally. And there were always women in the workforce who managed to

Table 2

Structure of employment in the EU, 1975-96 (percentages)

	1975	1985	1996
Employment rate – all	64	60	60
Employment rate – women	44	45	50
Employment rate – men	–	75	70
Part-time workers	–	10	16
Fixed-term contracts	–	9	12
Unemployment	4	10	11
Women as % of workforce	35	38	42

Source: European Commission, DG V (1997).

juggle the responsibilities of caring and paid work. Nevertheless, in most developed economies during the 1950s and 1960s, these groups were small enough to be regarded as aberrations.

As we near the end of the 1990s, however, not a single feature of this model remains unquestioned, as can be seen from Table 2. While a pool of unemployed people has emerged as a long-term feature of the labour market, women's economic participation has steadily increased while men's has declined. Meanwhile, there has been an inexorable decline in permanent full-time employment, while part-time and temporary work have grown.

Major changes in the structure of families can be added to this picture of major changes in the structure of employment. Figure 1 summarizes the

Figure 1

Changes in family structure in the UK, 1961-91

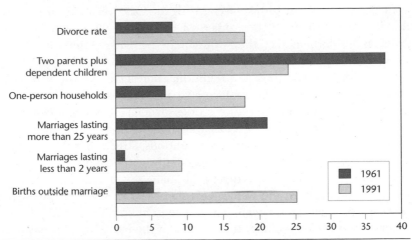

Source: Social Trends, HMSO, London, 1997.

changes that have taken place in the UK since the 1960s (not untypical of the rest of the EU, though perhaps more extreme in some cases). The divorce rate has more than doubled, and there has been a marked decline in households made up of two parents living together with their dependent children. The growth in single-parent households has been even steeper, as has the number of children born outside marriage and the proportion of marriages lasting less than two years, while the number of marriages lasting more than 25 years has dropped sharply despite increased life expectancy.

Taken together, these changes have major implications for work organization and training, suggesting that it will be necessary for both men and women to have ongoing access to training and education throughout their working lives. The traditional suppliers of such education and training – schools and colleges on the one hand, and employers on the other – cannot be relied on to deliver what is necessary, however. For a variety of reasons, a large and growing proportion of the workforce will be outside the reach of formal schemes, because they:

- have not completed formal education
- are alienated from educational institutions
- are self-employed (and therefore outside the scope of both employer- and state-provided training for the unemployed
- are geographically remote
- lack appropriate language skills
- have a disability.

It is therefore necessary to find alternative, accessible, community-based, and individualized forms of delivery.

Furthermore, when analysing the skills required in the labour market, it is no longer sufficient to take account of the local, regional, or even national demand. Many of the workers of the future will have to sell their skills on the world market; they will require the market intelligence, infrastructure, equipment, and training to enable them to do so.

Finally, the breakdown of the traditional bureaucratic form of work organization and control also entails the breakdown of traditional externally determined rule systems. In future, workers will be increasingly required to determine their own rules, whether this involves negotiating individually with employers over their pay and conditions, structuring their working time and developing self-discipline, negotiating with family and neighbours about when they can be interrupted, or laying down boundaries between work and nonwork in the home. This involves the development of new skills and competencies as well as a change in mind-set.

For both men and women, the collapse of the old certainties has introduced a considerable measure of stress and economic insecurity into working life, and it is tempting to seek to recover the stability and permanence of the postwar model. It is worth remembering, however, that this model was flawed. It created an experience of work that was rigid, alienating, and infantilizing for a large proportion of the workforce. It also discriminated against anybody who did not fit the (white, male, able-bodied) model of the "normal" worker. To succeed in this system, women had to "behave like men," including, in many cases, foregoing the right to have children. For all its precariousness, the new model offers a number of possibilities for making work more autonomous and creative, and giving each individual greater scope for designing a flexible work pattern that fits around his or her personal and family needs. At present, it offers these possibilities to only a small and privileged minority. The challenge is to use the potential of ICTs to bring opportunity to the majority – to make the knowledge society one that genuinely enhances equality of opportunity for men and women.

Notes

1 I have discussed these concepts in greater detail in Huws (1999).
2 The relationship between gender bias in benefit systems and flexible employment patterns under four contrasting EU policy regimes is discussed in Huws (1998).
3 Data from Statistics Sweden/NTO, supplied by NUTEK (Swedish National Board for Industrial and Technical Development), 1998.
4 An early commentary on this development can be found in Grossman (1979).
5 In one European example of this, the Northern Ireland Development Board in 1998 advertised Northern Ireland as a desirable location for call centres with a photograph of a smiling young woman wearing a telephone headset and the slogan "the smile on the phone."

References

Call Center News. 1998. *International Call Center Statistics*. Available online at <http://callcenternews.com/resources/statistics.htm>.
Datamonitor. 1997. *Call Centre Outsourcing in Europe: The Market Opportunities for Call Centre Service Provision*. London: Datamonitor plc.
Dives, S. 1997. "Customer Service in Call Centres." In *Training Officer* (October 1997). Available online at: <http://www.ukhrd.com/trainingofficer.html>
European Commission, DG V. 1997. *Employment in Europe, 1997*. Luxembourg: Office for Official Publications of the European Communities.
Fernie, S. 1998. *Call Centres – the Workplace of the Future or the Sweatshops of the Past in a New Disguise?* London: London School of Economics, Centre for Economic Performance.
Fernie, S., and D. Metcalf. 1998. *(Not) Hanging on the Telephone: Payment Systems in the New Sweatshops*. Discussion Paper 390. London: London School of Economics, Centre for Economic Performance.
Grossman, R. 1979. "Women's Place in the Integrated Circuit." In *Changing Role of South East Asian Women. South East Asian Chronicle* (January-February) and *Pacific Research* 9: 5-6 (joint issue).
Gunnarsson, E. 1997. "Gendered Faces?" In E. Gunnarsson and U. Huws, eds., *Virtually Free, Gender, Work and Spatial Choice*. Stockholm: NUTEK.
Holderness, M. 1996. "The Internet: Enabling Whom?, When? and Where?" Paper presented at the UNU/INTECH Workshop "The Information Revolution and Economic and Social Exclusion in the Developing Countries," Maastricht, 23-25 October 1996.
Huws, U. 1984. "The Runaway Office Jobs." In *International Labour Reports* (March-April).
–. 1993. *Teleworking in Britain*. Employment Department Research Series No. 18. Sheffield.

–. 1990. "Pinning Down the Mobile Worker." *Practical Computing.*

–. 1998. *Flexibility and Security: Towards a New European Balance.* London: Citizens Income Trust.

–. 1999. "Material World: The Myth of the Weightless Economy." In L. Panitch and C. Leys, eds., *Socialist Register.* Rendlesham, UK: Merlin Press.

Huws, U., S. Honey, and S. Morris. 1996a. *Teleworking and Rural Development.* Swindon: Rural Development Commission.

Huws, U., S. Podro, E. Gunnarsson, T. Weijers, K. Arvanitaki, and V. Trova. 1996b. *Teleworking and Gender.* Brighton: Institute for Employment Studies.

IDS (Incomes Data Services). 1997. *Pay and Conditions in Call Centre.* IDS Report 739. London: Incomes Data Services.

ITU (International Telecommunication Union). 1995. *World Telecommunications Development Indicators.* Geneva: ITU.

McLouchlin, U. 1997. "Call Centre Staff Development." *Training Officer* (October). Available online at <http://www.ukhrd.com/trainingofficer.html>.

Office of National Statistics. 1998. *Labour Force Survey Data, 1997* and *1998.* London: Office of National Statistics.

Reardon, G. 1996. "Externalising Information Processing Work: Breaking the Logic of Spatial and Work Organisation." Paper presented at the conference on *Globalised Information Society: Employment Implications,* Maastricht, United Nations University Institute for New Technologies.

Rees, T. 1994. "Feminising the Mainstream; Women and EU Training Programmes." In R. Franceskides and C. De Troy, eds., *A Wider Vision: Reflections on Women's Training.* Brussels: IRIS.

Soares, A. 1991. "The Hard Life of the Unskilled Workers in New Technologies: Data Entry Clerks in Brazil." In H.J. Bullinger, ed., *Human Aspects in Computing.* Amsterdam: Elsevier Science Publishers.

TELDET (Telework Developments and Trends). 1994. *Pan-European Telework Surveys* (funded under the European Commission's Telework Stimulation Program, DG XIII-B). Bonn: TELDET.

18
Lifelong Learning for the Knowledge Society: Demand, Supply, and Policy Dilemmas

Kjell Rubenson and Hans G. Schuetze

Introduction

It is difficult to find a Canadian policy document on education and training that does not in one way or another refer to the concept of lifelong learning. This is not specific to Canada. Policy documents from various nations, as well as reports from intergovernmental organizations such as the European Union (EU), the Organization for Economic Cooperation and Development (OECD), and the United Nations Educational, Scientific, and Cultural Organization (UNESCO), uniformly promote lifelong learning as the foundation for educational and training policy. In 1994, UNESCO chose "Lifelong Learning for All" as its midterm strategy covering the period 1996-2001. In the same year, the OECD conference of ministers of education proposed that member countries adopt "making lifelong learning a reality for all" as a priority for the ensuing five-year period, and the EU declared 1996 the "Year of Lifelong Learning." Success in realizing lifelong learning is broadly seen as an important factor in promoting employment, economic development, democracy, and social cohesion in the years ahead (OECD 1996).

With broad promises to solve the economic and social problems facing the industrialized world, lifelong learning has become something of a "New Jerusalem." As Rubenson (1997) notes in a review of the OECD's *National Reviews of Educational Policies,* however, the most striking revelation is an almost absolute absence of lifelong learning as a master concept, in either national educational policy or as a perspective in the examiners' assessment of national policies. This absence is in stark contrast to the prominence and promotion of lifelong learning in national and international policy documents and by the private sector and the educational establishment.

Following the OECD's policy initiative on *Lifelong Learning for All,* some countries have taken initiatives to concretize, at least in part, the principle of lifelong learning. Still, recent initiatives to establish national lifelong learning strategies, although containing important reforms in selected areas, lack not only a cohesive strategy to implement the idea of lifelong learning but also an understanding of what the concept means and entails. With the exception of the OECD document *Lifelong Learning for All,* there seems to be little interest in engaging in a more serious analysis of the viability of various policy options.

The most probable explanation for this lack of concrete policy initiatives is that the concept is so broad that it encompasses everything. Many factors can be related in one way or another to lifelong learning. Because everything from everyday learning at the workplace to formal education is included, there is also a temptation to move public policy into the background as policies are sector-specific and there are few mechanisms for policy coordination. It is therefore easy to lose sight of overall developments towards lifelong learning by being preoccupied with parts of the system. Moreover, the danger of putting old wine in new bottles is evident in many of the discussions on lifelong learning.

In order to seriously address the issue of lifelong learning for all, we believe that a policy analysis and discussion must apply a constructivist approach: that is, a theoretical position informed by a combination of normative and empirically founded theories (Rothstein 1998, 17). Our analysis of policy dilemmas in designing strategies of lifelong learning begins with an attempt to clarify the concept from these two perspectives. Against the background of a brief demand analysis, we then discuss the central issues of this chapter: opportunities for lifelong learning; the readiness of adults to engage in such opportunities; and the barriers that adult learners face. In the final part, we discuss the role of public policies in enhancing lifelong learning strategies, and the need to link parts of these strategies to private sector interests, initiatives, and resources.

The Concept of Lifelong Learning

The concept of lifelong learning is based on three fundamental attributes: lifelong, life-wide, and motivation (Cropley 1981). First, "in lifelong education all people should continue a process of further learning and continuous self-education throughout their lives" (Cropley 1981, 189). Thus it is no longer possible, as it was during the period of recurrent education, to concentrate only on post-compulsory education. Instead, the formative years are considered of crucial importance, and pre-primary and primary education are very much in the frame. The lifelong aspect raises questions about the structure and interrelationship between different sectors of the educational system. A crucial prerequisite for lifelong education is a system that promotes smooth progression, with no programs leading to dead-ends. Mechanisms for transition from school to work and repeated later transitions between work and education and training are highlighted.

Equality is a core issue. It is no longer sufficient to consider equality from a front-end perspective; it must be seen from the lifelong, i.e., life cycle, perspective. This shift implies far-reaching consequences for research on educational, learning, and life opportunities. If we want to measure progress towards a lifelong learning system, there are also consequences for the type of educational statistics to be collected.

Second, the fact that lifelong learning must also be "life-wide" implies that learning occurs not just in schools but in many different settings. It recognizes that many important learning influences are found outside the formal educational system. Embracing life-wide learning carries far-reaching consequences for educational policy. The essentials of educational services must be reconsidered, and increased value allocated to learning events and opportunities outside the formal educational system (Pineau 1981). In such a system of life-wide learning, coordination becomes a major practical problem, as all forms and kinds of education are treated as a single whole (Schiefelbein 1981). The issue of life-wide learning raises certain questions: Does a coordinated policy exist between sectors? Are there mechanisms for coordination between ministries with responsibilities for different segments of lifelong learning? With more and more nonformal adult education occurring at the worksite, the relationship between publicly and industry-financed adult education and training is a crucial strategic issue. How efficiently are resources used? Financing must be addressed differently within a perspective of lifelong learning and/or a more diversified system of adult education.

As people increasingly engage in various forms of nonformal education, discussions will occur on how these activities should be recognized. The OECD education ministers' communique, *Making Lifelong Learning a Reality for All*, points out that this problem requires improved mechanisms for assessing and recognizing skills and competencies, whether acquired through formal or nonformal learning (OECD 1996, 21). Ultimately, one would look for forms of evaluation independent of the context under which the learning occurred. An example of this is the International Adult Literacy Survey (IALS), a joint initiative by Statistics Canada and the OECD to assess functional literacy in the adult population (OECD 1995), which we will discuss below.

The life-wide aspect is not confined to formal and nonformal educational activities. Thus, for example, the OECD has replaced its former concept of recurrent education with the broader idea of lifelong learning. This coincides with a noticeable change in the OECD's interpretation: from a narrow focus on the education and training system to a broader perspective that "focuses on how to make learning a process extending from early age through retirement, and occurring in schools, the workplace and many other settings" (OECD 1996, 3). To think about learning in this broad all-encompassing way is a change of almost Copernican magnitude, with enormous consequences for how we address lifelong learning for all. It raises enormous challenges for public policy when the very core of lifelong learning is the informal or "everyday" learning, positive or negative, occurring in day-to-day life (Dohmen 1996). The issue is the nature and structure of everyday experiences, and their consequences for a person's learning processes, ways of thinking, and competencies. What challenges do people face? What possibilities do these challenges create, not only for restrictive forms of learning but also for investigative learning promoting new ways of acting (Engeström 1994)? While all of these parameters are embraced by the concept of lifelong learning, one has to question whether it is possible to fruitfully approach policy on lifelong learning from such a broad understanding of the concept.

The third element of lifelong learning is individual motivation to engage in learning beyond compulsory schooling. Lifelong and life-wide learning depend on the individual's possession of the personal characteristics necessary for the process. In the literature, this principle is commonly discussed in terms of fostering the motivation and capacity for learning to learn, which brings into focus the quality of pre-primary and primary education. From a lifelong angle, and in accordance with the broader understanding of lifelong learning, it becomes important to observe how, during the course of a life cycle, motivation is closely related to the structure and processes of day-to-day situations.

Demand for Lifelong Learning

Demand for continuing learning opportunities comes from several sources. Probably the most important is the ongoing structural change taking place in the Canadian economy. Over the last 60 years, a gradual shift can be observed. The dominance of resources-based and goods-producing sectors has given way to the production of high value-added products and the provision of services. Judging from statistics on the economy's industrial and occupational structure, during the last 10 to 15 years the pace of change towards a more knowledge-based economy with a higher-skilled workforce has accelerated. In addition to its effects on the aggregate demand for skilled workers, this change also has consequences for people in the labour force, who need to expand their knowledge base and skills to adjust to new jobs and tasks.

Canadian census data provide a broad overview of these structural changes. Between 1981 and 1996 overall employment has grown by roughly 2.5 million jobs, but some 280,000 jobs have been lost in the resource-extracting and manufacturing sectors. Thus almost all the job gains have been in the services sectors. Not all of these are white-collar jobs requiring higher skill levels, but especially in education, health, communications, and financial services many do require enhanced skills.

Structural change is even more obvious from shifts in occupational structures and levels revealed by census data. Thus, while management positions decreased, the demand for those with senior management functions increased. In business and finance, health, education, and arts and culture, the share of professional positions has increased more than proportionately. In most cases, this upgrading of the workforce has entailed an increased demand for advanced skills.

Related to these structural changes are the organizational changes taking place in many firms, as they redirect their business strategies, structures, and behaviour to cope with changing markets, intensified competition, and rapid technological change. These changes entail more job complexity, multitasking and multi-skilling, greater horizontal communication, and distribution of responsibility (see the chapters by Betcherman, Leckie, and McMullen and by Bosch in this volume). For the individual worker, for work teams, or for a firm's workforce as a whole, there is a need for ongoing learning, both formal and nonformal, organized or incidental, whether on or off the job.

Various reports from business underline the view that to meet the demand for increased levels of skills companies themselves need to provide learning opportunities for their workers, either alone or in cooperation with educational or other business organizations. Thus, for example, a strategy report for the business community in British Columbia advocated that business should set up "a lifetime learning program ... to encourage all workers to upgrade their skills" (BC Chamber of Commerce 1994, 68).

A third source of demand is the growing educational attainment of the Canadian population. The demand for continued learning opportunities and advanced educational credentials is steadily growing as the postsecondary education system expands and absorbs larger numbers of learners. Since to a large extent demand for and participation rates in further education are dependent on a person's cultural and social upbringing and formal education, it follows that participation in workplace-related training is dependent on the status and prior attainment of workers. Thus, Labour Force Survey data show that 40 percent of workers with a university degree participate in job-related education and training, compared with 5.9 percent of people with less than eight years of previous education (de Broucker 1997).

Opportunities for Lifelong Learning

Canada devotes a considerable share of its total financial resources to education and training. Taking into account both public and private sources of funds, Canada invested 7.2 percent[1] of gross domestic product (GDP) in support of its educational institutions, more than in any other OECD country. Of this only about 7 percent came from private payments to educational institutions. In relation to other OECD countries, Canada's investment in tertiary education is particularly high at 2.6 percent. The participation rates in 1995 among 18- to 21-year-olds and 22- to 25-year-olds, respectively, were 37.9 percent and 21.7 percent. With these rates, Canada was second in the OECD for the 18- to 21-year-old age group and fourth for the 22- to 25-year-olds. Looking at the entire 17- to 34-year-old age span, Canada led the OECD with 16.3 percent (OECD 1997a).

The high level of education in the Canadian population further supports the importance of public education to Canadian society. In 1995, 47 percent of the 25- to 64-year-old population had completed some form of tertiary education (see Table 1). This is a substantially higher proportion than in any other OECD country.[2] The US had the second highest rate, at 32 percent, while the country mean is 22 percent. The high level in Canada stems mainly from the large segment of the population that has completed non-university tertiary education (30 percent).

These figures might be considered a proxy for the basic cognitive capabilities prerequisite for the knowledge-based economy (see the chapter by Gingras, Massé, and Roy in this volume). They also indicate the degree of civilization and cohesion in Canadian society, which provides the foundations for civic participation and responsibilities, work ethics, and life and social skills deemed necessary for social and economic well-being (OECD 1997a, 33).

A more disturbing picture emerges if, instead of educational attainment, we use the distribution of functional literacy as a measure of the population's capability (Table 1). According to the results of the IALS,[3] a considerable proportion of Canadians are able to do only tasks that demand a low level of functional literacy. Thus, on documentary literacy (success in processing everyday documents), 44 percent of those aged 25 to 64 scored below the level 3 capability deemed necessary for success in the knowledge economy. The situation for the 19 percent who performed at the most basic level is most problematic. As Table 1 shows, this is not a specifically Canadian problem but something that all countries struggle with. However, the discrepancy between educational attainment and actual literacy distribution is particularly noticeable in Canada and the US. In fact, estimating the number of Canadian adults likely to be in need of basic education and training on the basis of actual literacy scores yields a much higher number than estimates based on educational attainment. One might think that literacy deficiencies like this would be a concern only for older adults, and it is true that the problem is most severe for those over 55 years. But the troublesome fact is that 39 percent of those 26-35 years, 36 percent of those 36-45 years,

Table 1

Level of education and functional literacy in selected countries, 1995

	Canada	US	Germany	Netherlands	Sweden
Highest completed education[1]					
Not completed high school	25	14	16	39	25
High school	28	50	61	39	46
Non-university tertiary	30	8	10	–[2]	14
University	17	25	13	22	14
Level of functional literacy (document)[1]					
Level 1	19	24	10	11	7
Level 2	25	25	33	27	19
Level 3	32	32	39	43	40
Level 4/5	24	20	19	19	35

Sources: OECD (1997a, b).
1 Percentage of the population aged 25 to 64.
2 The category does not exist for the Netherlands.

and 54 percent of those 46-55 years are in need of help, according to the estimates.

It is interesting to note that the majority of those with low scores did not rate their literacy skills as poor or even moderate for their current job, or feel that their skills limited their opportunities (OECD 1995, 101ff). In Canada, just two in five of those with only the most basic skills reported that poor skills limited their job opportunities. Among those who scored at level 2, fewer than one in five expressed a concern.

Readiness of Adults to Engage in Lifelong Learning

A crucial issue for a strategy on lifelong learning for all is how the distribution of educational attainment and functional literacy impact on the readiness of adults to engage in lifelong learning. The IALS data show clearly that readiness to learn as an adult can be explained by "the long arm of the family." There exists a strong link between an individual's level of functional literacy and the literate culture of the family in which they grew up. While roots are established during childhood, readiness for learning is further fostered by the educational system. The same social and cultural forces that lie behind the relationship between early literacy and family background also link the distribution of educational attainment across different socioeconomic groups, as well as reading and writing habits as an adult (OECD 1997b).

Figure 1

Percentage of population aged 16 to 65 participating in adult education and training, by level of educational attainment, 1994-95

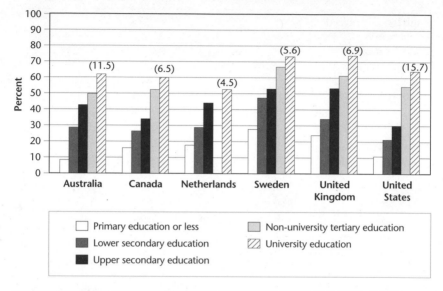

Source: OECD (1997b).
Note: Figures in parentheses show adjusted odds ratios comparing university education with primary education.

Not surprisingly, participation in adult education and training increases with the level of education: the higher the educational attainment, the more likely a person is to participate. As Figure 1 shows, compared with some other countries, the inequalities in Canada, although substantial, are moderate.

While the long arm of the family – as reflected in the relationship between social background, educational attainment, and participation in adult education – is noticeable in each of the countries, it seems stronger in some than in others. Thus, Figure 1 shows that the differences in likelihood of participating in adult education between the least educated and those with a university degree are particularly large in the US and Australia. The likelihood of Americans with a university degree to participate in some form of adult education and training is 15.7 times higher than for Americans with only a primary education, when controlled for age and gender. In Canada, the difference in likelihood is "only" 6.5 times. In the Netherlands and Sweden, the differences between those with little previous education and those with extensive education are smaller than in Canada or any of the other countries. In Sweden, the high level of participation and somewhat lower level of inequality might be explained by the country's long history of adult education. Other important factors are a large publicly funded voluntary sector and funding earmarked for recruiting groups with low readiness to participate. This involves funds for outreach activities at work and in the community, and study assistance for long and short courses. In the Netherlands, there has been an attempt in recent years to strengthen the adult education sector and to find new ways to combine private initiatives with the committed involvement of social partners. Thus, the data suggest that while the long arm of the family will always be present, public policy can reduce its impact on readiness to participate in adult education and training.

Further, a realistic policy on lifelong learning for all must be based on an understanding that, because of the long arm of the family, not all adults are ready to make use of existing opportunities for education and training. If a strategy's point of departure is the notion that adults are completely self-directed individuals in possession of the tools necessary to seize on adult education opportunities, then that strategy is doomed to widen, not narrow, the educational and cultural gaps in society.

IALS data on participation and everyday learning confirm another influence perhaps best characterized as "the long arm of the job." This "arm" has two different yet related components. The first is the deskilling effect of work settings where opportunities or incentives are lacking for workers to continue learning or to use the gamut of skills acquired during schooling and initial vocational training (Rubenson and Schuetze 1995). The second is the increased importance of adult education and training as an investment. The increase in employer-supported activities has dramatically altered the landscape of adult education over the last two decades.

While about half of all Canadian participants attend an employer-supported course, the importance of the employer is not as striking as in the United Kingdom and the United States. In the UK, two out of three participate in a course supported by the employer. Although employer-supported education reaches a large number of people, the duration is substantially shorter than for non-employer-supported activities. In Canada, as in most countries, women benefit less often than men from employer support for their education. They must instead rely on alternative sources, which means they must study on their own time as well as self-finance their studies or training. The strong influence of the world of work is also evident in the motivations Canadians give for engaging in education and training. Those in courses supported by their employer almost exclusively give job- and career-related motives for participating. But so do an overwhelming proportion (71 percent) of participants in courses not sponsored by their employer. The figure is similar in other Anglo-Saxon countries but lower in continental Europe.

As adult education becomes increasingly linked to work, lifelong learning strategies must recognize the inequality inherent in receiving employer support for education and training. It is also important to consider how the work setting frames the nature and quality of everyday learning taking place, and the extent to which it fosters a readiness to seek education not supported by the employer. The analyses show that the likelihood of an employee receiving some employer support for education and training is related to the size of the company, the employee's occupational status, and the engagement in literacy activities at work.

In general, workers in a small or medium-sized company benefit less from employer-supported education and training than those employed in large companies. This is true even though studies of small firms show that learning in smaller workplaces is often less formal and more part of a work organization conducive to learning than of an organized training effort (Schuetze 1988). Other important indicators are the sector of industrial activity, which affects differences in the organization of work, and advances in human resources policies and practices and hence employee access to organized education and training opportunities. There are also important regional differences due to the availability and proximity of educational and training institutions, and suitable programs as well as, more generally speaking, an infrastructure for collaboration, networking, and exchange between firms in human-resources related matters. The Adult Education and Training Survey (AETS), as well as all other studies, show that there is also a clear relationship between occupational status and employer support for education and training. Professional and technical staff, as well as managers, tend to get all the support they need or request. Other workers, unless they are covered by legislative requirements or collective bargaining clauses that specifically provide for training, normally receive none.

Largely, factors such as size of company and occupational status are proxies for work situations that influence training decisions. They do not say anything, however, about the actual nature of the job and the training needs associated with it. The AETS reveals a strong connection between reported use of literacy at work and the extent of employer-supported education and training. The more demands are made on the use of literacy skills, the more likely it is for the employer to invest in an employee's education and training. This is where the two elements of the "long arm of the job" combine.

These findings shift the discussion on lifelong learning for all strategies from a narrow supply question to a demand issue. Both the employer's willingness to support an individual's learning activities and the person's own incentive for investing in learning are strongly influenced by the actual opportunity to use literacy skills at work. Persons outside the labour market or in undemanding jobs clearly experience a barrier with regard to both learning and their learning-readiness. Combined with the fact that publicly funded adult education is increasingly related to work and employer support, this is the reality in which a strategy for "lifelong learning for all" must be grounded. Before we go deeper into the policy issues, we offer a few words on barriers to participation in adult education and training.

Barriers to Lifelong Learning for All

In her pivotal work *Adults as Learners,* Cross (1981, 98) classifies obstacles to participation under three headings:

- *situational barriers* – those arising from one's situation in life, such as lack of time because of work, family responsibility, and so on
- *institutional barriers* – practices and procedures that hinder participation, such as fees, lack of evening courses, entrance requirements, or limited course offerings
- *dispositional barriers* – attitudes and dispositions towards learning.

Like similar large-scale data collections, the IALS almost exclusively concentrates on situational and institutional barriers. Initially people were asked whether they had ever failed to pursue some education and training they had wanted to take for work- or non work-related reasons. Those responding affirmatively were then given a list of possible reasons for not having participated. The assumption that there are no dispositional barriers is implicit, as the respondent had indicated an interest in participating. Asking those *not* interested in further education and training about barriers is seen as irrelevant and inapplicable. We find this approach highly problematic and would argue that it runs counter to a true acceptance of lifelong learning for *all*.[4]

Looking at responses to the list of reasons for nonparticipation, the picture that emerges corresponds well to that found in previous studies on barriers (e.g., Cross 1981; Rubenson and Xu 1997; Jonsson and Gähler 1995). It was more common to state situational barriers than institutional. A general lack of time was the major reason given for not having started a course one needed or wanted to take; around 60 percent of Canadian respondents cited this as the reason for not having started non work-related education. For work-related education and training the figure was around 45 percent. Less common were references to specific situations, such as being too busy at work or family responsibility. Very few cited a lack of employer support as the reason they had not started.

Among institutional barriers, financial reasons ("too expensive" or "no money") were by far the most prevalent, cited by around one in three Canadian respondents as the reason for not enrolling in work-related education. This ratio is high compared, for example, with Switzerland and the Netherlands, where the corresponding figure is just one in seven. To an even greater extent, this applies to high school students making the decision whether or not to go on to university. According to a recent longitudinal study, the cost of tuition was cited as a negative influence by 31 percent and the problem of getting financial assistance by another 10 percent of high school students (Looker 1997).

Not only the cost but also the financial mechanisms supporting learning opportunities can constitute barriers for lifelong learners. Currently, financial mechanisms are mostly specific to the sector, program, or institution in which a student enrolls. For educational institutions, this means that levels and modes of revenues differ depending on factors such as full-time or part-time study, field of study, or whether a student belongs to a specific group targeted for support. For the student or trainee, this fragmentation of educational finance means that different rules govern eligibility, level of support, and the terms and conditions under which grants or loans are awarded and paid back. Thus, for learners, accessibility and the choice of what to learn, and where and by which mode to learn, will often be determined by the availability of financial support. This is especially the case when income from work diminishes or disappears while they are undertaking organized education or training.

Many studies have found that specific institutional hurdles particularly prevent adults with work, family, and social obligations from participating in formal postsecondary education. Many institutions still maintain rather rigid regimes and schedules. Universities, in particular, are traditionally organized to cater to the full-time, younger student coming directly from high school. Arrangements more suitable to adults, such as alternative access routes or admission rules, provision for distance and independent learning, easy portability of learning credentials from one sector to another, and other flexible forms of organized learning are still the exception. This is gradually changing, as postsecondary institutions have started to see the adult learner as part of their regular clientele, and continuing education as part of their mission (Schuetze 1987). Consequently, in Canada, where part-time students constitute approximately 45 percent of overall student enrollment, inconvenient scheduling is now rarely seen as a hindrance to engaging in non work-related education. Also, according to the Labour Force Survey, only around 10 percent mentioned the lack of appropriate courses as a reason for not engaging in work-related education. Flexible schedules and relevant programs for working students are not yet the norm throughout all institutions, however, or in all fields of study. They are still the exception in university-level programs that require the use of laboratories and other specialized equipment or settings, such as medicine or engineering.

Among the stated barriers, the lack of time is fairly dominant for both sexes. It was, however, somewhat more common among men (67.2 percent versus 59.7 percent for women in Canada). On the other hand, women were more prone to refer to family responsibilities, which also have a time component. Gender inequalities in family responsibilities are also evident in work-related education and training. Canadian women who had wanted to participate mentioned lack of money more often than men. Not surprisingly, those in higher income brackets ($31,000 and above) mention financial barriers less often.

While lack of time emerges as the dominant barrier in almost all studies of this nature, it is a vague concept. Time is not an endless resource, so people have to make choices about how they want to spend their spare time. This is not to deny that, because of work and family, some people may have very little discretionary time. For many, however, mentioning "lack of time" is mainly a statement of the value they ascribe to education and training, and the expected outcome of such an activity. The same applies to the cost barrier. It cannot be denied, however, that some people do face major barriers such as child care and cost that prevent participation. The fact that fewer people in higher income brackets mentioned financial reasons is an indication that the answers reflect not only the willingness to pay but also the ability to do so.

Thus, it is interesting that participants and nonparticipants mention situational barriers to about the same extent. Jonsson and Gähler (1996, 38) found that for people with "objective" barriers such as disabilities, young children, working hours, and so on, as many participated in adult education as did not. Therefore, "instead of barriers, that might have to do with cost, lack of time, it is probably differences in expected rewards that can explain why some choose to participate while others remain outside" (Jonsson and Gähler 1996, 38). This is why Cross (1981, 97) states that "it is just as important to know why adults do not participate as why they do." Nevertheless, it is doubtful to what extent answers to questions regarding barriers shed light on the processes of nonparticipation. In order to reach this insight, we also have to look at the structural situation as a form of barrier that affects the usefulness ascribed to education and training by the individual.

Beyond the individual and structural barriers already discussed, institutional barriers affect accessibility and mobility across different types of learning opportunities. In Canada, the lack of portability of credits across institutional and provincial boundaries severely limits learners' choices and mobility. There is no Canadian postsecondary education "system." Postsecondary institutions do not form an integrated whole. They do not work together within well-defined relationships, governed by established rules, and coordinated in a consistent fashion; rather, there are 12 provincial and territorial quasi-systems. Although sharing a few comparable features and using much of the same terminology, they have quite different rules and arrangements concerning access, curriculum, student transfer, and

financing. While this makes the Canadian "system" one of the most diversified in the OECD (Dennison 1995), it also negatively affects interprovincial
mobility, as many credentials for formal learning are not portable across
provincial borders. This not only is an obstacle to the mobility of professionals and people with vocational certificates but also affects students who
have not yet completed their initial education but want to continue their
studies or training in another province.

This lack of nationwide standards with respect to admission, transfer of
credits, recognition of degrees, and so on is not a technical problem that
could be easily addressed by a federal policy initiative. Rather, it is in the
North American tradition that favours diversity between the provinces and
rejects a federal role in the coordination of the system of higher education
(Cameron 1992). Neither has the Council of Ministers of Education, Canada
(CMEC), an interprovincial body with no federal representation, assumed
such a coordinating role. In a recent attempt to increase student mobility,
the CMEC proposed a recognition of credit transfer for the two first years of
undergraduate study. However, respectful of university autonomy, the ministers were careful to point out that such an agreement would not infringe
upon "the right of universities to determine programme design and delivery, to determine academic prerequisites and to establish admission criteria
and certification requirements of academic achievement" (CMEC 1994, 6).

While the problem of geographical mobility points to a deficit of interprovincial coordination and articulation, there is also a lack of clearly established rules for transfer between the different parts of the postsecondary
education system and of effective coordination mechanisms within the provinces themselves (with the notable exception of Quebec). Public PSE in most
provinces has two or, in some provinces, three distinct sectors, governed by
different laws and funded according to different formulas. Although the
main features of universities are similar across the provinces, the role and
mandate of non-university institutions vary. In only three provinces (Quebec, British Columbia, and Alberta) do community colleges have an explicit
role in preparing students for university or providing the first two years of
four-year degree programs (Skolnik and Jones 1993, 59). So far, coordination between the different institutions in most provinces has been "spas-
modic at best and in some regions virtually non-existent" (Dennison 1995,
123). Even the transfer between universities in the same province is complicated – as the CMEC statement quoted above (CMEC 1994, 6) indicates –
because of their autonomy in setting their own standards for admission and
recognition of credit for coursework done at other universities.

Some provinces have set up special coordination mechanisms or bodies,
such as the Councils of Admission and Transfer in British Columbia and
Alberta, which convince institutions to negotiate what is considered as
"credit equivalents." This process is both cumbersome and time consuming

since, given institutional autonomy, transfer agreements for programs or individual courses are voluntary. These problems and obstacles to accessibility and student mobility across provincial borders not only create substantial confusion but also often result in actual barriers to access or transfer for the lifelong learner (Schuetze 1995). Thus, Canada has no integrated educational system or "seamless web" that would permit easy movement from one sector to another.

The Role of Public Policy

Like other countries, Canada faces major challenges in extending lifelong learning to the least qualified. With literacy skills becoming increasingly important in recruitment and screening practices, low-skill adults, young as well as old, are at risk of being routinely excluded from the labour market (Holzer 1996). The large number of adults with low literacy levels (IALS levels 1 and 2) is thus a ticking time bomb. Worse, analyses reveal that these people – those most in need of expanding their learning – seldom participate in adult education and training and spend little time engaged in everyday reading, either at or outside work. The problem goes beyond disadvantaged groups not participating in the type of learning that can improve their situation. These groups also tend to find themselves in contexts, at or outside work, that do not stimulate a readiness to learn. Thus, before discussing policy options it is necessary to begin with a basic assumption: lifelong learning for all can be achieved only in a society that actively engages and makes demands on the literacy skills of *all* its citizens. It is conditional on a working life organized in a way that promotes the use of literacy, and a society where people are encouraged to think, act, and be engaged.

In terms of adult education and training, the link between societal processes and structure and institutional processes depends to a large extent on the possibilities and limits of the state. Carnoy (1990, 3) argues that there are crucial differences in what adult education attempts to do and can do in different sociopolitical structures. Public policy on funding regimes and provision of lifelong learning opportunities can be understood in terms of various forms of welfare state (see Esping-Andersen 1989). The liberal welfare state, with its means-tested assistance and modest universal transfers that cater mainly to a clientele of low-income dependents, tends to see adult education mainly as way of getting people off welfare. Participation is left mainly to market forces, and entitlements are strict and often associated with stigma. In contrast, according to Esping-Andersen, rather than tolerate a dualism between state and market, between working class and middle class, a social democratic welfare state is likely to promote equality oriented to the highest standard, not just to minimal needs. In such a scenario, the state will take a more active role in adult education and be more

concerned about inequalities in participation. In order to overcome the institutional barriers discussed, one has to look at the politics of adult education and training opportunities. From this perspective, as the above
discussion indicates, the fact that adult education and training is only slowly
being recognized as an important and integral component of a strategy for
lifelong learning for all can be seen as a major barrier.

Financial support is crucial for any viable policy. A vital issue, therefore,
is how existing funding regimes affect the recruitment of those traditionally not participating. In a market-driven system, it is obvious that advantaged groups will strongly influence patterns of provision. Evidence also
suggests, however, that even organizations with pronounced ambitions to
reach disadvantaged groups actually make a provision that corresponds best
to the demands of the advantaged (Nordhaug 1991). This is because existing funding regimes do not compensate for the increased costs involved in
recruiting the underprivileged. When government policies seek to increase
efficiency through the adoption of more market-oriented approaches and
outcomes-based funding, the likelihood is that organizations will cater to
those students who are easiest to recruit and most likely to succeed (McIntyre
et al. 1996). Swedish adult education policies over the last 25 years shed
some light on the influence of funding regimes on recruitment effects. Experience shows that general policies are not effective when it comes to recruiting disadvantaged groups, as traditionally strong groups are consuming
the resources. Instead, earmarked funding for targeted strategies, such as
outreach and special study aid, have been most effective (Rubenson 1996).

A further complication is that few employers contribute to the general
education of workers with limited literacy skills. Canada is no exception.
This leaves the public sector with the task of providing the foundation for
lifelong learning to a large segment of the adult population. The cost sce-
narios for undertaking this provision are staggering. The discrepancy between available public funds, present funding regimes, and the extent of
the task is a major barrier to lifelong learning for all.

This brings up crucial issues around the relationship between the state
and its citizens, and what understanding of democracy should inform state
intervention (see Rothstein 1998). Dworkin (1977, 180ff) argues that the
state should treat citizens not only with concern and respect but with equal
concern and respect, making the point for justice in the allocation of resources. As Amartya Sen (1982) stresses, however, equitable resource allocations are not a sufficient condition for a just society. Instead, he introduces
the concept of "basic capability equality." This refers to the need to take
into account, among other things, differences in those abilities that are
crucial for citizens to function in society. Nussbaum (1990) discusses the
fundamental problem that people living under difficult conditions tend to
accept their fate because they cannot imagine any reasonable alternative.

She argues that instead of accepting this situation, it is the duty of the state, with due respect to citizens' right to choose different ways of life, to see to it that citizens are in a position to make well-considered choices.

Understanding that the role of the state is to provide its citizens with equitable, not just equal, life chances means that it is not sufficient to provide a compartmentalized approach to developing a strategy for lifelong learning. The various problems and solutions cannot be dealt with in isolation from each other. A new, coordinated approach is called for, one that would involve the cooperative efforts of policy sectors such as the labour market, education, welfare, and cultural institutions. Presently, there is not only a lack of cooperation between various sectors but also fragmentation within specific sectors. Thus, for example, when addressing the worsening labour market situation for those with low literacy skills, it is not sufficient to concentrate on those already unemployed; the broad strategy needed would also include those at risk of being made redundant.

Of particular importance to Canada, although not the only central issue, is the balance between private and public responsibilities and initiatives. With its demand for a better skilled workforce, the changing economy has created new conditions for adult education and training. This amplifies the old issue of divided responsibilities between public and private sectors for educating and training adults in Canada. Regardless of political colour, governments so far have been cautious about interfering in the "training market." It is becoming clear, however, that private sector involvement is increasingly crucial for human resources development, and is central to a strategy for lifelong learning for all. Of particular interest here, as shown in the analyses above, is the link between educational credential stratification and the way the work role encourages or discourages readiness to engage in learning. The present situation calls for a renewed discussion of the role of the state and public (or publicly supported) education and training, in relation to education and training initiated and financed by employers. It is all too common to avoid this thorny issue when dealing with strategies for lifelong learning. From the IALS research, the message emerging is that a fruitful Canadian strategy for lifelong learning is as much an issue of labour market policy as of educational policy.

The question of an appropriate financing system for a system of lifelong learning has been occasionally discussed in the literature (e.g., Levin and Schuetze 1983; Schuetze and Istance 1987) and by international organizations (e.g., OECD 1996), with most authors concentrating on postsecondary education or its specific parts. Proposals include comprehensive schemes that would tie financial support of students to financing schemes for social security (Rehn 1983) or unemployment insurance (Emmerij 1983), and provide comprehensive financing for individual students, independent of age or the type of program or institution chosen. Most of these schemes propose that support from the public purse would be supplemented from a variety of sources, including individuals and employers. The appropriateness of these various forms of financing for a system of lifelong learning for all, their impact on education and training institutions, and their cost cannot be discussed here in any detail (for an overview, see Timmermann 1995), but this omission should not belie the importance of financing as a key element in realizing a lifelong learning strategy.

Since the discussions of the 1980s, there has been a constant debate on how to pay for lifelong learning, and particularly on how to deepen the involvement of the private sector (see, for example, OECD 1996; Timmermann 1995). Although different strategies have been suggested and some of them tried – for example, training levies, parafiscal schemes, and individual entitlements – there is no agreement between or within the scholarly and policy communities on what really works. The 1970s saw a strong push for direct state involvement in regulating industry education and training. This emphasis was replaced in the 1980s by the neoliberal conviction that if only matters were left to the market, an efficient "system" would evolve. The analyses of participation in education and training presented earlier reveal serious problems with a mainly market-driven approach; consequently, the state cannot totally abandon its responsibility. This does not suggest a return to the strategies of the 1970s but rather a search for new workable solutions. One interesting and promising possibility is parapolitical boards and parafiscal systems of financing. Under this scheme, the major task of the state is to get the central partners together and help foster a common understanding of the underlying issues, which can then form the basis for a cooperative working strategy and a sharing of responsibilities among these partners and the state.

The strong link between the long arm of the job and reasons people give for participating in adult education has to be recognized by the educational sector. It is not sufficient merely to be critical of what some see as a vocationalization of adult education. Instead, a strategy for lifelong learning for all must take account of what seems to motivate an adult to learn. This does not imply that the education ought to be some form of narrow, very specific vocational training. On the contrary, what those with limited literacy skills need is a broad general education that will better equip them to be fully involved, both at work and in society. The findings suggest, however, that it is difficult to recruit adults to the model of general adult education offered high school students. It is necessary to search for new models that can provide a broad general upgrading while at the same time being relevant and connected to the world of work. This would mean a blurring of the boundaries between company/industry-specific training and general education.

In order to reach those most in need, a workplace strategy will have to utilize the community and the volunteer sector. The OECD's *Reviews of National Policies of Education* over the last decade send a strong message about the current and future importance of the voluntary sector in delivering adult education. According to some country reports, this sector is more flexible and adapts to new demands more quickly than the formal system. Also, it seems to reach adults who otherwise would not enroll in adult education. The voluntary sector has played a significant role in the promotion of civil society – an important task not only in the former Eastern European bloc but also in a Western world searching for a new social contract (see the chapters by John Richards and Tom Wall in this volume).

Conclusions

In this chapter we have addressed some of the issues that need to be analysed by research and addressed by policy if a strategy for lifelong learning for all is to succeed. In doing so, we have challenged the general enthusiasm and uncritical hype about the necessity and inevitability of the advent of the "learning society," as well as the neoclassical credo that reliance on market mechanisms will achieve what the welfare state has failed to achieve – as long as the latter takes care of those who cannot compete in the (global) market.

The difficulties of designing an equitable and efficient strategy for a learning society – characterized not only by access to learning opportunities throughout life but also by the enhanced capacity of all members of that society to take advantage of them – is underlined by the fact that no country has developed a realistic strategy to make lifelong learning a reality. In order to achieve a concerted effort, a number of different initiatives would have to be designed for the different policy sectors and fields of practice; they would also need to be coordinated. We have tried to make clear that formal education and training are but a small, although important, part of such an effort, and that industrial and labour market policies; fiscal and tax policies; cultural, communication, and regional policies; as well as others would need to be redefined to accomplish the task. The problem is not the realm of policy alone, however. In fact, policy can act only on the basis of general rules, guidelines, incentives, partnerships, and good examples with respect to the public sector. Society as a whole, in its various parts, and the economy in particular, are main actors. Their active involvement and co-operation is required if a strategy for lifelong learning for all is to be designed and implemented, and succeed.

If markets are a necessary component of a system of lifelong learning opportunities – and we think they are – employers have a major role to play. Since they now require a more literate and sophisticated workforce, employers must be prepared to invest more than in the past. While continuing to rely on literate graduates supplied by the public school and postsecondary system, they must do more to organize work in a way that utilizes and further develops the skills of workers, and sets free the creativity and sense of commitment that well-qualified and motivated workers are able to contribute to their work. If such a workplace strategy were aimed at all workers, not just those at the top of the firm's hierarchy, the "long arm of the job" could become a positive rather than negative element in a lifelong learning strategy.

For those outside the workforce or who do not have the necessary skills to find employment, the state has a specific responsibility that goes beyond income maintenance at the minimum level and stopgap training measures. As we have pointed out, welfare rules, special provision of education and training, and financial support for learners must not simply be equal but also equitable. They must address the specific needs, handicaps, and barriers to be overcome if disadvantaged individuals are to join the majority and become an active part of working, social, and civic life. Such a policy is not just a matter of social justice and social cohesion but is also the only efficient way of investing public funds with a realistic expectation of gaining a benefit.

A few lessons for building a "learning society" can be learned from abroad. Canada would benefit especially from analysing foreign examples that show how a commitment to large investments in public education and infrastructures can be turned into effective learning opportunities for the entire population, not just its upper half. Canadian governments might also benefit from considering examples from jurisdictions where effective mechanisms secure the coordination of various sectoral policies, not least between federal and regional governments and between governments and social partners. Such a view from abroad may encourage industry to invest more in the active participation of employees in work-related learning opportunities, and to consider training and learning not just as "fringe benefits" to appease their workforce or the unions but as investments in their own economic future.

The educational sector itself may prove to be a proponent or an obstacle to such a strategy. The educational establishment – institutions and the various internal stakeholders – might well be tempted by the promise, implicit in the strategy, of another massive expansion of its reach. But it may also be an impediment if it fights for more and continued control over access, standards, and the proper definition of legitimate knowledge. Such control is threatened by the life-wide attribute of lifelong learning, and compromises will have to be struck if the strategy is to succeed.

Notes

1 Six percent in direct public expenditure on educational institutions; 0.67 percent in total public subsidies to household and other private entities, excluding public subsidies for student living costs; and 0.49 percent in private payments to educational institutions, excluding public subsidies to household and other private entities.
2 It should be noted that cross-country comparisons suffer from the fact that the application of the Standard Classification of Education might differ. Countries may not always classify diplomas and qualifications at the same International Standard Classification of Education (ISCED) level.
3 The International Adult Literacy Survey (IALS) is a collaborative effort by 12 countries with the support of the OECD, UNESCO, and the European Union. The IALS dataset consists of a large sample of adults (ranging from 1,500 to 8,000 per country) in Belgium, Canada, Germany, Ireland, the Netherlands, New Zealand, Poland, Sweden, Switzerland, the UK, and the US. The persons involved in the study were given the same wide-ranging test of their literacy skills and a questionnaire collecting information about family background and literacy practices in the home, work situation, leisure activities, and involvement in everyday learning activities as well as organized forms of adult education and training. Using multivariate analysis (logistic regression), these data have been used to critically examine who is involved in different forms of lifelong learning, the barriers to lifelong learning, and the structural inequality in learning opportunities.
4 For a more in-depth discussion of the limitations of the traditional way of measuring barriers, see Rubenson and Xu (1997).

References

BC Chamber of Commerce. 1994. *Moving Forward: The Vision of BC Business.* Vancouver: British Columbia Chamber of Commerce.
Cameron, D. 1992. "Higher Education in Seven Federal Systems: A Synthesis." In D. Brown, P. Cazalis, and G. Jasmin, eds., *Higher Education in Federal Systems,* 29-43. Kingston, ON: Institute of Intergovernmental Relations, Queen's University.
Carnoy, M. 1990. "Foreword: How Should We Study Adult Education?" In C.A. Torres, *The Politics of Nonformal Education in Latin America.* New York: Praeger.
CMEC. 1994. *Pan-Canadian Protocol on the Transferability of University Credits (Draft).* Brochure. Toronto: Council of Ministers of Education, Canada.
Cropley, A.J. 1981. "Lifelong Learning and Systems of Education: An Overview." In A.J. Cropley, ed., *Towards a System of Lifelong Education,* 1-15. Oxford: Pergamon Press.
Cross, K.P. 1981. *Adults as Learners.* San Francisco: Jossey-Bass.
de Broucker, P. 1997. "Job-Related Education and Training – Who Has Access?" *Education Quarterly Review (Statistics Canada),* 4: 10-31.
Dennison, J.D. 1995. "Organization and Function in Higher Education." In J.D. Dennison, ed., *Lifelong Learning and Opportunity – Canada's Community Lifelong Learning at the Crossroads,* 121-40. Vancouver: UBC Press.
Dohmen, G. 1996. "Lifelong Learning – Guidelines for a Modern Education Policy." Bonn: Federal Republic of Germany, Ministry of Education, Science, Research and Technology.
Dworkin, R. 1977. *Taking Rights Seriously.* London: Duckworth.
Emmerij, L. 1983. "Paid Educational Leave: The Dutch Case." In H. Levin and H.G. Schuetze, eds., *Financing Recurrent Education – Strategies for Increasing Employment, Job Opportunities, and Productivity.* Beverly Hills, CA: Sage.
Engeström, Y. 1994. *Training for Change.* Geneva: International Labor Organization.
Esping-Andersen, G. 1989. "The Three Political Economies of the Welfare State." *Canadian Review of Sociology and Anthropology* 26: 10-36.
Holzer, H. 1996. *What Employers Want.* New York: Russell Sage.
Jonsson, J., and M. Gähler. 1995. "Folkbildning och Vuxenstudier. Rekrytering, Omfattning, Erfarenheter." SOU 1995:141. Stockholm: Fritzes.
–. 1996. "Folkbildning och Vuxenstudier. Rekrytering, Omfattning, Erfarenheter-Sammanfattning." SOU 1996:159. Stockholm: Fritzes.

Levin, H., and H.G. Schuetze, eds. 1983. *Financing Recurrent Education – Strategies for Increasing Employment, Job Opportunities, and Productivity.* Beverly Hills, CA: Sage.

Looker, D.E. 1997. "In Search of Credentials: Factors Affecting Young Adults' Participation in Postsecondary Education." *Canadian Journal of Higher Education* 27,2/3: 1-36.

McIntyre, J., A. Brown, and F. Ferrier. 1996. *The Economics of ACE Delivery.* Sydney: BACE.

Nordhaug, D. 1991. *The Shadow Educational System: Adult Resource Development.* Oslo: Universitetsforlaget.

Nussbaum, M. 1990. "Aristotelian Social Democracy." In R.B. Douglass, G.M. Mara, and H.S. Richardsson, eds., *Liberalism and the Good,* 203-52. New York: Routledge.

OECD (Organization for Economic Cooperation and Development). 1991. *Reviews of National Policies for Education – Netherlands.* Paris: OECD.

–. 1995. *Literacy, Economy and Society: Results from the First International Adult Literacy Survey.* Paris: OECD.

–. 1996. *Lifelong Learning for All.* Paris: OECD.

–. 1997a. *Literacy Skills for the Knowledge Society.* Paris: OECD.

–. 1997b. *Education at a Glance: 1997.* Paris: OECD.

Pineau, G. 1981. "Organization and Lifelong Education." In A.J. Cropley, ed., *Towards a System of Lifelong Education,* 98-133. Oxford: Pergamon Press.

Rehn, G. 1983. "Individual Drawing Rights." In H. Levin and H.G. Schuetze, eds., *Financing Recurrent Education – Strategies for Increasing Employment, Job Opportunities, and Productivity,* 67-79. Beverly Hills, CA: Sage.

Rothstein, B. 1998. *Just Institutions Matter. The Moral and Political Logic of the Welfare State.* Cambridge, UK: Cambridge University Press.

Rubenson, K. 1996. "The Role of Popular Adult Education: Reflections in Connection to an Analysis of Surveys on Living Conditions, 1975 to 1993." In *Parliamentary Commission on Popular Adult Education. Three Studies on Popular Adult Education,* 4-63. Stockholm: Fritzes.

–. 1997. *Adult Education and Training: The Poor Cousin. An Analysis of Reviews of National Polices for Education.* Paris: OECD.

Rubenson, K., and H.G. Schuetze. 1995. "Learning at and through the Workplace: A Review of Participation and Adult Learning Theory." In D. Hirsch and D. Wagner, eds., *What Makes Workers Learn? The Role of Incentives in Workplace Education and Training,* 95-116. Cresskil, NJ: Hampton Press.

Rubenson, K., and G. Xu. 1997. "Barriers to Participation in Adult Education and Training: Towards a New Understanding." In P. Bélanger and A. Tuijnman, eds., *New Patterns of Adult Learning: A Six-Country Comparative Study,* 77-100. Oxford: Pergamon Press.

Schiefelbein, E. 1981. "Planning Implication of Lifelong Education." In A.J. Cropley, ed., *Towards a System of Lifelong Education,* 68-96. Oxford: Pergamon Press.

Schuetze, H.G. 1987. *Adults in Higher Education.* Paris: OECD.

–. 1995. "Funding, Access and Teaching: The Canadian Experience of a Mass System of Higher Education." In T. Schuller, ed., *The Changing University?,* 161-76. Buckingham, UK: Open University Press/SRHE.

–. 1998. "How Do Small Firms Innovate?" In J. de la Motte and G. Paquet, eds., *Local and Regional Systems of Innovation,* 191-209. Boston: Kluwer.

Schuetze, H.G., and D. Istance. 1987. *Recurrent Education Revisited – Modes of Participation and Financing.* Stockholm: Almquist & Wickse International.

Sen, A. 1982. *Choice, Welfare and Measurement.* Cambridge, MA: MIT Press.

Skolnik, M., and G. Jones. 1993. "Arrangements for Coordination Between University and College Sectors in Canadian Provinces." *Canadian Journal of Higher Education* 23,1: 56-73.

Timmermann, D. 1995. *Problems in the Financing of Recurrent Education.* Paris: OECD.

19

Learning to be a Citizen of Cyberspace

Vincent Mosco

This chapter addresses the need to focus on the content of education in cyberspace and, specifically, is about teaching people to be citizens, not just consumers, in this new arena. I begin by reviewing three general conclusions from research on education in cyberspace. First, most of it takes place in the developed world; cyberspace is empty space for most of the world's people. Second, in the West the emphasis is primarily on technical education, on teaching people how to use technology. Third, where attention is paid to content, most is directed to teaching people how to be consumers of products and services. Notwithstanding the value of technical and consumer skills, this chapter calls for a stronger commitment to teaching people to be citizens of cyberspace. This includes the ethical value of treating cyberspace as a public space or "new commons" to which all people have rights of access and participation, reasonable expectations of privacy and security, and, along with these rights, civic responsibilities of participation and mutual respect for fellow cyber-citizens. The chapter concludes by identifying examples of programs that promote this new form of citizenship.

Most researchers agree that the growth of a knowledge-based society will bring about fundamental changes in the production, distribution, and exchange of information and that most social and cultural institutions will be changed in some way, but none more than education (Negroponte 1995; Oppenheimer 1997; Stevenson 1997; Upitis 1997). This is because, more than any other social institution, education is fundamentally about knowledge, information, and communication. Although it certainly makes use of material tools and sometimes results in the production of material goods, these are ancillary to the fundamental process of education: *people use knowledge to create more knowledgeable people.*

It is therefore not surprising to find considerable support for transforming education so that it is as fully independent as possible from geographic location and physical space. If education does not require a specific spatial location or a building, then it can be delivered from anywhere to anywhere.

This will, some argue, transform the fundamental infrastructure of education at every level, starting particularly at the postsecondary level, and will fundamentally erode local community, or even national, control over education. The development of online courses, libraries, and other information resources, and the marketing of distant or online education by businesses and schools eager to profit from opportunities to expand their horizons, are the beginning of what some see as a revolution in learning (Veccia 1998; Wilson 1997).

These developments hold significant policy implications for Canada. If education can be produced from anywhere and delivered to anywhere, to what extent can it or will it continue to be Canadian? This question alone provides sufficient grounds for making this a policy-research agenda item on the meaning of a knowledge-based society (KBS). In addition to overcoming geographical constraints on the delivery of education, however, new technologies promise to expand the basic nature of education. In quantitative terms, computer communication is opening up vast new sources of information and learning by enabling online access that frees schools from complete dependence on paper delivery. Associated with this is the ability to link written with audio and visual material that can enrich the full range of the learner's senses. The technology also creates a qualitative expansion in the means of education by taking a process rooted in the one-way delivery of knowledge and making it more participatory and reciprocal. Education moves from an emphasis on transmitting information to the active creation of knowledge. Moreover, according to this view, computer communication takes a system of learning based on narrow linear, narrative forms and opens it up to a wide range of nonlinear, exploratory processes that allow the learner to make full use of his or her own multiple cognitive maps. As a result, students mutually constitute their learning environments, all of which grow in the learning process (OECD 1997, 120; Veccia 1998; Wilson 1997).

Researchers, however, are increasingly acknowledging that the reality of computer-mediated education is sadly falling far short of the promise. As one generally supportive Organization for Economic Cooperation and Development (OECD) report concluded: "the classroom revolution foretold decades ago has failed to materialize. Overall, the school system has not kept pace with the rest of society in terms of IT use" (OECD 1997, 134). Indeed, some argue that the promises themselves have been clouding our ability to see the reality – and especially to see that, in our rush to realize the dreams of leading advocates, we have neglected important values, particularly the values of citizenship, that have historically grounded traditional education.

Several tendencies in computer-mediated education support these conclusions. Almost all of it takes place in the developed world or in those pockets of the less developed world that are urban and rich. This is largely because, in spite of much talk and some action to provide vital network infrastructure, the vast majority of the world's peoples are without the means to learn in cyberspace. According to the International Telecommunication Union (ITU), only 34 percent of the world's households have telephone service, and most of this is concentrated in the developed world. At the beginning of 1997, 62 percent of all main telephone lines were installed in just 23 developed countries (Australia, Canada, the European Union, Iceland, New Zealand, Norway, Switzerland, and the United States). Africa, including South Africa, has 2 phone lines per 100 population, while the US and Europe have 65 and 35 lines per 100, respectively. Fully 97 percent of all Internet hosts are found in developed countries. Regarding the gap between the level of service provided in the richest and poorest countries, progress has been made but there is still a considerable way to go before equality will be reached. For example, there are more Internet hosts in Estonia than in Sub-Saharan Africa (excluding South Africa) (ITU 1998; see also Press 1998). In 1996 the US, Western Europe, and Japan accounted for about 73 percent of all computers shipped, while the developing world has gone from 19 percent (1993) to 14 percent (1996) of all shipments (OECD 1997, 21). One might argue that we are in the early stages of computer development and that we are likely to see the gap narrow as costs decline. The consistent failure to overcome substantial historic inequities in telephone penetration does not inspire optimism about expanding equity in cyberspace, however. According to a United Nations Children's Fund (UNICEF) report, nearly one-sixth of the world's people cannot read or write, and it is expected that the number will rise steadily because only one in every four children in the poorest nations is now in school (UNICEF 1999).

Moreover, there are also significant gaps within the developed world, with the US and UK averaging about nine students per computer and Japan and Portugal averaging about 50 students per computer (OECD 1997, 118). Even within the United States, the gap between the information haves and have-nots is substantial and growing. So while the technology-fuelled "new economy" is driving up stock prices and expanding job opportunities, the so-called digital divide between the technological haves and have-nots is growing at an equally fast pace. According to a US Department of Commerce report (1998), even though 50 percent more Americans owned computers in 1997 than in 1994, the digital divide has widened between the upper- and lower-income segments of society. People living in rural areas at the lowest income levels are the least likely to be connected to the Internet. The disparity has also grown among racial groups, as African Americans and Latinos buy computers and get online less frequently than whites. The report found that white households were more than twice as likely as African American and Latino homes to own a computer: 40.8 percent for white,

19.4 percent for Latino, and 19.3 percent for black households. Computer ownership levels are lower for minorities living in rural areas. Studies carried out by the Canadian government point to a similar gap between the rich and poor in access to computer communication technology and services (Dickinson and Sciadas 1997).

There is thus considerable research literature on differential access to the technology and content of media and information and communication technology (ICT). We know that income differences map precisely onto a chart of the penetration of ICTs. Higher-income people are more likely to have computers, telephones, cable television, CD players, and so on. Additionally, higher-income people are more likely to read newspapers, go to the movies, buy books and CDs, and so on. Indeed, there is also extensive discussion of how to devise remedies by providing greater access to both technology and content to groups such as the poor, women, ethnic minorities, and others who are left behind in the KBS (Castells 1996; Gandy 1998; Information Highway Advisory Council 1995, 1997; Mosco 1996; Schiller 1996; Sussman 1997).

Some demur and call for simply waiting for the market to lower price barriers to access (Compaine 1986). Nevertheless, there is general agreement that, at least in the short term, we are facing a substantial gap in access that is likely to have widespread implications for education, employment, and general participation in the KBS. One finds some, but not much, discussion of corollary problems: how do people know what they should have access to in the KBS, and what should they do with it? It is one thing to have access to a computer or to a store of information, but it is another to know what to do with these resources. In essence, how do we know what we need to know, and what should we do with the knowledge? As the KBS grows in importance and as technologies and information resources spread, we face a problem more fundamental than getting machines into people's homes, schools, and offices, or even of getting information into those same places. We will confront the gap between those who are skilled in knowing what to do with the technology and its resources and those who may have increasing access but lack the capabilities to act on that access.

This is a more difficult problem than what is traditionally associated with access because it involves considerably more than providing price and distributional mechanisms to bring people in closer contact with the tools of the KBS. It means providing training in what technologies and information resources can and cannot accomplish. It also requires the creation of bridging institutions, technologies, and software materials that not only ease the process of figuring out the best uses for access but help users make the most of that access. In the absence of these, we may think we have closed the gap between the information rich and poor without actually having done so. We will have figured out how to get a technology or a data resource into the homes, schools, and workplaces of the poor and otherwise disadvantaged without making much progress in demonstrating their value sufficiently to make a difference. We are beginning to see the impact of this problem today, as surveys report that there is little mass interest in access to the Internet and ICTs. This is generally because people have little sense of how their lives might be enriched by learning how to use the technology (Earnscliffe Research 1995; Ekos Research Associates 1998; Gallup Canada 1994).

The current business interest in marketing computers as advanced versions of television, mainly a device to provide more entertainment and information, does little to help broaden people's interest or desire to extend their capabilities. As a result, we face the same problem that radio enthusiasts confronted in the 1930s when a medium that promised to make every receiver a transmitter became instead a largely one-way conduit for mass entertainment. Educational institutions can provide some help, but schools are severely constrained to meet basic educational goals and remain overwhelmingly geared to providing instruction to children and young adults. We need the educational equivalent of high-tech firms that design bridgers and routers to ease the flow of data over a network. What is called for are institutions that bridge users and the technology or database in such a way that users learn what the technology can do for them and develop their own new ways to use the technology (Mansell and Silverstone 1996; Garnham 1997).[1]

Research is needed on precisely how to measure the extent of the capabilities gap. This is certainly a more challenging task than determining the relationship between income and the presence of a home computer or between income and Internet use. First, we need historical research on patterns of technology adoption and use, including, for example, telegraph, telephone, electrical power and lighting, and broadcasting. Again, what is required is more than how long it took for innovations to be taken up; we need to know what it took for people, particularly disadvantaged groups, to learn (or fail to learn) how to use them effectively and to willingly and satisfyingly incorporate them into their daily lives (Martin 1991; Marvin 1988; Nye 1990). What sort of learning was required? How was this accomplished? Second, we need contemporary ethnographic research on the role of ICT in the lives of disadvantaged people, on their attitudes about it, and about what sorts of learning they are now receiving in its use. Finally, we need best-case research on successful programs that have had positive consequences, for example, in enhancing learning, job skills, and creative thinking among disadvantaged groups.[2]

In addition to the concern about the quantitative gap in access, there is also cause for reflection on the type of training that is taking place in cyberspace and on the type of content that is most heavily emphasized. Specifically, although there are exceptions, much of the learning in

cyberspace is technical training that reflects the one-way, linear, and passive approaches that have characterized traditional education. According
to one multimillion-dollar US study, schools use networks for teaching and
learning in what the researchers concluded were the most obvious and pe-
destrian ways (Kaye et al. 1996). Experts in instructional design worry that
educators are seduced by the sheer amount of information available on the
Internet, and administrators, attracted by the potential to save on instruc-
tor costs, conclude that it is only necessary to point students to the data
and learning will follow. Instructional design expert M. David Merrill de-
murs: "We need to wake up and recognize that information is not instruction. There is this belief that all you need for learning is information and
collaboration: Put enough people and enough information on the Web,
and learning will happen ... There isn't enough guidance and structure there
[on the Internet] for someone to learn a systematic body of knowledge" (in
Zemke 1998; see also Noble 1997).

A Harvard professor of education agrees, noting that "the most mindless
use of computers is at the elementary level" (Bronner 1997). Relatedly, there
is significant concern that we are moving ahead with computer applications in schools (US spending on technology in schools is expected to grow
to $5.2 billion in 1999 from $4.3 billion in 1997) without conducting serious research on their impacts. In comments on a multimillion-dollar study
funded by three US government departments, the Dean of the Faculty of
Education at Queen's University in Ontario provides a sobering summary
of what we do know about the impact of information and communication
technology on education (Upitis 1997, 4; Kaye et al. 1996; cf. Stevenson
1997):

> The overarching conclusions were that school districts had not evaluated
> the impact of computer networks on student achievement ... with scant
> attention being paid to their effectiveness. The critical question remaining
> was stated as such: "Do computer networks improve student education?"
> – ironically the very question the study sought to answer. But what is
> startling – inconceivable, in fact – is that the researchers nevertheless recom-
> mended that government policies, supported by the private sector, should
> be established to ensure stable and long-term funding for computer net-
> works, so that school district networks might become more widely accessi-
> ble to teachers, students, parents, school staff, and computer members at
> large.

It is unfortunately easy for this form of logic to win out, however, because
another form of logic – the logic of the marketplace – has made the business
of education and its cost-effective delivery by technological means a very
attractive option for firms like Microsoft, now one of the major forces in

what is increasingly called the education industry (Newman 1997; Noble 1997). As a result, there is growing concern that cyberspace is evolving into a largely commercial space, an electronic mall whose main activity is electronic commerce rather than public debate and education (Stoll 1995; Sussman 1997). By 1997, one-fourth of all Internet sites were fully commercial and many of the rest were partially commercial sites that used national or other domain names (OECD 1997, 36). Although information retrieval and electronic mail helped the Internet to a remarkable beginning, the fastest-growing uses of the Net are now electronic commerce and advertising. Anyone contemplating the use of cyberspace for genuine education must confront an increasingly commercial environment, whose goal is to teach new generations of consumers how to shop electronically (*The Information Society* 1997; Hansell 1997).

Notwithstanding the value of technical and consumer skills, it is important to make learning how to become a *citizen* of cyberspace an ethical imperative of online education. Indeed, citizenship education is a necessary grounding for learning how to fully use the Internet, and the Internet itself can be an important tool for developing effective citizenship. It is absolutely essential to invoke citizenship today because citizenship elevates human activity beyond the commonly accepted view that the best way to define human activity is by its marketplace value – its worth as a consuming or labouring commodity. The widely accepted view of citizenship is that elevation has also been accompanied by extension. Here, it is common to invoke the work of T.H. Marshall (1964), who charted the progress of citizenship in modern Western society starting with basic legal rights and protections, such as habeas corpus, due process, the presumption of innocence, and the right to trial by a jury of one's peers. From here, citizenship was extended to encompass political rights, particularly the right to vote and to public assembly. Finally, social citizenship stretches the notion to include the right to employment, housing, health care, and other social welfare benefits.

Citizenship in the new electronic age means treating cyberspace as a public space or "new commons." Here, all people have rights of access and participation, reasonable expectations of privacy and security, and, along with these rights, civic responsibilities of active involvement and mutual respect for fellow cyber-citizens (Garnham 1997). Genuine education for an information society starts by teaching these principles and uses the Net as one among the many means to implement them.

Unfortunately, most of the research and policy thinking about the KBS and culture invokes people as consumers in markets. One might argue that this is an important start because so much of our involvement in the KBS is as consumers. This includes purchasing hardware and software and using it to extend our roles as consumers, by banking, shopping, and enjoying leisure pursuits in cyberspace. There is no shortage of research on the economics of the computer communication market and on factors that enhance and retard consumer preferences. For example, considerable attention has been directed to the need for guaranteed security and privacy before electronic commerce, or e-commerce, takes off.[3]

There is less research about and policy attention to the sociocultural dimensions of the KBS that invoke people as citizens of communities. Nevertheless, this attention is warranted because the application of ICTs is spreading beyond the economy, extending throughout society into political, religious, and sociocultural institutions. Furthermore, to the extent that we have thought about issues of citizenship in the virtual age, attention is almost completely directed to citizenship as a bundle of rights, some or all of which should be extended into cyberspace. There is little research or policy interest in what constitutes the *responsibilities* of citizenship in the KBS. Although it is widely recognized that citizenship brings with it both rights and responsibilities, one searches without success for sustained research or reflection on the latter. This is particularly unfortunate because it is widely recognized that fundamental aspects of the social contract that held societies and their communities together in the industrial era have withered. They require rethinking if we are to maintain social cohesion in a era that is marked by powerful forces, including ICTs, that are not congenial to strong, stable, and long-lasting community ties. Can we devise social policies that overcome the tendencies to fragmentation and extreme individuation in the KBS?

One place to start is with research on the meaning of citizenship in the KBS. Historically, citizenship has comprised a set of primarily national rights (such as voting) and responsibilities (such as national service) (Riesenberg 1992; Miller 1993). Since national borders are more transparent in the KBS, we may find that the meaning of national citizenship is subject to new interpretations. The rise of the European Community (EC) has certainly changed the meaning of citizenship in the European context. Much of this development has been advanced by growing contacts across Europe that erode distinct national cultures and lead to a significant sense of European citizenship. What implications do similar tendencies in North America have for Canadian culture and for our sense of citizenship?

Citizenship is also changing at the local level as governments in fiscal restraint cede some of their powers to private sector organizations. For example, New York City has pioneered in the formation of Business Improvement Districts (BID). These give basic municipal powers and responsibilities such as security, sanitation, recreation (the BID manages parks and local civic and entertainment activities), and signage to area businesses, which collect a levy from one another to fund their activities (Zukin 1995). There are now more than one thousand such districts in the United States and they are expanding to other parts of the world, such as the United Kingdom. One of the inspirations for the BID is the need to attract high-tech workers to districts that lack government support for the amenities that professionals demand. For example, one of the most successful and prosperous BIDs is located in lower Manhattan, where a government-business partnership has created Silicon Alley, a centre for software engineering and Web-based content production (Mosco 1997).

On the other side of the world, Malaysia's planned Multimedia Super Corridor, a massive high-tech complex south of Kuala Lumpur, proposes a new "private form of citizenship" that would, among other things, limit government control over cultural and entertainment activity, which, in this Muslim country, is quite restrictive. The intent is to attract multinational high-tech firms that would use the region to test new products; government control, including censorship, is viewed as a major impediment (Mosco 1997; see also Madon 1997). Finally, the development of export-processing zones, which provide incentives for businesses to locate production in developing countries, brought with it significant changes in citizenship rights, including the reduction of national environmental and occupational safety and health standards (Sussman 1997, 240-44).

One of the primary consequences of the flexibility that ICTs provide the KBS is that national standards of rights and responsibilities for citizenship are more difficult to maintain and require rethinking. The central challenge facing governments here is their ability to take the lead in helping forge a new social contract for the KBS. We need a new social contract because the old one has withered with changes in the global political economy. It consisted of political support for national institutions, including businesses, that were owned outright or tightly regulated by the state. In return for accepting this level of control, as well as partnerships with labour and with consumers, businesses were assured stable control over their markets, near-guaranteed rates of return on investment, and strong state support in the international arena. The state ensured that the balance between profits for business, jobs and wages for labour, and prices and quality for consumers remained relatively stable. It also guaranteed basic rights and responsibilities for citizens, oversaw their universal application within national borders, and defended the social contract in the international arena. In a global economy, national states can no longer make that guarantee; in fact, they have recognized that the fundamental vesting of power in states and nationally dominant businesses is ending. That power is now shifting to the global marketplace, and a nation's businesses, workers, and consumers are now subject to its decisions.

What would a new social contract begin to look like? Like the old social contract, it would protect rights and define responsibilities in areas that lie outside the market mechanism. Like the old social contract, which made possible universal access to the vote, to education, and to basic information services like the telephone, it would have to address universal standards. Finally, like the old social contract, it would have to define individual rights and responsibilities. It would have to do so, however, in a world where the application of ICTs has fundamentally altered our basic relationships to space and time, introducing entire new levels of flexibility and transparency. It is no wonder that many governments have tended to avoid the challenge. It is far easier to put off thorny issues like citizenship and national identity, and leave it to the market to sort out new relationships among people defined as consumers and audiences (Karim 1997; see also Dahlgren and Sparks 1991).

The cost of avoiding the challenge to rethink citizenship and rebuild a social contract is quite high, however. The pressures to promote economic development with ICTs will continue to erode traditional mechanisms. These have historically ensured that market power alone would not determine access to what is necessary to participate in society, and that market power alone would not determine responsible conduct by individuals and social institutions. The latter include institutions based upon universal access to information, including the public postal service, public education, public libraries, and public broadcasting. They also include programs such as lower pricing, grants to cultural producers, and Canadian content regulations. Research in Europe and in the United States demonstrates that the shift in government activity from providing public services to advancing the market is reinforcing the singular reliance on the market and diminishing opportunities for countervailing or balancing powers, thereby favouring those with market power (Kuttner 1997). Absent policy consideration of the rights and responsibilities of citizenship, we will increasingly invoke people as consumers and audiences rather than as active participants in building the KBS. This is particularly unfortunate because research has demonstrated numerous opportunities for people to make independent use of ICTs for a wide range of purposes, including advancing their involvement in civic life (Doheny-Farina 1996).

A research agenda on rethinking citizenship in the KBS should start with analysis of how citizenship is changing. This should begin with an international assessment of shifting laws and regulations involving who can hold citizenship, changing rights and responsibilities, and trends towards multiple citizenships. It would be useful to pay particular attention to how ICTs and related global trade agreements have changed citizenship, including the extent to which people are freer to move across borders and exercise citizenship from a distance. This would also include research on what might usefully be called electronic citizenship; that is, the extent to which and how people are making use of ICTs to exercise basic public rights of participation in political affairs in their own or other nations.

Moreover, it would be useful to assess modifications of citizenship at the local level. The growing role of the private sector in local governance, whether through Business Improvement Districts or export-processing zones, and the rise of privately controlled "gated" communities call for research on the implications of these "local" citizenships for the KBS. Citizenship has traditionally been identified with rights, and it would be useful to examine how these rights are evolving in the KBS. But citizenship also means responsibilities, including requirements to uphold the law, in letter and in spirit, and to participate in the political process, including supporting or opposing established policies (Etzioni 1996). We are beginning to recognize that the use of ICTs is creating the need for research and debate on the specific responsibilities of individuals and groups in the KBS. This is primarily because of the recognition that, notwithstanding the enormous potential of ICTs for improving society, ICTs also pose significant risks – primarily by their sheer power to overcome space and time constraints on the delivery of both socially useful and damaging material.

For example, ICTs and a host of economic incentives (such as the business of targeted marketing) contain the potential for enormous violations of privacy in both the public and private sectors (Sopinka 1997). Moreover, ICTs can instantly deliver to any Internet user the fullest range of pornography and hate propaganda that has ever been available (Mehta and Plaza 1997). We have research on privacy and on the extent of its socially harmful use, but we would benefit from research on what societies are doing, for example, establishing codes of responsible conduct. What are public and private sector organizations doing to set standards for responsible use and for dealing with abuse of ICTs? What do we know about what others are doing and what we might do to develop a set of standards for the specific rights and responsibilities of citizens in the ICT-intensive KBS?

There has been considerable discussion of the importance of civil society in the KBS. This is partly inspired by the apparent growth of local, national, and particularly international organizations and social movements, whose links to government and business are tenuous at best, and which aim to represent constituencies before or in opposition to the state and to the private sector. Research has suggested a close connection between the rise of such movements, their success, and the use of ICTs (Witheford 1996; Mazepa 1997). We need a systematic analysis of this phenomenon. Have we seen a resurgence of civil society in the KBS? What is the role of ICTs in civil society? Can civil society provide countervailing weight to the market? Given the diminished or changed role of government in the KBS, does civil society offer an alternative foundation for a renewed social contract in the KBS?

Finally, we need research on how ICTs are changing the political process in the KBS (Putnam 1995). Specifically, what is the impact of ICTs on political participation, including voting, involvement in political organizations, and expressions of public opinion? How are political organizations responding to the use of ICTs? How is government responding? Are ICTs a source of increased participation in public life or an entertaining distraction that occupies time that might be spent in public activity?

We are beginning to accumulate a body of examples that provide important guidance for developing the practice of citizenship in cyberspace. One of the most important is the establishment of community nets or freenets, which bring together people in a city, town, or neighbourhood, providing essential information about public services besides all of the material normally found on the Internet. Freenets provide two essential elements missing in most of the commercial networks. First, because they make use of servers provided by educational, nonprofit, or other donor organizations, freenets offer low-cost access for users. This is particularly important for low-income people, who, even in the most developed societies, have little chance of making use of the Internet. Second, they locate terminals in public places such as post offices, libraries, schools, and markets, enabling people to make use of the Net without having to purchase a computer (Noack 1998; see also Doheny-Farina 1996).

With regard specifically to education, several countries have initiated programs to provide hardware, develop content, establish public networks, provide teacher training, initiate research on educational innovation, and promote distant and adult education (OECD 1997, 122-34). For example, the Canadian government has established the Computers for Schools program that channels surplus computer equipment and software from public and private sector partners to needy schools. Its joint federal and provincial School-Net program connects libraries and schools to the World Wide Web. Human Resources Development Canada conducts research and supports demonstration projects across the country on learning applications in schools and employment training. The federal and provincial governments have also pioneered delivery of distance education to the scattered populations of the Canadian North (Industry Canada 1995, 1997). Canada provides just one of several national examples of a commitment to the principles of citizenship in cyberspace. Nevertheless, as with other nations, Canada's commitment is under constant challenge, particularly from those interested in making cyberspace a private space, largely oriented towards commercial activity and open only to those who can pay for access and security.

Conclusion
There is considerable potential in the educational uses of cyberspace, but there are also many challenges and dangers. Computers can provide the means to explore new forms of learning that break out of the traditional hierarchies of educational bureaucracy, and to develop genuine alternatives to rigid, passive approaches to learning. They can, however, also reify those

hierarchies if they are applied without a commitment to the principles of equality, participation, privacy, mutual respect, and responsibility that historically have provided the foundation for many of our systems of public education. New technologies can also entice us into thinking that the technology alone will overcome problems of equity and excessive commercialization. Experience suggests that this is not the case and calls for a commitment to the principles of citizenship, including strong support from the agencies of civil society and the public sphere, in order to make cyberspace a rich community itself and an instrument to enrich our existing communities.

Unfortunately, like the research on community, the analysis of ICTs and education has little to say about the meaning of education. As a result, supporters and opponents of ICT applications tend to talk past one another, with the former viewing education as an information distribution problem and the latter as a problem of social relations and communication. If you believe that education is about producing, packaging, and distributing information, then you are more likely to see the virtual classroom or university by and large as a benefit. But if you view education as a social experience requiring communication between people using their senses as fully as possible, then ICTs are at best an adjunct to the classroom and at worst a distraction that drains valuable human and material resources. The policy debate on ICTs in education calls for a discussion of what amounts to the many different forms and functions of education, so that we know what might and might not be enhanced with the application of ICTs. Once we have a reasonable sense of that, then it would be appropriate to assess the costs and benefits of actually applying ICTs. These strategies would appear to make more logical sense than simply pursuing ICTs in education strategies because they might save money or because technical experts have touted the technical capabilities of online systems.

Sensible policy discussion about the meaning of education and the role of ICTs within it would go a long way towards setting a balanced tone in debates about technology and the KBS. It would also help the discussion of the specific national issue: how to preserve Canadian education in the KBS. For now, we need two kinds of research on this pressing cultural policy issue. First, it would be useful to do a survey of virtual education in Canada that provides information on the extent of Canadian content and on the balance of Canadian versus foreign production. Second, we need to assess the responses of other national governments to the cultural implications of virtual education. What protections, from subsidies to restrictions, are being discussed and implemented outside Canada?

Finally, despite considerable investment in the educational uses of ICT, we know very little about the consequences for learning, about when it works and when it does not. We need research on the shift meaning of education in the KBS, particularly on the question: "Is virtual education, indeed, education?"

Notes

1   Examining the economist Amartya Sen's "capabilities" approach to welfare, Garnham (1997, 32) perceptively comments: "But what the capability approach highlights is that access is not enough. In evaluating levels of entitlement we need to take into account both the range of communication options made available, and these must be real options not mere choices between products and services with minimal real differences, and the ability of people actually to make use of these options, to achieve their relevant functionings. We can have real reasoned disagreements as to what range and type of service can now be regarded as necessary and about how to equalize the level of achieved functionings. But the first crucial point, from the capability perspective is that this cannot be justified simply in terms of either the metric of exchange – that is, what people actually buy – or the metric of utility – that is, what people actually enjoy."

2   One of the best sources of online information and discussion on this subject is the group Techedge – Technology at the Margins of Society, hosted by Professor John Freund of St. John's University in New York City: <http://www.Techedge@maelstrom.stjohns.edu>. See also the Web sites <http://www.stjohns.edu/vincentianctr> and <http://www.cptryon.org/vdp>.

3   For a thorough treatment of commerce, markets, and marketing in the KBS, see *The Information Society* (1997).

References

Bronner, Ethan. 1997. "High-Tech Teaching Is Losing Its Gloss." *The New York Times*, 30 November, section 4, p. 4.

Industry Canada. 1995. *Connection, Community, Content: The Challenge of the Information Highway*. Ottawa: Industry Canada.

–. 1997. *Industry Portfolio: Information Highway*. Ottawa: Industry Canada.

Castells, Manuel. 1996. *The Rise of the Network Society*. Oxford: Blackwell.

Compaine, Benjamin M. 1986. "Information Gaps: Myth or Reality?" *Telecommunications Policy* (March): 5-12.

Dahlgren, Peter, and Colin Sparks. 1991. *Communication and Citizenship*. London: Routledge.

Dickinson, Paul, and George Sciadas. 1997. *Access to the Information Highway: The Sequel*. Ottawa: Statistics Canada.

Doheny-Farina, Stephen. 1996. *The Wired Neighborhood*. New Haven, CT: Yale University Press.

Earnscliffe Research. 1995. *Proceed with Caution*. Ottawa: Earnscliffe.

Ekos Research Associates Inc. 1998. *The Information Household and the Canadian Communications Household*. Ottawa: Ekos Research Associates.

Etzioni, Amitai. 1996. *The New Golden Rule: Community and Morality in a Democratic Society*. New York: Basic Books.

Gallup Canada. 1994. *What Canadians Think About the Information Highway*. Toronto: Gallup.

Gandy, Oscar H., Jr. 1998. *Communication and Race: A Structural Perspective*. London: Arnold.

Garnham, Nicholas. 1997. "Amartya Sen's 'Capabilities' Approach to the Evaluation of Welfare: Its Application to Communications." *The Public: Journal of the European Institute for Communication and Culture* 4,4: 25-34.

Hansell, Saul. 1997. "Money Starts to Show in Internet Shopping." *The New York Times*, 1 December, D-1.

Information Highway Advisory Council. 1995. *Connection, Community, Content: The Challenge of the Information Highway*. Ottawa: Industry Canada.

–. 1997. *Preparing Canada for a Digital World*. Ottawa: Industry Canada.

The Information Society. 1997. "Special Issue: Theory and Practice of Electronic Commerce." 13,1.

ITU (International Telecommunication Union). 1998. *World Telecommunications Development Report,* 4th ed. Geneva: ITU.

Karim, Karim H. 1997. "Relocating the Nexus of Heritage, Citizenship, and Technology." *The Public: Journal of the European Institute for Communication and Culture* 4,4: 75-86.

Kaye, J.C., D.B. Jacobs, P. Aschbacher, and B. Judd. 1996. *Model Nets: A National Study of Computer Networking in K-12 Education.* Los Alamos, CA: Los Alamos National Laboratory.

Kuttner, Robert. 1997. *Everything for Sale: The Virtues and Limits of Markets.* New York: Alfred A. Knopf.

Madon, Madon. 1997. "Information-Based Global Economy and Socioeconomic Development: The Case of Bangalore." *The Information Society* 13,3: 227-43.

Mansell, Robin, and Roger Silverstone, eds. 1996. *Communication by Design.* New York: Oxford University Press.

Marshall, T.H. 1964. *Class, Citizenship, and Social Development.* Garden City, NY: Doubleday.

Martin, Michele. 1991. *Hello Central? Gender, Technology and Culture.* Montreal: McGill-Queen's University Press.

Marvin, Carolyn. 1988. *When Old Technologies Were New.* New York: Oxford University Press.

Mazepa, Patricia. 1997. *The Solidarity Network in Formation: A Search for Democratic Alternative Communication.* M.A. thesis, School of Journalism and Communication, Carleton University, Ottawa.

Mehta, Michael, and Dwaine Plaza. 1997. "Content Analysis of Pornographic Images Available on the Internet." *The Information Society* 13,2: 153-61.

Miller, Toby. 1993. *The Well-Tempered Self: Citizenship, Culture, and the Postmodern Subject.* Baltimore: Johns Hopkins University Press.

Mosco, Vincent. 1996. *The Political Economy of Communication: Rethinking and Renewal.* London: Sage.

–. 1997. "Citizenship and the Technopoles." *The Public: Journal of the European Institute for Communication and Culture* 4,4: 35-45.

Negroponte, Nicholas. 1995. *Being Digital.* New York: Vintage Books.

Newman, Nathan. 1997. "From Microsoft Word to Microsoft World." A NetAction White Paper. San Francisco: NetAction (<http://www:netaction.org>).

Noack, David. 1998. "Try Taking a 'Free' Ride on the Internet." *Investor's Business Daily,* 24 April, A1.

Noble, David. 1997. "Digital Diploma Mills." Toronto: York University (<http://www.journet.com/twu/deplomamills.html>).

Nye, David. 1990. *Electrifying America: Social Meanings of a New Technology, 1880-1940.* Cambridge, MA: MIT Press.

OECD. 1997. *Information Technology Outlook 1997.* Paris: OECD.

Oppenheimer, T. 1997. "The Computer Delusion." *Atlantic Monthly* 280,1: 45-62.

Press, Larry. 1998. "Tracking the Global Diffusion of the Internet." *Communications of the ACM* 40,11: 11.

Putnam, Robert D. 1995. "Tuning In, Tuning Out: The Strange Disappearance of Social Capital in America." *PS: Political Science and Politics* 28: 664-83.

Riesenberg, Peter. 1992. *Citizenship and the Western Tradition.* Chapel Hill: University of North Carolina Press.

Schiller, Herbert I. 1996. *Information Inequality.* New York: Routledge.

Sopinka, John. 1997. "Freedom of Speech and Privacy in the Information Age." *The Information Society* 13,2: 171-84.

Stevenson, D., ed. 1997. *The Future of Information Technology in UK Schools.* London: McKinsey and Co.

Stoll, Clifford. 1995. *Silicon Snake Oil: Second Thoughts on the Information Highway.* New York: Doubleday.

Sussman, Gerald. 1997. *Communication Technology and Politics in the Information Age.* Thousand Oaks, CA: Sage.

UNICEF. 1999. *The State of the World's Children 1999.* Oxford: Oxford University Press.

US Department of Commerce. 1998. *Falling Through the Net, II.* Washington, DC: Department of Commerce.

Upitis, Rena. 1997. "The Impact of the Communications Revolution on Education." Paper presented at the Canada–United Kingdom Colloquium on the Communication Revolution, Keele University, Staffordshire, UK, 23-26 November 1997.

Veccia, Susan. 1998. "Will Schools Become Irrelevant." *Multimedia Schools* 5,1: 6, 8.

Wilson, Jack M. 1997. "Distance Learning for Continuous Education." *Educom Review* 32,2: 12-17.

Witheford, Nicholas. 1996. *The Contest for General Intellect: Cycles and Circuits of Struggle in High Technology Capitalism.* Ph.D. dissertation, Department of Communication, Simon Fraser University, Burnaby, BC.

Zemke, Ron. 1998. "Wake Up! (And Reclaim Instructional Design)." *Training* 35,6: 36-38, 40, 42.

Zukin, Sharon. 1995. *The Culture of Cities.* Cambridge, MA: Blackwell.

Part 5
Measuring the Knowledge Society

20
Measuring Human Capital: Data Gaps and Survey Requirements
Albert Tuijnman

Introduction

The purpose of this chapter is to review salient aspects of human capital theory, especially insofar as these have implications for the measurement of skills and competencies. A second purpose is to describe the so-called direct and indirect approaches to the measurement of human capital. The third aim is to examine advances and new directions in the measurement of human capital. Recent innovations, such as the ongoing International Adult Literacy Survey (IALS) and the planned International Life Skills Survey (ILSS), are also reviewed.

Variants of Human Capital Theory

Human capital theory has roots extending far back in history, but the formal representations current today are usually traced to scholars writing in the early 1960s (Schultz 1961; Kristensen 1962; Mincer 1962; Becker 1964). A recent Organization for Economic Cooperation and Development (OECD) publication offers the following definition: "Human capital ... [refers to] ... the knowledge, skills, competencies and other attributes embodied in individuals that are relevant to economic activity" (OECD 1998, 9). The emphasis on "economic activity" is important because it focuses attention on the intangible assets and attributes of individuals that can improve or support productivity, innovation, and employability.

The claim that human capital is a major ingredient in productivity and economic competitiveness has found a large and receptive audience among policymakers and researchers. In recent years, it has helped once more to propel the issue of human capital formation to the fore of the policy debate. The renewed interest in human capital theory derives from a debate about whether, and why, Western economies have performed below expectation since the mid-1970s. Some economists have postulated that skills mismatches explain, at least in part, why the cumulative inputs of financial capital, labour, and technology have produced below-expected economic growth in Western economies. Productivity growth, the argument goes, depends not only on the optimization of primary input factors but especially on their optimal allocation and use, given the stock of available human capital.

Human capital, which is thought to confer scale economies to capital and labour inputs, is associated with people and organizations. Hence, productivity growth cannot be separated from worker skills and other relevant individual attributes, such as attitudes towards work, information, and the quality of interpersonal relationships that occur as micro-phenomena in the workplace (Eliasson 1993). Variants on the human capital theme differ in the weight they accord to these individual attributes. Three theories seem particularly salient: the human capital perspective, screening theory, and job-matching theory.

The individual rate of return to education is central to the human capital approach, using personal income as the criterion. The relationship between educational attainment and productivity is considered straightforward: more formal education results in a higher wage because education confers knowledge and skills that increase the capacity of workers to perform efficiently on the job. Two distinct relationships are hypothesized: (1) an effect of formal education on labour productivity, and (2) an effect of productivity on individual income. Studies conducted in the human capital framework focus on the relationship between education and income; the relevance of education for productivity is often taken for granted.

Screening or signalling theory hypothesizes a different connection between education and individual earnings. The theory proposes that people undertake an education not primarily because it makes them more productive at work but because the conferred qualifications and credentials can be used to inform employers that the person possesses certain scarce skills and other desirable traits that are likely to make him or her more productive in a given job than competitors who lack these specific characteristics. In this view, formal education thus presents a means to identify and select workers with a high expected marginal productivity. Self-selection rather than productivity forms the basis for the observed relationship between education and earnings. In this theoretical perspective, education is not necessarily a strategic investment that will raise productivity.

Information is a central variable in both screening and job-matching theories. The two approaches are therefore closely related. In screening theory the emphasis is on the comparative advantage of the individual who holds vital information, vis-à-vis the employer who lacks such information. In job-matching theory both workers and employers are considered to derive useful information from the fact that a given person has gone through a particular educational program. This information is used by both parties to improve the efficiency of the "match" between workers and jobs. In this perspective, education raises productivity and income only if it improves the job match of an employee. The job match depends on whether the knowledge and skills acquired by means of additional education are actually utilized on the job. If more education leads to mismatches in skill demand and supply, however, the effect on productivity may be nil or even negative.

Screening and job-matching theories thus call into doubt the idea that additional education necessarily represents a productive investment, because more education can also lead to overschooling (Bishop 1996). Human capital theory, in contrast, provides a powerful justification for the belief that education is more investment than consumption. It has provided a rationale for the rapid expansion and growth of systems of formal education throughout the world. The theory also features importantly in the current advocacy of lifelong learning policies by international organizations and national governments. The validity of the lifelong learning approach, however, hinges on a number of assumptions about the relationships between costs and various types of benefits, and the conditions under which the benefits are optimal for individuals, work organizations, and whole societies. (See the discussion in the chapter "Lifelong Learning for the Knowledge Society: Demand, Supply, and Policy Dilemmas," by Rubenson and Schuetze in this volume).

The success of a lifelong learning strategy, insofar as this is geared towards achieving economic objectives such as improved productivity, innovation, and employability thus depends partly on obtaining better information and understanding about the costs and benefits of human capital investment. This in turn makes the improved measurement of human capital stocks and flows a critical issue for analysts and policymakers.

Types of Human Capital Measures

There are different approaches to measuring human capital, defined as the economically useful knowledge, skills, competencies, and attitudes held by individuals or, in the aggregate, as the stock of knowledge and skills present in whole populations. A distinction can be made between direct and indirect approaches to measurement (Jones 1997). These approaches and their associated problems of measurement are described below.

Indirect Measurement

The indirect approach to measuring human capital is based on the assumption that educational attainment can serve as a useful, low-cost proxy measure of human capital stock because of the observed high correlations between education, skills, and income from work. Sociologists and economists have long used measures of educational attainment in models of status attainment and analyses of private and social rates of returns to education. The most commonly used measures are years of schooling obtained or highest attained educational qualification or level, in accordance with either the national qualification structure or the so-called International Standard Classification of Education (ISCED).

A serious threat to validity can arise, however, if years of schooling, initial educational attainment, and knowledge or skills do not correspond. Such a situation can occur for a variety of reasons. For example, people who enter the labour market with similar educational qualifications do not necessarily have the same level of proficiency in assorted skills and competencies. Discrepancies can also arise because people do not stop learning and acquiring new skills upon leaving school. Because opportunity to learn varies depending on a host of personal, situational, and economic variables, the relationship between educational attainment and stocks of human capital is not necessarily linear. Whether educational attainment nevertheless can be used as a proxy of acquired human capital depends on the specific questions that are addressed and the chosen method of analysis.

Educational attainment is conventionally employed as a variable predicting the individual, social, and economic outcomes of schooling. The possible effects of education on life, career, and earnings can be measured in different ways and at different levels. Micro studies tend to focus on variables that carry meaning for individuals, such as the incidence of unemployment, occupational opportunity, sex differences in the labour market, worker productivity, or earnings from work. In contrast, macro studies are concerned with the effects of education on the supply of skilled workers, the functioning of labour markets, and aggregate economic growth. In both cases, empirical work is guided not only by the hypothesized relationship between the dependent variables and educational attainment per se but also by an assumption concerning the relationship between the dependent variables and the knowledge, skills, and competencies thought to be associated with educational attainment.

In most economically advanced countries, schooling has long been compulsory until at least 14 years of age. Completed upper-secondary education, or even a few years of postsecondary educational experience, is rapidly becoming the norm for youth and young adults in Europe and North America. Notions about what constitutes a minimum level of competency are changing, in line with the continued expansion of formal education early in life. Until fairly recently, primary schooling was generally assumed to be congruent with proficiency in foundation skills such as literacy, numeracy, and civics. This minimum threshold was gradually upgraded with the expansion of secondary education. Today, a full cycle of upper-secondary education or high school is considered by many observers as a suitable minimum level for entry into the world of work beyond school. In parallel with this development – and with the first empirical results of international skill assessments in hand – the awareness is gradually spreading that measures of completed years or levels of schooling are at best poor substitutes for measures of human capital stock.

A positive correlation between individuals' schooling attainment and earnings has been demonstrated by hundreds of statistical studies (Psacharopoulos 1985). These findings leave some fundamental questions unanswered, however. As pointed out above, schooling attainment per se is not a measure of knowledge or skill. Arrow (1973), Spence (1973), and Layard and Psacharopoulos (1974) demonstrated that labour markets might reward higher educational attainment even if schools contributed nothing to individual productivity. Ever since then, the extent to which schools operate as a screening mechanism has remained an open question. If ability is assumed to be a one-dimensional construct, then schools in theory might only be certifying individuals' ability to employers, who are willing to pay more to persons so certified, even if nothing they learned in school increased their productivity. In contrast, if ability is multidimensional (Gardner 1985) – and if certain jobs require more of some abilities than of others – then schools may be helping individuals sort themselves into different kinds of jobs (Willis and Rosen 1979) without necessarily adding to their productive knowledge or skill. How much the monetary return to schooling represents payment for competence acquired there remains an open question.

Adult education and training complicate the issue even further. When measures of adult education and training are specified as mediating variables in a model sequencing the effect of schooling on occupational attainment and individual earnings, the size of the parameters associated with the influences of schooling decreases substantially. Moreover, the specification of measures of adult education and training changes the shape of the curves associated with the schooling effect; in both cases, the capacity of initial schooling to predict occupational status and earnings from work decreases at an earlier age than would be the case if such variables were ignored (Tuijnman 1989). Thus, the effect of formal schooling on earnings is partly spurious, since omitted variables such as post-initial learning evidently also influence this relationship. This evidence provides strong support for theories of lifelong learning (OECD 1996). It also suggests that it is necessary to go behind simple measures of educational attainment and to assess more directly the knowledge, skills, and competencies that may be associated with productivity and earnings growth.

A further reason why the correlation between earnings and schooling fails to tell us much about the relationship between skills and productivity is that earnings and productivity are by no means synonymous. Lazear (1981), for example, demonstrated that competitive labour markets might award higher pay to individuals with more seniority, even if their productivity remained absolutely constant over time. The prospect of higher pay later in life would keep young noses to the grindstone, and would keep more senior workers from shirking because they would not want to risk dismissal while in their highly paid years (Stern and Tuijnman 1997). Individuals are therefore more productive than they would be if they were paid exactly the value of what they produced as they went along, and the resulting gain in lifetime productivity would benefit both employers and employees. In general, then, it cannot be assumed that individual earnings are highly correlated with productivity (Brown et al. 1993).

The above discussion precludes a simple interpretation of the association between educational attainment and individual earnings. In order to understand whether, how, and to what extent workers' knowledge, skills, and competencies affect their productivity, studies of initial educational attainment and earnings will not suffice. It is necessary to measure the independent and dependent variables – productivity and competence – directly. This line of reasoning offers arguments for looking very carefully at the dimensions of adult basic skills, how they are acquired and possibly lost, and how they bear on production.

In sum, there are at least four good reasons why the indirect approach to measuring human capital using educational attainment proxy variables is insufficiently robust and may lead to spurious conclusions about the relationships between schooling and competence, productivity, and earnings (Tuijnman 1995; Stern and Tuijnman 1997; OECD 1998):

- Requirements for completed educational levels vary across countries. Similar levels of educational attainment do not guarantee, therefore, that relevant skills have been mastered to the same extent.
- Educational attainment based on cycles of completed formal education neglects the knowledge and skills people acquire in the post-school years through nonformal or informal learning at home, at work, or in the community.
- Similarly, educational attainment measures are based on the false premise that the knowledge and skills acquired through formal schooling keep their value over time. This is untrue insofar as skills can be lost through obsolescence and disuse.
- Educational attainment should be measured dynamically and not statically because knowledge and skill requirements in the economy and society evolve with time.

Direct Measurement
Direct measures of knowledge, skills, and competencies can be used to shed new light on the relationships between individual abilities, productivity, and various social and economic outcomes. Direct measurement is a relatively new development, however. It is also expensive and very demanding on both theory and the science of assessment.

International comparative studies of student achievement were the precursors of today's direct approaches to the measurement of human capital. Comparative studies of student achievement have been undertaken under the auspices of the International Association for the Evaluation of Educational Achievement (IEA) since the early 1960s (see Husén 1967).

The IEA surveys have measured dimensions of student performance and their determinants in a range of school subjects, such as mathematics, science, reading literacy, and civics education. From a human capital perspective, a drawback has been that the studies typically sampled young students around the ages of 10 and 14. Comparative data on student achievement at these young ages have proved valuable for many analytical purposes, but the data have only limited applicability for the analysis of human capital stocks. For the latter, populations of working age are of more immediate interest. Previous IEA studies have also collected assessment data for samples of 17- to 18-year-old students. At this age, the assessment data could have more relevance for the benchmarking of human capital, at least potentially, because in the economically advanced countries this age marks the transition from secondary education to the world of work or higher education. Problems of self-selection, however, have tended to limit the usefulness of these data as well. Selection bias has occurred because enrollment was used as a primary criterion for the sampling of 18-year-olds, even though in different countries different proportions of 18-year-olds were still enrolled in secondary education. This bias has limited the applicability of the data to the comparative analysis of human capital.

In the absence of available population data on actual abilities or real educational performance, researchers have used data on gross population enrollment in primary, secondary, and tertiary education, or some other measures of overall educational attainment. For the reasons mentioned previously, these indirect approaches to measurement have been inadequate.

The conclusion to be drawn from the above is that population assessment data are needed for the comparative analysis of human capital stocks. What is required is information about the actually observed rather than inferred levels of knowledge, skills, and competencies in the population. Further, because the information should be relevant to the analysis of economic activity, it would be necessary to sample adults in the workforce.

The best level at which to study the relationship between workers' knowledge and skills and productivity is neither the individual nor the whole population but the intermediate level of the firm, establishment, or work group. These are the actual units of production, where knowledge and competence are combined with other factors to produce goods or services. Surveys of workers' competence are being conducted in an increasing number of countries. Although this development represents a big step forward, there still remains the issue of benchmarking and interpretation.

For this, internationally comparable data on the stocks of relevant skills are needed.

From the viewpoint of human capital analysis, it would be important to collect the data on workers' knowledge, skills, and competencies in such a way that it is at least possible to gather the related productivity evidence for the same workers or a subsample of them (Stern and Tuijnman 1997). In order to test the relationship between human capital and productivity, the samples for these international surveys should be designed to measure both competence and productivity for the same respondents. This implies collecting data in actual work settings, where productivity can be observed and measured. The primary sampling units would be firms or establishments, and individuals would be sampled within them.

The main alternative would be to take households as the primary sampling units, from which individual respondents would then be drawn. But earnings is the only proxy measure of productivity available for individuals in a household survey, and this is an unsatisfactory measure for the reasons mentioned earlier. Despite this drawback, the household survey approach to the measurement of human capital stocks has offered some exciting new avenues in recent years.

Recent Advances in the Measurement of Human Capital Stocks

At the international level, three new avenues of work on the direct measurement of human capital stocks have been explored in recent years. The first is the International Adult Literacy Survey (IALS), through which data have become available for 12 economically advanced countries so far. The second approach is the collection of new and comparative data on the formal education and informal learning of adults in the workforce. For this, national labour force surveys have typically been employed, although new data have also been collected as part of international skill assessments. A third approach, so far only in the planning stages, entails a further elaboration and extension of the literacy assessment surveys to measure other relevant skill domains. Some of the more salient aspects of these three approaches are described below.

The International Adult Literacy Survey

The IALS started out with two underlying goals. First, the aim was to develop an assessment framework, measurement instruments, and reporting scales that would permit valid and useful comparisons of one important element of human capital, namely the literacy performance among people with a wide range of abilities. If such an assessment could be produced, the second aim was to describe and compare the demonstrated literacy skills of people from a range of different countries. This second aim presented the challenge of comparing literacy performance across cultures and across languages. In some respects this represented a break with practice at the time.

During the postwar years, the level of literacy was usually inferred either from a simple question added to the population census or from survey data showing the percentage of the population that had received at least four years of primary schooling. In all countries, four years of schooling was considered enough to learn to read and write at a basic level. This indirect approach to the measurement of one important aspect of human capital, namely literacy, is still current in many countries. Not surprisingly, it leads to the conclusion that literacy is almost universal in the economically advanced countries of the world. Using this definition, the United Nations Educational, Scientific, and Cultural Organization (UNESCO) routinely reports statistics suggesting literacy rates of close to 100 percent for most OECD countries.

In recent years the relevance of these literacy statistics has been called into question, for three principal reasons. First, required standards of education and skill have increased gradually, so that four or even six or eight years of schooling is no longer considered an adequate foundation level in many countries. Second, a school-based measure denies the dynamic nature of literacy and lifelong learning. Because people learn on the job and develop in their adult roles in the community and at work, it is misleading to rely on initial schooling as a proxy measure of literacy skills. For the same reasons, using initial educational attainment as a measure of human capital stock is certain to misrepresent the actual pool of knowledge and skills available to the labour market. Third, the statistics are based on the questionable notion that literacy can be expressed as a dichotomy: either you have it or you don't. Instead, current understanding of literacy refers to a complex and multidimensional set of traits, dispositions, and competencies that must be measured on continuous scales.

The IALS venture, first conducted in 1994 and 1995, sought to assess literacy performance along a continuum – like a distance scale used to map a journey. Along this continuum, adult proficiency at using written information to function in society ranges from quite limited to very high. This reporting framework recognized that everyone has some level of proficiency, which may or may not be sufficient, given the skills demanded. The framework built on the seminal work of Kirsch, Jungeblut, and Mosenthal (for an overview, see Murray et al. 1997) with respect to the factors that underlie difficulty in adult reading. Previous empirical work had employed theories and models that offered little predictive value or differentiation of level of ability. In contrast, the new framework opened the way to the efficient assessment of adult literacy proficiency.

Literacy was assessed in three domains, each encompassing a common set of skills relevant for diverse tasks. The use of these three parallel literacy scales made it possible to profile and compare the various types and levels of literacy demonstrated by adults in several countries, and by subgroups within those countries. In each domain a scale from 0 to 500 was constructed, upon which tasks of varying difficulty were placed. For analytical purposes, the ranges of scores achieved on each of the three scales were grouped into five proficiency levels (OECD and Statistics Canada 1995, 14). The three domains are:

- *prose literacy* – the knowledge and skills needed to understand and use information from texts, including editorials, news stories, poems, and fiction
- *document literacy* – the knowledge and skills required to locate and use information contained in various formats, including job applications, payroll forms, transportation schedules, maps, tables, and graphics
- *quantitative literacy* – the knowledge and skills required to apply arithmetic operations, either alone or sequentially, to numbers embedded in printed materials, such as balancing a chequebook, figuring out a tip, completing an order form, or determining the amount of interest on a loan from an advertisement.

The same wide-ranging literacy test was administered to a large but representative sample of adults in Europe and North America during the autumn of 1994. In all, more than 23,000 respondents aged 16 to 65 years were interviewed for about 20 minutes and then took a 45-minute literacy skill test in their national languages, in their homes. Because it was thought that adults would be more interested in answering open-ended questions, the instruments did not include any multiple-choice items. All questions were open-ended and taken from "real life" stimuli; they reflected the literacy requirements encountered in everyday life and work.

Testing adult literacy directly necessitates going to people's homes to assess their abilities, in a manner reminiscent of the testing usually done in schools. Thus the IALS was unusual because it combined the techniques of household-based surveys and research with those of educational testing. In each case, the test was accompanied by a background questionnaire to obtain detailed information on demographic and other characteristics of the respondent. The background interview was devoted to obtaining demographic information from the respondents. These data provide a means of exploring how literacy is connected to social, educational, economic, and other variables, and of exploring the extent to which these relationships are similar across cultures.

Each country was obliged to draw a probability sample from which results representative of the civilian, non-institutionalized population aged 16 to 65 could be derived. All samples excluded full-time members of the military and people in institutions such as prisons, hospitals, and psychiatric facilities. Countries were free to sample older adults too, and several did so. Given the length of the interview, as well as the fact that a part of the interview involved the administration of a test to adults, response rates were expected to be low in certain countries, and this was borne out.

The development and management of the IALS were coordinated by Statistics Canada, the statistical arm of the Canadian government, and by the Educational Testing Service, the leading private testing organization in the United States, with crucial extra support provided by the National Center for Education Statistics of the US Department of Education. These organizations were guided by national policymakers and research teams from the participating countries, who agreed on the scope of the survey and helped draw up the definitions adopted and develop the survey design. Three international organizations – OECD, UNESCO, and EUROSTAT, the statistical arm of the Commission of the European Communities – also supported the survey.

The IALS data have enabled researchers and policy analysts to examine for the first time the distribution and determinants of human capital stocks in populations, employing an international comparative dataset containing direct measures of economically relevant skills. In every country surveyed to date, results provide clear evidence of the strength of, and discrepancies in, the relationship between formal educational attainment and literacy skills. Key findings obtained to date include the following (OECD et al. 1997; the chapter "Lifelong Learning for the Knowledge Society: Demand, Supply, and Policy Dilemmas," by Rubenson and Schuetze in this volume):

- Important differences in the levels and distribution of literacy skills exist within and between countries.
- Literacy skill deficits are found not just among socially or economically marginalized groups; they also affect significant groups of adults in all countries surveyed.
- Literacy is strongly related to individual life chances and opportunities.
- Literacy skills, like muscles, are maintained and strengthened through regular use.
- Adults with low literacy skills do not usually acknowledge or recognize that their limited skills can pose problems for participation in social or economic activity.

The micro dataset now available will enable researchers to explore the relationships between formal education, skills, and individual earnings in much more depth. Still lacking, however, are good measures of productivity. It is in linking the evidence on individual skills and earnings with measures of the value added in workplaces that future survey cycles could make an invaluable contribution. Given the necessity of employing the workplace rather than the individual as the unit of data collection and analysis, however, it will be some time before such work can be undertaken at the international level. In the short term, progress in collecting empirical information on skills and productivity is more likely to be made if workers are sampled within specific firms or labour market sectors within countries. Another open question concerns the quality of the relationships between literacy skills and other competencies assumed to carry relevance for economic activity. Exploring these relationships will require testing individuals with instruments designed to measure multiple skills. Achieving this is one of the goals currently being pursued as part of the planned International Life Skills Survey (see below).

Comparative Surveys of Adult Education and Training

Until recently, support for the conviction that adult education and training are complements to initial formal education and can supplement the knowledge and skills acquired there has come mainly from inferences based on the concavity of age-earnings profiles, or from other indirect evidence based on general work in the economics of education, which showed that increased levels of education are associated with, on average, higher personal income (Tuijnman 1989). Direct evidence showing that adult education and training increase productivity has been largely lacking so far. Micro studies of the nature and strength of the relationships between initial schooling and adult education, productivity, and income were generally not available until the late 1980s (see Stern and Tuijnman 1997).

The dearth of empirical information greatly limited the possibility of examining the validity of hypotheses concerning the economic value of investment in adult education and training. Only when adult education and training became more central to the policy concerns of governments in the economically advanced countries did interest in its measurement begin to rebuild. The gradual increase in interest culminated in the early 1990s, when a number of countries finally made funds available to undertake large-scale and even comparative surveys of adult education and training markets. Until then, empirical work on the supply and demand of adult education and training had been based mainly on institutional statistics derived from a variety of administrative sources. Alternatively, studies had used statistics derived from sample surveys that had not been designed as a primary means of collecting adult education or training data.

Not only at the national level but also at the international level, more and better datasets have become available in recent years. At present, at least three datasets hold much promise for analysts interested in the relationships between initial and further education, and the economic and labour market outcomes of human capital investment later in the life span. The first is the Continuing Vocational Training Survey (CVTS) undertaken by countries of the European Union. While still somewhat restricted in coverage and limited in data quality, the CVTS offers a good starting point for developing specific international surveys of adult education, training, and learning more broadly defined. A second advance worth mentioning concerns the development of standardized modules for the collection of adult education and training data; the modules can be administered as part of regular labour force surveys, to yield adult education data that can be related to many other demographic and socioeconomic characteristics of the respondents. Labour force survey data from different countries have also been employed with some success in developing a set of internationally comparative indicators of continuing education and training. Finally, comparative adult education data have been collected as part of the IALS, and work is currently under way to build on and strengthen the available instruments for use in future comparative survey cycles.

The International Life Skills Survey (ILSS)

Currently being designed by survey-design and skill-assessment specialists in North America and Europe, the ILSS is a response to the interest expressed by several countries in building on the success of the IALS. Until now, the work has been financially supported mainly by Canadian and US agencies, although some European countries appear increasingly ready to join the effort.

The ILSS international study team has four short-term objectives related to the validation of the instruments currently under development. First, it hopes to receive feedback on the conceptual framework documents developed for each proposed skill domain. Second, the team hopes to establish a truly international consortium to further refine the measurement protocols and develop the actual test instruments. Third, the team planned to field-test an item pilot survey in a limited number of countries during the first half of 1999. An item pilot is required to provide information on the psychometric performance of the test items. The final short-term goal is to secure the necessary funding for the international and national study teams.

In the medium-term perspective, the goal is to undertake data collection in a limited number of countries to profile the distribution of selected life skills in a sample of the adult population, and to determine the relationships among these skills as well as their associations with aspects of literacy performance. To achieve this, the ILSS aims to extend the measurement protocols used for the IALS in order to assess a range of additional skills thought important to the social and economic success of individuals, firms, and nations. Patterned on the IALS approach, the survey would see the administration of direct performance tests to representative samples of adults aged 16 to 65. Respondents would be interviewed and tested in their homes, using their national languages and paper-and-pencil testing protocols. Current design parameters call for a 16-booklet spiral design in order to make optimal use of the available – but restricted (because of high costs) – testing time.

The survey design currently assesses four skill domains directly and two domains indirectly. Besides the assessments, the survey also includes administration of a background questionnaire to collect information on a number of important socioeconomic and demographic covariates. A module featuring adult education and training questions will also be included in the background questionnaire. Direct assessment will be used to gauge the performance of adults in the following skill domains: prose literacy, document literacy, numeracy, and problem solving. The two skill domains to be measured indirectly are interpersonal skills and teamwork, and computer familiarity.

The long-term objective of the ILSS is to contribute to the knowledge base on human cognition. In pursuing this objective, the survey is expected to also shed new light on the determinants and social and economic consequences of the observed skill distributions. Although this will not in itself ameliorate the problem associated with insufficiently developed productivity measures, the survey will provide researchers and policy analysts with much-improved tools for measuring and understanding human capital.

Concluding Observations

Indirect measures of human capital based on initial educational attainment have limited application in studies of the relationships between knowledge and skills, productivity, and earnings. The two main problems are (1) that educational attainment is not synonymous with acquired competence, and (2) that earnings at best constitute only a poor proxy measure of productivity. Rather than continuing to specify such poor measures of human capital and productivity in econometric models, researchers would do well to employ direct measures of human capital based on assessed life skills and of productivity based on the observed output of work units, in terms of the quantity and quality of goods and services produced.

From a general survey of workers' knowledge, skills, and competencies, we might gain first of all the possibility of discovering how the various skill domains are related – to each other, as well as to predictor variables such as initial education, continuing training, and work experience. Second, there is the possibility of measuring directly how skills are related to productivity. This kind of information would begin to fill the void in the research base to date. Such information would also begin to create a more solid basis for decisions concerning education policy.

Unfortunately, most countries currently lack the financial, scientific, and operational basis for fielding a large-scale and internationally comparative survey that would *both* assess the levels and distributions of life skills of a nested sample of workers within firms, *and* collect information on their productivity. Rather than advocating that countries make a quantum leap into this kind of unknown territory, a more gradualist approach is recommended. Such an approach will take more time but is expected to yield new knowledge and insights at considerably lower risk and cost. In such a gradualist approach, the next logical step would be field-testing and refinement of the instruments and survey designs proposed for use in the International Life Skills Survey.

References
Arrow, K.J. 1973. "Higher Education as a Filter." *Journal of Public Economics* 2: 193-216.
Becker, G.S. 1964. *Human Capital.* New York: Columbia University Press.
Bishop, J.H. 1996. "Overschooling." In A.C. Tuijnman, ed., *The International Encyclopedia of Adult Education and Training,* 2nd ed., 258-65. Oxford: Pergamon Press.
Brown, C., M. Reich, and D. Stern. 1993. "Becoming a High-Performance Work Organization: The Role of Security, Employee Involvement and Training." *International Journal of Human Resource Management* 4: 247-75.
Eliasson, G. 1993. *The Market for Educational Services: A Micro-Based Model of Macro-Economic Growth* (restricted document). Paris: OECD, Centre for Educational Research and Innovation.
Gardner, H. 1985. *Frames of Mind: The Theory of Multiple Intelligences.* New York: Basic Books.
Husén, T. 1967. *International Study of Achievement in Mathematics: A Comparison of Twelve Countries, Vols. 1-2.* Stockholm: Almqvist and Wiksell International.
Jones, S. 1997. "Measuring Adult Basic Skills: A Literature Review." In A. Tuijnman, I.S. Kirsch, and D.A. Wagner, eds., *Adult Basic Skills: Advances in Measurement and Policy Analysis,* 115-38. Cresskil, NJ: Hampton Press.
Kristensen, T. 1962. "Preface." In *Policy Conference on Economic Growth and Investment in Education,* Washington, DC, 16-20 October 1961. Paris: OECD.
Layard, R., and G. Psacharopoulos. 1974. "The Screening Hypothesis and the Returns to Education." *Journal of Political Economy* 82: 985-98.
Lazear, E.P. 1981. "Agency, Earnings Profiles, Productivity, and Hours Restrictions." *American Economic Review* 71: 606-20.
Mincer, J. 1962. "On-the-Job Training: Costs, Returns, and Some Implications." *Journal of Political Economy* 70: S50-S79.
Murray, T.S., I.S. Kirsch, and L. Jenkins, eds. 1997. *Adult Literacy in OECD Countries: Technical Report from the First International Adult Literacy Survey.* Washington, DC: National Center for Education Statistics, US Department of Education.
OECD (Organization for Economic Cooperation and Development). 1996. *Lifelong Learning for All.* Paris: OECD.
–. 1998. *Human Capital Investment: An International Comparison.* Paris: OECD.
OECD and Statistics Canada. 1995. *Literacy, Economy and Society: Results of the First International Adult Literacy Survey.* Paris and Ottawa: OECD and Statistics Canada.
OECD, Human Resources Development Canada, and Statistics Canada. 1997. *Literacy Skills for the Knowledge Society: Further Results of the International Adult Literacy Survey.* Paris and Ottawa: OECD, Human Resources Development Canada, and Statistics Canada.
Psacharopoulos, G. 1985. "Returns to Education: A Further International Update and Implications." *Journal of Human Resources* 20: 584-604.
Schultz, T.W. 1961. "Investment in Human Capital." *American Economic Review* 51,1: 1-22.

Spence, M. 1973. "Job Market Signaling." *Quarterly Journal of Economics* 87: 355-74.

Stern, D., and A.C. Tuijnman. 1997. "Adult Basic Skills: Policy Issues and a Research Agenda." In A.C. Tuijnman, I.S. Kirsch, and D.A. Wagner, eds., *Adult Basic Skills: Advances in Measurement and Policy Analysis*, 1-16. Cresskil, NJ: Hampton Press.

Tuijnman, A.C. 1989. *Recurrent Education, Earnings, and Well-Being: A 50-Year Longitudinal Study of a Cohort of Swedish Men*. Acta Universitatis Stockholmiensis. Stockholm: Almqvist and Wiksell International.

Tuijnman, A.C. 1995. "The Importance of Literacy in OECD Countries." In *Literacy, Economy and Society: Results of the First International Adult Literacy Survey*, 21-6. Paris and Ottawa: OECD and Statistics Canada.

Willis, R.J., and S. Rosen. 1979. "Education and Self-Selection." *Journal of Political Economy* 87: S7-S36.

21

The Development and Use of a Canadian Linked Employer-Employee Survey

H. Krebs, Z. Patak, G. Picot, and T. Wannell

Introduction

The 1990s have witnessed a bumper crop of buzzwords for anyone interested in the economy in general and the labour market in particular. We are working in a *new competitive environment,* making the transition to a *knowledge-based economy.* To thrive in this environment, firms must be *flexible* or *adaptive;* they should develop *high-performance workplace practices.* Employees too must be *adaptive;* they can *empower* themselves by adjusting their *skill set.* Otherwise, they risk becoming *disposable.*

Annoying as they may be, clichés don't reach that status without some underlying truth. Canadian firms and their employees have always faced a competitive, changing environment. Some types of change – particularly those related to microprocessor technologies – have probably accelerated in recent years. The development of a North American free-trade zone has certainly heightened awareness of the competitive environment. And the growing disparity among workers (and would-be workers) – in terms of both earnings and hours – has been well documented. These trends contribute to a general sense that economic change is increasingly difficult to understand, that the costs of change fall mainly upon less adaptable workers, and that even among the "winners" in the labour market, employment is becoming less stable.

Looking at these and other problems, analysts in Statistics Canada and elsewhere have reached the conclusion that two key elements are missing in our understanding of firm performance and worker outcomes. The determinants of how well firms respond to change can be properly studied only in a longitudinal setting that covers many of the firm characteristics and behaviours related to performance. Of particular importance are the practices and policies related to employees, since employees must be the agents of change in the firm. Conversely, the fortunes of employees are intricately tied to what they do on the job and how they interact with the internal forces of change in a firm. Thus the ideal survey instrument would follow an integrated sample of employers and employees over an indefinite period. Some of these elements exist in other Statistics Canada surveys, but not in an integrated design.

The Workplace and Employee Survey (WES) is a new Statistics Canada undertaking designed to provide an integrated view of the activities of employers and their employees. A large-scale pilot of the WES was conducted in 1996, with a production survey scheduled for 1999. In the rest of this chapter we provide an overview of the objectives of the survey, discuss what was learned from the WES pilot study, look at some of the methodological problems, discuss future plans, and provide a summary of some research findings.

Research Objectives:
Why Have a Linked Workplace and Employee Survey?

Advanced economies are constantly evolving. The key stimuli for this evolution are new technologies (particularly information technologies), increasing international competition, and the continued expansion of transnational enterprises. Firms respond in a number of ways: increasingly embracing new technologies, reorganizing or re-engineering their workforces, or resorting to downsizing or other elements of numerical flexibility. For firms, these trends create challenges in the management and development of human resources. For policymakers, education and training are central policy prescriptions for increasing prosperity.

In this evolving environment, firms are thought to have undergone dramatic change in the areas of technology adoption, organizational change, training patterns, business strategies, levels of competition, and the manner in which they engage labour. Workers, on the other hand, experience this evolution through changes in job-creation rates, job stability, wages and wage inequality, training, the use of advanced technologies, and the type of employment contracts available.

Because of a well-developed set of household (worker) surveys, we in Canada have a good understanding of workers' outcomes regarding wages and wage inequality, job stability and layoffs, training, job creation, and unemployment. What is missing on the employees' side is the ability to link these changes to events taking place in firms. Such a connection is necessary if we hope to understand the association between labour market changes and demand-side pressures, which stem from global competition, technological change, and the drive to improve human capital, among other things. Thus, one primary goal of the WES is to establish a link between events occurring in establishments and the outcomes for workers.

The advantage of a linked survey is depicted in Figure 1. This chart displays the main content blocks in the two surveys. Note the reference to establishment and worker outcomes. Analysis of these events can be informed not only by the characteristics of the establishment – as in other firm surveys – but also by the characteristics of the workers. Similarly, worker outcomes can be informed not only by data on the workers themselves, as has always been the case, but also by new establishment data.

Such a link would, for example, allow changes in the levels and distributions of wages of workers to be associated with events occurring in

Figure 1

The link between the establishment survey content, the employee survey content, and outcomes

Employee outcomes:

- wage/earnings/hours polarization
- wage levels by worker type
- training received
- use of technologies
- job tenure

Establishment characteristics:

- technology implemented
- operating revenues and expenditures, payroll, and employment
- business strategies
- unionization
- compensation schemes
- training provided
- mix of full-time/part-time, contract, and temporary employees
- organizational change
- subjective measures of productivity, profitability, etc.
- type of market in which firm competes

Worker/job characteristics:

- education
- age/gender
- occupation, management responsibilities
- work history, tenure
- family characteristics
- unionization
- use of technology
- participation in decision making
- wages and fringe benefits
- work schedule/arrangements
- training taken

Establishment outcomes:

- employment growth
- growth in revenues
- organizational change
- implementation of technologies
- changing human resource practices

establishments, such as the adoption of technology or competing in international markets. Much of the literature on earnings inequality suggests that technology and rising international trade are major contributors to inequality. Research on many other labour market issues would be enhanced by the existence of such a link. Issues that have formerly been considered primarily from the supply side, often within the context of a human capital model, could be viewed increasingly from the demand side of the labour market. This might include issues such as job stability, the determinants of wages, the creation and destruction of different types of jobs, training levels among different types of workers, and so on.

An establishment-worker link would also contribute enormously to improved measurement of a number of establishment-level variables. The characteristics of an establishment's workforce are often an important determinant of the behaviour of a firm. Data on workforce characteristics has been lacking or poorly measured in establishment surveys, however. The link would allow establishment variables – such as training incidence and intensity, occupational and educational distribution of the workforce, use of technology by the workers, various workplace practices such as quality circles, fringe benefit levels, the distribution of wages, and a host of others – to be better measured than in the past. Workers can provide more reliable and detailed data on these variables than can establishment-level respondents.

Hence, an establishment-worker link at the micro level would allow the inclusion of demand-side factors (events occurring in establishments) in research on labour markets. The reliance on primarily supply-side theories and data would be reduced. It would also result in much-improved estimates of many establishment-level variables.

The second goal of the survey is to develop a better understanding of what is indeed occurring in companies in an era of substantial evolution. Just how many companies have implemented new information technologies? On what scale? What kind of training is associated with this? What type of organizational change is occurring in firms? What types of business strategies are firms relying on to thrive during this period of change, and do they vary dramatically across firms? How important are human resource development activities and strategies, or are they largely ignored by most establishments? Do firms that adopt one set of strategies in fact adopt many (e.g., adoption of technologies, innovation, human resource development, and organizational changes)? Is there a set of high-performance workplaces that tend to move on many fronts? These are the kinds of issues addressed in the WES.

While the available household surveys inform us about significant labour market changes, there is no corresponding set of establishment surveys that deal with new concerns. Some limited survey work has been done. The WES is an attempt to extend this in the context of a general worker-workplace survey.

Finally, the third objective is to extend surveying infrastructure. Given the uncertainty regarding some of the new variables being developed, it is likely that the WES content will change during the early years. To a considerable extent, the WES is seen as the development of the infrastructure necessary to conduct integrated establishment-household surveys. The content can be altered through time, although some core content is desirable in order to take advantage of the longitudinal nature of the survey.

There are a number of issues for which integrated data sources such as the WES would be useful. Many relate to technology and innovation, processes that play an increasingly important role in the production process. These in turn influence the outcomes of firms and their workers. Following are some of the related research areas:

- incidence of information technology adoption and innovation in different industries, different size classes, and so on
- training associated with technology adoption
- association between technology adoption and downsizing, the use of contingent labour, organizational change, unionization, and so on
- innovation, technology adoption, and the outcomes for establishments
- innovation, technology adoption, and the outcomes for workers.

These examples relate to technology and competition. There are numerous other areas of possible research based on a longitudinal data source such as the WES, including:

- research on employment dynamics
- extending the human capital model of wage determination to include firm characteristics
- labour unions and their effects on workers and establishments
- nonwage compensation
- training and its impact on firms and workers
- the incidence and effects (on workers and establishments) of new workplace practices
- the incidence and effects of differential business strategies of firms
- job vacancies and skill shortages, and job and worker turnover.

Many of these topics would benefit from the use of longitudinal integrated establishment-household data. Dynamics will become a central research focus when longitudinal data become available.

Overview of the WES Pilot Survey

To test both the feasibility and efficacy of a dual survey to address some of the issues noted earlier, both pre-testing and a large-scale pilot were conducted. Early pre-testing confirmed that employers were able to answer the types of questions proposed and provide lists of employees from which intra-establishment samples could be drawn. Human Resources Development Canada (HRDC) provided funding for a large-scale pilot to test more fully the operational, methodological, and analytical feasibility of the project.

The pilot aimed to interview approximately 1,000 employers in selected strata from a production-scale sample of 5,500 employers. Up to seven employees would then be sampled within each selected establishment. The rest of this section outlines some basic issues addressed in the development of the WES and the content of each of the surveys, sketches the frame creation and sampling methodology, and summarizes the operations.

Some Issues in the Development of Integrated Surveys such as the WES

While administrative (taxation) data have been used by Statistics Canada to link workers and establishments (Picot 1998a), it was decided that such a source would not be capable of addressing the vast majority of issues of interest to Canadian researchers. Thus, the decision was made to proceed with a pilot survey or, in reality, two surveys – one establishment, the other household – to obtain data on both workers and establishments. This has the tremendous advantage of being able to accommodate the necessary content, subject of course to response burden constraints. It also has the advantage of being able to collect the data at the most appropriate level in the enterprise structure for the type of research at hand. These are tremendous advantages, but there are also a number of important issues that must be addressed, as in any new venture.

Cost

Developing surveys is more costly than developing administrative data. If, however, the administrative data are incapable of providing the information needed, then the decision is not between choosing a survey or administrative data approach but rather whether the information that can be provided from a survey warrants the cost.

Response Rates

Achieving high response rates in both the establishment and worker surveys is an issue, perhaps the central issue in the conduct of linked surveys. This appears to be true whether the establishment is the first level in the survey and then workers in the establishments are sampled, or whether it is done the other way around. The response rate issue seems to appear at the interface between the workers and the firm, no matter which way the survey is done. This issue was encountered in the WES pilot survey, where the worker response rate was 55 percent. This low rate was due primarily to the process used to make the connection between the worker and the interviewer, and steps are being taken to raise this rate to acceptable levels. This is discussed in the next section.

Which to Sample First: Worker or Firm?
There are substantive reasons for sampling either the worker or the firm first. For example, in developing a longitudinal survey, the unit sampled first is likely to become the primary longitudinal unit in the survey, and this has substantive implications. There are also cost implications. Suppose one is seeking a sample of, say, 30,000 workers. If establishments are sampled first, this could be achieved by sampling 5,000 establishments and picking an average of six workers per establishment. If the worker is selected first, the 30,000 workers may work for almost as many establishments, resulting in a very large (and expensive) establishment sample. This outcome is due to the manner in which workers are distributed among establishments. There will be relatively few cases where multiple workers in the sample work for the same establishment.

To test this, we used a linked company-worker administrative data source. Thirty thousand workers were selected at random, and they were found to work in 18,200 different companies. The number of separate establishments would have been even greater under such a sampling approach. Likely in the order of 20,000 establishments would have had to be sampled to achieve a random sample of 30,000 workers. Since an establishment survey is more expensive to conduct than a worker survey (if one uses personal visits to obtain high-quality data), having such a large number of establishments in order to achieve a sufficiently large sample of workers can increase costs tremendously.

One could reduce the number of workers and establishments, but for any given amount of money, a smaller sample is possible if workers rather than firms are sampled first. One could cluster the worker sample by establishment to reduce the number of establishments in the sample, but this is in essence the opposite approach, where the establishment is sampled first. Furthermore, the high worker separation rate (20 percent per year) means that in a longitudinal survey, a large number of new establishments would have to be added to the survey each year, as large numbers of workers move to new establishments. Hence, for both cost and substantive reasons, establishments were sampled first in the pilot WES, and workers selected within establishments.

Making the Surveys Longitudinal

The real gains from such surveys will be the extent to which they focus on dynamics. What is the association between a change in an establishment practice and the outcomes for the workers or the establishment? Longitudinal data are required to answer such questions. Should the surveys be longitudinal in the establishment, the workers, or both? Complexity in the sample design and increased costs are associated with the latter alternative, and it is likely unrealistic. Making the worker the primary longitudinal unit of analysis and then sampling the establishment entails the cost implications mentioned above. Making the survey longitudinal in the establishment allows changes in establishment practices to be associated with worker or firm outcomes. This is the approach proposed for the WES. The survey will also track workers for two years and will include retrospective questions for recent hires. This will provide data on one transition, thus making the use of "fixed-effects" models and other similar longitudinal analytical approaches possible.

Introducing New Content

The opportunity to collect a wide range of data on workers and firms leads to the introduction of a number of new variables that have been little used in other surveys. Technological change in establishments, the types of technologies employed, and workplace practices as they affect workers are examples of difficult-to-measure concepts that are central to many of the research issues that one would like to address using such integrated worker-firm data. Furthermore, traditional measures such as operating revenues and expenditures and training expenditures may also be difficult to measure accurately at the establishment level. Thus, there are difficult challenges in operationalizing the content of the surveys, particularly the establishment survey.

Providing Measures of Establishment Performance

The ultimate goal of the integrated surveys is to focus on the association between worker and establishment characteristics on the one hand and worker and establishment outcomes (performance) on the other. Worker outcome variables such as wages, fringe benefits, training, hours worked, job stability, and so on are measured in a relatively straightforward manner. Establishment performance measures can prove more difficult. Employment-related outcome measures could be relatively easily provided at the establishment level. In multi-establishment enterprises, however, financial measures are typically not available at the establishment or location level but rather at the company or enterprise level. Information on operating revenues and expenditures can be sought, but some establishments have difficulty providing such information. Obtaining quantitative estimates of productivity at the establishment level economy-wide (outside of manufacturing and related industries) can prove difficult. Some effort is needed to obtain reliable establishment performance measures. Links to administrative data such as corporate taxation data can assist in the production of performance measures, and this approach will be used in the Canadian survey.

Survey Content

Two separate questionnaires were developed for the pilot: one for employers and another for employees. The employer questionnaire contains a broad range of information. So broad, in fact, that we anticipated that several respondents might be required to answer it completely, particularly in large establishments. As such, the questionnaire was parcelled into blocks – each with a separate cover sheet – so that each block could be directed to the appropriate respondent. A brief description of each block follows.

- *Workforce Characteristics and Job Organization:* The work arrangements of employees (full-time/part-time, permanent, seasonal, on-site/off-site, etc.), recent hiring and separations, and the presence of unfilled vacancies. All questions in this section were broken down into five occupational groups.
- *Compensation:* Variable pay plans, gross payroll, nonwage benefits, and the distribution of earnings in the company. Most questions captured occupational detail.
- *Training:* The presence of formal training programs, which occupational groups received training in the past year, how training was funded, and how much was spent on training.
- *Human Resource Function:* Who has responsibility for human resources; the level of employee involvement in decision making; and the incidence, type, extent, and effects of recent organizational change.
- *Collective Bargaining:* The presence and membership (by occupation) of collective bargaining groups, treatment of "flexibility" issues in contracts, work stoppages and grievances.
- *Establishment Performance:* Operating revenues and expenditures, change from the previous year, variability in revenues by quarter, and foreign ownership.
- *Business Strategy:* Respondents rate the importance of elements of business strategy, estimate their distribution of sales by market area, and specify the number of competitors in their market.
- *Innovation:* Major innovations introduced in the past three years.
- *Technology Use:* Overall computer usage in establishment, specific major technology implementations in the past three years (hardware/software, computer-controlled technologies, other technologies), and the effects of the implementations.

- *Use of Government Programs:* Establishment use of grants and loans, employee-related programs, tax provisions, information services, and other ventures with government.

The employee questionnaire was not as clearly blocked as the employer questionnaire, since it involved only a single respondent. The questionnaire covered: job characteristics, requirements when hired, hours of work, pay and benefits, working off-site, leave, promotions, technology, training, participation in decision making, work stoppages, recent work history, education, family situation, and membership in designated employment equity groups. While the questionnaire covers a fairly wide range of topics, the pilot demonstrated that it was not overly burdensome for respondents.[1]

Survey Frame and Sampling

The WES is based on the notion of a workplace as the microdata unit where labour supply and demand is resolved. Although the responsibility for staffing is included in this concept, it more importantly includes the organization of a group of employees to achieve a common purpose. Our ultimate target population includes workplaces in all industries and geographic areas of the country. Ideally, the WES would operate as a two-stage survey. The first stage would involve drawing a sample of workplaces large enough to produce estimates for industries with similar characteristics at the provincial level. The second stage would draw a large enough sample of workers within each workplace to permit variance calculations. In conducting a survey, however, our concepts and intentions are tempered by operational constraints and the availability of data.

Statistics Canada's Business Register (BR) – a registry of all businesses in Canada – is the primary frame resource for business surveys. The BR organizes business entities into a hierarchy of four statistical levels: enterprises, companies, establishments, and locations. Although the location level is conceptually the closest to a workplace, several factors led us to sample from the establishment level for the pilot survey.[2] An establishment can be thought of as the smallest organizational unit, consisting of at least one physical location, that can provide a complete set of input and output statistics. For most businesses, establishments and locations are one and the same. However, establishments in many larger enterprises – particularly those in the financial, communications, and utilities sectors – may include separately managed operations in a number of locations.[3] For these complex units, the WES sampled smaller units within the establishment using information from the BR, from auxiliary files, and, in rare cases, from contact with respondents. Thus the employer survey evolved into a two-stage sample and the employee survey a three-stage sample.

At the first stage of sampling, the frame is stratified by region, industry, and employment size. Sampling fractions vary by size group so that larger employers have a greater probability of being included in the sample. In the second stage, complex establishments drawn in the first stage are subdivided into smaller units and a sample of these units is drawn. In the third stage, a sample of workers is drawn from employer-provided lists in each workplace.

Operations

The unique content and methodology of the WES placed unusual demands on survey operations. Many of the required operations had no recent precedents at Statistics Canada. What we provide here is a thumbnail sketch of the survey operations without too much detail on the logistical permutations involved.

Preparation for fieldwork began with the examination of the sample (primary sampling units, or PSUs) for potentially complex establishments, that is, those with multiple workplace locations. Complex establishments were subdivided into secondary sampling units (SSUs). In the sample the SSUs were selected at a rate of one per stratum. This process was necessary to overcome the problem of having "establishments" in the sample that had multiple workplace locations.

Interviewers in the regions contacted employer respondents to schedule on-site interviews. Interviewers had a number of tasks to perform during these visits:

- Complete all possible sections of the employer questionnaire with the available respondents. Document any problems regarding survey content or procedures.
- Leave appropriate sections of the questionnaire behind when required respondents are not available.
- Take sample of employees from employer list according to methodologist's written instructions.[4] Record names of sampled employees and, at interviewer's discretion, other information about them.
- Transmit sampled employees' names to Winnipeg Regional Office.

Sampled employees were to fill out the contact/consent forms – which asked for information on convenient times and numbers for a telephone interview – and return them by fax or prepaid mail. About two-thirds returned the forms and about 85 percent of those agreed to participate. Employees were then interviewed by phone.

Methodological Problems and Responses

Primary and Secondary Sampling Units

The employer portion of the WES was originally conceived as a stratified single-stage design with establishment as the PSU. It became apparent that, for approximately 10 percent of the sample, the target unit of interest – secondary sampling unit – corresponding to a physical location was different from the PSU. This came about as a result of many larger establishments having multiple workplaces (locations on the Business Register).

Collecting data from every location of a complex establishment was not feasible due to sample size constraints imposed on the pilot survey. A second stage was added to the survey design to facilitate the subsampling of PSUs. Each in-sample complex establishment was stratified by type of SSU (e.g., head office, typical bank branch). For the pilot, one location was selected from each SSU stratum.

The employee portion of the WES added a second/third stage to the employer survey. After a workplace reporting unit (WRU) had been sampled, a list of employees was obtained from the employer, followed by the selection of a systematic sample of six (or seven) employees.[5] SSUs with fewer than seven employees were sampled exhaustively. The employee sample size of six was a somewhat arbitrary compromise among a number of factors: employer sample efficiency (fewer employees, more employers), the desire for at least rudimentary within-establishment variance estimates (more employees in each workplace), employer response burden (fewer employees in each workplace), and the overall sample sizes of employers and employees needed to make inferences about meaningfully disaggregated groups of each (experience with other surveys indicated about 6,000 employers and 20,000 to 40,000 employees).[6] The pilot sample consisted of approximately 3,500 employees, of whom 1,960 responded to the survey, representing 544 SSUs.

Thus, the response rates in the pilot survey were approximately 80 percent among establishments and 55 percent among the workers. The establishment response rate was acceptable, but many linked surveys appear to have low response rates at the second stage of the survey. In this case, the low worker response rate was due to the process used to contact the workers (through the establishments), rather than the content of the survey itself. Other Canadian surveys have used similar content and registered response rates in the 80 to 95 percent range. In the pilot, employers forwarded an information slip to the workers, and the workers were asked to contact Statistics Canada so that a telephone survey could be conducted. This is asking a lot of respondents, and the low response rate is not surprising.

Other approaches are being currently tested. In one case, workers are asked to complete a small questionnaire (of perhaps five questions) and return it to Statistics Canada, along with their phone number. They are then contacted and a larger telephone interview conducted. It has been found in testing that asking for workers' active participation through the completion of a small survey could raise response rates to the 70 percent range.

Other approaches are also being tested. Employers will be asked to provide the employees' work telephone number. Statistics Canada interviewers could then actively seek an interview, rather than passively waiting for potential respondents to contact them. The possibility of the interviewer speaking to the employees while conducting the employer interview at the establishment to obtain the employees' consent and telephone number is also being considered. It is believed that these approaches, possibly taken together, will bring the worker response rates to an acceptable level, matching those of the establishments.

Multistage Estimation
In a typical multistage survey, the total estimated variance can be decomposed into components computed individually for each stage of sampling, provided that at least two units have been selected in each stratum at each stage. Failure to satisfy this criterion (the WES sampled one unit per stratum in the second stage of selection) forced us to find an alternative to estimating proper multistage variances. To this end, we made the simplifying assumption that the first-stage units had been selected with replacement and proceeded to compute the corresponding variances.

The Statistics Canada Generalized Estimation System (GES) was used to compute the design weights for the sampled locations (SSU) of complex establishments. Locations of simple establishments were assigned a weight of 1. Second-stage estimates were produced using the combined ratio estimator. The auxiliary variable, establishment employment, was not collected directly; it was derived from either the information available on the Business Register or data collected by SEPH.

A second run of the GES produced the first-stage design weights for the sampled establishments. The parameters of interest were computed using the combined ratio estimator. The auxiliary variable was once again employment. It was first computed using data carried by the BR and later adjusted to agree with SEPH estimates deemed to be more current and sufficiently reliable. Auxiliary information was applied at the industry/region level, with an exception discussed in the subsection "Pilot Meta Results" below.

The GES was also used to compute the design weights for employee records. Each selected individual was given a weight, ignoring nonresponse, equal to the number of employees in an SSU divided by the number of employees in the corresponding sample. This was also the calibrated weight, since the number of employees in the SSU was taken directly from the employer questionnaire.[7] The final employee design weight, then, is the product of the SSU weight and the employee's calibrated weight. In the production survey, the employee weights will be post-stratified to match known characteristics of interest (e.g., gender, education, occupation) from the Labour Force Survey.

Pilot Meta Results

The employer sample consisted of 1,006 live, 53 dead, 54 inactive, 1 receivership, 11 holding company, and 169 out-of-scope PSUs. Estimates of totals for some 897 variables were computed using 1,025 establishments (all except "live/complete refusal"). At the national level, the coefficients of variation (CV) for *Gross Operating Revenue, Gross Expenditures,* and *Total Gross Payroll* were 0.0887, 0.0654, and 0.0201, respectively, indicating good reliability.[8] Overall, still at the national level, two-thirds of the estimates had a CV between 0 and 0.33.

On the employee side, 1,960 persons provided either partial or complete responses. As an example of the reliability of the totals computed from the employee portion, the CVs at the national level for *Family Income* and *Salary* were 0.0236 and 0.0230. Overall, still at the national level, three-quarters of the estimates had a CV between 0 and 0.33.

Future Plans

Cross-sectional surveys of workplace practices and outcomes – the WES pilot included – suffer from some common methodological problems that hamper workplace research. First, in a cross-section it is quite difficult to establish the timing of the introduction of workplace practices, their dissemination throughout the workplace, and the lag time necessary to have an impact on workplace performance. Thus it is difficult to infer the causal direction between performance and practice, even though the relationship may appear very strong. Second, the estimates of cross-sectional relationships may be affected by a survival bias. In effect, the cross-section represents a truncated distribution of workplace performance: failed businesses are not observed. It is entirely probable that a number of practices will increase both the probability of improved performance and the probability of workplace death. Without being able to account for past deaths, cross-sectional surveys will tend to overestimate the returns to relatively risky practices, such as product innovation, reorganizations, and technological investment.

These methodological issues can be overcome by true panel data – a starting cohort of workplaces that is followed over time. Reinterviewing the panel at regular intervals would allow researchers to follow the introduction of workplace policies and practices and infer their effect on workplace outcomes, while properly accounting for the effects of deaths within the cohort. Current plans are for the WES to treat its first cross-section in April 1999 as the starting cohort of an ongoing workplace panel. The rest of this section outlines in greater detail our plans for the survey.

Inaugural Cross-Sectional Survey

The initial production survey was scheduled to be in the field in April 1999.

The planned usable sample for this survey was about 6,000 workplaces and about 25,000 employees. Unlike the pilot survey strategy of sampling establishments and then subsampling locations within complex establishments, the production sample would be drawn from the location level of the Business Register. This more efficient sampling design has been enabled by increased BR profiling efforts in the banking and insurance sectors. The final sample was to be selected in January 1999. Sample restrictions will be similar to those described for the pilot survey.

Basic Elements of the WES Longitudinal Design

Workplace

Our working assumption is to follow locations for a minimum of five years from their selection into the sample. One of the reasons we chose to sample at the location level is the stability of the statistical unit at this level. While ownership changes can trigger deaths and rebirths at higher levels (enterprise, company, and establishment), location deaths can be triggered only by the location actually closing up shop or through a major change in the products or services produced at the location. No matter how stable the statistical unit, there will still be sample attrition over time – due to both location deaths and refusals. In the third year and in each subsequent odd-year sample, attrition by death will be handled by selecting new entrants from a pool of births.

This design yields a cross-sectionally representative sample in odd years. In addition, these cross-sections form the basis of overlapping panels: locations active in year 1, locations active in year 3, and so on. Each subsequent panel could, in principle, run indefinitely. In practice, we will monitor response burden and refusal attrition carefully after year 3 to determine our sampling strategy for year 5 and beyond. The sample will not be cross-sectionally representative in even years due to the lack of information on new births.

Employee

An "ideal" employer-employee survey would follow employers and employees for long periods of time. Employees, however, change employers with some frequency. To follow them from employer to employer and collect data from each subsequent employer would be very costly. Accordingly, our original plan was to follow employees for as long as they were with the establishment they were originally sampled in and for one period thereafter. Similar to the establishment sample, sample attrition would be handled by selecting new employees from a pool of new hires since the first sample. A follow-up to our pilot showed, however, that not all employers could put together lists of new employees. Rather than continue with an asymmetrical sample, a different strategy was developed.

Employees sampled in the first year will be interviewed for two consecutive years. An "exit" questionnaire will be administered to those employees no longer with the same employer in the second year regardless of the reason for exit. The employee sample will be redrawn in the third year using a pool of all current employees, yielding a new cohort of employees. The two-year cycle would then be repeated for the selected employees in the third year. Under this design, a set of retrospective questions for recently hired employees had to be added to the first-cycle questionnaire so that transitions into and out of the employer would be covered by the survey.

Operational Features and Cost
As a result of the workplace and employee plans outlined above, the WES collection will alternate between relatively easier and relatively more difficult years. In odd-numbered years all the operations outlined above will be carried out. In even-numbered years, we will not be sampling any new locations or employees so there is no need to send interviewers into the field. All the information will be collected by telephone using contact information captured the previous year.

Starting in the 1998-99 fiscal year, the WES will be funded directly from the government's main accounts as part of a package of new survey initiatives. The WES program, including in-house analysis, will cost an average of $3.2 million (approximately US$2.2 million) per year over the first full cycle.

A Summary of Some Preliminary Findings from the Pilot Survey
In order to assess the quality and relevance of the pilot WES data, a number of research projects were undertaken. This section provides a summary of some findings from one such project: the association between computer use and training. Because of space considerations, the details of the research, including the econometrics, cannot be reported. Such details are available in a separate paper (Picot 1998b).

Why Focus on Computer Use and Training?
The extensive adoption of information technologies and the increase in international competition has focused attention on training as a means of increasing the skills of workers in this more technological and competitive environment. There is particular concern regarding the level of training in Canada because of this country's low incidence, by international standards, of employer-provided training (Lynch 1994). This section uses the new linked pilot employer-employee database to address issues regarding the use of computers, training, and the acquisition of skills related to their use.

The analysis that follows makes use of the linked employer-employee data in a number of ways. When posing questions regarding the association between technology use and training, past research has employed data from establishment surveys. Hence, little was known about the characteristics of the workforce. Here, we are able to focus on training and technology information from the establishment survey, and control for the characteristics of the workers (education, age, and occupation). Data on such characteristics can be reasonably collected only from a worker survey; firms are usually unable to reliably provide such data. Our controls are not restricted to characteristics of the employees from the worker survey; we can also incorporate controls related to the firm from the establishment survey. Furthermore, we are not confined to training measures provided only in the establishment survey. Questions on the worker survey can provide much more detail on the training taken, and be matched with questions on technology use from the establishment survey. With questions on training from both the employer and employee surveys, we are able to compare results when using each, to determine the robustness of the associations and whether measurement is an issue.

Technology use and human resource development are increasingly seen as interrelated. It has been argued by Mincer (1989) that technological change and the demand for human capital are complementary. Firms that have as a business strategy the adoption of higher-level technologies will demand higher-skilled workforces, both of which are associated with a higher level of training. Using primarily industry-level data, the association between higher rates of technological change and increased training levels has been noted in a number of studies (McMullen 1996; Betcherman et al. 1997; Lillard and Tan 1986; Bartel 1989; Bartel and Sicherman 1995; Baldwin et al. 1995). More generally, Lynch and Black (1995) have found that employers who have made large investments in physical capital (relative to employment) are more likely to train their workers.

This study differs from many of the earlier ones in a number of ways. We focus on computers and computer-based technologies (CBTs) exclusively, not technology in a more general sense. We can also control for worker and establishment characteristics, something that is possible because of the linked nature of the data. Such data have not previously been available in Canada. Furthermore, the information on training used here is provided by the worker; we do not employ the training data from the establishments in this analysis. The worker survey provides more training detail; many firms know little about the training taken by their workers. Workers are more likely to be able to provide an accurate picture of both incidence and intensity of training. Finally, the analysis is conducted at the micro level, not at the industry level as in some earlier work. Industries consist of a very heterogeneous set of firms – some adopt technologies while others do not; some have high levels of training while others do not (Baldwin 1998). It is more appropriate to test the notion that technology use and a firm's training patterns are complementary at the level of the establishment rather than the industry.

The introduction and use of computers and CBTs may lead to higher training levels for two reasons. First, firms adopting technologies generally have more highly skilled and educated workers, and earlier studies have indicated a strong association between education level and training (Picot 1987; Simpson et al. 1993; Lynch and Black 1995; de Broucker 1997). Second, the adoption and use of a new technology is likely to lead to increased training requirements if companies wish to maximize the benefits of the technology. These training requirements would likely exist no matter what the education level of the employees. The latter point is of particular interest in this chapter. We want to know whether, after controlling for the educational and other characteristics of workers, establishments that adopt computer-based technologies and workers that use computers train at higher levels than other workers.

Computer Use on the Job: General and Specialized Applications

While more than half of the workers in the sample used computers, they use them for many different applications. About 85 percent of users focused on short-time or general applications and 15 percent on specialized applications. Women are much more likely than men to be "general" users. There is a general consensus that technology is skill-biased. In this work, the probability of using a computer rises with educational attainment. However, users employing "general" applications were found at all educational levels above elementary school. This is because clerks, as well as managers, use computers for general applications. Specialized applications are concentrated among those with postsecondary education, so that increased use of these applications would lead to a higher (relative) demand for more highly educated workers.

The Association Between Computer Use and Training

The use of a computer increased significantly (by up to a factor of 2) the likelihood that a worker will undergo training, even after controlling for differences in education, age, and so on. This result was derived from a logistic model where the unit of analysis was the worker and where the dependent variable was 1 if the worker had taken training during the past year and zero otherwise. It was found that the more intense or specialized the computer use, the greater the probability of training and the longer the duration of training. There was also a positive association between the likelihood of training and many workplace practices, such as the use of quality circles, self-directed work groups, and total quality management. This supports the notion that establishments implement a series of human resource practices besides training in the drive for increased productivity.

The establishment data on the adoption of computer technology informed us that most establishments that implement a computer-based technology provide some training to the workers affected. Formal employer-based training is by no means the primary method by which users of computer technologies acquire the skills necessary for particular applications, however. Data from the worker survey indicated that informal and on-the-job training play a much larger role. This held true for both general and specialized applications. It is clear that when considering the process whereby workers acquire the skills necessary to use computer technology, on-the-job training and self-learning have to be central, and one cannot focus only on formal employer-based training or any type of formal training. It is not clear whether the importance of informal training is due to the lack of formal training being provided by the employer or because this is the most efficient way to acquire the skills.

It is evident, however, that the use of a computer or the adoption of a computer-based technology does lead to increased training levels. This is consistent with earlier work. These increased levels are due not only to the characteristics of workers who use computer-based technologies or the types of establishments that implement them. There is an additional kick to training levels even after controlling for such characteristics. One would expect such an increase to raise productivity levels associated with the implementation and use of the technologies.

The goal of the projects, including the one briefly reported here, was to provide demonstrative, not definitive, research. All of the findings are preliminary. The sample used in the pilot was quite small (750 establishments and 2,000 workers) and not representative of the Canadian economy. It consisted of a number of industry-region combinations that can be thought of as case-study in scale. The pilot data, however, did provide the opportunity to control for both worker and establishment characteristics when addressing various issues, something that is quite important for the reasons discussed in the text, and not previously possible in Canada. When the production version of this survey is run in early 1999 and is analysed, the research necessary to validate and extend these results will be possible.

Notes

1 Typically employee interviews lasted about 25 minutes. Employer interviews averaged about one and a half hours, including the sampling of employees.
2 For more details, see "Frame Allocation for the Workplace and Employee Survey," Sharon Wirth, Business Surveys Methods Division.
3 The subestablishment units sampled were not necessarily statistical locations. Please see the section on Workplace Reporting Units for more details.
4 Interviewers were provided with a look-up table that provided starting numbers and selection intervals for specific employment size ranges of workplaces. In the pilot, no allowance was made for ordered lists (e.g., alphabetically or by seniority) in the selection procedure. Ordering of the lists will be a moot point in the production survey, since a truly random sampling routine will be included in the interviewers' capture application.
5 Within an establishment, employees were selected using a random starting point followed by equal intervals to reach the desired sample size for the size of the establishment. For

example, in an establishment of 50 employees with an indicated starting point of 3 and an interval of 8, the interviewer would select the 3rd, 11th, 19th, 27th, 35th, and 43rd employees from the list.

6   In studies subsequent to the pilot, an average employee sample of six proved to be optimal in terms of minimizing the variance of employer and employee estimates given the relative cost of each type of interview. One problem that did emerge was the high variance of employee estimates in several strata with very large workplaces. For these, the maximum employee sample size will be doubled to 12 for the production survey.

7   The reported SSU employment could, conceivably, be different from the number of employees on the list used by the interviewers for sample selection. Unfortunately, this number was not recorded; it could have provided a measure of nonsampling error.

8   As a point of reference, Statistics Canada policy allows estimates with CVs of up to 0.16 to be published without qualification; estimates with CVs between 0.16 and 0.33 may be published with some indication that the estimate is highly variable; and estimates with CVs greater than 0.33 are to be suppressed.

References

Baldwin, J. 1998. "Are There High-Tech Industries or Only High-Tech Firms?" Mimeo. Analytical Studies Branch. Ottawa: Statistics Canada.

Baldwin, J.R., T. Gray, and J. Johnson. 1995. "Technology Use, Training and Plant-Specific Knowledge in Manufacturing Establishment." Research Paper No. 86, Analytical Studies Branch. Ottawa: Statistics Canada.

Bartel, A. 1989. "Formal Employee Training Programs and Their Impact on Labour Productivity: Evidence from a Human Resources Survey." National Bureau of Economic Research Working Paper No. 3026. Cambridge, MA: NBER.

Bartel, A., and N. Sicherman. 1995. "Technological Change and Skill Acquisition of Younger Workers." National Bureau of Economic Research Working Paper No. 5107. Cambridge, MA: NBER.

Betcherman, G., N. Leckie, and K. McMullen. 1997. *Developing Skills in the Canadian Workplace: The Results of the Ekos Workplace Training Survey.* CPRN Study No. W/02. Ottawa: Canadian Policy Research Networks.

de Broucker, P. 1997. "Job-Related Education and Training – Who Has Access?" *Education Quarterly Review (Statistics Canada),* 4: 10-31.

Lillard, L., and H. Tan. 1986. "Private Sector Training: Who Gets It and What Are Its Effects." Road Monograph R-3331-DOL/RC.

Lynch, Lisa M. 1994. "Payoffs to Alternation Training Strategies at Work." In R.B. Freeman, ed., *Working Under Different Rules.* Chicago: Russell Sage Foundation.

Lynch, L., and S. Black. 1995. "Beyond the Incidence of Training: Evidence from a National Employers Survey." National Bureau of Economic Research Working Paper No. 5231. Cambridge, MA: NBER.

McMullen, Kathryn. 1996. *Skill and Employment Effects of Computer-Based Technology; The Results from the Working with Technology Survey II.* Ottawa: Canadian Policy Research Networks.

Mincer, J. 1989. "Human Capital Responses to Technological Change in the Labour Market." National Bureau of Economic Research Working Paper No. 3207. Cambridge, MA: NBER.

Picot, G. 1987. "Unemployment and Training." Research Paper No. 2, Analytical Studies Branch. Ottawa: Statistics Canada.

–. 1998a. "Integrating Establishment and Household Data: Development Work Underway in Canada." Mimeo. Presented at the International Statistical Meetings, Mexico, for Analytical Studies Branch, Statistics Canada.

–. 1998b. "Computer Technologies, Training, and International Competition." Paper presented at the Linked Employer-Employee Conference, Washington, DC, for Analytical Studies Branch, Statistics Canada.

Simpson, W., R. Sproule, and D. Him. 1993. "Specification of On-the-Job Training Incidence." Mimeo. Winnipeg: University of Manitoba.

22
Monitoring Workplace Change in the European Union
Kevin P. O'Kelly

Introduction

The European Foundation was established in 1975 to advise the institutions of the European Union (EU) on medium- to long-term developments in living and working conditions, develop ideas and policy proposals in the light of practical experience, identify factors that lead to change, and contribute to the planning process within the EU.

In the context of the workplace, this mandate means monitoring developments and trends in the organization of work and job design, and identifying problems arising in the employment relationship. The work of the Foundation over almost a quarter-century has included comprehensive studies of industrial relations, occupational health and safety, the impact of technology, and employee participation.

The Foundation does not undertake research itself but, through its Administrative Board, identifies topics and trends of key importance and contracts academic and research institutions within the member states to undertake studies on these developments. The Foundation brings together the results of these studies and, working with researchers, provides EU policymakers with information on which to base their decisions. The Foundation, therefore, acts as a central repository of information and ideas for the European Commission, the Council of Ministers, the European Parliament, the social partners, and the governments of the member states.

Since the beginning, employee participation has been a key focus of the Foundation's work, but in more recent years the whole issue of workplace change and new forms of work organization has come to the fore. Over the past few years, a number of relevant research studies have been undertaken to monitor changes in work organization, working conditions, and trends in employment.

Recent Research Projects

During the 1990s, the Foundation commissioned a number of research projects related to work organization and working conditions. In this chapter, I discuss three EU-wide surveys in particular. These three projects used different methodologies for the field work and are examples of the range of approaches taken by the Foundation.

European Survey on Working Conditions

In 1991 and 1996, the Foundation carried out two surveys into the working environment across the EU, in cooperation with the national statistical agencies and as part of the EUROBAROMETER household survey in all member states. A representative sample of the total active population was selected, either employed or self-employed. The survey was based on interviews with individuals in their homes. The target sample was 1,000 cases per country, except 500 in Luxembourg and 2,000 in Germany (1,000 each in the former East and West parts of that country). In fact, close to 16,000 interviews were conducted; some 60.5 percent of these were kept in the sample for analysis.

At the national level, samples were generally shown to be over-representative of some sectors, such as services and public administration, whereas other sectors, such as agriculture, were underrepresented. As the respondent selection was done on a random basis, there was a greater rate of refusal among the underrepresented categories, and this had to be corrected through weighting.

The survey questionnaire had some 40 questions covering a range of thematic topics: physical environment and design of workplace, organizational environment, social environment, and occupational risks. The results were analysed around these topics by country, sector, occupation, form of employment, gender, age, and company size. The results of the two surveys were also compared.

Limitations to the methodology used in this survey call for some caution in interpreting the data. First, a difference in the workplace structures and distribution of business sectors between the member states means that the results differ from one country to another. Second, the sample size of 1,000 workers in each member state is small in the context of the overall EU workforce, and the number of cases in each group may be small in some countries. Third, legal and cultural differences between the countries may influence the way the questions are understood and answered. For example, in some northern member states, the concept of the working environment is well understood and is an accepted part of normal work, whereas in other countries less emphasis is placed on it in the daily work situation. Fourth, the survey describes working conditions as perceived by the individual, so there is an element of subjectivity in the responses. Taking these limitations into consideration, however, the survey does provide a comprehensive picture of working conditions.

Some Key Results

The survey showed that absenteeism due to work-related health problems affects almost a quarter of the EU workforce (23 percent). Stress (28 percent) and back pain (30 percent) are the two most common work-related health problems, and such problems are often connected with poor working conditions.

Comparing the two surveys, the pace of work has increased during the 1990s and repetitive and monotonous work is still very common – 37 percent of workers perform short repetitive tasks while 45 percent work at monotonous jobs. Worker autonomy over the pace of work increased from 64 percent (1991) to 72 percent (1996), which still left 28 percent of workers with little or no control.

Computers and automation are now important features of the workplace. Some 38 percent of all workers use computers occasionally (41 percent of employees) and they are a permanent feature for 18 percent of workers (20 percent of employees). More than a third of Dutch workers use computers all or almost all the time, compared with only 5 percent in Greece. These numbers on computer use increase when gender and occupations are considered, with 22 percent of female workers using computers all the time. Naturally, white-collar workers are also frequent users; computers are a permanent feature for almost 50 percent of clerical workers.

Finally, the survey found that 45 percent of employees were involved in organizational issues within their production unit or work team; 50 percent were consulted by their manager on changes in work organization or on working conditions. There are considerable differences between countries in employee involvement, ranging from almost 70 percent for the Netherlands and Finland to 31 percent for Portugal. A third survey in this series will be undertaken in 1999.

Employment Options of the Future

While a lot is known about the situation in European workplaces, little is known about the sort of work people want and their preference for the organization of work. This new survey project set out to fill the information gap.

The survey was carried out in 1998 and results are being analysed at the time of writing. A different methodology from the working conditions survey was used: field work consisting of telephone interviews based on a structured questionnaire.

The target groups were: (1) the employed, (2) women/men returning to work after a break, (3) young first entries, and (4) the unemployed. For the employed, a series of questions related to actual working time: whether full-time or part-time, on temporary contracts, or self-employed; and levels of overtime worked. For all groups, questions covered preferences for new working time arrangements and new forms of work organization.

For the five larger member states, the target population was 2,000 from the employed group and 1,000 from the other groups. For the 10 smaller countries and Norway, the sample was 1,000 and 500, respectively.

The questions focused on:

- *Groups* – who wants to work?
- *Flexibility* – how do they want to work?
- *Working time* – when do they want to work?
- *Location/teleworking* – where do they want to work?
- *Motivation* – why do they want to work?

No results are available yet, but the initial indications show a greater desire for flexibility in working time and in the organization of work than there are opportunities.

Employee Participation in Organizational Change (EPOC)

Third, and most relevant to the focus of this volume, is the research undertaken by the European Foundation into aspects of employee involvement in changing work organization.

Over the years, the European social model has given workers a degree of protection, rights, and job security. The globalization of markets, however, requires enterprises to respond quickly to changing demands, and to have greater flexibility in the organization of the work process. The dilemma of policymakers and the social partners in the European Union – identified in the European Commission Green Paper *Partnership for a New Organisation of Work* – is: how do we provide job security while at the same time ensuring greater workplace flexibility?

As enterprises strive to protect their market share and survive in an increasingly competitive business environment, management – in many cases with the cooperation of unions – are searching for ways to achieve greater efficiencies and increase productivity. Part of this trend is the increased use of new employment arrangements, resulting in the reduction of core jobs, a growth in peripheral employment, and a decrease in job security. It is argued that these arrangements provide enterprises with greater flexibility to deal with fluctuations in demand for products or services.

Much of the recent debate on work organization has, to some extent, focused on how enterprises can respond to competitive pressures through greater operational flexibility, and how this can be achieved through the implementation of employee involvement arrangements, such as direct participation. A large number of enterprises, however, continue to meet flexibility needs through reduction in jobs, while others achieve flexibility through the use of insecure forms of employment, such as part-time work and temporary contracts. This approach is changing the nature of the employment relationship and the employment contract from long-term employment to short-term, project, or demand-related jobs.

Through its EPOC Program, the Foundation has for the past five years undertaken a study of these issues and of direct employee participation in organizational change in particular. Projects included a review of the attitudes and approaches of the social partners, and a literature review of research in the United States, Japan, and Europe. In the autumn of 1996, a survey in 10 EU member states was carried out to establish the nature and extent of direct participation arrangements, including levels and forms of consultation with, or delegation of decision making to, the individual or the work group. The survey concentrated on the largest occupational group within the establishment, and the first results were published by the Foundation in late 1998.

The survey, by a postal questionnaire, was representative of the economic/ business structures of the 10 countries, by population and by number of employees in the workplace and sector. It covered not only private sector manufacturing but also private services, public administration, state-owned utilities, and nonprofit organizations. The gross sample comprised 5,000 workplaces for the large countries (France, Germany, Italy, Spain, and the United Kingdom), 2,500 for medium-sized countries (Denmark, the Netherlands, and Sweden), and 1,000 for the small countries (Ireland and Portugal), for a total population of 34,500. There was a threshold of 20 or more workers in the smaller member states, and 50 in the larger countries.

The response rate was 18 percent, ranging from 9.5 percent for Spain to 39 percent for Ireland – a total of 5,800 workplaces with an estimated workforce of 4 million. The questions ranged around two key issues: (1) consultation with the individual worker or work group and (2) delegation of decision making to the individual or the group. The focus of the survey was the "Largest Occupational Group" within the workplace.

Some Results from the EPOC Survey

There is cause for both optimism and concern in the results. The survey shows a significant level of both direct participation and new forms of work organization. In four out of five of the workplaces in Europe surveyed (81 percent), management either encourages employees to make their views known on work-related matters or gives employees increased responsibility for organizing their work. On the other hand, a significant minority of workplaces in the EPOC survey, one in five, do not practice any form of direct participation.

Optimism is based on the fact that managers who responded to the EPOC survey believe that direct participation in organizational change is effective.

Each of the forms of direct participation was viewed as having positive effects on a range of key indicators of economic performance. For example, 60 percent of managers saw a significant cost reduction as a result of group work; 94 percent said that there was an improvement in the quality of the service/product, and 60 percent said that there was a reduction in through-put time. Overall, respondents on direct participation believe it to be a successful strategy in improving the economic performance of the enterprise. Workers indicate greater job satisfaction by a 37 percent reduction in absenteeism, increasing to 50 percent when the entire workplace is team-based.

An important element of success is the involvement of employee representatives, either trade unions or works councils, in the introduction of direct participation. Survey results confirm that it is important for employee representatives to be involved in the regulation of direct participation, in order to improve both the quality of the participation itself and its economic and social effects. Our survey shows that in Europe, far from being a barrier to progress, employee representatives and trade unions are agents of change. The more they were involved, in terms of both form and extent (and this applies particularly to negotiation and joint decision making), the more the indicators of business performance were positive.

Workplace Representation

Of those European workplaces with direct participation, 44 percent involve worker representatives in the introduction of direct participation, either by "extensive consultation" or through "joint decision making/negotiations" (Table 1). Among those enterprises that involve worker representatives, the process was considered "useful" or "very useful" by 88 percent of managers. In a quarter of firms in the survey sample, however, there is no participation by employee representatives in the introduction of direct participation, and this is cause for concern. Figures are very close to the employee-based working conditions survey, even though the methodology was different.

What about the workers themselves? In some 80 percent of workplaces, the employees affected by the changes are involved in the introduction of direct participation. More surprising is the reverse side of this finding – employees were not involved in the introduction of direct participation in 10 percent of workplaces, and received only limited information in another 8 percent.

Concerns for European Enterprises

The results of the EPOC survey give grounds for concern. Results show that European enterprises are slow to take the participation route to greater competitiveness. It is difficult to make comparisons with other surveys because of the different methodologies, but it seems that while there has been an increase in the incidence of direct participation in Europe in recent years,

Table 1

Extent of employee representative involvement in the introduction of direct participation (percent of all workplaces with direct participation)

	No participation	Limited information	Extensive information/ limited consultation	Extensive consultation	Extensive joint decision making/ negotiations
10-country average	25	9	22	20	24
Denmark	22	3	10	21	44
France	22	8	37	16	17
Germany	29	5	15	18	34
Ireland	40	8	16	22	14
Italy	25	18	22	17	17
Netherlands	39	8	18	19	16
Portugal	44	8	15	19	14
Spain	19	13	23	24	22
Sweden	3	7	17	29	45
UK	19	12	24	27	19

Source: EPOC Survey, 1996.

the gap with Japan and the US identified in previous EPOC research has not yet been closed. This is especially so in the case of Japan, where group work, for example, was found to be practiced by more than 90 percent of large companies in industry and more than 80 percent in services, compared with 25 percent in Europe. Another comparison of integrated forms of group work (i.e., more than 50 percent of the workers working in teams) shows the US at 41 percent (1994) and Europe at only 19 percent (1996).

The vast majority of European companies, therefore, miss the opportunities to utilize new forms of work organization to improve their competitiveness, and European enterprises lag significantly behind their main competitors in the US and Japan. More importantly, many of those that do take the participation route are pursuing a partial approach. Relatively few – around one in seven – report a policy of integrating forms of direct participation. When we examined the levels of "high" scope (issues on which employees are consulted or are given decision-making rights), we found that only 6 to 12 percent of establishments fell within this category (Table 2). Furthermore, when we applied our "intensity of DP" measurement (i.e., scope plus autonomy), we found that much of the direct participation practiced by European enterprises is very limited – from 5 to 11 percent.

The EPOC survey results confirm the view that the problem of finding a balance between job security and workplace flexibility is likely to be an

Table 2

Workplaces achieving high scores for scope for each form of direct participation (percent of all establishments)

	Individual face-to-face consultation	Individual arms-length consultation	Temporary group consultation	Permanent group consultation	Individual delegation	Group delegation
10-country average	6	6	6	8	12	6
Denmark	4	7	8	7	12	7
France	8	5	9	12	11	4
Germany	4	4	5	8	17	6
Ireland	8	4	7	9	20	3
Italy	2	2	2	2	3	3
Netherlands	10	15	9	11	12	8
Portugal	2	0	5	7	3	5
Spain	6	4	3	4	5	0
Sweden	8	10	10	11	15	15
UK	6	5	6	9	13	5

Source: EPOC Survey, 1996.

especially sensitive one. In the EPOC survey, many of the workplaces introducing direct participation (around one-third) reported that one effect was a reduction in the number of employees in general and managers in particular. The more extensive the practice, it seems, the more likely that this reduction will occur. In half of these cases, however, short-term reductions seem to have been compensated or overcompensated for by stable or increased employment in the medium term. Furthermore, and more important, workplaces *without* direct participation were more likely to report a reduction in medium-term employment than those *with* direct participation.

Along with the findings of our earlier research (European Survey on Working Conditions), the EPOC survey results suggest that not just the workplace is important. The wider national context is also significant. The Netherlands and Sweden stand out on a number of counts, including the incidence, scope, intensity, and effects of direct participation. It is difficult to escape the conclusion that this phenomenon reflects the wider context of social-partner and political support. In both countries, the interest in new forms of work organization is long-standing and is rooted in a wide variety of institutional arrangements.

In particular, two features of the Dutch and Swedish experience appear to be especially relevant: an overarching understanding or framework agreement between the social partners, giving legitimacy to implementation projects, and major public campaigns of practical support. At the very least, careful study of the recent experience of these countries, taking account of

Table 3

Level of innovation in Europe

	Percent of workplaces
None	30
Very little	34
Little	23
Medium	10
Intense	3
Total	100
$n = 5,786$	

the failures as well as the successes, would benefit enterprises interested in going this route.

Innovation and Employment

During 1998, we undertook further analysis of the data to find out more about the link between innovation, organizational flexibility, and employment levels. The definition of innovation we applied included the application of new information technology, automation, and product and process innovation, together with the effects on workers of changes in work organization involving new plant/machinery/automation.

We found very little innovation in Europe (Table 3). The research shows that innovation is influenced by sector and by country. Industry is the most innovative sector, whereas construction and public services are the least likely to be innovative. Our findings show that Denmark and Italy (21 percent) appear to be the most innovative, while France and Sweden are the least (6 percent and 9 percent of workplaces, respectively).

Table 4

Innovation and functional flexibility in Europe (percent of workplaces)

	Functional flexibility		
Innovation	None	Some	High
None	33	28	25
Some	54	57	62
High	13	15	14
Total	100	100	100
n	*2,432*	*2,062*	*1,291*

Table 5

Workplaces in Europe with different combinations of functional flexibility and innovation

Levels of innovation AND functional flexibility	Percent of workplaces
None	14
Both low	53
Both medium	10
High innovation	6
High functional flexibility	15
High both	2
Total	100

$n = 5,786$

Source: EPOC Survey, 1996.

When we linked innovation to direct participation, a combination we labelled as "functional flexibility" (Table 4), we were unable to support the hypotheses that innovative firms are also participative firms and vice versa. Very few European workplaces take the "high road" of innovation and participation (2 percent), while 14 percent are neither innovative nor participative (Table 5).

When we examined the link between functional flexibility, innovation, and employment trends in enterprises, we came up with better news. Innovative firms create jobs. In workplaces where innovation is most intense, employment increased. Add functional flexibility (direct participation) and 54 percent of workplaces showed an increase in employment. In contrast, where there was innovation without direct participation, employment decreased in one-third of the workplaces in the sample.

Looking at the data in another way, we find that workplaces with "no innovation" and "no functional flexibility" tend not to increase employment (-8 percent), in contrast to the enterprises that do both intensely (27 percent) (Table 6).

Further Analysis

A number of other work organization issues require examination and further study. During 1998, we undertook secondary analysis on three other topics: direct participation in the public services, gender, and the nature and extent of team work.

While a number of interesting results emerged, one is particularly interesting in the context of the current discussion: the use of team work or "group delegation," as it was termed in the questionnaire, defined as "rights and responsibilities that are granted to groups of employees to carry out

Table 6

Functional flexibility, innovation, and employment change in European workplaces

	10-country average
Stable employment: % of establishments reporting no increase or decrease in employment	40
Net employment change: difference in % of establishments reporting increase or decrease in employment	+5
Level of functional flexibility and innovation	
None	–8
Both low	+2
Both medium	+14
High innovation	+12
High functional flexibility	+14
High both	+27
n = 5,528	

Source: EPOC Survey, 1996.

their common tasks without constant reference back to managers – most often known as 'group work.' "

Using this definition, the survey results showed that in a quarter of the workplaces covered, group work was practiced to some extent. The analysis set out to establish how intensive group work was practiced. Two criteria were applied: (1) the percentage of employees working in teams (coverage), and (2) the range of issues on which teams are entitled to make decisions, without reference to management (intensity).

Using the definition and the criteria from the EPOC study, only 3.8 percent of all establishments in Europe have serious team-based workplace arrangements.

This reluctance of European management to devolve decision making to teams is further confirmed by the results of a question to managers asking which form of direct participation they considered most important. In most countries, the consultative forms (e.g., quality circles, problem-solving groups) were regarded as more important than group delegation. Indeed, many managers who have group work in their enterprises did not necessarily regard it as the most important form of direct participation.

Conclusion

Taking their different purposes, target groups, and methodologies into consideration, many of the European Foundation research projects confirm results from a number of national surveys, such as the ISI survey on flexible work organization in Germany, the Swedish National Board for Industrial and Technical Development (NUTEK) workplace survey in Sweden, or the Aalborg workplace survey in Denmark. They also confirm what has been found in some cross-national research, such as the Price Waterhouse-Cranfield Project on International Strategic Human Resource Management in Europe or the European Commission (DG XIII) European Innovation Monitoring System (EIMS) studies on innovation and employment.

The objective of this chapter was to demonstrate that the monitoring of the European workplace is a key part of the European Foundation's mandate. An ongoing program of study, research, and observation monitors the impact of globalization, workplace change, and new approaches to work organization on workers and enterprises in Europe. The Foundation will continue to play a key role in providing EU institutions with the necessary information to make informed policy decisions.

Contributors

Gordon Betcherman has been Senior Economist, Labor Markets, at the World Bank in Washington, DC, since 1998. Prior to this appointment, he directed the Work Network at Canadian Policy Research Networks, a non-profit think tank, and the Human Resource Group at Ekos Research Associates, a private research company. He has held a Senior Fellowship at the School of Industrial Relations at Queen's University, Kingston, Ontario, and was a Research Director at the Economic Council of Canada until 1992. Dr. Betcherman is a director of Canadian Policy Research Networks, and a member of the Statistics Canada Advisory Committee on Labour Statistics and the editorial board of the *Canadian Business Economics* journal. He has published widely on labour economics, industrial relations, and public policy. He obtained his Ph.D. from the University of California at Los Angeles.

Gerhard Bosch is Professor of Sociology at the University of Duisburg, Germany, and vice president of the Institute of Work and Technology, Science Centre, North Rhine-Westphalia, in Gelsenkirchen. He is an expert on labour markets and has published several books in German and English, including *Retraining Not Redundancy: Innovative Approaches to Industrial Restructuring in Germany and France*, with P. Dawkins and F. Michon (editors); *Times Are Changing: Working Time in 14 Industrialized Countries*, with D. Anxo, D. Bosworth, D. Taddei, and T. Sterner (editors); and *Work Patterns and Capital Utilization: An International Comparative Study*.

Nicola De Michelis, who has a background in economics, administers the Directorate General for Regional Policy and Cohesion at the European Commission. He is responsible for telecommunication, information society, research and development, innovation, and industrial policies. Previously, he worked on urban policies at the Organization for Economic Cooperation and Development (OECD) in Paris, where he focused on energy management, urban transport, and information and communication technologies. Before starting his international career, he worked for six years in the private sector in Italy.

Charles Edquist is a professor in the Department of Technology and Social Change at the University of Linköping, Sweden. He received an M.A. in Economics from the University of California, Berkeley, and a Ph.D. in Economic History from the University of Lund, Sweden. In November 1986 he was appointed to a chair in the Department of Technology and Social Change, University of Linköping. During 1996-98 he coordinated Innovation Systems and European Integration (ISE), a research project funded by the European Commission that involved nine research groups in nine European countries. His fields of research include socio-economic and political aspects of technological change, organizational innovations, technology and productivity, R&D policy and innovation policy, and systems of innovation.

Yves Gingras received an M.A. in Economics from Laval University, Quebec, in 1992. He joined the Federal Public Service through the Accelerated Economist Training Program in 1992, first as an analyst in the Labour Market Policy Analysis Group of Human Resources Development Canada (HRDC), then as a policy advisor in the Privy Council Office. In 1997 he returned to the HRDC as a senior economist in the Applied Research Branch, where his work concerns labour market trends in Canada.

Ronald Hirshhorn is an Ottawa-based economic consultant specializing in industrial organization. He has published a wide range of reports and studies on individual Canadian industries, on government policies influencing industrial performance, and on governance issues. Before establishing his own consulting practice, Ronald Hirshhorn was a senior economist and project director with the Economic Council of Canada.

Ursula Huws is the director of Analytica Social and Economic Research and an Associate Fellow of the Institute for Employment Studies in the United Kingdom. Details of her research and publications can be found at <http://dspace.dial.pipex.com/analytica>.

Howard Krebs is Chief of the Workplace and Employee Survey (WES) Section in the Labour Statistics Division of Statistics Canada. He is currently spearheading a feasibility study to develop a Labour Cost Index for Canada. He has concentrated on developing new survey instruments and products mainly from the WES, the Survey of Employment, Payrolls and Hours, and administrative data sources. He has published research on income adequacy for the elderly, consumer behaviour, inflation, firm behaviour, and labour compensation. He has a strong interest in changing workplace issues, such as relationships among competitiveness, innovation, technology use, and human resource management practices on the employer side and technology use, job stability, and earnings on the employee side. He is developing an infrastructure to support other special surveys and information production activities.

Norm Leckie is currently Senior Consultant, Human Resource Group, at Ekos Research Associates, an Ottawa-based consulting company. Since joining Ekos in 1994, Mr. Leckie's work has included studies of workplace training, youth issues and school-to-work transition, self-employment and small business, labour-management cooperation, innovative work practices and organizational change, and technological change and skill trends. Before joining Ekos, Mr. Leckie was an economist at the Economic Council of Canada.

Brenda Lipsett is Senior Economist in the Applied Research Branch, Human Resources Development Canada. Her recent research on the changing nature of employment includes flexible work arrangements; job insecurity; hours of work preferences; entitlement to employer-sponsored pension, health, and dental plans; and the role of work arrangements in women's entitlement to workplace benefits. She holds an M.A. in Economics from Carleton University.

Richard G. Lipsey, FRSC, OC, is Professor Emeritus of Economics at Simon Fraser University, Burnaby, British Columbia, and Fellow of the Canadian Institute for Advanced Research. He received his Ph.D. from the University of London (at the London School of Economics) in 1957, where he held a chair in Economics from 1960 to 1964. Several of the 10 textbooks authored by Dr. Lipsey are in use worldwide. He has published more than 200 articles and books on various aspects of theoretical and applied economics, and three volumes of his selected essays have recently been published. Dr. Lipsey is an officer of the Order of Canada, a Fellow of the Royal Society of Canada and the Econometric Society, and past president of the Canadian Economic Society and the Atlantic Economic Society. He holds several honorary doctorates.

Since 1996, **Kathryn McMullen** has been Network Leader and Senior Research Associate with the Work Network of Canadian Policy Research Networks. Previously, she was a senior consultant with Ekos Research Associates in Ottawa and an economist with Queen's-University of Ottawa Economic Projects and the Economic Council of Canada. Kathryn McMullen has researched and written extensively on issues relating to technological and organizational change, changing skill requirements, and the transformation of work.

Philippe Massé obtained his M.A. in Economics from the University of Ottawa in 1993. He is Senior Research Officer with the Human Capital and Workplace Studies Division of the Applied Research Branch, Human Resources Development Canada. He has been with the Branch since 1993. His primary research interests include determinants of change in the structure of employment and skill requirements; determinants and effects of investment in human capital; and international mobility of skilled workers.

Vincent Mosco is a professor in the School of Journalism and Communication at Carleton University, Ottawa. He received his Ph.D. in Sociology from Harvard University and conducts research with the Harvard Program on Information Resources Policy. He has held research positions with the White House Office of Telecommunication Policy, the National Research Council, and the Office of Technology Assessment in the United States, and with the federal Department of Communication in Canada. He has also served as a consultant to governments, universities, corporations, and trade unions in Canada, the United States, Malaysia, and South Africa. His current work addresses the rise of post-industrial high technology districts, and communication and social science.

Kevin O'Kelly is a research manager with the European Foundation, Dublin, Ireland, with responsibility for research projects on employee participation, industrial relations, and work organization. He is a graduate of University College, Dublin, in politics and economics, and of Trinity College, University of Dublin, in industrial relations. A former political advisor to the Irish Minister for Labour, he has worked in the public and private sectors in a range of consultancy positions. Mr. O'Kelly is chairman of the Irish Association for Industrial Relations and a member of the Executive Committee of the International Industrial Relations Association.

Luigi Orsenigo is Associate Professor of Economics at Bocconi University, Milan, Italy. His work mainly concerns the economics of innovation and industrial dynamics. Publications include *The Emergence of Biotechnology: Institutions and Markets in Industrial Innovation* (Pinter Publishers, London, 1989) and several articles in major international journals.

Zdenek Patak is a senior methodologist in the Business Survey Methods Division of Statistics Canada. He is currently working on the Workplace and Employee Survey (WES). His responsibility is to oversee the methodological aspects of the survey from sample design to estimation and confidentiality. His main area of interest lies in the domain of outlier detection and estimation using auxiliary information such as that available on the Statistics Canada Business Register. He is involved in researching methods for longitudinal imputation using what one might call a "cookbook" approach, where one gives general guidelines to users as to the most efficient approach in the presence of item data missing at random.

Pascal Petit is CNRS Director of Research in Economics at CEPREMAP, the Centre d'études prospectives d'économie mathématique appliquées à la planification, in Paris. His work focuses on the issues of growth and employment in open economies experimenting with new technological systems and information and communication technologies. His most recent publication is "L'économie de l'information" (1998).

Garnett Picot is Director of the Business and Labour Market Analysis Division at Statistics Canada. His recent research has been primarily in the area of labour economics, on topics such as worker displacement, layoffs, job creation and destruction, earnings and income inequality, child poverty, and training. He has led the content development for a number of new surveys, most recently the longitudinal Workplace and Employee Survey. In addition to a number of positions with Statistics Canada, he has held positions with the University of British Columbia, the provincial Department of Industry and Commerce in British Columbia, Canadian General Electric, and the federal Secretary of State for Education.

Someshwar Rao is Director of the Strategic Investment Analysis Directorate in the Industry and Science Policy Sector at Industry Canada, where he is responsible for research publications. He also directs research in productivity, trade and investment, connectedness metrics and the information revolution, and sustainable development. Before joining Industry Canada in 1992, Dr. Rao was with the Economic Council of Canada.

John Richards grew up in Saskatchewan and served as a member of that province's legislature from 1971 to 1975. He still works closely with the Saskatchewan government on aspects of social policy. Trained as an economist, he currently teaches in the business faculty at Simon Fraser University, Burnaby, BC. He is also an adjunct scholar at the C.D. Howe Institute. His latest book, *Retooling the Welfare State*, was published in early 1999 by the C.D. Howe Institute.

W. Craig Riddell is a professor in the Department of Economics at the University of British Columbia and an associate of the Canadian Institute for Advanced Research. His research interests are in labour economics, labour relations, and public policy. Current research focuses on unemployment and labour market dynamics, the role of human capital in economic growth, experimental and non-experimental approaches to the evaluation of social programs, unionization and collective bargaining, gender differences in labour market behaviour and outcomes, unemployment insurance and social assistance, and education and training.

His recent publications include "Qualifying for Unemployment Insurance: An Empirical Analysis" (with David Green, 1997); "Wages, Skills and Technology in the United States and Canada" (with Kevin Murphy and Paul Romer, 1998); and "The Measurement of Unemployment: An Empirical Approach" (with Stephen Jones, 1999). Professor Riddell is past president of the Canadian Economics Association.

Since 1991, **Henri Rouilleault** has served as general director of France's National Agency for the Improvement of Working Conditions (ANACT). Earlier, he worked as a macroeconomist at the French National Institute for Statistics and Economic Studies (INSEE) and the Ministry of Finance.

Richard Roy holds an M.Sc. degree from the Université de Montréal and is ABD in Economics at the University of British Columbia. He directs the Applied Research Branch of Human Resources Development Canada. Before joining HRDC in 1994, he worked with the International Monetary Fund in Washington, DC, the Economic Council of Canada, and the Bank of Canada. His current research interests include occupational labour markets, returns to human capital, and the effect of technology on labour requirements.

Kjell Rubenson is a professor of adult education in the Department of Educational Studies at the University of British Columbia. He received his education and academic degrees from Göteborg University (Sweden), and held the chair of adult education at the University of Linköping before coming to Canada in 1986. He is the long-term director of UBC's Centre for Policy Studies in Higher Education and Training (formerly the Centre for Policy Studies in Education). His main academic interests and publications concern the relationship between education, learning and work, adult education and learning, and educational policy studies. He is a consultant to the Organization for Economic Cooperation and Development (OECD) and the United Nations Educational, Scientific and Cultural Organization (UNESCO).

Educated at the universities of Göttingen and Bonn (Germany), Grenoble (France), and California at Berkeley (USA), **Hans G. Schuetze** worked as a policy analyst and advisor for the Centre for Educational Research and Innovation of the Organization for Economic Cooperation and Development (OECD) in Paris and for the province of Niedersachsen (Lower Saxony) before joining the University of British Columbia in 1991 as a research fellow at the Centre for Policy Studies in Higher Education and Training. His research interests include private sector innovation, university-industry collaboration, higher education, labour market issues, comparative and international education, and the role of human resources in economic and social development.

Albert Tuijnman received his Ph.D. from Stockholm University in 1989. He was with the Faculty of Education, University of Twente, before joining the Organization for Economic Cooperation and Development (OECD) in 1992 as an administrator (and later principal administrator). He was appointed Special Professor at the University of Nottingham in October 1997 and, after taking leave from the OECD, returned as a visiting professor to the Institute of International Education at Stockholm University in August 1998.

Albert Tuijnman has published extensively in his fields of interest: comparative education, education economics, and adult education and training, and consults widely in these areas. He was scientific secretary of the Royal Swedish Academy of Sciences, and rapporteur of an Academia Europaea task force on schooling in the new European society. He also served as an officer of the International Academy of Education and a member of the editorial board of the *International Encyclopedia of Education,* second edition.

John Van Reenen is a professor in the Department of Economics at University College London and a Research Fellow at the Institute for Fiscal Studies, where he leads the IFS work on innovation, labour markets, and company performance. He is the coordinator of the TSER Network on Innovation, Research and Development, and Productivity. A member of the editorial board of the *Review of Economic Studies,* the *European Economics Review,* and the *Journal of Industrial Economics,* he has published widely in the areas of industrial economics, labour economics, and applied econometrics.

Tom Wall is Assistant General Secretary of the Irish Congress of Trade Unions, where he has worked since 1972. He has represented his organization and the European Trade Union Confederation on a number of bodies. These include the European Foundation for the Improvement of Living and Working Conditions; the European Health and Safety Agency; the European Social Dialogue Committee; the (Irish) National Economic and Social Forum; and the National Occupational Health and Safety Authority and Labour Relations Commission in Ireland.

Ted Wannell is a senior research analyst in the Business and Labour Market Analysis Division of Statistics Canada. Besides working on the development of the Workplace and Employee Survey, Ted has published research on the earnings of women and minorities, labour market outcomes of young people, changes in the earnings distribution, self-employment, distribution of firms by employment size, career advancement in the public service, and a number of other labour-related topics. He has also managed the development of a personnel microsimulation model (PERSIM) used to support long-term human resource planning in Statistics Canada and a number of other government departments.

Caroline L. Weber holds a Ph.D. in Human Resource Management from Cornell University. Her main research interests include compensation, strategic human resource management and planning, health and safety, and the overall effectiveness of human resource management systems. Her written work has appeared in refereed journals such as *Relations Industrielles,* the *Academy of Management Journal,* the *Journal of Applied Psychology,* and *Compensation and Benefits Review.* An associate professor in the Schools of Industrial Relations and Business at Queen's University in Kingston, Ontario, she is currently on leave to serve as Director of the Women's Bureau at Human Resources Development Canada.

David A. Wolfe is Professor of Political Science at the University of Toronto, where he earned his Ph.D. His past research has examined the implications of technological change for skills, occupational requirements, and education and training. He is currently completing a multiyear project on "The Rise of the Region State in Canada and the Role of Interstate Networking." In 1997 he co-founded the new Program on Globalization and Regional Innovation Systems (PROGRIS) at the Centre for International Studies, at the University of Toronto. PROGRIS is a node in the Innovation Systems Research Network and acts as the national secretariat.

Index